The Everyday Science Sourcebook

Revised 2nd Edition

Ideas for Teaching in Elementary and Middle School

The Everyday Science Sourcebook

Lawrence F. Lowery

Revised 2nd Edition

Ideas for Teaching in Elementary and Middle School

NSTApress

National Science Teachers Association

Arlington, Virginia

National Science Teachers Association

Claire Reinburg, Director
Jennifer Horak, Managing Editor
Andrew Cooke, Senior Editor
Wendy Rubin, Associate Editor
Agnes Bannigan, Associate Editor
Amy America, Book Acquisitions Coordinator

ART AND DESIGN
Will Thomas Jr., Director

PRINTING AND PRODUCTION
Catherine Lorrain, Director
Jack Parker, Electronic Prepress Technician

NATIONAL SCIENCE TEACHERS ASSOCIATION
Francis Q. Eberle, PhD, Executive Director
David Beacom, Publisher
1840 Wilson Blvd., Arlington, VA 22201
www.nsta.org/store
For customer service inquiries, please call 800-277-5300.

NSTA is committed to publishing material that promotes the best in inquiry-based science education. However, conditions of actual use may vary, and the safety procedures and practices described in this book are intended to serve only as a guide. Additional precautionary measures may be required. NSTA and the authors do not warrant or represent that the procedures and practices in this book meet any safety code or standard of federal, state, or local regulations. NSTA and the authors disclaim any liability for personal injury or damage to property arising out of or relating to the use of this book, including any of the recommendations, instructions, or materials contained therein.

eISBN 978-1-936959-84-6

Library of Congress Cataloging-in-Publication Data
Lowery, Lawrence F.
  The everyday science sourcebook : ideas for teaching in elementary and middle school / By Lawrence F. Lowery. -- Rev. 2nd ed.
      p. cm.
  Includes bibliographical references and index.
    ISBN 978-1-936959-09-9
  1. Science--Study and teaching (Secondary)--Handbooks, manuals, etc. 2. Science--Study and teaching (Elementary)--Handbooks, manuals, etc. I. Title.
    Q181.L872 2012
      507.1'2--dc23
                          2012002282

Table of Contents

Entry Section

Table of Contents

Preface

As a human endeavor, science is a quest for knowledge about the world in which we live. We observe and describe objects; we act upon them to see what happens; we take notes of what takes place. We organize our observations, test what we think we know, and then reorganize our observations. We make inferences about what we cannot determine directly, and some of us apply what we have learned to construct new objects or invent new combinations of ideas.

"Doing" science is not significantly different from normal human behavior. For example, very young children observe the objects of their environment by looking at them, touching them, tasting them, smelling them, and manipulating them. Similarly, the scientist places a space probe on the surface of a distant planet and turns on the TV eye to see what it can see. A mechanical hand touches the surface and explores its composition. Sensors "smell" the atmosphere. With each of these sensory actions, the child and the scientist gather knowledge about our world.

It is important for teachers to realize that science is not solely the accumulation of information over the centuries, but rather it is the simultaneous relationship between the information and the ways by which it is obtained. Science is, at once, the *processes* by which we gather and think about information and the *knowledge* that results from such actions.

The Need to Improve Science Instruction

In April 1983, one of the more important educational reform publications of the last century, *A Nation at Risk*, was released (National Commission on Excellence in Education). It warned that if our educational enterprise continues to develop a citizenry that is illiterate in the areas of mathematics, science, and technology, our nation would lose its influential position among other nations and become a second-rate power in the 21st century.

It was not long before several efforts were initiated to bring about change in science education. Project 2061 under the guidance of the American Association for the Advancement of Science (AAAS) made recommendations for basic learning goals in *Science for All Americans* (1989) and *Benchmarks for Science Literacy* (1993). The *National Science Education Standards* (1996), developed under the auspices of the National Research Council (NRC), outlined the minimal expectations for science programs in schools and described important aspects for curriculum change. Both efforts involved collaboration among scientists, mathematicians, engineers, psychologists, and educators to outline the knowledge and inquiry skills K–12 students needed to understand

and apply to become scientifically literate citizens. Although the documents provided a fundamental set of outcomes for students and educators, they did not, and still do not, prescribe a curriculum. It is expected that states and local districts use the standards as guidelines for planning and implementing science instruction through all grade levels.

The documents emphasize that it is not sufficient to just read about science or demonstrate and lecture in a show-and-tell manner. Rather, they emphasize that learning the essence of the enterprise (the modes of inquiry and the procedures for gathering, organizing, and analyzing data in intellectually honest ways) is more important than memorizing facts. This sourcebook was created because science should be memorable, not memorizable.

This Sourcebook and National Science Standards

The content in this sourcebook was selected to build upon and extend the science standards outlined in the AAAS and NSES documents. All the activities contribute to those standards that can best be learned through direct and indirect observations of natural phenomena. Because the major standards are broad and inclusive, this book restates them in teachable terms that combine the content to be learned with ways by which students can explore and inquire. Since many textbook and kit-centered science programs do not provide engaging activities for all the science standards, the activities in this book can fill gaps in programs and extend and enrich experiences where programs have minimal or shallow activities.

This sourcebook is a thesaurus. It enables the user to quickly locate numerous experiences related to particular scientific standards and thinking processes. Users will be pleased by the many fresh ideas for teaching. The book can make instruction valid, powerful, and enjoyable.

It is important to know that this sourcebook is not a science program, and it is not a methods book. You will not learn from this book how to teach science. As a storehouse of ideas, it will not tell you how to work through activities in a prescribed way. How you instruct depends upon your own training and philosophy about learning. Each activity can be taught didactically or by an inquiry technique. Because this is not a methods book, the activities are intentionally brief. Creative and well-prepared individuals will use the suggestions as springboards for their own ideas and will adapt the activities in many ways to meet the goals of their curriculum and the needs of students.

This book is also not a source of scientific knowledge and not intended to supply all the factual background and explanations for science concepts. However, the entries do supply the generalizations inherent in each activity, and each contributes to a standard and contains sufficient information pertaining to the instructional conditions that enable the teacher to prepare and introduce the activity to students.

Remember: The main purpose for this book is to enable you to easily find hands-on experiences that directly engage students with phenomena in our world.

Safety

With hands-on, process, and inquiry-based activities, today's teaching and learning of science can be both effective and exciting. The challenge of securing this success needs to be met by addressing potential safety issues. Teachers can reinforce safety for students and themselves by adopting, implementing, and enforcing legal standards and best professional practices in the science classroom, laboratory, and out in the field. In this sourcebook, *610 Safety Precautions* (p. 448) includes both recommended basic safety practices and resources for activities. It is designed to help teachers and students become aware of relevant standards and practices that will help make activities safer. Doing science makes the learning come alive; doing science safer makes it a successful experience.

For additional safety regulations and best professional practices, go to:

NSTA: Safety in the Science Classroom:
www.nsta.org/pdfs/SafetyInTheScienceClassroom.pdf

NSTA Safety Portal:
www.nsta.org/portals/safety.aspx

How to Use This Sourcebook

It is easy to use this sourcebook. Look up a topic in the Index Guide, note the entry, or activity number for that topic, and then use that number to find one or more activities in the Entry section.

Let us try an example. Suppose your students have found some rocks that interest them and they bring them to class. You might want to do some activities with rocks to extend their interest.

If you look up the word *Rocks* in the Index Guide, you will see the following:

Rocks
    breakdown of, 141.18
    characteristics of, 141.01–12
    classification of, 141.22–24
    collecting, 651.03
    definition of, operational, 141.10
    identification of
        color sorting key, 141.14,–15
        hardness sorting key, 141.22
        size sorting key, 141.23
    magma, 141.01–04
    minerals in, 141.13–15
    plant growth, effect of, 142.28
    porosity of, 142.27
    in soil formation, 141.16–18
    temperature change, effect of, 142.26–27
    tests for
        cleavage, 141.11b
        hardness, 141.10
        streak, 141.11a
    types of
        igneous, 141.01–04
        metamorphic, 141.08–09
        sedimentary, 141.05–07

From the listing under *Rocks*, you can see that you have a lot of choices. Pick the one that best fits the interest of the students and the resources you have available.

Suppose you decide it would be best for your students to learn something about how rocks can be identified. Note that, in the Index Guide, a set of numbers accompanies the topic *identification of: color sorting key, 141.14, 141.15; hardness sorting key, 141.22*; and *size sorting key, 141.23*. These numbers mean that in section 141 of this sourcebook, there are several activities related to learning about the identification of rocks.

Suppose you decide to look up *hardness sorting key, 141.22* in the Entry section of this book. The activity numbers are printed at the top of each page for the activities on that page—much in the way that a dictionary and an encyclopedia list entries at the top of their pages. When you look up the *identification of rocks, 141.22* in the Entry section, you will find a page that looks like the following:

Inorganic Matter / Earth Science   141.21–141.23

daily records of what happens. Students will find that the plants in the glass without soil cannot sustain growth, and that the soil must be a contributing factor for continued growth.

b. Fill one flowerpot with sand, another with clay (or subsoil), and a third with loam (or topsoil). Plant five lima beans in each pot and place the pots side by side where they will receive the same amount of sunshine. Add the same amount of water to each pot daily and keep a record of the growth for a month. Decide which kind of soil is best for growth. (The topsoil is usually best.)

Generalization IV. Rocks can be organized by their physical characteristics.

Contributing Idea A. Rocks can be seriated.

Seriating rocks by hardness. Rocks vary in hardness and can be ordered from soft to hard. Table 141.22 is a commonly used hardness key. Students can set up their own hardness scale using the rocks they find by seeing if one will scratch another. (A rock that scratches another rock is harder than that rock.) They can then order their rocks by relative hardness. **22 Ab Da**

Seriating rocks by size. Have students bring to school rocks of different sizes. Line up all the collected rocks in a row from smallest to largest. Table 141.23 shows standard categories for the various **23 Aa Da**

Table 141.22. Hardness Sorting Key—Rocks

Hardness Scale (Soft to Hard)	Hardness Test	Rock Example
1	Scratches easily with a fingernail	talc
2	Scratches with a fingernail	gypsum
3	Scratches with a pin or copper penny	calcite
4	Scratches easily with a knife	fluorite
5	Scratches with a knife	apatite
6	Knife will not scratch rock and rock will not scratch glass.	feldspar
7	Scratches glass easily	quartz
8	Scratches quartz easily	topaz
9	Scratches topaz easily	corundum
10	Scratches all other rocks	diamond

This is one of several pages that list activities related to the identification of rocks. If you skim across the pages in this section, you can choose one or more of the other activities in which to engage your students.

Here is another example. Suppose you are looking for an activity that would help students understand the science content standard that expresses that water washes away topsoil.

If you look up in the Index Guide the word *erosion*, you will find several possible subtopics listed.

Erosion
    glacial, 142.24–25
    plant, 141.18, 142.28
    prevention of, 242.02
    temperature, 141.08b, 142.26–27
    water, 142.17–23
    wave, 142.23, 152.16–17
    wind, 142.05–06

The most suitable reference to your idea might be subtopic *water 142.17–23*. Look up the numerical reference in the Entry section, and you will find many activities, one or several of which are applicable to your particular situation and goal.

Observing how rain carries away soil. 17 Aa
Fill several flower pots or cans with loose soil until the soil is just level with the edges. Place some small stones or bottle caps on the surface of the soils and set the containers outside or in a sink. Water them with a watering can to represent rain, gradually increasing the flow. When finished, let students notice how the unprotected soil is splashed away, leaving columns of soil under the stones. After a rain, have students look for the same effect in an unplanted area.

When you locate a numerical reference, you will see that the scientific content is clearly stated as *Contributing Idea*. In the erosion example, you will find *Contributing Idea C: Water carries and deposits materials*. When you look at the subsequent activities 142.18–22, you will find many more ideas concerning erosion by water.

Thus the activities listed for Contributing Idea C relate to the common content that water washes away topsoil. Yet each activity is different in terms of possible experiences for students. Students may observe how rain carries away soil (entry 142.17), collect samples of waterborne materials (entry 142.18), observe how water-carried materials are deposited (entry 142.19), and so forth. Note that the activities are generally sequenced from simple to complex or from directly experienced to abstract. Such sequencing will help you identify the most appropriate activity for your students.

Also note that if you glance over the total structure of this section, other contributing ideas will provide you with additional related activities that might be useful. The other ideas may suggest preliminary experiences that you might not have thought about. Or they might suggest branching experiences for further exploration.

There is another aspect of this book that you will find useful. You probably noticed the letters beneath the activity numbers. These letters indicate the major problem-solving and thinking processes that are part of the activity. The letters are a simple code that is outlined inside the cover of this book. For example, the letter *A* indicates the various sensory observations students will make during the activity:

Aa = looking and seeing
Ab = touching and feeling
Ac = hearing and listening
Ad = smelling
Ae = tasting (within safety guidelines)
Af = multisensory, using several senses

When you use the chart of thinking processes, you will find that each corresponds to the thinking process that researchers have found are the ways by which humans naturally think when given a chance.

The letter codes are easy to remember and use. The sequence of the letters corresponds to developmental stages. The ability to observe begins early in our lives and continues as other abilities are added over time. Inferring (i.e., the thinking about things that are remote in time and space) begins with adolescence and takes many more years to fully develop.

Let us now examine how the thinking processes are a part of an activity. In the erosion example that you looked at earlier, you can see that below the activity numbers, the letter code tells you the major thinking students will do during each activity.

142.17 Aa   Students will observe erosion.
142.18 Ca and Ge   Students will collect and compare samples.
142.19 Ec   Students will test variables.

Contributing Idea C. Water carries and deposits materials.

Observing how rain carries away soil. **17 Aa**
Fill several flower pots or cans with loose soil until the soil is just level with the edges. Place some small stones or bottle caps on the surface of the soils and set the containers outside or in a sink. Water them with a watering can to represent rain, gradually increasing the flow. When finished, let students notice how the unprotected soil is splashed away, leaving columns of soil under the stones. After a rain, have students look for the same effect in an unplanted area.

Using this sourcebook is easy! Now enjoy enabling your students to learn science concepts through interesting hands-on experiences.

Features of This Sourcebook

This sourcebook is a thesaurus. In contrast to a dictionary or encyclopedia, which format content alphabetically, a thesaurus is a reference work that arranges its content according to conceptual similarities. Its purpose is to enable readers to find specific ideas and to see how the ideas relate to other ideas.

As a thesaurus of science concepts, this book provides easy access to science activities that teach science concepts that correspond to national standards. And it does much more because of the way the science content is organized.

Organization: Science Content

The Entry section of this book comprises a number of interlocking science content groupings organized by numerical code system. Entries are arranged in broad science categories to match the Standards. These are subdivided into topics, subtopics, and specific activities, all related to the content being taught.

Broad Science Content Categories

Six broad content categories are used to provide a framework for the Entry section—the main body of this book. Each of the content categories is coded by numerals in a decimal system.

100–199: Inorganic Matter

Matter, one of the two great divisions studied by scientists, includes all the materials that occupy space in the world around us. The scientist subdivides the materials into two kinds: inorganic and organic. Inorganic matter is the subdivision that comprises all nonliving materials (e.g., the rocks and minerals above and below the surface of the Earth). This content category includes such directly observable aspects as the physical and chemical properties of matter and the changes in the states of matter (i.e., solid, liquid, gas).

200–299: Organic Matter

The other subdivision of matter studied by scientists is organic matter. Organic matter is found in all living materials (e.g., the various forms of plants and animals). This content category contains entries that pertain to the directly observable physical and chemical properties of living organisms, their growth and response to environmental conditions, and the interrelationships among them.

300–399: Energy

Energy is the second great division studied by scientists. Energy means the ability to do work. This content category includes entries that pertain to the various forms of energy such as light, sound, and heat.

400–499: Inference Models

In scientific terms, a model is a theory that describes or explains a phenomenon that cannot be directly observed (e.g., atomic structures, the solar system). This fourth category contains entries that serve to explain phenomena and pertain to ideas derived through indirect means.

500–599: Technology and Engineering

Technology is the blend of science and invention that aims to increase productivity by rearranging the environment and producing goods. As such, technology is sometimes called *applied science* or *engineering*. This category contains entries pertaining to inventions (e.g., simple machines) developed from the application of scientific principles that, in turn, can be used to further understand basic scientific laws and principles.

600–699: Instructional Apparatus, Materials, and Systems

This sixth category contains entries dealing with the preparation of various materials useful in teaching science that have wide application throughout the content categories. This category includes such topics as techniques for cutting and bending of glass to making certain apparatus and construction plans for the construction of measuring devices (e.g., balance and spring scales).

The content numbering system is presented in the Table of Contents.
100 ← Inorganic Matter
200 ← Organic Matter
300 ← Energy
400 ← Inference Models
500 ← Technology and Engineering
600 ← Instructional Apparatus, Materials, and Systems

Topics

Each of the six broad science categories is divided into specialized topics. For example, the category *100 Inorganic Matter* is subdivided into six topics that are coded by the second numeral in the series of three numerals.

100 Inorganic Matter
  110 ← Solids
  120 ← Liquids
  130 ← Gases
  140 ← Earth Science
  150 ← Oceans
  160 ← Weather

Subtopics

Within the topical categories, scientific knowledge is subdivided into four subtopics.

1. Characteristics: This subtopic contains knowledge that relates to the characteristics or attributes of objects (e.g., size, shape, color, texture, and so on). Generally, this knowledge is descriptive of physical properties of objects.
2. Interactions: This second subtopic contains interactive knowledge. Such knowledge describes causes and effects between and among objects.
3. Theory: The third subtopic contains knowledge that is speculative (e.g., theories and explanations for observed phenomena).
4. Applications: The final subtopic contains activities that are applications of knowledge.

These subtopics are identified by the third numeral in the series of three.

300 Energy
  340 Heat
    341 ← Characteristics
    342 ← Interactions
    343 ← Theory
    344 ← Applications

Knowledge of Characteristics

When we observe, compare, or organize our observations and then describe the results, we make statements such as "insects have three body parts and six legs," "sea water is salty," and "leaves are green." Observing, comparing, and organizing processes always produce information that is largely organizational in character. Objects are described for specific attributes that define them as members of a particular class or function: Fish have fins (class), birds have feathers (class), the flower is the part of the plant where seeds develop (function), and machines are devices that make work easier (function).

Knowledge of Interactions and Relationships

When we observe, compare, or organize objects to determine relationships between and among them, or when we determine the cause and effect of phenomena, we produce knowledge that is largely relational in character: Whales are mammals because they have internal skeletons, hair on their skin, glands that produce milk, and because they bear their young alive (relational); fungi live off animals, dead organic matter, and other plants (relational); adding heat to solids causes them to expand (interactive); and the direction of an object's motion is a straight line unless the object is acted on by other forces (interactive).

Inferential, or Theoretical Knowledge

Inferring is a thinking process that allows us to conceptualize ideas that are not directly observable. This process often leads to explanatory or predictive statements about objects or phenomena: All matter is composed of tiny particles in constant motion (inference); the Earth and other planets revolve around the Sun (inference); cross pollination of particular plants will produce particular results (prediction); and given the rate of water flow from the pipe, we calculate a loss of 4,000 gallons by 7 a.m. (predictive).

Applied Knowledge

Inventing, problem solving, and determining probabilities are ways of using knowledge that leads to further knowledge. To a great extent, usage and invention-technology principles are representative of the knowledge statements obtained from applying knowledge. Some examples are the following: Instruments that are run by heat energy can be built to do work (invention-technology), the electromagnet is an instrument that can be used in the operation of many electrical systems (invention-technology), the principles of sound can be incorporated into instruments to produce music (usage), and selective breeding of plants and animals that have desirable characteristics can cause these characteristics to occur more frequently in offspring (usage).

Applied ideas can also be organizational ideas: The scientist can develop taxonomy, or blueprint based upon a logical rationale, concerning the relationships among the objects or ideas comprising the taxonomy, while at the same time realizing that the arrangement is tentative. That is, the arrangement is one of many possible arrangements that may be changed based upon fresh insights.

Specific Activities

Specific activities are listed for each of the subtopics of knowledge. For example, the Earth Science topic *142 Interactions* includes activities that are listed sequentially and enumerated as decimals:

100 Inorganic Matter
  140 Earth Science

142 Interactions
    142.**01** ← Observing wind moving across soil
    142.**02** ← Observing how wind carries and deposits materials
    142.**03** ← Measuring the distances wind carries and deposits different materials
    142.**04** ← Collecting and comparing samples of wind-borne materials

Organization: Thinking Processes

An additional feature to the structure of this sourcebook is the identification of the thinking processes by which we derive knowledge. These processes are part of the nature of inquiry and are listed on the chart inside the cover of this book.

The thinking processes have been carefully selected to be appropriate to all fields of science, and they have been sequentially ordered to be compatible with developmental learning theory. In this book, each subsequent process in the listing is built upon and inclusive of the previous process. Thus each process is enhanced and continually used in more advanced and complex ways. Chart 1 inside the front cover of this book shows how the processes correspond with the developmental stages of students. This arrangement matches the suggested order of content outlined as *Benchmarks for Science Literacy* in Project 2061 and as documented in the *National Science Education Standards*.

The organization for the thinking processes uses a letter code system. Capital letters represent broad superordinate thinking-process categories. The first four categories tend to encompass process activities that are most appropriate for young students (preschool through grade three), while the latter three categories tend to be most appropriate for older students (grade four and above). The broad categories of thinking processes are the following:

    A ← Observing
    B ← Communicating
    C ← Comparing
    D ← Organizing
    E ← Relating
    F ← Inferring
    G ← Applying

Lowercase letters are used to represent more specific types of thinking related to the broad categories of processes:

    A Observing
      A**a** ← Seeing
      A**b** ← Feeling

Ac ← Hearing
Ad ← Smelling
Ae ← Tasting
Af ← Using Several Senses

Each activity in the Entry section is accompanied by the coded capital and lowercase letters indicating, respectively, the general thinking process and the specific thinking expected in the activity. For example, the letter code *Ec* indicates that the main purpose of the activity involves relating (*E*) and specifically requires the student to control and manipulate variables (*c*). Naturally, other science thinking processes and actions are required in any given activity. This code simply indicates the processes of greatest emphasis in an activity.

Every activity relates thinking processes to scientific knowledge. The arrangement of the processes suggests the best age levels at which to introduce particular scientific knowledge so that it can be learned in a meaningful way.

The following examples provide another view of the content and process structure of this sourcebook. The following section shows several pages from the Entry section. The topic for the examples is *350 Electricity*. Pages xxiv–xxvii show the content structure for the topic *without* the activities. From this you can see the logic to the Generalizations and Contributing Ideas that correspond to standards related to Electricity. Pages xxvii–xxxi show the content structure again but with the *thinking processes* added. These labels indicate what the activity is about. From this, you can see the relationship between how humans come to know something and the content that is derived from that experience.

Example 1
Content Organization Without Activities
Topic: Electricity

350   Electricity

351   Characteristics

Generalization: Electricity has identifiable characteristics.

Contributing Idea A: Electrical energy can be stationary (static electricity).

Contributing Idea B: Electrical energy can move (current electricity).

352   Interactions

Generalization I: Electricity is a form of energy produced by different sources.

    Contributing Idea A: Chemical reactions can be a source of electricity (electrochemical propagation).

    Contributing Idea B: Motion can be a source of electricity (mechanical propagation).

Generalization II: Current electricity produces a magnetic field.

    Contributing Idea A: An electric current carried by a wire produces a magnetic field around it.

    Contributing Idea B: A compass is an instrument that can be used to detect magnetic fields.

Generalization III: Current electricity moves when there is a complete circuit.

    Contributing Idea A: Current electricity can be detected.

    Contributing Idea B: A circuit is a continuous path through which electricity can move.

    Contributing Idea C: Current electricity takes the shortest and easiest circuit back to the place where it started.

    Contributing Idea D: Switches are used to open and close circuits.

Generalization IV: Current electricity travels through some materials better than others.

    Contributing Idea A: Some materials allow electricity to pass through them easily (conductors); other materials tend to block the movement of electricity (insulators).

    Contributing Idea B: Thinner wires have more resistance than thicker wires of the same material; longer wires have more resistance than shorter wires of the same material.

    Contributing Idea C: Some metals have more resistance to electricity than others.

    Contributing Idea D: Overloading a circuit with too many resistors can overheat the wires.

Generalization V: Current electricity can be controlled.

Contributing Idea A: Series circuits channel all the electricity through a single pathway; parallel circuits channel all the electricity through a main pathway and branching pathways.

Contributing Idea B: Electric cells can be arranged to produce different voltages.

Contributing Idea C: Switches can be used to control circuits and voltages easily and safely.

353   Theory

Generalization I: According to theory, all matter is made up of atoms that contain tiny particles of electricity.

Contributing Idea A: Atomic particles can be accumulated into electrical charges.

Contributing Idea B: Unlike electric charges attract; like electric charges repel.

Contributing Idea C: Models can be used to explain the movement of electrons.

Generalization II: Electrical energy can produce electromagnetic radiation.

Contributing Idea A: Electrical energy can produce heat and light.

Contributing Idea B: Electrical energy can produce radio waves.

354 Applications

Generalization I: A magnetic field is generated around a wire carrying electricity; the strength of the magnetic field can be increased or decreased several ways.

Contributing Idea A: The electromagnet is an instrument used in the operation of many electrical systems.

Contributing Idea B: Electric circuit breakers and door chimes can operate using electromagnets.

Generalization II: Many household appliances use highly resistant wires to produce heat and to control electric currents.

Contributing Idea: Highly resistant metal wires are commonly used to produce heat in such appliances as electric irons, toasters, and heaters.

The following example provides more detail about the features of this book. The example repeats a portion of the previous example but adds the descriptors for each of the content statements.

Example 2
Content–Process Organization
Topic: Electricity

350   **Electricity**

351   **Characteristics**

Generalization: Electricity has identifiable characteristics.

Contributing Idea A: Electrical energy can be stationary (static electricity).
- **01 Seeing, feeling, and hearing evidence of electrical charges**
- **02 Observing that rubbing charges some materials**
- **03 Determining what materials can produce electrical charges**
- **04 Determining that not all electrical charges are alike**

Contributing Idea B: Electrical energy can move (current electricity).
- **05 Generating a direct current**
- **06 Generating an alternating current**

352   **Interactions**

Generalization I: Electricity is a form of energy produced by different sources.

Contributing Idea A: Chemical reactions can be a source of electricity (electrochemical propagation).
- **01 Making an electric cell**
- **02 Producing electricity from a "wet" cell**
- **03 Producing electricity from a "dry" cell**

NATIONAL SCIENCE TEACHERS ASSOCIATION

354 Applications

Generalization I: A magnetic field is generated around a wire carrying electricity; the strength of the magnetic field can be increased or decreased several ways.

Contributing Idea A: The electromagnet is an instrument used in the operation of many electrical systems.

01 Studying the presence of a magnetic field produced by an electric current

02 Making an electromagnet

Contributing Idea B: Electric circuit breakers and door chimes can operate using electromagnets.

03 Building a simple circuit breaker

04 Building a simple electric bell

Generalization II: Many household appliances use highly resistant wires to produce heat and to control electric currents.

Contributing Idea: Highly resistant metal wires are commonly used to produce heat in such appliances as electric irons, toasters, and heaters.

05 Observing the application of the idea that a greater electrical resistance results in a greater production of heat

It is hoped that these features will be useful to researchers, curriculum developers, and others interested in not only the relationships among scientific knowledge but also how that knowledge can be learned.

Acknowledgments

In various ways, many friends and colleagues have contributed throughout the years to the gradual collection and classification of appropriate activities in this sourcebook. Countless teachers and classroom students have added to the collection by suggesting activities, testing activities, and providing refinements. A very loud thank you goes to those scores of individuals who contributed directly and indirectly in so many different ways.

Mathematicians have contributed to the metric measures in the activities in this book. Following their advice, some activities purposely do not give precise conversions to metric measures due to the intent of the activity. For example, sometimes the metric measure is rounded to an easily measured unit. Sometimes the ratios of sequential units are more important than precise equivalents. Another example: If an activity requires the measurement of 5 in., 10 in., and 15 in., the suggested metric measurements might be 10 cm, 20 cm, and 30 cm, because the second unit must be twice the first and the third unit must be three times the first. In addition, many industrial conversions are not yet clear. Although liter containers can substitute well for quart containers, gallon equivalents are not established among different industries. Thus a 10-gallon aquarium remains so until an industrial decision is made on an equivalent size. Finally, some of the activities have no metric equivalents because they would make the activities awkward and confusing. This is especially apparent for graphs and certain tables. Hopefully, all activities will eventually be presented in the metric system. Until then, this book tries to help the reader toward this end as much as possible.

Much appreciation also goes to the specialists who submitted activities and kept information scientifically accurate and classroom related. To the following science educators, thanks for years of fruitful professional interactions: Carl Berger, dean of education, University of Michigan; Jane Bowyer, dean of education, Mills College, California; Diane Conradson, professor of science education, California State University at San Jose; Lawrence Hovey, professor emeritus of science education, Texas Tech University; Professor Roger Johnson, University of Minnesota; Bill Leonard, professor emeritus of science education, Clemson University; Vince Mahoney, professor emeritus of science education, Iowa Wesleyan; Richard Merrill, director emeritus of science education, Mt. Diablo Unified School District, California.

And thanks to the following scientists who read portions of the manuscript, contributed current scientific knowledge, and corrected for accuracy: Stuart Bowyer, professor of astronomy, University of California at Berkeley; Gordon Chan, professor of marine ecology, College of Marin, California; Joseph Hancock Jr., professor of

Acknowledgments

plant pathology and environmental studies, University of California at Berkeley; Alan Friedman, director of astronomy, Lawrence Hall of Science, Berkeley, California; Robert Karplus, professor of physics, University of California at Berkeley; Richard White, professor of electrical engineering and computer sciences, University of California at Berkeley; Robert Stebbins, professor of zoology, University of California at Berkeley; Bonnie S. Wood, professor of biology, University of Maine at Presque Isle; Christine Anne Royce, associate professor of education, Shippensburg University; Eula Ewing Monroe, mathematics educator, Department of Teacher Education, Brigham Young University.

References

American Association for the Advancement of Science (AAAS). 1989. *Science for all Americans: Project 2061* report on goals in science, mathematics, and technology. Washington, DC: AAAS.

American Association for the Advancement of Science (AAAS). 1993. *Benchmarks for science literacy*. Washington, DC: AAAS.

National Commission on Excellence in Education. 1983. *A nation at risk: The imperative for educational reform.* Washington, DC.

National Research Council (NRC). 1996. *National science education standards.* National Academy of Science. Washington, DC: National Academies Press.

100–199
Inorganic Matter

110 Solids

111 Characteristics

Generalization I. Solid is one of three states of matter.

> *Contributing Idea.* Solids melt into liquids; liquids freeze into solids.

Observing melting and freezing (solid ↔ liquid). Caution: The procedure of melting solder or lead should be demonstrated by the teacher and not done by the students. With guidance and appropriate safety precautions, students can see solder or lead (fish weight) melt in a tin can held with pliers. After letting students describe what happens in each case, you might tell them that whenever a solid changes to a liquid, it is said to be melting. When each pan is removed from the heat and placed in a bowl of ice water, students will see the liquid change back to a solid. Tell them that this change is called freezing, even though the substance might not feel cold to the touch. You might want to demonstrate that some organic solids can also melt and freeze: a piece of paraffin; a cube of sugar; a pat of butter or margarine. **01 Aa Bb**

Determining the melting point of different solids. Students can harden some olive oil in a jar by placing it in a refrigerator for one day. When hard, set the jar of oil in a sunny place. As the oil starts to melt, tip the jar so that the students can take the oil's temperature. Have them record the melting point, then follow the same procedure using margarine, butter, lard, ice, and **02 Ce Da**

ice cream. The different materials can be seriated by their melting points.

Observing changes of state: ice (solid ↔ liquid). Have students watch ice cubes melt in dishes placed in different parts of the classroom. After seeing which melts fastest, students should try to explain why (usually the cause is heat). Challenge the students to bring a solid ice cube to school from home. (They will have to be inventive to keep it from melting.) Discuss factors that contributed to those that were brought successfully to school. Next, challenge students to devise ways to make ice cubes that are spherical, hollow, or various other shapes. They might discover that the shape (i.e., amount of surface area) influences the rate at which each melts. For controlled comparisons, differently shaped ice of equal volumes can be made by pouring equal amounts of water into paper cups with flat bottoms and pointed bottoms, various candy cups, cookie molds, round lids or covers, or tall cylinders. Set the frozen shapes on dishes in the same locations to keep temperature conditions the same. Students can record and compare the time it takes each to melt. **03 Aa Gb**

Generalization II. Solids have identifiable characteristics.

> *Contributing Idea A.* Our senses can be used to identify solids.

Seeing and describing some characteristics of some solids. The visual properties of objects that can be selected and **04 Aa Ba Ca**

controlled in instructional situations are size, shape, color, and pattern. Although students might begin with grossly different objects, fine discriminations can be later used to sharpen perceptual awareness. Fine discriminations might involve examination of closely matching lengths of sticks, serrations or venation of leaves, complex designs, or shades or tones of colors.

a. *Clue Given*: Show students a leaf. Have them find a matching leaf (on the basis of shape) from a collection of differently shaped leaves.

b. *Clue Given*: Buttons, coins, or other small objects can be glued to heavy cardboard. Ask students to find the two objects that are alike. Finer discriminations among the objects can be developed by selecting ones that are more closely alike.

c. *Clue Given*: String beads (identical in size and color but different in shape) on a string. Every time you string a bead, have a student string a matching one.

d. *Clue Not Given*: Prepare a collection of polished, colored stones of similar size (include two stones that are identical in color). Ask students to find the two that look the same on the basis of color.

e. *Clue Not Given*: Prepare a set of objects that vary in size but that are the same in shape and color.

Have students match identical objects by size.

Feeling and describing some characteristics of some solids. Tactile properties have the greatest range of instructional possibilities. Materials can be selected to emphasize such aspects as size, shape, or textures (e.g., roughness, stickiness, softness, sharpness, etc.). **05 Ab Ba Ca**

a. *Clue Given:* Prepare about eight squares of sandpaper, identical in size, but different in grade (i.e., roughness). Place the squares in a Feely Box (see Figure 111.05). Give students another square that matches the roughness of those in the box. Ask them to find the matching square. For finer discriminations, you might try using different grades of emery paper.

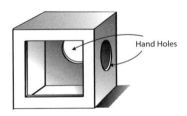

Hand Holes

Figure 111.05

b. *Clue Not Given:* Place about six wooden dowels of equal length but of different diameters within a Feely Box. Include two dowels of identical diameters. Have students use their sense of touch to locate the two that feel the most alike.

Hearing some characteristics of some solids. Sounds produced by certain solid objects are sometimes a characteristic of that object. The primary auditory properties are pitch, intensity, and rhythm.

06
Ac
Ba
Ca

  a. *Clue Given:* Have students listen as you play a single note on a musical instrument. Ask them to identify a matching note from a number of notes played in a series.

  b. *Clue Given:* Using a pencil, tap simple rhythms on a desk. After students listen to the rhythms with their eyes closed, have them use pencils to repeat the rhythm that you tapped.

  c. *Clue Not Given:* Before playing a series of seven notes on a musical instrument, ask students to listen and record the numbers of the two notes among the seven that sound alike. (You might have to repeat the series several times.)

  d. *Clue Not Given:* Record various household sounds. As students listen to the recording, let them describe the characteristics of each sound before identifying the object that makes the sound (e.g., ticking clock, turning egg beater, vacuum cleaner, washing machine).

Smelling some characteristics of some solids. Our sense of smell is not as acute as that of many other animals, and smells are generally described by naming a

07
Ad

potential source of the smell (e.g., It smells like a skunk; It has a mint smell).

  a. *Clue Given:* Place six to eight bars of differently scented soaps into different containers. The bars should be identical in size and shape, and wrapped so that they cannot be distinguished on the basis of color. Place one more bar matching one of the scents in another container and ask students to find, by smelling, the matching container within the set.

  b. *Clue Not Given:* Wrap differently scented candles that are identical in size and shape. Place six to eight into boxes or cans. Add one additional box containing a candle that matches one of the others on the basis of its smell. Mix the boxes and ask students to find the two that smell alike.

Tasting some characteristics of some solids. Generally our sense of taste is influenced by our sense of smell. Other than the basic tastes of sweet, sour, bitter, and salty, flavors become complex combinations interwoven with our sense of smell. **Caution: Tasting unknown materials can be dangerous. Warn students against this practice, and let them discuss reasons for the caution.**

08
Ae
Ba
Ca

  a. *Clue Given:* Give each student his or her own set of four small cups containing salt water, sugar water, quinine water, and water with lemon juice. Hand each student a fifth cup containing a liquid that matches in flavor one of those in the other four cups. Have the student find the matching flavor.

b. *Clue not given:* Blindfold students. Let them taste four or five different foods (e.g., slice of lemon, cherry, orange, lime, pineapple). Next, give each a hard candy that matches one of the previous flavors. Ask students to identify which of the previous flavors it matches.

Contributing Idea B. Indicators can be used to identify solids.

Using indicators to identify unknown solid materials. Various tests can be performed on known materials to see what reactions take place. Unknown materials can then be compared to known materials for similarities. Such tests serve as indicators that show the presence of known materials. To introduce students to some simple indicators, prepare five numbered envelopes for each student or for small groups of students. In each envelope, place 1 tsp. (5 ml) of the following materials:

- **Envelope 1.** Granular dextrose or glucose (available at drugstores) Note: Ordinary sugar cannot be used. It contains a small amount of starch to keep it from caking. It will not produce satisfactory results in Tests 1–5.

- **Envelope 2.** Powdered starch (available at grocery stores)
- **Envelope 3.** Baking soda (available at grocery stores)
- **Envelope 4.** An equal mixture of dextrose (or glucose) and starch
- **Envelope 5.** An equal mixture of dextrose (or glucose) and baking soda

Have students place one teaspoon (5 ml) each from the numbered envelopes 1, 2, and 3 on a piece of waxed or foil paper. Let them describe the materials without naming them using sight, touch, smell, but *not* by taste. **Caution: Tasting unknown materials can be dangerous. Any tasting must be done by following safety guidelines.** Observations can be recorded on a table, similar to Table 111.09 (p. 6). Have students discuss limitations of the senses in trying to identify materials. When finished, the materials can be named. Now give students numbered envelopes 4 and 5. Tell them they are mysteries to be solved. Each contains a mixture of two of the known materials. Students can then perform the following tests and record their observations. When finished, they can deduce what materials make up the mystery mixtures.

Test 1—Water as an indicator.

Water dissolves some solid materials. Students can fill three test tubes half-full with water, put 1 level tsp. (5 ml) of the known materials in them, shake the tubes

Table 111.09. Identifying the Characteristics of Solid Materials

Material	Sight	Touch	Smell	Other
1. sugar				
2. starch				
3. baking soda				
4. unknown				
5. unknown				

to mix the materials, allow them to stand for a few minutes, and record observations. Students need not agree on descriptive words. It is best to let each record in his or her own terms. Next, test the mystery mixtures and record findings.

Test 2—Heat as an indicator.

Heat melts or burns some solid materials sooner than others. Students can put 1 level tsp. (5 ml) of each of the known materials into three dry test tubes. Holding them with a test tube holder, heat over a flame by moving the tube in a small circular motion to distribute the heat evenly. **Caution: Keep the open end of the test tube pointed away from faces and other people.** Record observations, and then repeat the test using the mixtures.

Test 3—Iodine as an indicator.

Iodine, available at drugstores, indicates the presence of starch by turning a blue-black color. Students can put 1 level tsp. (5 ml) of each known material into dry test tubes or place materials in three piles on a piece of waxed or foil paper. Using an eyedropper, put a few drops of iodine solution on each material. Record observations, and then test the mystery mixtures. **Caution: Iodine solution is poisonous and stains are difficult to remove. Have students wash their hands after using it.** A dilute solution of sodium thiosulfate, available at drugstores, in water can be used to remove stains. Students can use the iodine to test for the presence of starch in various other materials, such as slices of apple, bread, candy, potato, banana, butter, and cheese.

Test 4—Vinegar as an indicator.

Vinegar (white or red) indicates the presence of a carbonate by bubbling and fizzing. Students can put 1 level tsp. (5 ml) of each of the known materials into three dry test tubes or in three piles on waxed or foil paper. Add a few drops of vinegar to each with a clean eyedropper. Record observations, and then test the mystery materials. Vinegar is acetic acid and reacts in the presence of a carbonate by releasing carbon dioxide gas. Students can use vinegar to test various other materials, such as slices of apple, flour, ground chalk, limestone rock, marble rock, bones, egg shells, or sea shells.

Test 5—Benedict's solution as an indicator.

Benedict's solution (or Fehling's solution, both available at drugstores) indicates the presence of simple sugars (sucrose or dextrose). (Note: It does not react to complex sugars such as table sugar.) Demonstrate this indicator by placing 1 level tsp. (5 ml) of each known material into dry test tubes. Add one-half tube of water and 10 drops of the Benedict's solution. Heat gently, holding the mouth of the tube away from yourself and others. Students will see the color change from blue to green to yellow to orange to brick red, depending upon the concentration of sugar present. Next, test the mystery mixtures for the presence of sugar.

Using their own version of Table 111.09 as a guide, students can now deduce the materials that make up materials in envelopes 4 and 5. Following this experience, other materials can be tested in similar ways: try powdered plaster of paris; granulated sugar; biscuit, pancake, or cake mixes; powdered milk; flour; powdered potatoes. After characteristics are identified, mixtures can provide new mysteries to solve.

Contributing Idea C. Some solids can be identified by their shapes.

Examining the shapes of crystals. **10** **Aa** Enlarge, reproduce, and distribute a set **Ba** of the basic crystalline shapes as shown **Ca** in Figures 111.10a through 111.10g (pp. 8–9). If possible, provide samples of actual crystals. When the shapes are cut out, their tabs can be glued. Have the students sort the completed shapes by similarities and differences. They can also count the number and types of surfaces (sides) and corners (angles) on each. A table, such as Table 111.10 (p. 10) but without the columns filled in, could be used to guide observations. Students will find that each crystal has a definite shape, a certain number of flat surfaces, sharp edges, and pointed corners.

Contributing Idea D. Some solids dissolve and some do not.

Testing the solubility of different solids. **11** **Db** Obtain a variety of solid materials **Ec** such as sugar cubes, marbles, salt, nails, soil, coins, or soap. Place a small amount of each into glasses or jars of water. Stir or shake the contents, and let stand for several minutes. Students can categorize the materials that dissolve (e.g., sort the materials in terms of those that dissolve, those that do not, those that partially dissolve). Similar tests can be performed using warmer water.

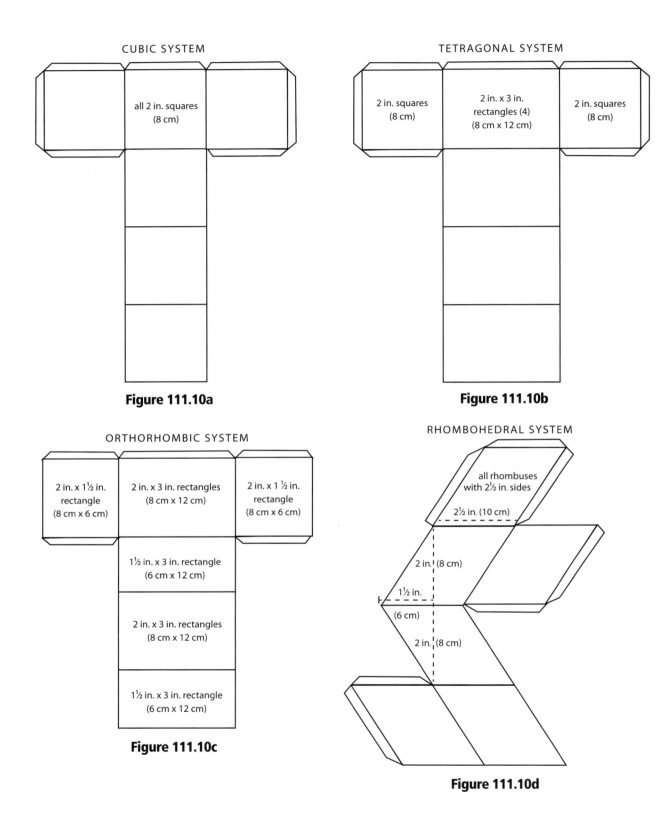

CUBIC SYSTEM

all 2 in. squares
(8 cm)

Figure 111.10a

TETRAGONAL SYSTEM

2 in. squares
(8 cm)

2 in. x 3 in.
rectangles (4)
(8 cm x 12 cm)

2 in. squares
(8 cm)

Figure 111.10b

ORTHORHOMBIC SYSTEM

2 in. x 1½ in.
rectangle
(8 cm x 6 cm)

2 in. x 3 in. rectangles
(8 cm x 12 cm)

2 in. x 1 ½ in.
rectangle
(8 cm x 6 cm)

1½ in. x 3 in. rectangle
(6 cm x 12 cm)

2 in. x 3 in. rectangles
(8 cm x 12 cm)

1½ in. x 3 in. rectangle
(6 cm x 12 cm)

Figure 111.10c

RHOMBOHEDRAL SYSTEM

all rhombuses
with 2½ in. sides

2½ in. (10 cm)

2 in. (8 cm)

1½ in.
(6 cm)

2 in. (8 cm)

Figure 111.10d

MONOCLINIC SYSTEM

Figure 111.10e

HEXAGONAL SYSTEM

Figure 111.10g

TRICLINIC SYSTEM

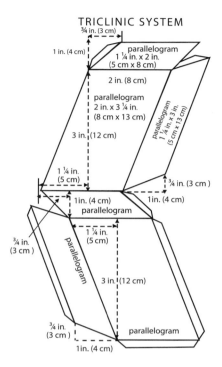

Figure 111.10f

Contributing Idea E. Solids occupy space and have weight.

Observing that solids occupy space. **12** **Aa** Half-fill a glass of water and mark the level on the glass. Place a rock, marble, nail, or other object into the water so that it is submerged. Let students note how far the water level rises. They will realize that the solid object has taken up some space in the glass and has pushed some of the water out of the way. To measure solid objects by displacement, see entry 122.23.

Measuring solid objects by size and **13** **weight.** Have students measure the dimen- **Cd** sions of a variety of objects such as blocks **Cf** of wood, desktops, or doors. Be sure they

Table 111.10. Examining the Shapes of Crystals

Type	Number of Surfaces	Shape of Surfaces	Crystalline Examples
Cubic	Six	All are square.	alum, pyrite, garnets, gold, sodium chloride, silver, diamond
Tetragonal	Six	Four are rectangles. Two are squares. Corner angles are right angles.	white tin, zircon
Orthorhombic	Six	All are rectangles. Three pairs of rectangles, each pair a different size. Corner angles are right angles.	topaz, Epsom salt, rhombic sulfur
Rhombohedral	Six	All are rhombuses (i.e., equilateral parallelograms). No right angles.	calcite
Monoclinic	Six	Four are rectangles. Two are parallelograms. Sixteen angles are right angles. Eight angles are not right angles.	sugar, gypsum, borax
Triclinic	Six	All are parallelograms. No right angles at corners.	boric acid, copper sulfate
Hexagonal	Eight	Two are regular hexagons. Six are rectangles. Angles of rectangles are right angles.	ice, ruby, sapphire, quartz, emerald, apatite

measure the objects in each dimension. After they have practiced, challenge students to measure objects such as pieces of a jigsaw puzzle, a jack, or a marble. Ask in what other way objects can be measured (by weight). Students can practice weighing objects on an equal arm balance scale. Let them keep records of the objects measured or weighed and seriate the objects by size or weight.

Contributing Idea F. Nearly all solids expand when heated and contract when cooled.

Observing that solids expand and contract when heated and cooled. Have **14 Aa** students find metal washers made of different materials (e.g., steel, copper, iron) that will just fit through the mouth of a glass bottle. Hold each washer with a pair of pliers and heat it over a flame until it is very hot. Now try to drop the washer through the mouth of the bottle. Students will realize that each washer expands from the heat and will not pass through the mouth. Cool the washers with water or an ice cube to let students see that the washers contract and again fit into the bottle. Students can also note the spaces in concrete walks, bridges, and railroad tracks to see how the structures have been prepared to take care of expansion.

Contributing Idea G. Some solids conduct heat better than others.

Sensing that solids conduct heat. Have **15 Ab** students fill a glass with very hot water, place a spoon from kitchen cutlery into it, and hold the end of the spoon for a few minutes to feel it increase in temperature. Students will realize that the heat has been transferred from the water and conducted through the spoon. Let them test other solid objects in the same way and compare how well each conducts the heat.

Contributing Idea H. Some solids transmit sounds better than others.

Listening to sound through solid materials. Have a student hold a wristwatch in his or her hand at a distance of about 5 ft. (2 m) from another student. Let the first student gradually bring it closer until the ticking can be heard by the second student. Measure the distance between the students. Repeat with other individuals. Next, place the face of the watch at one end of a board, and have the students take turns listening. Move the watch toward a student until he or she hears the ticking. Measure this distance and compare it with the earlier measurements. Students can discuss what happens to the volume of sounds when they are transmitted through a solid substance. Try this again using other solid materials. Compare differences. **16 Ac Cd**

Contributing Idea I. Some solids respond to magnetic forces, and some do not.

Magnetizing some solids. Obtain some short hard steel rods from a hardware store, and have students stroke one end of each with one end of a magnet (about 50 times) from the center to the tip of the steel. Stroke the other end of the steel rod with the other end of the magnet in the same way. When finished, test for magnetism in the steel rod by using it to pick up tacks, paper clips, or pins. Have students test other solid objects to see if they can be magnetized. **17 Gc**

Testing the transparency of some solids to magnetism. Have students pick up different objects with a magnet, then place a sheet of paper between the magnet and the objects and try again. Test various thicknesses of the paper (i.e., add more sheets) to see what limit there is to the magnetic force. Students can test other materials to see which allow the magnetic force to pass through. **18 Ec**

Generalization III. Solids can be classified on the basis of their physical characteristics.

Contributing Idea A. Some characteristics of solids can be seriated.

Seriating solid objects by sight. Have students order or sequence objects on the basis of shape (e.g., one-sided to **19 Aa Da** many-sided), size (e.g., small to large), or color (e.g., light to dark). Collections of insects, rocks, leaves, etc. can also be seriated. Have students give rationales for the arrangements they make.

Seriating solid objects by touch. Students can use a Feely Box (see entry 111.05) to order samples of papers by their textures (e.g., smooth to coarse), nails by their sizes (e.g., short to long, or small to large), bags of sand by their weights (light to heavy), and so forth. When finished, give them another object, and have them place it in the series they have arranged. **20 Ab Da**

Contributing Idea B. Some characteristics of solids can be classified.

Classifying solid objects by sight. Give students an assortment of buttons. Tell them to sort them in any way they wish. Some may group them by color, size, shape, or other characteristic; some may use combinations of characteristics. Let the students give a rationale for their arrangement and share the different ways of sorting. Stress that none of the ways is incorrect; all are correct as long as the buttons are sorted on the basis of some rationale. When finished, take the groupings apart, and have them regrouped on another basis. This activity can be repeated using mixtures of breakfast foods, parquetry blocks, or natural objects such as rocks or leaves. **21 Aa Dc**

Classifying solid objects by touch. **22**
Prepare a Feely Box (see entry 111.05). **Ab**
Let students sort objects that might be **Dc**
grouped in more than one way. For example, if the certain objects were placed in
the box, a student might group them by
shape (e.g., all circles in one pile, squares
in another, etc.). When finished, let the
students give their rationales, then take
the groupings apart and ask the students
to group them again but in a different
way. This time they might be grouped by
size, for example.

Classifying solid objects on the basis **23**
of tests. Indicators can be used to test the **Bb**
properties of some solid objects, and the **Dc**
objects can be grouped by the way they **Ec**
react (e.g., dissolve versus do not dissolve; acid, neutral, or alkaline). Other
tests pertaining to the strength of solids
can be tried as follows:

    a. Students can roll sheets of paper
into a tube, holding the tube
together with a piece of tape.
Stand the tube on a bathroom scale
and push straight down on it with
a hardback book to see how hard
they must push before the paper
crumples (Figure 111.23a). Students can experiment by rolling
skinny, fat, square, triangular, and
rectangular tubes. They can try
several tubes at once to see if quantity makes a difference. Let them
keep records of their judgments.

They can test and classify objects
on the basis of findings (e.g., weak
versus strong). You might tell
them that the measurement of a
solid's ability to withstand crushing is called compression strength.
Finally, give them two challenges:
(1) ask them to find and discuss
pictures of human-made structures that make use of columns for
support; (2) ask them to test if it
takes twice as much compression
to collapse two tubes half the size
of one tube.

Figure 111.23a

    b. Students can cut ¾ in. × 8 in.
(2 cm × 20 cm) strips of different
papers. Make loops of the strips
and hold them in place with glue
or a piece of tape. Attach a strong
rubber band to the top of a ruler
with a tack. From the band, hang
a paper clip. Note where the lower
end of the paper clip is on the
ruler; then attach one of the loops
and slowly pull it downward until

it breaks (Figure 111.23b). When it breaks, have students record how far the paper clip moved.

Rubber Band

Bent Paper Clip

Ruler

Loop of Paper

Tape

Figure 111.23b

Repeat the test for other loops of paper to see which is the strongest and which is weakest. Students can sequence or classify papers on the basis of strength or compare brands advertised on television to see if strength claims are correct. You might tell them that the measurement of a solid's ability to withstand breaking is called tensile strength. To extend this activity, cut ¾ in. × 8 in. (2 cm × 20 cm) strips of different shapes but from the same kind of paper (Figure 111.23c). Students can guess where each strip will break when pulled, and then check their

guesses by pulling the strips apart by tugging on the ends. Finally, ask students to find pictures of manufactured structures that make use of strands for strength (e.g., cable supports on bridges).

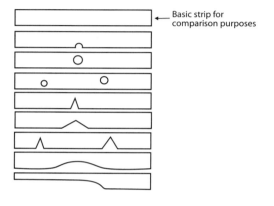

Basic strip for comparison purposes

Figure 111.23c

112   Interactions

Generalization. Certain dissolvable and colloidal solid materials can pollute water and air.

> *Contributing Idea A.* Some solids dissolve in water, and some do not.

Observing some solids that dissolve. **01** After students examine the characteristics **Aa** of solid pieces of salt and sugar with a hand lens, let them place 1 tsp. (5 ml) of each in different jars of water. (The materials will dissolve.) Next, set the jars in the sunlight or near a heat source to allow the water to evaporate. When the water has evaporated, the students can examine the solid materials again with a hand lens. They will realize that water can contain unseen, dissolved solid materials. Encourage them to test other solid materials to see which dissolve and which do not.

Contributing Idea B. Solid impurities can pollute water.

Detecting solids in water. Students can collect running water from a stream or gutter after a rainfall. Set the water in a widemouthed shallow pan, and allow the water to evaporate. Examine the residue with a hand lens to see what materials the water was carrying. Identify any manufactured materials found. **02 Aa**

Comparing the effects of some solids upon water. Obtain several jars with lids. Place a small amount of various solid materials into the jars (e.g., salt, sugar, coffee, soap, pieces of food). Label each jar for its contents, and then cover the jars. After several days, open the jars, and let students smell, feel, and look at the contents. They can discuss how some materials readily pollute the water. **03 Af Ca**

Contributing Idea C. Solid impurities can pollute air.

Detecting solids in air. Students can make devices for collecting airborne particles in several ways: **04 Bc Ca**

    a. Coat baby food jars with petroleum jelly, set them inside large cans, and suspend or place them in various locations. Particles will adhere to the petroleum jelly, and

the cans will protect the jars from ground dirt.

    b. Bend a heavy wire, such as a coat hanger, into the shape in Figure 112.04a. In the lower loop of the wire, fasten a strip of tape to write on. To the sticky side of the tape, fasten a glass slide that has been thinly coated on one side with petroleum jelly. Hang the device somewhere for several weeks. This device can be weighed before and then weighed after several weeks when particles have collected. The area of the exposed surface and the accumulated weight can be computed to indicate the amount deposited per square mile (kilometer).

    Wire
    Tape
    Glass slide

Figure 112.04a

    c. Cut a 2 in. × 6 in. (5 cm × 15 cm) strip of heavy tag board and fold it lengthwise. Punch five holes through one side of the tag with a standard hole punch. Place a long strip of transparent tape, sticky

Figure 112.04b

side up, on a flat surface and set the tag on the tape so that the sticky surface shows through each hole (Figure 112.04b). Make the strip of tape longer than the tag so that the top half can be sealed over the lower half to keep particles from adhering to the tape before it is ready for use. The device can also be placed in an envelope to protect it further. Students can expose one or more of the devices to the air in different locations. The exposure time and location of sampling can be recorded for each device along with other conditions such as the relative wind velocity or number of days since the last rainfall. Samples can be taken in a variety of places (e.g., indoors, on windowsills, or outdoors, in trees, on porches, etc.) and in different positions (e.g., high, low, horizontal, vertical). A table such as Table 112.04 can be helpful in organizing observations. Students can determine the hours of the day or the days of the week when most pollution occurs, the area in which most pollution is collected, and the amount produced by people or natural means. Students can also examine the collected particles with hand lenses or identify the particles under the low power of a microscope. Let students discuss how pollution might be reduced.

Observing particles being added to the air. Have students collect pictures of factories, furnaces, fireplaces, and so on, that spew smoke into the air. Have students identify such contributors in their hometown, discuss the problems that are created by such pollution, and plan how the problems might be solved.

05
Aa

Table 112.04 Detecting Air Pollution

Location	Time Exposed	Description of Particles	Amount of Pollution

120 Liquids

121 Characteristics

Generalization I. Liquid is one of three states of matter.

Contributing Idea. Liquids evaporate into gases when heated; gases condense into liquids when cooled.

Observing evaporation (liquid → gas). **01** **Aa** **Bb**
Have some students keep a daily check on the water level of a room aquarium or other container filled with water. Others can mix paints with water, paint a picture, and check its wetness several hours later. You might explain that the term used to describe what happened is *evaporation*.

Graphing evaporation rates. Students **02** **Bf** can measure how fast a liquid evaporates from a material by hanging a wet piece of the material from an arm balance. Balance the arm and observe at regular intervals. As the water evaporates, the material end of the balance arm will rise. At the regular intervals students can rebalance the arm and keep track of how many units it takes to balance the arm each time. When the material is dry, the data can be graphed as shown in Graph 121.02. To extend this experience, test and graph other materials or make tests to speed up the evaporation (e.g., fanning, heating). Different graphs can be compared and generalizations can be made.

DETERMINING EVAPORATION RATES

Graph 121.02

Observing condensation (liquid ← gas). **03** **Aa** **Bb**
Fill a quart or liter jar with ice water, let it stand out in the room, and have students observe the moisture that collects on the outside of the jar. Add some food coloring or ink to the water in the jar, and they will realize that because the moisture on the outside is clear, it probably did not come through the glass. Students can also exhale against the glass and watch the moisture form. Tell them what they observed is called condensation. You might make analogies to common phenomena such as the formation of moisture on mirrors and windows.

Generalization II. Liquids have identifiable characteristics.

Contributing Idea A. Our senses can be used to identify liquids.

Observing some physical characteristics of some liquids. Students can com- **04** **Af** pare and describe the appearance of separate jars of water obtained from different sources (e.g., pond, lake, sea, or stream water; distilled water; tap water). Note the colors and materials in the waters. Similarly, small quantities of various liquids (e.g., orange juice, tomato juice, apple juice, etc.) can be placed into clear glasses and compared using other senses, such as smell and touch. Or several liquids with similar appearance but of different densities and viscosities (e.g., white syrup, mineral oil) can be put in identical jars for students to observe characteristics other than color.

Feeling some characteristics of liquids. **05 Ab Ba** The sense of touch can be used to explore the properties of liquids by having students feel various liquids (e.g., alcohol, water, shampoo, molasses) with their fingers. Students can describe what they feel to develop useful vocabulary words (e.g., wet, sticky, slippery).

Comparing liquids by taste. **06 Ae Ca** Have students taste various liquids (e.g., sugar water, salt water, lemon juice, quinine water). **Caution: Students should be made aware of the danger in tasting unknown liquids.** Group the liquids by similarities in taste or classify them by the following headings: sweet, sour, salty, and bitter. Taste other liquids and add them to the classifications.

Contributing Idea B. Indicators can be used to identify liquids.

Using litmus paper to identify liquids. **07 Fb** Obtain some blue and red litmus paper.

Have students first use the blue litmus paper to test different liquids such as water, orange juice, lemonade, and vinegar. Let them also test as many other liquids as possible, making one list of the liquids that changed the color of the litmus paper and a second list of the liquids that did not change the color. Retest the same liquids using the red litmus paper and make new lists. When students compare the lists, they will discover substances that turn the blue litmus paper red do not affect the red litmus paper and vice versa. They will also discover the neutrality of water. (Also see entry 121.24.)

Contributing Idea C. Liquids generally take the shape of their container.

Describing the shape of liquids. **08 Ba** Pour some water into a tall container and ask students to observe and describe the shape of the water. Pour the water from the container into a low, flat container; ask for another description, then pour the water into a third, dissimilar container. From their descriptions, students can generalize that water has no shape of its own.

Contributing Idea D. Some liquids have the ability to dissolve certain other materials; some materials dissolve in liquids and some do not.

Identifying materials that dissolve in liquids. **09 Aa Bc** Fill four beakers each with ½ c. (100 ml) of water. Let students put 1 level tsp. (5 ml) of different materials (e.g., sugar, salt, iron filings, dirt) into different beakers. (Note: A level spoonful can be obtained by scraping off any excess with the edge of a ruler.) Separate spoons should be used to stir each beaker. Stir thoroughly and observe the contents. (Some materials will "disappear" or dissolve; some will remain visible.) Test other materials to see which dissolve and which do not. Students can compile lists under such headings as "dissolves," "partially dissolves," and "does not dissolve." Let them test other liquids.

Contributing Idea E. Liquids occupy space and have weight.

Determining that liquids occupy space and have weight. Obtain two empty half-pint (half-liter) milk cartons. Ask students to fill the cartons with a liquid such as water. Hang the cartons from an arm balance and adjust until it balances. Let one student hold an empty container under one carton and, with a small nail, puncture the bottom of the carton. As the water runs out, students will observe a change in the balance and realize that the water has weight.

10 Cf

Contributing Idea F. Nearly all liquids expand when heated and contract when cooled.

Comparing the expansions of different liquids. Fit three or four bottles with one-hole rubber stoppers. Place 12 in. (30 cm) lengths of glass tubing in each

11 Cd

stopper. Fill each bottle completely with a different liquid (e.g., water, alcohol, liquid detergent). Place the stoppers into the bottles so that some of each liquid rises in each tube. With a medicine dropper, add some liquid to the tubes making the liquids equal in height. Mark the heights with a piece of thread, string, or rubber band. Immerse the bottles in a large pan of hot water. Students can observe the rise of the liquids inside the tubes and make some judgments about the differences in expansion. Next, place the same bottles in a pan of ice cubes, and observe them again. (The liquids will contract and their height in the tubes will be below the markers.) Students can compare the contractions.

Contributing Idea G. Liquids have surface tension.

Comparing the shapes of droplets of different liquids. Using various liquids such as water, honey, cooking oil, and alcohol, have students compare the appearances of single drops of each on waxed paper. (From the side, drops approximate a hemisphere.) Students can make profile charts (Graphs 121.12a and 121.12b, p. 20) of what they see. Two drops of the same liquid can be pushed together with a pin or toothpick. Results can be compared with the action between two drops of water. Students will notice that there is a tendency for each liquid to pull in its open surface so that the surface

12 Bb Be Ca

PROFILE CHARTS

Graph 121.12a   **Graph 121.12b**

is as small as possible. Tell them that this characteristic is called surface tension.

Picturing the shapes of droplets on different surfaces. Have students experiment with different nonabsorbent surfaces (e.g., aluminum foil, glass, paraffin, waxed paper) to see what effect each has on the shapes of drops. Profile charts as suggested in the previous activity can be made and used for descriptive comparisons.

**13
Be
Ec**

Observing surface tension in soap films. Make various copper wire forms such as in Figure 121.14. Have students dip the forms into a thick soap solution. (Place 4 level tsp., or 20 ml, of soap flakes or powder into 4 c., or 1 L of hot water. Let stand for several days before using.) As the wire forms are withdrawn from the solution, the students can observe the films that stretch between the wires. Repeated dipping can cause more than one film to form. Students can observe the shapes and behaviors of the films, then state explanations for any regularities they see. (Note: If a slider is attached to the

**14
Aa**

square form (Figure 121.14h), the slider can be pulled gently, and the film will be stretched. When the slider is released, it will be pulled back by the strength of the surface tension.) Students can be encouraged to invent other wire forms.

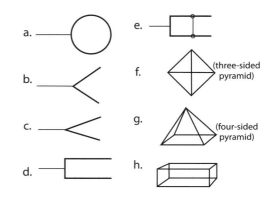

a.

b.

c.

d.

e.

f. (three-sided pyramid)

g. (four-sided pyramid)

h.

Figure 121.14

Observing that the surface of a liquid acts like a skin and can support weight. The surface tension of water can be used to float some objects that would normally sink. Each of the following activities can be done using different liquids, although water is used for descriptive purposes. If various liquids are tried, comparisons can be made.

**15
Aa
Ca**

    a. A student with a steady hand can, from a very low height, drop a paper clip or needle upon the surface of some water in a widemouthed glass or similar container. The object will seem to float on the surface. (Actually it will be supported by the surface tension.) Students can observe the skinlike surface bending under the weight of the object.

b. A student can float a piece of tissue paper upon some water, then carefully place an object to be floated upon the paper without sinking it. As the paper absorbs the water, it becomes heavy and sinks, leaving the object at rest on the surface.

c. Objects can be gently lowered onto the surface of some water with the aid of a fork or bent paper clip.

Observing that surface tension allows liquids to build up without overflowing. Each of the following activities can be tried with different liquids. **16 Aa**

a. Give each student a small paper cup, a medicine dropper, and a glass of water. Ask each student to put as much water into the cup as he or she can without having it overflow. Students will find that the water will rise considerably higher than the rim of the cup. Let them describe and discuss what they see. (The surface seems to have a skinlike appearance.) A sheet of dark paper held behind each cup will improve the observations.

b. Students can fill paper cups with water until the water is level with the edge. Using medicine droppers, they can find out how many drops of water it takes to make the level cups of water overflow. As drops are added, have them observe the rise of the water above the edge.

Making and using a tensiometer. Students can realize, in a physical sense, the concept of surface tension by preparing a paper device called a tensiometer. The tensiometer is made by cutting and folding a piece of wrapping paper (Figure 121.17a). Thoroughly moisten the base of the device (keeping the stem dry), and bring its lower edge close to the surface of a liquid such as water. Students will see the base being drawn to the water. The student holding the device will sense a definite "pull." Other students can make tensiometers and test the pull of various liquids in the following ways. **17 Bf Ga Gc**

a. Attach tensiometers to one end of an equal-arm balance. The base of each tensiometer should rest horizontally (i.e., flat) on the surface of

10 in. (20 cm)

2 in. (4 cm)

3 in. (6 cm)

Figure 121.17a

the liquid in a container. Students can count how many washers or other units of measurement it takes to pull the tensiometer from the surface (Figure 121.17b). (Note: With repeated trials the number of washers may vary: The base of the

Figure 121.17c

Figure 121.17b

tensiometer might have touched the edge of the container; air bubbles might have been trapped under the flat base; etc. Such variables can be explored and discussed with the students.) Other tests can be carried out using tensiometers made from other materials such as tagboard, cardboard, stiff plastic, or glass. The latter can be attached to the balance arm with thread glued or taped to each base (Figure 121.17c).

b. Students can design tests to answer many of their own questions concerning tensiometers and surface tension. Variations on the previous activities are almost

limitless. For example, if a student wonders whether all liquids have the same "pull" (surface tension), different liquids can be tested and compared by washer weight to see which has the greater tension. If a student wonders whether the shape of the tensiometer makes any difference, differently shaped bases can be prepared, tried, and compared. The liquids can be seriated and the results can be graphed as shown in Histogram 121.17. (Note: Differently shaped bases should have identical surface areas so that valid comparisons can be made.) Other graphs

MEASURING SURFACE TENSIONS
USING DIFFERENTLY SHAPED TENSIOMETERS

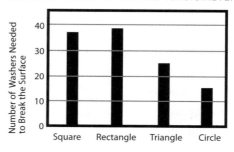

Histogram 121.17

can be made to compare matching shapes that increase in area (e.g., 2 in. × 2 in. or 2 cm × 2 cm square; 3 in. × 3 in. or 3 cm × 3 cm square).

Testing the surface tensions of water and soapy water. Several of the following activities can be done using liquids other than water. **18 Ea Eb Ec**

a. Give students large (8 in., or 20 cm, across or more) plates (not paper). Be sure the plates are clean and soap-free. Fill them with water, and give each student a strand of lightweight thread about 4 in. (10 cm) long. Tie the thread into a loop and set the loop on the surface of the water near the center of the plate. Touch the water in the center of the loop with a bar of soap or place a drop of soapy water in the center of the loop. Discuss observations. (The loop will enlarge to form a nearly perfect circle because the surface tension within the loop is reduced.)

b. The previous activity can lead to a large number of experiments that can answer questions the students raise. For example, a student might wonder if the thread loop was pushed or pulled out in a circle. To find out, the activity can be repeated and the soapy water can be added outside the loop. The observed result can be compared to the original procedure by placing soapy water in the plate and adding plain water to the loop.

c. To make a comparison of the surface tensions of water and soapy water clearer, sprinkle some fine powder onto the surface of a layer of water in a large, open-faced plate. Various powders work well: facial powder, talcum powder, pepper, cinnamon, nutmeg, or powdered tempera paint. When the water is calm, have the students use a medicine dropper to place a drop of soapy water onto the surface. Observe what takes place on the surface. (The surface tension of the water will break up and draw together away from the drop.)

Observing that the surface tension of a liquid can be reduced. Fill a wide-mouthed container with cold water. Allow the water to become calm, and then sprinkle the surface with a fine powder to make viewing easier. Place a small piece of soap into the center of the container. Let the students observe what happens. **19 Aa**

Reducing surface tension to propel small boats. Students can observe and make use of the reduction of surface tension by making surface tension boats out **20 Ga**

of cardboard. Cut the tiny boats (about 1 in. × 2 in. or 2.5 cm × 5 cm) from cardboard or stiff paper. Along the stern of each boat, spread a thin line of airplane glue (Figure 121.20a). Place the boats in a container of water. (The depth is not important.) Students will observe that the glue reduces the surface tension behind the boats. (Less force is exerted at the rear of the boat than in front.) If a fine powder is sprinkled on the water in front of the boats, the action will be more apparent. For a variation, a drop of glue can be placed on the end of a wooden or plastic toothpick. If several toothpicks are placed on a large surface of water at the same time, some interesting interactions can be observed (some toothpicks will seem to repel others). If a slot is cut in the stern of each boat, the boats can be "refueled." Into a chamber in the slot, place some soap, detergent, rubbing alcohol, or small piece of gum camphor. Slots can also be cut in various ways to cause different boat movements (Figure 121.20b).

Glue

Figure 121.20a   **Figure 121.20b**

Generalization III. Liquids can be classified on the basis of their characteristics.

> *Contributing Idea A.* Some characteristics of liquids can be seriated.

Seriating liquids. Have students use medicine droppers to place drops of different liquids upon waxed paper. Let them seriate the liquids on the basis of the physical appearance of the drops. Liquids can also be seriated on the basis of other characteristics such as color, oiliness, stickiness, viscosity, solubility, or density. **21 Da**

Seriating liquids on the basis of surface tension. Fill several identical containers with various liquids (e.g., vinegar, milk, alcohol). Make sure each container is filled until the liquid is level with the edge. Students can use medicine droppers to add drops of each liquid to the containers, compare the "piling up" of the liquids above the rims, and order the liquids by the number of drops needed past the level point to make each overflow. Tensiometers can be used to seriate the liquids more accurately. To make a tensiometer, see entry 121.17. **22 Da**

> *Contributing Idea B.* Some characteristics of liquids can be classified.

Grouping liquids by sight, smell, and taste. Present students with six sealed transparent vials, two vials each **23 Af Db**

of three different clear liquids such as white vinegar, water, and sugar water. Ask students to match the vials—first without opening them, then by using only their sense of smell, and finally using their sense of taste. **Caution: Students should be told about the danger of tasting unknown liquids. Follow safety guidelines for any tasting activity**.

Classifying liquids. Although liquids **24 Dc Fb** can be classified in numerous ways (e.g., color, smell, taste, viscosity, density, solubility), most are classified as acids (e.g., vinegar, citrus fruits, tomato juice), bases or alkaline liquids (e.g., washing soda), or neutral liquids (e.g., water). Blue litmus paper tests for acids by turning various shades of red. Red litmus paper tests for bases by turning various shades of blue. To give students an opportunity to use such indicators as an aid in identifying and classifying liquids, have them bring various liquids from home to test. After testing, group the liquids according to the results of the tests. When varying shades of color change are considered, the liquids can be ordered by degrees of acidity or alkalinity.

122 Interactions

Generalization I. The volume of a liquid is a measure of the space it occupies.

     Contributing Idea A. The space a liquid occupies can be measured.

Measuring liquid volumes. The volume **01 Cg** of a liquid can be measured in a number of ways by using any small container to fill a larger one. Each filling from the small container represents a unit of measure.

   a. Arrange containers of various sizes and shapes for students to see. Fill a drinking glass to the brim with water or another liquid (the liquid should be colored so that it can be easily observed). Ask students to estimate how high the liquid would be if it were poured into one of the other containers. Empty the contents into one container, refill the glass, and repeat for several containers. Discuss the various levels observed. (Note: Liquids take on the shape of the containers that hold them. This fact often misleads children, because a tall, narrow, container seems to contain more liquid than a shallow, wider one.) Ask how the different levels might be measured. (The amounts have already been measured; the same tumbler was used in each case.)

   b. Fill a large container to see how many tumblers, or other units of measurement, it will hold.

   c. Partially fill a large bucket with water or other liquid. Ask students to determine how much water is in the bucket. They can use tumblers or other containers to find out the volume of the water (the water can be withdrawn in equal units). Possible measuring containers range from thimbles to buckets. Students can choose the best size unit to use. (A thimble might take all day to empty a large container, while a bucket might be too large to give useful information.)

Making instruments for measuring liquid volumes. To measure the volumes of liquids, each student can make his or her own measuring device by obtaining a tall bottle. Each bottle can be turned into a graduated cylinder by scratching a scale on its side with a file. Each mark on the scale can represent any small measuring unit of liquid (e.g., a thimble, a jigger glass, a top from an aerosol can). **02 Gc**

Using standard liquid volume measuring instruments. Obtain several common measuring containers (e.g., baby bottles, measuring cups, various milk cartons). Fill each container with water or some other liquid. Let students pour the liquid back and forth among different containers to find the relationships of amounts each holds. **03 Ga**

Contributing Idea B. Liquid volumes have weight.

Feeling the weight of water. Have students heft several differently sized, empty milk cartons. Fill them with water and **04 Ab**

heft again. Discuss the differences felt. Similarly, have them lift a dry wash rag, then soak it in water and lift again. Students will realize that water has weight. They can also look at the weight printed on bottle labels of different liquids such as syrup, soda, and oil.

Weighing liquids. To help students realize that any weighing is a comparison of a known amount (i.e., mass) whose weight has been decided against an unknown amount (i.e., mass), ask them to determine the actual weight of an amount of water in a carton that is filled to the brim. They can use arbitrary units of measurement (e.g., washers, nails, pennies, marbles) or standard units. Compare results with the weights of other liquids in identical cartons. **05 Cf**

Comparing the weight of water to the weights of other liquids. Compare the relative weights of various liquids to water by obtaining six or more plastic pill bottles with tight-fitting caps, filling an aquarium one-fourth full of water, then filling one plastic bottle with water and capping it so that no air remains in the bottle. Set the bottle in the aquarium and observe the level at which it floats. (The water level in the bottle may be slightly below the surface of the aquarium water level due to the weight of the plastic bottle.) Now fill the other bottles with different liquids (e.g., vinegar, alcohol, soda, milk) and float them in the aquarium. **06 Cf Da**

Students can compare the level at which each floats with the level of the floating bottle of water. Order the liquids from the lightest to heaviest on the basis of observations. Weigh each container to see if the observations agree with the actual weights.

Generalization II. The specific gravity of a liquid is a comparison of its density to the density of water.

> *Contributing Idea A.* Each liquid has a different density.

Determining the density of liquids. The weight of a volume of one liquid differs from the weight of an equal volume of another liquid. The density of water (equal to one) is used as a standard for measuring the densities of other liquids. (e.g., Alcohol is less dense or lighter than water; molasses is denser or heavier than water.) Several activities provide students with comparisons. After one or more of the experiences, explain that the relationship between a material's weight and its size is called density.

07
Bb
Cf
Da

a. Students can measure and compare the weights of a pint or half-liter of water with pints or half-liters of alcohol, syrup, milk, oil, etc. Order the liquids from lightest to heaviest.

b. Place equal volumes of various liquids into identical plastic pill containers. Measurements can be made with a commercial or homemade arm balance scale. Order the containers from lightest to heaviest.

c. The density of liquids can be measured fairly accurately by placing each container of liquid on one side of an arm balance. The weight of the liquid and its container can be balanced by adding units of weight to the other side of the balance arm. To find the weight of each liquid, the students must weigh the containers *before* adding the liquids, and then subtract this weight from the total. You might explain that the ratio between the density of a material and the density of water is called specific gravity.

Contributing Idea B. The hydrometer (nonmercury) is an instrument used to measure specific gravity.

Making a hydrometer. Simple hydrometers can be made in several ways.

08
Gc

a. Put a thumbtack in the eraser end of a pencil. Stand the pencil vertically in a beaker of tap water. Mark the water level on the pencil. Remove the pencil and dissolve 3 tsp. (15 ml) of salt in the water, and float the pencil again. Compare the water level with the mark made on the pencil. (The pencil should float higher in the salt water because it has a greater density.) Test other liquids with the pencil hydrometer. (See Figure 122.08a.)

Figure 122.08a

b. Seal one end of a waterproof drinking straw with melted wax and place some sand into the straw until it stands in a vertical position. A drop of melted wax or glue placed in the straw above the sand will keep it in place. Float the straw in ordinary tap water and mark the water level on the straw. Other liquids can now be tested and compared with the water mark. (Note: The water-mark line represents the specific gravity of water; the specific gravity of any other liquid tells how its density compares with the density of water.) If the specific gravity of water is considered to be one (unity), the submerged part of the straw to the mark can be considered as a whole unit (one), and

this unit can be scaled into tenths. Another unit can be extended above the water line and scaled into tenths. Other liquids can be tested and compared very accurately with this scaled hydrometer. (See Figure 122.08b.)

Figure 122.08b

Comparing liquids by their specific gravity. Place glass tube (with ¼ in. or 1 cm diameter or more) into a glass container of water. Pour a liquid that is lighter than water into the tube until it forces the water to the lower end. Students can compare the height of the liquid in the tube to the height of the water outside the tube. (Note: The difference in height is a measure of the specific gravity of the water, as shown by the water level.) If a liquid heavier than water is used, fill the container with the liquid and pour water down the tube until the liquid is forced to the bottom. The tube can be marked and scaled similarly to the hydrometer in the

09 Cg

previous activity. Measurements taken by the two devices can be compared. **Caution: Follow safety guidelines when handling glass tubing**.

Generalization III. Liquids exert pressure.

> *Contributing Idea A.* The pressure of a liquid increases with depth.

Observing that the pressure of water increases with depth. Punch three holes with a small nail, equidistant and vertical to each other, in the side of a 1 qt. (1 L) or 1 gal. milk carton. Cover the holes with tape and fill the carton with water. Hold the carton over a sink or large container and quickly pull the tape away. Have students observe the flow of water from the holes. (The flow will be improved if small pieces of glass or metal tubing approximately $\frac{1}{3}$ in. (0.3 cm) in diameter, ½ in. (1.2 cm) long are tightly fitted into the holes.) Repeat the activity several times. Let students draw inferences about what they see. (The pressure of the water at the base of the container is greater than at the top.) If the carton is held high enough above the sink, so that the streams of water have a chance to fall through their full trajectory, the streams will appear as they do in Figure 122.10.

**10
Ca
Fa**

Figure 122.10

Measuring the pressure created by the weight of water. Remove the top only of one milk carton. Remove both the top

**11
Bc
Cd
Fa**

and bottom from two other milk cartons. Tape two cartons together, one on top of the other that has only the top removed. Punch three holes in the side of the bottom carton, equidistant and vertical to each other. Place tape over the three holes, fill the lower carton with water, hold over a sink, and then quickly remove the tape. Use rulers to compare how far each of the three water jets travel. Now retape the holes, fill both cartons and repeat the activity. Next, tape the third carton on top of the other two and repeat. If the lower cartons bulge from the weight, put tape around them. Now tape each of the three holes separately. Place a meterstick against the bottom carton so that it extends away from it below the holes. Fill the three cartons and remove the tape from the bottom hole. Students can check and record the length of the jet. Cover the bottom hole, fill the containers again, remove the tape from the second hole, measure the jet, and record the measurement. Repeat for the third hole. A table can be kept of the data. Next, remove the top carton and repeat the activity. Remove the second carton and do the same. From their observations and the data recorded in Table 122.11, students can draw inferences about the height of a column of water and its relationship to the pressure the water exerts.

Contributing Idea B. The manometer is an instrument used to measure the pressure liquids exert.

Comparing water pressures at different depths. A simple pressure bottle can be made by students for experiencing the relationship of water pressure to depth. Stretch a piece of rubber (balloon rubber works well) across a small, widemouthed bottle. Make sure the rubber is tightly stretched. Fasten it securely with a rubber band. The bottle can now be submerged to different depths in a tank of water. Students can observe differences in the rubber membrane at different depths. (The deeper the bottle, the greater the pressure.) They can also turn the pressure

12
Ca

bottle in various directions at the same depth and observe what happens. (The pressure at any particular depth is equal in all directions.)

Making a manometer. A manometer is a U-shaped tube pressure gauge that can measure the pressure that liquids exert. To make a manometer, connect two transparent soda straws (or straight glass tubing) with a short piece of rubber tubing. Attach the arrangement to a stand as shown in Figure 122.13. Fill the tubing with colored water until it rests at the same level in each straw. To one straw, fasten approximately 1 yd. or 1 m of rubber tubing. On the end of the tubing, attach a small funnel, thistle tube, or pipette with a piece of rubber stretched tightly across its face (balloon rubber can be used). Have students press on the rubber and observe the liquid in the U-shaped tube. (It should rise when pressure is applied.) Place the funnel end of the rubber tubing just below the surface of some water in a large, deep container. Students can observe the change in the liquid level in the manometer. Move the funnel deeper, and observe again. Next,

13
Gc

Table 122.11. Measuring Water Pressure

Number of Cartons	Length of Jet 1	Length of Jet 2	Length of Jet 3
3			
2			
1			

Figure 122.13

Table 122.14. Measuring Water Pressure

Depth of Funnel	Rise of Water in Open Tube
0 in.	__ in.
1 in.	__ in.
2 in.	__ in.
3 in.	__ in.
↓	↓

put the funnel to the bottom of the container. Students will realize that the pressure increases with depth.

Using a manometer. To make accurate measurements with a manometer, a scale can be added to the device described in entry 122.13. First, mark the level of the colored water in the U-shaped tube on the tubing itself or on a card set behind the open-ended tube. Submerge the funnel below the surface of some water and measure, in in. or metric units, how deeply the funnel is submerged. For every unit in depth, mark the change in level on the U-shaped tube. A record can be kept as shown in Table 122.14. After the scale is completed, other liquids can be tested and compared with the pressure of water. The data should produce a straight line graph from which students can predict the pressure at other depths by extrapolation. (The information will also indicate that the pressure of water is directly proportional to its depth.) By extending the length of the rubber tubing and replacing the open-ended tube with several ft. of glass tubing, the manometer can be used

14 Bc Ga

to test depths in a swimming pool. From graphed data, students can predict the pressure at a particular depth, and then use the revised manometer in a swimming pool to check their predictions.

Contributing Idea C. The pressure exerted by a liquid depends upon the density of the liquid.

Comparing the pressures of different liquids. Obtain two 1 gal. size containers into which the funnel end of a manometer will fit. Fill one container with water and one with alcohol or some other liquid less dense than water. Measure and compare the pressures at the bottom of each liquid. Repeat with a liquid that is heavier than water. **Caution: Alcohols are inflammable and should be kept away from open flames.**

15 Cg

Contributing Idea D. The pressure of a liquid is the same in all directions at any given depth.

Comparing pressures of liquids in all directions. Fill an aquarium with water. Use a manometer to measure the pressure

16 Cg

of the water in all directions. A depth mark on the side of the aquarium will enable students to hold the manometer in different positions at the same depth (Figure 122.16a). Since an immersed hand will change the depth of the water greatly, tape or tack the manometer funnel to a small, thin board that is attached to a ruler or meterstick with a bolt and small screw or wing nut. Figure 122.16b shows the front and the back of the manometer attached to a ruler or meterstick. The funnel position can then be adjusted easily and immersed.

Figure 122.16a   **Figure 122.16b**

Generalization IV. Buoyancy is the upward force exerted upon an immersed or floating object by a liquid.

Contributing Idea A. Buoyancy is an upward force.

Feeling and describing buoyancy. Objects float because water pushes up against them. Several activities can let students feel the push or buoyancy of a liquid.

17
Ab
Ba
Bb

a. Students can hold a block of wood under water, and then describe what they feel. You might tell them what they feel is called buoyancy.

b. Float an empty can in a pan of water. Have students put one hand in the can and push downward without sinking the can. Ask them to describe what they feel.

c. Obtain a large cork. Have students push it to the bottom of a bucket or other suitable container filled with water. Have them describe how it feels and the amount of force (push) needed to hold it under the water. Put the cork in a bottle and repeat the activity to see if any difference is made in the effort needed to hold the cork under water.

d. Blow up a balloon and have a student push it to the bottom of a bucket of water. Compare the force needed to hold other objects under water.

e. Obtain an empty coffee can (or small plastic pill bottle) with a tight-fitting lid. Have students push the covered container, top down, to the bottom of a bucket of water. Have them describe how the can feels, then quickly release it and observe what happens. Repeat this action at different depths and compare differences.

Contributing Idea B. Buoyancy makes objects seem lighter.

Feeling how buoyancy affects an object. Students can feel the lightness of an object due to the buoyancy of water by filling a coffee can with water and covering it. Cut a string or cord approximately 1 yd. or 1 m long. Double the string for strength and attach it to the can so that it can be held by the loop. Have several students lift the can of water (it should feel heavy), then lower the can into a bucket of water and describe how it feels (it will feel much lighter).   **18 Ab**

Weighing objects in water. Several activities help students realize that objects in water seem to weigh less due to buoyancy.   **19 Cf**

    a. Obtain a small empty jar (or plastic pill bottle) with a tight-fitting lid. Fill the jar with water and put the lid on it. Suspend the jar from a spring scale or rubber band. Lower the jar into a container of water and record any change in the spring scale or in the stretch of the rubber band. Students will see that the buoyancy of the water

pushes up on the jar and lessens the weight (see Figure 122.19).

Figure 122.19

    b. Weigh a large stone with a spring scale. Record the weight and let students suspend the stone from the scale into a container of water. Record the "new" weight. (The stone will seem to weigh less in the water due to the buoyancy.)

    c. Test the materials in the previous activities again, using other liquids such as alcohol, salt solutions, or sugar solutions. Compare the buoyant effect each has upon objects.

Contributing Idea C. Buoyancy of a liquid is related to the density of the liquid.

Increasing the density of water. Place an egg in a glass of tap water. Increase the density of the water by stirring in 3 to 5 tsp. (15 to 25 ml) of salt. Let students observe what happens to the egg.   **20 Ca**

(The density of the water is increased in relation to the density of the egg, and the water becomes more buoyant.) A similar way to increase the density of water would be to empty two tea bags and fill them with salt. Fill a beaker with warm water. Drop four or five unshelled peanuts into the beaker. (Peanuts have different densities, thus some will sink while others float.) Hang the two tea bags on opposite sides of the container and have students observe what happens. A sheet of black paper can be placed behind the container to make observations clearer. (Students should see the salt going into solution near the bottom of the beaker. A layer of the denser solution can be seen rising in the beaker. As it rises the peanuts will rise with it, supported by the buoyant force.)

Contributing Idea D. Buoyancy is related to the weight and volume of objects.

Comparing and sorting floating objects by weight and volume. Collect objects such as paper clips, bottle caps, spoons, cans, candles, corks, and marbles. Sort them by weight (light, medium, and heavy categories). Sorting can be done with a weighing device or by letting students heft each piece to make a judgment about its placement. Drop the objects, one at a time, into an aquarium filled with water. Let students describe what they see. (Some objects will float; others will sink.) Keep a record of what each object **21 Cf Cg Db**

does, and then compare with the weight groupings made earlier. Ask if weight has any relationship to whether objects sink or float. Students can make other inferences by sorting the same objects by size (small, medium, and large categories).

Contributing Idea E. An object will float if it displaces a volume of water whose weight is the same as its own; an object will sink if it weighs more than the volume of water it displaces.

Comparing the weight of displaced water to the weight of an object that floats. Weigh a large dishpan and record its weight, then place a 1 qt. (1 L) can in the dishpan. Fill the can to the very top with water. Wipe the outer surface of the can and the dishpan dry. Weigh a large block of wood or other object that floats. Place it in the can. Students can observe what happens. (The water will be displaced and overflow into the dishpan.) Now weigh the dishpan with the water in it. Calculate the weight of the water by subtracting the weight of the dishpan and compare it to the weight of the object. (The two weights will be the same. An object floats when it weighs less than an amount of water that it displaces.) Repeat this activity with several other objects that float. **22 Cf**

Making and using an overflow container. An overflow container can be made from a large plastic bucket or tin **23 Ga Gc**

can fitted with a rubber tube or a troughed spout made from a 3 in. (8 cm) piece of metal. Seal the spout securely to the container with wax or silicon rubber. Fill the overflow container until the water barely runs out the spout. (It should then be level with the spout.) Weigh and record the weight of this filled bucket. Place a second smaller container underneath the spout to catch overflowing water. Now obtain a piece of wood or other object that will float in water. Weigh the piece of wood on a spring scale and record the weight. Let the block of wood float in the water while suspended from a spring scale. (If the object floats, the weight is 0.) Find the weight of the overflow water and compare the loss of weight on the spring scale with the weight of the overflow water. (They will be the same; the buoyant force is equal to the weight of the water an object displaces.) Students can repeat the activity using other objects that float (e.g., different woods such as cork, maple, mahogany, or ebony cut to the same size and shape) or liquids other than water.

Comparing the weight of displaced water to the weight of an object that sinks. Hang an object, such as a heavy rock, from a spring scale. Record the weight of the object, and then immerse it in the water of an overflow container. Students can observe and record the object's "new" weight on the spring scale. Let **24 Cf**

them weigh the water in the container and find the weight of the overflow water by subtracting the container's weight from the total weight. Have students make some judgments about the apparent loss of weight of the object in relation to the weight of the water in the overflow container and about the original weight of the object in relation to the weight of the water displaced. (Objects sink when they weigh more than the water they displace.) In the same way, students can test other objects that sink. (Note: Any material, no matter how heavy, can be made to float if it can be shaped to displace enough water.)

Generalization V. Moving liquids have identifiable characteristics.

> *Contributing Idea A.* Some characteristics of liquids can be observed as the liquids fall.

Listening to moving water. Whenever possible, have students listen to and describe the sounds made by various kinds of moving water, such as ocean waves, waterfalls, running brooks and streams, light and heavy rainfalls, and dripping and flowing faucets. **25 Ac**

Observing and measuring columns of falling liquids. Obtain several clean, empty, plastic glue bottles. With a hot needle, make one small hole in the base of each bottle. Hold one finger over the hole and fill the bottle with water. Place the cap **26 Af Cd Da**

on the bottle and turn it upside down over a sink or large container. Remove your finger from the hole and have students observe the column of water as it streams from the opening in the bottle cap (see Figure 122.26). Students will first see a

Figure 122.26

column of water that tends to break up and bead some distance from the bottle opening. They will hear the difference in the continuous or broken portion of the column if the bottle is raised and lowered above the container. Repeat the activity using other liquids, and have the students compare what they see and hear. Next, draw a line near the top of a chalkboard so that a bottle can be held at the line. Fill one bottle with water, hold it at the line, release the hole, and let students mark on the chalkboard the place where the column of water breaks up into beads. Label the mark on the board, and then test other liquids such as alcohol, molasses, honey, syrup, and soapy water. Compare the marked columns. The data can be ordered from the shortest column to the longest.

Students can compare these observations with observations made during surface tension activities 121.12–121.20. **Caution: Students must wear protective garments during this activity and wash hands when activity is finished.**

Contributing Idea B. Viscosity is the characteristic of a liquid that makes it resist flowing.

Observing and describing viscosity. Obtain several small plastic pill bottles with tight-fitting caps. Fill one bottle with oil, one with water, and one with a thick shampoo. Cap the bottles, leaving a small air bubble in each. Invert the bottles simultaneously. Students can observe how long it takes the bubbles to rise in each bottle. Ask them to explain what this tells them about each liquid. (They may describe some liquids as being "thicker" than others.) You might introduce the term *viscous*, and have the students test other liquids. The tested liquids can be ordered on the basis of their viscosities. **Caution: Students must wear protective garments during this activity and wash hands when activity is finished.**

27
Aa
Ba
Bb
Da

Comparing viscosities. Fill several small identical jars half-full with liquids that differ greatly in viscosity. Cap each jar and roll the jars down a slightly inclined plane (see Figure 122.28). Students can observe what happens. Ask them to explain what their observations tell them about each liquid. (The more

28
Ch
Da

Figure 122.28

viscous the liquid, the more slowly it rolls.) It is possible to time the rolling of each jar if start and finish positions are set up and if care is taken that each jar starts its roll with equal force. This can be done by slightly raising a 3 ft. (1 m) long board. A starting line can be drawn near the top and a finish line near the base. (A good distance between the lines would be 2 ft. or 60 cm.) A small stick can be held across the starting line with the jar resting against it. At a signal from a timer, using a stopwatch or a watch with a second hand, the stick should be raised and the jar will begin to roll. As the circumference of the jar first touches the finish line, the timing stops. The liquids can be compared and ordered by the recorded times. The times will vary in relationship to the viscosity of each liquid. (Note: It is best to take an average of several trials.)

Generalization VI. Moving liquids have force and can do work.

Contributing Idea A. Liquids flow from higher to lower levels.

Observing that water flows from higher levels to lower levels. Prepare the apparatus that is shown in Figure 122.29. **29 Aa Fc**

Remove the top of a 1 qt. (1 L) milk carton. Make a hole near the bottom and insert a 1 yd. (1 m) length of rubber tubing to fit snugly. Place the free end of the tubing in an empty aquarium. Use a clothespin to pinch the tubing closed near the carton. Fill the carton with water. Remove the clothespin. Students can test the carton at various levels to see which level is best

Figure 122.29

for water to flow from the carton to the aquarium. (The flow will diminish as the height of the water column decreases.) Since water in most city water systems flows under the influence of gravity, an analogy might be made between the parts of this apparatus to water tanks or dams (carton), valves (clothespin), and pipelines (tubing).

Observing that a liquid will cease to flow when it reaches its own level. Place two-hole stoppers in two bottles. Fill one bottle with a colored liquid and attach the two bottles with rubber and glass tubing. Hold the bottle of colored liquid above the empty bottle, place a finger over the **30 Aa**

hole without the tubing, and invert the bottle. As soon as the liquid flows into the empty bottle, set the full bottle beside it. (Students will observe that the liquid continues to flow until it reaches the same level in each bottle.) This activity can be repeated with bottles of different sizes. As a variation, a simple siphon can be started by sucking upon the tubing in a bottle of liquid. When the liquid enters the mouth, the tube is transferred to an open pan or jar *below* the water level. The water will then flow until the level is the same in each container or until the jar is emptied. **Caution: Follow safety guidelines when using rubber and glass tubing.**

Measuring and making predictions about the flow of water from a steady source. A marked vessel (in one-half ounces or metric units) can be used to collect a volume of water at a drinking fountain. Measurements can be made of the collected amounts in 10-second intervals. After five or six measurements, the data can be graphed and predictions made of the time needed to fill the vessel or other container. Drinking fountains in different locations can be compared.

31
Bf
Cg
Ch

> *Contributing Idea B.* The force of moving liquids can be used to do work.

Feeling and using the force of moving water. Let students feel the force of water flowing from a faucet, a drinking fountain, or a carton filled with water.

32
Ab
Ga

This force can be put to work to move an object by preparing a simple waterwheel as illustrated in Figure 122.32a and 122.32b. Place the cardboard pieces together and tie them; then mount the nails through the cardboard pieces as an axle. Have students work in pairs, one holding the waterwheel at the axle while the other pours water against the blades to turn the wheel.

Figure 122.32a

Figure 122.32b

Using a waterwheel to do work. Wind the end of a string around one of the nails in the center of a waterwheel. Pass the other end of the string through two eye screws on a board at the edge of a table. Tie a weight (e.g., paper clip or fish

33
Ga

weight) to the string so that it rests on the floor. By pouring water on the wheel, the weight will be lifted from the floor (see Figure 122.33). As a variation, the wheel can be used to pull a plastic toy car or wagon across the table.

Figure 122.33

Generalization VII. Capillarity is the action by which the surface of a liquid, in contact with a solid, is elevated or depressed.

> *Contributing Idea A.* Capillary action is primarily due to narrow spaces in a material and the attraction between the liquid and the material.

Observing capillary action. Using such **34** material as a sponge, blotter paper, or **Aa** cloths, have students observe how the **Bb** material soaks up water. The water can be colored to improve observations. To observe the fibers and narrow tubes in materials that absorb liquids, obtain hand lenses. Students can examine closely the

torn edges of blotter paper, cloths, and other absorbent materials, and describe what they see. (They should see tiny, closely packed fibers.) If a microscope is available, use it to observe colored liquid rising through the fibers. You might tell them that what they see is called capillary action.

Comparing influences on capillarity by **35** **the amount of spacing in a material.** **Cd** Obtain two clear pieces of glass or plastic (lantern slide size or larger). Spread a film of water over one side of one piece and place the other piece on top. Secure one end with a rubber band. Separate the pieces at the other end with pieces of tag board so that the separation is not more than 1/32 in. (0.2 cm) thick. Set the pieces of glass in a pan or saucer of water (see Figure 122.35) Have students observe what happens over a period of time. (The water will rise by capillary action, but it will rise higher on one side of the apparatus than the other due to the change in closeness of the pieces of glass.) Students can try this activity using other liquids

Figure 122.35

and making comparisons of the heights to which the liquids rise. A grease pencil can be used to trace the waterline on one sheet of glass. This line can be used for making comparisons with other liquids. **Caution: Follow safety guidelines when using glass. Clean up any spillage immediately to avoid slipping.**

Generalization VIII. A solution is a homogeneous liquid containing more than one material.

> *Contributing Idea A.* Some materials dissolve in liquids; some do not.

Observing materials dissolving in water. Have students bring several tea bags to school. Cut a hole in the top of each bag and remove the tea. Pour dissolvable materials into each tea bag (e.g., salt, sugar, photographic hypo). Place each bag in a separate beaker of warm water. Let students observe and describe what they see. (Note: A sheet of black paper placed behind the beakers will aid the observations.) Test other materials in a similar way. Students will find that some dissolve and some do not.   **36 Aa**

Determining how much of a material will go into solution in a given amount of water. Measure ½ c. (120 ml) cold tap water into each of four beakers. To each beaker, add 1 level tsp. (5 ml) of one of the following: salt, sugar, photographic hypo, or dirt. Stir vigorously, label the beakers, and observe the results. Students   **37 Bb Cc**

will see that some crystals are more soluble than others—they dissolve completely—and that none of the dirt seems to go into solution. (Some small particles may remain in suspension for a long time, and the water will appear cloudy.) Continue to add spoonfuls of salt, sugar, and hypo to the appropriate beakers, stirring after each entry, and observing the results until the salt no longer goes into solution. (Some salt will remain at the base of the beaker after about 7 tsp.) At this point, students can infer that there is more salt in the container than can go into solution and the salt is less soluble than the other materials. You might introduce the term *saturation* at this time. Students can continue adding spoonfuls of the other materials until they find the saturation point for each. A table of data can be kept.

> *Contributing Idea B.* Some materials can dissolve in one liquid but not in another.

Identifying solvents. Have students try to dissolve small but equal amounts of various materials such as salt, sugar, grease, petroleum jelly, cocoa, flour, and soda. Have them observe and compare the rates at which the materials dissolve in water, then let them try dissolving the same materials in other liquids such as alcohol, milk, oil, and vinegar. They can infer that water might be the most universal solvent and that some materials will dissolve in some liquids, but not in others   **38 Fa**

(e.g., grease will not dissolve in water, but it will in alcohol).

Contributing Idea C. Hard water contains dissolved materials.

Making hard water. Hard water contains minerals dissolved from rocks. It can be obtained from a stream or prepared artificially in the classroom as in the following procedures: **39 Gc**

a. Drop lime tablets, available from drugstores, into water or mix some lime from a hardware store with water. Let it stand overnight. Siphon off the clear lime water. When carbon dioxide is bubbled through lime water, temporary hard water will be produced.

b. Stir some plaster of paris, Epsom salts, or flakes of gypsum into water and let it stand overnight. Permanent hard water will be obtained when the solution is filtered.

Making hard water soft. Removing dissolved minerals from hard water will produce soft water, as soft water contains few or no dissolved minerals. To make soft water from temporary hard water, simply boil it. To make soft water from permanent hard water, add sodium carbonate (washing soda) or borax to the water. **40 Gc**

Testing the washing power of soaps in hard water and soft water. Prepare two identical dirty cloths. Have students keep track of how much time it takes to wash one cloth in soft water with soap until it is clean. Wash the other cloth in hard water with the same soap for the same amount of time; then hang both to dry. Compare the differences between them. Samples of different detergents can be brought from home and their effects on hard and soft water can be compared. **41 Ec**

Contributing Idea D. Some minerals in solution affect the freezing and boiling temperatures of liquids.

Comparing the times at which different liquids freeze. Place a jar or beaker of each of the following liquids in the freezing compartment of a refrigerator: water, alcohol, and syrup. Wrap each container in newspaper or plastic bags, in case the containers break when they freeze. Have students observe the containers every half-hour for a four-hour period. List the liquids in the order by which they froze. (Note: Some materials may not freeze.) **42 Ch Da**

Comparing the times at which different solutions freeze. Give students four or five unsealed jars or beakers containing water in which different amounts of salt have been dissolved (e.g., 0 tsp., 1 tsp., 2 tsp., or use 5 ml spoonfuls). Have them place the jars in plastic bags and set the bags in a freezer. Compare the times it takes for the different solutions to freeze by checking them at half-hour intervals. (Note: Some may never freeze.) Remove the jars after four hours and record the results. The jars **43 Ch**

can be left in the classroom to see which frozen solution melts first. Students will see whether or not a salt solution inhibits the melting of water. This activity can be repeated using different solutions such as sugar or photographic hypo.

Contributing Idea E. Temperature affects the solubility of most materials.

Determining the effect of heat upon solubility. Fill a beaker with half a cup (120 ml) of water. Add salt, stirring in 1 tsp. (one 5 ml) at a time until you cannot get any more salt to dissolve. (At approximately 7 tsp., some salt will remain at the bottom of the beaker.) Place the beaker over a heat source and slowly heat it. Let students observe what happens to the salt at the bottom of the beaker. (It will dissolve.) Allow the beaker to cool and observe again. (Some salt will reappear.) Repeat this activity with sugar. Students will realize that when a liquid is heated, more material will dissolve in it. **44 Ca**

Contributing Idea F. Crystals can be made from solutions.

Observing the formation of crystals. It is possible to remove some or all of the water from a solution and leave the dissolved substance. To do this, have students pour a small amount of salt solution into a saucer and place the saucer on a sunny window ledge. Put a beaker of the solution on a heating unit to evaporate **45 Aa**

the water. Check the saucer periodically until all the water is gone. Students will see that salt crystals remain in both instances. Compare the appearance of the crystals in both containers. (There will be a difference due to the speed at which the water evaporated.) Repeat the activity using sugar or photographic hypo.

Making crystals. Students can prepare a saturated solution of sugar—about 26 tsp. (130 ml) in ½ c. (120 ml) of water. Suspend a nail, nut, or other such object midway in the solution (see Figure 122.46). Set the container on a sunny window ledge. As the water evaporates, observe the formation of crystals on the object. Dissolved substances tend to crystalize on objects within a solution. Another container can be prepared with a sugar solution sprinkled with a very small amount of fine dust or sand. Let students observe where the crystals form. **46 Gc**

Figure 122.46

Growing large crystals. It is possible to grow large single crystals in a solution. To do this, fill a beaker with 2 c. (475 ml) of **47 Bb Gc**

water. Saturate the water with salt (approximately 7 tsp.). Heat the solution until it boils, and then add more salt until the water is again saturated. Allow the solution to cool. Students can observe salt crystals formed at the base. To remove the crystals, pour the solution through a filter or a piece of cloth folded over several times. Collect the liquid in several small jars. The cloth will catch the crystals, and the liquid in each jar will be a saturated solution. Now have students collect several of the largest crystals, called seed crystals, and drop one in each of the jars. If the lids are kept off the jars, the crystals will grow larger in the next few days due to the evaporation of some water. Still larger crystals can be made by filtering the solutions again to collect the large crystals. Tie a thread to each of them to provide a base on which other crystals can grow. Heat a beaker of the saturated salt solution and add several more teaspoons of salt. As the beaker is allowed to cool, suspend the crystals in the solution from their threads. Observe them daily. They will grow in size equal to the "added" amounts of salt. If foreign particles have entered the solution, clusters of crystals will form. The crystals can be made larger by repeating this process several times—reheat the saturated solution, add more salt, and allow it to cool with the crystals in suspension. Some students might try placing the beaker in a refrigerator to see what happens. (As the temperature drops, more salt will come out of

solution and form crystals.) Students can hold a contest to see who can grow the largest crystal in a certain amount of time. Other crystals can be made by the same procedures using different materials. The resulting crystals of sugar, copper sulfate, Epsom salts, alum, photographic hypo, or Rochelle salt can be compared by their characteristic shapes. (See Figure 122.47.)

Figure 122.47

Generalization IX. Certain materials can pollute liquids.

Contributing Idea A. Impurities can pollute liquids.

Determining how water can become polluted. Obtain a dozen baby food jars with lids. Place small quantities of many different materials into different jars (e.g., salt, sugar, sand, ink, oil, beans, coffee, wood, soap, candy, chalk, carrots). Have students half-fill each jar with water and label the contents. Let them keep records of the sealed jars for one week. At the end of the week, open the jars to observe,

48
Ad
Ga

smell, and feel the contents. **Caution: Do not let students taste the water.** Pour all the contents into a 1 qt. (1 L) jar. Let students look at and smell the mixture. An analogy can be made to polluted rivers and lakes and to the problems facing living organisms from the spreading contamination of water. Students can speculate whether or not they would like to drink the liquids.

Contributing Idea B. Impurities can be removed from liquids.

Making a device to remove some impurities from water. Put a wad of cotton in the base hole of a flower pot and cover the cotton with several in. (10 cm) of clean sand. Pour some muddy water into the pot and collect it in a container. Observe the liquid as it emerges, and compare it with some remaining muddy water. **49 Gc**

Making a filter. An efficient filter can be made by sequencing the following materials in a funnel, tall tube, flower pot, or inverted bottle that has had the bottom removed. Put ½ in. (1 cm) of cotton in the base (or a layer of filter paper) to retain the sand. Add 2 in. (5 cm) of pebbles, then 1 in. (3 cm) of coarse, clean sand (see Figure 122.50). (Note: Charcoal can aid the filtering process—pieces of charcoal can be added in a layer beneath the pebbles or it can be made into a paste by grinding up wood charcoal and mixing it with **50 Gc**

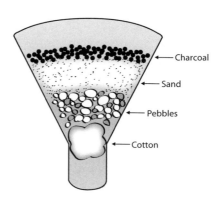

Figure 122.50

a little water and spreading it over the top layer of sand.) Pour muddy water through the filter. Collect and observe the filtered water. **Caution: The collected water might not be pure enough to drink.**

Using filter paper. Filter paper can be used to filter some suspensions, but not solutions. Commercial filter paper can be obtained or ordinary paper toweling can be cut into circles with 6 in. (15 cm) diameters. Fold a circle in half, then in half again (see Figure 122.51). Place the quarter-circle into a funnel. Spread one leaf of the paper against one side of the funnel and three leaves against the other side. The paper will tend to pop out until it is wet. Slowly pour a liquid to be filtered into the funnel and collect it below. If different liquids are tested, students will see that in a solution, the substance that dissolves cannot be separated by filter paper. (Note: Use a different filter paper for each test.) **51 Ga**

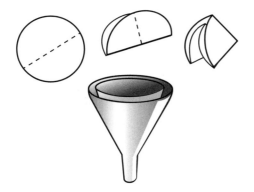

Figure 122.51

Separating materials from water by evaporation. Place a salt or sugar solution in a tea kettle. Heat the kettle to a boil and collect the steam from its spout on a flat pan. If the pan is tilted, the water vapor will collect and run off the pan. It can be caught in another container.

52 Ga

130 Gases

131 Characteristics

Generalization I. Gas is one of the three states of matter.

Contributing Idea. Gases condense into liquids when cooled; liquids evaporate into gases when heated.

Observing condensation. Have students watch water condense on the outside of a jar of water that you seal after adding ice to it. Ask where the water comes from. If students think that the droplets come from the ice water through the glass, prepare an identical jar, but fill it with warm water. They will see that droplets do not form on this jar. They will realize that there is water in the air in the form of an invisible gas and that when the gas cools, as it does against the glass, it takes on the form of a liquid. You can explain that the term *condensation* describes what they saw. Some students might describe dew that they have seen and recall the time of day and conditions when it was observed (usually on cool mornings). Others can describe the droplets that form on windows, mirrors in bathrooms, and eyeglasses. Challenge them to recall the conditions that might have caused the droplets. The surface upon which the droplets formed was probably cool. Students will begin to realize that water in a gaseous state will condense as a liquid against cooler surfaces.

01 Aa Bb

Observing evaporation. Students can take turns dipping a finger or hand in water and waving it until it dries. Let them describe what they feel, and ask them where the water went. Explain that when liquids, like water, seem to disappear, they have changed into an invisible gas. You might tell them that the term *evaporation* describes what they observed. Next, set a saucer of water in direct sunlight and have students check it periodically as the water evaporates.

02 Aa Ab Bb

Observing changes of state: water (gas ↔ liquid). Place a saucer of water inside a large glass jar or aquarium. Put some Vaseline around the rim of the container, and cover it with a pane of glass. Be sure it is tightly sealed. Students can observe the saucer periodically to see what happens to the water. (It will evaporate.) Ask where the water went. (It can be seen as droplets on the glass sides of the container.) Ask if anyone saw the water move from the saucer to the glass. Students will begin to understand that when water disappears (evaporates), it becomes an invisible gas, and when it reappears (condenses), it usually becomes a liquid again. Students can repeat this activity using other liquids such as oil or solids such as cubes of ice.

03 Aa

Observing changes of state: Dry ice (solid → gas). Let students observe a piece of dry ice over time as it changes directly from a solid to a gas (sublimation).

04 Af

Caution: Dry ice is extremely cold and dangerous to handle; handle with care.

Generalization II. Gases have identifiable characteristics.

Contributing Idea A. Our senses can be used to detect and identify gases.

Inferring the presence of a gas: air. **05** **Fc** Obtain two identical sheets of typing paper and ask students if one is heavier than the other (the weights are identical). Crumple one and leave the other flat, then ask again if one is heavier than the other (the weights are still the same). Now stand on a chair and drop both papers at the same time. Challenge students to explain why one takes longer to fall when both are the same weight (one has more surface area and must push more air aside as it falls). Since air offers resistance to objects moving through it, students can have fun playing with a whirlybird. Cut the whirlybird from mimeograph or similar paper and fold as shown in Figure 131.05. By tossing the heavy end into the

Figure 131.05

air, students will see that air affects the whirlybird's fall.

Observing some physical characteristics of a gas: air. **06** **Af** Let students catch some air in a plastic sandwich bag by holding the mouth of the bag open and swishing it through the air. Quickly close the mouth and twist it tightly to trap the air. Fasten the bag with a rubber band. Students can (1) squeeze the trapped air and describe how it feels; (2) sit on the bag or on several bags at a time to see if the bags can support weight; (3) look through the bags to see if they can see each other; (4) open their bags a little and smell the air to see if any odor can be detected that is different from the plastic bag; (5) take the bag outdoors, open it, empty out the air, fill it with outdoor air, bring it back inside, and explain how they can be sure it is filled with outside air and not inside air; (6) collect samples of air from other places around the school (e.g., in the basement, closet, hallway) and do all the things with the bag that they did with the classroom air.

Seeing some characteristics of a gas: air. **07** **Aa** Students can "see" air in several ways:

a. They can blow through a straw into a large jar or aquarium of water and watch the bubbles coming from the end of the straw. If they fill a glass with water and invert it in an aquarium, they can blow bubbles and catch them in the glass.

b. Students can fit a rubber tube over the end of a glass funnel, hold it upside down on the bottom of an aquarium, and blow air into the tube to slowly force the water out of the funnel. Other students will be able to "see" the air pushing the water out.

c. Students can quickly submerge an empty soda pop bottle, top up, into a large jar or aquarium of water. As the air bubbles rise from the bottle, the students will realize that the bottle was not "empty," but that it was filled with a gas that we call air.

Feeling some characteristics of a gas: air. Have students swing their hands through the air quickly and describe what they feel. Next, have them hold stiff sheets of cardboard and swing their hands again. They will sense that the cardboard pushes against something. Now have them fill a balloon with air and hold the neck closed with one hand. With the other hand, squeeze and knead the balloon and describe how the contents tend to push back, but the balloon moves if pushed hard enough. When the neck of the balloon is released, they can feel the air rush out.
08 Ab

Smelling some characteristics of gases. Show some liquid perfume in a sealed bottle. Uncap the bottle when the air in the room is still and have students raise their hands when they smell the aroma.
09 Ad

They will realize that a gas comes from the bottle. (The gas cannot be seen, but it can be detected by the sense of smell.) Students can note the order in which hands are raised and see that the aroma is gradually diffused throughout the room. Have them note other smells that indicate the presence of a gas (e.g., fumes near a gas station pump; aromas of flowers).

Contributing Idea B. Indicators can be used to identify gases.

Producing carbon dioxide. Carbon dioxide is an odorless, colorless gas. It does not burn or explode. It is not poisonous. It is heavier than air, used to carbonate soft drinks, and is important to the life of plants. Students can produce carbon dioxide easily by several methods.
10 Bb Gc

a. Pour approximately 2 in. (6 cm) of vinegar into a soda pop bottle, flask, or other container. Add 2 tsp. (10 ml) of baking soda. Students will see that bubbles are produced. Baking soda is the common name for a chemical compound called sodium bicarbonate. It consists of the elements carbon, hydrogen, oxygen, and sodium. Vinegar consists of a mild acid called acetic acid. When the two are mixed, a chemical action occurs which sets free the gas called carbon dioxide.

b. Cover the bottom of a soda pop bottle or other container with a layer of eggshell pieces or broken bits of limestone or marble. Fill the container about three-fourths full of vinegar. Students will see bubbles (carbon dioxide) being produced.

c. Dry ice is a solid form of carbon dioxide. **Caution: Dry ice is extremely cold and dangerous to handle; handle with care.** Pick up a few small pieces of dry ice with gloves or tongs and place them in water. Observe the bubbles (carbon dioxide) coming from it. (Note: The fog that is produced is condensed moisture in the air and not carbon dioxide.) Students can do research on dry ice to learn how it is made and its uses.

d. Mix yeast with sugar and water. The gas produced is carbon dioxide.

e. Drop an Alka-Seltzer tablet in a glass of water to produce bubbles of carbon dioxide.

Collecting carbon dioxide. Carbon dioxide can be collected by several methods, the selection of which depends upon what is to be done with the gas.

11 Ge

a. As soon as some carbon dioxide is produced in a soda pop bottle or flask by any of the methods described in entry 131.10, have students immediately pull the neck of a balloon over the mouth. The balloon will inflate. When

filled, tie off the neck. Students now have a quantity of carbon dioxide gas in the balloon.

b. Produce carbon dioxide in a flask and collect it by placing a one-hole rubber stopper tightly into the flask. Extend from the stopper, a short glass tube to which is attached about 18 in. (50 cm) of rubber tubing (long enough so that it can be placed under test tubes or bottles as shown). Students will see the carbon dioxide as it bubbles through the water. (See Figure 131.11.)

Glass Tube — Rubber Tube
Water
One-Hole Rubber Stopper
Vinegar and Bits of Limestone

Figure 131.11

c. Vinegar added to baking soda, eggshells, or limestone can be sealed in plastic sandwich bags. The bags will inflate and can be sealed with a rubber band.

d. An Alka-Seltzer tablet can be placed at the bottom of a balloon or plastic sandwich bag. Tie it tightly in a corner of the bag with rubber bands or string, then fill the remainder with water and seal it. The gas can be produced by loosening the bands and allowing the water to reach the tablet.

Using an indicator to test for the presence of carbon dioxide. Several tests may be performed to detect the presence of carbon dioxide.

12
Fb
Ga

a. Collect some carbon dioxide in a test tube, place a thumb over the tube, and hold the tube upright. Carefully pour a small amount of clear limewater into the tube and observe what happens. (The limewater will turn milky indicating the presence of carbon dioxide.) To show that carbon dioxide is present in air, place a few spoonsful of clear limewater in an open container for several days and note that white deposits of limestone form around the edge of the container at the surface of the limewater. (This is the result of carbon dioxide in the air combining with the limewater.) To have students see that their own breath contains carbon dioxide, have them exhale through a straw into a glass of clear limewater. Students will find that it takes a great deal of blowing to turn the liquid milky. (Exhaled breath contains very little carbon dioxide—approximately 3% to 4%.) Students can also invert a jar over

a burning candle or germinating seeds, then test the candle and seed "airs" to see if they contain carbon dioxide.

b. Collect carbon dioxide by letting dry ice sit in a widemouthed container for several minutes. A glowing splint or lighted wooden match placed into the container will go out because carbon dioxide does not support combustion and can keep air from a fire.

c. A balance can be used to indicate different amounts of carbon dioxide in carbonated drinks. Place an unopened diet soda bottle on one side of the balance and a nondiet equivalent (same brand, bottle, and amount) on the other. Balance the bottles then open each to see if the scale dips to one side. If it does, what is learned? Comparisons can be made among different brands. If the scale has gram weights, the weight of the carbonation in a soda can be determined.

Producing oxygen. Oxygen is an odorless, colorless gas. It makes up about 20% of the air. It is slightly heavier than air and is a necessary component in supporting life. Whenever anything burns, it unites with oxygen. Oxygen can be produced by students in several ways.

13
Bb
Gc

a. Place 1 tbsp. (15 ml) of dry yeast in the bottom of a heat-resistant bottle or flask. When 1 tbsp. (15 ml) of hydrogen peroxide (6%) is added, a bubbling of oxygen gas will result. The gas can be collected in quantity by the collecting procedure described in entry 131.11b. If bubbles cease to be generated, simply add more peroxide. (Note: The peroxide should be fresh. Since it is light sensitive, it may decompose within a few weeks and become primarily water.)

b. Put a heaping spoonful of pieces of activated charcoal into a container such as a heat-resistant baby bottle. Cover the charcoal with 6% hydrogen peroxide and cover the bottle with a sheet of cardboard to trap the oxygen that is produced.

Testing for the presence of oxygen. Several tests and activities can be performed to detect the presence of oxygen.

14
Bd
Fb
Ga

a. Hold a container of oxygen right side up and keep it sealed until ready to test. Blow out a flaming splint of wood so that only a tiny spark remains. Remove the cover on the container and insert the glowing splint. (It will glow more brightly or burst into flame, thus indicating the presence of oxygen.) For a variation, twist a small piece of steel wool, hold it with a pair of tongs in a candle flame to bring it to a glow, and then drop the wool into a bottle containing oxygen. (Note: To keep the bottle from cracking during the burning, add a small amount of sand after the oxygen has been collected, but cover the bottle quickly to keep the gas from escaping.)

b. Iron can be used as an indicator for the presence of oxygen because it chemically interacts with the gas and produces rust (a form of burning). To prepare the testing conditions, obtain a box of steel (iron) wool from a grocery store. Remove one roll, find its loose ends, and gently unroll it. **Caution: Use gloves to protect hands from steel wool slivers.** Clip the knotted ends away with scissors and divide the remainder into fourths. Cut each fourth into fourths and roll each piece into a loose ball about ¾ in. (2 cm) in diameter. Soak the balls in white vinegar overnight to remove the coating that protects them from rusting, and then rinse them with tap water. Now wedge a ball of wet steel wool into the bottom of a test tube or other gas-collecting container. Wedge it just tightly enough to hold it in place when the tube is inverted. Collect oxygen in the container as described in entry 131.13a and leave the container inverted in a pan of water for 48 hours. If the steel wool rusts, oxygen was present in the container. An estimate of the amount of oxygen can be made by measuring how much water moved into the container from the pan and subtracting this volume from the total volume of the container. If three or four identical collecting containers can be obtained, students can do experiments to answer most questions that naturally arise from this test. For example, if students think that the distance between the steel wool and the water made a difference in the rise of the water, let them put a steel wool ball in the base of one container, three-fourths of the way into another, one-half of the way into a third, and one-fourth of the way into a fourth. Leave the containers inverted for 48 hours, and then observe the water levels. If students want to know if two steel wool balls would cause the water to rise higher than one, let them place two balls in two containers and one ball in each of two other containers. Observe after 48 hours.

Contributing Idea C. Gases have no shape of their own.

Observing the shape of a gas. Fill a balloon with air and seal the neck of it with a rubber band. Squeeze and make different shapes with the balloon. Ask students what shape the air inside has. They will realize that air can be compressed, and its shape can be changed. (Every time the balloon undergoes a change in shape, the air in it does, too.) If students repeat this activity with a balloon filled with carbon dioxide, they will realize that all gases are shapeless but take on the shape of their container. **15 Aa**

Contributing Idea D. Gases occupy space and have weight.

Observing that gases occupy space. Turn a glass full of air upside down and push it down into a pan or wash basin which contains 3 or 4 in. (8–10 cm) of water. Students will see that the air in the glass takes up space and holds the water from entering the glass. Now let them slowly tip the glass and observe the air bubbles as they leave it. When placed down again, they will see that the water has now entered the glass. Several variations of this activity can be performed. **16 Aa**

a. Push a piece of dry, crumpled, paper toweling into a dry glass. Be sure that the toweling cannot fall out. Invert the glass and push it to the bottom of the water in the pan. The toweling will remain dry because the air kept the water from entering.

b. Float a small cork in the pan and invert the glass over it. Note the level of the floating cork and let students explain why it changed. If a bottomless glass or jar can be obtained, it can be set over another floating cork next to the first glass, and the levels of the two corks can be compared side by side. Challenge students to give explanations for the differences they see.

c. Hold two inverted glasses, one filled with water, one with air, underwater in an aquarium. Pour the air back and forth between the glasses by tipping one to the side and trapping the rising air bubbles with the other.

Weighing a gas: air. Using a balance scale, have students weigh a balloon before they blow it up. Record the weight. Blow up the balloon and weigh it again. Compare the two weights and have students explain what the measurements tell them about air. Similarly, the weights of inflated and deflated playground equipment (e.g., footballs, basketballs, volleyballs) can be compared. **17 Cf**

Weighing a gas: carbon dioxide. Use a commercial balance scale with glasses balanced on each side, or balance a meterstick with two small empty paper bags of identical size as shown in Figure 131.18. Fill a jar with carbon dioxide and slowly **18 Cf**

Figure 131.18

pour it into one of the glasses or bags. Students will see the balance tip as the container receives the carbon dioxide, and realize that this gas is heavier than air.

Using a heavy gas to put out a fire. Use tongs or wear gloves to place several pieces of dry ice in a dry beaker. **Caution: Do not handle dry ice with bare hands.** Stand a short candle in another beaker and light it. Be sure the candle is below the top edge of the beaker. After a few minutes, hold the beaker containing the dry ice over the candle and tilt it as if to pour something out (Figure 131.19a). Students will see that the candle flame is extinguished. You might tell them that the dry ice is frozen carbon dioxide. As it changes to a gas, it remains in the beaker because it is heavier than air. When poured on a burning candle, it pushes the air out of the way and smothers the flame. Similarly, a jar containing vinegar and soda solution can be tipped so that the gas produced (carbon dioxide) will flow down a creased strip of paper aimed directly at the candle flame (Figure 31.19b, p. 54). An alternative method would be to light **19 Ga**

a candle that is set in a widemouthed jar that contains 1 in. (3 cm) of water (Figure 131.19c). Add several teaspoons (approximately 15 ml) of baking soda to the water, and then pour vinegar into the solution. As the bubbles rise and the amount of carbon dioxide collects, the candle will go out. Students will realize that the carbon dioxide not only puts out fires, but it is heavier than the surrounding air. Many fire extinguishers use carbon dioxide to put out fires. If possible, ask the school custodian to demonstrate one to the class.

Figure 131.19a   **Figure 131.19b**

Figure 131.19c

Contributing Idea E. Gases expand when heated and contract when cooled.

Observing that gases expand and con- **20** **tract when heated or cooled.** Cut a piece **Aa**

of rubber from a balloon and stretch it across the mouth of a flask or bottle. Secure it with a rubber band and place the container near a warm radiator or in a pan of warm water. Students can observe changes in the rubber membrane and discover that when the air inside is heated, it expands and forces the balloon outward. Now cool the container in a bowl of ice cubes and observe what happens. Similarly, several bottles of different sizes can be cooled in a refrigerator for about an hour, then capped with balloons and returned to the classroom. Judgments concerning expansion in relation to volumes can be made. A reverse procedure can be carried out by heating the bottles over a radiator, capping them with the balloons, and allowing them to come to room temperature.

Measuring the expansion and contrac- **21** **tion of a gas when heated and cooled.** **Cd** Blow up a balloon, measure its circumference with a tape measure, and place it over a radiator (or by some other heat source) for approximately 10 minutes, then measure its circumference again. Remove it from the heat source for approximately 10 minutes (or place the balloon in a bowl of ice cubes or refrigerator) and measure its circumference. By comparing the three measurements, students will be able to judge that the heat caused the air inside to expand and when the heat was removed, the air contracted.

132   Interactions

Generalization I. The volume of a gas is a measure of the space it occupies.

Contributing Idea A. The space a gas occupies can be measured.

Observing that gases occupy space. **01**
Aa
Carefully push a funnel through a one-hole stopper and place the stopper tightly into a bottle. Slowly pour some water into the funnel and observe what happens. Repeat using a funnel in a two-hole stopper (Figure 132.01a). Challenge students to explain the reason for the differences they note. (In the first test, air occupied the space in the bottle and the water could not enter; in the second test, the air was able to escape through the second hole as the water entered.) For a variation of this activity, insert a U-shaped tube or piece of plastic tubing in the second hole of the two-hole stopper. Fit a balloon over the end of the tube and tie it securely. Slowly pour water into the funnel until the bottle is filled (Figure 132.01b). Ask for explanations of the balloon's size increase as the water is poured. Remove the balloon, empty the bottle, and let a student hold a finger over the end of the tube. Fill the funnel with water again. Move the finger to open and close the tube and observe what happens. Ask students to tell about experiences they have had trying to pour or drink liquid from a can with only one hole punched. They will begin to realize

Figure 132.01a

Figure 132.01b

that two materials cannot occupy the same space at the same time.

Measuring and graphing air volumes **02**
in relation to burning times. Bring **Bf**
Ca
to school several jars of different sizes. **Cg**
Divide the class into groups, each with a birthday cake candle and a lump of modeling clay. Have one student be responsible for lighting the candle properly. (Note: Have a can of water available for the matches after the candle has been lit.) Let another student be a timer, using a watch with a second hand. Have each student, in turn, set the jar over the lighted candle when the timer says "go." Let each record how long it takes to burn,

then measure the volume of space in the jar by filling it with water from a measuring cup. Each test should be repeated several times to check on measurements. (Note: It is best to swing the jar through the air a few times before each test to fill it with fresh air.) The collected information can be placed on a graph similar to Graph 132.02. Students should place their measurements for their own jars on the grid. From the final graph, they will be able to predict how long a candle will burn for any size container.

MEASURING VOLUMES AND BURNING TIMES

Graph 132.02

Contributing Idea B. Gases have weight.

Comparing gases by weight. Collect carbon dioxide in a balloon, and then blow up a second balloon with air to the same size. Toss the balloons into the air and let students observe what happens. If helium can be obtained from a chemical supply house, fill one balloon with it, another to the same **03 Cf**

size with carbon dioxide, and a third with air. Release all three at the same time. Students will be able to judge that different gases have different weights.

Comparing gases by weight and volume. Inflate a balloon and set it over a radiator or other heat source. After 10 minutes, measure its circumference. Inflate a second balloon to the same size, but keep it at room temperature. Place the two balloons side by side and ask which contains more air and which is heavier. Let students check their guesses by placing the balloons on each side of a balance scale. Next, let the warm balloon cool and have the students compare the sizes. Students will realize which contained the most air and why one was heavier, even though both were once identical in size. (Identical gases of the same volume may differ in weight due to temperature differences.) **04 Cf Cg**

Generalization II. Gases exert pressure.

Contributing Idea A. The pressure of a gas increases with depth.

Feeling the weight of air. Let each student fill a plastic sandwich bag with air, either by blowing up the bag or by pulling it through the air quickly with the mouth held open. They may help each other tightly tie the air-filled bag upside down over the mouth of a jar with a string or rubber band. Have them press down on the bag, lean on it, rest a book on it, and **05 Ab Cf**

describe what happens. Now ask them to remove the bag, empty it of air, and tie it again—but this time with the bag inside the jar. When the bag is secure, have them hold the jar and try to pull the bag out. They will find that they cannot do this. (The plastic bag has air resting in it; this air weighs much more than the students can lift.)

Measuring the amount of air weight (air pressure) upon a surface. Place a meterstick, a slat from a wooden crate, or other very thin piece of wood approximately 1 yd. (1 m) long and 2 in. (6 cm) wide on a table, allowing approximately 1 ft. (30 cm) to extend over the edge. Have a student strike the end of the stick with his or her hand just hard enough to knock the stick off the table. **Caution: Do this activity away from other students, and be sure no one is in front of the stick.** Now replace the stick in the same position and lay an open section of newspaper over the part that is on the table. Let the student strike the end of the stick as before. Students can discuss what caused the stick to break. Next, fold the newspaper into a small bundle, approximately 6 in. × 4 in. (16 cm × 12 cm) and tape the edges so that the bundle lies flat. Let the student repeat the test using the folded paper. Challenge students to explain what might account for the results this time. As an alternative or supplementary experience, mark off one side of the

06 Bb Cf

open newspaper into 1 in. (3 cm) squares before placing it on the stick. When the paper is folded, fewer squares or surface areas are exposed to the air. By reminding students that air has weight (at sea level, the weight of the air on 1 square in. or 3 square cm of area is about 15 lbs. or 7 kg—all the air directly above 1 square in. or 3 square cm of surface), they can compare the weights on the squared surfaces. You might tell them that this weight is called air pressure. Next, mark off a piece of notebook paper into 1 in. (3 cm) squares, then have students draw an outline of their hands on the paper and calculate how many pounds of air are pressing down on their hands. Have students estimate how many 1 in. squares could fit on the outside of their bodies and how many pounds (kilograms) of air they think their bodies support. If students wonder why they are not crushed by all this pressure, you might explain that our bodies, like most objects, have air in them and this air pushes outward with the same force. When the forces are equal, we cannot feel the pressure. When they are unequal, we feel the pressure. Students can relate the sensation of their ears "popping" to this experience. (The sensation occurs when either the outside or the inside pressure in their ears is different.)

Contributing Idea B. The altimeter is an instrument used to measure the pressure air exerts at different altitudes.

Making an altimeter. Draw a line lengthwise across the middle of a white card and mark off ¼ in. (1 cm) spaces along the line. Insert the short arm of an L-shaped tube through a one-hole stopper and place a drop of colored water in the center of the long arm. Hold a finger over the end of the long arm while students insert the stopper into the mouth of a gallon plastic jug. Be sure the stopper is air-tight (some clay or petroleum jelly will seal the stopper). Now tape the card to the long arm of the tube and tie a string around the neck of the bottle leaving a loop so that it can be carried without fingers touching the jug (Figure 132.07). If your school has several floors, students can carry the altimeter to the highest floor and notice any change in the water marker. (Variations in air pressure upon the jug will cause the water to move in the tube.) You might tell them a device that indicates the weight or pressure of the air at different altitudes is called an altimeter. If possible, let them carry the altimeter in an elevator to observe what happens.

07
Bb
Gc

One Drop
Colored
Water

Figure 132.07

Contributing Idea C. The pressure of a gas is the same in all directions at the same altitude.

Testing to see if air pressure is the same in all directions. Cover the top of a funnel with a piece of rubber from a balloon. Be sure the rubber is stretched tightly and held in place with a rubber band. Students can take turns placing a finger over the small open end of the funnel and turning it in different directions to see if the rubber membrane remains level. Ask what would happen if the outside pressure was greater than the inside pressure. Now suck some air from the funnel and quickly cover the end with a finger. Ask why the membrane is depressed. (The air pressure inside the funnel is less than the air pressure outside.) Again turn the funnel in different directions to see if there is a change in the rubber membrane (Figure 132.08a). Students will realize that if the outside pressure were less at any position, the membrane would be less depressed or would bulge. If possible, test this device at different altitudes to see if air pressure is the same in all directions. Similarly, students can fill a glass to the brim with water and press a plastic dish cover over it (Figure 132.08b). A thin piece of cardboard can be used, but a dish cover is impervious to water. Let one student carefully turn the glass upside down over a sink or large pan and slowly remove his or her hand. (The cover will remain in place due to the outside air pressure pressing upward

08
Ec
Fa

Figure 132.08a

Figure 132.08b

against it.) Now hold the glass sideways and turn it in various directions. Ask students what this tells them about air pressure and what would happen if the pressure inside the glass were greater than the pressure outside. As an extension to this experience, you might ask if less water in the glass would make any difference in the test; then let students find out by retesting with the glass only partially filled with different amounts of water. They will discover that no matter how much or how little the amount of water, the cover will not fall off. The reason involves a factor that might be explained to the students: with a partial amount of water, the cover sags slightly from the weight of the water inside, the weight of the cover, and the pressure of the air inside. The sagging slightly enlarges the

space the air inside occupies, the almost imperceptible enlargement being enough to reduce the pressure inside the glass (pressure decreases as volume increases), and the greater outside air pressure being enough to stabilize the situation and hold the cover in place.

> *Contributing Idea D.* The pressure of a gas decreases as the amount of space available for the gas increases; the pressure of a gas increases as the amount of space available for the gas decreases.

Observing that the expansion and contraction of a gas increases and decreases its pressure. Invert a bottle or jar over a burning candle that is set in a tray of water. The candle is used to heat the air inside the container. As the air is heated, bubbles will be driven from the mouth of the container. (The air inside expands and the increased pressure forces some of the contents out.) When the candle is extinguished and the air inside cools, water will enter the container. Students will realize that this is caused by a reduction in pressure (The outside air pressure was greater than that inside the jar, thus its push on the surface of the water forced some of it into the container.)   **09 Aa Fa**

Using the pressure of a gas to extinguish fires. Students can make simple fire extinguishers that work from the pressure created by the production of carbon dioxide.   **10 Gc**

a. Clean an ink bottle that has a well inside. Put a small hole in the cap and insert a glass tube or plastic straw (the smaller the opening, the better). Let the tube extend no more than ¼ in. (0.5 cm) into the bottle and seal the fitting with clay, candle wax, or several coats of sealing wax. Now fill the well inside with sodium bicarbonate (baking soda) and the remaining portion approximately one-quarter full of vinegar. Screw the cap on tightly (Figure 132.10a). A small fire or burning candle can be extinguished by tilting the bottle upside down and aiming the tube or straw at it.

Figure 132.10a

b. Empty a tea bag and fill it with sodium bicarbonate. Suspend it in a bottle that is half-filled with vinegar water (50% vinegar and 50% water). Insert a one-hole stopper into the bottle. Extend from the stopper a piece of glass or plastic tubing with a short piece of rubber tubing attached (Figure 132.10b). The rubber tubing can be used as a hose to direct the spray when the bottle is inverted. To be effective, all fittings must be tightly sealed. Nozzles made from medicine droppers can be used on the end of the rubber tubing to increase the range of the spray, and different amounts of baking soda and vinegar can be tried to see which produce the strongest stream of water.

Figure 132.10b

Observing the effects of increasing air pressure. Blow up a balloon until it is slightly larger than the mouth of a large empty bottle. Tie the neck of the balloon with a rubber band, and then wet the balloon and the mouth of the bottle to make them slippery. Have students take turns trying to force the balloon into the bottle without letting the air out of the bottle. Now deflate the balloon and place it inside the bottle, a cup, or a glass with the neck up. Blow up the balloon as much as you can and lift it by its neck. Students will see that the sides of the bottle compress

11 Aa

the balloon which, in turn, increases the air pressure inside. The pressure is great enough to hold the object firmly so that it can be lifted.

Observing the effects of reducing air pressure. Blow up a balloon part way, tie it with a rubber band, and squeeze it into a transparent plastic jug. Prepare a stopper with a glass tube approximately 10 in. (25 cm) long and place it in the mouth of the jug. Attach a piece of rubber tubing to the glass tube and tighten the stopper in the jug. Have a student suck some air from the jug using a clothespin to squeeze the rubber tube together whenever the student stops to exhale. While the student continues sucking the air, have the others try to explain what causes the balloon inside to enlarge.

12 Aa

Contributing Idea E. Changes in air pressure can be measured.

Observing that air can support a column of water. Have students fill an olive jar or other tall thin jar with water and place a piece of cardboard over the open end. While keeping the cardboard in place, invert the jar in a bowl of water. When the open end of the jar is below the level of the water, remove the cardboard. Ask students to explain why the level of the water remains higher in the jar than in the bowl. (The weight of the air pressing upon the surface of the water in the bowl is sufficient to support a column of water in the jar.)

13 Aa

Making and using a water barometer. Place a bottle with a long slender neck (e.g., wine bottle) inverted in a quart or liter size jar that is half-full of water. Let a student warm the bottle with both hands until several large bubbles of air escape. Let the bottle sit undisturbed for several minutes. Students can be challenged to explain why the water rises in the bottle as it cools. Place the jar and bottle in a spot where the temperature remains constant. (A thermometer might be placed nearby to make sure the temperature is constant.) Number a large index card lengthwise with lines ¼ in. (1 cm) apart. Tape the card, lined side against the glass, on the side of the jar. Students can periodically read and record the level of the water inside the bottle and realize that the water level is an indicator of the pressure of outside air (providing the pressure inside the bottle does not vary as a result of temperature changes). You might tell them that the device they have made is called a water barometer (Figure 132.14).

14 Bb Ga Gc

Figure 132.14

Making and using an air barometer. **15**
Obtain a large, clean, dry bottle and place **Bb**
it in warm water for a few minutes. Be **Ga**
careful not to let any water enter the bot- **Gc**
tle. Over the top of the bottle, stretch a
piece of rubber from a balloon and secure
it tightly with rubber bands. Glue a straw
to the rubber top so that the straw extends
horizontally from the center. Hold the
straw firmly against the glue until it
dries, then flatten the free end by pinch-
ing it. Set a white card behind the straw
and place a mark on it at the level where
the straw touches it. Mark this position
0, then at ⅓ in. (0.5 cm) intervals mark
1, 2, and 3 above and below the 0 (Figure 132.15). Ask students to figure out in

Figure 132.15

which direction the straw will move when
air pressure increases or decreases. Since
the bottle contains a closed volume of air
under a certain pressure, any changes in
the outside pressure will cause the rubber top to move in or out slightly, causing
a rising or dipping of the straw that can
be noted on the scale. Now set the bottle
away from direct sunlight, radiators, or
other heat sources so that heat will not

influence the operation of the instrument.
You might tell them that this device is
called an air barometer. Keep records of
changes in air pressure. If a water barometer is also constructed, comparisons of
readings between the two can be made.

Generalization III. Heat causes gases
to move.

   Contributing Idea A. The movement
   of gases can be detected.

Detecting the diffusion of gases. Put a **16**
spoonful of inexpensive cologne in a jar. **Aa**
Inflate a balloon, secure it with a rubber **Bb**
band, and push it inside the top of the
jar just enough to seal it. After 24 hours,
remove the balloon and take off the rubber band. Let students describe the smell
of the escaping air. They will realize that
the cologne, as a gas, moved without the
aid of wind currents through the air in the
jar and through the balloon. You might
explain that this type of movement is
called diffusion. Next, close all the classroom windows and when everyone is still,
open a bottle of perfume or other material
of strong scent. Have students raise their
hands when they detect the smell so they
can see how the gas diffuses throughout the room. **Caution: Some students
might be allergic to certain perfumes
and other vapors.**

Constructing devices to detect air **17**
movements (currents). Have students **Bb**
observe the movement of leaves on trees, **Ga**
Gc

dust on the ground, or flags on poles. Ask them to notice other indicators that show when air is in motion. You might tell them that moving air is called wind. Students can construct various kinds of air movement indicators.

a. On a white card, make three concentric circles with diameters of 2½ in., 2¼ in., and ½ in. (6 cm, 5 cm, and 1 cm). Set the ends of a compass so that they are 1¼ in. (3 cm) apart. Place the point of the compass anywhere on the outer circle, and make six consecutive marks around the outer circle. Using a ruler, connect opposite marks with a straight line (Figure 132.17a). Carefully cut out wind foils along the dark lines and fold along the dotted lines as illustrated. The detector can be mounted on the eraser end of a pencil with a pin (Figure 132.17b). Be sure it spins freely. The device can be used to detect wind currents in different parts of the school grounds or classroom.

Figure 132.17a   **Figure 132.17b**

b. Stick a pin through the middle of a plastic straw and attach it to a

cork. Turn the straw on the pin a few times so that it rotates freely. Next, pinch together one end of the straw and fasten a paper clip to it. On the other end, glue or tape a light index card in a horizontal position. Level and balance the straw by moving the paper clip. Use a protractor to make a scale like the one illustrated in Figures 132.17c and 132.17d.

Figure 132.17c

Figure 132.17d

Attach the scale to a large side of a small breakfast cereal box. Glue the cork to the center of the scale. When the box is held in a vertical position, students will see that the detector arm moves up and down and indicates the relative force of the rising or falling air. When held in a horizontal position, it measures air that moves horizontally.

Hold the detector in various locations (e.g., over lighted bulbs, below open refrigerator doors, over radiators, below open windows). Measurements can be recorded and compared.

Contributing Idea B. The exchange of heated and less heated gases creates convection currents in gases.

Observing that warm air rises and cold air falls. Blow some soap bubbles or bring a burning candle flame near a hot radiator. Students can observe the movement as the bubbles or flame are placed in different positions. They will realize that the air above the radiator seems to travel upward while the air near the floor moves toward the base of the radiator. Similarly, the bubbles or flame can be brought near an open window to see which way the air moves. If observations are coupled with temperature measurements, the students will find that hot and cold air tend to trade places. (Note: The detector described in entry 132.17 can be used instead of the soap bubbles or candle flame.)

**18
Aa**

Generalization IV. Moving air has force and can do work.

Contributing Idea A. Moving air has force.

Observing that moving air has force. The force of moving air can be observed in many ways.

**19
Af**

a. Have students cut a hole in one end of a shoe box or similar cardboard box. Squeeze the sides of the box and feel the air coming from the hole. Squeeze the box to blow bits of paper or feathers with it.

b. Float a cork, a piece of wood, or a matchbox in a pan of water. With a sheet of cardboard or a fan, fan the object and move it across the water.

c. Fill a balloon, and then let it go. Students will realize that when the gas moves out of the neck, the balloon is forced in the opposite direction.

d. Smooth a paper bag and put it near the edge of a table with the opened end over the side. Place a book on the bag and blow the bag up. Students will see that the air has enough force to lift the book.

Contributing Idea B. The force of moving air can be used to do work.

Finding examples of the force of air being put to use. For each of the experiences in entry 132.19, let students find pictures in magazines that show how people have made use of the force of air to do work. For example, air compressors and vacuum cleaners would exemplify the first experience, sailing vessels the second, rockets the third, and air pumps the fourth. Students can also make various pinwheels and study how windmills can do work much like waterwheels.

**20
Ga**

140 Earth Science

141 Characteristics

Generalization I. Rocks have identifiable characteristics.

Contributing Idea A. Igneous rocks are formed from hardened magma.

Identifying the characteristics of magma. Obtain a stick of red sealing wax. Let students feel it, then set it in a hot place (near a heater or sunlit windowsill). When warmed, let them examine it again, and describe what changes took place. Now hold one end of the sealing wax in a candle flame, and let the wax drop onto a sheet of cardboard. Point out that the characteristics of the sealing wax are similar to those of thick, hot, molten, pliable rock within the Earth. You might tell the students that the hot plastic rock within the Earth is called magma, but when it comes to the surface it is called lava. Explain that when magma cools, it hardens (like the sealing wax) and forms masses of hard rock.

**01
Aa
Bb
Fc**

Making models to show how magma rises to the Earth's surface. Obtain a partly used tube of toothpaste, screw the cap on tightly, and flatten the tube so that the toothpaste is evenly distributed inside. Provide the analogy that the side of the tube represents the hard crust of the Earth, and the toothpaste represents the molten rock or magma beneath. Demonstrate how magma flows under pressure by pressing on the lower half of the tube. Students will note how the upper end enlarges under the pressure. After you explain that magma sometimes finds breaks or weak places in the crust, puncture the end near the cap with a pin. Students will realize that the toothpaste flowing up through the hole due to pressure is similar to magma flowing from the Earth and forming volcanoes. This idea can be further explored by making a volcanic cone from a sheet of paper and placing it over the open end of the toothpaste tube. Cut the point from the cone, and squeeze the tube. The toothpaste will flow from the cone like magma from a volcano. You might tell students that when magma flows on the surface of the Earth, it is called lava.

**02
Fc**

Identifying the characteristics of igneous rocks. Bring to class several examples of each of the following igneous rocks: granite, basalt, obsidian, pumice. Explain that because each was formed from magma, some people call them "fire rocks." You might tell students that scientists call such rocks igneous rocks. Students can describe the characteristics of each—their shapes, colors, and textures. Some students can break pieces of each kind with a hammer for closer examination with a hand lens and to see if each breaks in a regular way. **Caution: Place each rock in a bag or wrap it in a cloth to keep pieces from flying.** Some of the following information on each type might be helpful:

**03
Aa
Bb**

a. *Granite.* Granite forms under the ground when magma cools and hardens in spaces between layers of rock. Students can note that this type of rock is coarse and contains large crystals. It varies in shading from white to gray, and is sometimes pinkish. If possible, show examples of the use of granite in making statues, monuments, and buildings.

b. *Basalt.* Basalt forms when magma pours out of the Earth slowly and cools and hardens slowly. Students may note that this rock contains very small crystals. It is usually a dark, greenish-gray color. Some pieces have holes made by escaping gases.

c. *Obsidian.* Obsidian forms when magma pours out of the earth slowly like tar, but cools quickly. The students may note that this rock has no visible crystals. It has a black, glassy appearance. When fractured with a hammer, note what pattern the chips make. Hold pieces up to the light to see if light shines through. If possible, show examples of arrowheads made from obsidian.

d. *Pumice.* Pumice forms when magma spills out of the Earth so quickly that it is foamy. You might shake and squirt the foam from a soda pop bottle to illustrate how magma sometimes spills out. When cooled quickly, it forms pumice. Students can note that the grayish rock is very light, porous, and will float in a container of water.

Comparing crystalline differences in igneous rocks. 04 Ca Fc Obtain several examples of granite, basalt, and obsidian rocks. Let students compare samples of each with a hand lens. They will see that granite contains large crystals, basalt very tiny crystals, and obsidian no observable crystals. Ask why such differences might occur, then prepare solutions of powdered alum in two test tubes (two spoonsful of alum in water—shake to dissolve). Sugar, salt, Epsom salt, or borax can be used in place of the alum. Boil the solutions over a candle flame and add another spoonful to each. Explain that the solutions represent magma in the Earth. Now hang small nails from strings and suspend them in the test tubes. Set one test tube in a holder and allow it to cool slowly. Place the second test tube upright in a bowl of ice cubes to cool it quickly. In 24 hours the students will see differences in the formation of crystals—large crystals in the container that cooled slowly, small crystals in the one that cooled quickly. Students can make the analogy to rocks: slowly cooling rocks contain large crystals, and quickly cooling rocks contain small crystals. Let them order their rock samples by the speed at which they probably cooled.

Contributing Idea B. Sedimentary rocks are formed through the depositing of sediments that are pressed and cemented together.

Making a model of sedimentary deposition. Half fill a quart-size glass jar with water and add several handfuls of sand, gravel, and soil. (An alternative mixture might be made of powdered clay, sand, iron filings, and small brads.) You might point out that the mixture represents materials that a river might deposit in an ocean, sea, or lake. Shake the jar, and then set it on a table where it will not be disturbed. Observe the jar periodically throughout the day until the water clears. Students will note the layered appearance of the settled materials and can determine which materials are on top, in the middle, or on the bottom. The action is analogous to that of natural materials being added to old layers year after year. Many mineral deposits are thought to have been formed in this way.

05 Fc

Feeling and seeing the effect of the buildup of subsequent layers of sediment. The compaction of layers of sediment can be shown by having several students put one hand, palm down, flat on a tabletop and placing a book on it. The hand and the book are analogous to layers of sediment. Now place a second and a third book on top of the first. Students can describe how the hand feels, and realize the analogy to the pressure placed on

06 Af Bb

lower layers of earth as subsequent layers are placed on top. Similarly, students can experience compaction by pressure by having several take a handful of wet soil and squeeze it as tightly as they can. They will notice that the material seems to hold together, is harder, and is more compacted after the pressing. You might tell them that when small pieces of material are pressed and cemented together, they form a kind of rock called sedimentary rock. To make models of fossils in sedimentary rocks, see entries 151.15 and 243.06.

Identifying the characteristics of sedimentary rocks. Bring to class several examples of each of the following sedimentary rocks: conglomerate, sandstone, shale, and limestone. Explain that each was formed underwater as a result of layers of deposited materials. Differences in kind depend upon the materials deposited. Tell students that particles that settle are called sediments, and that when they harden, they are called sedimentary rocks. Have them describe the characteristics of each—shapes, colors, and textures—and note whether or not each breaks in a regular way. Examine the broken pieces with a hand lens. To identify the samples, some of the following information might be helpful:

07 Aa Bb

   a. *Conglomerate* forms underwater, made up of stones and pebbles cemented together. Students can see these pieces in the rock and can probably break some away from the specimen. Look closely at a sidewalk (an artificial conglomerate) to see how similar it is in composition.

b. *Sandstone* forms underwater, made up of tiny grains of sand cemented together. Students can clearly see the sand grains with a hand lens. By rubbing two pieces of sandstone together over a sheet of black paper, they can collect and study some of the grains. Sandstone may be of various shades of gray, yellow, or red. If it is brown or orange, it contains some iron.

c. *Shale* forms underwater, made up of clay or mud that is cemented together. By rubbing two pieces of shale together over black paper, the students can collect and study some of the tiny fragments with a hand lens. If a few drops of water are placed on the shale, it will give off an odor of mud or clay. Shale varies greatly in color and may be shades of gray, green, yellow, red, or black.

d. *Limestone* forms underwater, made up of shells and skeletons of animals that lived long ago. Often the shells are worn, making them difficult to recognize, but a vinegar test can be used to

identify limestone. To do the test, set a piece of limestone in a dish and put two other rocks which are not limestone in two other dishes. Pour some vinegar on each. Students will see bubbles and hear a fizzing sound in the limestone dish, and realize that such a reaction takes place only with forms of limestone rock. To further demonstrate how vinegar can be used as an indicator of limestone, pour some on a piece of classroom chalk and note the reaction. Explain that chalk is a very fine-grained limestone. Natural samples of limestone may be white, gray, or red in appearance.

Contributing Idea C. Metamorphic rocks are formed when pressure and heat change igneous and sedimentary rocks.

Identifying the characteristics of metamorphic rocks. Bring to class several examples of each of the following metamorphic rocks: gneiss, schist, quartzite, slate, and marble. Explain that each was formed from igneous or sedimentary rocks that were subjected to great pressures and heated over long periods of time. Tell students that scientists call such rocks *metamorphic rocks*. Have them describe the characteristics of each—shapes, colors, textures, and hardness—and then cover samples with a cloth or

08 Aa Bb

bag and break each with a hammer. Students can note whether or not each breaks in a regular way. Examine fragments with a hand lens. If possible, compare the metamorphic rock form with an example of the igneous or sedimentary rock form from which it was made. The following information might be helpful:

a. *Gneiss* is formed by pressure and heat from igneous granite. The crystalline fragments within the two kinds of rock can be compared.

b. *Schist* is formed by pressure and heat from sedimentary conglomerate.

c. *Quartzite* is formed by pressure and heat from sedimentary sandstone. With a hand lens, students can note how the sand grains have been reduced in size through the crushing action of great pressures.

d. *Slate* is formed by pressure and heat from sedimentary shale. Ask students to find out if wet slate smells like wet shale. (It does, but faintly.) Some blackboards are made of slate. If you have access to a slate blackboard, your students can examine the school blackboard to see if it is made of slate.

e. *Marble* is formed by pressure and heat from sedimentary limestone. Compare a piece of marble with a piece of limestone to note similarities and differences. Each can be subjected to a vinegar test. If the marble is first crushed with a hammer, it will react visibly in vinegar.

Making models of pressure and heat sources in the Earth. Models of pressure and heat sources can be shown in several ways.   **09 Fc**

a. Have students open books on their desks. Tell them that the pages represent layers of sediment in the Earth. Let them hold the center of the book with one hand while they push on the edges of the pages with the other. Explain that the bulging in the middle is similar to the building of layers of sediment in the earth when pressure is applied. You might explain that pockets formed beneath the layers sometimes fill with magma creating more pressure and heat on the layers.

b. Students can crumple a piece of paper, unfold it, and place it flat on a desk. When they push the ends of their papers toward each other, they will see that the pressure causes the surface to wrinkle up along certain crease lines. This suggests how mountains were formed along fault lines in the Earth and that as they were formed, the extreme pressures may have changed the surrounding rocks.

c. Wrap alternate color slices of white and brown bread together in waxed paper to make about six sedimentary layers. Place several very heavy books on the slices. Unwrap the slices after one day, and note what changes took place. Students can realize that in a similar way, sedimentary layers of rock are sometimes compacted by extreme pressures in the Earth.

Contributing Idea D. Rocks can be identified by certain physical characteristics.

Identifying rocks by size, hardness, and weight. Bring a variety of rocks to class for students to observe, handle, and compare. Different activities emphasize certain physical characteristics of rocks.

10 Bb Ca Da

a. *Size.* Set out some rocks ranging in size from sand to large stones. Have students sort the rocks by size. You might tell them that small pieces are *sand,* the next size rocks are *pebbles,* the next are *stones,* and the very large are *boulders.* (See entry 141.23.)

b. *Hardness.* Show that some rocks scratch or crumble easily and some do not. Try scratching one rock on another to see which is the hardest. Students can sort the rocks by degrees of hardness. (See entry 141.22.)

c. *Weight.* Show that some rocks are heavy and sink in water while others are light (e.g., pumice) and will float. Explain that despite differences in size, hardness, and weight, all are called *rocks.* Ask in what ways all the rocks are alike or why they are all called rocks. Some guidance in deriving a definition might be provided by asking the following questions: "Do rocks rust, rot, or burn?" "Do they move on their own, breathe, or grow?" Ask how they can be sure about answers to the guiding questions (e.g., place a rock and an iron nail in jars of water for several days to see which rusts; place a rock and a piece of fruit on a strip of waxed paper on a windowsill for a week to see which rots; place a rock and a piece of wood in a flame to see which burns). After such tests, ask again in what ways all the rocks are the same.

Identifying rocks by color and composition. Bring a variety of rocks to class and have students describe them by physical characteristics such as color and composition.

11 Ba Ca Db

a. *Color.* The colors of opaque rocks are best observed if the rock is scratched across a piece of unglazed tile. (Note: The streak that is left may be different from the rock's color.) Transparent and translucent rocks can be tested for their color or lack of color. Students can sort the rocks on the basis of colors.

b. *Composition.* Study the surface of the rocks with a hand lens, and note if they are made up of one or more kinds of material. If a rock is covered with a cloth or bag, it can be broken with a hammer, and the inside of the rock can be compared with the outside. Rocks can be sorted by the size of the particles they contain, or whether or not the particles are crystalline. In breaking rocks, you may find that some break in certain ways (e.g., along cleavages). Note the directions of breakage, if any (e.g., number of parallel sides or faces).

Contributing Idea E. Indicators can be used to identify some rocks.

Using indicators to identify some characteristics of rocks. Some rocks can be identified and sorted because they respond in certain ways to magnets or chemicals. Rocks that contain iron will respond to magnets. Rocks that have magnetic properties (e.g., magnetite, lodestone) will attract pieces of iron. Limestone and marble react to the vinegar test (see entry 141.07d). **12 Db Fb**

Generalization II. Minerals have identifiable characteristics.

Contributing Idea A. Rocks are composed of minerals.

Observing minerals within rocks. Using a hammer, pulverize a piece of granite that is wrapped in a cloth or in a bag. Pour the fragments on a piece of paper and observe them with a hand lens. Have students sort some of the fragments. There are three main kinds of minerals: feldspar (may be many colors), mica (may be black or light), and quartz (may be many colors). Tell students that all rocks are made up of materials called minerals. Explain that all the rocks of the world are made up of various combinations of minerals and that minerals have a definite, unchanging composition while rocks may contain varying amounts of different minerals. Pulverize other rocks and sort out the different minerals that are found. (Some will be made up of only one mineral while others will be made up of many.) **13 Aa Bb Db**

Contributing Idea B. Minerals can be identified by certain physical characteristics.

Identifying the characteristics of some minerals. Divide the class into small groups and provide each group with several hand lenses, a small bag of sand, and some black paper or a paper plate. Have each group examine its sand and sort the pieces by colors. After sorting, students can use Table 141.14 (p. 72) to identify some of the minerals that commonly make up sand. Have different groups compare **14 Aa Db**

findings, and then compare the composition of a sandstone rock with their sand samples. Students will realize that the various kinds of rocks are determined by the kinds of minerals within them.

Table 141.14. Color Sorting Key—Minerals in Sand

Color	Mineral
white or colorless	usually quartz
pink	usually feldspar
black	hornblend
green	serpentine
black and flat	black mica
shiny and flat	light mica

Identifying minerals by a streak test. Rub a sample of pyrite or chalcopyrite across a piece of unglazed porcelain tile. Tell students that the greenish-black powder is from the mineral in the rock and that it is often different from the color of the rock. Rub other rocks against the tile

**15
Aa
Ca**

and compare the color differences. Students will begin to understand that a color streak is useful in the identification of some minerals, but that white streaks are not. Table 141.15 lists the external coloring and the mineral streak made by some common minerals.

Generalization III. Soils have identifiable characteristics.

> *Contributing Idea A.* Soils are made up of small pieces of rock mixed with plant and animal materials.

Observing the nonorganic and organic components of soil. Gather a handful of dry leaves and sticks. Have students note how easily the materials can be crumbled to resemble soil. Let them feel some rich topsoil and compare the feel with soil from a barren spot. Tell them that dead plant and animal matter decays and builds in thickness to become what

**16
Af
Bb**

Table 141.15. Color Sorting Key—Minerals in Rocks

External Color	Streak Test	Mineral
blue-green	white	apatite
blue or white	white	calcite
brass yellow	greenish-black	chalcopyrite
green, purple, white	white	fluorite
lead gray	lead gray	galena
gray, red-brown	red-brown	hematite
brown	ochre yellow	limonite
gray or green	white	talc
black	black	magnetite
bright green	pale green	malachite
pale yellow	greenish-black	pyrite

is called humus. Mix some humus with the soil taken from a barren spot and note how the humus changes the color of the soil. If possible, take a nature walk, and have students notice where topsoil is built up and where it has been washed away. Ask in what kinds of places it seems to be deepest. Use rulers to see how deep the topsoil is. (It takes about 300 years to produce 1 in. (3 cm) of good topsoil.) Students can note that topsoil is darker than subsoil.

Sorting and identifying the nonorganic and organic components of soil. **17 Aa Db** Place several handfuls of soil in a large widemouthed jar. Let students cover the soil with approximately 1 in. (3 cm) of water, cap the jar, and shake it thoroughly. As the materials settle, students will note that the heaviest settle first and the lightest last. (The layers will be in the order of the weight of the particles.) After the materials have settled, carefully pour off the water, disturbing the sediments as little as possible. Examine a small sample from each of the layers with a hand lens. Identify and list how many objects other than grains of sand, pebbles, and rocks can be found in a sample of soil (e.g., crumbled bits of plant material, insects).

> *Contributing Idea B.* Rocks are broken down in the formation of soil.

Making models to show how rocks are broken down to make soil. **18 Fc** The wearing of rocks into smaller particles that make up soils takes place in a variety of ways. Depending upon the locality of the school, students can (1) observe the wind carrying and depositing dirt and dust; (2) observe a stream wearing away the earth, carrying sediments, and depositing them in other places; (3) observe how ocean shores are continually being worn away by water action; (4) observe how plants crack rocks. Some specific activities are suggested below.

a. *Wind and Water.* Bring to class different kinds of rocks varying in degrees of hardness. Have students scratch one rock with another to see how rocks can be worn into soil. They can rub various other rocks together over a sheet of black paper and observe the soil-like grains as they fall. They can realize that wind and water carry abrasive materials that wear away softer materials in a similar way. You might have them find pictures of areas eroded by wind or water.

b. *Temperature Changes.* Soak a rough piece of sandstone in water for about one hour, and then pour the rock and water into a milk carton. Set the carton in a freezer. When frozen, tear away the carton, and let the ice melt naturally in a fine sieve or cotton cloth. Examine the remaining rock and particles. Students can make the analogy to rocks that get wet naturally, freeze, and thaw. Now have them heat small pieces of soft rock such as sandstone in a pan over a hot plate for several minutes, turning them to distribute the heat evenly. Drop the heated rocks into a bowl of cold water and observe changes. Explain that the changes in temperatures in each activity were to simulate natural (slower) changes between night and day or winter and summer. Help them realize that temperature changes break down rocks, contributing to the building of soil. **Caution: Follow safety guidelines when using a hot plate or other heat source**.

c. *Plants.* Soak some seeds in water overnight, and then pack them tightly in a small plastic bottle with a screw cap. Cap the bottle and observe it daily. Students will see that as the seeds grow, the pressure exerted by them is great enough to break the bottle. Look for places in rocks, cement, or asphalt to find plants that are breaking down materials in a similar way.

Contributing Idea C. Plant and animal matter is broken down in the formation of soil.

Observing decay. Decay of organic materials can be observed in several ways.   **19 Aa**

a. Push a small pointed stick into the ground in a shady spot near small plants or grasses. Affix an apple onto the stick so that it cannot be carried away by animals. Observe it day by day and keep a record of what happens (e.g., the first signs that something had been eating it, the first break in the skin, the first indication of decay odors, the appearance of insects or worms and where they came from, the appearance of molds or fungi). The record will indicate how many days it takes the apple to almost disappear and how many different agents worked on the cleanup job.

b. Place a ½ in. (1½ cm) square of sliced ham on the playground where it will not be disturbed. Mark the spot and watch from a short distance to note if the meat gets moved, how, and by what.

c. Have students explore the school yard to list all the discarded objects that they can see. A table such as Table 141.19 may be used. Determine what fraction of the trash will not return to raw materials for future life, what

Table 141.19. Observing Trash

Substance Found	Decays Easily	Decays Slowly	Does Not Decay

fraction will help to make up new soil, and what fraction will provide food for animals or plants. Discuss the problems caused by materials that do not decay.

Manipulating conditions that affect the rate of decay. Half-fill two jars with dry soil and leave a third jar empty. Add equal amounts of leaves and grass cuttings to each jar. Moisten the soil in one jar, cover the jars; then after one week, students can compare the contents. Under which conditions did the materials seem to be changing into soil fastest?

20 Ch Ec

Contributing Idea D. Some soils contain nutrients that contribute to plant growth.

Testing to see how soil influences plant growth. Several kinds of activities can be carried out to enable students

21 Ec

to understand that some soils are very important for plant growth.

a. Line two glasses with blotting paper. In one glass, hold the blotting paper in place with paper toweling. In the other, hold it in place with rich garden soil. Place radish or lima bean seeds between the blotting paper and the glass (Figure 141.21). Add equal amounts of water and set in a warm sunny location. Keep both moist during the growth, and keep

Figure 141.21

daily records of what happens. Students will find that the plants in the glass without soil cannot sustain growth, and that the soil must be a contributing factor for continued growth.

b. Fill one flowerpot with sand, another with clay (or subsoil), and a third with loam (or topsoil). Plant five lima beans in each pot and place the pots side by side where they will receive the same amount of sunshine. Add the same amount of water to each pot daily and keep a record of the growth for a month. Decide which kind of soil is best for growth. (The topsoil is usually best.)

Generalization IV. Rocks can be organized by their physical characteristics.

Contributing Idea A. Rocks can be seriated.

Seriating rocks by hardness. Rocks vary in hardness and can be ordered from soft to hard. Table 141.22 is a commonly used hardness key. Students can set up their own hardness scale using the rocks they find by seeing if one will scratch another. (A rock that scratches another rock is harder than that rock.) They can then order their rocks by relative hardness. **22 Ab Da**

Seriating rocks by size. Have students bring to school rocks of different sizes. Line up all the collected rocks in a row from smallest to largest. Table 141.23 shows standard categories for the various **23 Aa Da**

Table 141.22. Hardness Sorting Key—Rocks

Hardness Scale (Soft to Hard)	Hardness Test	Rock Example
1	Scratches easily with a fingernail	talc
2	Scratches with a fingernail	gypsum
3	Scratches with a pin or copper penny	calcite
4	Scratches easily with a knife	fluorite
5	Scratches with a knife	apatite
6	Knife will not scratch rock and rock will not scratch glass.	feldspar
7	Scratches glass easily	quartz
8	Scratches quartz easily	topaz
9	Scratches topaz easily	corundum
10	Scratches all other rocks	diamond

Table 141.23. Size Sorting Key—Rocks

Name	Size (in in.)
Boulder	more than 10 in. across
Cobble	2½ to 10 in. across
Pebble	1/8 to 2½ in. across
Granules	1/16 to 1/8 in. across
Sand	1/64 to 1/16 in. across
Silt	As fine as scouring powder
Clay	Particles can only be seen with a microscope.

sizes. A set of rocks representing the different sizes can be kept in the classroom for comparative purposes.

Contributing Idea B. Rocks can be classified.

Sorting and classifying rocks. Bring to class a variety of rocks. Let students group them in as many ways as they can (e.g., by size, shape, color, texture, or other properties). They can use screens with openings of diminishing size to sift rocks by size, and then compare the kinds of rocks that comprise each size grouping. With knowledge gained from activities with igneous, sedimentary, and metamorphic rocks, students may be able to classify rocks on the basis by which they were formed. Young children can use egg cartons to separate specimens on the basis of simple observable characteristics (e.g., smooth or rough, flat or round, shiny or dull). Let the children decide where each new rock they bring to class should be placed.

24 Dc

142   Interactions

Generalization I. Wind physically changes the Earth's surface by carrying and depositing soil, sand, and other debris.

Contributing Idea A. Wind is air moving over the Earth's surface.

Observing wind moving across soil. Carry a vacuum cleaner outdoors and attach the hose to the end that blows air. Explain that the air from the vacuum represents wind that might blow across the Earth's surface. Point the nozzle at a spot of dry ground and turn the vacuum on. Students will see how the vacuum blows the loose particles of dirt, leaving a small depression. They can realize that wind erodes the land in much the same way— blowing dust and small particles from place to place. Have them look around the school's grounds to find where wind blows up dirt and dust. See if they can also find places (e.g., in corners of buildings) where the wind deposits the dirt, dust, and other debris.

01 Aa Ga

Contributing Idea B. Wind carries and deposits materials.

Observing how wind carries and deposits materials. Make a mixture of materials ranging in size from clay to coarse sand. Set several shallow pans outdoors at different distances from an electric fan. Turn the fan on at a slow speed and slowly pour a small steady stream of the mixture

02 Ca Fc

into the wind from the fan. Students will see how wind blows the particles. Let them note what kinds of particles are collected in the different pans. (There will be a pattern with the heavier particles being nearer the fan.) Repeat the activity using faster fan speeds to see if the force of the wind makes any difference. Students will realize how this activity is similar to the way particles are actually moved across the Earth's surface by the wind.

Measuring the distances wind carries and deposits different materials. Mark a 20 in. × 30 in. (50 cm × 75 cm) sheet of paper or cardboard into 1 in. (2 cm) squares and tape it tightly to a table in front of an electric fan. Place a spoonful of rice on the edge of the paper directly in front of the fan. Hold a large sheet of cardboard between the fan and the rice. Turn the fan on. When it reaches a steady speed, remove the cardboard for 15 seconds, and then turn the fan off. Students can measure how far the rice moved across the paper in that time and record their findings. Let them repeat the activity using puffed rice. Record measurements and compare differences between the two kinds of rice. Students might want to try an equal mixture of puffed rice and rice. Challenge students to find out if it is the size or the weight of the rice that makes a difference. Many variations of this activity can be tried. Students can test different kinds of materials (e.g., sand, sugar, salt, talcum powder, dry soil); they can try varying the wind power by using a larger or smaller fan, by increasing or decreasing its speed, or by changing its distance from the test material. After reaching some conclusions about size and weight and wind force, have them recall the greatest distance the rice (or other substance) moved in a previous test. At half the distance, place an eraser, and then repeat the activity. Students will see that the rice collects against the object. Have them find examples around the school that show when something gets in the way of the wind, it lessens the wind's speed and the wind deposits some of the material it was carrying. You might explain that sand dunes are formed in this way.

03 Cd Ec

Collecting and comparing samples of wind-borne materials. On a windy day, set up a wide board in a field or open space on the school grounds so that the wind blows against it. Let students coat the board with some glue, paste, or strips of double-sided tape, and observe what collects against the board in a half hour. Note any differences in the kinds of particles found at the top of the board and those at the bottom. Comparisons can also be made by repeating the activity on a less windy day. You might let students describe the stinging sensation they have felt on their faces when walking into wind-whipped sand or dust.

04 Ca Ge

Contributing Idea C. Wind-carried materials carve and erode land surfaces.

Finding examples of surfaces worn by wind-carried materials. 05 Ga Have students look at sand under a hand lens, and note that the edges of the grains (especially quartz) are sharp. Explain that these grains can be blown through the air by wind and that they can scratch and wear away rocks. Ask students to comment on how wind-blown sand and dirt feels against hands and faces. If any student has been in a sandstorm, let him or her relate the experience. Explain that the long-time effect of wind-carried particles gradually wears down the Earth's surface. Have students find pictures from magazines of wind-worn desert rock formations. In some pictures, students might note that the wearing seems to be greatest near the base. Let them hypothesize why. If possible, observe sandblasting to see how wind-driven sand is used to clean buildings or to take paint from surfaces.

Observing how soft rocks can be worn by hard rocks. 06 Aa Rub a piece of sandstone with a piece of limestone over a sheet of black paper. Students will see that tiny particles of rock are rubbed from the softer rock. Similarly, rub pieces of hardwood and softwood with sandpaper and collect the particles on separate sheets. Students will understand that these experiences are examples of how rocks can be eroded and

that particles carried by the wind erode softer materials in a similar way.

Generalization II. **Water physically changes the Earth's surface by carrying and depositing soil, sand, and other debris.**

Contributing Idea A. Some water is absorbed into the Earth's surface and stored in porous soils and rocks.

Observing the porosity of soil and rocks. 07 Aa Bb Cf Absorption of water can be shown by dipping one end of a slice of bread or sugar cube in colored water. Explain that materials like these contain many empty spaces and are said to be *porous*. Now fill a glass three-quarters full of dry soil. Pack it in tightly, and then quickly fill the rest of the glass with water. Observe the bubbles coming from the soil. Ask students to explain the derivation of the bubbles. (Soil is porous and filled with air pockets; as water fills the pockets, the air is driven out.) Next, show how individual rocks can absorb water by weighing a piece of granite and/or marble and a piece of sandstone and/or limestone, recording the weights, and then placing the rocks in a jar of water. After one day, weigh each rock again. Students will find that some rocks are more porous than others, indicated by the increased weight of the absorbed water. For fun, let students try to wipe the rocks dry.

Measuring amounts of airspace in different soils. 08 Cg Put some soil in a glass jar and carefully, but quickly, pour in some water. Let students note the air bubbles that come from the soil as the water seeps through. Students can use this procedure to visually compare amounts of air in different soils. They will realize that the amount of space (porosity) influences the drainage and retention of water on land. More precise measurements of airspace can be made by several methods.

a. Fill a large glass jar with dry pebbles from a beach or creek bed. Let students estimate how much space there is between the pebbles, then see how near their estimates are by filling the jar to the brim with measured amounts of water. Other soils such as sand or gravel can also be measured. **Caution: Follow safety guidelines when glass is used.**

b. Place 8 fl. oz. (237 ml) of water into a quart (liter) jar, then add dry sand, 1 fl. oz. (30 ml) at a time, to the water until the sand's surface is even with the water's surface. Count the fluid ounces (milliliters) of sand that were added and compare the two measurements. For example, if there are 8 fl. oz. (237 ml) of space in 32 fl. oz. (948 ml) of sand, then 25% of the sand is airspace.

c. Put a two-hole stopper into a widemouthed jar filled to the brim with a soil sample. Try samples of subsoil as well as topsoil. Tap the jar to settle the soil, and then insert the stopper, leaving no airspace above the soil. In one hole of the stopper, place a thistle tube that extends to the bottom of the jar. In the other, place a U-shaped tube that has some rubber tubing attached to it. Invert a second jar of water in a pan of water and place the end of the rubber tubing under it. Add water to the thistle tube until the jar of soil is filled to the stopper (see Figure 142.08). Compare the amount of air collected in the second jar with the amount of water poured into the first. Keep a record of the amounts, and let students test other soils in the same way.

Figure 142.08

Measuring amounts of water in different soils. Place some soil in a tin can and cover it with a glass jar. Set the can in   09 Cf sunlight or in a pan on a hot plate and heat it. Have students note the moisture that collects inside the jar. Using this procedure, they can visually compare amounts of water in different soils. A more precise measurement of amounts can be made by weighing one pound of garden soil on a scale, then placing it in sunlight for several days or in an oven for several hours to dry out. When dry, reweigh it to see how much weight was lost due to the evaporation of water. Similarly, students can take samples of different kinds of soil and make small, wet mud balls (about the size of a pea). Let them weigh each mud ball sample on a scale, record the weight, and set it aside on a piece of waxed or foil paper to dry. When dry, weigh the balls again and figure out how much water each held. Students can examine the characteristics of the different soils with a hand lens to judge why some hold more water than others.

Testing the compaction of different soils. **10 Ec** Fill several large juice cans with soil, each with a different type. Press a sharpened ¼ in. (1 cm) diameter dowel into each can to see how far it can be inserted. Let students keep records of the results. Next, have them wet the soils and try this again. When the soils dry, try a third time. Students can make comparisons among the soils and among the three tests, and make judgments on which types of soil were the most or least compact.

Making a soil compaction gauge. Have **11 Gc** students sharpen one end of a 10 in. (25 cm) dowel in a pencil sharpener. With a ruler, measure 1 in. (2 cm) from the point, and make a ring around the dowel. Measuring from the unsharpened end, mark and number 10 lines ½ in. (1 cm) apart. Fasten a wide rubber band to the top of a wooden spool with tacks or staples. Slip the dowel into the spool and pull down on the spool forcing the point of the dowel into the soil up to the ring line (see Figure 142.11). The number at the top edge of the spool will indicate the relative compaction of the soil. Students can try the gauge in other places (e.g., lawns, gardens, baseball infields, paths, sloped hillsides), find where the soils are most and least compacted, and observe how the relative compaction compares with the number and kinds of plants growing nearby.

Figure 142.11

Comparing and measuring the absorp- 12 tion of water by different soils. Have **Cb Ch** students tie a piece of cloth over one end of each of several lamp chimneys. Fill each chimney three-fourths full with a different type of soil (e.g., sandy, loamy, fine gravel, clay). Place the lamp chimneys in a flat pan of water and observe the type of soil in which the water rises the highest or fastest. Have students make some judgments about the types of soil and their ability to absorb water. Rates of absorption can be determined by timing the absorption for one minute and measuring the height of the water in each lamp. The relationship of height to time will provide the absorption rate (e.g., 1 in. in 30 seconds). Clear plastic drinking straws can be used as substitutes for the lamp chimneys.

> *Contributing Idea B.* Water accumulates and flows from high places to lower places over the Earth's surface.

Making a model to show the cumulative flow of water. Place a large plate in a sink; crumple up some waxed paper and put it on the plate. Place a small object under one edge of the plate so that it is slightly tilted. Tell students that the waxed paper represents a mountain range, and then pour a little "rain" in different places on the uphill end of the waxed paper. Let students observe where the water goes. They will see that each trickle of water tends to collect and to work its way downhill to the lowest point. They will realize that, similarly, the water on mountains

13
Fc

collects to form streams, and streams collect to form rivers that collect and eventually empty into oceans and seas.

Measuring the speed of flowing water. **14**
The speed at which water flows can be **Ch**
determined by several methods.

a. Students can float an object in moving water (e.g., a stream or gutter flow) and measure the distance it travels in one minute or in some specified number of seconds. For example, a leaf or piece of paper placed in moving water might travel 88 ft. (16.5 m) in one minute. This information can be calculated to determine the speed in miles (k) per hour (88 ft. × 60 minutes = 5,280 ft./hr. or 1 mi./hr.; or 17 m × 60 minutes = 1,020 m/hr., approximately 1 km/hr.).

b. Mark a 100 ft. (50 m) distance along a straight-flowing portion of a stream. Float an object between the marks and record the time. If the object travels 100 ft. (50 m) in 25 seconds, then dividing by 25 equals 4 ft. (2 m), which is the number of ft. or meters traveled in one second. The speed per hour can be calculated: 3,600 seconds (number of seconds in one hour) × 4 ft. (2 m) = 14,400 ft. (7,200 m) (approximately 2.7 mi. or 7.2 km/hr.).

Making a clinometer. A clinometer is an instrument used to measure the slope of a hillside. One can be made by obtaining a plastic protractor or drawing a protractor on an index card and mounting it on a wooden ruler or stick. An indicator line made from a thread and weight (e.g., a paper clip) can be suspended by a thumbtack from the center of the protractor's diameter (see Figure 142.15). When the instrument is tipped upward, the number of degrees from the horizontal can be read on the protractor. A straw attached to the top of the ruler aids sighting of some object at the top of a hill. The angle read on the protractor indicates the slope of that hill. **15 Gc**

Figure 142.15

Determining the steepness of a slope. Have one student stand at the bottom of a hill and, through the straw on a clinometer, sight an object or another student standing at the top of the hill. Have another student read the angle indicated on the clinometer. If students compare the slope of a hill to the speed of water flowing down it and the amount of materials carried by the water, they will discover a relationship between the steepness of the **16 Cd Ch**

slope, the speed of flow, and the amount of erosion taking place.

> *Contributing Idea C.* Water carries and deposits materials.

Observing how rain carries away soil. Fill several flower pots or cans with loose soil until the soil is just level with the edges. Place some small stones or bottle caps on the surface of the soils and set the containers outside or in a sink. Water them with a watering can to represent rain, gradually increasing the flow. When finished, let students notice how the unprotected soil is splashed away, leaving columns of soil under the stones. After a rain, have students look for the same effect in an unplanted area. **17 Aa**

Collecting and comparing samples of waterborne materials in different locations. After a heavy rainfall, have students take samples of running muddy water in glass jars. Label the jars with the location of the water. Let the water stand for several hours until the contents have settled. From their observations, students will realize that moving water carries materials, and that the materials settle out of the water at different rates. Compare the kinds of sediments collected from the different locations. **18 Ca Ge**

Testing to see how water carries and deposits materials. Prepare a long U-shaped cardboard trough filled with coarse sand. Hold the cardboard in a **19 Ec**

slanting position over a pan and pour water, a little at a time, on the sand at the upper end. Have students note that as the water flows slowly, it carries small grains of sand with it into the pan while the larger and heavier pieces stay behind. Now pour the water with a greater force. Students will see that both the sand and larger pieces are washed downstream and will begin to realize that moving water carries objects. Students can experiment with the trough by raising and lowering it to see what effect the slope has upon the carrying and depositing of materials. They can experiment by placing a large object, such as a rock, in the flow of the water to see what effect it has on the deposition of sediments.

Testing to see how waterborne materials are deposited to build up landforms. Cut a V-shaped notch in one end of an aluminum foil pan. Weigh some dry soil and fill the pan with it. Set the pan at one end of a larger pan and raise the uncut end by resting it on a small block of wood. Each day for a week, let students sprinkle a half cup of water over the soil at the top of the pan. At the end of the week, have them examine the soil that was washed into the larger pan. They will see that the smaller, lighter materials fan out the farthest from the opening. Explain that this happens because the flowing water slows down as it fans out, thus depositing the heavier materials first

20
Bb
Ec

and the lighter ones last. Tell students that the materials deposited from rivers as they slow down are called sediments. If possible, show pictures of delta regions (e.g., the Mississippi River) to help students realize that such deposits take place at the mouths of rivers. You might challenge them to hypothesize what happens to sediments that are blocked by dams. To check hypotheses, build a dam in a gulley or gutter of running water or block it by curving a large sheet of cardboard. As the water rises behind the dam, observe what happens to the materials it carries. Students can make the analogy to actual dams that span rivers. Discuss the problems of sediment buildup and possible solutions.

Contributing Idea D. Water and waterborne materials carve and erode land surfaces.

Using a model to test the erosive power of raindrop splashes. Have students fasten a sheet of white paper to a piece of cardboard. Set it on the floor, and from a foot above the paper, drop colored water (to represent raindrops) from a medicine dropper. Note the size and shape of six splashes. Carefully remove the paper and replace it with a fresh sheet. Tilt the board slightly and repeat. Students can compare these splashes with the others. Continue the activity by gradually increasing the slope of the surface, using a new sheet of paper each time. When dry, the papers

21
Ec
Fc

will be a visual record for display. Other tests can be made by varying the height of the falling drops and by varying the height and the slope at the same time.

Measuring differences in soil erosion caused by raindrops. 22 Cd Make several splash boards out of shingles or similar board pointed at one end. A covering over the top will keep sheets of graph paper attached to the splash boards from being hit directly by raindrops. When the weather forecaster predicts rain, have students drive the pointed ends into the soil in several different locations (e.g., under trees, on lawns, on bare paths). Be sure the graph paper is level with the Earth's surface (see Figure 142.22). After a rain, measure the height to which the soil splashed in the different locations. Students can judge which surface seems to protect the soil best from being carried away by raindrops.

Figure 142.22

Making a model to show wave action along a shoreline. 23 Fc Obtain a large, 10 in. × 15 in. (25 cm × 30 cm) baking pan, about 5 in. (12 cm) deep. Mix some soil with water to make mud. Fill about one-third of the pan with mud at one end to a height of 4 in. (8 cm). When it dries, place a 2 in. (4 cm) layer of sand in the remaining portion of the pan and add enough water to submerge the sand. Place a wooden board into the pan at the sandy end and move it back and forth to make small waves. Explain that the model represents the ocean battering a shoreline. Students can observe the waves as they splash against the land mass and note how a beach gradually forms, how the particles are tumbled by the waves, how the land mass is eroded, and how the eroded portions are distributed (see Figure 142.23).

Figure 142.23

Contributing Idea E. Glacier-carried materials carve and erode land surfaces.

Making a model to show that pressure melts glaciers. 24 Fc Have students arrange two groups of ice cubes (four in each group) and place a square of cardboard on top of each group. Place a brick or a pile of heavy books on top of one group and observe which group melts faster. Students can decide whether or not pressure makes a difference. Explain that, similarly, the bottoms of glaciers melt due to the weight of the upper layers of ice. Although the movement of glaciers is very complicated, some theories suggest that the continuous process of melting, refreezing, and melting again contributes to the movement.

Making a model to show glacial erosion. 25 Fc Have students rub an ice cube across the painted surface of a board, noting that the ice is not hard enough to abrade the surface. Now let them press the cube into a dish of sand. When the ice melts a bit, place the dish and the cube into a freezer. After it refreezes, remove the cube and rub it across the board again. (It will have picked up pieces of sand and will scratch the board's surface.) Explain that glaciers similarly melt, pick up sediments, and refreeze. Ask what might happen when soil, sand, rocks, and boulders become frozen into the edges of a moving glacier. Ask what happens when a rock rubs against other rocks and soil. If possible, show pictures of glacial valleys. Students can note how sliding glaciers have ground away rocks and soils to deepen and widen the valleys through which they travel. Notice that the valleys are always U-shaped.

Generalization III. Temperature changes and plant growth physically change the Earth's surface by breaking larger materials into smaller ones.

> *Contributing Idea A.* The alternation of hot and cold temperatures breaks rocks.

Testing a model to show how a change from a hot to cold temperature can affect materials. 26 Ec Fc Heat several glass marbles on a plate in an oven or on a pan over a hot plate. Move them about to heat them as evenly as possible. When very hot, remove them with tongs and plunge them into a container of very cold water. Students can observe the results and hypothesize what will happen when you repeat this activity using small rocks. (Some rocks, like those containing large amounts of quartz, will break into various size pieces.) Students will realize that repeated heating and cooling (e.g., day–night; summer–winter) slowly causes rocks to break into smaller pieces.

> *Contributing Idea B.* Water breaks rocks when it freezes.

Testing a model to show how water freezes and expands to break rocks. 27 Ec Fc Fill two small jars to the brim with water. Cap one tightly, but leave the other uncapped.

Students can pretend the jars are rocks and that the water has filled cracks in them. Place the jars in plastic bags and seal the bags with rubber bands. Set them in a freezer overnight. (Be sure the open jar does not spill.) Have students examine the results the next day. (One jar may break while the water in the other may expand above the rim without breaking the jar.) Now have students soak several pieces of porous rock (e.g., sandstone, limestone, pumice) in water for an hour. Place the pieces in a plastic bag and set the bag in a freezer overnight. Challenge the students to hypothesize what will happen to the rocks, and then examine the rocks the next day. By analogy, students can realize that water from rain and melting snow flows into cracks and pockets in rocks during the daytime, then at night the liquid sometimes freezes, expands, and cracks pieces from the rocks.

Contributing Idea C. Growing plants break rocks.

Observing the breaking of rocks by plants. Cut one side from a milk carton, **28 Aa** and fill it halfway with moist soil. Plant some soaked corn or lima beans just under the surface of the soil, and pour approximately ¼ in. (1 cm) plaster of paris on top of the soil. Set the carton aside and examine it daily. Students will soon note that the germinating seeds push up under the plaster with enough force to break it. Similarly, students can plant the seeds and

place a sheet of heavy glass over them. They will soon see that the germinating seeds will push the glass upward. (The glass allows the students to observe the process directly.) Students will learn that germinating seeds can either cause rocks to move out of the way or crack them into smaller pieces. Explore the school's grounds to find places where plants have broken through asphalt or cement.

Generalization IV. Water chemically changes some materials on the Earth's surface.

Contributing Idea. Water dissolves and deposits some materials.

Observing that some materials are dissolved and deposited by water. The **29 Aa Fc** following activities demonstrate the formation of mineral deposits on the surface and interior of the Earth:

a. Salt deposits can be found in various locations on the Earth's surface. To show how deposits may be formed, have students put a small amount of salt in a jar of water and shake it. Ask what happens to the salt. (It seems to disappear as it dissolves.) Ask students to name other materials that dissolve in water. Now let them continue adding spoonfuls of salt until some remains in the bottom of the jar even after a thorough shaking. Pour the water into a shallow pan and set the pan in a sunny place to let the water evaporate naturally. Discuss the results. Ask where on the Earth's surface similar salt deposits have been found (e.g., Great Salt Lake, Utah). Explain that salts in the Earth are continually being dissolved by water. Ask where the water usually takes the salts (lakes, seas, and oceans). Let students describe the ocean's taste and relate their descriptions to this activity.

b. Stalactites and stalagmites build up in caves from the dissolving and depositing of minerals by water. To illustrate the formation of stalactites, which hang down from the ceiling of some caves, and stalagmites, which stand upright on some cave floors (usually beneath stalactites), have students dissolve as much Epsom salt in a container of water as they can. Fill two smaller containers with the solution, set them on paper towels, and suspend a thick string between them, one end in each container. Let the string remain for several days. Students will see that water soaks the entire string and drips off at the low point between the containers. They will also see that deposits form where the water drips—both from the string and on the towels. They can infer that the deposits are carried

in solution to the drip point and that through evaporation of the water, the mineral is left behind. They will realize that this formation is similar to the slow formation of stalactites and stalagmites in some caves.

143   Theory

Generalization. Unbalanced forces above and below the Earth's surface cause mountain formations.

> *Contributing Idea A.* The formation of the Earth's surface took place very slowly over a long period of time.

Making a model to explain a theory of how the Earth was formed. Have students pour some red and orange dye into a pot of hot wheat cereal. Add water, stir and bring to a boil on a hot plate. Observe the bubbling action. Tell students that magma in volcanoes looks similar when it surfaces as lava. Explain that some scientists theorize that the Earth's surface was much like this many years ago. Now turn off the heat, allow the material to cool, and let students observe the changes that take place on the surface. They can realize that the Earth may have cooled in a similar way and that the cooling took a very long time. **01 Fc**

Making a model to explain a theory of the composition of the Earth's interior. Prepare a model to represent what some scientists theorize the interior of the Earth **02 Fc**

to be. To do this, place a pea in the center of a ball of Plasticene clay approximately 1¼ in. (3 cm) in diameter. Place this ball within another ball of clay (a different color), making the total diameter 2½ in. (6 cm). Dip the ball in plaster of paris to give it a thin coating. When dry, cut the sphere in half and explain the components (see Figure 143.02).

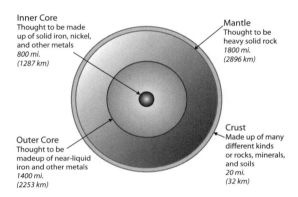

Inner Core
Thought to be made up of solid iron, nickel, and other metals
800 mi.
(1287 km)

Mantle
Thought to be heavy solid rock
1800 mi.
(2896 km)

Outer Core
Thought to be madeup of near-liquid iron and other metals
1400 mi.
(2253 km)

Crust
Made up of many different kinds or rocks, minerals, and soils
20 mi.
(32 km)

Figure 143.02

Contributing Idea B. Pressures in the Earth cause blocks of crust to shift along fault lines causing earthquakes.

Making a model to show how blocks of Earth can shift along cracks. Set several strips of colored clay (alternate the colors), one on top of the other, to represent sedimentary layers of earth. Cut through the layers with a knife. Tell students that the line or crack between the two portions is called a fault line. Now set the two blocks side by side and press them together by slowly increasing the **03 Bb Fa Fc**

pressure. Students can observe the folding, breaking, and shifting of the layers in each block and realize that mountains and valleys might be similarly created by shifting blocks.

Making a model to show that earthquakes are vibrations. Have students hold a piece of thin wood (about ¼ in. by 2 ft. × 1 in. or 1 cm × 75 cm × 3 cm) by the ends. Let them slowly bend the wood until it breaks. **Caution: The bend should be away from the body and other students.** Explain that, in a similar way, layers of rock in the Earth bend until they can bend no more and they suddenly break. Have students describe what they felt in their hands when the wood broke (a slight tingling sensation). Tell them that what they felt were vibrations caused by the break. Explain that when rocks break or shift in the Earth, their movements cause vibrations that are sent through the Earth, and these vibrations are called earthquakes. **04 Bb Fc**

Making a simple seismograph. Tie a short pencil with a sharp point to a pound weight, such as a fish weight, that has been suspended from a support. Adjust the height of the weight and pencil so that the point just touches the surface of a sheet of paper (see Figure 143.05, p. 90). Let students jump up and down on the floor of the room and note what happens. (The pencil will vibrate and make marks on the paper.) Tell them that the **05 Bb Ga Gc**

instrument is called a seismograph and that it works on the same principle as the seismographs used by scientists. Students can see how sensitive their instrument is by jumping up and down at greater and greater distances from it. They will realize how a seismograph can be used to detect earthquakes.

Contributing Idea C. Pressures in the Earth force magma, rocks, and gases to the surface to form volcanic mountains and great lava fields.

Weight

Pencil

Figure 143.05

Making a model to observe some of the characteristics of magma. Students can thin some clay soil with water until 06 Fc

it flows like mud. Have them fill a plastic bag with the material and tie the bag securely to the mouth of a small funnel. Now let them invert the funnel and press on the bag. If possible, compare what is observed with pictures of lava flowing from volcanoes. Explain that magma (melted rock deep within the Earth) is called lava when it comes to the surface. The consistency of the material can be varied and differences compared.

Making a model of a fault line eruption. Fill an 8 in. (20 cm) cake pan with thick mud. Cut a square of cardboard to fit the pan, and make two slits in the cardboard (6 in. long and ¼ in. wide or 15 cm × 5 cm). Press the cardboard down onto the mud evenly and observe what happens. Students will begin to understand that not all volcanic eruptions are spectacular; sometimes magma flows out on the surface as lava from long cracks in the Earth. If possible, have them find pictures of land masses formed by this type of volcanic activity (e.g., the Columbia and Snake River Plateau in the northwest United States). 07 Fc

150 Oceans

151 Characteristics

Generalization I. Ocean water has identifiable characteristics.

> *Contributing Idea A.* Ocean water is a solution of many dissolved gases and solids.

Observing that ocean water contains dissolved materials. Obtain a quart (liter) of ocean water, or simulate ocean water by dissolving 1 oz. (28.35 g) of table salt in a quart (liter) of water. Pour the water into a clean, shallow pan. Allow it to evaporate by placing the pan in the sunlight or by gently heating it over a hot plate. When the water is gone, let students inspect the residue. If simulated ocean water is used, students can weigh the residue to see if the original amount of salt remains. (Note: By weight, ocean water is about 3.5% salt.)

**01
Aa
Cf**

Making a model to show how rainwater dissolves materials in the Earth. Wash some aquarium sand several times, and then set the sand out to dry. When dry, mix 1 tsp. (5 ml) of table salt for each 4 c. (1 L) of dry sand. Simulate an inclined river bed with aluminum foil and pour the sand and salt mixture into it. Place a bowl at one end to catch the river water. Pour some rainwater or distilled water at the top of the river bed. Students can taste the collected water to see if it contains salt or set the collected water out to evaporate. They will realize that in a similar way,

**02
Af
Fc**

rainwater dissolves salts in rocks and soil, carries them from the land by way of rivers, and deposits them in the oceans. Thus, the oceans now contain materials that have drained off the land for millions of centuries.

Removing dissolved materials from ocean water by freezing. Obtain some ocean water or dissolve 1 oz. (28.35 g) of table salt in a quart (liter) of water. Pour the water into ice cube trays and place them into a freezer. Do the same with an equal amount of plain water. Students can record the appearance of the water in each tray at 10-minute intervals until each is frozen. Next, take several cubes from each tray, melt them in saucers, evaporate the water, and inspect the residue. Students will find that very little residue remains. (When salt water freezes, it forms crystals of nearly pure ice—most of the salt is left behind in unfrozen water.)

**03
Ca**

> *Contributing Idea B.* Ocean water exerts more pressure than freshwater.

Comparing equal volumes of ocean water and fresh water by weight. Have students weigh two 1 qt. (liter) containers. Fill one with tap water and the other with an equal amount of ocean water. If ocean water is not available, dissolve 1 oz. (28.35 g) of table salt in the quart (liter) of water. Now weigh the containers again. By subtracting the weight of the empty container from the weight of

**04
Cf**

the container with water in it, students will find out how much weight each volume of water has. Similarly, two large balloons can be attached to the ends of two 10 ft. (3 m) lengths of rubber tubing. While outdoors, one tube can be filled with tap water and the other with ocean or salt water. Hold the balloons closed so that the water does not enter them. When each tube is filled to capacity, allow the water to flow into the balloons. The tube containing ocean water will expand its balloon to a greater extent. Because of the weight difference brought about by dissolved salt and other materials, water pressure is greater 10 ft. (3 m) deep in ocean water than it is 10 ft. (3 m) deep in freshwater.

> *Contributing Idea C.* Ocean water has greater buoyancy than freshwater.

Comparing the weight of an object suspended in air with an object suspended in water. Tie a string around a large rock and suspend it from a spring scale. Record the weight of the rock out of the water. Now hang it in a container of tap water and record the weight. Next, hang it in a container of ocean water or water that has 1 oz. (28.35 g) of table salt dissolved in 1 qt. (liter) of water. Let students look for differences in the recorded weights. You might explain that water has a force that pushes up on objects and that this force is stronger with ocean water.

**05
Cf**

Observing the above-surface and below-surface configurations of floating ice. Place an ice cube in a clear glass of tap water and an identical cube in a glass of ocean or salt water. Students can observe how much of the ice is above and how much is below each surface. (Although the ice floats somewhat higher in the ocean water, about two-thirds remain submerged.) Some students might be interested in researching the tragic story of the *Titanic*, which struck an iceberg in the Atlantic Ocean.

**06
Bd
Ca**

> *Contributing Idea D.* Ocean water transmits, absorbs, and scatters solar radiation.

Observing the penetration of light through ocean water. Fill an aquarium with ocean water or a solution of salt water—1 oz. (28.35 g) of table salt per quart (liter) of water. Beam a light from a 35 mm slide projector through the length of the aquarium, and let students measure the diameter of the beam where it shines against a screen 1 ft. (30 cm) from the aquarium. Now shine the beam above the aquarium, across the same distance to the screen. Compare this diameter to the previous one. The difference in density between air and ocean water will cause a difference in the refraction of the beam and thus produce images of different diameters. You might tell students that solar radiation in the form of light disseminates in a very short distance after entering water (approximately 15 m).

**07
Ca
Cg**

Observing the effect of water on depth perception. 08 Aa Suspend several corks from strings of different lengths and tie identical weights to them. Arrange the corks in a line in an aquarium. Let students take turns looking straight down through the water at a cork and, while looking, place a mark on the outside of the aquarium with a grease pencil to show the point where they think the top of each cork is. After several students try this, compare the marks with the actual heights of the corks when viewed through the side. (The marks will tend to be above the actual heights of the corks and the difference in distance will increase toward the lower corks.) Students will realize that water affects depth perception. (Visibility is distorted because of the refraction of light in the water.) Air also affects depth perception, although to a lesser extent. Because we become adjusted to the effect, we find it difficult to judge distances when air is absent. (Astronauts report that they have some difficulty judging distances while on the Moon.)

Contributing Idea E. Ocean water conducts electricity better than freshwater.

Measuring the electroconductivity of freshwater and salt water. 09 Ca Set up a simple 6-volt circuit with a lightbulb as shown in Figure 151.09. Separate the free wires and dip the ends in freshwater, then in a salt water solution. Students will see that the salt water allows the light to light up.

Now repeat the activity by beginning with freshwater and adding salt spoonful by spoonful until the light comes on and gets brighter and brighter. Next, let students slowly move the free ends farther apart in the salt solution. You might explain that salinity (i.e., the amount of salt) in water is sometimes measured by the brightness of the light. If possible, obtain some ocean water and compare the brightness of the light to the brightness in one of the previous tests. (Note: In some areas, hard water will conduct electricity; thus, distilled water should be used in the initial tests.)

Figure 151.09

Contributing Idea F. Ocean water contains living organisms.

Observing small organisms with a microscope. 10 Aa Obtain some ocean water. Use a wet mount slide with a cover slip to let students observe the small organisms with a microscope. (Binocular microscopes are especially good for viewing these organisms.) You might explain that the small organisms are part of a food chain upon which other organisms are dependent. In the ocean, diatoms (algae and plankton) are the primary food producers and the beginnings of all food chains.

> *Contributing Idea G.* The surface of the ocean is made up of waves.

Observing waves at the seashore. If possible, take several field trips to a coastal region, and have students record observations of waves at different seasons of the year. They can determine the relationship between waves and a shore's appearance by observing how the waves approach the beach. They can determine approximate wave heights and breaker heights by references to the height of people on the beach and the height of fixed objects such as pilings.

11
Aa
Bc
Cb

Measuring some wave characteristics. Place approximately 8 in. (25 cm) of water in a large aquarium. Roll a hand towel around the horizontal bar of a wire hanger, then bend the top of the hanger and hook it over one end of the aquarium so that the towel is just at the water level to lessen the bouncing back of waves. Measure 6 in. (18 cm) distances along one side of the aquarium and vertically mark them with a wax pencil or with strips of masking tape. To produce waves, place a flat board or your hand palm down, at the water level and move it up and down about 2 in. (6 cm) in a rapid but steady rhythm. Students can estimate the wavelength of the waves by referring to the 6 in. (18 cm)

12
Cb
Cc
Ch

marks. They can use a stopwatch to count the number of waves made in 10 seconds. (The number of waves will be the same as the number of downward motions.) They can divide the number of waves into the time (10 seconds) to determine the wave period, then calculate the velocity of the waves in ft. (or cm) per second:

$$\text{velocity} = \frac{\text{wave length}}{\text{period}}$$

Determining a relationship between waves and water depth. Place approximately ½ in. (1 cm) of water in an aquarium or large, flat, deep baking pan. Set up a series of waves through the water by tapping or otherwise jarring the container. Students can observe and describe the waves they see, especially the heights and the spacing between them (e.g., the distance between the top of one to the top of the next). Make the water twice as deep and repeat. The students will discover that the waves are now of a different size and wavelength. Explain that within certain limits, the distance between one wave and another *decreases* as water in oceans, seas, and lakes becomes shallower and *increases* as water becomes deeper. This experience can also be tried in a bathtub. If possible, let students examine aerial photographs of shorelines for further evidence. Some may wish to see what effect waves have below the surface of the water. To find out, attach a number of small corks to weighted strings so that they float at different depths

13
Ec
Fc

in a large aquarium. Students can make waves by raising and lowering a flat board on the surface at one end of the aquarium. Have them note any movement of the corks as they observe through the side of the aquarium.

Observing wave action. Add a shallow amount of water to a rectangular heat-resistant baking dish and set it on an overhead projector. Make waves in the pan by tapping the container. Students can observe the patterns of waves by the projection on a screen or wall, and experiment by putting obstructions into the pan to represent wharves or jetties. They will discover that waves seem to move around obstructions and change direction after striking, thus producing a sheltered or calm area on the surface.

14
Aa
Ec

Generalization II. Some characteristics of ocean water can be organized.

> *Contributing Idea A.* Fossils in ocean sediments help scientists sequence events of the past.

Making a model of a fossil. Obtain sea-shells or snail shells. Working individually or in small groups, have students coat one side of each shell with petroleum jelly, and press the coated side into a block of modeling clay that is about twice as large as the shell. Next, mold a thin rim around the top edge of each block of clay, then remove the shell, leaving a mold. Prepare some

15
Bb
Fc

plaster of paris. (Follow the directions on the package or add water until the mixture is thick.) Using small brushes, paint petroleum jelly on the top of the block and inside the mold. (The jelly will prevent the plaster from sticking to the clay.) Fill the mold to the top with plaster and let it dry for 24 hours. Gently peel off the rim, remove the block of clay from the plaster, and you will have a good cast of one side of each shell. (The edges of the plaster may have to be trimmed with a dull knife.) You might explain that in a similar way, marine organisms with shells are buried at the bottom of oceans and pressed into the mud, silt, and ooze. When their soft bodies decay and their shells dissolve, a hole or *mold* is left showing the exact shape of the outside of the organism. Tell students that the mold is sometimes filled with other materials that form a *cast* (like the plaster) that is the exact shape of the original organism. Both the mold and the cast are fossils. As an alternate or supplementary activity, students can make a complete fossil shell by pressing the shell between two blocks of clay. (Be sure to coat the entire surface of the shell with petroleum jelly as well as all surfaces of the blocks.) When pressing the blocks together, try to have only half the shell impression in each block. Separate the blocks, remove the shell, and then hold the blocks tightly together with rubber bands. Cut a funnel-shaped hole into the top of the blocks to pour plaster into the mold. Tap the mold gently several times to remove any trapped air, and add more plaster. If any plaster leaks from the mold, press the blocks together where the leak occurs. When the plaster has hardened, open the mold and trim the fossil's edges to produce a good model. Discuss with students how fossils provide knowledge of past ocean life and how fossils in layers of sediments help scientists order sequences of events over geological periods of time. **Caution: Students must wear protective gear during this activity.**

Contributing Idea B. Some characteristics of ocean water can be seriated.

Making and using a Secchi disk. One of the most widely used instruments for measuring water transparency is the Secchi disk. Such an instrument can be made in several ways.

**16
Bb
Da
Gc**

a. Students can place adhesive tape on the edge of a metal coffee can lid, spray white paint on one side and black on the other (or each side can be sprayed half and half or in quarters), tie a string to a horseshoe magnet, and hold the lid with the magnet (see Figure 151.16a).

Figure 151.16a

b. Students can insert a weighted eyebolt through a metal disk that is approximately 8 in. (25 cm) in diameter and suspend the disk from a chain or calibrated line (see Figure 151.16b). Prepare two or three

Figure 151.16b

aquariums, one with tap water and the other(s) with water and different amounts of powdered milk to make cloudy. Lower the disk into one aquarium, then another. When the disk disappears from view, the depth of visibility can be recorded by marking the line at the water surface and measuring the length to the disk. Students can order the three aquariums by the measurements they obtain. Tell them that the device they used is called a Secchi disk, used to determine the cloudiness or *turbidity* of water. Use it to test other liquids (e.g., baking soda and water, adobe clay and water). (Note: Rinse out the aquariums when finished; some materials, such as powdered milk, decay quickly and become difficult to remove.)

Measuring and comparing the transparencies of bodies of water. Secchi disks can measure the transparency of water, expressed as the depth or limit of visibility, of lakes, ponds, estuaries, oceans, or other bodies of water. Lower a Secchi disk on a calibrated line every 3 in. (10 cm) into a body of water until the disk disappears from view. (Be sure the disk remains horizontal with the water surface at all times.) Have a student take a line reading (the distance from the surface of the water to the disk) when the disk disappears from view, then raise the disk until it reappears and take another reading. The limit of transparency can be determined by finding the arithmetical mean between the depth at which the disk disappeared and the depth at which it reappeared. Now let several students take different measurements. (They may find that many variables can influence the readings: the distance the observer's eye is from the surface, the degree of roughness of the water, the time of day, etc.) Students can standardize their procedures to obtain consistent readings. (Consistency of the data can be improved if the disk is viewed with the observer's eye at a fixed distance from the surface and if the observations are made in the shade during the middle of the day.) Have students keep other records such as the date, time, place, and name of observer. For additional activities they can use the disk to (1) determine to what extent water transparency differs for the same body of water from day to day and season to season; (2) investigate what differences there are in the water transparency of local lakes, estuaries, or other bodies of water; (3) find out if water transparency varies significantly with distance from industry or sewage treatment plants. The various bodies of water can be ordered by their degrees of transparency. **Caution: Depending on the water area investigated, provide life vests for students.**

17 Cd Db Ec

Making and using a cloudiness indicator. Cut six or more rectangular windows in a heavy piece of cardboard. Cover half of each window with strips of plastic from overhead transparencies. The first window might be covered with four strips, the second with eight, and so on (see Figure 151.18). Students can hold collected samples of water in clear glass

18 Db Gc

Plastic Transparencies

Figure 151.18

jars behind windows to find the number of layers of plastic that best matches the cloudiness of each sample (the more plastic sheets, the greater the cloudiness of the sample). This device can be used to identify possible water pollution areas.

Contributing Idea C. Some characteristics of ocean water can be classified.

Making and using a water sampler. Obtain water samples from different depths with a water sampler. To make one, let students tape nails or fish weights to the outside of a small bottle to make it heavy, and then twist an eye screw into the top of a cork fitted into the bottle. Mark a string or nylon cord at 6 in. (15 cm) intervals, and tie it to the eye screw. Now tie a 1 ft. (30 cm) length of another string from the eye screw to the neck of the bottle, letting the loop of the string hang loose. Insert the cork just tightly enough so that it will stay in place when the bottle is lifted by the first string (see Figure 151.19). Carefully lower the bottle into the water to a depth from which a sample is to be obtained. Next, jerk the string to remove the cork, wait for the bubbles to stop rising to the surface, then pull up the bottle. Students can pour some of the sample into a baby food jar and label it in terms of location and depth. This sample can be compared with others obtained at different depths and locations. The samples can be classified

19 Ca Dc Gc

Figure 151.19

by color or cloudiness by placing them next to each other to view them from the side against an area of clear blue sky. Students should look carefully for differences in shades and colors.

Contributing Idea D. Some ocean sediments can be classified.

Making and using sorting screens. Students can build a set of sieve screens by constructing three identical square frames using twelve 2 in × 2 in. × 12 in. (5 cm × 5 cm × 30 cm) pieces of lumber. Use tacks to cover one frame with ¼ in. (0.5 cm) mesh hardware cloth, another frame with window screening, and a third with material from an old nylon stocking. Use the screens to separate mud samples by stacking them so that the hardware cloth screen is on top and the stocking screen is on the bottom. Place a mud sample on the top screen, and then sprinkle it with a watering can until the soil has been washed through. When the screens are separated,

20 Dc Gc

various materials, plants, and animals can be found and studied. Some can be organized by texture, color, and size. Live organisms can be kept in pill vials with some water. Be sure to label samples with location and type.

Collecting and organizing mud samples. **21**
Dc
Gc
Ge
If the water bottom along a shoreline is soft, students can go wading to collect mud samples at low tide with a long handled shovel. A dredge must be used for deep water specimens. Construct a dredge by making holes in the center and around the edge of a coffee can. Find a second can, slightly smaller in diameter, with a plastic lid. Place rocks, nails, or fish weights in the smaller can, then attach the smaller can to the bottom of the coffee can by threading a nylon string through center holes in the cans and tying knots in the string so it won't slip through the holes. Tie a second string (the lifting string) to the open end of the coffee can (see Figure 151.21). Drop the dredge into the water so

Lowering String

Lifting String

Fill With Weights

Small Can With Lid

Small Holes

Coffee Can With One End Removed

Figure 151.21

that the coffee can will embed itself into the mud. By pulling on the lifting string, the coffee can will scoop up a mud sample. The dredge should be pulled out of the water by the lifting string. (Note: If the cord is marked in ft. or decimeters, the sample collection depth can be recorded.) Use a set of sieves, as described in entry 151.20, to sort the materials that are found. Collect samples from different locations and keep a record for each (e.g., location, depth, number of specimens, number of each type of specimen).

Contributing Idea E. Ocean life can be classified.

Identifying and classifying some ocean **22**
Bc
Bd
Dc
life. If possible, take students on a field trip to study the plant and animal life washed up on the shore. Let them keep a record of where and when particular organisms were found. Reference books can help to identify and classify the organisms.

Collecting and classifying small plant **23**
Dc
Gc
Ge
life in ocean water. Students can construct a net to collect small organisms such as plankton. To do this, use string to lace the opening of a nylon stocking to an embroidery hoop or looped coat hanger wire. Place a small bottle in the stocking toe, and use two rubber bands to secure it in place with the mouth toward the hoop. After attaching a towing string or nylon cord to the hoop, tow the device through the water or let a current flow through it (see Figure 151.23, p. 100). After the device has

Hoop or wire

Rubber Bands

Tow String

Nylon Stocking

Small Bottle

Figure 151.23

been in the water for several minutes, pull it out and remove the small bottle. Examine its contents under a microscope. Collect samples from other locations. (Note: If green material (algae) is collected, place some into a baby food jar. Label jars to show where samples were obtained. Jars can be arranged according to the amount of green material each contains. Generally, the greater the amount of algae, the greater the nutrients in the water.)

152 Interactions

Generalization I. Ocean currents are produced by different sources.

Contributing Idea A. Heat can be a source of ocean currents.

Observing that cold water is heavier than warmer water. Put some food coloring into water and freeze it in an ice cube tray. After the water is frozen, place a cube into an aquarium of water. Students can draw a picture of the currents as indicated by the flow of the color (analogous to a cold current) from the cube. From their observations, students can infer that cold water is heavier than

**01
Aa
Be
Fc**

warmer water. You might tell them that the temperature of oceans may vary by as much as 65°F (18°C) between the equator and polar regions. They might infer that the cold, polar water constantly descends because it is heavier and tends to move toward the equator, while the warmer surface waters at the equator tend to stay at the surface and flow toward the poles.

Observing that warm water is lighter than colder water. Put a one-hole stopper in a small bottle filled with hot water colored with food coloring. Submerge the bottle into an aquarium of cold water. Students can draw a picture of how the water circulates.

**02
Aa
Be
Fc**

Observing a current caused by heat. Place a transparent coffee pot of water on a hot plate. As it starts heating, place a few drops of food coloring or washable black ink into the water. Observe the flow patterns. Next, put the pot on only one side of the heating unit and add a few more drops. Students will see a definite current in the water. Explain that what is seen illustrates vertical currents (from ocean depths to the surface) that move north and south toward the Earth's poles (cold) from the equatorial region (warm). You might also discuss why the movement takes place. (Heated water is less dense and lighter than cooler water; thus it rises and is replaced by the cooler water.) **Caution: When working with aquarium heaters, use only ground**

**03
Aa
Fc**

fault interrupter (GFI) protected electrical circuits to help prevent an electrical shock hazard.

Measuring the temperature of water currents and layers of water. Have students measure and record the temperature of water at various places (top, sides, bottom, corners) in a 5 gal. (20 L) or larger aquarium. They will find that the temperature of the water is much the same throughout the container. Along the same side but at opposite ends, tape two identical thermometers so that the bulb of one is near the surface of the water and the bulb of the other is near the bottom. Now place a row of ice cubes at the end with the thermometer whose bulb is near the surface. (Be sure the cubes are at least 1 in. or 3 cm from the thermometer.) At one-minute intervals, read the temperatures on both thermometers. (The thermometer farther away from the ice will soon show a lower temperature.) If you let students try to explain why this happens, some may suggest that the cold water traveled downward and along the bottom. Let them check such an explanation by using a medicine dropper to put several drops of food coloring just below the melting ice. (They will see a colored current of water traveling downward from the ice cubes and along the bottom of the aquarium.) (Note: The greater the temperature differential between the ice and the water, the faster the current.) Explain

04
Ce
Fc

that, in a similar way, temperature differences between equatorial and polar ocean waters and between surface and subsurface waters cause a circulation. (Equatorial waters average about 80°F or 27°C, and polar waters average about 30°F or –2°C; ocean water temperature decreases with depth and is very cold at extreme depths.) A supplementary or additional experience can be set up using an aquarium heater. Attach the heater to one end of the aquarium, and arrange the bulbs of two identical thermometers so that the one nearer the heater is at the bottom of the aquarium and the other is at the top. Students can predict what will happen, then turn on the heater and note the temperatures at one-minute intervals. (The thermometer farther away from the heater will change first.) The movement of the current can be seen by adding food coloring near the heater. (Note: If the heater is placed near the surface, students will be able to identify thermal layers in the water; if it is placed near the bottom, they can identify movements or currents in the water.) Other variations to this experience can be created. For example, several thermometers and/or ice cubes can be placed at different levels and/or locations; food coloring can be introduced at different locations; and various water temperatures can be used. **Caution: When working with aquarium heaters, use only ground fault interrupter (GFI)** protected electrical circuits to help prevent an electrical shock hazard.

Contributing Idea B. Wind can be a source of ocean currents.

Observing and testing the effect of wind upon the surface of water. Fill a long baking pan with water, place it on a flat surface, and then wait until the water surface is calm. Without touching the pan, let each student take a turn putting his or her mouth at the water level and blowing gently over the surface of the water using one long breath. Observe any movement in the water and repeat several times. Next, let students experiment with various types of blowing to see what happens (e.g., very strong puffs at regular intervals). They will be able to relate observations of the effect that various winds have upon the ocean's surface.

05 Aa Bd Fc

Observing a water current caused by wind. Set up an electric fan so that it blows across a long, wide container of water. If some sawdust or pepper is sprinkled onto the water, students will see that the water moves in a large, circulating path. Explain that in a similar way, wind tends to drive water ahead of it until a continuous current is generated. Tell them that such prevailing winds are the most important causes of ocean currents. Some students might be interested in researching wind and ocean currents in an encyclopedia or other reference source. **Caution: When working with**

06 Aa Ec

fans near water, use only ground fault interrupter (GFI) protected electrical circuits to help prevent an electrical shock hazard. Caution students to never place hands or other objects in the fan blades.

Contributing Idea C. Salinity can be a source of ocean currents.

Observing a water current caused by salinity. Fill four identical bottles, two with salt water (4 spoonfuls of salt per cup) and two with tap water. Use food coloring to color one bottle of tap water and one bottle of salt water. Place a card over the mouths of these colored-water bottles and invert them over the bottles containing uncolored water (see Figure 152.07). Carefully remove the cards and let the students observe what happens. (Because there is no temperature difference between the salt and tap waters, students will realize that the mixing is caused by a difference in salinity.) Explain that in a similar way, salinity causes parts of the ocean to move as currents.

07 Aa Fc

Figure 152.07

Generalization II. Waves are produced by different sources.

Contributing Idea A. Wind can produce waves.

Observing water waves. Fill a large, widemouthed container such as an aquarium or deep, flat baking pan with water. When the surface is calm, have a student blow across the water to produce waves. Students can take turns trying to produce different kinds of waves. Some will discover that the height of the waves depends upon the velocity of the wind and the distance over which the wind blows. Tell them that ocean waves behave similarly—those that rise and sink and become regular are *swells;* those that approach the shore, form a steep front, and break are *surf* or *breakers.* Now float a cork on the surface. When the surface is calm, have a student try to move the cork by making waves but without blowing directly on it. After several tries, students will find that they cannot move the cork even though they create waves in the water. (Only the form of the waves moves forward and the cork does not move with a wave.)

08 Aa Bb Ec

Observing waves caused by wind. Fill a long, widemouthed container, such as a deep baking pan or heat-resistant dish, halfway with water and blow a current of air across the water with an electric fan. Students can note the spacing and height of the waves that are produced. Let them

09 Aa

experiment by varying the depth of the water and the speed of the fan. From their tests, they will better realize that ocean waves are caused by wind in a similar way. **Caution: When working with fans near water, use only ground fault interrupter (GFI) protected electrical circuits to help prevent an electrical shock hazard.**

Contributing Idea B. Earthquakes can produce waves.

Using a model to explain the cause of earthquake waves. Place a brick at one end of a large container. Elevate one end of a second brick to just rest on the first one, and then fill the container with water until there are about 2 in. (6 cm) of water above the leaning brick. Explain that the bricks represent two blocks of rock beneath the Earth and that movement of the blocks can sometimes cause earthquakes. Now use a stick with a small diameter to gently push the leaning brick from the other one (see Figure 152.10). Students will realize how a similar movement under the ocean might cause a wave. You might tell them

10 Aa Bb Fc

Figure 152.10

that such a wave is called a tsunami (\tsoo nah' me\), a Japanese word meaning "big wave in the harbor."

Generalization III. **Tides are produced by the relationship of the Moon to the Earth.**

> *Contributing Idea A.* Tides are indicated by the rise and fall of the water level at shorelines.

Determining changes in water levels at shorelines. If possible, have students place sticks or other markers at the edge of a large body of water such as a very large lake, estuary, or ocean. After several hours, check the markers in relation to the water's edge. Students can compare what they observed with their own seashore experiences. (Sand castles may be washed away as the water level rises.) Tell them that the natural rising and falling of water levels in a large body of water is called tides. Some students might be interested in looking up tidal information in the daily newspaper, almanacs, or tide books available at sporting goods stores.

11
Bb
Bd
Cb

> *Contributing Idea B.* The Moon produces tides.

Using a diagram to explain tides. Draw a 20 in. (50 cm) diameter circle on a chart or chalkboard. Tell students that the circle represents the Earth, and have them imagine that they are above the North Pole looking down upon it. Now draw a 5 in. (12.5 cm) diameter circle 4 ft.

12
Ca
Fc

(125 cm) away to represent the Moon. Tell students that the Earth and Moon attract each other, that the Moon's attraction causes the ocean to bulge directly outward toward the Moon, and that there is another bulge on the opposite side of the Earth. Draw the bulges and letter the high and low positions of the ocean. Put several numerals on the Earth and ask students to describe the various tides from those positions as the Earth turns (see Figure 152.12). For example, they

Figure 152.12

might say that from position 1, the tide seems to be coming in or rising (because the Earth is moving into the bulge) and from position 4, the tide seems to be going out. Students should be able to tell that there are 12 hours between one high tide and the next high tide and 6 hours between changes in tides.

Using a globe and a smaller sphere to explain tides. Obtain a globe of the Earth and a table tennis ball to represent the Moon. Demonstrate that as the Earth rotates on its axis, the Moon goes around the Earth in the same direction, but much

13
Fc

more slowly. As you turn the globe and move the ball, show with your hand how the water on the globe is pulled toward the Moon. (Although it is pulled almost directly in line with the moon, the tides lag just a bit.)

Making a model of a tidal basin. Have a student try to carry a shallow pan of water across the room. (This will be very difficult to do without spilling.) The sloshing motion is similar to the motion set up in great ocean basins around the world (e.g., Bay of Fundy). You might use models of the Sun, Moon, and Earth to show that when the Sun and Moon are in line, their gravitational influences combine to produce the highest possible tides (spring tides); when they are at right angles to each other, their influences divide to produce lower tides (neap tides).

14 Fc

Generalization IV. Oceans are both constructive and destructive forces as they build up and wear down the Earth's surface, creating characteristic shoreline features.

> *Contributing Idea A.* Ocean water physically changes the Earth's surface by building up materials.

Observing the relationship between the size of materials and the rate at which they settle in water. Obtain a large test tube that can be corked. Mix at least three sizes of gravel, some sand, and mud. Place the mixture into the tube and fill it with water. Cork and invert the tube. Students

15 Aa Fc

will see that as the materials fall through the water, the larger materials settle quickly at the bottom, the medium sizes in the middle, and the fine silt slowly at the top. Explain that rivers, streams, and oceans carry sediments and deposit them on the basis of weight and size.

> *Contributing Idea B.* Ocean water physically changes the Earth's surface by wearing down materials.

Observing the effects of waves on a model beach. Have students make a model beach of sand or dirt at the far end of a large rectangular pan or tray. Be sure the edge of the beach is parallel to the end of the pan. Fill the pan about half full of water. Produce a wave by lifting the near end of the pan approximately 1 in. (3 cm) above the tabletop and returning it quickly to its original position. Repeat this every five seconds for two minutes. Students can observe and discuss what gradually happens to the model beach. Next, repeat the activity after rebuilding the beach so that its edge is at an angle of 30 degrees to the end of the pan. Discuss the differences in the results.

16 Aa Fc

Collecting and examining seashore sand. If possible, visit a seashore and let students collect samples of sand from different locations. The sand can be placed in small vials or bottles and labeled with its location and date of collection. Upon returning to the classroom, scatter a few grains from each sample onto light green

17 Ca Ge

or blue paper. (The color aids viewing of the grains.) Students can examine the grains with a hand lens or binocular microscope if one is available and identify and classify the differences in types of grains that make up each sample. Some students might work out the percentage of each kind and hypothesize where the various grains came from. If possible, return to the seashore at a later date and collect samples from the same locations. Compare these samples with the previous ones to see if changes have taken place.

Generalization V. The oceans affect climate and weather.

> *Contributing Idea A.* Ocean water evaporates into the atmosphere as moisture; moisture in the atmosphere may condense and return to the ocean.

Making a water cycle model. Inflate a **18** large transparent plastic bag and fit it over **Fc** a widemouthed jar or aquarium containing ocean or salt water. Prop up or suspend the bag as shown in Figure 152.18. Let students observe the bag from time to time. They will see that droplets of moisture appear on the top and sides of the bag, collect, and run down into the aquarium. Explain how what is seen is analogous to the natural water cycle.

Figure 152.18

> *Contributing Idea B.* Storms such as hurricanes and typhoons originate over the oceans.

Researching ocean storms. Have stu- **19** dents research in encyclopedias and other **Bd** sources to find differences and similarities between land storms (e.g., tornadoes) and ocean storms (e.g., hurricanes). They will find that both originate over heated surfaces and blow toward a low pressure center but that the hurricane originates over warm water (the tornado over land in temperate zones), has a path width of hundreds of miles or kilometers (the tornado seldom has a width of more than 2 miles or 3 km), and generally moves at a rate of 12 miles (18 km) per hour (the tornado moves more rapidly, however).

Simulating a waterspout. Fill a jar three-quarters full with water. Place a lid on the jar. Holding the jar in both hands, have a student move it very rapidly in a circular motion, then quickly stop. Students will see a cyclonic water current that tapers downward like a funnel. Explain that what is seen is analogous to a *waterspout*, a rotating, funnel-shaped column of whirling winds and water extending upward from an ocean or large body of water.

20
Bb
Fc

153   Theory

Generalization. According to the continental drift theory, land masses were once joined, and then some gradually drifted apart.

> *Contributing Idea A.* The continents were once joined together.

Matching continents. Using a Mercator projection of the world, have students trace the outer edge of the continental shelf, and then cut out the continents that bound the Atlantic Ocean. Now ask students to use the pieces like a jigsaw puzzle to put the continents together so that the margins match without the Atlantic Ocean between them. Explain that the high degree of fit tends to support the theory that the continents were once joined (during the Mesozoic era some 120,000,000 years ago) but gradually drifted apart. Ask the students to hypothesize what one might expect to find in

01
Bd
Eb
Fc

animal life and the stratification of rocks between the two continents; then let them research reference sources to check out their hypotheses.

> *Contributing Idea B.* Some continents are drifting apart.

Comparing shorelines on the leading and trailing edges of the North American continent. Ask students to hypothesize how a large moving body like a continent might look along its forward moving edge and its trailing edge. Now obtain maps of the eastern and western portions of the United States and have students trace the shoreline along both coasts. Let them describe and discuss similarities and differences between coastlines. (They should find a relatively straight Pacific coastline and a highly irregular Atlantic coastline with numerous islands and waterways.) Explain that the west edge, the forward moving edge of the continental block, is thought to be ramming against and riding over the eastern edge of the Pacific Ocean floor, while the eastern edge is dipping and trailing behind. Two bricks on blocks can be used to demonstrate how the North American continent block might be riding over the Pacific Ocean block. As the bricks are moved, tell students that breakage occurs in the boundary zone between the two blocks, and internal stresses build up and are periodically released as earthquakes.

02
Ca
Eb
Fc

Using a model to observe and map submerging and emerging land areas. Build a plaster of paris or clay land model in a large, very deep pan. The model should depict various levels of ground (e.g., hills, valleys, river beds, lakes, etc.), but the greatest height should not exceed the side of the pan. After the plaster has hardened, slowly pour water into the pan. Students will see that some hills become islands, shorelines change, and some areas become flooded. Explain that what is seen is much like the trailing edge or submerging portion of a continent. Now use a drinking straw to dip out the water. Explain that what is seen is similar to the leading or emerging edge of a continent. As an extension of this activity, students can develop a contour map of the land model. To do this, one student can hold a ruler vertically against the bottom of the pan while another pours in water until it reaches the ½ in. (1.5 cm) mark. Now, with a soft pencil, another student can mark the water level in a continuous line wherever the water touches the land. When finished, add another ½ in. (1.5 cm) of water and mark again. Repeat until the highest part of the model is submerged. When the water has been poured off, students can look straight down on the model and draw a picture of the lines just as they see them. The water levels can be marked on the lines. From their pictures, students will be able to tell the heights of each hilltop, which way rivers flow, where level areas are, and which slopes are steepest. If

**03
Be
Cg**

possible, let them compare their pictures with geological survey maps.

Plotting concentrations of earthquakes, volcanic activity, and recent mountain chains. Have students research information on the positions of (1) mountain ranges, (2) areas of volcanic activity, and (3) zones of earthquake activity, and then plot them on a globe or map of the western hemisphere. They will discover that nearly all such features are concentrated along the Pacific coastline. Have them explain how this information might provide support for the theory that both North America and South America are drifting westward. You might follow the discussion with a demonstration: gently and slowly push a small rug across the floor from the trailing end. (The rug will develop folds along the leading edge.) Explain that in a similar way the upper rock layers along the western edge of the North and South American continents buckle and deform into mountain ranges as drifting takes place.

**04
Bd
Be**

154 Applications

Generalization. People explore and use the oceans.

> *Contributing Idea A.* Diving bells and submarines are instruments that allow people to live beneath the surface of the ocean.

Making a model of a diving bell. Float a cork on some water, and then place a transparent plastic container or glass over

**01
Ba
Fc
Ga**

the cork. Tell students that the cork represents a person and the container represents a diving bell. Push the diving bell down into the water. Students will see that the water does not go into the diving bell. (As the bell descends, the air inside keeps the water out.) Discuss how the diving bell makes it possible for people to explore the ocean floor.

Making a model of a submarine. Cover the bottom of a widemouthed bottle with pebbles. Pour melted paraffin over them to hold them in place. Put a U-shaped glass tube through one hole of a two-hole stopper and a short straight glass tube through the other hole. Attach a length of rubber tubing to the straight tube, insert the stopper in the bottle, and float the bottle in an upright position in a large container of water. Have a student suck air from the rubber tube. (Water will enter the bottle, and it will start to sink.) Now blow air into the tube. (The water will be driven from the bottle, and the bottle will rise.) Use this model (Figure 154.02) to explain how a submarine submerges and rises.

02
Fc
Ga

Contributing Idea B. Oceans can supply people with natural resources.

Recovering salt from ocean water. Put some ocean water or a saturated solution of salt in a flat pan. Set the pan in a warm room until the water has evaporated. Explain that this is one method used to recover salt from the ocean.

03
Fc
Ga

Extracting pure water from ocean water. Place ocean water or a solution of salt water into a small plastic container, and set it on a large saucer. Roll a blotter, put rubber bands around the roll, and stand it in the salt water. Cover the small container with a larger clear plastic container and place the apparatus in the sun. When the water collects on the sides of the larger container, tilt it carefully and collect the water in the saucer (see Figure 154.04). Explain that this is one method used to extract pure water from ocean water.

04
Ac
Ga

Figure 154.04

Figure 154.02

160 Weather

161 Characteristics

Generalization I. Temperatures on Earth vary from time to time and place to place.

> *Contributing Idea A.* The thermometer is an instrument used to measure temperatures.

Making a liquid thermometer. Put a length of glass tubing (approximately 1 ft. or 30 cm long) through a one-hole stopper using a twisting, rotary motion. Fill a bottle or flask to the top with water and add a drop of red ink to make the water more visible. Force the stopper into the bottle so that the water rises into the tube approximately 3 in. (10 cm). Mark the position of the water, then let a student warm the bottle with his or her hands. Students will note that the colored water rises in the tube. Now cool the bottle with an ice cube or a sponge soaked in cold water and note that the water level drops. To calibrate this instrument, place the bottle into a deep bowl filled with ice cubes. When the liquid in the tube stops descending, tie a string or slip a rubber band around the tube to mark the level of the liquid. Next, place the bottle in a pan of water and heat it. Boil the water in the pan until the level of the colored liquid stops rising. Mark the level with another piece of string or rubber band. The two marks represent the high and low points. A card divided into tenths and hundredths can be placed behind the tube for a scale. This instrument works similarly to commercial liquid thermometers; the liquid expands when heated, contracts when cooled. Commercial liquid thermometers use alcohol or mercury instead of water, since these liquids respond uniformly to temperature changes and do not freeze at temperatures below 32°F (0°C). Other types of thermometers can be compared to this one.

01
Gc

Measuring and graphing air temperatures. Attach a thermometer outside a classroom window. Be sure it is shielded from direct sunlight. (A thermometer will show a higher temperature than the air if it is placed in sunlight.) Have students record the temperature twice each day by checking it at the same time each morning and each afternoon. A record can be kept on a table similar to Table 161.02. The information can be graphed (see Graph 161.02, p. 112) to represent the general directions of temperature change throughout the week. Several interesting variations of this activity can be explored: One student can record the temperature every hour for one day to see how the temperature changes; a

02
Bf
Ce
Ch

Table 161.02. Measuring Temperatures

Week of	Morning	Afternoon
Monday	41°F (5°C)	48°F (9°C)
Tuesday	32°F (0°C)	45°F (7°C)
Wednesday	43°F (6°C)	50°F (10°C)
Thursday	45°F (7°C)	59°F (15°C)
Friday	48°F (9°C)	68°F (20°C)

Graph 161.02

group of students can keep records for several months to note temperature changes during the year—weekly or monthly averages can also be computed; individuals or groups can study contrasting temperatures in (a) sun and shade, (b) moving wind and calm air, (c) surface soil and subsoil, (d) shallow water and deep water, (e) shallow snow and deep snow, and so on.

Measuring the temperature of air at different altitudes. Record the temperature of a thermometer outdoors, then tie the thermometer to a large kite. Let students sail the kite as high as they can. In about 30 minutes, pull the kite in as quickly as possible and record the temperature. Compare the two temperatures.

03 Ce

> *Contributing Idea B.* The Sun's radiant energy is converted to heat energy when it reaches the Earth.

Observing that the Sun is a source of heat energy. Put equal amounts of ice in two glasses. Place one in the shade and one in the sunlight. Let students observe in which glass the ice melts

04 Aa

more quickly. They will realize that the deciding factor is the heat from the Sun.

Measuring the conversion of solar energy to heat energy. Obtain two small identical flasks and coat one with candle soot or cover it with aluminum foil to prevent sunlight from entering. Insert thermometers into one-hole stoppers, and place them into the flasks. Set the flasks in a place that is shaded from direct sunlight until they become cool, and then record the thermometer readings. Next, set both flasks in the direct rays of sunlight, and record the thermometer readings every minute until the same reading appears at least three times in a row for each thermometer. The results can be plotted on a graph. Students will readily realize that the Sun's radiant energy easily enters the uncovered flask and is converted into heat energy that is measured by the thermometer. The experimental flask remains cool because the radiant energy could not enter. You can make an analogy to the radiant energy that penetrates the Earth's atmosphere, strikes the Earth, and is converted into heat energy. As a supplementary activity, let students repeat the above procedure after covering the experimental flask with various materials such as colored cellophanes or paint or by filling it with various solid or liquid substances such as soil or water.

05 Ce Ec

> *Generalization II.* Air pressures vary from time to time and place to place.

Contributing Idea A. The barometer is an instrument used to measure air pressure.

Making an air pressure indicator (barometer). **06 Bb Gc** Remove the cork from a small thermos bottle and drill a hole through the cork just large enough to insert a plastic straw or glass tube. Seal the cork in the thermos by dripping candle wax on all connections, and then mount the thermos upside down on a stand so that the end of the tube is approximately ¼ in. (1 cm) from the base. Wrap the thermos in some insulating material, and fit a cardboard box snugly around it. The insulation will help to keep the instrument from acting more like a thermometer than a barometer. Now have students color some mineral oil with food coloring. Set a cup of mineral oil beneath the tube on a day that the air pressure is low (listen to weather forecasts; the low should be below 29.90 in. or 76 cm). Have students observe that whenever the air pressure rises, the mineral oil is pushed up the tube. A scale can be placed behind the tube to note changes (see Figure 161.06). Barometers will work indoors as well as outdoors since the air pressures are about the same.

Measuring and recording the pressure of air. **07 Bc Cd Fb** Use a commercial or homemade barometer to keep twice-daily records of changes in air pressure. Note what weather changes take place outdoors with each recording on a table similar to Table 161.07 (p. 114). Some weather predictions can be made if wind direction and wind speed information are also obtained.

Contributing Idea B. The movement of air affects air pressures.

Observing that low pressure areas can be created when air flows swiftly. **08 Aa** There are several activities that will help students realize that air pressure can be reduced by rapidly moving air.

a. Place a table tennis ball in a funnel, hold it stem downward, and blow up through the stem. Students will be surprised to find that they cannot blow the ball out of the funnel. Next, turn the funnel stem upward while holding the ball inside with one hand. While blowing, release the ball. (The ball should not fall as long as the student is blowing.) Students

Cardboard Box
and Insulation

Thermos

Scale

Wood Stand

Colored
Mineral Oil

Figure 161.06

Table 161.07. Measuring Air Pressure

Week of			
	a.m.	p.m.	Observations
Monday	rising	falling	
Tuesday			
Wednesday			
Thursday			
Friday			

can realize that the quickly moving air over the ball creates a low pressure area behind it, and the normal air pressure is enough to hold the ball in place. Explain that when air moves rapidly across the surface of the Earth, low pressure areas result in a similar way.

b. Put a pin through the center of a 3 in. (8 cm) square of cardboard. Insert the pin into the hole of a spool of thread, and hold the cardboard beneath and flat against the spool. Blow through the spool and remove the hand holding the cardboard. (The card is held in place due to the decreased pressure above the card; the normal air pressure is sufficient to hold the card to the spool.)

Generalization III. Water on Earth evaporates into the atmosphere as moisture.

Contributing Idea A. The hygrometer is an instrument used to measure the relative amount of water in the air (humidity).

Making a humidity indicator (hygrometer). There are two basic ways to build an instrument that can measure the amount of moisture in the air.

a. Open two paper clips partway (Figure 161.09a) and press them approximately ½ in. (1 cm) apart into a block of soft wood about halfway down one side (Figure 161.09b). The block of wood should be approximately 10 in. (25 cm) high and sturdy enough so that it will not tip over easily. Glue a fine wire or piece of straw into the eye of a needle (Figure 161.09c), then set the needle on the two paper clips so that the straw or wire sticks out past the edge of the block (Figure 161.09d). Wash a long strand of hair in hot soapy water to remove the natural oils. When dry, tie the hair to a pin placed at the top of the block (Figure 161.09e). Wrap the free end once around the needle in a counterclockwise loop (Figure 161.09f), and then tie a

09
Gc

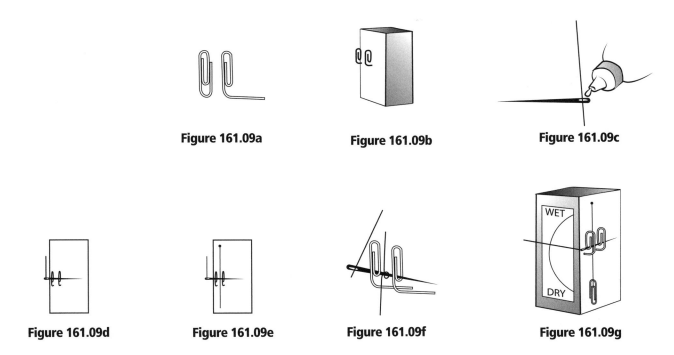

Figure 161.09a   Figure 161.09b   Figure 161.09c

Figure 161.09d   Figure 161.09e   Figure 161.09f   Figure 161.09g

paper clip onto the end of the hair so that it pulls tightly around the needle. Make a measuring scale on a card and mount it on the side of the block (Figure 161.09g). Set the straw so that it is at the center of the card. The scale can be calibrated by draping the hygrometer with a cloth soaked in very hot water. Hair stretches when wet and contracts when dry. This action is at an exact rate and is proportional to the amount of water in the air. The humidity under the cloth will cause the hair to stretch and the pointer to rise. When it stops rising, the humidity will be very close to 100%. This position can be marked on the card. Other positions can be calibrated by comparing this hygrometer with a commercial one.

b. Mount two identical thermometers on a milk carton or side by side on a board. Cut the tips from a clean white cotton shoestring and slip the loose fibers of one end over the bulb of one thermometer. Tie it in place with a piece of thread, then place the other end into a small container of water. In operation, the two thermometers will produce two different readings. The wet bulb thermometer will give a reading based upon the evaporation of the water from the shoestring. Evaporation has a cooling effect; the reading will

Table 161.09. Relative Humidity Table

		Difference Between Dry Bulb and Wet Bulb Temperatures in Degrees Fahrenheit																					
		1	2	3	4	5	6	7	8	9	10	11	12	14	16	18	20	22	24	26	28	30	32	34
	10	78	56	34	13																				
	15	82	64	46	29	11																			
	20	85	70	55	40	26	12																		
	25	87	74	62	49	37	25	13	1																
	30	89	78	67	56	46	36	26	16	6															
	35	91	81	72	63	54	45	36	27	19	10	2													
	40	92	83	75	68	60	52	45	37	29	22	15	7												
	45	93	86	78	71	64	57	51	44	38	31	25	18	6											
Dry Bulb Temperature Degrees Fahrenheit	50	93	87	80	74	67	61	55	49	43	38	32	27	16	5										
	55	94	88	82	76	70	65	59	54	49	43	38	33	23	14	5									
	60	94	89	83	78	73	68	63	58	53	48	43	39	30	21	13	5								
	65	95	90	85	80	75	70	66	61	56	52	48	44	35	27	20	12	5							
	70	95	90	86	81	77	72	68	64	59	55	51	48	40	33	25	19	12	6						
	75	96	91	86	82	78	74	70	66	62	58	54	51	44	37	30	24	18	12	7	1				
	80	96	91	87	83	79	75	72	68	64	61	57	54	47	41	35	29	23	18	12	7	3			
	90	96	92	89	85	81	78	74	71	68	65	61	58	52	47	41	36	31	26	22	17	13	9	5	
	100	96	93	89	86	83	80	77	73	70	68	65	62	56	51	46	41	37	33	28	24	21	17	13

be lower than that of the dry bulb thermometer. The rate of evaporation depends upon the amount of water already in the air. When there is a great deal of water in the air, the evaporation is slowed down; thus the temperature reading is higher and closer to that of the dry bulb thermometer. By comparing the readings of the two thermometers, students can determine the relative humidity of the air. Generally a difference in temperature of 15°F (9°C) or more is considered to be an indication of low humidity while a difference of less than 15°F (9°C) indicates high humidity. Table 161.09 can be used to determine the relative humidity more precisely. For example, if the dry bulb thermometer reading is 65°F and the wet bulb thermometer reading is 56°F, the difference in temperature would be 9°F. By reading down the left-hand side of Table 161.09 to 65°F and across the top of 9°F, the intersection of the two columns is at 56. The numeral in the intersection indicates that the relative humidity is 56%.

Measuring and recording the amount of moisture in the air. Have students use hygrometers to measure the amount of moisture in the air. Have them use Table 161.10 to keep a weekly record of their measurements.   **10 Bc Cg**

Contributing Idea B. Water evaporates.

Observing that water evaporates. Have students observe saucers filled with water over a period of several days. Discuss what happens to the water.   **11 Aa**

Measuring the amount of water that evaporates from soil. Fill a flower pot with soil and pour some water into the soil until it begins to drip from the bottom. Weigh the pot, and then do not water   **12 Cf**

Table 161.10. Measuring Humidity (Wet and Dry Bulb Hygrometer)

	Week of _____		
	Wet Bulb	Dry Bulb	Humidity
Monday	58°F (15°C)	65°F (19°C)	High
Tuesday	49°F (9°C)	65°F (19°C)	Low
Wednesday			
Thursday			
Friday			

it again for a week. After a week, weigh the pot again. Students can compare the before and after weights and infer what caused the difference.

Experimenting to see how different factors affect evaporation. Challenge students to design tests to find out how each of the following factors affects the rate at which water evaporates: temperature, movement of the air, amount of liquid exposed to the air, type of liquid, amount of moisture in the air (humidity). If needed, help students prepare at least two conditions for each test so that results can be compared (e.g., to test the effect of air movement, place some liquid in front of an electric fan and an equal amount in another place where the temperature and humidity are the same, but where there is no wind).

13 Ec

162   Interactions

Generalization I. As land and water are warmed by the Sun, the air above them is heated, becomes lighter, and rises; cooler air, being heavier, moves to replace the warm air.

> *Contributing Idea A.* The wind vane and the nephoscope are instruments used to determine wind direction.

Making a wind direction indicator (wind vane). There are several kinds of instruments that can be made to indicate wind direction.

01 Gc

a. Cut a notch approximately 1 in. (2.5 cm) deep in each end of a 1 ft. (30 cm) long piece of wood. Cut a small arrow head and a large tail piece from aluminum pie plates. Insert them into the slits, and nail them into place (Figure 162.01a). Find the point along the stick where it balances, then drill a hole at that spot just large enough for a small test tube or medicine dropper tubing to fit through. The medicine dropper tubing can be prepared by holding it by the rubber bulb, placing the tip of the dropper into a flame, and rotating it slowly until the opening is completely closed and rounded (Figure 162.01b). When the glass is cool, remove the rubber and insert the tubing through the wood. You might need to use some friction tape to keep the wood from slipping off the tubing (Figure 162.01c). Now bend a coat hanger to form a bracket (Figure 162.01d), and mount the wind vane on a post or fence where winds blowing from many directions will strike it (Figure 162.01e). Be sure students note that the arrow points in the direction *from* which the wind comes. Tell them that winds are named for the direction *from* which they come (e.g., a north wind comes from the north, and the arrow will point north). Students can use a compass to determine from which direction the winds come.

b. The wind sock is another instrument that is used at airports as a wind direction indicator. It can be made by bending a section of light wire into a circle and attaching some thin cloth to it. It can then be attached to a stick with strings and placed outdoors where the wind will blow freely into it. (See Figure 162.01f.)

Making a cloud direction indicator (nephoscope). 02 Gc The lower part of a moving air mass is usually obstructed and influenced by trees, houses, and other objects; thus, wind vanes (usually near the ground) do not always indicate the true direction of the moving air. To observe movement higher in the atmosphere, have students glue a round mirror to a piece of cardboard, and mark the points of the compass around the mirror. Paste a small paper circle about the size of a dime in the center of the mirror. Set the cardboard on a level spot outdoors with the *N* pointing north (a compass can be used to orient the mirror). Have students look down into the

Figure 162.01a   Figure 162.01b   Figure 162.01c

Figure 162.01d   Figure 162.01e   Figure 162.01f mirror. When they see a cloud passing over the dime-sized circle, have them follow it with their eyes until it reaches the edge of the mirror. At that point they will see a wind direction indicated on the cardboard. This is the direction *toward* which the wind is blowing. You might remind them that winds are named for the direction *from* which they come.

Table 162.03. Recording Wind Direction

Week of _____			
	a.m.	p.m.	Observations
Monday			
Tuesday			
Wednesday			
Thursday			
Friday			

Recording wind directions. Use a commercial or homemade wind vane or nephoscope and record the wind direction twice a day at the same times each day as shown in Table 162.03. Note if there seems to be any relationship between the direction of the wind and the kind of weather that follows.

03
Bc
Fb

> *Contributing Idea B.* The anemometer is an instrument used to measure wind speed.

Making a wind speed indicator (anemometer). There are two basic kinds of instrument designs used to measure the speed of winds.

04
Gc

   a. The first design requires the student to turn the instrument into the wind. To make such an instrument, clean a milk carton and remove both ends. Thumbtack it to a block of wood to hold it steady. Cut an *H* in the middle section of the top side and open the flaps (Figure 162.04a) Push a cork to the center of a long knitting needle; then push the needle through the flaps (Figure 162.04b). Mount a small needle vertically into the cork to serve as a pointer. Cut a square piece of cardboard so that it fits inside the carton. Attach a second, smaller needle to it with tape or glue and stick the needle into the bottom of the cork (Figure 162.04c). Students may have to adjust the cork, knitting needle, or the card so that the card swings smoothly within the box. When the wind is blowing, point the indicator into the wind so that it blows through the box. The wind will push against the square card, tilting the cork and moving the needle pointer. The distance the needle tilts indicates how fast the wind flows through the carton. A card can be attached to the carton to make a gauge. When attached, draw a line on it parallel to the needle when it is straight up (Figure 162.04d). The gauge can be calibrated using the Beaufort scale (see entry 162.06).

Figure 162.04a

Figure 162.04b

Figure 162.04c

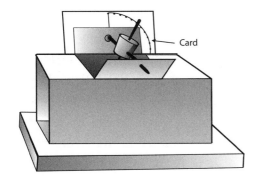

Figure 162.04d

b. A second type of anemometer rotates as the wind strikes it. To make this type, attach two 1½ in. (4 cm) square sticks, 18 in. (½ m) long (Figure 162.04e, p. 122). After the sticks have been nailed together (leaving room for a hole in the middle), drill through their

centers so that a small test tube or medicine dropper will fit snugly into their holes (see entry 162.01a, for the preparation of a medicine dropper) (Figure 162.04f, p. 122). Attach four paper cups, halved rubber balls, tin cans, or other cupped objects to the ends of the sticks (Figure 162.04g, p. 122). The instrument can be mounted on a coat hanger (Figure 162.04h, p. 122) or a hole can be drilled into a block of wood, a pencil placed in the hole, and the instrument set over the pencil (Figure 162.04i, p. 122). Paint one of the cups so that students can easily count the number of times it goes around in one minute. The instrument can be calibrated by comparing the number of turns with observations on the Beaufort scale (see entry 162.06). Another way to calibrate the instrument is to hold it out the window of a moving car on a calm day. This is done by sitting next to the front right window while the driver drives the car at a steady 5 miles (kilometers) per hour. The number of turns is counted for one minute. (This should be done several times and an average taken.) Repeat for 10 mph (kph), 15 mph (kph), etc. The information can be graphed (see Graph 162.04, p. 122). When the instrument is

Figure 162.04e   **Figure 162.04f**

MEASURING WIND SPEED

Graph 162.04

Tin Cans

Paper Cups

Figure 162.04g

Figure 162.04h

mounted on the school grounds, the speed can be determined by counting the number of turns in one minute.

Measuring and recording the speed of wind. Students can keep a daily record of wind speed on a table similar to Table 162.05. Measurements should be made at the same time each day, and students should note whether the sky is sunny, cloudy, rainy, and so on. Have them study their table after several weeks to see if there is any relationship between the speed and direction of the wind and the kind of weather that follows.

**05
Bc
Ch
Fb**

Figure 162.04i

Table 162.05. Measuring Wind Speed (Rotary Anemometer)

Week of _____			
	a.m.	p.m.	Observations
Monday			
Tuesday			
Wednesday			
Thursday			
Friday			

Estimating wind speed without an anemometer. The speed of the wind can be estimated without complex instruments simply by using the Beaufort scale (see Table 162.06). The scale allows students to estimate fairly accurately the speed of wind by observing the motions of leaves on trees, chimney smoke, etc.

06
Cb

Contributing Idea C. Air is heated primarily by contact with the ground.

Measuring the temperature of air near the ground. On a windless day, have students find a place in direct sunlight and drive a 6 ft. (2 m) stake into the ground.

07
Ce

On the shadow side of the stake, let them place one thermometer on the ground so that the bulb is in direct contact with the ground. Place a second thermometer on the stake near the ground and directly above the first thermometer. Attach a third thermometer at least 5 ft. (1.5 m) above the second. Be sure that each thermometer is on the shadow side so that it is not in the direct rays of the Sun. At 10-minute intervals, check the readings on the thermometers. Students will find that the temperatures are higher nearer the ground. Explain that when cold air moves near the warm land or water, it becomes warmer and begins to rise.

Table 162.06. The Beaufort Scale of the Speed of Wind

Scale Number	Observation	Name of Wind	Miles Per Hour
0	Smoke goes straight up	Calm	Less than 1
1	Direction shown by smoke but not by wind vanes	Light Air	1–3
2	Wind vane moves; leaves rustle	Light Breeze	4–7
3	Flag flutters; leaves move constantly	Gentle Breeze	8–12
4	Raises dirt, paper; flags flap	Moderate Breeze	13–18
5	Small trees sway; flags ripple	Fresh Breeze	19–24
6	Large branches move; flags beat	Strong Breeze	25–31
7	Whole trees sway; flags are extended	Moderate Gale	32–38
8	Twigs break off; hard to walk against	Fresh Gale	39–46
9	Slight damage to buildings	Strong Gale	47–54
10	Trees uprooted; windows break	Full Gale	55–63
11	Widespread damage to buildings	Violent Storm	64–75
12	General destruction	Hurricane	Over 75

As the air rises, it becomes cooler and heavier, and then moves down toward the land and water again.

> *Contributing Idea D.* Winds are caused by unequal heating of the Earth's surface.

Comparing the absorption and release of heat by soil and water. Fill one coffee can with dry soil and another with water. Let each remain in the classroom overnight so that they will be equal in temperature. Students can then put thermometers to the same depth in each and place both cans outdoors in the sunlight. After two hours, check the temperatures to see which is warmer and which is cooler. (The water should be cooler.) Have students share experiences they have had walking barefoot from hot pavement or land to a puddle or from a sandy beach to the water. They should deduce that soil heats up more rapidly than water. If they next set a can of soil and a can of water of equal temperatures in a refrigerator and check the temperatures every 10 minutes, they will find that the soil cools more quickly than the water. Such data can be easily graphed. Explain that soil or water temperatures influence the air above them. That is, land areas generally warm more rapidly during the day than water areas; thus the air above the land tends to be heated and rise while the cooler, heavier air over the water areas pushes inland to replace it. At night the land areas generally cool more quickly, thus the exchange of air is reversed.

08 Ce

Detecting warm and cool air currents. Small wind currents in the classroom can be detected using simple wind current detectors. The detector in Figure 162.09 can be made by folding a square piece of paper up on the solid lines and down on the dotted lines, then attaching a thread to the center. If held by the thread over a radiator or lightbulb, the device will move and indicate the direction of the current. If temperature readings are taken in different places in the room (e.g., at the ceiling and the floor; at the bottom and top of an open window), students will see that the movement corresponds to the exchange of warm and cool air. Explain that warm air weighs less than cold air, exerts less pressure—thus creating an area of low pressure. The heavier cold air creates an area of high pressure and pushes the warm air upward.

09 Aa

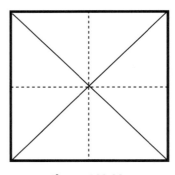

Figure 162.09

Generalization II. Water on Earth evaporates into the atmosphere as moisture.

Contributing Idea A. Temperature change affects evaporation.

Testing to see if an increase in temperature affects evaporation. Pour ½ c. (100 ml) of water into each of two identical shallow pans. Place one in a warm location and the other in a cool place away from any breeze. Compare the time required for the water to evaporate from each pan. Students can make some judgment about the relationship of heat to evaporation. The test can be repeated and speeded up by placing the experimental pan over a heat source such as a hot plate or radiator. Similarly, two cloths of the same size and same material can be substituted for the pans. Soak each thoroughly in water. Set one in a cool location and one in a warm location. An analogy can be made to clothes on a line on a sunny day and on a cloudy day. In each of the above tests, be sure that the heat factor is the only influence.

10 Ec

Testing to see if a great reduction in temperature affects evaporation. Thoroughly wet a cloth on a sunny day when the temperature outside is below freezing. Suspend the cloth and observe it every half hour until it is frozen stiff. After several hours, bring the cloth indoors and let students examine it. They will find that the cloth is dry. The time required for

11 Ec

the frozen water to leave the cloth will depend upon the relative humidity of the air, the wind, and the temperature. (Note: The water in the cloth actually sublimes from a solid state to a gaseous state.)

Contributing Idea B. Moving air affects evaporation.

Testing to see if moving air affects evaporation. If you have access to a chalkboard or one in the classroom, wet two identical areas of a chalkboard and fan one with a piece of cardboard or an electric fan. Students will realize that the moving air was the influencing factor in making one area dry faster. Similarly, they can thoroughly wet two cloths of the same size and material, and hang one outdoors in a windy location and the other in a sheltered spot. If students touch the cloths periodically, they will find that the water evaporates from the cloth in the wind more quickly. Let them discuss how clothes dry on windy days. **Caution: Follow safety guidelines when using the electric fan.**

12 Ec

Testing to see if moving moist air affects temperature. Have students use thermometers to find the temperature of moving air (outside when the wind is blowing or in front of an electric fan). Hang some wet straw, newspaper, or cloth strips in the breeze. Leave a little space between the strips so the air can pass between them. Use thermometers to find out what happens to the temperature of the air after

13 Ec

it passes through the wet material. An analogy can be made to air conditioners and how they work.

> *Contributing Idea C.* Surface area affects evaporation.

Testing to see if surface area affects evaporation. Pour 1 c. of water into a wide, shallow dish and another cup into a tall, narrow jar. Place both in direct sunlight. Students will see that the one with the wide mouth evaporates faster than the other. Discuss the differences in evaporation from small puddles and large lakes.

14 Ec

Generalization III. Moisture in the atmosphere can condense into various forms that return to the Earth.

> *Contributing Idea A.* The rain gauge is an instrument used to measure rainfall.

Making a rainfall indicator (rain gauge). Any open container with straight sides can be used to measure amounts of rainfall. When the rain is collected, simply have students stick a ruler into the container to see how deep the water is. If the water is 1 in. (3 cm) deep, then 1 in. (3 cm) of rain

15 Gc

has fallen. Since most rainfall is less than an inch, a true rain gauge is designed to catch a relatively wide area of rainfall and to funnel it into a narrow area so that it will be deeper and can be measured more easily. (Note: Measurements must be taken very soon after a rainfall or evaporation will give inaccurate readings.) Attach a test tube beside a strip of paper on a block of wood. Fill a widemouthed, straight-sided jar with 1 in. (3 cm) of water. Pour this water into the test tube and mark the height on the strip of paper. Repeat this procedure using ¾ in., ½ in., and ¼ in. (or 2.5 cm, 2 cm, 1.5 cm, 1 cm, and 0.5 cm) of water. Now the jar can be placed outdoors in the open. When rain is collected in the jar, pour it into the test tube to measure how much rain fell.

Measuring and recording rainfall. Use a rain gauge in conjunction with a wind vane. Information can be recorded on Table 162.16. A graph of the data (Graph 162.16) will reveal how much rain falls in your area in a month and which winds bring rain.

16 Bc Bf Cd

> *Contributing Idea B.* Water condenses.

Table 162.16 Measuring Rainfall

Date	Direction of Wind During Rainfall	Amount of Rainfall

Graph 162.16

Observing condensation. Have students observe the condensation of water on glasses of ice water. Let them discuss where the droplets come from. Let them also describe personal experiences that are examples of condensation (e.g., moisture on a mirror in bathroom, moisture on windows inside a closed automobile). **17 Aa Ga**

Contributing Idea C. Temperature change affects condensation.

Observing condensation by cooling through contact. On a very cold day, have students go outside and notice how the moisture from their breath can be seen when it comes in contact with the cold air. Similarly, have them exhale across **18 Aa**

an ice cube tray or into an open freezer compartment and observe the condensation in the air. They will realize that this phenomenon takes place when moist air comes in contact with cooler air or a cooler surface.

Observing condensation by cooling through rising. Boil some water in a pot, beaker, or tea kettle on a hot plate. When it is boiling, let students describe what they see. **Caution: Be careful of the steam.** Students will see clouds of moisture forming as the heated moist air rises into the cooler air of the room. Encourage them to imagine how warm moist air near the Earth may rise and cool in the **19 Aa Fa**

atmosphere in a similar way. (Note: Rising air cools at the rate of 1°F every 300 ft. in the atmosphere.)

Observing condensation by cooling through expansion. Pour a cup of hot water into a transparent widemouthed gallon (4 L) jar. Put a plastic bag inside the jar and fold its edge over the rim, fastening it tightly with rubber bands. Have one student hold the jar firmly on the table, and let another pull upward on the bag quickly. Have them describe what they see inside the jar. (When the bag is pulled upward, the pressure inside the jar is reduced and the warm moist air inside expands. It cools with expansion and a cloud forms inside. When the bag is released, the cloud disappears.) This activity can be repeated several times. The cloud is best seen when the light source is behind the viewer. Students should be able to generalize that clouds can form in a similar way.

20 Aa Fa

> *Contributing Idea D.* Dew and frost are formed by the condensation of water vapor on the surface of the Earth.

Observing how dew is formed. Remove the label from a tin can. Take some water that has been allowed to stand until it has reached room temperature, and fill the can about halfway. Add a few ice cubes to cool the water. After several minutes, students will see droplets of water forming on the outside of the can. Tell them that

21 Aa Bb Fa

the formation is called dew. Explain the parallel formation of early morning dew that they may have seen. They will realize that when moist air contacts a cooler surface, such as the side of the can or blades of grass, the moisture in the air condenses on the surface. (Note: In very dry areas, this activity may not work because there may not be enough water vapor in the air for droplets to form.)

Measuring dew points. Remove the label from a tin can, and half-fill it with water. Place a thermometer in the water, and record the temperature. Add chips of ice, stir, and record the temperature again when droplets form on the outside of the can. Tell students that the temperature reading when the droplets form is called the dew point for the temperature of the air in the room. Explain that water droplets or dew on blades of grass or flowers in the morning is formed in a similar way, and the temperature at which it forms is the *dew point*. Let students repeat this activity in different locations and on different days to compare dew points. If other observations are recorded (e.g., room temperature, humidity), factors influencing dew point will be discovered. After several tests, ask students what conclusion they would make if the temperature of the room and the dew point were within a few degrees of each other. (There would be a very high relative humidity.)

22 Bb Ce

Observing how frost is formed. Remove the labels from two tin cans and half-fill one can with water, chips of ice, and a handful of salt to make it very cold. Half-fill the second can with water only. Use two thermometers to record the temperature of each can, and then stir the contents of both rapidly. Students can observe the outside of the cans. Tell them that the formation they observe on the first can is called frost. Explain the parallel formation of early morning frost on the ground. They can then compare the two temperature readings and realize that when the surface of an object (e.g., the ground) is below the freezing temperature of water, the water vapor in the air condenses on the surface as frost.

23
Aa
Bb
Fa

Contributing Idea E. Fog is formed by the condensation of water vapor near the surface of the Earth.

Observing how fog is formed. Fog is the condensation of moisture in the atmosphere near the surface of the Earth. For any of the following experiences, help students realize that real fog is formed in an analogous way through the rapid cooling and condensation of water vapor in the air near the Earth's surface.

24
Aa
Fa

   a. Heat some water in a container until it boils, and then fill a beaker slowly to prevent it from breaking. Next, empty all but 1 in. (3 cm) of water from the bottle and hold it so the light source (e.g., window,

electric light) comes from behind the viewers. Now, set the bottle on a tray of ice cubes, and let students describe and discuss what happens inside. They will realize that in a similar way fog forms at night when the Earth cools rapidly (represented by the ice tray) and the air next to it cools in turn and comes in contact with the warmer moist air above.

   b. Take a large fruit juice can, put some ice in it, and add a handful of salt to make it very cold. Set a smaller can on the ice so that the tops of both cans are even. Pack more ice and salt into the space between the two cans and let a student exhale into the smaller one. The class will see fog form and remain in the smaller can. Point out the parallel to real fog that clings in valleys when the ground is cooled.

Contributing Idea F. Clouds are formed by the condensation of water vapor in the atmosphere.

Observing how clouds are formed. Clouds are condensations of moisture in the atmosphere. For any of the following experiences, help students realize that real clouds are formed similarly through the cooling and condensation brought about by the expansion of rising air.

25
Aa
Fa

a. Pour 1 c. (200 ml) of warm water into a transparent widemouthed gallon (4 L) jar. Hold a lighted match in the jar, blow it out, and let it remain briefly. Now place a plastic bag inside the jar, turn its edge down over the rim of the jar, and fasten it securely with rubber bands. Have a student hold the jar firmly on the table, and let another quickly pull upward on the plastic bag. They will see a cloud form inside; when the bag is released, it will disappear. The cloud forms for several reasons: (1) the air in the jar contains invisible water vapor; (2) the air pressure inside the jar is reduced; (3) there are many small particles from the match in the air. As the air inside the jar expands, it cools, and the water vapor condenses as liquid around the smoke particles form the minute droplets that make up the cloud. Students can test to see if a cloud can be made: (1) without putting water in the jar; (2) with cold water instead of warm water; (3) with water but without smoke, and so on.

b. Obtain two identical widemouthed jars. Line half the inside of each with soft, black cloth. Add glue to hold the cloths in place, and then soak the cloths with water. Cover each jar with a square of glass and set them upright, one in a pan of cold water, the other in a pan of very hot water. Leave the jars for 15 minutes. Remove them from the pans and set the cold jar upside down over the warm jar leaving the glass squares over the openings (see Figure 162.25). Hold a flashlight to shine down through both jars, and then carefully remove the glass squares. A cloud will form as the warm moist air rises and comes in contact with the cooler air above. Students can experiment by repeating the activity and reversing the positions of the jars. Tiny tissue paper streamers can be placed inside the jars to indicate the direction the air flows. If possible, observe cloud formations outdoors, and let students judge the relationship of hot and cold air masses based upon their experimental models.

Identifying cloud types. Have students keep records for a week of the kinds of clouds that they see. Help them recognize some of the common types. **26 Ba Bb**

a. *Cirrus*, *cumulus*, and *stratus* are the basic types of clouds. Cirrus are very high in the atmosphere. They generally look feathery and are composed of tiny ice crystals. They are usually a sign of clear weather. Cumulus clouds are

Flashlight

One-Gallon Jar

Cold Jar

Black Cloth
Cemented to
Sides of Jars
and Saturated
With Water

Glass
Plates

One-Gallon Jar

Warm Jar

Figure 162.25

lower than cirrus clouds, and airplanes often fly above them. They look like white puffs in the sky and usually indicate fair weather. Stratus clouds are much lower and foglike. They form gray layers across the sky.

b. *Nimbus* describes basic clouds containing a great amount of water. They are usually very low in the sky and look thick and black. They generally bring rain, snow, sleet, or hail.

c. *Alto* is a prefix meaning "high." It is used to describe high forms of basic clouds.

Students can study events that bring about the formation of each type of cloud. They

might group cloud types on the basis of the events (clouds that usually follow in sequence with an approaching cold front: altocumulus, cumulonimbus, stratus, stratocumulus; clouds that usually follow in sequence with an approaching warm front: cirrus, cirrostratus, altostratus, nimbostratus, stratus).

Contributing Idea G. When the moisture in clouds continues to condense, it may fall as rain or snow.

Observing how rain is formed. After students have seen how clouds can be formed, have them hold the flat bottom of an ice cube tray slightly tilted but close to steam escaping from a boiling teakettle. **Caution: The steam is very hot.** Be sure they observe how the water droplets collect, enlarge, and drip off the edge of the tray because of their increasing weight. It should be noted that although the formation of rain is not fully understood, scientists believe that droplets form upon minute particles in the air and continue to increase in size as water vapor cools. Students can try this activity again using two ice cube trays—one empty and one filled with ice cubes. Explain that as the moist air rises (from the teakettle), it cools rapidly against the filled tray and less rapidly against the empty tray. Take care to hold the trays at equal distances from the spout of the teakettle and record the time taken for drops of "rain" to fall

**27
Aa
Fa**

from each. They can compare the times. Students can relate their findings to actual events in the atmosphere.

Measuring the size of raindrops. On a rainy day, pour some flour through a sifter into a pie pan until it is ½ in. (1 cm) deep. Cover the pan with a large plate and take it outdoors. Hold it in the rain, uncover it, and let the rain fall into the flour for three seconds. Cover the pan with the plate and return indoors. When the pan is uncovered again, students will see wet round lumps where the raindrops fell. Let the lumps dry for about three hours, and then use the sifter to separate the lumps from the flour. Measure the lumps with a ruler or seriate them by size to learn something about the relative size of raindrops. (Note: The lumps are slightly larger than the actual raindrops.) If records are kept (Table 162.28), the sizes of raindrops can be compared during different parts of a storm or between different storms. Another way to measure the size of raindrops is to prepare hoop screens by stretching pieces of discarded **28 Cd Da**

nylon stockings over embroidery hoops. When each screen is stretched tightly, staple or tack it in place, then trim away the excess stocking. On a rainy day, press the screens into a large pan with some sprinkled powdered sugar. Tap off any excess sugar, cover the screens, take them outdoors, and hold them horizontally in the rain. When ready, uncover the screens and allow raindrops to fall on them for a timed period (e.g., 30 seconds). Cover the screens again and bring them into the classroom. If the screens are held up against a dark background, students will see darkened spots where each drop removed the sugar as it fell through the screen. Diameters can be compared with a ruler. Samples taken from different locales or at different times during the rainfall can also be compared.

Observing how snow is formed. Obtain some dry ice. **Caution: Do not touch dry ice with bare hands. Keep it in a closed container when not in use.** Prepare a cloud as in entry 162.24b, and then chip a few small pieces from the dry ice, and **29 Aa Bb Fa**

Table 162.28. Seriating Raindrops by Size

	Small Drops	Medium Drops	Large Drops
Number of drops in 3 seconds at the beginning of the storm.			
Number of drops in 3 seconds in the middle of the storm.			
Number of drops in 3 seconds near the end of the storm.			

drop them into the cloud. Hold a flashlight into the small can and exhale gently into the cloud at two-minute intervals. Have students describe what happens. Explain that snow is formed directly from water vapor to ice crystals in a similar way (no liquid state between the two), and that the crystals may fall to the ground as snowflakes. You might explain that if rain freezes when it contacts an object or the ground, the result is called *sleet*, and when frozen particles in the air have additional layers of water frozen to them before they fall to the ground, the result is called *hail*.

Observing how obstacles affect snow-drifts. On a snowy day, prop some cardboard sheets upright on old snow. Set the sheets so they face in different directions. When it stops snowing, students can examine the distribution of the snow around each sheet. They will be able to describe where the drifting takes place. On the basis of their observations, ask them how they would place a snow fence if they wanted to keep snow from a walkway.

30 Aa

Measuring snowfall. Although snow-fall depth is reported on newscasts and is important to skiers, the snowfall measurement by weather bureaus has more meaning when the water content of the snow is determined. To do this, remove the top and bottom from a straight-sided can and push the can straight down into the snow until

31 Cd

its rim is even with the Earth's surface. Let one student reach under the can and cut the snow even with the bottom edge with a piece of cardboard. Remove the cylinder of snow and dump it into a second can of the same size but that has only one end removed. Melt the snow slowly to avoid too much loss of water by evaporation. Measure the depth of the water that remains. Compare the depth of the water to the depth of the snow that produced it. Since snows are different, students can try this activity with dry, light, fluffy, and packed snows. They will find that some snows are drier than others (the ratio of water to snow depth is less). They can seriate or rank the snows by the amount of water each produces; and if temperature measurements are taken during snowfalls, a relationship between temperature, the type of snow that is formed, and the water content will be discovered.

163   Theory

Generalization I. Many factors act together in complex ways to keep the forces that control weather constantly out of balance.

> *Contributing Idea A.* The tilt of the Earth affects the balance of temperatures.

Making a model to show how solar energy strikes the Earth's surface. On lined paper, have students trace and cut out a large circle. Have them print *North*

01 Fc

Pole on the top of the circle and *South Pole* on the bottom. Draw a heavy horizontal line through the middle of the circle to represent the equator. Place two sheets of lined paper on a flat surface, and mark an *S* in the center between the two sheets to represent the placement of the Sun. Tell students that the lines on the paper represent rays of solar energy, some of which become converted into heat. Place the cut-out Earth on the left-hand lined sheet so that the North Pole is at the top and the lines on the circle match those on the sheet. Ask students which part of the Earth receives the most radiation from the Sun when in this position, then move the North Pole to the right as if the Earth were tilted toward the Sun (the Earth tilts 23½°), and ask which part of the Earth now receives the most radiation from the Sun. They will see that more rays strike the northern regions than the southern. (Arrow heads can be added to the parallel lines to emphasize how the rays strike the Earth.) Next, move the Earth so that it travels around the Sun to the other side (place it on the right-hand sheet of lined paper). Be sure the Earth remains in the same tilted position. Again ask which areas on the Earth receive more and less solar energy. Students will see that the polar regions alternate in receiving more or less solar energy due to the tilt of the Earth and realize the angle of the Sun's rays cause the changing seasons. In winter (in the Northern Hemisphere) the Sun is low in the sky. In the summer it is more directly overhead.

Contributing Idea B. The curved surface of the Earth affects the balance of temperatures.

Using a model to observe the effect of solar energy upon a curved surface. 02 Ce Fc
Shine a flashlight through a cardboard tube (to keep the rays from spreading outward). Aim the tube horizontally at the equator of a globe, and let students describe the spot of light that is projected. Move the flashlight gradually toward the North Pole while holding the tube horizontally. (Note: The parallel lines in entry 163.01 can be used to supplement this experience.) Students can describe the spot of light that is now projected. (It is larger because the rays strike the surface at more and more of a slant as the light is moved toward the pole.) They can make the analogy to the radiant energy reaching the Earth from the Sun. Now attach several small thermometers to the globe. Place a lamp 8 in. (20 cm) from the globe so that the thermometer on the equator is in the center of the lighted half of the globe. After three minutes, compare the thermometer readings. Students will find that the temperature readings decrease toward the poles.

Comparing temperature differences of soils receiving direct and slanted solar energy. 03 Bc Ce
Fill identical cardboard boxes or milk cartons with equal amounts of soil

or sand. Insert thermometers into each box to equal depths. Set both boxes in the sunlight, but prop one so that the Sun's rays strike it directly. Record temperature readings every 10 or 15 minutes. Results can be graphed. Students will see that the temperature rises more quickly and higher where the Sun's rays strike the soil directly. Analogies can be made to various places on Earth.

Contributing Idea C. Some materials absorb more heat energy than others.

Comparing differences in heat energy absorbed by differently colored materials. Obtain two dowel sticks of the same diameter and length. Sharpen one end of each so that it can be driven or pressed into packed snow. Paint one stick black and the other white. On a sunny day, when there is a good snow cover, press the two sticks upright into the snow to the same depth, and check them every few hours while observing the snow around each. Students will observe that the snow area around the black stick melted more than the snow area around the white stick. Have them look for everyday examples of the same phenomenon (e.g., the area around tree trunks, weeds, and posts sticking through the snow and around various objects that people drop onto the snow). Students can also cut several identical squares from different colors of construction paper. On a sunny day, place

04
Ca

the papers on a clean snow surface and observe every hour to see which shows the least effect from exposure to the Sun.

Measuring the heat energy absorbed by differently colored materials. Fill two glasses with equal volumes of water. Wrap a sheet of white paper around one glass and a black sheet around the other. Set identical thermometers in each, and place the glasses in direct sunlight. Have students take temperature readings every 10 minutes. The data can be graphed. Students will find that the water in the glass wrapped in black paper warms more quickly. Next, let them try papers of various colors and compare the results. They may wish to discuss the advantages and disadvantages of wearing certain color clothes at different times of the year.

05
Bf
Ce

Contributing Idea D. The atmosphere affects temperatures by shielding the Earth from solar radiation and by trapping heat energy that is reradiated from the Earth's surface.

Using a model to observe that solar energy can be shielded from a surface. Hold a thermometer directly beneath a lighted bulb at a distance of 8 in. (20 cm) for three minutes. Record the temperature, then let the thermometer return to room temperature. Next, repeat this procedure after inserting a sheet of paper between the bulb and the thermometer. After three

06
Ce
Fc

minutes, record the temperature and compare readings. Let students feel the paper and ask them how the atmosphere might affect heat and light from the Sun in a similar way. Explain that clouds, dust, and other impurities in the air reflect and absorb some solar energy much like the sheet of paper and that some of the Sun's energy is turned back by the atmosphere, some is absorbed by the atmosphere, and some goes clear through the atmosphere and warms the Earth. As a supplemental or alternative activity, tape two thermometers on directly opposite sides on a globe at the equator. Hold a lamp about 8 in. (20 cm) from the globe so that one thermometer is in the center of the lighted half of the globe. After three minutes compare the two thermometer readings. Students can discuss the temperature differences between night and day and relate their finding to personal experiences. Next, have them hold a piece of paper between the bulb and the thermometer for another three minutes and compare the readings. They can make analogies between this experience and days that are overcast, foggy, or smoggy.

Using a model to observe that heat can be trapped in the atmosphere. Fill a plastic bag with soil, and place a small thermometer on top of the soil. Tie the bag securely. Place another thermometer on an identical type of soil outside the bag. Leave both in the bright sunlight and **07 Ce Fc**

record the temperature readings every 10 minutes for an hour. Compare the readings of the two thermometers. The data can be graphed. Ask why one reading is higher than the other. (Although both received the same amount of solar energy, the energy absorbed by the soil in the bag heated the air confined in the bag. The trapped air, in turn, kept the soil warm.) Similarly, the students can fill two pans with equal quantities of soil or sand and set them in a warm place for several hours. Let them insert thermometers, each one-half inch (1 cm) beneath the surface of the soil or sand in each pan. Place both pans outdoors and away from any buildings on a sunless, windless day. Place a cloth or canvas covering a few in. over one of the pans and take temperature readings of the soil every 10 minutes for an hour. The data may be graphed. The students should see that the uncovered pan cools more rapidly, as heat energy strikes the canvas over the covered pan and reflects some back, retaining some of the heat.

> *Contributing Idea E.* Air moves because of unbalanced temperatures.

Observing that warm air rises and cooler air moves in to replace it. Make a tube of lightweight cardboard, and fit it loosely around an uncovered lightbulb (Figure 163.08a). If you have access to chalk and chalkboard erasers, rub chalk or erase chalk to create dusty erasers. **08 Aa**

Turn the bulb on and darken the room. Have one student clap together two dusty chalkboard erasers near the bottom of the tube (Figure 163.08b), and let others observe what happens. (The chalk dust will rise through the tube and out the top.) Ask what happens to the air that is warmed. (It rises.) Ask what happens to the air over warm parts of the Earth. (Warm air creates a low pressure area.) Next, hold the tube under a tray of ice cubes, shine a flashlight at the bottom of the cubes, and hold a smoking piece of clothesline rope or string near the top. Ask what happens to the air as it is cooled. (It falls.) Ask what happens to the air over cold parts of the Earth. (Cooler air forms a high pressure area and replaces warmer air as the warmer air rises.)

high and just slightly larger than a square-shaped hot plate. Cut the bottom from the box so that it can be set over the hot plate. Next, cut out large openings on two adjacent sides of the box, cover them with heavy clear plastic, and paint the inside of the box black. Next, cut a 4 in. (10 cm) hole in the top and insert a 3 ft. (1 m) long cardboard chimney. Be sure to tape the chimney securely and seal it with melted wax so that no air can leak into the box. Now, cut ½ in. (2 cm) slots in the four corners, starting 1 in. (3 cm) from the top and extending to within 1 in (3 cm) from the bottom. Place on the hot plate a shallow square tray of water that is about the same size as the hot plate. Cover them with the box. Shine a flashlight through one window, and let the class observe (Figure 163.09). They will see the formation of a vortex, like a miniature tornado,

Figure 163.08a   **Figure 163.08b**

Chalk Dust

Making a model tornado. Find a cardboard box that is at least 1 ft. (30 cm)

09
Fc

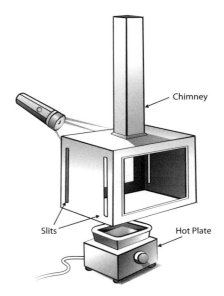

Chimney

Slits   Hot Plate

Figure 163.09

above the boiling water. (A real tornado is formed similarly due to convection currents.)

Observing that high pressure areas move into low pressure areas. Air generally moves from a high pressure area to a low pressure area; thus, winds blow from high to low. There are several activities that help students realize this.

**10
Aa
Bb**

   a. Students can hold two sheets of typing paper approximately 3 in. (10 cm) apart and blow between them. As long as the students blows, the sheets of paper will be forced together. (The rapidly moving air current between the papers creates a low pressure area as the greater surrounding pressure outside forces the papers together.)

   b. Students can attach threads to two table tennis balls with cellophane tape or drops of glue. Suspend the balls about an inch apart and, using a soda straw, blow between them. Students will realize that as the stream of air passes between them, a low pressure area results as indicated by the balls being pushed together. Tell them that weather forecasters call low-pressure areas *lows* and high-pressure areas *highs*. If possible, show weather maps, indicate the high and low symbols, and discuss what they mean in terms of moving air masses.

Using a model to observe how winds are affected by the rotation of the Earth. Spin a globe in a counterclockwise direction (west to east) as viewed from above the North Pole. Let one student try to draw a straight line on the spinning globe by pressing lightly on it with a piece of chalk or wax pencil. The line drawn should extend from about 35°N latitude to the equator (Figure 163.11a). When the globe stops spinning, students can observe the line that was made. Tell them that the line could represent a wind blowing from the north. Explain that such winds are twisted to their right (west) as was the drawn line. Because winds from the north constantly come in contact with the Earth's surface, whose speed of rotation is greater than the winds' speed, the wind currents lag behind, causing them to turn a little from their straight course. Students will realize that the Earth's rotation influences all winds in the Northern Hemisphere to shift to their right (i.e., north winds become easterly and south winds become westerly) (Figure 163.11b). Explain that winds that push toward a low pressure area are also twisted to the right, creating a counterclockwise swirl of air, while winds pushing out from a high pressure area are all twisted to their right, creating a clockwise spiral of air (Figure 163.11c). This can be demonstrated three-dimensionally by cutting

**11
Fc**

Figure 163.11a   **Figure 163.11b**

Figure 163.11c

a rubber ball in half and painting rings around the outside of each half. Place one cup of the ball open-side down on a map at a place where a high pressure area might be indicated. Place the other cup open-side up where a low might be. Explain that the cups represent the pressure areas, and then trace with a pencil how the air will spiral up one cup and spiral downward into the other.

Generalization II. **According to theory, the air above the Earth can be thought of as masses that are separated by zones of rapidly changing conditions.**

Contributing Idea. Air masses transport complete sets of weather conditions that change as the air masses move over the Earth's surface.

Using models to demonstrate weather fronts. An aquarium can be structured to show what generally takes place when differently heated air masses come in contact. To do this, use plastic-model cement or contact cement to glue plastic rib binders, such as the type used by students to hold report papers together, along the bottom and sides of the aquarium (Figure 163.12a). Be sure the ribs are glued securely to form a watertight guide for a glass partition. Now make a parti-

12
Bb
Fc

Figure 163.12a

tion from a sheet of glass. Cut it so it will just slide in the plastic guides, but higher than the top edge of the aquarium. Several different demonstrations pertaining to the contact of warm and cold air masses (weather fronts) can be observed.

a. *Warm and Cold Fronts.* Place warm water in one side of the aquarium and cool water in the other. Use food coloring to color the warm water red and the cool water blue. Add half a spoonful of salt to the cool water. Explain to students that the red water represents a warm air mass and the blue represents a cool air mass (Figure 163.12b). Such air masses are like huge invisible flat bubbles—often over 10 miles high and hundreds of miles across. Now remove the partition and let students describe what they see. Tell them that the dividing line between the masses is called a front. When a cold mass (blue water) moves against a warm mass there is a *cold front*. Students will see that the warm mass is forced upward over the cold mass (Figure 163.12c).

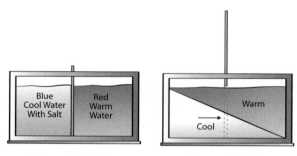

Figure 163.12b   **Figure 163.12c**

Let them predict what warm moist air would do under such circumstances. Generally a sequence of cloud types progress along the front bringing a sequence of weather events (Figure 163.12d). (1) A general haziness, light fog, or fairly low clouds appear due to the chilling of the warmer moist air near the ground. Near the ground the air

Figure 163.12d

is warmer than it will be as the cold front progresses. (2) Somewhat higher thunderclouds (cumulonimbus) appear due to the rapid rising and cooling of the warm moist air over the cold mass front. Heavy rains fall and on the ground strong winds blow. (3) Diminishing numbers of cumulus clouds can be seen high in the sky. On the ground, the wind is calmer and the air is cooler or cold. Some variations take place in this sequence, depending upon the degree of difference in temperatures between the cold and warm masses. If the difference is slight, the stormy portion is less violent— possibly just changing from mild to light rains and to slightly cooler temperatures. In the winter, the cold front may bring snow or sleet instead of rain.

When a warm mass (red water) moves against a cold mass there is a *warm front*. In the same demonstration students can imagine (Figure 163.12e) how the warm mass can advance over the cold mass and bring a sequence of weather events (Figure 163.12f):

clouds increases in altitude. They decrease in altitude when a warm front progresses. By knowing what type of air mass is approaching and how fast, the meteorologist can generally predict the type of weather and when it will arrive.

Figure 163.12e

Cold Air Mass

Warm Air Mass

1   2   3   4

← Direction of Movement

Figure 163.12f

(1) Feathery bands or rows of cirrus clouds appear approximately 8 miles (13 km) up where the air is so cold that water vapor freezes. The clouds are made up of ice crystals due to the warm mass being chilled by the cold mass. (2) Thin sheets of altostratus clouds appear at a lower altitude. (3) Nimbostratus clouds appear and steady rains fall. The clouds seem to come lower and lower as the front progresses, and may touch the ground as fog. (4) The sky clears and the air is warmer and damp. Many variables can affect this general sequence. Students should note that when a cold front advances, the progression of

b. *Occluded Fronts.* Insert the glass partition after finishing the previous activity. Stir one side, and then remove the partition (Figure 163.12g). Explain that the three colors of water now represent three different air masses: warm, cold, and colder (Figure 163.12h) Students will see the air mass of the intermediate

Warm and Cool Water Mixed   Warm   Cool

Warm   Mixed →   Cool

Figure 163.12g   **Figure 163.12h**

temperature forcing its way between the warmer and colder layers to form three distinct layers. Tell them that this relationship forms an *occluded front*. In a sequence of events, this triple-mass system passes high above the ground, the clouds move downward (e.g., cumulus, stratus, nimbostratus), then back up again (e.g., nimbostratus, altostratus, cirrus). The lowest clouds are almost always some distance above the ground. The weather changes from clear and cool to stormy, to clear and cool again (Figure 163.12i).

Figure 163.12i

Let students use the aquarium to see what would happen if no salt was used in the beginning or if the two compartments contained water of the same temperature. They might find the temperature differences among the three layers in an occluded front. Other liquids, such as white syrup or glycerin, might be tried to slow down the changes that take place.

164 Applications

Generalization. Changes in weather can be predicted.

Contributing Idea A. Weather is the temporary condition of temperature, wind, and moisture of the atmosphere in a given place at a given time.

Using instruments to predict changes in weather. Many factors such as temperature, wind, air pressure, and moisture make up what is called weather. The following are a few very general suggestions for obtaining information and making predictions from some of the factors.

**01
Fb
Ga**

  a. *Wind.* Students can use a wind vane to find patterns of wind direction and the subsequent changes in weather (see entry 162.01). For example, on the west coast of the United States, winds from the south, southwest, west, and northwest usually bring rain because they blow from the ocean; winds from the northwest, north, northeast, and east usually bring fair and cooler weather because they come from cooler land areas; winds from the east, southeast, and south usually bring fair and warmer weather because they come from warmer land areas; winds coming from the west, northwest, or north usually bring fair and cooler weather

Table 164.01. Relating Humidity to Weather Changes

	Before Front	During Front	After Front
Warm Front	Increasing	very moist	slight decrease
Cold Front	Steady	very moist	rapid decrease

because they come from cooler land farther north or from dryer land farther west; winds from the northeast, east, southeast, and south usually bring rain because they blow from the ocean. Students might also use an anemometer to determine how long it takes for certain types of weather to move into their locale (see entries 162.04, 162.05).

b. *Air Pressure.* Until weather satellite photos became available, the barometer was the major instrument to forecast changes in the weather days in advance. Students can use a barometer to identify patterns between readings and subsequent weather changes (see entries 161.06, 161.07). Students will find that a rising barometer usually means the approach of a high pressure air mass that generally brings increasingly cool, heavy air and better weather. A falling barometer usually means the approach of a low pressure air mass that generally brings increasingly warm, light air, and stormy weather.

c. *Moisture.* Students can use a hygrometer to measure the amount of water (humidity) found in the air (see entries 161.09, 161.10) In general they will find that the humidity of the air increases before a rain and decreases afterward. In terms of approaching weather fronts, the humidity will usually change as shown in Table 164.01.

Preparing a weather station. Several **02** instruments are important in a weather **Gc** station: thermometer, barometer, anemometer, hygrometer, rain gauge. Such instruments should be placed outdoors in a protected and shaded location for best results. The instruments may be sheltered in an open box; or a station can be built (Figure 164.02). This station can house

Figure 164.02

both the instruments and several visual aids to provide easy access as well as protection. If the central panel is constructed of ½ in. (1 cm) hardware screening, various weather instruments can be mounted to it. The opening will allow the air to circulate around the instruments. The two panels on either side can be used as bulletin boards and data recording boards. One board might hold a map of the local area or the United States, covered with acetate so that students can sketch weather fronts on it with grease pencils. It might also hold pictures of cloud types, relative humidity tables, or wind speed scales. The other board might hold data sheets, tables, charts, and graphs that the students prepare. Data tables should be kept current by recording instrument readings twice a day at the same hours.

Recording data and predicting weather changes. There is a great variety of forms that can be used to record data. The selection depends upon what information is sought. A few examples are given here in hope that they will stimulate other ideas (e.g., each activity can be altered by substituting an hygrometer or barometer for the wind vane). All of these data sheets may be similarly prepared using the metric and Celsius systems.

03
Bc
Bf
Fb

  a. *Determining the relationship of wind direction to weather.* Make or obtain a wind vane. Using the instrument, keep a record for a

Table 164.03a

month on a table similar to Table 164.03a. On a daily basis, mark the wind direction and the type of weather observed by using symbols. Next, label the mark with the day of the month (e.g., on the third day the wind was from the northeast, and the sky was cloudy; on the tenth day the wind was from the northeast, and it rained). When completed, students will have a graph representing one month of data. Let them decide what winds brought what weather into their locale. Using the knowledge gained from the patterns, they will be able to make more rational predictions in sub-sequent months.

b. *Determining the relationship of wind direction to temperature.* Make or obtain thermometers and wind vanes. A graph similar to Graph 164.03a can be used to compare wind direction and temperature simultaneously. Students can thus determine that winds from particular directions generally bring certain temperatures.

c. *Determining the relationship of wind direction to rainfall.* Use a rain gauge and wind vane to gather data for a table like Table 164.03b. Amount of rainfall can be recorded in tenths of in. in relation to wind direction. At the end of one month, students can determine which direction brought the most rain.

d. *Comprehensive weather table.* Using all the instruments important to a weather station, students can take readings twice daily and record them on a table like Table 164.03c.

Graph 164.03a

Table 164.03b

From the data, predictions can be made as to what weather to expect. The predictions can be compared with those made by weather forecasters. From such data, students will realize that

Table 164.03c. Collecting Weather Information

Date	Time	Temperatture	Barometer Reading (air pressure)	Hygrometer Reading (humidity)	Air Direction	Air Speed	Rainfall	Types of Clouds	Weather Prediction

today's weather was brought on by something that took place earlier and that today's weather, in turn, will be an influence upon the future weather. Students can also discuss the importance of predicting weather (e.g., hurricane warnings, frost warnings).

Contributing Idea B. Climate is the long range condition of temperature, wind, and moisture of the atmosphere in a given place over a long period of time.

Determining local climate. Students can keep monthly graphs of weather conditions in their locale. Averages may be kept on a table like Table 164.04. After several months, students can make some judgments about trends in the weather conditions. Have students recall what the weather was like during the same periods of time in previous years to see if they **04 Bb Bc Fa** can determine some pattern. Explain that similar weather conditions over long periods of time are called climate. If graphs of data are kept for subsequent classes, in a few years students will have much data to help them determine climatic conditions for their area.

Determining climates in other parts of the world. Find maps showing the principal climatic conditions found in various countries of the world. Students can infer what factors may cause the conditions (e.g., they can use their knowledge of wind systems and precipitation to explain the climate of certain geographic regions). Have students also infer how the conditions might affect people (e.g., in terms of where they can live or how they must adjust their clothing and shelters to live in certain areas; where they can grow certain food crops). **05 Fa**

Table 164.04. Collecting Monthly Averages of Weather Factors

Month _____	
Average Temperature	
Average Humidity_____	How many times "high"
	How many times "low"
Average Rainfall	Number of days it rained
Average Snowfall	Number of days it snowed
Sunny Days	Number
Cloudy Days	Number
Windy Days	Number

200–299
Organic Matter

210 Zoology

211 Characteristics

Generalization I. Animals have identifiable characteristics.

Contributing Idea A. All animals reproduce their kind.

Observing that animals reproduce their kind. Have students find pictures of animals and their young (e.g., deer and fawn, bear and cub, horse and colt, bird and fledgling). They can describe the characteristics of the adults and the young. Have them make a list of the traits that are present in both parents and offspring. **01 Aa Bc**

Observing the reproduction of guppies. Guppies reproduce easily under most classroom conditions and can be used to help students realize that subsequent generations maintain the characteristics of the parents. A pair of guppies will live well in a 1 gal. (4 L) aquarium, but the tank will become too small as offspring arrive. The offspring should be placed in other containers. Stock the aquarium with a male and female guppy (the adult female will be larger and less colorful than the male) and some aquatic plants. Keep the temperature above 72°F (22°C). Feed the guppies daily with commercial food from a pet shop or brine shrimp and daphnia. Students can see the male court the female as he swims around her and turns his body into an S-shape. A pregnant female will produce a brood in 21 to 28 days and can continue to do so up to **02 Aa**

eight months from one mating. The tiny fish are easy prey for the adults, therefore some floating plants should be provided as hiding places for them. Compare the characteristics of the young to those of the adults. Let students tell of experiences they have had in seeing or knowing of the birth of kittens, puppies, hamsters, or other animals. They should realize that in each case, adult animals produce young that carry characteristics of the adults.

Observing inheritance of some physical characteristics. Obtain pictures of the parents (blood relatives) of students and put them on a bulletin board without any identification. Let students study the pictures and guess whose parents are shown. Compare the physical characteristics of the students with those of their parents. Pictures of brothers and sisters can also be used. **03 Aa**

Contributing Idea B. All animals grow.

Describing growth in animals. Let students tell of experiences in raising pets, specifically observable indications that the animals being raised were growing. They might describe changes in size, weight, appearance, habits, or behaviors. If they compare a variety of animals (e.g., birds, fish, hamsters, snails), students can generalize that all types of animals grow. **04 Ba Fa**

Measuring the growth of an animal. Keep a small young mammal as a pet in the classroom (e.g., a mouse or a **05 Bf Cd Ch**

hamster). Provide it with an appropriate, clean cage and feed it a proper diet. Weigh the animal once a week by placing it in a tall coffee can or cardboard oatmeal carton and setting it on a balance scale. Determine the weight of the animal by subtracting the weight of the container. The weekly measurements can be recorded on a graph to depict the animal's growth over time. Other animals can be measured in the same way. It would be interesting to weigh portions of the food during the study. **Caution: Always keep an animal's habitat clean. Wash hands after handling.**

> *Contributing Idea C.* All animals need food, water, and oxygen to grow.

Observing that animals eat. Place a snail and some green leaves in a jar, and cover it with a piece of nylon stocking. Observe the snail as it locates and eats the leaves. Now place other animals in an appropriate environment (grasshoppers, caterpillars, earthworms, hamsters, and so forth), feed them properly, and observe what, when, and how each feeds.

06 Aa Fa

Sorting animals by the types of food they eat. Explain that there are three general types of food-eating animals in nature: plant eaters, meat eaters, and those that eat both. Have students collect pictures of animals from magazines and bring them to class. The pictures can be

07 Db Fa

pasted on charts, one for each of the three types of food eaters. To do this, look in encyclopedias or other reference books for physical characteristics that indicate the type of food each animal eats. (In mammals, plant eaters have flat, grinding teeth; meat eaters have sharp, pointed teeth for cutting and tearing; plant/meat eaters have both kinds of teeth; in birds, beaks and ft. are indicators.)

Observing that animals breathe. Let students count the number of inhale–exhale movements of their chests in one minute. Now have them exercise for a few minutes by jumping up and down on one foot. Let them sit down and count their breathing rates again. Discuss the effect of exercise upon the body's need to obtain more air (oxygen). Next, see if they can detect breathing in other animals such as dogs, cats, fish, birds, frogs, and lizards. Determine the breathing rates for the different animals and, if possible, do so again after the animal has been active. Students will realize that animals seem to need more air (oxygen) after exercising.

08 Cc Fa

Generalization II. There is a great variety of physical characteristics among animals without backbones.

> *Contributing Idea A.* Most segmented worms have soft, round, segmented bodies with no legs (although they have appendages), are cold-blooded, and hatch from eggs.

Observing common characteristics of segmented worms. Observe several earthworms to determine similarities among them. Students will find that the animals (1) have soft, elongated, round, segmented bodies; (2) have a moist skin for body covering; (3) have no legs; (4) hatch from eggs. When touched, they feel cool. (They are cold-blooded; their body temperature is nearly the same as the temperature of their environment.) Animals with these characteristics are *segmented worms*. About 10,000 species have been identified, most living in water.

09 Aa Bb

Collecting earthworms. After a habitat has been prepared for keeping earthworms, collect them by digging into some rich garden soil covered with dead leaves. At night with a flashlight, in early morning, or after a heavy rain, earthworms can be easily picked up at the surface of the soil.

10 Ge

Housing and caring for earthworms. Fill a small wooden box with approximately 5 in. (13 cm) of rich garden soil. Dampen the soil and keep it moist but not wet. Place earthworms in the box and set some damp black construction paper or six sheets of newspaper loosely onto the soil. Place the box in a dark location. Earthworms should be fed twice a week by lifting the paper and placing bits of lettuce, moist oatmeal, or moist bread on the surface of the soil. Other foods can be tested to see which ones the worms

11 Gd

consume. Another type of container can be built by fastening two pieces of glass on wood strips (Figure 211.11a). Cover the glass sides with black paper and set the container in a dark place for a few days. When the paper is removed, students will see how the earthworms burrowed underground (Figure 211.11b). An aquarium or large widemouthed jar can also be used.

Figure 211.11

Contributing Idea B. Most arthropods have segmented bodies (protected by an external skeleton) with segmented legs, are cold-blooded, hatch from eggs, and live on land (some live in water).

Observing characteristics common among arthropods. Examine various animals from this group (phylum) to determine similarities among them. Students might observe a sow bug (crustacean), a spider (arachnid), and an insect. They will find that most of the animals in

12 Aa Bb

this group (1) live on land (although some live in water); (2) have a hard exterior body covering; (3) have pairs of jointed, movable appendages for locomotion; (4) have pairs of antennae; (5) hatch from eggs. Animals with these characteristics are called arthropods. About 900,000 species have been identified.

Observing characteristics common among crustaceans. Crustaceans are a subgroup or class of arthropods. Students can examine various animals from this class to determine similarities among them. They might observe water fleas, a crab, shrimp, and lobster. They will find that most animals in this class (1) live in water; (2) have two pair of antennae; (3) have one pair of legs per body segment; (4) hatch from eggs laid in water. Animals with these characteristics are called crustaceans. Crustaceans include barnacles, crayfish, and sow bugs. **13 Aa Bb**

Collecting crayfish. Crayfish are freshwater crustaceans often found under stones or in the mud of freshwater streams and ponds. They can be caught by dragging a dip net over the muddy bottom or by fishing with a small piece of raw meat attached to the end of a string. When the crayfish grabs the meat, slowly pull the string from the water. Usually the crayfish will be pulled out with it. Place the crayfish in a container filled with the pond water. **14 Ge**

Housing and caring for crayfish. Crayfish are fairly large, and they demand much food. For these reasons they are better suited to a pond habitat than to a classroom aquarium. Plastic wading pools work well with small plant pots for hiding places. For a short period of time they can be kept in large jars or aquariums equipped with aerating pumps. Remove the crayfish to another container when feeding so that the water in which it lives will not become polluted. Feed them small pieces of raw meat or earthworms. **Caution: Follow safety guidelines when handling crayfish.** **15 Gd**

Collecting daphnia. Daphnia are freshwater crustaceans most often found in quiet sections of streams or stagnant pools that are green with algae and free from fish. They are easy to see but are so small that they can only be caught with a very fine mesh dip net. Place them into a jar filled with the pond water. **16 Ge**

Housing and caring for daphnia. Daphnia can be kept in jars filled with water containing algae. Daphnia eat bacteria and algae, but can also be fed once a week with boiled bonemeal or mashed hardboiled egg yolk at the ratio of 1 oz. (28 g) of dry material to every 2 qt. (2 L) of water. Adding pulverized manure and placing the jar in sunlight will aid the growth of algae. **17 Gd**

Collecting sow bugs. Sow bugs are land crustaceans found in dark, moist environments under boards, logs, and stones. They are related to pill bugs and wood lice. Pill bugs will roll into a ball when touched, but sow bugs will not. **18 Ge**

Housing and caring for sow bugs. Sow bugs can be kept in almost any type of container, but are best suited for a woodland environment containing sticks and small rocks under which they can hide. They can be fed very small bits of apple, lettuce, raw potato, bread, or small insects. **19 Gd**

Observing characteristics common among arachnids. Arachnids are a subgroup or class of arthropods. Students can examine various animals from this class to determine similarities among them. They might observe spiders. They will find that most of the animals in this class (1) live on land; (2) have no antennae; (3) have four pairs of legs for locomotion; (4) hatch from eggs laid on land. Animals with these characteristics are called arachnids. Arachnids include scorpions and mites. **20 Aa Bb**

Collecting spiders. Spiders are arachnids and can be found almost everywhere: close to or far from structures, on or about shrubbery, smaller plants, and lawns, and near the soil. The easiest way to find them is to first look for a web. It has been estimated that there are thousands of spiders **21 Ge** per acre of woodland and meadow and hundreds per house and garden. Different kinds live in different environments. Most can be captured by allowing them to crawl on a stick, then transferring the stick to a container. An orb-web spider (one that constructs a suspended, round web) can be trapped by placing a bag beneath the web then gently tapping the spider so that it drops into the bag. A funnel-web spider (one that constructs its web in the shape of a funnel) can be caught by inverting a jar quickly over the spider when it is at the front of its web and sliding a card under the mouth of the jar. Sweep netting a grassland area will gather hundreds of spiders. A collection of weeds, rotted leaves, or loose soil in autumn will probably turn up many small spiders. To see them, put the materials in a white pan. The spiders will show up against the light background. In the fall, egg cases can be found. These are often brownish and look like small balls of silk, similar to a round cocoon. **Caution: Follow safety guidelines when gathering organisms from the field.**

Housing and caring for spiders. Most spiders can be kept in widemouthed jars for fairly long periods of time. Cover each jar with a piece of cheesecloth or nylon stocking and hold it in place with a canning ring or rubber band. Spiders should be kept in separate jars. They have difficulty climbing on glass, so add some **22 Gd**

debris to the jar along with a few twigs for them to climb on. Spiders will usually not eat unless their food is alive, so be sure to feed them live meal worms, flies, or other small, soft-bodied insects. You can catch insects in a net swept over a weedy place or trap small flies, beetles, moths, and midges that are attracted to outdoor lamps at night and feed them to spiders. In the winter, you can raise insects such as flies, fruit flies, and mealworms in the classroom for food. Moisture is very important to a spider, so place a small moist piece of sponge or ball of cotton in the jar, and keep it damp.

Observing characteristics common among insects. Insects are a subgroup or class of arthropods. Students can examine various animals from this class to determine similarities among them. They might observe ants, butterflies, grasshoppers, beetles, and flies. They will find that most of the animals in this class (1) live on land; (2) have one pair of antennae; (3) have three pairs of legs for locomotion; (4) have one or two pairs of wings; (5) hatch from eggs laid on land. If students watch them over time, they will see that most go through several stages to become adults. Ladybug larva are good to work with and easy to collect. Animals with these characteristics are called insects. Insects include termites, wasps, moths, crickets, and earwigs.

23
Aa
Bb

Housing and caring for insects. Almost any container can serve as a cage to keep insects for short periods of time. The size of the container should depend upon the size and number of insects collected. Always keep the habitats clean.

24
Gd

   a. *Containers for Land-Dwelling Insects.* Insects can be housed in terrariums or various cages that are quickly and inexpensively made. Figure 211.24 (p. 154) gives several suggestions from which others can be invented. The climate inside a container is important. Try to make the temperature and humidity conditions similar to those where the insect naturally lived. Be sure the container is not placed in direct sunlight or near a heat source. Food can be placed in the bottom of most containers. Leaf-eating insects tend to need fresh food regularly; add fresh leaves every day or so. Other insects might eat fruit, pieces of meat, or fermenting materials. All containers should be kept clean, and any food that has not been eaten after a day should be removed and replaced. Water can be provided in most containers in several ways: a jar inverted on a sponge in a small dish or lid; a vial full of water plugged with cotton and lying on its side; a water-soaked sponge.

Overhead Transparencies, Cellophane Wraps, and Nylon Stockings Make Very Good Windows.

Windows

Box With Screening or Netting Cover

Box With Lid

Box With Flap

Jars or Cartons With Screening or Nylon Stocking Covers

ICE CREAM

Cellophane Bag

Rubberband

Milk Carton Inside Nylon Stocking

Lid

Cake Tins

Coffee Can

Rolled Screening (Staple or Sew Overlap)

Dirt or Plaster of Paris Base

Figure 211.24

b. *Containers for Water-Dwelling Insects.* Almost any glass container can be used to keep water insects. To keep insects such as mosquitoes or water boatmen from escaping, cover the container with a piece of nylon stocking, mosquito netting, or wire screening. The climate inside a container should be kept cool. Keep it from direct sunlight, and set it where there is a free circulation of air. As the water evaporates from the container, replace it with more water from the same pond or stream, or tap water that has been set aside for 24 hours. Water-dwelling insects can also be kept in an aquarium.

Contributing Idea C. Most mollusks have soft, shapeless bodies (protected by a limestone shell) with no legs, are cold-blooded, hatch from eggs laid in water, and live in water.

Observing characteristics common among mollusks. Observe a variety of animals from this group (phylum) to determine similarities among them. Possibilities are limpets, mussels, and clams. Students will find that most animals in this group (1) live in water; (2) have soft, shapeless, nonsegmented bodies protected by an external shell of limestone; (3) have a broad single foot for locomotion; (4) hatch from eggs. Animals with these characteristics are called mollusks. Mollusks include the common garden snail. About 80,000 species have been identified.

25 Aa Bb

Collecting snails. Snails are tiny mollusks that can be found in water or on land. Water snails can be found in streams, ponds, or lakes. They can be picked from water plants or dredged from the bottom with a net. Land snails can be found feeding on plants almost anywhere. Look for them in gardens in the early morning or early evening.

26 Aa Ge

Housing and caring for snails. Water snails can be kept in any widemouthed jar or aquarium filled with pond water and many water plants. Three snails for every 1 gal. (4 L) of water make a

27 Gd

balanced aquarium. Water snails will eat algae from the sides of the aquarium and some water plants. Students can watch them move across the glass and see their mouthparts work as they eat algae from the sides. Land snails can be kept on damp peat moss or soil in a glass jar or terrarium. One snail per quart (liter) container is best for balance. Land snails will eat many kinds of leaves. **Caution: It is important to wash hands after handling animals. Keep the habitat clean.**

Generalization III. There is a great variety of physical characteristics among animals with backbones.

Contributing Idea A. Most fish have scales on their bodies, are cold-blooded, hatch from eggs laid in water, and live in water.

Observing characteristics common among fish. Examine various animals from this group to determine similarities among them. Students might observe guppies, goldfish, and various tropical fish in an aquarium. They will find that most of the animals of this group (1) live in water; (2) have interior skeletons and scales for body covering; (3) have fins for locomotion; (4) breathe by gills; (5) hatch from eggs laid in water. They feel cool to the touch because they are cold-blooded; their body temperature is nearly the same as the temperature of their environment. Animals with these characteristics are called fish. Explain that most live in salt

28 Aa Bb

water, some in freshwater, and a few in both types of water. About 20,000 species have been identified. **Caution: Follow safety guidelines when maintaining an aquarium.**

Housing and caring for fish. Tropical, freshwater and saltwater fish each require special aquariums (see entry 241.01). Most fish can be fed commercial fish food, small pinches of oatmeal or cornmeal, or live food such as worms and brine shrimp. Do not overfeed the fish (three times a week is usually sufficient). If a fish becomes sick, immediately remove it, and place it in a separate bowl so that it will not contaminate the other fish.

29 Gd

> *Contributing Idea B.* Most amphibians have smooth or bumpy skin on their bodies, are cold-blooded, hatch from eggs laid in water, and live in water and on land.

Observing characteristics common among amphibians. Examine various animals from this group to determine similarities among them. Students might observe frogs, toads, newts, and salamanders. They will find that most of the animals in this group (1) live part of their lives in the water and part on land; (2) have an internal skeleton and a moist skin (without scales) for body covering; (3) have two pairs of legs for locomotion; (4) hatch from eggs laid in water. When touched, they feel cool because they are

30 Aa Bb

cold-blooded; their body temperature is nearly the same as the temperature of their environment. Animals with these characteristics are called amphibians. About 2,800 species have been identified.

Collecting salamanders. Salamanders can be found in damp, wooded areas under rotting logs, rocks, and matted leaves. After a rain they can be seen on the rocks and logs. Pick them up by hand on land or scoop them from ponds with a net. Place them in wide-mouthed jars filled with damp leaves and moss. **Caution: Some salamanders have poison glands on their skins. Wash hands after handling.**

31 Ge

Housing and caring for salamanders. Place salamanders in a woodland terrarium made in a large jar or aquarium tank. Plant it with small ferns, moss, and woodland plants. Add rocks for cover and climbing and a container of water at soil level. A weighted wire screen over the top is necessary to keep the salamanders in the terrarium. Salamanders will eat small aquatic life, small insects and their nymphs, earthworms, and meal worms. If some do not eat, return them to where they were found.

32 Gd

Collecting the eggs and tadpoles of frogs and toads. During spring and early summer, eggs can be found floating on or near the surface among plants in shallow ponds and marshy places close to shore. Frog's eggs are in jumbled masses of jelly,

33 Ge

while toad's eggs are in jellylike strings often wrapped around plants (see Figure 211.33). Use widemouthed jars or nets to scoop up the eggs. Add several small water plants to the jars. Do not collect too many eggs, for many will die in crowded conditions. In the spring and summer, frog and toad tadpoles can be found feeding among thick plant growths in calm water. Tadpoles move quickly, thus a large net and a quick hand are needed to scoop them with an upward motion from the water. They can be placed in large jars filled with water and plants taken from the location where they were found.

Frog Eggs   Toad Eggs

Figure 211.33

Housing and caring for the eggs and tadpoles of frogs and toads. Place eggs or tadpoles in large, widemouthed glass jars or in a fishless aquarium filled with pond water. Include clumps of floating plants and several other water plants. These will serve as places for newly hatched tadpoles to hide. A large rock that extends above the surface of the **34 Gd**

water or other type of ramp must be available for tadpoles to crawl upon as they develop. Place screening over the top of the aquarium; hold in place with books or rocks. It might be necessary to change the water every few weeks and to clean out the container. Replace the water with more pond water or aged tap water. (Let tap water sit for several days so that the chlorine will evaporate.) Tadpoles will feed on algae in the aquarium or on small bits of lettuce.

Collecting frogs and toads. Frogs and toads can be caught by hand or with a net at night near plants in shallow, calm waters. They can be located by listening for their calls. If they are in the water, scoop them from underneath with a large widemouthed net. Both animals can be kept temporarily in a wet burlap sack. **35 Ge**

Housing and caring for frogs and toads. Keep frogs in aquariums that have places for them to climb on dry land. Keep toads in a woodland terrarium. Both will eat live worms, roaches, caterpillars, insects, and small aquatic life. Let students describe the frog as it eats. (Its tongue is hinged at the front of its lower jaw and is flipped out quickly; its eyes retract and bulge because the food is forced down the throat by an inward movement of the roof of its mouth.) **Caution: Be sure to keep the animal's habitat clean. Wash hands after handling an animal.** **36 Gd**

Contributing Idea C. Most reptiles have dry, scaly skin on their bodies, are cold-blooded, hatch from eggs laid on land, and live on land.

Observing characteristics common among reptiles. Examine a variety of animals from this group to determine similarities among them. Students might observe turtles, tortoises, snakes, and lizards. They will find that most of the animals in this group (1) live on land; (2) have an internal skeleton and a scaly skin for body covering; (3) have two pairs of legs for locomotion; (4) have claws on their toes; (5) hatch from shelled eggs laid on land (rattlesnakes and garter snakes bear their young alive). When touched, they feel cool because they are cold-blooded; their body temperature is nearly the same as the temperature of their environment. Animals with these characteristics are called reptiles. Reptiles include alligators and crocodiles. About 7,000 species have been identified. **37 Aa Bb**

Collecting snakes. Snakes can be found in fields, woods, and near creeks. **Caution: Some snakes are poisonous, so be sure they are properly identified before handling.** Nonpoisonous snakes are easily caught by hand. Those easiest to handle are garter, ring-necked, and hognose. A snake can be gently, but firmly held just behind the head with one hand while the rest of its body is supported with the other hand. Snakes can be temporarily **38 Ge**

placed in old pillowcases with the tops tied securely.

Housing and caring for snakes. Nonpoisonous snakes can be kept in large aquariums covered with weighted wire mesh that folds over the sides. Put a 2 in. (5 cm) layer of sand or gravel at the bottom, and embed a pan of water in the sand. Add some rocks and a sturdy branch on which the snake can climb. Place the container where the snake can receive sunshine, but do not let it get too hot. Snakes will not feed regularly, and some will not eat at all in captivity. If a snake does not eat for several weeks, release it in the area where it was found. Most snakes will eat live insects, worms, grubs, or frogs. Be sure to clean the container frequently to avoid unpleasant odors. **39 Gd**

Collecting lizards. Lizards can be found under logs or among rocks. They are fast runners and a net is helpful in catching them. They can be placed in an old pillowcase temporarily. **40 Ge**

Housing and caring for lizards. Lizards can be kept in woodland or desert terrariums. Be sure they contain rocks, twigs, and living plants to climb on, and embed a small container of water in the soil. Lizards will not drink from a dish, but they will take water from the leaves of plants. Spray the leaves of growing plants in the terrarium each day. (Spray the lizard's skin, too.) Lizards feed on living flies, **41 Gd**

moths, and mealworms. Keep the terrarium clean of uneaten food, and place it so that it receives sunlight or artificial light during part of the day and maintains a temperature range between 70°F (21°C) and 80°F (27°C).

Collecting turtles and tortoises. Turtles can be found in or near ponds, slow streams, and swamps. Tortoises are generally found in more arid regions. Both can be caught by hand. **Caution: Some turtles and tortoises bite; some turtles carry diseases.** (Note: The desert tortoise is protected by law in some areas. Check local restrictions. Turtles purchased in pet stores should be certified as healthy and free from salmonella. Other turtles should be checked by a vet.) The animals can be placed in a box temporarily. **42 Ge**

Housing and caring for turtles and tortoises. Most turtles can be kept in an aquarium tank filled with 3 in. (7 cm) or 4 in. (10 cm) of water. Include a flat rock or other ramp in the tank so the turtle can crawl onto it. Box turtles and tortoises can also be kept in a terrarium (woodland for some, desert for others). Embed a pan of water in the soil of the desert terrarium. Set the terrarium where it gets some sunshine and some shade. Do not let it get too warm. Feed turtles once a day with commercial turtle food, insects, earthworms, or bits of raw hamburger. Most turtles will eat out of the water, but the painted turtle must feed in water. **43 Gd**

Tortoises are vegetarians and eat less often. They will feed on slices of apple, berries, leafy vegetables, and lettuce. Be sure to change the water twice a week, and clean out uneaten food regularly. **Caution: Unclean turtle environments can cause serious illnesses in humans. Also see caution note in entry 211.42.**

> *Contributing Idea D.* Most birds have feathers on their bodies, are warm-blooded, hatch from eggs laid on land, and live on land.

Observing characteristics common among birds. Observe a variety of animals from this group to determine similarities among them. Students might observe local birds as they feed. They will find that most of the animals in this group (1) live on land and can fly; (2) have an internal skeleton and feathers for body covering; (3) have one pair of legs and one pair of wings for locomotion; (4) have bills (without teeth); (5) hatch from shelled eggs laid in nests. If live birds can be handled, they will feel warm because they are warm-blooded; they maintain a steady body temperature different from their environment. Animals with these characteristics are called birds. About 8,600 species have been identified. **44 Aa Bb**

Housing and caring for birds. It is not advisable to confine birds in the classroom; however, if a cage is temporarily necessary, the size is of great importance. For two small birds such as canaries, **45 Gd**

budgies, or finches, the minimum size should be approximately 20 in. × 10 in. × 15 in. (50 cm × 25 cm × 40 cm). For larger birds such as mynas, the minimum should be 25 in. × 20 in. × 15 in. (65 cm × 50 cm × 40 cm). Tame birds will eat commercially prepared bird foods, lettuce, carrots, apples, and pieces of bread. Provide fresh water daily. Caged birds also need a separate container for mixed grit and cuttlefish bone for roughage. Remove all perishable food at the end of each day. The cage floor should be covered with fine sand or paper and changed frequently. (Note: It is illegal to disturb wild birds or their nests.)

Making bird feeders to attract wild birds. Bird feeders are easy to build and offer students many opportunities to observe and study wild birds (see Figure 211.46). Stock the feeders with commercially prepared wild-bird food, various seeds, grains, apples, bread, raisins, cracked corn, oats, peanuts, sunflower seeds, or suet. A bread pudding can be prepared by heating suet until it liquefies, stirring in raisins, unsalted peanuts,

**46
Ec
Gc**

and various kinds of seeds as it cools, then pouring it into paper cups or over pinecones as it thickens. The cups or pinecones can be suspended from trees to attract birds.

a. *Simple Feeders.* Hang pinecones, coffee cans, gourds, shallow boxes, half a coconut, or a whole coconut. Imagination will enable students to create other simple feeders.

b. *Tray Feeders.* Place food on open trays by windows or on stands. Tray feeders should have upturned edges to keep the food from falling off. Water containers can be placed on tray feeders. A covered tray on a pulley clothesline makes a feeder that can be brought in for restocking.

c. *Log Feeders.* Drill holes in an old log or block of wood to contain food. Add pegs on which birds can perch.

d. *Basket Feeders.* Tape two slotted soap dishes together or fold wire mesh into a box shape and fill the interior with suet.

Students can keep records of the number and types of birds feeding each day and/or the time of day each type feeds. They can also keep longitudinal records to see which kinds of birds are attracted to the feeders during different seasons of the year. Experiment by varying the food

Log   Soap Dishes   Wire Mesh

Figure 211.46

to see which kinds of birds are attracted to particular types of food (e.g., seed-eating birds such as sparrows are attracted to chicken feed, weed seeds, and bread crumbs; fruit-eating birds such as robins and cedar wax wings are attracted to berries and various fruits; insect-eating birds such as chickadees, jays, and creepers are attracted to suet, nuts, peanut butter, and sunflower seeds). Also experiment by coloring the food used to see if birds show a preference for certain colors. (Note: If you start a feeder in the fall, continue through the winter because birds will depend upon it.)

> *Contributing Idea E.* Most mammals have some fur or hair on their bodies, are warm-blooded, bear their young alive, provide milk for their young, and live on land.

Observing characteristics common among mammals. Observe a variety of animals from this group to determine similarities among them. Students might observe mice, hamsters, dogs, cats, and rabbits. They will find that most of the animals in this group (1) live on land; (2) have internal skeletons and hair or fur on their skin for body covering; (3) have one or two pairs of legs for locomotion; (4) have glands that produce milk to feed their young; (5) bear their young alive. Animals with these characteristics are called mammals. Mammals include deer, horses, elephants, monkeys, and people.   **47 Aa Bb**

Housing and caring for small mammals. Guinea pigs, hamsters, white rats, rabbits, and similar small animals can be raised in the classroom. It is best to obtain such animals from a reliable source (e.g., laboratory) to be sure they are not diseased. Also be sure to check any local restrictions on keeping such animals in the classroom. For most, a large wooden box with a wire mesh cover is sufficient. (Hamsters will gnaw their way out of a wooden box and are better kept in a wire cage.) Cedar shavings or shredded newspapers should be placed in the bottom of the cage and replaced daily. Water should be placed in a heavy dish to keep it from being overturned or a water-drip bottle can be made or purchased from a pet store. Most small mammals will eat commercial pellets, lettuce greens, and carrots. Hamsters will also eat grains such as corn, oats, wheat, and fresh fruit. Provide straw, hay, or cotton for animals that like to nest.   **48 Gd**

Generalization IV. Animals can be organized by their characteristics.

> *Contributing Idea A.* Animals can be seriated.

Seriating animals. Obtain a number of seashells of the same kind. Have students arrange the shells from smallest to largest or by some sequence in their color patterns. Some students might research factors about animals to seriate them. For example, animals can be ordered from   **49 Da**

slow moving (snail or slug) to fast moving (cheetah or swift), from small land animal (shrew) to large land animal (elephant), small water animal (goby) to large water animal (whale or shark), and small flying animal (hummingbird) to large flying animal (eagle or condor).

Contributing Idea B. Animals can be classified.

Classifying animals by observable characteristics. Prepare a set of 10 pictures of birds or sets of other animals. Ask students to note differences in coloring, marking, size, shape, and other features. Next, ask them to note at least three ways in which the animals are alike. Now ask each of them to bring one picture of some animal to school. Divide a bulletin board into four sections with a picture of one animal in each (selected for diverse characteristics). Ask the students to place their pictures in the section where the posted animal is most like theirs. As pictures are placed, have students give their rationales. They can discuss the characteristics of the animals in each group. When finished, have them divide one group of pictures into two or more groups. The subdividing process can continue as long as the characteristics of the animals suggest further groupings.

**50
Ca
Dc**

212   Interactions

Generalization I. Reproduction is a process by which animals produce offspring.

Contributing Idea A. Some animals hatch from eggs.

Observing the eggs of animals. The eggs of many animals such as frogs, toads, snails, and insects can be kept in aquariums or terrariums in the classroom and watched over time. Under the proper conditions, the eggs will hatch, and students will be able to see the development of the young animal.

**01
Aa**

Contributing Idea B. Some animals do not hatch from eggs.

Researching animal reproduction. Have students tell of experiences they might have had observing or hearing about the birth of kittens, puppies, rabbits, or other mammals. It is possible for students to observe the birth of guinea pigs, gerbils, or white rats kept in cages in the classroom. You might wish to discuss human birth, and let students research information about various animal live births. Guppies are among the few fish that give birth to their young alive. Although it is difficult to see the actual live birth of guppies, students can realize that the new babies in an aquarium were born alive.

**02
Bd**

Generalization II. Animals respond to certain environmental conditions.

Contributing Idea A. Animals respond to touch.

Observing that earthworms respond to touch. Tap the head of an earthworm

**03
Aa**

gently with a finger or pencil eraser. (The worm will contract and move backward.) Students will realize that the worm seems to be sensitive to things that touch it. Let them try touching other parts of the worm to see if it is equally sensitive in all places. They can also set an alarm clock with its face side against the soil where worms are located. When the alarm is set off, worms will come from their burrows. Explain that earthworms do not hear sound as we do; they feel the sound vibrations from the ringing. (Students can touch the clock lightly to feel the vibrations.) Explain that the vibrations make the earthworm feel uncomfortable, and it attempts to get away from the feeling.

Observing that snails respond to touch. 04 Aa
With a pencil, gently touch the eyes at the ends of the extended stalks of a snail. (The stalks will retract.) Touch the snail in various places and observe what happens. If the snail is overly disturbed, it will retreat into its shell. Now prepare a board by cutting three or four holes in it. The largest hole should be able to accommodate the snail's shell easily. The smaller holes should accommodate the snail's body, but not the shell. Place the board in the path of a moving snail, and let students see how the snail is able to select the right-sized hole to travel through.

Contributing Idea B. Animals respond to sound.

Observing that some animals respond to sound. 05 Aa Fa
Set two snails near each other and make a loud noise (e.g., suspend an alarm clock in the air and ring it). Observe the behavior of the snails. This can be repeated using other animals such as fish (use a cricket clicker in and out of the water), insects, amphibians, and so on. (Note: Some animals will "feel" the sound vibrations rather than "hear" the sound as we do. See entry 212.03.)

Contributing Idea C. Animals respond to smell.

Observing that earthworms respond to smell. 06 Aa
Dip a piece of paper into vinegar or household ammonia. Bring the paper to within 1 in. (2 cm) of an earthworm's head but do not touch the worm. Students will see an immediate reaction and can realize that the worm seems to sense odors. Try bringing the paper near other parts of the worm to see what happens. Also, try other aromatic substances.

Observing how well people detect smells. 07 Ad
Hide an aromatic substance, such as an open perfume bottle, in the classroom. Have students use their sense of smell to track it down. Next, have them pretend they are bloodhounds. Sprinkle a trail of 1 in. (2 cm) squares of blotter paper, soaked in clove oil, across a field. Blindfolded students can take turns trying to follow the trail on their hands and knees. Others can watch, and discuss the problems the "bloodhound" student has.

You can vary this activity by letting the trail circle across itself or by crossing it with a different scent. Make analogies between this experience and the tracking done by animals such as dogs.

Contributing Idea D. Animals respond to gravity.

Observing that snails respond to gravity. Let snails climb a board, and observe whether or not the snails always climb upward. When a snail reaches the top of the board, turn the board over, and observe again. Keep the board vertical, and test by rotating it 45° or 90° each time. Next, tilt the board various degrees to see what effect the angle of tilt has upon the direction the snail travels. For each test, students can record observations and draw conclusions.

08
Aa

Contributing Idea E. Animals respond to light.

Observing that some animals respond to light. If students look carefully, they will find that worms do not have eyes, yet they seem to be sensitive to light. For example, if worms are kept in a damp box of soil and covered with moist newspapers for several hours, some worms will be found on the surface of the soil when the newspapers are removed. Students will see them move rapidly into burrows or begin burrowing when the light strikes them. Try placing a worm on a sheet of damp newspaper and cover it with a box

09
Aa
Fa

so that it is in complete darkness for an hour. Darken the room, remove the box, and turn a flashlight with a small beam on the head end. To create a small beam, place a cone-shaped piece of paper over the flashlight, snipping off the pointed end (Figure 212.09). Students will see an immediate reaction and a movement away from the light. Let them test the light beam against other parts of the worm's body. Test other animals in a similar way to see which are most sensitive to light.

Figure 212.09

Contributing Idea F. Animals respond to temperature changes.

Observing that some animals respond to cold. Chip a piece of ice and use a pointed tip to touch an earthworm in various places to see which parts of its body seem most sensitive and least sensitive to cold. Next, chill the worm in a container of soil in a refrigerator for 10 minutes and observe how it moves on the surface of the soil. Students can determine how cold influences the worm's movement. Challenge them to create ways to test the effect of cold on other animals such as grasshoppers or crickets.

10
Aa
Fa

Observing that some animals respond to heat. Near one end of a terrarium, place a heating unit or lamp with the bulb turned away from the interior. Put two snails near the heat source, two midway in the terrarium, and two as far from the heat as possible. Observe whether the snails move toward or away from the heat. Other animals can be observed in a terrarium in a similar way. Water snails can be tested by placing one in a can of water, lighting a candle, and holding it beneath the snail. Observe the snail's reaction. Do not leave the heat source in one position too long, because the heat might injure the snail.

11
Aa
Fa

Experimenting to see the effect of temperature changes upon fish. Place a goldfish into a widemouthed jar half-filled with water. Place a thermometer in the jar so that it can be read without disturbing the fish. Record the temperature of the water and the number of gill beats of the fish in one minute. Add crushed ice to the water very slowly to avoid exciting the fish. Continue adding ice until the temperature is near freezing (32°F or 0°C). Again count the number of gill beats in one minute. Next, add warm water to the jar (slowly, to avoid exciting the fish) until the temperature is raised by 5°. Record the gill beats per minute. Continue adding warm water by 5° intervals until the temperature reaches 86°F or 30°C. By studying the

12
Cc
Ce
Ec

gathered data, students will be able to tell what happens to the fish's respiration rate as temperatures increase or decrease.

Observing hibernation. Place a frog in a large jar of water. When the frog floats at the surface, count the number of moves its throat makes in a minute to determine its rate of breathing. Now add ice to the water, one piece at a time. As the water cools, students will see the frog move to the bottom and become less active. When this happens, determine the rate of throat movements again. When nearly all motion stops, tell students that the frog is in a state of *hibernation*. (The heartbeat and respiration are very slow.) Explain that, to avoid being frozen, frogs hibernate during the cold winter by digging beneath the soft mud of a pond or stream. They breathe under the water by taking in small amounts of oxygen through their skin. For an additional experience with hibernation, put a different frog in a jar containing a small amount of water. Set the jar in a refrigerator (not the freezer) overnight. When the frog is removed, it can be turned onto its back and its movements observed. Keep track of the time it takes the frog to become active again. Some students might be interested in researching reference books to find out what other animals hibernate during winter.

13
Aa
Bb
Fa

220 Botany

221　Characteristics

Generalization I. Plants have identifiable characteristics.

Contributing Idea A. All plants reproduce their kind.

Observing seeds produced by plants grown from seeds. Let students examine several different kinds of seeds (e.g., bean seeds, tomato seeds) and draw pictures of them. Plant the seeds in potting soil. After germination, continue growing them until they flower and produce new seeds. Examine the new seeds and compare them with the pictures drawn previously. Students will realize that the plants reproduced their own kind. Plant the new seeds and observe their growth. (Note: Direct sunlight or a special artificial lighting system is necessary if plants are to be grown in the classroom.)

**01
Aa
Be
Ca**

Observing plants grown from spores. Fern spores can be planted on the outside of a moist flowerpot to let students see how new ferns develop. Begin by letting a fern frond that has spores on it dry out for several days. Obtain a clay flower pot and wash it thoroughly. Next, soak it for several hours, changing the water several times to remove minerals in the clay that might keep the fern spores from developing. Fill the pot with wet newspapers or paper toweling, and invert it in a saucer of water. (The newspapers will keep the flowerpot moist.) Shake the dry leaf over

**02
Aa
Bb**

the pot so that some of the spores drop off. Cover the pot and saucer with a glass jar and set it in a dimly lit place at room temperature. Add a little water to the saucer whenever the surface of the pot begins to dry out. In three to four weeks, the spores will form small green spots. Tell students that these are the sexual plants and are called the prothallia. The larger *prothallus* will be about ¼ in. (0.5 cm) in diameter. These structures contain the egg-producing and sperm-producing parts of the fern. As each egg is fertilized by a sperm cell, it begins to grow into a new fern plant. In about eight weeks, the prothallia will shrivel, leaving a small fern in their place. The fern can be transplanted to a pot of rich soil if care is taken not to damage its fragile roots.

Contributing Idea B. All plants grow.

Germinating seeds and measuring growth. Sprinkle grass seeds in a small box of potting soil. Be sure the seeds are spread sparely. Soon after they germinate, have students note that the plants are thinly spaced. Continue observations for several weeks. Students will find that the grass not only grows taller but also grows more blades over time. Challenge them to devise a way to measure the increase in density of the grass (e.g., blades of grass might be counted periodically within a small defined area).

**03
Aa
Cc**

Observing growth from spores. Obtain a fern frond that has spores on it. Let it dry out for several days. Place some rich soil into four pots, and cover the soil with ½ in. (1 cm) of fine, washed sand. Pour boiling water over the sand and pots to sterilize them. (Bacteria and mold spores are difficult to keep out of the developing fern spores; sterilization and four pots increase the probability of success.) Shake spores from the fern frond over the soil, and cover each pot with a sheet of glass. Set the pots in saucers of water and keep them moist in a shady location. Students will see the plants develop through two stages in the following two to eight weeks.   **04 Aa**

> *Contributing Idea C.* All plants need food, water, and oxygen to grow.

Experimenting to see the effect of nutrients in soil upon plant growth. Prepare five soil containers. Into the first, put only garden soil. Into the second, put soil plus fertilizer in the quantity recommended by the manufacturer. Fill the third, fourth, and fifth with soil and one-fourth, one-half, and three-fourths the amount of fertilizer, respectively. Plant three pea seeds in each container and water them equally. If the heights are measured daily, the data can be graphed. Continue taking measurements past the seedling stage. Students will find that the amount of nutrients in the soil influences the growth of the plants. Many variations of this activity   **05 Bf Ec**

can be tried. For example, students can compare the addition of nutrients to sand, vermiculite, or sterilized soil (soil that has been baked in an oven), compare soils from different locales, or compare different types of fertilizers.

Comparing the growth of watered and unwatered plants. Plant equal amounts of radish and lima bean seeds in potting soil in each of six pots. Place all but one pot in quart (liter) milk cartons. Prepare one pot so that it gets no water and increase the amount of water in several increments in each of the four other pots so that the soil in the last pot is standing underwater. For the last pot, seal the drain holes in the bottom of the pot, or set the pot into a larger container filled with water. Cover the tops of each carton with a plastic bag held in place with rubber bands. (This will keep the water from escaping and reduce the need for watering during the test.) Place all the containers where light can enter them. Set the uncovered plant near the others for comparative purposes. Give this plant normal watering. Observe the plants on a regular basis. Students will find that water is necessary for growth, but that too much water is harmful. Explain that too much water blocks the flow of air to the plant's roots, and plants need oxygen in the soil for growth.   **06 Ca Ec**

> Contributing Idea D. All plants are sensitive to their surroundings.

Experimenting to determine the environmental factors to which plants are sensitive. Grow seed or seedless plants in a terrarium. Let students devise ways to find out the effect of different factors on the growth of the plants. Some factors they might test are temperature, light, water, soil nutrients, and wind. As they devise their tests, help them to control all factors except the one they are testing. If numerical data are kept regularly (e.g., height of growth each day), the results can be placed on a graph.

07 Ea Eb Ec

Generalization II. There is a great variety of physical characteristics among seedless plants.

> *Contributing Idea A.* Fungi live off other plants, animals, and dead organic matter.

Observing mushrooms. Mushrooms are the best known fungi and can be found in woods, fields, and orchards. They appear quickly after warm spring and autumn rains. Students can see that a mature mushroom consists of a stalk and a cap, the latter opening after the fungi pushes through the soil or decaying log. If they examine the underside of the cap, they will frequently see numerous plates, called gills, radiating from the center. On the outside of each gill are hundreds of cases containing *spores*. These spores can be examined with a microscope. It has been estimated that a single mushroom produces as many as 10 billion spores.

08 Aa Bb

Caution: Explain that some mushrooms are poisonous and that there is no certain rule to tell which are edible. Students might compare mushrooms with other types of fungi, such as mold and mildew.

Making mushroom spore prints. Students can make prints from mature, fresh mushrooms. After picking, a mushroom should be placed in a plastic bag and printed as soon as possible. To print, carefully remove the stem from the cap and place the cap with its spore-bearing side down over a piece of paper. Since spores are usually the same color as the underside of the cap, it is best to use white paper if the underside is pink or brown and dark paper if it is light-colored. For the best results, cover the cap and paper with a glass bowl, cake cover, or jar to keep the spores from being blown off by air currents. Let it stand overnight. When the cap is removed from the paper, a spore print should remain. Spray immediately with clear hair spray or other spray fixative to preserve it. (Note: Do not hold the spray can too close to the spores or the force will disturb the print.)

09 Gd

> *Contributing Idea B.* Ferns and mosses are simple plants.

Collecting ferns and mosses. Ferns and mosses are primitive seedless plants found in wooded areas, near streams, and in other damp, shady places. When collecting mosses, it is important to dig out

10 Bb Gd

their rootlike structures along with some soil. These structures, called *rhizoids*, absorb moisture and nutrients from the soil. Wrap them carefully in damp paper toweling to prevent drying, and keep them from direct sunlight until they can be transplanted.

Housing and caring for ferns and mosses. A variety of ferns and mosses will grow with a minimum of attention in a classroom terrarium. Prepare the terrarium in a large jar or aquarium tank. Place a 1 in. (3 cm) layer of gravel or crushed rock on the bottom to provide proper drainage. Add ½ in. (2 cm) of sand, then a generous layer of garden soil or humus. Arrange the soil to provide a higher terrace at one end. Rocks can be placed on top of the soil, and then the ferns and mosses can be planted. When transplanting, firmly embed the plants into the soil. Let students create their own landscaping patterns. Now add water to the low end of the terrarium until the gravel is nearly covered. (This should provide adequate moisture for the soil.) Next, cover the terrarium with a sheet of glass to prevent evaporation and to maintain a humid condition inside. Check occasionally to be sure the terrarium remains moist. If it becomes too wet or if molds appear, remove the cover to let it dry out for a while. (Powdered sulfur sprinkled into the container will help prevent the growth of molds.) Set the terrarium where it will

11 Gd

receive a medium amount of light; avoid direct sunlight and overheating. A closed terrarium will maintain itself for a very long time.

Generalization III. There is a great variety of physical characteristics among seed plants.

> *Contributing Idea A.* Seeds have similar and dissimilar characteristics.

Examining the external parts of seeds. Remove lima beans or peas from their pods, and notice the rough portion on the seeds where they were attached to the pod. Tell students that this marking is called the seed scar. Have them find the seed scars on other seeds. Now place the seeds in warm water, and note the air bubbles coming from a tiny hole near the seed scar. You might tell them that this tiny hole is called the micropyle and that it is the main point through which water can enter the seed to enable it to begin its growth. Other seeds can be tested in a similar way to locate their micropyles. From their observations, students should infer that seeds contain air. Let the seeds continue to soak, and observe them at one-hour intervals. As the water enters the micropyle, the seed swells. A lima bean seed will be well soaked in about three hours. Compare the soaked seeds with dry ones in terms of size, color, shape, and texture. **Caution: Do not eat seeds after handling. Wash hands when the activity is completed.**

12 Aa Bb Fa

Examining the internal parts of seeds. **13 Bb Ca** Soak various seeds overnight, and then let students dissect them. They will find two main classes of seeds. Most seeds divide into two parts and are called dicotyledons (e.g., beans, peas, peanuts). Those that do not divide are called monocotyledons (e.g., corn, oats, coconuts). **Caution: Do not eat seeds after handling. Wash hands when the activity is completed.**

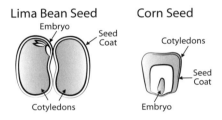

Lima Bean Seed   Corn Seed

Figure 221.13

a. *Dicotyledons.* Distribute soaked lima bean seeds to each student. Place the seeds on paper towels or plates so that the parts will not get lost. With a pin, toothpick, or dissecting needle have each student carefully peel the cover (*seed coat*) from the seed. The protective-covering purpose of the coat can be discussed. Now open the seeds into two portions. (Each portion is called a cotyledon.) Find the tiny plant (*embryo*) inside. Hand lenses can be used to observe the leaves, stem, and root of the embryo (Figure 221.13). Similar seeds can also be soaked and compared with the lima bean seed. For example, the familiar unshelled peanut can be dissected to find the same parts: the reddish brown seed cover, the two seed halves, and the plant.

b. *Monocotyledons.* Distribute soaked corn seeds. The seed coat can be removed with a sharp implement. Beneath the coat, students can see the embryo.

Contributing Idea B. In most seed plants, the root grows at the base of the stem.

Determining the location of root growth on stems. **14 Aa Bb Fa** Germinate various seeds in a soilless garden (see entry 641.01). Observe the root growth, and have students note that it is at the base of the plant stem. By examining many kinds of plants, they can infer this commonality among most plants. In their observations they may note one root that appears larger than the surrounding or branching roots. Tell them that this is the main or *primary root*, but that not all plants have primary roots. Have students describe how the primary root differs from the other roots in location, appearance, and texture. The three basic groupings for root systems in Key 221.14 can be used as a guide for students as they identify and match roots in the classroom. As a supplemental activity, break open a pot in which a plant has been growing for some time. The mass of roots can be studied. Also, seeds can be planted in soil next to the side of a glass jar. The jar can be wrapped in black paper to keep sunlight from the roots. After a week, the paper can be removed and the roots observed.

Key to Root Patterns

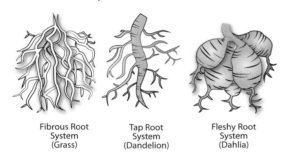

Fibrous Root System (Grass)   Tap Root System (Dandelion)   Fleshy Root System (Dahlia)

Key 221.14

Contributing Idea C. The external characteristics of a stem imply an order to its parts and appendages.

Observing stems. With careful observation, much can be inferred from the details of the external characteristics of a woody stem. Distribute a woody stem, such as a willow or horse chestnut, to students. Let them observe and describe all the characteristics they see. Although the important characteristics are labeled in Figure 221.15, the students' discoveries of the parts and the descriptive words they use are of utmost importance. Among the significant points that can be realized from the examination of a number of different stems might be the following: The roots are found at the base of the stem, stems usually grow upward, and

**15
Aa
Ba
Fa**

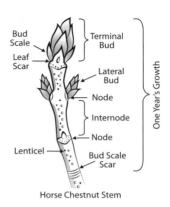

Bud Scale
Leaf Scar
Terminal Bud
Lateral Bud
Node
Internode
Node
Lenticel
Bud Scale Scar
One Year's Growth

Horse Chestnut Stem

Figure 221.15

a large bud (*terminal bud*) is found at the tip; there are usually enlargements on the stem (*nodes*) where leaves occur; there are spaces between leaves (*internodes*) of various lengths; where leaves have fallen, leaf scars remain on the stem (students can remove leaves to observe the place where the scar will form); there is a tiny bud (*lateral bud*) above each leaf or leaf scar (the bud remains when a leaf falls); pores (*lenticels*) can be seen on the internodes of some stems such as birch, horse chestnut, and cherry; the bud scale indicates where new growth began (students can tell the age of a branch by counting the growth areas between the bud scales). From observing these characteristics of various stems, students might be able to draw some inferences and generalizations about the parts of stems: Between the base and tip of most stems are enlargements (nodes) separated by smooth stem sections (internodes); between the base and tip are leaves and buds with the bud always preceded or followed by a leaf or leaf scar; a leaf scar always denotes the place where a leaf has been; a bud scale marks the place where new growth began.

Determining order in stem characteristics. By observing various stems, students **16 Fb** will realize that all plants have an ordered relation of parts. A base, denoted by roots (*R*), precedes a leaf or leaf scar (*L*), which precedes a bud (*B*), which precedes a tip or terminal bud (*T*). Using this formula (*RLBT*), students will be able to determine the direction of any stem. To check their understanding of the relationship of the parts, bring to class a willow or other woody stem with the leaves removed. See if students can determine the direction of the stem and provide evidence for their judgment.

Contributing Idea D. Stems have definite external characteristics.

Comparing the external characteristics of stems. Have students remove new plants **17 Bf Ca Fa** from the soil and observe them to determine where a stem begins (e.g., above the ground or below the ground). Then bring to class a variety of stems to compare for

similarities and differences (e.g., size, covering, etc.). The various stems can be grouped by tallying characteristics on a histogram. Encourage students to use their senses of touch and smell as they observe. When the tallies are completed, they can interpret the results to see which shape is most common, which texture is least common, which color is the rarest, and so on. (See Histogram 221.17.)

Contributing Idea E. Stems have definite internal characteristics.

Observing the annual rings in woody stems. A Christmas tree stem can be cut **18 Aa Fa** into segments and distributed to students, or a freshly cut tree stump can be used for this purpose. From observations and inferences, students can discover the following: woody stems increase in diameter; growth slows down or stops during cold and dry seasons (variance in spacing between rings indicates climatic effects upon the growth of the plant); rings that are not concentric (wider on one side than the other) indicate that the plant grew on a slope or hill with the wider rings being on the downhill side; light and dark portions

COMPARING THE EXTERNAL CHARACTERISTICS OF STEMS

Count	Color			Texture				Length		Shape				Support				Straight	
	green	brown	other	smooth	rough	fuzzy	other	short	long	round	flat	oval	other	leaves	flowers	branches	other	yes	no
25																			
20																			
15																			
10																			
5																			

Histogram 221.17

within the same ring indicate seasonal differences.

Comparing grains in different woody **19** **stems.** Gather samples of various kinds of **Ca** wood such as pine, ash, birch, and redwood. Cut some of them crosswise and some lengthwise to let students observe and compare the grains and color differences. Cut ends can be shellacked for preservation.

> *Contributing Idea F.* Leaves are appendages of the stem and are arranged in different ways upon the stem.

Determining the location of leaf growth **20** **on stems.** To help students realize the **Aa** positional relationships between the leaf **Ca** and stem parts, have them observe pot- **Fa** ted plants, plants growing in the school area, or cut stems with leaves attached. Many different kinds of plants should be observed so that patterns can be realized. A few suggestions concerning possible observations are given here. By carefully observing, students will see the following (see Figure 221.20):

a. The leaf is usually supported by a stalk (*petiole*). In a few plants (all grasses) the leaf may be attached directly to the stem.

b. At the base of the petiole, on either side of some plants, there are two appendages (*stipules*). In most plants these are absent.

c. Leaves occur at the nodes of a stem. If there is one leaf at each node, the leaves form a spiral or alternate pattern. If two leaves are at a node, they are always opposite. If there are more than two leaves, they are whorled. It is not unusual for plants to have combinations of the different leaf arrangements shown in Key 221.20.

Key to Leaf Patterns on Stems

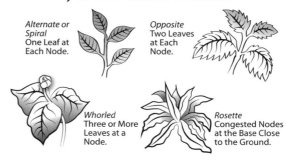

Key 221.20

d. Buds are always above where the leaf meets the stem, but some buds may be so underdeveloped that they cannot be seen. Although botanists use certain

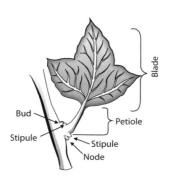

Figure 221.20

terms for the various observable parts and arrangements, it is best to let students describe what they see in their own terms.

Contributing Idea G. Flowers are appendages of the stem and are arranged in different ways on the stem.

Observing the structures of flowering plants. Students can discover that leaves and flowers each appear at a node on a stem; thus the two can be related as both being appendages. Closer examination will reveal, however, that the flower appendages differ from leaf appendages in having no buds in their axils. If observations and measurements can be made periodically, students will realize another difference—that the internodes of leaf appendages elongate over time, while the internodes of flower appendages do not.

**21
Aa
Cd**

Comparing the arrangements of flowers on stems. Bring to class different kinds of flowers from the eight types shown in Key 221.22. Often local dry weeds will best show the various structures. Students can work in small groups for this activity. Although they generally realize that some flowers are produced only at the tip of a flower stalk (e.g., poppy), they will readily discover other common arrangements (types of inflorescences) from observations of the many examples. The inflorescence types can be used as a basis for grouping or classifying other flowers that

**22
Ca
Dc
Fa**

are brought to class. You might explain that inflorescence, or flower arrangement on a stem, is thought to be an advantage to a plant, for the grouping together of many tiny flowers increases the coloration or brightness (e.g., geranium). The bright coloring tends to attract animals, aiding in pollination.

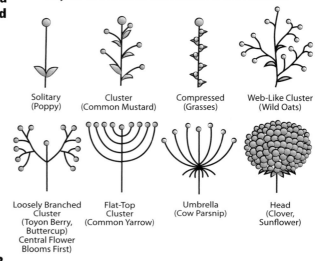

Key to Inflorescence Patterns on Flowers

Solitary (Poppy)   Cluster (Common Mustard)   Compressed (Grasses)   Web-Like Cluster (Wild Oats)

Loosely Branched Cluster (Toyon Berry, Buttercup) Central Flower Blooms First   Flat-Top Cluster (Common Yarrow)   Umbrella (Cow Parsnip)   Head (Clover, Sunflower)

Key 221.22

Generalization IV. Plants can be organized by their characteristics.

Contributing Idea A. Plants can be seriated.

Seriating seeds. Have students collect fruit of different types. Count the seeds contained in each, and arrange the findings in some numerical order. In some fruit, there may be only one or two seeds (e.g., carrots produce only two seeds per fruit),

**23
Cc
Da**

in some there may be several (e.g., peas, beans), while in others there may be many seeds (e.g., tobacco produces more than 40,000 seeds per fruit). Students can also determine whether all fruit from the same plant produce the same number of seeds.

Making a histogram of the numbers of seeds in pods. Obtain a large bag of pea pods from a grocery store. Have each student remove two pods from the bag. Open each pod and count the number of peas in each. Paper plates are helpful in keeping pieces of the pods off the desks. Ask who found the least number of peas in a pod and write the number on the chalkboard. Ask who found the most and write the number. Draw a horizontal base line between the two numbers and divide the space into equal segments. For example, if the range for the number of peas in the pods was from 3 to 12, prepare a base line with equal segments labeled *3, 4, 5, 6, 7, 8, 9, 10, 11, 12*. After the line has been prepared, open a pea pod and count the number of peas in it. Put an *X* on the board above the numeral that represents the number of peas in that pod. Repeat for a second pea pod. After this demonstration, let students come to the board and mark the number of peas found in each of their pods. The result will form a histogram similar to Histogram 221.24. From the results, questions that will lead to inductive thinking can be asked: "If you were to pull one more pea pod from the bag, what is the most likely number of peas in the pod?"; "Is there a relationship between the length of a pod and the number of peas in the pod?" The activity can be continued with string bean pods or other types of seed pods. If fresh pods are not in season, two large cans of whole beans will provide enough bean pods for a class of thirty students. Apples in season can be cut in half between the stem and blossom ends, the seeds can be counted, and a histogram made of the count. (Note: Seeds from plants in the same family produce identical numerical seed patterns.)

24
Bf
Da

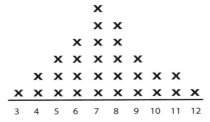

Tallying the Number of Peas in Pods

Histogram 221.24

Contributing Idea B. Plants can be classified.

Classifying seeds. Let students bring to school seeds that they find. Have them classify the seeds in as many ways as they can. Classifications will depend upon the seeds that are collected and are best if they are invented by the children. They need not agree with scientific classifications; however, students should be able to provide rationales for their groupings.

25
Dc
Fa

For example, they might group seeds by shapes (triangular, circular, egg-shaped, curved, coiled), by colors (orange, purple, striped, spotted, black, white), by sizes or weights (small or large), or by textures (horns, wings, tails). If fairly large numbers of seeds from the various classifications are obtained, students can set them outside, observe, and keep records concerning the animals that eat the seeds. Judgments about which animals eat which seeds can be made. Students can hypothesize why some seeds are not eaten by any animals.

Classifying seeds by types of dispersion. Divide the class into several small groups. Pass one envelope containing various seeds to each group. Ask students to divide the seeds into sets by the way they think the seeds might travel from one place to another. Encourage group discussion and experimentation to see how seeds might travel (e.g., seeds can be dropped or blown to see what air or wind does to them). Reclassify the seeds on another basis such as texture, shape, size, or color. Reclassify them several times. This will help students realize that there are multiple ways to classify and that some objects can belong to several classifications at one time. **26 Dc**

222   Interactions

Generalization I. Germination is the process by which an embryo starts to grow into a new plant.

Contributing Idea A. Some plants grow from seeds.

Observing that some plants grow from seeds. Have students take a shallow wooden box approximately 1 ft. (30 cm) square and approximately 4 in. (10 cm) deep and fill it with topsoil from a place where many plants have been growing, such as a vacant lot, garden, or nature area. Keep the soil in the classroom for several weeks or more, moistening it frequently. Students can observe and record the different kinds of plants that grow. Similarly, dig up a square foot (25 cm) of soil in the winter. The soil should be approximately 4 in. (10 cm) deep. It can be placed in a container in the classroom and kept moist. Observe the emergence of plants and make some judgments about seeds in winter. **01 Aa Cd Fb**

Contributing Idea B. Not all seeds germinate.

Recognizing that not all seeds germinate. Let each student plant two dozen radish seeds in a flower pot. Keep the soil moist. In about one week, they can count the plants to determine what fraction of the planted seeds germinated. **02 Cc Fb**

Comparing the germination ratios of different kinds of seeds. Students can make seed testers to help them determine how many seeds germinate in a given example. **03 Cc**

a. Fold in half a long piece of paper toweling or cloth such as muslin or gauze. Mark equal-size squares on one side. Number the squares and, using different seeds for each square, place 10 within each square. Fold the other half of the towel over the seeds and carefully roll it up. Tie it loosely with string, moisten it, and set it in a saucer of water. Keep it moist and in a warm place for three days, then carefully unroll it and tally how many of each kind of seed germinated. The tester can be rerolled and opened after another three-day interval. A histogram showing the number that germinated can be tallied (Histogram 222.03).

b. Percentages of germinating seeds can be obtained by dividing a 10 in. × 10 in. (25 cm × 25 cm) cloth into 1 in. (2 cm) squares. Place a seed in the center of each square. Place a second piece of cloth over the seeds and sprinkle it with water. Set the cloths and seeds on several sheets of newspaper. Carefully roll them up. The newspapers will help keep the cloths moist. Fasten the ends loosely with string, and keep the papers moist. After one week, carefully unroll the tester, and count the seeds that germinated. A percentage or ratio can be obtained easily. For example, if 78 seeds germinated, the sample of seeds would be rated at 78%.

Contributing Idea C. Different seeds germinate in different lengths of time.

Measuring the germination times of different seeds. Use small containers filled with clean sand and plant various seeds such as orange, lemon, apple, pumpkin, barley, oat, corn, or bean in different containers. Plant two or three of a kind in a container, and make sure that all seeds are planted at the same depth and receive the same amount of water. Keep a record of the germination times. The selected seeds can be ordered by the sequence in which they germinate. (Note: Some seeds can **04 Ch Da**

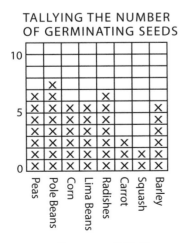

TALLYING THE NUMBER OF GERMINATING SEEDS

Histogram 222.03

be defective and will never germinate; others can take several months or more. For example, apples, peaches, plums, and many other kinds of fruit seeds will not grow immediately after taking them from a fruit. Such seeds generally need time to ripen in a cool, moist location.)

Contributing Idea D. Germinating seeds can be observed and measured.

Drawing pictures of germinating seeds. 05 Be Ca
Have students draw pictures of seeds during stages of germination. To aid their observations and drawings, place a sheet of ¼ in. (1 cm) graph paper behind the seeds in a soilless garden. Observations can be copied on another sheet of graph paper. Pictures of the germination stages of monocotyledons and dicotyledons can be compared (Figure 222.05).

Measuring the rate at which various 06 Bf Cd Fa
parts of a germinating seed grow. Select a seed, such as a pea or bean, that has just broken through its seed coat. Place an ink mark at the tip of the root and at the tip of the stem (see Figure 222.06). Let the seed continue to germinate in a soilless garden. Mark the root and stem daily or every other day in the same manner. A simple bar graph (Graph 222.06) can be prepared to depict the growth of the root and stem side by side. Students can be asked to make some judgments about the results (e.g., "Which part grew the most after one week?").

Figure 222.06

Figure 222.05

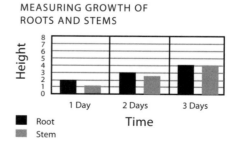

Graph 222.06

Observing and measuring the strength **07** **of a germinating seed.** Plant seeds 2 in. **Aa** (5 cm) apart in a large flat box. Place two **Cf** equal-sized cigar boxes or trays over the seeded areas. Weigh one of the boxes down with a few light objects. Observe the results after several days. Similarly, weigh several kinds of large seeds and record their weights. Plant each seed at the same depth. Weigh several quarters (they are approximately ¹/₅ oz. or 6.25 g each) and place one over each seed. Students can observe what happens to the quarters after several days and compute the ratio of the seed's weight to the weight it could lift. Now find out the maximum amount of weight a seedling will lift by weighing 50 cent pieces, silver dollars, or other similar objects. Over each seed, place a differently weighted object, observe, and compute ratios. The strengths of other seeds can be measured in the same way, and then ordered by their relative strengths.

Generalization II. Somewhat specific conditions are needed for seeds to germinate.

Contributing Idea A. Seeds need some water to germinate.

Experimenting to see the effect of water **08** **on germination.** Plant four bean seeds in **Ec** wet soil and four in dry soil. Make sure that one container is kept moist and the other dry. Other factors such as temperature, light, and ventilation should be normal and equal for both containers. Let students observe what happens. Similarly, place folded paper towels in the bottoms of two glasses. Sprinkle some seed on each, cover them with another paper towel, and label the glasses *A* and *B*. Soak the towels in glass *A* and keep them moist. Keep the towels in glass *B* dry. The other conditions should be the same for both containers.

Measuring how much water is absorbed **09** **by a seed.** Use a balance scale to weigh 12 **Bf** lima bean seeds and record their weights. **Cf** Soak them in water overnight, and then **Db** weigh them again. Compute the percentage of increase. The results can be compared with similar measurements taken of corn, beans, peas, or oats. Kinds of seeds can be ordered by their average percentages.

Contributing Idea B. Seeds need some warmth in order to germinate.

Experimenting to see the effect of tem- **10** **perature upon germination.** Prepare **Ec** two identical soilless gardens with four identical seeds in each. Place one garden in a very cold place and the other in a relatively warm place. If a refrigerator can be used, the second garden should be placed in a warm dark location because the interior of the refrigerator is dark. Students can observe which seeds germinate first.

Experimenting to see the effect of **11** **extreme temperatures upon the ger-** **Ec** **mination of seeds.** Boil 10 seeds for

10 minutes or heat them in an oven at 150°F (65°C) for 15 minutes. Place the same number of seeds in dry ice for the same amount of time, or place them in the freezer of a refrigerator overnight. Do not alter a third set of 10 seeds. Allow all the seeds to return to room temperature, and then place them in a soilless garden to let them germinate. Have students observe the results.

> *Contributing Idea C.* Light is not needed for seeds to germinate.

Experimenting to see if light is necessary for germination. 12 Ec Plant equal numbers of several kinds of seeds in two identical soilless containers. Place one container in the dark (e.g., a closet, cabinet, or drawer) and one in indirect sunlight. Keep the temperature normal and equal for both. Have students compare the growths. As an alternate approach, a cover can be placed over one container to keep out light.

Experimenting to see if the amount of light has an effect on germination. 13 Ec Have students keep all conditions the same for different soilless seed containers except for the amount of sunlight. A light meter can be used to check the amount of light in different locations. Patterns in germination can be compared among the different locations.

> *Contributing Idea D.* Soil is not needed for seeds to germinate.

Experimenting to see if soil is necessary for germination. 14 Ec Obtain some sand and wash it clean to remove all the soil. Plant seeds in several containers of the sand, keeping the sand moist and warm. Plant identical seeds in soil for comparisons. The seeds in the sand will grow up through the sand and continue growing for a short period of time (as long as the cotyledons provide food for the plant). Other material such as vermiculite can be used in place of the washed sand, or seeds can be grown in soilless gardens. Students will realize that soil is not necessary for germination to take place but it is necessary for growth to continue.

> *Contributing Idea E.* The depth of a seed in soil will not affect germination.

Experimenting to see the effect of depth on germination. 15 Ec Fill a straight-sided glass container with good garden soil. Plant seeds at different depths next to the glass. Plant two seeds 1 in. (2.5 cm) deep, two seeds 2 in. (5 cm) deep, two at 3 in. (7.5 cm), and two at 4 in. (10 cm). Keep the soil moist and fasten a sheet of black paper around the jar. Remove the paper daily to observe which seeds germinate. Students can keep a record of which seeds sprout and how long it took each to sprout. They can also record how many plants grew above the surface of the soil and from which depths they came. They can realize that deeply planted seeds will germinate, but will have used their food material before reaching the surface. (Note: The black paper in this activity is to keep light from the seeds until they break through the soil's surface, thus simulating the lack of light underground.)

> *Contributing Idea F.* The position of a seed in soil will not affect germination.

Experimenting to see if the position of a seed affects germination. Soak some seeds overnight, and then mount them on needles so that they point in various directions. Mount the needles on a cork, and set it in a shallow dish of water. Cover the cork with a glass and observe. Similarly, students can place seeds sideways, upside down, right side up in a soilless container. Students will find that seeds will germinate from any position. **16 Ec**

Generalization III. Plants respond to certain environmental conditions.

> *Contributing Idea A.* Gravity influences roots to grow down and stems to grow up (geotropism).

Experimenting to determine the effect of gravity upon roots and stems. Let students germinate seeds (e.g., lima bean, radish) between a blotter and glass. Several days after germination, turn the apparatus on its side, and observe the roots and stems for several more days. (The roots will change direction and grow downward; the stem will change **17 Ec Fa**

direction and grow upward.) Repeat the turning every several days or try various partial turnings. For example, move the apparatus one-eighth turn each day in the same direction or move it one-fourth turn every four days, alternating the direction at each turn. The roots and stems will always respond to gravity in the same way. To compare the effect of gravity upon different plants, prepare six soilless containers with three bean, three radish, and three corn seeds in each. As the seeds germinate, set two containers on their sides and invert two containers. Keep the remaining two unchanged. Let students compare the roots and observe the direction of growth. They can infer that the roots of plants will always grow downward, and the stems will always grow upward. Similarly, gravity's effect upon just the stems of plants can be seen by growing some seeds in a soil container and turning it on its side after the plants have grown to sufficient heights.

Observing the effect of artificial gravity on the growth of plants. Attach soilless containers (see entry 641.01) to the turntable of a phonograph (record player), and observe the directions of growth of the roots and stems as they are rotated for several days. Different speeds can be tested. **18 Aa Ec**

Observing that twining plants only grow upward. Grow a twining plant along an upright string or wooden **19 Aa**

support. After it has grown sufficiently, let students gently remove the support from the soil without detaching the plant. Set the support horizontally, and observe the plant for several days. (It will stop twining.) Turn the support upside down and observe again. (The last coils will unwind, and the plant will start to climb upward again.)

Contributing Idea B. Roots grow in the presence of water.

Observing that roots grow in the presence of water. Several activities indicate that roots develop and grow in relation to the amount of water present. **20 Aa**

a. Half-fill a shallow box with soil. Using adhesive tape or oil-base clay, plug the holes in two porous flower pots. Set the pots in diagonal corners of the box. Plant seeds evenly throughout the box. Fill one of the pots regularly with water but not the other. Do not water the soil. Over several weeks, have students note the order of germination and the appearance of the plants nearest the watered pot. (The plants will be taller and healthier looking.) After about two weeks, carefully remove both pots, and notice the mat of roots around the water-filled pot. Remove several plants from various sections of the box and observe the direction of root growth. As a variation, one flower pot can be placed in the center of a box with seeds evenly planted around it. Fill the pot with water and observe.

b. Plant soaked seeds evenly in soil next to the glass side of an aquarium. Set a small, plugged, porous flower pot in one corner of the aquarium next to the glass. Add water to the pot regularly, but do not water the soil. Over several weeks, students can observe the roots growing next to the glass and see that they extend within the moist area.

Contributing Idea C. Stems above the ground, leaves, and flowers are affected by light (phototropism).

Observing that some stems bend toward light. Plant a number of bean seeds in a box and water them as needed. When the plants have reached a height of approximately 5 in. (15 cm), students can change the position of the box in relation to the angle of the sunlight. In a short time, the stems of the plants will bend back toward the Sun's rays, but the bending will be in a different place on the stem. Students can change the box's position in relation to the sunlight any number of times, observing the change in direction of stems. (They will always bend toward the light.) **21 Aa**

Observing that some leaves and flowers turn toward the light. Place a well-grown geranium or coleus plant in a sunny window, and observe that the leaves seem to follow the light throughout the day. (Actually sunlight inhibits growth; the shaded side of the plant continues to grow and causes it to elongate on one side and bend away from the shade.) After watching the plant for several days, turn it so that the leaves point away from the light at midday. Observe what happens. Students can keep a record of how long such turning takes. Several kinds of plants can be compared by their turning times. The blossoms on plants can be tested in the same way.
22 Aa

Observing that some leaves open and close in response to light. Have students observe clover leaves to see how they are affected by sunlight. During the day they can see that the three clover leaflets are spread out and change their positions. At night the leaflets close. (The two side leaflets move together until they are facing, while the top leaflet folds over them.) The effect of night can be simulated by covering a clover plant with anything that will keep out the light such as a large can or box. In about half an hour, the leaves will start to close. In an hour, the leaves will be folded in their nighttime positions.
23 Aa

Experimenting to see which colors influence the growth of plants. Have students grow a patch of grass in the classroom or use a patch of lawn in the school yard. Divide a fairly thick section of the grass into four sections. This can be done by placing cardboard walls around the sections to keep light from leaking from one section to another. Cover one section with blue cellophane, another with red, and a third with green. Leave the fourth section uncovered, or cover it with clear cellophane (Figure 222.24a, p. 184). Let students record their observations as the days pass. Note the length of the stems, color of the plants, and other general appearances. Students should be able to make some judgments as to which colors of light seem to be the most important for plant growth. (Red is best.) As an alternative, the open ends of several shoeboxes can be covered with different colors of cellophane. Several holes should be punched in the sides of each box near the bottom for adequate air circulation. Unless the plants are large, they will fit easily into the shoeboxes when placed on end. The boxes make it easy to water the plant and to take daily measurements (Figure 222.24b). A graph can be kept to show any changes in the growth rates of plants. Comparisons can be made, and students will find that not all colors affect growth in the same way.
24 Bf Ec

Contributing Idea D. Some plants respond to touch.

Observing that roots react to obstacles in their path. Plant some seeds in glass
25 Aa

Figure 222.24a

Figure 222.24b

containers filled with soil. Make sure the seeds are placed next to the glass for observation. Add pieces of wood, rocks, or other obstacles to the soil beneath the seeds and under the root tip. Students will see that the roots grow around the objects. Similarly, germinate seeds on blotting paper or a sponge, and place small pieces of wood or other obstacles at the tip of the roots. Observe on a daily basis how they react.

Observing that stems react to obstacles in their path. Set a plant directly under some blockage, such as a low shelf, and observe it for several days. **26 Aa**

Observing that some plants react dramatically when touched. Obtain a mimosa plant from a nursery. Let students touch the narrow leaves with a **27 Aa**

pencil. (The leaves will fold together and droop rapidly.) The plant will not be harmed, but it may take several hours for it to regain its original shape.

Observing that twining stems respond to touch. Observe a climbing plant such as a sweet pea, morning glory, pole bean, or moon flower. Note that the narrow tendrils on such plants precede the rest of the plant and curl around sticks or strings. Also note the direction in which the tendrils turn. (The mentioned plants all turn in a counterclockwise direction.) Have a student carefully unwrap a tendril from another plant, and gently wrap it several times around a support in a clockwise direction. In a short time, the tendril will unwind completely. (Tendrils of a plant turn only in one direction.) **28 Aa**

Contributing Idea E. Some plants respond to heat and cold.

Observing that some plants respond to heat. Bring a lighted match near a terminal leaflet of a mimosa plant. The entire leaf will respond immediately. After a few hours, the original shape will be regained. Other plants can be tested in the same way. Students can also notice that the leaves on many plants become limp on hot days. **29 Aa**

Observing that some plants respond to cold. Place a mimosa plant in a cold place for about 10 minutes. Have a student gently touch a terminal leaflet and note that the plant no longer responds to **30 Aa**

touch rapidly. When the plant returns to room temperature, its sensitivity to touch also returns. Other plants can be tested in the same way.

Contributing Idea F. Some plants respond to seasonal changes.

Experimenting to see what causes leaves to change color. Set twigs with **31 Ec** leaves (e.g., red maple, sugar maple, poplar, oak) in glasses filled with different solutions such as salt water, sugar water, vinegar water, or combinations of these. Place some in a refrigerator at night and others near a heater. Be sure to keep identical twigs in plain water and under normal conditions as controls. Keep notes on what happens and try other tests.

230 Other Organisms

231 Characteristics

Generalization I. Microorganisms have identifiable characteristics.

> *Contributing Idea A.* All microorganisms reproduce their kind.

Observing that microorganisms reproduce their kind. Microorganisms are very diverse. They include bacteria, fungi, protists, microscopic plants (green algae), and animals such as plankton and the planarian. Some microbiologists include viruses, but others consider these as nonliving. Have students culture protozoa, mold, yeast, and algae. As each culture develops, they will easily see that the increases in populations involve new organisms that are like the parent.

01
Aa
Fa

> *Contributing Idea B.* All microorganisms grow.

Measuring the growth of microorganisms. Microorganisms are too small for the growth of an individual organism to be measured in the classroom; however, growth of populations can be measured.

02
Cd
Cg

   a. *Protozoa.* Throughout history, protozoa have been defined as single-cell organisms with animal-like behavior. They are a diverse group of single-cell organisms. Obtain some pond water and develop a culture (see entry 231.11). The number of protozoa in a drop of pond water can be counted and compared with a later sample. Students can keep count of each type of organism that they see. A few drops of gelatin or methyl cellulose added to the water will slow the animals down for better viewing.

   b. *Molds.* Molds are fungi. There are thousands of known species of molds. Grow mold on bread (see entry 231.14). Students can cut paper strips each day to represent the distance each mold grows. *Aspergillus elegans* is a relatively slow growing mold that grows on bread. It leaves a ring of spores with each day's growth, making it easy to measure on a daily basis.

   c. *Yeasts.* Yeasts are fungi. There are thousands of known species of yeasts. Culture some yeast (see entry 231.15). Students can estimate the number of plants in one-fourth of a viewed area, and then multiply the number by four to obtain an estimate of how many there are. Recount later, after the yeast has risen.

   d. *Algae.* Algae are a large and diverse group of simple organisms. Students can see the increase in green algae in an aquarium kept in strong but not direct sunlight (see entry 231.18).

Contributing Idea C. All microorganisms need food and water to grow.

Observing that microorganisms need food in order to grow. As students culture various microorganisms, they will realize the importance of providing the proper food source for each kind. For example, students can culture yeast in one container, but not add molasses to the recipe for a second container (see entry 231.15). Similarly, they can try to grow bacteria in a petri dish that does not contain a culture medium.

03 Aa Fa

Observing that yeasts require food for growth. Put 1 tsp. (5 ml) of cornstarch in a pint (500 ml) of water. Remove a spoonful of the mixture and add a little dilute iodine. (It will turn blue indicating the presence of starch.) Add a yeast cake to the jar. Repeat the iodine test several times a day. (The color will show less and less starch until none is left.) If students test for the presence of sugar during this activity, they will realize that the yeast uses the starch for food and turns it into sugar.

04 Aa Fb

Experimenting to see the effect of moisture upon the growth of molds. Place a piece of white bread in each of two coffee cans. Moisten the bread in one can, but not in the other. Leave both uncovered for three hours, then cover and place both in a warm dark place for a week. Compare the growth of molds on each piece of bread. Students will find that the dry bread shows much less growth than the moistened bread and conclude that moisture is important for the growth of molds.

05 Ec Fa

Contributing Idea D. All microorganisms are sensitive to their surroundings.

Observing that some microorganisms are sensitive to light. Place a culture of euglena in a long test tube sealed with a cork or rubber stopper. Hold the test tube in a horizontal position. Using hand lenses, students will see that the animals become evenly distributed in a short time. Now hang a piece of dark cloth over half the test tube. Do this gently so as not to disturb the animals. After an hour, remove the cloth and immediately observe again. Students will find that the euglena tend to be in the lighted portion of the tube, and realize that the animals sense light and seem to have a preference for it. They can test the influence of light on one-celled plants by placing cultures of them in locations with different lighting conditions.

06 Aa Ec Fa

Observing that microorganisms are sensitive to temperature changes. Place a culture of protozoa in a long test tube sealed with a cork or rubber stopper. Hold the test tube vertically. Using hand lenses, students will see that the animals become evenly distributed in a short time. Now place the base of the tube against an ice cube. Students will find that the protozoa tend to move to the top of the tube,

07 Aa Ec Fa

and realize that the animals sense cold and seem to avoid it. Students can test the influence of heat and cold upon one-celled plants by placing cultures of them in locations of different temperatures.

Generalization II. There is a great variety of physical characteristics among microorganisms.

Contributing Idea A. The microscope is an instrument used for viewing objects that are very small.

Using a compound microscope. Show students that microscopes have at least two curved lenses that work together. See Figure 231.08, which identifies the lens and other parts of the microscope. The

08 Bb Ga

Figure 231.08

lens nearest the object being viewed is the *objective lens*. The lens nearest the viewer's eye is the *eyepiece*. Have students locate the *platform* or *stage* beneath the objective lens. The *clips* hold glass

slides on the platform. Beneath the platform is a *mirror* that can be turned to reflect light from a lamp or window onto the viewed object. **Caution: Warn students to not look at the Sun or reflected images of the Sun.** The mirror can be adjusted until a uniform circle of light without shadows is seen. This circle is called a field. Place a small drop of water in the center of a clean, dry glass slide. Cut a small letter *e* from a newspaper and lay it right-side up in the drop of water. Slowly place the cover glass over the water by placing one edge down first (to prevent air bubbles from being caught between the glasses). Now place the mounted slide on the platform, clip it into place, and move it with thumbs and forefingers until the letter *e* is in the center of the platform opening. Turn the *course adjustment knob* to move the objective lens down as far as it will go, but be careful not to touch the slide. (Look at the slide from the side to be sure the objective lens does not touch or break the slide.) Students can take turns looking through the eyepiece, watching the field as they turn the coarse adjustment knob slowly toward them. This will raise the body of the tube and the lenses, and students will see the letter *e* appear. The adjustment can be moved slowly up and down to focus the letter. Let students move the slide to the right, left, up, and down. They will find that everything seen through the eyepiece is reversed. Some students might be interested in looking up the work of Anton von Leeuwenhoek (1632–1723), a Dutch merchant, the first person to perfect the microscope.

Preparing microscopic slides. Place **09** a culture or specimen in the center of a **Ga** clean, dry glass slide. If the specimen is liquid, a cover glass can be placed over the top by placing one edge down first to prevent bubbles from becoming trapped beneath the glass (Figure 231.09a). If the water begins to dry up while viewing, use a medicine dropper to place a little more water along the edge of the cover glass. If a middle school science laboratory is available, bacterial cultures can be fixed to slides by spreading a drop so that it forms a thin film on the glass. Allow it

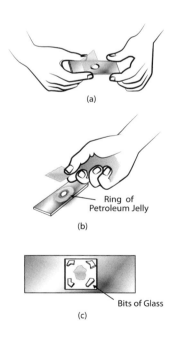

(a)

Ring of
Petroleum Jelly

(b)

Bits of Glass

(c)

Figure 231.09

to dry, and then pass it through a flame three or four times to kill the culture and fix it to the slide. Now put several drops of methylene-blue stain on the culture to improve viewing. Leave it for two minutes, and then dip the slide in water to wash off excess stain. Blot gently with a paper towel and view under a microscope. Sometimes it is best to not press the object being viewed with the cover glass. Special slides with indentations in them can be purchased or the cover glass can be raised by making a ring of petroleum jelly slightly smaller than the cover on the slide. Place a drop of a culture in the ring and add the cover glass (Figure 231.09b). An alternative method is to break a cover glass into several pieces, place them on a slide, cover them with an unbroken cover glass, and glue the pieces in place (Figure 231.09c). A culture can be dropped between the slide and the raised cover. **Caution: Follow safety guidelines when working with bacteria cultures.**

> *Contributing Idea B.* Protozoa are organisms that are too small to be seen with the unaided eye.

Collecting protozoa. Protozoa can be **10** found primarily in water. Although they **Bb** can be collected from puddles of standing **Ge** water almost anywhere, the best source is unpolluted ponds. Students can collect jars of pond water, including some mud from the bottom. Let the water settle.

After two days, stir the water without disturbing the mud, fill a medicine dropper with the water, and place a few drops in a watch glass or test tube. Students can use hand lenses to observe the contents. They will see some of the larger protozoa such as the *paramecium.* Tell them that some protozoa cause diseases in people: one causes malaria, carried by the anopheles mosquito; another causes sleeping sickness, carried by the tsetse fly. Some students might be interested in researching information on the prevention of such diseases.

Culturing protozoa. Place plant material such as dry grass, hay, or leaves in a quart (liter) widemouthed jar. Fill it three-fourths full with tap water that has been standing for two days to allow the chlorine to evaporate. Cover the jar and set it in a well lighted place, but away from direct sunlight. In two days, students can observe drops of the water under a microscope. The population and varieties of protozoa will increase for several weeks.

11 Gd

Observing the physical characteristics of protozoa. Although there are about 15,000 species of protozoa, most are too small to be seen without a microscope. To see some protozoa, prepare a microscope slide by placing a large drop of pond water on it and carefully covering it with a cover glass. Set the slide on a microscope or a microprojector platform. When focused, move the slide slowly until an animal is

12 Aa Bb

viewed. The protozoan most likely to be observed is the *paramecium.* A diagram of this animal can guide students' observations (Figure 231.12a). Students will see that the paramecium has a definite, permanent shape and moves rapidly by the coordinated beating of a great many fine, hairlike structures on its body. You might tell them that the structures are *cilia* and that the dark spots in the animal are *nuclei.* (The smaller nucleus controls reproduction, and the larger controls most of the animal's other functions.) As the animal swims, food is swept into the oral groove and eventually is passed out through the anal pore. Students might also observe an *amoeba*—a slow moving, clear animal with a constantly changing

PARAMECIUM

(a)

AMOEBA

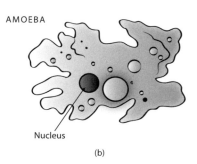

(b)

Figure 231.12

body shape (Figure 231.13b). It has one nucleus and obtains food by engulfing it. Now obtain several samples of water from a pond, stream, puddle, and faucet. Make a slide for each type, label the slides so they will not get mixed up, and then look for similarities and differences in the kinds and numbers of protozoa in the samples.

Contributing Idea C. Fungi are simple plants, some of which are too small to be seen with the unaided eye.

Culturing fungi. Fungi vary in size from microscopic plants to larger forms such as mushrooms; molds are a common form of microscopic fungus that cannot make their own food (they do not contain chlorophyll). To grow mold, place a moist blotter or paper towel on the bottom of a jar. Set a piece of white bread on the blotter and leave the jar open for thirty minutes. Put a lid on the jar, label it, and store it in a dark place for a week. At the end of that time, students will see how the mold has grown. You might tell them that there are more than 85,000 known kinds. Some are beneficial in the manufacturing of beverages and cheese and in the production of penicillin. Some are a nuisance, such as those that grow on leather; others are harmful and cause disease in plants (mildew on grapes, rot on peaches) or in people (ringworm, athlete's foot). Now have students compare cultures grown on different kinds of bread: homemade,

13 Gd

commercial white, whole wheat, rye, and so on. (Commercial breads include preservatives that will affect the growth of molds.)

Observing the physical characteristics of some molds. Culture some white-bread mold. After a week, students will see a variety of molds growing on the bread. Let them count the different colors. Explain that each color is a different colony. Black mold is a common variety that can be examined with a hand lens. Tell students that the small round balls they see on the end of the slender stalks are cases containing *spores*. Explain that when the cases ripen, they release the spores into the air, and some fall upon the bread to form new mold. Roquefort, blue, and Gorgonzola cheeses grow penicillin molds. These can be removed from the cheeses with a fine needle and placed on a microscope slide. Their structures can be seen under a microscope.

14 Aa Bb

Culturing yeasts. Yeast plants are a common form of microscopic fungi that cannot make their own food, and thus do not contain chlorophyll. More than 55,000 kinds are known. Yeast plants can be grown by mixing baker's yeast with warm water and a little molasses. Allow the mixture to stand for one hour. Place a drop of it on a glass slide and observe under a microscope or on a microprojector. Students can easily see the yeast plants. Ask students to estimate the number they

15 Cb Gc

see. One way to estimate is to divide the visual area into fourths, count the number in one fourth of the area, then multiply the number by four. Now let the mixture stand overnight. Look at it the next day and determine the number. Tell students that these tiny yeast plants are in the air almost everywhere.

Experimenting to see the effect of temperature changes on the growth of yeast. Make some bread dough with yeast. Divide the dough into three parts. Put the first in a refrigerator, the second in a warm place, and the third in a hot place. Students can examine the dough each hour and discuss the effect of the different temperatures. **16 Ec**

Making bread. Students can make bread by mixing 1¼ c. (300 ml) of flour with 3 tsp. (15 ml) of salt and 3 tsp. of sugar. Add 4 c. (1 L) of water and 2 packages of dry yeast. While making bread, be sure all equipment is clean and that hands are washed thoroughly. As students work with the bread dough, let them describe how it feels. Let the dough rise for 1½ hours, put it into small greased pans, and let it rise again. Bake for 10 minutes at 450°F (235°C). For a comparative experience, prepare two batches of dough—one using dry yeast and one without yeast. Compare the breads before and after baking in terms of color, smell, taste, and texture. **17 Ec Gc**

Contributing Idea D. Algae are simple plants, some of which are too small to be seen with the unaided eye.

Culturing algae. Algae vary in color and size from microscopic plants to larger forms such as seaweeds and kelps. Green algae are a common microscopic form that is widely distributed in ponds, lakes, streams, and on land in damp places. More than 6,700 kinds have been identified. Students can collect some green scum that forms on stagnant pools and transfer it to a large aquarium or jar. Algae can be cultured in an aquarium placed in strong but not direct sunlight. A stocked aquarium usually provides enough nutrients for the algae to grow. **18 Gd**

Observing the physical characteristics of algae. Place a drop of algae on a microscope slide and examine it under a microscope. Individual plants will be visible. Students can count the number of different forms they see and use reference books to identify them. They can observe a single plant for a while and perhaps see it reproduce by fission. **19 Aa Bd**

Generalization III. Microorganisms can be organized by characteristics.

Contributing Idea A. Some microorganisms can be seriated.

Seriating molds. Culture some mold. Students can measure the sizes of the different colonies on a daily basis for a **20 Da**

week, and then order the organisms by their growth rate.

> *Contributing Idea B.* Some microorganisms can be classified.

Classifying microorganisms. Some microorganisms can be classified by the substances they grow on, their colors, or the conditions under which they grow best. Let students research to identify each type in reference books. Molds are generally classified by color.

21 Bd Dc

232   Interactions

Generalization I. Reproduction is a process by which microorganisms give rise to new generations.

> *Contributing Idea A.* Some microorganisms reproduce by fission or conjugation.

Observing reproduction in protozoa and algae. Place a large drop from a rich culture of protozoa on a microscope slide and place it under a microscope or on a microprojector. Move the slide slowly until a large paramecium is found, then follow it. If the sample begins to dry, add more water. Rarely, students will see the paramecium divide to form two paramecia. Tell them that this type of reproduction is called fission (simple cell division). Explain the protozoa can also reproduce by joining together, then dividing (a process called conjugation), but the chances of seeing this in the classroom are slight. Algae

01 Aa Bb

can similarly be observed in hopes of seeing reproduction by fission or conjugation.

> *Contributing Idea B.* Some microorganisms reproduce by means of spores.

Observing reproduction by molds. Allow some moist white bread to become moldy in a coffee can. Students will soon see a black mold on the bread. This is a very common variety of mold called rhizopus. It can be examined with a hand lens to clearly see the stalks topped by black balls (Figure 232.02). Explain that the balls are *spore cases.* The cases can be broken open and the *spores* placed on a glass slide for observation under a microscope.

02 Aa Bb

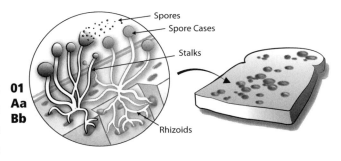

Figure 232.02

> *Contributing Idea C.* Some microorganisms reproduce by budding.

Observing reproduction by yeasts. Place a piece of baker's yeast into a small bottle and add a little molasses and warm water. Shake the mixture. Observe a drop of the mixture under a microscope

03 Aa Bb

(Figure 232.03). Students will see a small bulge grow out of a larger cell, remain attached for a short period of time, then eventually separate from it as an independent plant. Explain that this kind of reproduction is called budding.

Nucleus

Yeast Bud

Yeast Cell

Figure 232.03

Generalization II. Various microorganisms operate in special ways that keep the organism alive and growing.

Contributing Idea A. Certain bacteria break down proteins, carbohydrates, or other substances for their life functions.

Studying the growth of bacteria on different foods. Caution: This research is best done through various readings because of the dangers of growing bacteria in classroom settings. By checking book and internet references, students

04
Aa
Bb

can learn that protein is an important food that is present in cheese, meat, milk, and gelatin. Carbohydrate is an energy food present in bread, flour, starch, and sugar. When bacteria break down protein food in the absence of oxygen, the process is called putrefaction. When other bacteria break down carbohydrates in the absence of oxygen, the process is called fermentation. Some students might be interested in researching: (1) the uses people have made of fermentation; (2) the work of Louis Pasteur (1822–1895), the French chemist who studied fermentation.

Contributing Idea B. Certain molds grow only on certain foods.

Experimenting to see on what foods molds will grow. Bring to class several samples of moldy food such as an orange with green or blue mold covering part of it, an apple with a brown spot, a sweet or white potato with black mold on it, and a carrot with a soft, moldy area. Now scrape some mold from each sample onto healthy specimens of the same kind. Put the healthy specimens in sealed jars. Next, insert a sterilized needle or stiff wire into the moldy portion of one sample, then pierce the skin of healthy samples of different fruits and vegetables. Repeat this for each of the moldy samples, sterilizing the needle each time. Put all the inoculated, healthy specimens in sealed jars. Students can compare the results after several days. After examining the healthy

05
Ec
Fa

specimens that had mold scraped onto them, discuss how fruits and vegetables are structured to resist infections. Students will also realize that certain molds only grow on certain foods.

> *Contributing Idea C.* Some microorganisms produce carbon dioxide as they live and grow.

Testing the gas given off by some micro-organisms. Drop a piece of baker's yeast into a small bottle, add a little molasses and water, and then shake the bottle. Insert a piece of glass tubing through a one-hole rubber stopper and seal the bottle with the stopper so that the tubing does not touch the mixture. Pour some limewater into a second small bottle. Insert two pieces of glass tubing into a two-hole rubber stopper and seal the bottle with it. One piece of tubing should be long enough so it will be in the limewater, and the other should not touch the limewater. Connect rubber tubing from the first bottle to the longer tube of the second bottle. Now set up a second set of two bottles in the same way, but place moldy bread or another type of fungus (e.g., mushrooms) in place of the yeast mixture in the first bottle. Now set up a third set for control purposes by putting only molasses and water in the first bottle. After 24 hours, students will find that nothing happens in the control bottle; thus, the yeast or moldy bread must be responsible for making the limewater cloudy. Cloudy limewater indicates that

06
Fb

carbon dioxide is being given off by the mixtures. Explain that yeasts and molds are nongreen plants, and since they cannot manufacture their own food, they must live on other food sources. As an alternative experience, place a solution of yeast and water in small amounts in the bottom of a soda pop bottle. Add a few drops of syrup to one bottle, flour, gelatin, or grape juice to others. Firmly attach a balloon to each bottle and observe what happens. Students can see which substances mixed with yeast produce the most active results and test the gas that inflates the balloon. (It will be carbon dioxide.)

Observing fermentation by yeast. Follow a recipe to make bread dough (a mixture of flour, sugar, and water). Divide the dough into two parts. Mix some yeast into one part and set both in glass jars in a warm place for a few hours. Students will observe that the dough with yeast rises. By examining the dough, they will see that there are holes in it caused by gas bubbles. Explain that the gas (carbon dioxide) is produced by the action of the yeast on the sugar and that this process is called fermentation.

07
Aa
Bb

Generalization III. Natural and artificial conditions affect the growth of microorganisms.

> *Contributing Idea.* Temperature changes affect the growth of microorganisms.

Experimenting to see the effect of different temperatures upon the growth of protozoa. Pour equal amounts of pond water (or other water containing a protozoa culture) into three clean jars. Store one in a refrigerator, one in the classroom at room temperature, and one in a warmer location. After 24 hours, use a medicine dropper to place a large drop from each jar on different microscope slides. Place coverslips on them, and observe under a microscope or with a microprojector to see what effect the different temperatures had.

08
Ec
Fa

Experimenting to see the effect of different temperatures upon the growth of molds. Moisten two pieces of white bread and place them in two coffee cans. Leave them uncovered for three hours, and then cover both. Place one in a refrigerator and the other in a dark, warm place. Compare the growth after a week. Students will find that the bread in the refrigerator shows much less growth than the bread in the warm location. They should conclude that warmth is important for the growth of molds. A similar activity can be done with yeasts.

09
Ec
Fa

240 Ecology

241 Characteristics

Generalization I. Plants and animals can be found in a variety of environments; each kind exists only in certain environments.

> *Contributing Idea A.* Some plants and animals live in water. The aquarium is a simulated environment designed for observing marine plants and animals.

Building aquariums. Aquariums provide firsthand observations of marine plants, animals, and their relationships. The most useful aquarium simulates a particular environment and includes natural balances and ecological relationships. When properly set up, freshwater and saltwater aquariums need little attention.

01
Gc

    a. *Containers.* Commercially prepared tanks, preferably with slate or glass bottoms, are most satisfactory; however, almost any sturdy glass container from a drinking glass to a large container will work. Small-mouthed containers are not good, for they do not provide enough oxygen for most fish. It should be kept in mind that a commercial aquarium is fragile and tends to leak once it has been bumped, moved, or allowed to remain empty for a long time. It is also good to remember that the tank should never be lifted when it is filled with sand and water and that an empty tank should not be lifted by the top frame but should be supported by the bottom frame. Although cool freshwater aquariums might be covered or not covered, tanks used for tropical fish should include a cover that is slightly raised to allow air to circulate over the water. A cover will help keep the temperature constant and retain moisture. All-glass containers or containers with reinforced corners of stainless steel are best for saltwater environments. Be sure to spread several layers of waxed paper under the tank to protect the surface where it rests.

    b. *Sand.* If sand is placed in the aquarium first, water clouding can usually be avoided. The sand should be coarse and well washed before being placed into the container. To wash the sand, simply place it in a clean can, fill the can with water, stir, and pour out the dirty water, holding the sand in the can with your hand. It might be necessary to repeat this process several times. The layer of sand used in the aquarium might vary in depth, but 1 in. (3 cm) is sufficient. If it is piled higher toward one end, refuse will settle toward the other end, making it easier to remove. Ornaments such as castles and large stones should be avoided because they provide crevices in which refuse will collect. Refuse, if allowed to remain, will foul the water. Seashells should not be used in freshwater aquariums. They dissolve slowly, releasing too much lime into the water.

c. *Water.* If you do not use the water where the fish are found, ordinary tap water is fine. Remember, however, that tap water contains chemicals such as chlorine that will kill fish as well as the disease germs it was meant to destroy. To make tap water usable, let it stand (not in the tank to be used) for several days to allow the chlorine to evaporate. In order not to disturb the sand or gravel base (which might create a clouding that will take several days to clear), place a saucer or large piece of paper over the sand and pour the water directly over it. Fill the tank to half its capacity and then add plants. Anchor them securely, complete filling the tank, and remove the paper. Allow the water to stand for several hours to adjust to room temperature. The water temperature should be kept fairly constant and should be the same as the habitat that the aquarium represents. When the climate is extremely warm, an aerator will help to cool the water. If the climate is too cold, various heating devices can be obtained. The water temperatures for most freshwater fish are best between 65°F and 70°F (18°C and 21°C), but they can stand extremes from 50°F to 75°F (10°C to 24°C). Tropical fish survive best between 73°F and 78°F (23°C and 26°C), but will stand the narrow limits of 70°F to 85°F (21°C to 30°C). For saltwater aquariums, fresh seawater is best. Artificial seawater, however, can be made by dissolving 10½ oz. (300 g) of pure table salt, 1½ oz. (42 g) of magnesium chloride, 1 oz. (28 g) Epsom salts, and ½ oz. (14 g) plaster of paris in every 3 gal. (11 L) of water. The salts can be of a technical grade. It is possible to buy prepared mixes at some pet stores. Water that evaporates from saltwater aquariums should be replaced; otherwise the salt content that does not evaporate will become excessive and will lessen the oxygen content. A mark at the original waterline will help to keep track. A hydrometer can be floated in the container to check the salinity of the solution. The desired reading is 1025, but any point between 1020 and 1030 is satisfactory. Add more salt if the reading is too low. The hydrometer should be left in the tank so that a reading can be taken each day. The temperature for saltwater aquariums should be kept around 65°F (18°C). The water in a well-planned freshwater or seawater aquarium will seldom need to be changed, but if the need arises, remove the fish and place them in a container filled with water from the tank. Remove the remaining water with a siphon, clean the tank, and wash the sand. Rebuild the tank as previously described.

d. *Animals*. It is best to allow aquarium water to sit several days before introducing any animal life. When the aquarium is ready, place the fish and their water in a jar and float it in the aquarium for about an hour. The temperature of the aquarium and the water in the jar will gradually match, and the fish can be placed into the aquarium without shock. This precaution is necessary for the health and survival of the fish. Know your animals and plan for their proper food in advance. Foods will vary depending on the type of fish. Local pet stores carry products for all types. Feed the fish small amounts three times per week. The more varieties of animals in the same tank, the more interesting and varied will

be the observations. A cool freshwater aquarium can be stocked with goldfish, minnows, dace, and sunfish. There is a great variety of compatible fish appropriate for tropical aquariums, and saltwater aquariums might include such fascinating creatures as barnacles, corals, small crabs, sea anemones, and mussels. To create a balance in a freshwater tank, add scavengers such as snails and catfish. These housekeepers are active at night and clean up any refuse they find on the bottom, thus helping to keep the water from becoming foul. The snails will also eat algae off the glass. One medium-sized snail for every 1 gallon (4 L) of water is sufficient. Watch for dead snails, because their decaying bodies rapidly poison the water. Other animal forms, such as water insects and other invertebrates (beetles, hydra, copepods, ostracods) can also be placed in aquariums.

e. *Plants*. Plants can transform a plain-looking aquarium into an attractive one. They are also beneficial to the environment in practical ways, producing oxygen and consuming carbon dioxide. They use refuse as fertilizer, produce shade, and provide hiding places and egg-laying spots for the fish. There are many varieties of plants that might be chosen. Cool, freshwater aquariums might include sagittaria, ludwigia, water poppy, and nitella. Tropical freshwater tanks are colorful when arranged with anacharis, ludwigia, vallisneria, and sword plants. Saltwater containers can use enteromorpha, sea lettuce, rockweed, and ceramium.

f. *Equipment.* A great deal of equipment can be obtained to improve the efficiency of an aquarium: filters, bubblers, aerators, controlled feeders, and so forth. Most are unnecessary, but a few slightly improve the operation of the aquarium. A dip tube is essential for removing sediments that collect in the tank. Decaying matter, which soon fouls the water, should never remain in the container. Mechanical filtering of the water through glass wool and bone charcoal makes cleaning the tank a rare necessity. These filters are usually attached to the back of the tank. Sub-sand filters are also available and depend upon bacterial action to purify the water. Aerators have several advantages. They cause bubbles to rise through the water. The bursting bubbles break the surface tension, increase the air-to-water surface, and maintain more uniform chemical conditions. Saltwater tanks should be provided with aerators. Tropical fish tanks require heating units and thermometers.

g. *Problems.* All plants need light in order to manufacture their own food. Too much light, however, will cause green algae to form on the sides of the tank; and if the water is not fresh, too little light will cause brown algae to form. They will not hurt the fish, but algae are often unsightly. The condition usually clears by changing the amount of light on the tank. When the edge of the water becomes surrounded by bubbles or when the fish swim at the surface sticking their mouths out into the air, something is wrong. Usually the trouble is pollution or a lack of oxygen in the water. Check for dead snails, dead fish, or uneaten food.

After an aquarium is established, students can test the effect of changes in light or temperature upon the environment. They might observe that one or two animals dominate or become the "bosses" for other animals. Have them introduce a new animal into the aquarium to see how the others act toward it. They might also train fish to respond at feeding time to a tap, whistle, or other signal.

Contributing Idea B. Some plants and animals live on land, or in water and on land. The terrarium is a simulated environment designed for observing land plants and animals.

Building terrariums. Terrariums provide firsthand observations of land plants, animals, and their relationships. Basically there are three types of land environments, each with a particular set of environmental characteristics.

02
Gc

a. *Woodland Environment.* To create a woodland environment, cover the bottom of a container with a layer of gravel for good drainage, and then add several in. of fertile soil. Bury pieces of charcoal into the soil to absorb gases and prevent the soil from souring. Add a few rocks and a dish of water to provide the necessary moisture for this environment. With a glass top, the terrarium will maintain its own water cycle. Mosses, ferns, and other small woodland plants can be placed in the container and watered infrequently. If mold appears, remove the moldy plants and leave the top of the container open to allow some of the excess moisture to evaporate. Small animals such as frogs, turtles, toads, salamanders, newts, and snakes can be added. (Note: The animals must be compatible, and you should not put in too many. Be sure to remove any excess food that these animals do not eat.)

b. *Swamp Environment.* To create a swamp environment, use bog soil or make a base of sand, peat, and gravel in equal parts about 2 in. (5 cm) deep. Place a pan of water on a gentle slope of earth to make it easy for animals to climb in and out. Mosses, ferns, Venus flytraps, and pitcher plants can be placed in the container. Set the mosses in shallow soil and the other plants in deeper soil. To make an attractive display, place taller plants in the back and on the sides. Avoid overcrowding, but arrange everything so that no bare earth shows. After planting, sprinkle the terrarium with water. A glass top will help this terrarium maintain its own water cycle. Frogs, newts, baby alligators, tadpoles, salamanders, and turtles will live in this moist, marshy habitat if they are limited in number and type. Most of these animals will prefer live food such as insects, mealworms, caterpillars, worms, moths, and slugs.

c. *Desert Environment.* To create a desert environment, build a base with 2 in. (5 cm) of sand. Add rocks and a small dish of water. Plant desert plants such as cactus. Small desert snakes, lizards, and horned toads can be kept in this habitat. (Note: Desert plants decay from too much water, and molds might grow.)

After a terrarium is established, students can test the influence of changes in light or temperature on the environment. For example, they might turn it partway around for a few days to see what happens to the plants and animals. They might also try setting it under a 60-watt light all night for several weeks to see what happens.

242   Interactions

Generalization I. Plants are adapted to their environment for survival. Various structures of plants operate in special ways that keep the plants alive and growing.

> *Contributing Idea A.* Roots anchor plants and hold the soil in place.

Observing the anchoring power of roots. Have students pull up several different kinds of weeds from a lot near the school. Note and discuss the root structures of those with the strongest anchorage. Now find the same kind of weed growing in both a damp place and a dry place, noting the root structure and anchorage power of the weed in each place. If possible, obtain corn plants for observing their anchoring root systems. (Corn has *prop roots* that extend from the stem above the ground to the soil.) Students can look for other plants with **01 Aa Bb Ca**

prop root systems: mangrove trees grow in saltwater swamps and support the tree from both its trunk, and its branches; banyan trees grow in the tropics and have very visible prop root systems.

Generalizing that roots hold the plant in the soil and keep the soil from washing away. Grow some grass in moist soil on a board, in a shallow baking pan, or in a sand table. After the grass has grown to approximately ½ in. (1.5 cm) in height, clip the blades so that only the roots remain. Prepare a second pan with identical soil, but without grass. Slightly tilt the pans over a sink, and sprinkle water on them. Make comparisons to see which pan best retains the soil. Draw inferences about local surroundings where the soil is easily washed away during storms. **02 Fa**

> *Contributing Idea B.* Roots absorb water and dissolved substances from the soil.

Observing the importance of roots to plants. Obtain two identical leafy plants. Cut the roots from one and leave them on the other. Replant both, and observe their growth at daily intervals. Students will realize that roots provide an essential function for the growth of a plant. **03 Aa**

Observing that roots are the primary means by which a plant absorbs water. Obtain two closely matched plants. Water the soil of one normally, and keep track of how much water is used. Using the same **04 Aa Ec**

amount of water, water only the leaves and stem of the second plant. To prevent the water from dripping onto the soil, waterproof the pot opening by carefully wrapping aluminum foil or plastic wrap around the base of the plant. Let the foil extend over the sides of the pot. A tray underneath the pot can collect any runoff. Within a few days, observable results will be fairly conclusive: The plant whose leaves and stem were watered will be drooping; the soil-watered plant will be thriving.

Observing the path of the conduction **05** **tubes through a root.** Stand a carrot in **Aa** a glass of red-colored water. After two days, have students first cut the carrot crosswise to observe the colored tubes, then cut it again lengthwise to trace the path the red water has taken. It can be observed that the tubes go from the branch roots to the main root, then to the stem and leaves.

Generalizing that roots absorb dissolved **06** **substances, but not suspended solids.** **Ec** Insert three similar plants into test tubes **Fa** containing water, red ink, a suspension of congo red, respectively (Figure 242.06). After a few days, the plant with ink will have visibly absorbed the color, while the others will have absorbed only the water. This activity can be done with other solutions and suspensions (e.g., red dye, a solution, and tempera paint, a suspension). Students will be able to infer from several

tests that plants can absorb soluble materials but not nonsoluble materials.

Water   Ink   Red
                   Congo

Figure 242.06

Contributing Idea C. The stem is the part of the plant that supports other organs.

Comparing differences in stems. Let **07** students tour the school grounds or **Ca** neighborhood to see (1) if all plants have stems; (2) which portion of the plants are stems; and (3) what differences there are in the way stems grow and support appendages. They can observe that not all stems are rigid or upright (e.g., ivy, morning glory, water hyacinth, water lily), that some creep or twine, and that some that float on the surface of water are hollow and air-filled, while others beneath the surface are not (e.g., bladderwort).

Contributing Idea D. Stems conduct liquids and minerals from the roots to other organs.

Observing that stems transport liquids **08** **to the various parts of the plant.** Obtain **Aa** a white carnation and submerge its stem **Ca**

in water. While under water, cut off the end of the stem. (Holding it under water prevents air from entering and blocking the conducting tubes.) Place the carnation in a container half-filled with water with food coloring, vegetable dye, or washable ink. Set the container in sunlight for several hours. Observe the carnation at half-hour intervals. Students will see that the petals become colored and infer that the colored water rose up the stem through the conducting tubes. Several variations can be used as supplementary activities.

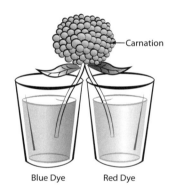

Figure 242.08

a. White lily or aster stems can be used in place of carnation stems to show the transportation of a colored liquid to the flower. Celery stalks with leaves attached can be used to show the transportation to the leaves.

b. Have the teacher split the stem of a white carnation into two or more parts with a razor blade. Extend the split several inches up

the stem and wrap the stem with tape above the cut to avoid further splitting. Gently spread the sections out and place them into containers, each filled with differently colored water (see Figure 242.08). Observe the plant at half-hour intervals.

Experimenting to see if stems carry materials dissolved in water. Obtain three healthy stalks of celery. Place one in a jar of sand and water, the second in a jar of sand and sugar water, and the third in sand and colored water. From observations over several hours, students will see that in the third stalk, dissolved material had been transported through the stem. By cutting the first and second stalks crosswise, students can taste the liquid droplets that form at the cut to see if any dissolved sugar was transported through the stem. **Caution: Students should not eat or drink any substances unless permitted to do so by the teacher.** Jar number 1 is used as a control to make sure that the dissolved sugar in jar number 2 was transported by the stem and not manufactured by the plant.

Contributing Idea E. Some leaves trap insects.

Observing leaves that trap insects. Many insect-trapping plants can be obtained from local nurseries. A hand lens is useful in observing them. Insect-trapping plants secrete liquids that dissolve

09 Ec

10 Aa

the soft body parts of insects and small animals and absorb them as food. These plants, however, also manufacture food in sunlight as other plants do.

  a. *Sundew Plant.* Students can see that the leaves of the sundew plant are covered with hundreds of tiny red hairs that look like pins on a pincushion. They can note that a drop of red liquid forms at the tip of each hair. Have them touch a droplet with a toothpick. The droplets are sticky and can be pulled away like a piece of gum. Students can infer how the sticky droplets capture small insects.

  b. *Butterworts.* Students can observe that the oval yellow leaves of butterworts are covered with a shiny, sticky substance that traps small insects. These leaves generally lie flat on the ground and the edges of the leaf roll inward to hold the victim.

  c. *Pitcher Plant.* This plant resembles a pitcher. Students can see that it retains rainwater and that many bristly hairs surround the mouth of the pitcher. They can note that these hairs all point down and inward. From these observations they can infer that insects attracted into the flower cannot leave and are drowned.

  d. *Venus Flytrap.* The leaves of this plant have two lobes, each fringed with bristles. On the surface of each lobe, students will see three hairs. A touch of a hair with a pencil point or toothpick will close the two lobes like a trap. Students can feed small insects to this plant.

Contributing Idea F. Reproduction in flowering plants is accomplished through pollination.

Generalizing that both male and female organs are necessary for reproduction in flowering plants. Let students examine the different parts of a simple, complete flower (one that has both female and male organs) such as the tulip or Easter lily. They can easily find the male organs (*stamens*) that produce a powdery substance (*pollen*). Let them touch the large tops of the stamen (*anthers*) and feel the yellow dust that sticks to their fingers. Let them blow the pollen from their fingers. Have them move the stamens of the flower with a pencil tip, and they will see the female organ (*pistil*), which looks like a slender vase. Touch the top of this organ (*stigma*) and feel its sticky surface. Describe the shape of its lower part (*ovary*). After blowing pollen from their fingers and feeling the sticky stigma, students will be able to infer one way by which pollen can reach a stigma (by being windblown). They will also be able to infer that the sticky stigma is built to receive the pollen.

11 Bb Fa

Observing that pollen must fall upon the stigma of a pistil before seeds can form. Keep a flower under unpollinated conditions for control purposes. This can be done by putting plastic wrap around the pistil of a new bloom. After the flower has wilted and dried, let students compare it (especially the ovary section) with a pollinated flower from the same plant. Through dissection, they can compare the differences in the ovules and the surrounding area.

12 Aa

Pollinating flowers. Obtain a plant, such as a tomato plant, that has been growing indoors and is now flowering. Wrap a small amount of absorbent cotton around one end of a thin piece of stiff wire. Make sure the cotton is firmly wound and not as thick as a commercial cotton swab. Select a full flower, and gently separate two petals so that the cotton tip can be inserted. Gently move it within the flower, touching first the stamens, then the tip of the pistil. Students will see the transfer of the pollen to the stigma. Tell them that when a plant is pollinated within its own flower, it is said to be *self-pollinated.* Using a fresh cotton-tipped wire for each flower, let students continue this process with other flowers, leaving some flowers unpollinated as controls for later comparisons. On a different plant, use the same cotton-tipped wire to touch all the flowers. Students will realize that this type of pollination is different from the previous

13 Bb Ec Ga

type. Tell them that when pollen is moved from one flower to the stigma of another flower, it is said to be *cross-pollinated.* Experiment with each type of pollination. After four or five days (for most flowers), observe the flowers. Compare them with those that were not pollinated.

Generalizing that pollination can take place naturally with the aid of wind. An analogy can be made to the traveling of pollen by wind if students lightly dust some flour inside the petals of a flower, then blow on it. They can see where the dust travels and note that some dust sticks to the stigma of the flower (self-pollination) and that some sticks to the stigma of other flowers that are close by (cross-pollination).

14 Fa Fc

Collecting wind-borne pollen. Coat glass slides with petroleum jelly and suspend them in various locations outdoors. Each day, note the pollen and dust that accumulates on them. Different pollen that is collected can be compared under a low-power microscope. Slides can be fixed by adding a bit of crystal violet and aniline oil to the pollen and placing the slide over a flame until the pollen is deeply stained. Students can also sort the pollen by physical characteristics such as shape, size, or color.

15 Db Ge

Comparing flowers pollinated by animals with those pollinated by wind. Have students look at the flowers of

16 Ca

grasses, grains, and weeds to see if they are colorful or fragrant. Compare the pollen from these flowers with the pollen from more colorful flowers. Explain that flowers that depend upon wind to transfer pollen are not usually colorful or fragrant. Students can infer how differences in pollen grains and flower appearance are appropriate to the way they are pollinated.

> *Contributing Idea G.* Seeds are dispersed in various ways that contribute to a plant's survival.

Collecting seeds. Because of their wide dispersal, seeds can be collected from many locations.   **17 Ge**

   a. Dip a hand in a creek or stream to collect any seeds floating there.
   b. Scoop up a spoonful of mud from around a drainpipe or a low place in a garden where seeds have been washed.
   c. Stroll across a field or lot, dragging a woolen cloth. Examine the cloth for seeds that have collected on it. The cloth can be compared to animal fur or clothing.

Collected seeds can be stored in cellophane bags or envelopes labeled with data concerning the location, description of the seeds, and the date they were collected.

Examining seeds by the way they are dispersed. Collect various kinds of seed   **18 Aa**
cases or capsules. Examine the capsules to determine methods of seed dispersal (e.g., columbines have a pitcherlike mouth at the top from which seeds are poured into the wind; poppies have tiny holes at the top with trap doors beneath them so that seeds are slowly scattered as the capsule shakes in the breeze; witch hazel, violet, touch-me-not, and jewelweed have capsules that swell and burst to pop their seeds in many directions). Depending upon locale, various seeds can be obtained and observed.

   a. Students can collect branches of Scotch broom that still carry pods. Allow the branches to dry. Listen and watch for signs of seed dispersal. Examine the pods before and after drying.
   b. Place wild geraniums or witch hazel fruits in a covered jar with moist cotton. Place others of the same kind in a dry, uncovered jar. Observe both for several days to see what happens as the fruits dry.
   c. Obtain two mature blossoms of poinsettia, thistle, and dandelion. Watch them as they dry and go to seed. Have one student blow on a dry dandelion head, and observe how the seeds travel.
   d. Collect pinecones. Heat them in an oven or set them in a warm place for several days. Students can observe the seeds as they pop out.

Generalization II. Animals are adapted to their environment for survival. Various structures of animals operate in special ways that keep the animal alive and growing.

Contributing Idea A. Animals are adapted to enable them to obtain and eat food in their environment.

Observing that the physical characteristics and actions of fish are related to their acquisition of food. Prepare an aquarium containing fish that feed in different ways (e.g., goldfish, catfish, and sunfish). Observe the feeding habits as commercial food is dropped into the container. Students will see that sunfish dart to the surface and snatch the food, goldfish take it more or less in the middle of the container, and catfish wait until it settles on the bottom. Let students describe the physical characteristics of the fish to see how they relate to each behavior (e.g., catfish have mouths on their undersides and long feelers for searching out food in crevices at the bottom of an aquarium). Research might be done on other fish to see how their characteristics enable them to obtain food.

19 Aa Bd

Observing that the physical characteristics of birds are related to the food that they eat. Select pictures of birds on the basis of their bills and/or ft.. Discuss how certain characteristics seem specialized for gathering and eating certain foods. The illustrations in Figure 242.20 will be

20 Aa Db

helpful in identifying the relationships. On the basis of bills and ft., students can tentatively sort bird pictures into such categories as seed-eaters, insect-eaters, and meat-eaters. Let them check their classifications by researching using various bird books.

Observing that the physical characteristics and actions of animals are related to their acquisition of food. Let students look at numerous pictures of animals and discuss the types of food each eats and whether or not each has a physical characteristic or ability that enables it to capture and eat the food. For example, meat-eaters and plant-eaters have teeth specially adapted for the type of food each eats; the long neck of the giraffe enables it to feed on high leaves in trees; the sacks on the legs of bees enable them to carry pollen to their hives.

21 Aa

Contributing Idea B. Animals are adapted to enable them to obtain oxygen from their environment.

Observing respiration in an earthworm. Obtain four identical jars. Leave two empty and fill two with water. Select four similarly sized earthworms, placing one in each jar. Set one empty and one full jar on a shelf out of direct sunlight where they will not be disturbed. Place the others in a refrigerator (not the freezer). After one day, take the earthworms from all the jars, and put them on a sheet of waxed paper. Students can look for pulses of

22 Aa Ec Fa

a. Bill is like a long, pointed nail—useful for digging into tough tree bark to pull out insects (woodpecker).

b. Bill is small, short, and pointed—useful for cracking open seeds and nuts (canary, meadowlark).

c. Bill is like a sharp hook—useful for tearing meat from the bones of animals (owl, hawk).

d. Bill is like a shovel—useful for scooping plants and small fish from water (duck, swan).

e. Feet have long toes, two forward and two backward—useful for holding onto vertical tree trunk (woodpecker).

f. Feet have short, curved toes, three forward and one backward—useful for perching on round tree limbs (robin, swallow).

g. Feet have sharp talons—useful for grasping and holding animals securely (eagle, hawk).

h. Feet are webbed—useful for paddling in water and walking on mud (duck, pelican).

Figure 242.20

blood in the large blood vessel on top of each worm's body. Count the number of pulses per minute for each and compare the rates. Explain that an earthworm has no special organ for breathing. It obtains the oxygen it needs directly through its skin to its blood. Because of this, it can live under water. If the skin becomes dry, gases cannot pass through it, and the animal will die. Since the worms from the refrigerator can be seen to breathe more slowly than the others and are less active, students can realize that greater activity requires more oxygen.

Observing respiration in an insect. **23 Aa Fa** Leave a jar of water outside when mosquitoes are plentiful. When students see little wigglers hanging from the surface or moving through the water, put a piece of screen across the top of the jar. Count the number of times per minute a wiggler comes to the surface for air and the number of seconds a wiggler will stay down without coming up for more air. Explain that a mosquito wiggler hangs head down in the water with an air tube just above the surface. Use a hand lens to find the openings along the sides of a large insect's body. Explain that these openings lead to tubes that go into the insect's body. Oxygen from the air slowly enters the body through these tubes. This method of taking oxygen is a characteristic among insects.

Observing respiration in a fish. Have **24 Aa Fa** students observe a fish in an aquarium.

Count how many times a minute it opens and closes its mouth, then count how many times the flap or gill covers just behind its head move per minute. Students will discover a relationship between the movements. (When the mouth is open, the gill covers are closed and vice versa.) Explain that a fish breathes by means of gills. As water enters the fish's mouth and passes over the gills, oxygen that is dissolved in water passes through thin tissues inside and enters the fish's blood. The water leaves the body by way of the gill cover. Now fill a beaker with water and boil it for five minutes to remove any dissolved air. When it cools to room temperature, place a fish into the water and observe. Return the fish quickly to the aquarium so that it does not die from lack of oxygen. Students will realize that fish depend upon oxygen in the water in order to live.

Observing respiration in an amphibian. **25 Aa Fa** Let students observe a frog in a terrarium. An indication that it breathes can be seen by the open nostril vents near its snout and the movement of its throat. Explain that a frog breathes by "swallowing" air. (The floor of its mouth raises and lowers, causing a pumping effect.) Frogs also absorb a good deal of oxygen through their skin. Count the number of times a minute its throat moves in and out, then hold the frog securely by its hind legs and submerge it completely in a jar of water for a minute. Students will see that the nostril vents close and the throat movements stop. **Caution: Do not hold the frog under water longer than one minute, for it will drown.** Tell students that frogs also have the ability to breathe through their skins.

Observing respiration in people. Have students exercise and note the effect it has upon their rate of breathing. They can determine the capacity of their lungs by filling a large jug with water, holding a hand over the mouth, and inverting it in a pan of water. Insert a plastic or rubber tube into the jug. Use a clean piece of glass tubing as a mouthpiece for each student. Have them take turns exhaling fully into the jug and measure the amount of water forced out each time by refilling the jug. Compare capacities to the rates of breathing before and after exercising.

**26
Aa
Fa**

243   Theory

Generalization I. According to Darwin's theory, evolution includes a process whereby plants and animals are naturally selected from generation to generation, producing descendants with different characteristics.

Contributing Idea A. Some plants and animals have been naturally selected and retain camouflage characteristics.

Playing a simulation game that depicts change in plants in terms of camouflage

**01
Fa
Fc**

characteristics. Divide the class into groups, five children in each. For each group, provide one hundred colored dots (10 dots of each of 10 different colors) that have been punched from construction paper with a large-hole hand punch. Give each group 1 yd.^{2} (1 m^2) of multicolored, patterned material. If possible, obtain differently colored yardages. Tell students that the material simulates an environment and that the dots represent seeds in the environment. Have them sprinkle the dots throughout the environment, making sure no dots are on top of other dots. Have students pretend they are birds that eat seeds in this environment. Let each student hunt and remove 10 seeds (dots). Take the remaining 50 seeds and place them on a sheet of paper in a long line. Tell them that each seed grows and produces another seed of its own kind; thus, they should place a new dot of the same color beside each of the 50 dots. Explain that this simulates the reproduction of certain plants, while those that were eaten could not reproduce. Now spread the new set of 100 dots into the environment as before, and repeat the simulation two more times. When finished, the dots can be glued to graph paper to produce a histogram of the results. Compare the histograms made by the different groups. Students will realize that the change in each seed population was due primarily to the natural selection of the "birds"; thus, those seeds that the "birds" did not see remained in the environment and reproduced their own kind. Since each group started with identical seed populations, differences in the end results can be attributed to differences in the coloration of the environment. Tell students that many other factors are also involved in such natural selection (e.g., the shape of the object, its fragrance, texture, or taste). Play the game again using colored dots of different shapes. Similarly, the game can be played by comparing the dots to whole plants that might be eaten by animals.

Playing a simulation game that depicts change in animals in terms of camouflage characteristics. 02 Fa Fc Obtain five hundred uncolored wooden cocktail toothpicks. Cut them in half. Select a vacant lot or lawn area and determine its general color (e.g., green, brown, yellow). Paint half the toothpicks so that they match the color of the lot. They can be painted by placing them into a can or jar of tempera paint, then setting them out to dry. When dry, use black ink to draw a stripe around the middle of 250 of the painted and 250 of the unpainted ones. Thoroughly mix all the toothpicks together, then scatter them thinly and evenly over an area of the lot before students come to school. When they arrive, tell them that they are to play the part of birds that will feed on worms in a lot. At a time signal, let the "birds" collect as many "worms" as they can by picking up each between a thumb and

forefinger and placing it in an envelope before picking up another one (analogous to a bird picking up a worm in its beak and placing it in its crop). After 10 minutes, return to the classroom and make a histogram of the results. Discuss aspects of the coloration (color to match a background and effect of stripe) as camouflage advantages to "worms." Have students think of other animals that match the background of their environment. Next, discuss what the appearance of the next generation of worms would be. Students will realize that those that remain will reproduce their own kind, while those that were eaten will not; thus, subsequent populations retain those characteristics beneficial to survival. Some students might be interested in researching information on the English oak moth whose color changed to match its background through natural selection.

> *Contributing Idea B.* Some plants and animals have been naturally selected and retain advertising characteristics.

Playing a simulation game that depicts change in plants in terms of advertising characteristics. 03 Fa Fc Play the game described in entry 243.01, but tell students that the dots represent flowers in an environment and that the students represent bees or other insects that fly to flowers to obtain nectar. To keep track of the flowers they fly to, have them each remove 10 dots. The removed dots now represent flowers that have been pollinated, while those left in the environment have not. Shake the remaining dots into a bowl, set the 50 pollinated ones in a line, and allow them to reproduce their own kind by matching each with an identical color. Return the new set of 100 dots to the environment, and repeat the simulation two more times. When finished, the dots can be pasted to graph paper to show the results. Students will realize that in this game, plants survive and reproduce because they attract animals who aid in their pollination. Explain that scientists believe that all organisms are naturally selected in similar ways, thus bringing changes in kind over time.

Experimenting to see if animals are attracted to particular flower colors. **04 Ec** Prepare a 16 in. × 16 in. (40 cm × 40 cm) board. Make 15 4 in. (10 cm) squares in different shades of gray from white to black and one 4 in. (10 cm) square of a primary or secondary color (e.g., red). Randomly arrange the squares on the board, and then place small paper cups on each square. In the cup on the colored square, place some sugar water. Be careful not to spill any on the squares. Set the board near a place where bees are gathering nectar. When (and if) the bees consistently come to the cup of sugar water on the colored square, remove the cups, rearrange the squares and replace all the cups except the one with sugar water in it. In its place on

the colored square, set an empty cup. Students will realize that if the bees return to the colored square, they are attracted by the square's color. From this they can infer that the color is one that the bees can see. By repeating this test using other colored squares, they will find that bees respond to yellow, yellow-green, blue, and violet. Following this activity, they can observe bees and note to what color flowers they naturally travel.

Researching information on advertising coloration in animals. **05 Bd** Some birds flash previously hidden colors (e.g., white tail feathers) as they take flight. Such colors probably serve for species recognition. Certain moths, lizards, butterflies, and frogs flash colors that apparently confuse a predator. These animals are colorless and difficult to see when at rest, but when they move, they expose bright body parts that apparently catch the eye of a predator who then seeks a brilliantly colored animal. Have students research information concerning the advertising colors of various animals: the English robin's orange-red breast that helps to keep robins in separate territories; the yellow-shafted flicker's black stripe by its beak that helps females identify their mates; the fire-bellied toad with its marblelike red and black underside that warns predators that it is distasteful and poisonous; the red mark on the herring gull beak that aids the chick in obtaining food; the bright eyespots on the underwing of the peacock butterfly that frightens predators. Have students seek examples of butterflies, moths, and fish that have eyespots on them. Discuss why these animals survive and reproduce while others might not.

Generalization II. According to Darwin's theory, evolution has been going on so long that it has produced all the groups and kinds of plants and animals now living, as well as others that have become extinct.

> *Contributing Idea A.* Fossils are indications of plants and animals that have lived in the past.

Making impressions of animal tracks or leaf forms. 06 Bd Fc Tell students that animals, such as dinosaurs, once walked on Earth but are now extinct. Explain that in addition to finding fossils of their bones, fossils of their footprints are sometimes found. Let students try to "capture" footprints of animals by setting up tracking areas with smooth patches of mud, sand, or flour dust. Check these areas each morning to see what animals traveled across them. Students can try to identify the animal by its footprint. If a good print has been left in the mud, place a cardboard hoop or wooden frame around it, pour plaster of paris into the print and the hoop. When it hardens, students will have a fossil-like image of the footprint. Tell them that footprints of prehistoric animals

remain today because their impressions were filled with materials that hardened like the plaster. Some students might be interested in researching information on dinosaurs. Similarly, leaves can be pressed into clay and plaster poured into the mold to represent how fossil impressions of leaves have been preserved.

> *Contributing Idea B.* Some animals are on the verge of becoming extinct.

Researching endangered species. 07 Bd Have students use reference books to find out what animals have become extinct since the turn of the century and which ones are on the endangered list. Let them discuss the reasons for the extinctions.

244 Applications

Generalization. The physical characteristics of plants and animals can be put to use.

> *Contributing Idea A.* People use plants for food, shelter, medicine, and clothing materials.

Tasting edible roots. 01 Ae Have students compare the appearances of a carrot, radish, turnip, beet, and sweet potato to other roots such as those of grasses, geraniums, and nasturtiums. Let them taste the edible roots, describe the flavors and textures, then discuss the importance of such roots to people. **Caution: Discuss with students the dangers of tasting unknown plants.**

Tasting edible flowers. Bring a cauli- **02** flower to class and let students study it **Ae** to see if it has all the characteristics of a flower. Let them taste this flower and other flowers that are used as food (e.g., artichoke, broccoli, clove).

Researching information about the use **03** **of flowers.** Have students read about the **Bd** cultural factors behind the bouquet, cor- sage, lei, funeral wreath, and the 50 state flowers.

Researching how people use stems. **04** Have students check reference books to **Bd** find out how people have used stems. Students will find that stems of many plants have been used as a source of heat through burning or as lumber for building shelters. In addition, useful products have been made from the protective barks. For example, nearly all cork is obtained from the bark of the cork-oak tree. The bark of the hemlock tree is used in tanning leather. Extracts from the bark of some trees are used for flavoring: sassafras pro- vides flavoring in root beer; cinnamon is made from a powdered bark from a tree that grows in India and Malaysia. Some barks are used in medicines: quinine is obtained from the bark of the cinchona tree that grows wild in South America.

Contributing Idea B. Some animals can be domesticated or trained.

Identifying the characteristics of **05** **domesticated animals.** Have students **Ba** **Bd**

make up lists of animals that are used by people for food, work, or companionship. Let them describe the characteristics needed by an animal to be placed into one of these categories. Compare the charac- teristics with those of wild animals. Some students might be interested in research- ing information on breeding dogs, cats, poultry, and so on to attain animals with highly specialized characteristics. Others might research the products they produce (e.g., wool, leather, eggs, ivory).

Discussing how animals are trained. **06** Let students discuss how dogs and horses **Ba** are trained for obedience and perfor- mance. Explain that other animals can also be trained (e.g., lions, tigers, and ele- phants for circuses). Invite dog or horse trainers to class to tell how such animals are taught.

Training earthworms. Obtain a tray **07** and build a T-maze in it with walls at **Ec** least 3 in. (8 cm) high (Figure 244.07a, p. 216). The first 4 in. (10 cm) of the T should contain a shelter where the worm can rest before each test. The shelter can be made from a folded piece of cardboard (Figure 244.07b, p. 216). To start a train- ing trial, remove the shelter and place it at the end of arm C. The light entering the maze will cause the worm to move. A clock with a second hand can time how long it takes the worm to find the shelter. Keep a record for each trial. The times can be charted on a histogram. (Note: It can take as many as 50 trials to train an earthworm. After a worm is trained, various experiments can be done using the T-maze.)

(a)

Cardboard Shelter

4 in. (10 cm)

(b)

Figure 244.07

a. When worms are trained to a particular side of the shelter, isolate the faster learners from the slower learners. Place them in separate containers of rich soil. Let them breed and test the offspring of the two groups to see if faster learning is inherited.

b. Put a trained worm in the shelter at A, then soak a piece of blotter paper in vinegar and place it at the end of arm C. Lift the shelter and place it at the end of arm

B. Observe whether or not the worm seems to "smell" the vinegar before actually touching the blotter, and determine how long it takes the worm to learn the new location of the shelter. Weaker vinegar (diluted in water) can be tried to see if the worm can tell the difference between a mild aroma and a stronger one. Similarly, try soaking blotter paper with other solutions: salt solution (1 oz. or 30 g of salt to 3 oz. or 90 g of water) or pine needle solution (mash up pine needles in water).

c. Put a 3 in. (8 cm) length of sandpaper, cotton, or crushed ice in arm C to see if a trained worm will travel over the various surfaces to get to the shelter.

Training fish. Place a T-maze of plastic or sheet aluminum into an aquarium of goldfish. Place food in one arm of the T while flashing a light. Do this for 15 minutes each day. In about three weeks the fish will be trained to respond to the light when hungry. Other fish can be trained and students can compare the rates of learning of each kind. Some students might be interested in reading about experiments in training chickens. **08 Ec**

Training small mammals. Prepare complex mazes. The walls should be at least 6 in. (16 cm) high and the paths 4 in. **09 Ec**

(10 cm) across. When a white rat or other small mammal is hungry, lead it through the maze by hand to where you place the food. Do this several times, but do not let the animal eat. Now let the animal enter the maze and close the opening. Students can record each day the number of trials the animal makes before finding the food. Reward the animal with extra food and petting each time it succeeds. Compare young animals' rates to older animals' rates or the rate of an animal fed a good diet to one that was fed a poor diet.

300–399
Energy

310 Motion

311 Characteristics

Generalization I. Motion has identifiable characteristics.

Contributing Idea A. Motion is the act of changing place or position.

Defining motion. Have students find evidence of motion they can see inside and outside the classroom. Have them then give examples that are not motion (e.g., thinking, static objects). From the examples, help students see that motion is always a coming or going from place to place. Let them use magazines to locate and collect pictures depicting motion. The pictures can be arranged on bulletin boards or in scrapbooks.
01 Bb Ga

Identifying distance and time as two characteristics of motion. Have students list examples of motion that clearly involve moving from place to place. Ask them if motion is possible without distance being involved. (An object cannot go from one place to another if there is no distance between the two places.) Ask if an object can travel a distance without time being involved. (No matter what is moved, the journey takes some time.) Give examples of motion that clearly involve distance and time, then ask students to find other examples (e.g., students travel some distance from school to home, and it might take 10 minutes, 20 minutes, or more to travel
02 Bc Ga

the distance). Identify in each example the parts that indicate that motion covers distance and also takes time.

Measuring motion in terms of distance and time. Let students work mathematical problems involving motion such as those given below.
03 Bb Cd Ch

    a. If you ride a bicycle 10 miles in two hours, how far can you travel in one hour (or at what rate does the bicycle move per hour)?

    b. If a man runs 100 yd. in 10 seconds, what is his average speed (or rate of distance covered per second)?

    c. If an airplane travels 600 miles in one hour, what is its speed (or rate of distance covered per minute)?

Tell students that rates of motion are called *speed*. Explain that speed involves distance and time. To figure the average speed of a moving object, one must find the rate at which it travels a known distance in a known time. For each problem, the average speed is obtained by dividing the total distance by the total time:

$$\left(\text{Speed} = \frac{\text{Distance}}{\text{Time}} \right)$$

Contributing Idea B. The direction of motion is a straight line unless acted upon by other forces.

Observing straight-line motion. While **04** students observe, place a checker on a **Aa** table and flick it with a finger, roll a toy **Bb** car in a straight line across the floor, and drop a ball from a table. Ask if each of the objects moved in a straight line. Repeat the experiences if necessary. Students will realize that each object moved in a straight line. Tell them that scientists call such motion regular straight-line motion. Recall other examples for the students: a bicycle continues moving in the same straight line if the front wheel is not turned, people lurch forward in a bus, train, or car when it stops quickly.

Observing influences on straight-line **05** **motion.** Roll marbles across a smooth, **Aa** level surface. Students will see that the **Ba** marbles always go in straight lines. Now **Ca** let them roll a single marble, and blow on it from the side as it travels. Discuss how the motion was changed. Next, hold a strip of thin cardboard on edge and curve it slightly. Roll a single marble into the curve of the strip, and discuss any change in its direction. Compare the effect of the cardboard to the blowing. Students will begin to realize that all moving objects travel in a straight line (e.g., bowling balls, hockey pucks, raindrops) unless influenced by other forces.

Observing periodic motion. Have stu- **06** dents work in small groups. Let each **Bb** group tie a string around a small weight **Ch** such as a fish weight, metal washer, or **Ec**

nut. Suspend the string from a stand or the edge of a desk. Pull the weight back, and let it go. Explain that the apparatus is a simple *pendulum*. Now use stopwatches or clocks with second hands to determine how long it takes for each pendulum to swing forward and back. After students have determined the time, tell them that one forward and back motion is called a period and that such repetitive motion is called periodic motion. (Grandfather clocks have pendulums with one-second periods.) Students might be asked to think of other examples of periodic motion (e.g., vibrating objects such as tuning forks, some clocks, swings on playgrounds, metronomes, some lawn sprinklers).

Measuring periodic motion. Suspend a **07** large metal washer from a 1 ft. (30 cm) **Bc** length of thread and determine the time **Ch** of its period with a stopwatch or a clock **Ec** with a second hand. One method for doing this is to count the number of periods (back and forth swings) in 30 seconds, then divide the number of periods by the number of seconds. For example, if one counts 60 periods in 30 seconds, then 60 ÷ 30 = 2 periods per second or 1 period per ½ second. Now provide students with rulers, scissors, more thread, and identical washers so that they can experiment to see what they must do to a pendulum to make its period twice as long as it was. Students might try varying the weight while keeping the length of the thread constant, or try varying the length of the thread while keeping the weight constant. Results can be recorded on Table 311.07. Students will find that the weight does not influence the period, but the length of thread does. If some students would like to see what effect the starting position of the weight has, let them rule a sheet of cardboard with horizontal lines 1 in. (1 cm) apart and stand the cardboard behind the pendulum. The weight can then be lifted to the 6 in. (12 cm) mark and released. (The height of the upward swing can be recorded as well as the period.) Repeat by starting the swing from different heights. (The height of the swing will have no effect on the period, however, the higher the starting point, the higher the swing.)

Observing rotary motion. Turn a bicy- **08** cle upside down and spin the front wheel. **Aa** Tell students that a continuous spinning **Bb** motion traveling in the same direction is called rotary motion. You might explain that rotary motion is similar to periodic

motion in repeating itself, but different because there is no change in the direction of rotary motion unless force is applied to change it. Ask students to think of other examples of rotary motion (e.g., rotary lawn sprinklers, Ferris wheels, merry-go-rounds, minute and second hands on clocks).

Measuring rotary motion. Turn a bicy- **09** cle upside down, mark one tire with chalk **Cd** or tie a white cloth around the wheel. **Ch** Spin the wheel, and let students count the number of complete turns in one second. Now have them obtain a smaller wheel, such as one on a wagon, and determine its speed or rotation. For both wheels, students can find out roughly how far the wheel would roll along the ground in one minute by measuring the distance around the outside of the wheel and multiplying by the speed. (Note: In actuality, the wheel will not rotate at the same speed when rolled on the ground due to other factors such as friction.)

Table 311.07. Testing the Influence of Length and Weight Upon a Pendulum

	Length	Weight	Number of Swings			
			Trial 1	Trial 2	Trial 3	Average
TEST 1	6 in. (12 cm)	1 washer				
	6 in. (12 cm)	2 washers				
	6 in. (12 cm)	3 washers				
TEST 2	8 in. (16 cm)	1 washer				
	10 in. (18 cm)	1 washer				
	12 in. (24 cm)	1 washer				

Contributing Idea C. Motion travels at a uniform rate of speed unless acted upon by other forces.

Graphing uniform rates of motion. **10 Bf Fb** Give students the following problems and tables of data. Help them transfer the data to a graph form, labeling the horizontal and vertical dimensions as shown. The result will be a straight-line graph that depicts a uniform rate of speed. The questions at the end of each problem will help students in reading graphs and extrapolating information from them.

a. Mr. Adams measured how long it took to fill a cup from the water tap in his sink. He then measured how long it took to fill a pint bottle and then a quart bottle (Table 311.10a). Make a graph of Mr. Adams's measurements and tell how long it would take water from the tap to fill a gallon-size container (Graph 311.10a)

b. Mr. Adams left home at 9 a.m. After he had been driving for one hour, he looked at his odometer and found that he had gone 50 miles. At noon he had traveled 150 miles, and at 2 p.m. he had gone 250 miles (Table 311.10b). Graph Mr. Adams's trip (Graph 311.10b). How far had he gone by 11 a.m.? What time was it when he had traveled 200 miles? If he kept traveling at the same rate of speed, what time would it be

Table 311.10a. Measuring the Flow of Water from Mr. Adams's Tap

Volume of Water	Time in Minutes	Volume in Pints
1 cup	¼	½
1 pint	½	1
1 quart	1	2
1 gallon	?	8

MEASURING THE FLOW OF WATER FROM MR. ADAMS'S TAP

Graph 311.10a

Table 311.10b. Mr. Adams's Trip

Time of Day	Distance in Miles
9 p.m.	0
10 a.m.	50
11 a.m.	?
Noon	150
1 p.m.	?
2 p.m.	250

MR. ADAM'S TRIP

Graph 311.10b

when he traveled 400 miles and how far would he have gone by 5 p.m.?

Defining uniform motion. Let students determine the average speed of vehicles in each of the mathematical problems given below.

11
Bb
Cd
Ch

a. Two speedboats, A and B, pass a rock at the same time, then travel directly north for one hour to a bridge. Boat A travels 5 miles in the first 20 minutes, 5 in the second 10 minutes, 15 in the third 10 minutes and 5 in the final 20 minutes. Boat B travels 5 miles in the first 10 minutes, 10 in the next 20 minutes, 5 in the next 10 minutes, and 10 in the last 20 minutes (See Table 311.11a and Graph 311.11a.) What is the average speed per hour of each boat and how would you describe the motion of boat B?

b. Two cars travel a long, straight highway across a desert for two hours until they reach the outskirts of a city 60 miles away. Car A has

SPEEDBOATS UP A RIVER

Graph 311.11a

car trouble and travels 20 miles per hour for the first hour, 60 miles per hour for the next 30 minutes, and 20 miles per hour for the last 30 minutes. Car B travels at exactly 30 miles per hour throughout the trip. (See Table 311.11b and Graph 311.11b.) What is the average speed per hour of each car and how would you describe the motion of car B?

In each of the above problems, the speed of vehicle A is not steady during the entire trip, while the speed of vehicle B is steady. Tell students that although each

Table 311.11a. Speedboats up a River

Boat A			Boat B		
Time in Min.	Distance Miles	Cumulative Miles	Time in Min.	Distance Miles	Cumulative Miles
20	5	5	10	5	5
30	5	10	30	10	15
40	15	25	40	5	20
50	5	30	60	10	30

Table 311.11b. Trip Across a Desert

Car A			Car B		
Time in Min	Miles	Distance Cumulative Miles	Time in Min	Miles	Distance Cumulative Miles
60	20	20	60	30	30
90	30	50	120	30	60
120	10	60			

Graph 311.11b

will see that the marble will not travel as far. Let them try other materials to see how each affects the speed of the marble.

Figure 311.12

vehicle had the same average speed, only vehicle B had a motion in a straight line and at a steady speed. Such motion is so regular that it is called uniform motion.

Increasing and decreasing rates of speed. Make a trough by taping two rulers together. Support one end so that it is raised ½ in. (1 cm) above a flat surface. Roll a marble down the trough and allow it to coast to a stop (Figure 311.12). Ask students to tell when the marble accelerates (down the slope) and when it decelerates (throughout the coasting distance). Try tipping the trough to see if the marble will travel faster. Now set a strip of cloth or strips of sandpaper along the coasting route, and roll the marble again. Students

**12
Aa
Ba
Ec**

Contributing Idea D. Descriptions of motion depend upon the frame of reference used.

Observing motions from different positions. Several activities will help students realize that the position of the observer is important to know when describing motions because all motions are relative.

**13
Ca**

a. On the playground, have a student sit in a wagon and throw a ball 8–10 ft. (2–3 m) in the air and catch it. Have another student pull the wagon in a straight path and continue having the first student toss the ball. Be sure the velocity of the wagon is not changed too quickly. Let the person in the wagon describe whether or not the ball goes straight up and comes straight down. (The ball appears to go straight up and down.) Let someone watching tell if the ball went straight up and straight back down. (The ball appears to arc forward.) Discuss differences in descriptions based upon the positions of the observers.

b. Use chalk to draw a large circle on the playground. Have one student stand in the center of the circle while another sits in a wagon parked on the circle. As the wagon is pulled along the line of the circle, let the students in the wagon and center of the circle play catch. Students will find that the one in the wagon must aim slightly to the right or left of the student in the center, depending on which direction the wagon is moving, to hit the target. The student in the center must throw ahead of the wagon so that it gets there just as the student in the wagon does. Because of positions of observers, the ball appears to go in a curved path to the observers on the side, but in a straight path to the student in the moving wagon. Again, students can note that the interpretation of motion depends upon the position of the observers.

Generalization II. Motions can be organized.

Contributing Idea A. Motions can be seriated.

Seriating motions by rates of speed. Since all motions involve distance and time, students can time the movement of several moving objects along a given distance and order them from fastest to slowest. For example, runners, horses, or cars in a race can be timed and their times seriated. Similarly, the speed of the wind taken at the same hour, but on different days, can be ordered. The amount of water running from a faucet can be compared to the amount from other faucets.

14 Cd Ch Da

Seriating motions by distances traveled. Roll objects such as marbles, skates, or racing cars down an inclined plane. Start each object at the same position and measure the distance it travels. Order the objects by the distance each travels. Challenge students to find an object that will travel farther than any of the others.

15 Cd Da

Contributing Idea B. Motions can be classified.

Classifying motions. Have students list examples of forces that cause motion. They will find that any force—living or nonliving—that starts something moving can be classified as a push or pull on something else.

16 Bc Dc

312   Interactions

Generalization I. Motion is a form of energy produced by unbalanced forces.

Contributing Idea A. A force is any push or pull action upon an object.

Feeling forces that put objects into motion. Have students put the palms of their hands together and push. Next, have them hook two forefingers together and pull. In each case, let them describe what they felt. Using these activities, explain that a force always has a direction. (When hands are placed together and pushed, the direction of the right hand force was to the left and vice versa; when the hooked forefingers are pulled, forces are exerted in opposite directions.) Now have students move various objects by pushing or pulling. Tell them that words such as *push, pull, shove,* and *tug* are often used to describe what makes objects move, and scientists use the word *force* to mean all of these actions.

01
Ab
Bb

Feeling forces that stop the motion of objects. Have every student stretch a rubber band tightly between two fingers of one hand and push against the rubber band with one finger of the other hand. Discuss what they feel. (The rubber band will seem to push back on the finger.) Now have them push harder, and ask what they feel. (It will seem to push back harder.) Explain that objects stop

02
Ab

motion by pushing back, even though this is hard to see. Have one student push against a wall and compare what is felt to the pushing of the rubber band. Have the student place a postal scale with a square platform top on its side with the dial up and its base against the wall. Place a second scale so that its platform is flush against that of the first scale. Now push against the wall again by pushing on the second postal scale. If the student pushes with a force of 3 oz. (100 g) indicated on the scale, the scale against the wall will push back with an equal force. By testing, students will find that the two scales will always push back with an identical force. (If one pushes against a wall or other surface, it will push back with equal force, thus stopping the forward motion.) This activity can be repeated by attaching a spring scale to a wall and pulling on it with another spring scale.

Applying forces to start, stop, and change the direction of a motion. Have a student place a ball on a table and push it with a finger. While the ball is rolling, push it from the side. Next, place a finger in front of the ball and apply only enough force to stop it. Point out to students that a force was used in each case. One force put the ball in motion, another changed the direction of the motion, and a third stopped the motion. Let students tell how the application of forces to change the direction of an object's motion takes

03
Af

place in various sports (e.g., kickball, baseball, football, tennis).

Contributing Idea B. Gravity is a force that can produce motion.

Feeling the force of gravity. Have a student hold an empty bucket out in front of her. Let another student pour sand or water into the bucket slowly. Have the student holding the bucket describe what is felt. (As the material is added, the bucket feels heavier and is pulled downward.) Explain that the more material there is, the greater the pull of the Earth upon it. Tell students that the pull is called gravitational attraction.

04 Ab Bb

Using gravitational attraction to produce motion. Tie a thread to a pencil and suspend the pencil from a tabletop by holding the thread in place with a book. When the pencil hangs motionless, two equal and opposite forces are being exerted upon it. Now ask students if they can put the pencil into motion without directly acting upon it themselves (the pencil might be held in the air then released; the book might be lifted from the thread; the thread might be cut). Students will find that in each case the gravitational attraction caused the pencil to move by pulling it toward the center of the Earth. Explain that this is a natural force and not a human force. Repeat this activity using other objects such as wads of paper, paper clips, or fish weights. Students will find that the force exerted

05 Bd Ga

by gravity is a constant and affects all objects. Some children might be interested in looking up the English mathematician, astronomer, and philosopher, Sir Isaac Newton (1642–1727) to learn more about gravitational attraction.

Contributing Idea C. Magnetism is a force that can produce motion.

Using magnetism to produce motion. Slowly bring a magnet close to an iron nail and observe as the nail is pulled toward it. Now hold the magnet under a thin board or sheet of paper and place the nail above it. By moving the magnet, the nail is also moved. Next, bring two like poles of two magnets close together. The magnets will move apart. One magnet can be used to push the other across a tabletop.

06 Ga

Contributing Idea D. Muscular activity can produce motion.

Using muscular activity to produce motion. Have students take a sheet of paper, crumple it into a ball, put the ball on top of a desk, and snap it gently with a finger. Discuss what made the ball move, whether or not it moved in a straight line, and what stopped its movement. Discuss how to make the ball move faster. Put the paper ball on a desk again; this time, blow on it and repeat the previous discussions. Through these experiences, students will realize that motion of an object takes place only when some force is applied.

07 Ga

They will realize that in these cases, muscular activity produced the motion.

Using muscular and mechanical activity to produce motion. Clamp a hook screw into a hand drill. Attach a 1 ft. (30 cm) length of string to the hook, and tie a large nail to the free end. Steadily crank the drill and let students observe what happens to the nail. Discuss how the nail was put into motion, and describe the type and direction of the motion. Other mechanical apparatuses can be constructed and used to produce motion (e.g., cranks, levers, pulleys, gears, windmills, waterwheels). **08 Ga**

Generalization II. The mass of an object affects the object's motion as long as the speed remains constant.

> *Contributing Idea A.* Mass is a measure of the quantity of matter present in an object.

Observing that mass is independent of size. Obtain two balls of different sizes, such as a bowling ball and a beach ball. Let students push each with a finger and tell which is harder to move. They will find that the bowling ball is more difficult **09 Af Bc**

to move and that it has the greater mass or quantity of matter. Next, ask students to bring balls of different sizes and masses to school. A table like Table 312.09 can be used to record observations. (Note: The only time there will be any correlation between size and mass is when the objects being compared are of the same material.)

> *Contributing Idea B.* Mass affects motion as long as the speed remains constant.

Measuring the effect of mass upon motion. Obtain two small boxes of equal size and shape. Label one box A and the other B. Fill to equal levels, box A with sawdust and box B with sand. Let students take turns pushing each box with one finger and discussing which was easier to move. Have them decide whether it was the shape, size, or mass (quantity of matter) that made the difference. They will realize that the mass must be the factor because the shape and size of the boxes were similar. Now let them measure this difference by placing each box on a roller skate, tying the skate to a spring scale, and pulling each box by the scale. **10 Aa Cc**

Table 312.09. Comparing Masses

Objects	Harder to Move	Greater Mass	Greater Size
Beach ball			X
Bowling ball	X	X	
Shot put	X	X	
Basketball			X

Defining acceleration. Let a marble or racing car roll down a track from a height of 1 in. (2 cm), and have students observe to see when the marble moves the most slowly and most rapidly. Tell them that when the speed of a moving object is increasing, scientists say that it is *accelerating,* and when it is decreasing, it is *decelerating.* Have students tell when they accelerate and decelerate while riding a bicycle or other vehicle.

11 Aa Bb

Applying the same accelerating force to objects of different masses. Obtain two identical lengths of brass curtain rods and two wooden dowels that equal the rods in length, shape, and diameter. Use heavy string to tie a clothespin so that it is held open (Figure 312.12). Set it on its side on the floor, and place the two wooden dowels against it. Let students observe as you cut the thread and the dowels are put into motion. Repeat, letting students mark the spots where the dowels come to rest. Tell them that when something is put into motion, it is said to be *accelerated.* Next, replace the dowels with the two rods and repeat. (The brass rods will move a shorter distance.) Students will realize, since the materials were of the same length, shape, and diameter, and only different in mass, that when given the same force, the difference in mass must have caused the difference in acceleration. Now have them prepare the clothespin again but this time place a wooden dowel

12 Aa Bb Cd

against one side and a brass rod against the other. Let them predict what will happen. (The wooden dowel with the lesser mass will have the greater acceleration.)

Figure 312.12

Generalization III. Factors that influence motion can be controlled.

Contributing Idea A. Friction is a resistance to motion.

Observing that friction impedes motion. Saw a 1 in. × 1 in. (2 cm × 2 cm) piece of lumber into cubes. Cut 1 in. (2 cm) squares of different materials (e.g., rubber, foam plastic, sandpaper, cloth, aluminum foil, leather) and glue them carefully on the faces of the cubes. Be sure the edges are trimmed so that each face rests on only one kind of material at a time. Set a cube on a smooth board resting on a flat surface and gradually raise one end of the board until the cube starts to slide (Figure 312.13). Students can measure and record the height of the raised end when the cube begins to slide. Repeat several times to obtain an average. Then repeat with the different faces of the cube resting on the board surface. Discuss why

13 Af Bb Cd

there were differences among the different materials. Tell students that there is a resistance to motion when surfaces are rubbed together, and the resistance is a force called friction. Let them rub each material with a finger to feel the frictional differences in the surfaces.

Cube Covered With Different Surfaces

Figure 312.13

Testing the effect of different surfaces on motion. Glue or tape light tagboard to make a pair of identical boxes like those shown in Figure 312.14a. Place one box on top of a flat table, and have a student blow on it. Let another student push it with one finger. Now put 10 identical pieces of chalk, crayons, or marbles into the box and push again. Students will feel that they have to apply more force to make the box move when it is heavier. Have them work in pairs to connect two paper boxes with 1 yd. (1 m) length of string (Figure 312.14b). Let one box hang over the edge of a table and place three crayons in the box on the table. Students can see how many crayons must be placed in the hanging box before the box on the table

**14
Aa
Bc
Ec**

starts to move. Repeat this several times, then increase the number of objects in the box on the table and repeat again. (Note: Be sure the students are careful that they do not give an extra push to the hanging box when they put the crayons in it.) Now test different surfaces to see what effect they have on the motion of the box. For example, students can set a large sheet of sandpaper with the rough side up on top of the table, place the box on the sandpaper and find out how many crayons in the hanging box are needed to move it. Repeat the procedure for other surfaces, then record the results in Table 312.14 (p. 232), and discuss the findings.

Figure 312.14a

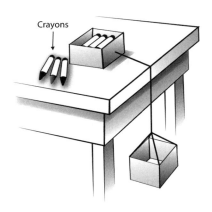

Crayons

Figure 312.14b

Table 312.14. Testing Different Surfaces

Surface	Number of Crayons in the Box								
	3	4	5	6	7	8	9	10	11
tabletop									
sandpaper									
waxed paper									
construction paper									
other surfaces									

Contributing Idea B. Friction can be reduced.

Reducing friction. Use a spring scale to pull a brick across the surface of a rough board. Record the force needed to pull the brick. Now rub the surface of the board with soap and repeat. Students will note a decrease in the friction. Next, have them arrange a row of round pencils or small dowels (approximately 6 in. or 15 cm long) on the board. Place the brick on the pencils and pull again. Some students may be interested in investigating early efforts in moving large stones to build pyramids, castles, cathedrals, and temples.

15 Cd

Comparing sliding and rolling motion. Place some blocks or fish weights in a shoebox, and pull it along a tabletop by a rubber band or spring scale. Now set the box on twenty-four parallel drinking straws and pull again. Students will realize that the difference in effort needed to pull the box is caused by substituting rolling motion for sliding motion. Similarly,

16 Ca Cd

they can compare sliding and rolling motion by

a. filling a tall, slender can with sand, setting it on a jar lid, and trying to spin it. Repeat after putting a circle of marbles in the lid.

b. rolling a skate down a playground slide, then fastening the wheels with tape so that they cannot turn and sending the skate down the slide again.

If possible, obtain samples of ball bearings to show how they are used to reduce friction.

Contributing Idea C. Circular motions tend to impel objects outward from a center of rotation.

Observing the effects of circular motion. Place a block of wood on a phonograph (record player) turntable. Turn on the phonograph at 78 rpm, and let students observe what happens to the block. (It flies off the turntable.) Now tie a string around the block and fasten the free end to the center post. Turn on the phonograph

17 Aa Bb

and observe again. (The block turns with the turntable.) Tell students that the force that keeps the object from flying off the turntable in a straight line is called *centripetal force*. Explain that in this experience the pull of the string on the block exemplifies the centripetal force. Try other objects of different masses and surfaces on the turntable. Students will find that different masses make no difference, although surface friction does in some cases. (Note: The tendency for objects to break away from centripetal force is sometimes called centrifugal force; however, the latter is really the inertial tendency of a body in motion to travel in a straight line and is not a force.)

Observing the tendency of objects to break away from circular motions. 18 Aa
Clamp a small hook screw into the bit of a hand drill. Attach two nails to the end of a ½ yd. (½ m) length of string hanging from the hook, then rotate the drill steadily (Figure 312.18a). Students will see that the nails have a tendency to fly straight outward from the center as the speed of rotation increases. Point out that the nails are held in place by the inward pull or centripetal force of the string. To show that liquids are similarly affected, punch several equidistant holes around the top of a can. Suspend the can from the hook screw with three strings (Figure 312.18b). Hold the can inside a larger container such as a bucket, filling the can

one-fourth full with water. As the rotation of the drill steadily increases, students will see the water rise in the can and fly out through the holes.

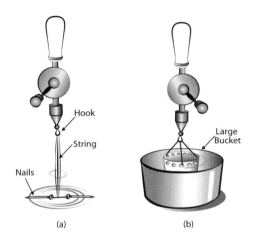

Hook

String

Nails

Large Bucket

(a)   (b)

Figure 312.18

Contributing Idea D. Some effects of circular motion can be controlled.

Observing how the inertial tendency of an object to travel in a straight line can be controlled. 19 Aa
Obtain three containers of similar diameter but of different depth (e.g., saucer, soup plate, deep bowl). Place a marble in the shallowest container and have a student hold the container in the palm of his hand and rotate it until the marble moves in a circle. Students will see that as the rotation increases, the marble moves faster and eventually leaves the container in a straight line. Repeat the activity with the other containers. Students will find that the deeper or more vertical the sides of the container, the better the confinement of the marble, even at increased

speed. Relate the effect on the marble to how people lean when they ride around curves (the tendency to continue traveling in a straight line). Tell how road engineers control this problem by banking the road around curves. If possible, find pictures of banked freeway curves designed to keep automobiles on the road at high speeds.

313   Theory

Generalization I. According to Newton's theory, a body at rest tends to remain at rest and a body in motion tends to remain in motion.

> *Contributing Idea A.* The inertia in an object at rest tends to keep the object from moving.

Observing the presence of inertia. Stack five or six blocks on a table and use a ruler to strike the lowest block abruptly. Students will see that the lowest block moves out from under the other blocks, and the remaining blocks do not move forward at all. Repeat striking each successive lowest block until only one remains. Tell students that the tendency of a body (blocks in the stack) to remain at rest is called inertia. (Note: Inertia is not a measurable quantity, but a property of matter.) Repeat by restacking the blocks and exerting a slow, steady push of the ruler against the bottom block. (The stack will move as a unit.) Students will realize that a slow, steady movement is not enough force to overcome the

**01
Aa
Bb**

small frictional force holding the blocks together. Now let them make stacks of five pennies on their desks. Set a sixth penny a short distance away and flick it with a finger against the stack. (The bottom penny will move out.) Encourage them to experiment with many kinds of materials that can be stacked. As a supplementary experience, obtain a rock or other object that weighs approximately 35 oz. (1 kg). Wrap a length of heavy string around it, and then attach ½ yd. (½ m) lengths of lighter string to the heavier string on two opposite sides of the object. Suspend the object from a hook by one of the lighter strings, and grasp the lower string firmly, pulling it with a quick jerk. (The lower string will break.) Now take hold of the remaining length of the lower string, and pull it slowly and steadily. (The upper string will break.) (See Figure 313.01.) Students will see that the steady application of force was enough to set the stone in motion.

Quick Pull   Slow Pull

Figure 313.01

Observing that an object at rest tends **02**
to remain at rest due to inertia. Various **Aa**
simple experiences demonstrate inertia, a
property of matter.

a. Pour sand into a widemouthed
bottle, place a piece of cardboard
over the mouth, and set a marble
or coin on it. Hold the bottle with
one hand and snap the edge of
the cardboard to knock it away.
Explain that the force was not
great enough to overcome the
inertia of the marble (the tendency of an object to remain at
rest); thus, the marble drops into
the bottle.

b. Spread a handkerchief out on a
smooth tabletop, place a glass
filled with water near one corner
of the handkerchief, then raise
the opposite corner and give the
handkerchief a quick pull. The
glass will remain still and no
water will spill because of inertia.

c. Fill a glass with water; let it sit
until the water is still, and then
suddenly twist the glass. The
water will not move when the
glass moves.

Contributing Idea B. The inertia in an
object in motion tends to keep the
object moving.

Observing that an object in motion **03**
tends to remain in motion. Place a ball **Aa**
in a shoe box that has one end removed.

With the open end forward, slowly push
the box, and then suddenly stop it. Students can observe what happens to the
ball. Explain that when an object is put
into motion, as the ball was, the object
tends to remain in motion; thus, the ball
rolled out of the box. Now set the ball
in the box, and give it a quick start with
the open end of the box toward the rear.
Explain that objects tend to remain at
rest, as the ball did, unless there is enough
force to overcome that tendency. Let students test various objects in the box in the
same way.

Generalization II. According to
Newton's theory, momentum is
directly proportional to both mass
and speed.

Contributing Idea A. When moving
at the same speed, an object
of great mass will have greater
momentum than an object of
smaller mass.

Defining momentum. Obtain a steel ball **04**
bearing and a marble that have the same **Bb**
diameter. Tape two rulers together to form **Cd**
a V-shaped track and raise one end of the
track with a book approximately 1 in.
(2 cm) thick. Let students determine if
the ball bearing or marble is heavier, then
roll each down the track from the same
height, measure the distance each travels,
and observe which goes faster. (Note: If
the floor is not smooth, cover it with a
large sheet of cardboard or heavy paper.)

Table 313.04. Comparing the Momentum of Two Objects

Height of Track	Distance Traveled Marble	(Avg of 5 Trials) Ball Bearing

Repeat the activity at least five times to determine an average distance for each object. (See Table 313.04.) Students will find that each travels at the same speed, but that the one with a greater mass travels a greater distance. Tell them that the combination of mass and speed equals an object's *momentum*. Objects with greater momentum take longer to stop. Students can lower and raise the track to see if the speed of the two objects remains the same and if the one with greater mass travels the greater distance each time.

Observing the relationship between mass and momentum. Prepare an inclined plane with books and a sturdy board approximately 1 yd. (1 m) long and 4 in. (10 cm) wide. Tie a brick to a roller skate and set it on the inclined plane so that when the skate is released, it will strike a block at the bottom. The block can be cubical or rectangular and almost any size. Measure the distance the block moves when hit. (This will be a measure of the amount of momentum transferred from one object to another.) Record the distance traveled. Students should repeat the procedure at least five times to obtain an average. Now replace the brick with

05
Cd
Fb

a block of wood the same size. Students will realize that the brick has a greater mass than the wooden block with the same dimensions, and can predict what will happen this time. Release the skate and again measure the distance the block is pushed when hit. Compare the average distance the block is moved with the previously obtained average. Students will realize that the greater the mass, the greater the momentum. (Note: The speed remained unchanged in the two situations.)

Contributing Idea B. The greater the speed of a moving object, the greater its momentum.

Determining the effect of mass and speed on motion. Tie a brick or other weights to a roller skate, then place one end of a sturdy board (approximately 3 ft., or 1 m long and 4 in., or 10 cm wide) on one book to form an inclined plane. Release the skate from the top of the board and note the speed at which the skate travels. Measure the distance the skate travels along the floor until it stops, and record the measurement. Repeat this at least five times to determine an average. Now increase the incline by placing two identical books under the board. Repeat the activity and

06
Bb
Bc
Ec

Table 313.06. Comparing Mass and Speed

Test	Speed	Height of Track	Weight on Skate	Distance Traveled (Avg of 5 Trials)	Momentum
1A	slow	1 in. (2 cm)	1 brick	2 in. (4 cm)	small
1B	fast	2 in. (4 cm)	1 brick	4 in. (8 cm)	great
1C	faster	3 in. (6 cm)	1 brick	6 in. (12 cm)	greater
2A	slow	1 in. (2 cm)	2 bricks	3 in. (6 cm)	small
2B	fast	2 in. (4 cm)	2 bricks	6 in. (12 cm)	great
2C	faster	3 in. (6 cm)	2 bricks	9 in. (18 cm)	greater
	etc.				

continue adding books. Results can be recorded on Table 313.06. The data can also be graphed. Students will discover that elevating the ramp causes an increase in speed of the same mass, making it travel farther. Tell them that mass and speed combined determine the *momentum* of an object and that the momentum is a measure of a quantity of motion—in this case, the distance the skate traveled.

Observing that momentum can be transferred from one object to another. 07 Aa Fb
Release one marble down an inclined track of taped rulers so that it hits a row of five marbles near the other end. Note how many marbles moved apart when the first marble hit them. Now release two marbles at the same time and observe again. After several trials, have students predict what will happen if they let four marbles roll down together. Let them test to see if their prediction was a good one. Explain that the marbles could represent any objects that bump into each other.

Any moving object has a given amount of momentum and can only transfer that amount of momentum (as seen by the collision between the moving marble or marbles and the stationary ones).

Generalization III. According to Newton's theory, for every action there is an equal and opposite reaction.

Contributing Idea A. The forces of action and reaction are equal and opposite.

Measuring the forces of action and reaction (pulling). Cut the loop of a 08 Aa Cd
broad rubber band, and staple one end to the end of a shoe box lid. Place the lid on a smooth surface and staple the other end of the rubber band to an identical shoe-box lid. Pull the lids apart so the rubber stretches a few in. (Figure 313.08, p. 238), and then release them at exactly the same instant. Do this several times and measure the distances the lids move. Students will see that the rubber band pulls equally on

each lid. Now firmly stick a large piece of clay to the inside of one lid and repeat taking measurements. As more clay is added and measurements are taken, students will discover that the clay acts with the lid as a single object with more mass (when the lids are empty, the rubber band pulls equally on both; when the masses are different, the pull is unequal). They might try taping nails inside the lid to increase its mass. They might also reduce the effect of friction by setting the lids on a series of parallel drinking straws.

Figure 313.08

Measuring action and reaction (pushing). Cut a 10 in. (25 cm) strip of steel band from around a packing case. Slip a loop of thread over the ends of the strip to form a U-shape. Set the strip between the bottoms of two identical shoe boxes (Figure 313.09), then snip the thread. Repeat this several times, each time measuring the distance the boxes moved. (The push will be equal on both.) Now add clay to one box to increase its mass and repeat. Continue adding weight to one box. Students will discover that when the masses of the two boxes are different, the push is unequal. They might try reducing the

09
Aa
Cd

effect of friction by setting the boxes on a series of parallel drinking straws.

Figure 313.09

Contributing Idea B. The forces of action and reaction can cause motion.

Causing motion by reactions to other actions. Use a paper punch to make a hole in one end of a light paper box, blow up a balloon, hold it closed, and put its neck through the hole, mouth outward so the lip is held firmly. Set the box on a row of parallel straws and release the balloon (Figure 313.10). You might discuss other examples of this idea: the movement of a rowboat when someone steps from it to a dock; the rotation of a lawn sprinkler (streams of water move in one direction and the sprinkler moves in the other); the propulsion of a rocket (the rocket moves forward as burning gases move backward).

10
Aa
Ba

Figure 313.10

314   Applications

Generalization. The principles of motion can be put to use.

Contributing Idea A. A clothes dryer makes use of an object's tendency to travel in a straight line.

Making a model to explain how a clothes dryer works. Poke a hole in the center of a round cardboard box cover and place it over the spindle of a record player so that it lies flat. Put a few marbles in the cover and start the turntable spinning at 78 rpm. Let students hypothesize what would happen if the rim was not there to push inward against the marbles. Now cut a few openings in the rim of the cover, holes that are just large enough for the marbles to fit through. Start the turntable again, put some marbles in the cover, and observe what happens at the openings. Compare this activity to the way a clothes dryer works. (The rim of the cover acts like the drum of the dryer, the openings are like the holes in the drum, and the marbles are like the drops of water.) Explain that in a dryer, the water is not pulled out of the clothes. Instead, the drum pushes inward on the clothes, keeping them from going outward in a straight line. The result is that the clothes are pushed away from the water. For a supplementary experience, wrap a narrow strip of cloth around the rim of a skate wheel, and hold it in place with a rubber band. Wet the cloth and lay the skate on its side on a sheet of colored construction paper. Spin the wheel rapidly. Students will see that the drops of water keep going in a straight line when they no longer adhere to the spinning cloth.

01 Eb Fc

Contributing Idea B. The forces of action and reaction can be used to move objects.

Building a boat to run by action and reaction. Construct a wooden boat and insert a loop of copper tubing through two holes in its stern as shown in Figure 314.02. Fill the tube with water and place the boat in a large container of water. Set a lit candle under the loop of tubing. As the water is heated, it will be driven out of one side of the tubing. The backward motion of the water will cause the boat to move forward.

02 Gc

Figure 314.02

320 Sound

321 Characteristics

Generalization I. Sounds have identifiable characteristics.

> *Contributing Idea A.* There are many kinds of sound.

Describing outdoor sounds. Take your class to different areas of the school grounds at different times of the day. Have students sit or stand quietly for 30 seconds with their eyes closed to listen to and remember each sound they hear. When the time is up, have various students report on the sounds they heard by describing them, identifying them, and telling where each came from.

`01 Ac Ba`

Describing household sounds. Prepare a recording of various household sounds (e.g., a whistling tea kettle, a typewriter, a vacuum cleaner, an alarm clock, an egg-beater, the winding of a clock, a washing machine and dryer). Play the recording and have students describe the sounds; then have them identify the objects that made the sounds.

`02 Ac Ba`

> *Contributing Idea B.* Sounds vary in volume; some are loud and some are soft.

Hearing variations in rhythm and volume. Play a tapping game. Students can listen with their heads lowered or their eyes closed while you tap evenly several times on the chalkboard or desk. Ask how many taps were made or have students repeat the number of taps on their own desk. With practice, they will be able to reproduce different rhythms and changes in volume. You might tell them that the loudness or softness of a sound is called volume.

`03 Ac Bb`

Making sounds louder or softer. Let students produce a sound by tapping a drinking glass or bottle with a pencil, by plucking a one-string instrument, or by blowing a whistle. Have them make the sound again, putting more effort into the tap, pluck, or blow. Next, repeat putting in less effort. After they describe differences in each sound, they will realize that because the object produces only one note, the difference must be primarily caused by the effort put into its production: loud sounds require more effort than soft sounds. Let them discuss the efforts they put into their voices when they whisper and when they call someone across a street.

`04 Ec`

Making sounds louder. Students can hold a comb in one hand and stroke its teeth with a thumb. Have them do this again by placing one end of the comb against different surfaces such as a cleared desk, doors, chalkboards, windows, bottoms of waste baskets, and so forth. They will find that certain materials and surfaces make the sound louder. You might tell them that a surface that makes a sound louder is called a sounding board. Ask them to find the sounding

`05 Bb Ec`

board portions of some musical instruments such as guitars and pianos.

Contributing Idea C. Sounds vary in pitch; some are high and some are low.

Hearing variations in pitch. There are several experiences in which students can hear differences in high and low sounds. After these experiences, you might tell them that the highness or lowness of a sound is called pitch. **06 Ac Bb**

    a. Have them run a fingernail over the fibers of a cloth-covered book or stroke a pencil or stick across the teeth of a comb, wood file, or corrugated cardboard. Students can note that the faster the movement, the higher the sound.

    b. Have them listen as you use a hand saw to cut through a board. They can note that the faster the teeth cut across the board, the higher the sound.

    c. Have them hold a playing card against a turning bicycle wheel and note the change in the sound as the wheel is speeded up or slowed down.

Making sounds higher or lower. Working in small groups, students can place a plastic ruler on their desks so that it extends approximately 10 in. (5 cm) beyond the edge. Holding one end of the ruler firmly on the desk, press down on the free end, then let go. Repeat with the **07 Ac Ec**

ruler sticking out 8 in., 6 in., 4 in., and then 2 in. (5 cm intervals) from the edge. Ask them what differences they heard, and how they relate to the extended length of the ruler.

Contributing Idea D. Sounds vary in quality.

Hearing variations in quality. To help students realize that the quality of a sound is neither its loudness nor pitch, prepare a tabletop barrier large enough so that different sound makers can be used behind it without being seen. Tell students to listen carefully as you make a sound behind the barrier. You can play music loudly while sounds are being made; thus, students will need to tune out the music to concentrate on other specific sounds. Follow this activity with a discussion of the fact that sometimes we hear things and sometimes we do not (e.g., a spoon dropped on the floor sometimes makes us jump, while at other times we hardly notice it). **08 Ac Bb**

Contributing Idea E. Sounds can be reflected and absorbed.

Hearing reflected sounds. Locate echo-producing areas in or around your school (e.g., auditorium, large assembly room, hallways). Place students where they can best hear reflected sounds, then make sounds from different positions around them. Ask if they can hear better in some places than in others. Explain that sound sometimes bounces off surfaces and **09 Ac Bb**

that if the sound returns to the sender it is called an echo. You might discuss the advantages and disadvantages of reflected sounds (e.g., people addressing audiences in large rooms can be hindered by reflected sounds that interfere with the direct sounds of their voices; ships rely upon reflected sounds to indicate the depth of water by bouncing sounds from the ocean floor).

Seriating materials by the way they absorb sounds. Strike a tuning fork with a rubber mallet and place its base against a wooden box. Repeat, but each time, place a different material between the base of the fork and the box. Students can compare the sound produced each time. They can test a variety of materials (e.g., squares of cloth, felt, paper, metal, an empty and a full can of water, Styrofoam) and seriate them by their ability to absorb sound.

**10
Ac
Da
Ec**

Generalization II. Sounds can be classified on the basis of their characteristics.

> *Contributing Idea A.* Some characteristics of sounds can be seriated.

Seriating sounds by volume. Have students collect pictures of machines. Let them order the pictures by the loudness of sound each produces. You might tell them that the intensity of sound is measured in units called decibels that are ordered along a logarithmic scale. Table 321.11 may help students seriate their pictures.

**11
Bb
Da**

Table 321.11. Volume Scale

Decibels	Examples
0	Threshold of hearing
10	Ordinary breathing
11–20	Whispers
21–30	Ordinary household sounds; Natural country settings
31–40	Ordinary classroom activities; Turning pages of newspapers
41–50	Automobile engines; Vacuum cleaners
51–60	Noisy offices or stores
61–70	Ordinary television sounds or conversations
71–80	Heavy street traffic
81–90	Trains; Subway cars
91–100	Boiler factories; Air drills; Riveters
101–110	Claps of thunder; Jet engines
120	Threshold of pain

Seriating sounds by pitch. Have students tap different objects and listen to the pitch each produces. Seriate the objects from the lowest to highest pitch. Students can also make simple musical instruments that require the seriation of sounds in order to produce a musical scale, or you might cover the frequency numerals (vibrations per second, or VPS) on a set of tuning forks with tape and have them

12 Bb Da

seriate the forks by pitch, then remove the tape so that the order can be checked. The numerals indicate the number of vibrations the fork makes per second (VPS); the higher the sound, the greater the number of vibrations. Tell them that *frequency* is the term used when describing how many vibrations there are for a particular tone. Table 321.12 can help students order various sounds on the basis of pitch.

Table 321.12. Pitch Scale

Frequency: Vibrations Per Second	Examples	
About 16	Lower limit of human hearing	
20–200	Deep bass tones (27 VPS = lowest note on the piano)	
256	"do" Middle C	
278	C-sharp	
294	"re" D	
312	D-sharp	
330	"mi" E	
349	"fa" F	
370	F-sharp	"Middle" Musical Scale
392	"sol" G	
416	G-sharp	
440	"la" A	
466	A-sharp	
494	"ti" B	
512	"do" C	
525–3,000	Normal adult conversation	
4,000	About the highest tone used in music	
8,000	High-pitched, shrill tones	
About 20,000	Upper limit of human hearing	
About 30,000	Upper limit of hearing for dogs and cats	
About 100,000	Upper limit of hearing for bats	

Contributing Idea B. Some characteristics of sounds can be classified.

Selecting categories for grouping sounds. Have students list some categories for sounds. Some headings might include pleasant sounds and unpleasant sounds, loud sounds and soft sounds, school sounds and home sounds, outdoor sounds and indoor sounds, sounds people make and sounds animals make. Let different groups of students use different headings as they listen for sounds around the school grounds. Compare listings for different locations and for different times of the day. Let them decide if some headings are more useful than others. **13 Db**

Grouping sounds. Various activities allow students to group sounds by similarities. **14 Db**

   a. Ask what the last sound was that they remember hearing before going to sleep last night. Ask what kind it was (e.g., machine made or natural), then ask what the first sound was that they heard this morning. Have them group the sounds by listing them under appropriate headings on a chalkboard.

   b. If you can obtain a collection of pictures of typical daytime sound sources (e.g., auto traffic, people working, people moving, dogs barking, wind blowing), students can group the pictures according to headings of their own choosing.

   c. Have them group pictures of various musical instruments according to the method used to produce sounds on them (e.g., striking for percussion instruments; plucking or bowing for string instruments; blowing for wind, reed, or flute instruments).

Classifying sounds. Have students prepare a table to keep a record of sound makers, the kinds of sound they produce, and the duration of the sound. When finished, let students devise sets of categories and subcategories for the sound makers. Figure 321.15 suggests sound makers that can be used, as well as possible sets of categories. **15 Bc Dc**

322   Interactions

Generalization I. Sound is a form of energy produced by vibrating matter.

   Contributing Idea A. Vibrations are the only source of sounds.

Sensing sound vibrations. There are many ways by which students can sense vibrations as sound is produced. For each of the following suggested experiences, have different groups of students describe what is felt, heard, and seen. **01 Af Ba**

   a. Fasten a rubber band to a door-knob, pull it taut, and then pluck it.

CLASSIFYING SOUNDS

Soundmaker	Description of Sound	Duration of Sound
Gong	Ringing, High	Continues After Efforts Stops
Flute	Shrill, High	Stop When Effort Stops

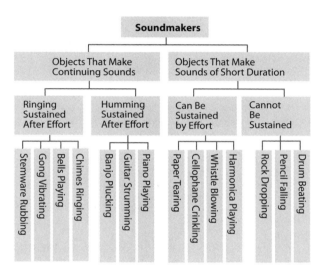

Figure 321.15

b. Touch the strings of a piano or stringed instrument as it is played.

c. Half-fill a drinking glass with water, wet a finger, and then rub it around the edge of the glass. For more consistent results, vinegar can be used in place of water. If the glass is steadied with the other hand, hold it near the base. (Note: Not all drinking glasses will produce a good sound.)

d. Place the tip of a spatula blade (or hacksaw blade) on a desk with the handle extending over the side. Pull the handle down, then let go.

e. Fold a 2 in × 6 in. (5 cm × 15 cm) strip of paper in half, cut a small semicircle in the fold, hold between two fingers, and blow hard through the semicircle.

f. Place some fine sand or salt on a drumhead, and then tap the drum gently and with a steady beat.

After these experiences you might explain that whenever something moves back and forth or up and down, it is said to *vibrate*. From these and similar experiences the students will realize that sound is produced by vibrations that are usually too rapid to see except as a blur.

Feeling vocal vibrations. Have students feel their lips and throats during each of the following experiences.   **02 Ab**

    a. Hum with mouths and noses open (air passes through them) while lightly touching throats and lips.

    b. Hum with mouths open and noses closed.

    c. Hum with closed mouths.

    d. Try to hum with both mouth and nose closed.

In each case, let them describe and discuss what they felt. They will realize that all vocal sounds are vibrations involving air passing out of the lungs.

> *Contributing Idea B.* Sound vibrations occur in wavelike patterns.

Making sound vibrations visible. Sound vibrations are usually too rapid to be seen as more than a blur. The following experiences suggest some ways students can more easily observe sound vibrations. From the experiences they will also learn that when an object stops vibrating, it no longer produces a sound.   **03 Gc**

    a. Stretch a rubber band tightly around three nails in a board. Hang several small strips of paper, creased in half, over one section of the band (see Figure 322.03). Pluck the section and observe

how the paper strips move. Similarly, strips can be placed over the different strings of string instruments. Students can note how long a string vibrates after it can no longer be heard.

Rubber Band

Strips of Paper

Figure 322.03

    b. Strike a tuning fork and place one of its tines into some water or against a suspended table tennis ball.

    c. Cut an opening in one end of a round cardboard carton and paste a thin sheet of onion skin paper over it. Glue a small mirror to the center of the paper. Have one student speak into the other, open end of the container while shining a light against the mirror so that the reflection is cast against a screen or wall. Let other students observe the reflected light as it dances on the wall as the sound of a voice causes the onion skin to vibrate. (Note: Different cartons perform in different ways; some require a strong voice or loud sound before the onion skin will vibrate.)

Changing sound vibrations into wave pictures. The teacher will smoke a piece of glass pane by holding it in a candle flame. Using a drop of wax or piece of clay, fasten a very fine wire to one of the tines of a tuning fork (Figure 322.04a). Attach the tuning fork to a ring stand or other upright structure to hold it in a constant position (Figure 322.04b). Have a student set the smoked glass under the point of the fine wire and gently bend the wire so that it just touches the pane (Figure 322.04c). Strike the tuning fork with a rubber mallet and observe how the fine wire moves back and forth as the tine vibrates. Students will see a streak appear on the glass as the wire scratches away the carbon. A similar apparatus can be prepared by firmly gluing sharpened, soft pencil leads to the tuning fork and suspending the fork over a sheet of paper (Figure 322.04d). Several tests can now be performed using the materials. (Note: The wave pictures should not be confused with transverse waves; sound waves are longitudinal waves.) You might explain that each sound produces a regular pattern of vibrations and that the number of vibrations that occur in one second is called frequency. **Caution: Window pane glass is fragile. Handle with care.**

04 Bb Ca

Figure 322.04a–d

a. Have a student slowly pull the glass away from the fork when it is not vibrating. (The fine wire should make a straight line on the glass.) Replace the glass under the wire at the starting position. Now strike the tuning fork and have the student pull the pane away again *at the same rate.* (A sequence of waves will be produced along the first line.) Discuss why this took place, and then repeat the procedure, this time striking the tuning fork with more force. As different intensities are tested, students will see that the number of waves remains the same over the same distance but that they rise higher on each side of the straight line.

b. Repeat the above test using different tuning forks. For each new test, different smoked pieces of glass should be used and labeled so that the wave pictures can be compared. With practice, students will be able to pull the pane of glass at a steady rate over one second of time. If the pulling time and the distance the glass travels are kept constant, comparisons will be more fruitful.

c. Each time the fork is struck, have a student pull a freshly smoked pane of glass away at a different rate. Be sure to strike the tuning fork with equal effort each time. Compare the wave pictures that are produced. (The heights of waves will remain the same on each side of the straight line, but some will appear to be more spread out.)

Contributing Idea C. Sound vibrations can be produced by striking, plucking, or blowing.

Producing different sounds. Have students tap on a variety of objects such as large and small pans, pans made of different materials (e.g., aluminum, cast iron, stainless steel), blocks of wood of various sizes, metal cans, glass jars or cereal boxes—filled, partially filled, and empty. Challenge students to find something that makes no sound when tapped. By testing many objects and keeping track of the sounds made, they will form some understanding of how size, shape, and the **05 Gc**

materials that make up the objects relate to the sounds produced.

Creating sound effects. Let students record and present a radio script or play. Have them select stories from their readers and library books, or let them make up stories of their own. Be sure that they select stories that allow many sound effects to be added. You might also challenge them to produce the sound of an egg frying, a freight train starting up, or a horse trotting. Here are some hints for producing some sound effects: birdseed falling on a table tennis ball—rain; beating coconut shells—horse trotting; cellophane being slowly crumpled—egg frying; cellophane being quickly crumpled—forest fire; sandpaper pieces being rubbed together in an accented rhythm—freight train; BB's being shaken in an inflated balloon—thunder. **06 Gb**

Contributing Idea D. The volume of sound vibrations depends upon the amount of energy input (intensity) and the distance the vibrations travel.

Listening to the effect distance has upon sounds. Place about 10 students at 10 yd. (10 m) intervals across the school playground. Have them turn their backs toward you so that vision will not influence their judgments. Now make various loud and soft sounds and have students raise their hands if they hear the sound. They will discover the distances **07 Ac Bb Fa**

that sounds of different intensities travel by the number of hands that are raised. You might tell them that the amount of energy a sound has when it reaches the ear is called loudness. Let each of the 10 students describe the same sound in terms of its loudness. (The loudness of a sound diminishes over distances.) From these experiences, they can theorize that loud sounds are produced by strong vibrations that travel for long distances, while soft sounds are produced by weak vibrations that travel shorter distances.

Testing factors that influence the volume of a sound. Wire a plastic or metal spoon to a mouse trap. Use a protractor to make a semicircle on a heavy piece of cardboard and mark it every 10 degrees. Paste the semicircle to the side of the mouse trap. Hold the apparatus so that the back of the spoon just touches the side of an empty glass (see Figure 322.08). Taps against the glass can be controlled by pulling back the spoon to a mark on the semicircle and letting go. Now have students listen for differences in volume and in the duration of the sound as they test weak to strong taps. Keep records for the following suggested tests.

08
Ec

Figure 322.08

a. Some students can produce taps of equal strength while others move measured distances from the glass. The sound will become fainter as the distance is increased. (Note: Some students will find that the pitch changes from low to high as the distance increases; scientists have discovered that the closer, stronger vibrations seem to affect the signal our ears send to the brain and lower sounds are realized.)

b. Experiment with the apparatus by tapping other objects or by placing the glass on different surfaces such as tin pans, porcelain plates, wood, or corrugated cardboard.

c. Systematically tap the glass with measured amounts of water added to it. (Note: Tapping makes the glass and the water vibrate, while blowing makes the air column in the glass vibrate.)

d. Study the ripples in the water for taps of different intensities. Heavier liquids (e.g., syrup) or lighter (e.g., alcohol) can be tested for visual and auditory comparisons. Students will discover that the weight of the material influences the sound.

e. Systematically dissolve measured amounts of salt or baking soda in measured amounts of water in the glass and note differences in the ripples and sounds that are produced.

Contributing Idea E. The pitch of sound vibrations depends upon the number of sound vibrations per second (frequency).

MEASURING FREQUENCIES

Graph 322.09

Comparing differences in the pitch of sounds. Have a student hold the tip of a spatula blade tightly against the edge of a table with one hand, pull down the handle with the other, then let go. (A low raspy tone should be heard.) Repeat the action several times, but each time, slide more of the blade onto the table. (The sound will become higher.) You might tell students that the change in sound from high to low or from low to high is called pitch. If they observe carefully, students will note that as the vibrating portion of the spatula is shortened, it vibrates faster. They might try counting the number of vibrations in a one-minute period for different lengths of the spatula. In place of the spatula, test plastic spoons, hacksaw blades, straightened-out bobby pins, and rulers. If a ruler is used, it can be clamped to the edge of the table, and then systematically shortened for each trial. Data can be recorded on a graph similar to Graph 322.09. Explain that the term *frequency* is used to describe the relative number of vibrations among sounds of different pitch.

09
Bb
Bf

Testing factors that influence the pitch of a sound. Pitch depends upon several factors—usually the composition of the

10
Bc
Ec

material, the tension it is under, its length, and its diameter or thickness. These factors can be tested for their influence upon the production of sounds by having students stretch three rubber bands of the same length around a small wooden box. The bands should range in width. If rubber bands of the same length and different width cannot be found, bands can be cut from an inner tube with widths of ¼ in., ½ in., and ¾ in. (0.5 cm, 1 cm, 1.5 cm). Students might explore the factors freely, or you might systematically guide them from one factor to another. Some suggestions follow:

a. Students can pluck each band, one at a time, while listening. Be sure they pluck each time with the same amount of effort. Have them describe in what ways the sounds differed and record their findings on Table 322.10. They will realize that since the length, effort, material, and other factors were identical, the primary factor influencing any difference was probably the width (the wider or thicker the material, the lower the sound; the narrower or thinner the material, the higher the sound).

Table 322.10. Comparing Pitch and Width (Thickness)

Factor	High Pitch	Medium Pitch	Low Pitch
Thin Band			
Medium Band			
Wide Band			

b. Twist a piece of wood near one end of one band to make the band tighter. Pluck the band, twist the wood, pluck, and twist again while noting changes in the pitch. Repeat for the other bands. Students will realize that the tension was the primary factor influencing the different sounds produced by the band.

c. Place a wedge under the rubber bands and have students pluck the longer portion of each. Move the wedge to make the length of each portion shorter or longer and continue plucking. Students will realize that the length was the primary factor in the production of the sound differences they heard.

d. Substitute wires, fishline, or other materials and test each of the above suggestions again.

e. Experiment by combining each of the factors in different ways to note what happens to the sound

production (e.g., tautness and length, thickness and length, thickness and tautness).

Generalization II. **Sound travels through solids, liquids, and gases at different speeds.**

Contributing Idea A. Sounds travel through solid materials.

Hearing sounds through solids. Have students listen to the sound made as they scratch or tap a leg of their desks. Have them repeat the action with an ear to the desktop. Compare the sound coming through the solid top to the sound coming through the air. You might have them discuss why Indians put their ears to the ground to listen for hoofbeats and why railroad maintenance workers place an ear to a rail to listen for an approaching train. Several other experiences can help students realize that sounds travel through solids; in each case they can judge that sounds can be heard better through solids than through air. **11 Ac Ca**

a. Place a watch in the center of a table and try to hear its ticking from a yard (meter) away. Next, rest one end of a meterstick on the watch and let students take turns placing an ear against the other end. (They should hear the ticking more clearly.) You might also let them experiment by holding the watch (or a tuning fork) against various parts of the head

(e.g., chin, teeth, jawbone) to discover that sounds may reach the
ear through solid parts of the body
(e.g., bones). This can also be
demonstrated by holding a pencil between the teeth, tapping it
lightly with another pencil while
holding the ears shut, and comparing the effect when the pencil
is held only by the lips.

b. Tie a spoon or coat hanger to the
center of a 3 ft. (1 m) length of
string. Suspend the object from
the ends of the string, strike it
against a chair or desk, and listen
to the sound. Now have students
wrap each free end of the string
around one finger on each hand,
and place the two fingers into their
ears (see Figure 322.11). Swing
the object so that it taps the chair
or desk again. Discuss differences
between the sound transmission
through the string and through the
air. Test the transmission using
one ear at a time. Also experiment
with spoons of other sizes and
shapes and materials (e.g., plastic,
wood, metal) and strings of various lengths and materials (e.g.,
short and long; fishline and wire).

c. Lightly scratch one end of a
broomstick with a fingernail while
students take turns listening at the
other end. To be sure the sound
is being transmitted through the

Figure 322.11

wood, the students can listen
while raising their ears from the
handle but keeping the same distance from the sound source so
that a comparison can be made.

d. Send International or Morse code
messages through pipes in the
school building, stair railings,
or metal fences by tapping them
with a piece of hardwood.

Contributing Idea B. Sounds travel
through liquids.

Hearing sounds through water. Fill
a large bowl, bucket, or aquarium with
water. Make various sounds under the
water (e.g., tap spoons together, strike
two rocks together, snap fingers, ring a

**12
Ac
Ca**

bell) or float a large block of wood on the surface and touch it with a vibrating tuning fork. Students can listen to the sound first through the air, then with their ears against a side of the container. They will find that sounds can travel through a liquid and judge that they travel better through water than through air. They might discuss sounds heard while swimming under water.

Contributing Idea C. Sounds travel through gases.

Hearing sounds through air. Students tend to take for granted the idea that sounds travel through the air because they hear people talk. A few experiences, however, will stimulate them into considering this assumption more carefully. **13 Ac**

    a. Stretch a piece of balloon rubber over the open end of a tin can, fasten it with a rubber band, and sprinkle some salt on it. Let one student strike a tuning fork with a rubber mallet and hold it approximately 1 in. (3 cm) over the salt. (Students will see the salt bounce and infer that the sound vibrations are transmitted from the fork through the air to the rubber.) Students can note that the effect does not take place if the fork is moved away from the rubber—indicating that the sound energy diminishes with distance.

    b. Suspend a piece of breakfast cereal from a string, bring a vibrating tuning fork close to, but not touching, the piece of cereal. (Students will see the cereal being moved and infer that the sound vibrations are being transmitted through the air.)

    c. Students can lay an empty wastebasket on its side, set a lit candle in front of the open end, tap the bottom of the basket to produce a sound, and watch the candle flame. (The flame will move as the sound vibrations are transmitted through the air.)

    d. Students can feel the sides of long paper tubes or empty cereal boxes as they speak through them. (The air inside vibrates and pushes with some force.) Discuss how some sound vibrations traveling through the air can cause damage (e.g., windows breaking from sonic booms or claps of thunder; glasses breaking from high-pitched musical notes).

Communicating through a tube of air. Have students add funnels to each end of an empty garden hose, and speak to one another. They will find that sounds coming through the hose, even when bent around a corner, are louder than identical sounds traveling through free air. They should especially note that the **14 Ba Gb**

hose contains a column of trapped air. Let them experiment with different lengths and diameters of tubes. You might tell them that ships sometimes use a similar device for communicating between sections and that some apartment houses use it between entryways and the apartments.

Contributing Idea D. Sounds travel through some materials faster than others.

Hearing that sounds take time to travel. **15** **Ac** **Ch** Lay out an empty 100 ft. (30 m) or more length of garden hose in a large loop so that the two ends are near each other. Students can take turns placing an ear to one end while tapping the metal portion of the other end with a pencil. They will hear two taps: one through the air and the other through the hose. Explain that the second tap is due to the distance the sound had to travel through the hose. Discuss similar experiences indicating that it takes sound time to travel across a distance (e.g., distant loudspeakers compared to close ones).

Hearing that the speed of sound varies through different materials. **16** **Ch** **Da** Pound a wooden stake into the ground at one end of a playground while students place their ears against the ground some distance away from the stake. They will hear the sound twice: first through the ground, then through the air. They should realize that it takes the sound longer to travel through the air than through the ground.

Repeat this activity at various distances to determine if sound always travels faster through the ground.

Contributing Idea E. The speed of sound through air can be measured.

Determining the speed of sound in air. **17** **Ch** Prepare a pendulum clock (see entry 632.09). On a day when there is no wind, set the timer in motion and have a student strike the bottom of a large can with a stick each time the pendulum is at one end of its swing. (This may take some practice.) When synchronized, have other students move away from the pendulum. They will notice that the sound does not remain synchronized with the swing. As they move farther and farther away, they will find that the sound again becomes synchronized, but a half-swing late. To determine the speed of the sound, measure the distance between them and the sound source. For example, if the distance is 550 ft. (168 m), then 550 ft. (168 m) in one-half second (a half-swing) equals 1,100 ft. (336 m) in one second or 750 miles (1,210 km) per hour. (Note: Sound travels at 1,087 ft. or 332 m per second at 32°F or 0°C. The speed increases 1.1 ft. per second for each degree of increase in Fahrenheit temperature, or 3 m/s for each 5°C.) If a very large open area is available, students can determine the speed of sound in another way by using a tape measure to carefully mark off a straight-line distance of

2,500 ft. (800 m). Let one student with a stick and large can stand at one end of the distance, while a group of students stand at the other end with a stopwatch. Have the first student strike the can with the stick. When the group sees the can being struck, start the watch. Stop it as soon as the sound is heard. To determine the speed of the sound, divide the distance by the time. This activity might be repeated several times to find the average time it took for the sound to travel the distance.

Contributing Idea F. The speed of sound through air is slower than the speed of light.

Comparing the speed of sound to the speed of light. Divide the class into two groups. Give one group a whistle and the other a flag, then station them approximately 500 ft. (150 m) apart. Have the whistle group blow the whistle loudly and have the flag group signal as soon as it hears the whistle. The whistle group will observe that it takes some time for the sound of the whistle to reach the second group. Interchange the flag and whistle and repeat. Similarly, one group can strike the bottom of a large can with a stick. The other group will see the action completed before it hears the sound.
18 Ca

Estimating the distance of a flash of lightning. Lightning and thunder are illustrations of the fact that light travels faster than sound. Even though they occur simultaneously, we usually see the
19 Cb

lightning bolt, and then hear the clap of thunder. The distance between the lightning and the observer can be computed by timing the interval between seeing the bolt and hearing the thunder. For example, since each second of delay between the flash and the sound indicates that the lightning is approximately one-fifth mile (320 m) away, students can simply count the seconds that elapse after seeing a flash until the thunder is heard (e.g., 15 seconds between flash and thunder—15 seconds ÷ 5 seconds per mile or meter = 3 miles or 4800 m).

Generalization III. Sounds can cause objects to vibrate.

Contributing Idea A. A vibrating object can force another object to vibrate.

Observing forced vibrations. Have a student strike a tuning fork and press its base against a tabletop or other flat, clear surface. Students will hear that the sound becomes louder and infer that the vibrations produced by the sound forced the larger surface to also vibrate at the same frequency. (If a larger surface is made to vibrate, the sound is louder.) Similarly, students can hear that the sound of their voices becomes louder when they talk into a waste basket or megaphone as the sides of the object are forced to vibrate at the same frequency. You might explain that when this happens, the transferred sound is called a forced vibration.
20 Ac Bb Fc

Examine the sound boxes of violins, guitars, and similar instruments and note that they are shaped to increase the loudness of musical sounds.

Using forced vibrations to amplify sounds. Have students use a hand lens to examine the groove on a phonograph record. Place a fingernail into the groove as it turns to sense the vibrations and to hear a faint sound. Now place the point of a toothpick, long cactus needle, or phonograph needle into the groove. (Students will hear the sound a bit louder as the object vibrates in the groove.) Repeat several times after placing the toothpick through the corner of an index card, then through the corner of an empty matchbox, and finally through the folded end of a paper megaphone. In each subsequent test, the sound will be amplified as the vibration of the toothpick forces the larger surfaces to vibrate at the same frequency. You might follow this experience by having some students find pictures of early phonographs that used horns to amplify sounds.

**21
Ac
Ec
Ga**

> *Contributing Idea B.* Sympathetic vibrations occur when a vibrating object is in tune with another object.

Observing sympathetic vibrations. Mount two tuning forks of the same frequency on two identical wooden boxes approximately 6 in. (15 cm) apart with the open ends facing each other as shown in Figure 322.22 (or have two students

**22
Ac
Bb
Fc**

hold them by their bases approximately 3 in. or 7 cm apart). Strike one fork with a rubber mallet, listen, and then stop the vibration with your hand. If students listen carefully to the other fork, they will hear a faint sound and realize that the second fork was put into motion by the vibrations of the first. You might explain that when this happens, the transferred sound is called a sympathetic vibration (another term is *resonance*). If this activity is repeated with tuning forks of different frequencies, students can discover that sympathetic vibrations can only be set up using identically pitched forks. Similarly, they can try blowing across the top of a jar or bottle near an identically pitched jar or bottle and listen for the sympathetic vibration.

Open Ends Facing
Each Other

6 in. (15 cm)

Figure 322.22

Generalization IV. Sounds can be controlled.

> *Contributing Idea A.* Sounds can be directed to a particular place.

Controlling the direction of sounds. **23 Ac Gb**
Have students put two funnels in a 1 yd. (1 m) length of rubber hose. Using the device, let them listen to their heartbeats, to themselves talking, to watches ticking (Figure 322.23), to engines running, or to a friend tapping his or her head. **Caution: Be sure children do not shout or blow into funnel when someone is listening at the other end.** Discuss how the sounds are funneled into the hose and through it in a controlled direction. Students can compare the same sounds being made without the hose and funnels or can make a two-ear stethoscope by connecting three funnels and rubber tubing to a Y-shaped glass or metal tube. This device can be compared to a one-ear stethoscope for effectiveness.

Figure 322.23

Contributing Idea B. Sounds can be reflected.

Observing that sounds can be reflected. **24 Ac Bb**
Have students hold a curved index card behind a ticking watch while listening. They can progressively move the card back and forth or change the curvature to hear how the sound is reflected. Similarly, a student can turn her back to the class as she speaks loudly (or sings one note without interruption for about 10 seconds) into the open end of a wastebasket that is alternately raised to her face and then lowered. The class will realize that the sound produced was reflected from the basket's base and sides. You might tell them that reflected sounds are called echoes.

Contributing Idea C. Sounds can be absorbed.

Determining that sounds can be absorbed. **25 Ac Cd**
Place a loudly ticking clock in a box with the open side toward the back of a student who is listening. Have the student walk away from the box in a straight line until the ticking becomes inaudible. Record the distance, then fill the box with some sound-insulating material such as cotton, and have the student walk away again. Mark the distance where the ticking becomes inaudible again. Compare the two distances and discuss reasons for differences.

Testing materials that absorb sounds. **26 Da Ec**
Pull a rubber band around a wooden box and pluck it. Next, place some cotton in the box and pluck again using the same amount of effort. (The cotton should deaden the sound.) Let students test other materials in the box (e.g., paper, sawdust, different cloths, sponges) to see whether

some absorb sound better than others. Compare the sounds produced and rank the materials from the best sound absorbers to the poorest. These tests might be followed with a discussion of sound controls used in homes and buildings (e.g., carpeting, drapes, building materials). If possible, have the students look for examples of soundproofing or the need for it in your school building.

323 Theory

Generalization. According to the wave theory, sound energy is thought of as vibrations that transfer energy in wavelike patterns through molecules.

> *Contributing Idea A.* Sound energy travels in longitudinal waves.

Sensing sound vibrations. Stretch a sheet of onion skin over an embroidery hoop, then strike a tuning fork and hold it near the hoop. Have students take turns touching the skin and describing what they feel. Some small seeds, such as poppy seeds, can be sprinkled on the hoop so that the vibrations will be visible. If an old radio can be obtained and the speaker exposed, students can feel how the speaker vibrates while the radio is playing.

**01
Af**

Making sound vibrations visible. Each sound has a particular vibration that can be made visible through the use of a brass plate (1 ft. × 1 ft. × ¹/₁₆ in. (30 cm × 30 cm × 0.2 cm). Obtain such a plate from a

**02
Ec
Fc**

hardware store, round its edges and corners, and then wash it with soap and water. When dry, set it on three ¼ in. (1 cm) square pieces of cork so that one side of the plate extends beyond the edge of a table (Figure 323.02). Now rub a 1 ft. (30 cm) length of bias-binding tape with powdered resin. Stretch the tape tightly between the thumb and forefinger of each hand, and using the smooth side of the tape, stroke it downward in a long motion against the extended side of the plate. (Note: You may have to try several times to locate the place where a sound can be heard best.) When a sound is heard, stop stroking and sprinkle some fine sand or seeds (e.g., celery, poppy) on top of the plate. Students will see that the vibration of the plate causes the seeds to move, but that the plate does not move as a single mass. (The seeds will form a pattern by moving to parts of the plate that are not in vibration.) As different sounds are produced, different seed patterns will appear. The various patterns can be preserved by photographing them or by spreading rubber cement over the entire face of a sheet of 1 ft. (30 cm) square paper and inverting it on the plate to pick up the seeds and preserve the pattern. When several patterns are obtained and labeled for the type of sound they represent, students can make comparisons of the patterns and judgments about what they represent. For example, well-defined sounds produce well-organized patterns—noise does not produce any pattern; the higher the pitch, the more intricate and delicate the spaces— the lower the pitch, the larger the spaces. Students can also try stroking the plate with other materials (e.g., a violin bow). As a supplementary experience to show that sound travels through the air in such patterns, students can sprinkle some fine powder (e.g., nutmeg) on the table under the plate. When the plate is struck sharply in the center with a stick, a definite pattern will be formed in the powder. Try altering the force of the blow, striking the plate in different places, and varying the width of the air gap between the plate and the table.

Figure 323.02

Using a spring model to represent sound vibrations as longitudinal waves. 03 Bb Fc Attach one end of a long spiral spring to a support. Let a student stretch the spring out a bit, holding it steady and off the ground. Have him quickly push his end in the direction of the support and quickly bring it back to its original position. (The coils should bunch up for an instant and travel along the spring). Let other students carefully observe and describe the

movement of the wave as it passes along the spring. (It appears to move back and forth.) Explain that the student's movement represented the source of a sound vibration and that the movement in the coil spring represented the manner in which a sound wave travels. (Sound waves consist of compressed particles as well as stretched or rarefied particles moving back and forth along the direction of the wave.) Now have the student pinch together about four coils of the spring and release them. (A wave of compression will be seen.) Next, pull apart and then release about four coils near the free end. (The "stretch" will be seen traveling to the attached end.) Explain that in each sound wave there is a similar crowding together of molecules followed by a thinning out of molecules. You might tell students that the crowding of molecules is called compression, and the thinning out is called rarefaction. When waves move in this way, they are called longitudinal waves (see Figure 323.03). Such waves can be compared with transverse waves. (Note: Observations of longitudinal

Figure 323.03

waves in the spring can be improved by attaching small colored strips of cloth to every tenth coil.)

Using a spring model to explain echoes. **04 Fc** Attach one end of a long spring to a support. Have a student stretch the coil out a bit, compress about four coils, then release them to send a longitudinal wave down its length. Observers will see the wave hit the support and return. Use the observation to explain that echoes are sound waves that bounce back from some surface.

Comparing longitudinal and transverse waves in a coil. **05 Bb Fc** Attach one end of a long spring to a support and stretch it out a bit. Ask one student to compress about 4 coils at the free end, and then quickly release them to send a wave through the spring. Now attach pieces of white adhesive tape or colored cloth to the coil at 10-ring intervals. When the coil is tapped again, the observers will see that as the wave moves along the coil, each portion of it merely oscillates (although the disturbance is transmitted, no part of the coil moves except to vibrate). Tell students that this kind of wave is called a longitudinal wave (Figure 323.05a). Next, have the student strike the coil at the free end, but at right angles to its length. The observers will see that the movements are now crosswise, at right angles to the motion of the wave itself. Tell them that this kind of wave is called a transverse wave (Figure 323.05b).

Longitudinal Waves

Figure 323.05a

Transverse Waves

Figure 323.05b

Producing longitudinal waves of various frequencies. **06 Bb Cc Ch** Suspend a long spring between two posts. Using a stopwatch, have one student call time at the beginning and end of one minute while another student makes a steady series of waves in the spring by tapping the post with a hammer. A third student can count the number of times the hammer taps during the minute to determine the number of waves produced. Tell students that the number of waves produced in a time unit is called the frequency. Relate the steady flow of longitudinal waves down the spring to the swing from side to side of a tuning fork. Now let students tap the post more or less rapidly to produce higher or lower frequencies. When coupled with activities on pitch, students will realize that the frequency determines the pitch of a sound.

Producing longitudinal waves of various amplitudes. Glue several sharpened pieces of soft pencil lead to a tuning fork. Strike the fork with a rubber mallet and hold the sides of the prongs against a sheet of paper. Tell students that the distance the prongs swing from side to side is called the amplitude. (See Figure 323.07.) Strike the tuning fork again, only harder, and hold it against the paper. Compare the lines that are made. Students will realize that amplitude is related to loudness; the greater the amplitude, the louder the sound.

**07
Bb
Cd**

Glued Pencil Leads

Amplitude

Figure 323.07

Contributing Idea B. Sound energy travels by the motion of molecules.

Observing that molecules must be present for sound to be transmitted. Suspend a ringing alarm clock within a bell jar or set it on a sound insulator under the jar. Pump the air from the jar. (Students will hear the ringing become fainter until it cannot be heard.) Let the air back into the jar (the ringing will again be heard). They will realize that the sound could only be transmitted when the molecules of air were present.

**08
Ac
Fa**

Using models to show how sound waves are transmitted by the motion of molecules. For each of the following activities, you might explain that there are billions and billions of molecules in the air of a single room, and that the objects used in each experience can be imagined representing a few of the air molecules.

**09
Fc**

a. Students can place four marbles, all touching one another, inside the middle of a tall open book (Figure 323.09a) or a 45° angled trough made from two yardsticks (Figure 323.09b). From one end, roll a fifth marble very hard so that it collides with the others. Let students describe and discuss what they see. (The marble at the far end of the row will move away from the others with almost the same amount of energy as the incoming marble.)

Marbles

Figure 323.09a

Yardsticks

Clay

Figure 323.09b

Repeat the experience several times to show that when energy is applied to produce a sound, the energy moves from molecule to molecule through the material in the same direction as the original disturbance.

b. Students can use four fingers of one hand to hold four checkers or coins in a row. Be sure the checkers touch each other. Now snap a fifth checker against the row and observe what happens.

c. Students can push a straight pin into each of six gumballs and suspend them from 6 in. (15 cm) lengths of thread attached to a horizontal support (Figure 323.09c). Have one student pull two gumballs at one end back, so when released, they will hit the others head on. Students will see what happens to the middle two gumballs when the first two are released. This model can help them imagine what happens to air molecules when they are crowded together by the pressure of a vibrating material and how that

pressure is transferred through other molecules. **Caution: Students should not eat the gumballs. They can become contaminated through handling.**

d. Students can stand a set of dominoes, approximately 1 in. (2 cm) apart, in four rows to form a cross, leaving enough space for a tennis ball to barely fit into the center (Figure 323.09d). Drop the ball into the center and observe what happens. Use the model to explain that sound waves are longitudinal and radiate in all directions from a source.

Figure 323.09d

(Note: In these experiences, the force of the impact will be transmitted from object to object, showing by analogy how sound energy is transmitted from molecule to molecule in a wave. The ejection of the end object, however, is not comparable to what happens in air.)

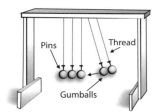

Figure 323.09c

324 Applications

Generalization. Instruments can be made to produce musical sounds.

> *Contributing Idea A.* Percussion instruments produce musical sounds when struck.

Producing sounds by striking solid surfaces. Obtain some cedar shingles, lattice, furring strips, or other hardwood from a lumber yard. Cut the wood into pieces approximately 1 in. (2 cm) wide and 8 in. (20 cm) long. Next, cut some of the strips to 5 in. (12 cm) lengths, some to 6 in. (15 cm) lengths, and so on. When finished, let students gather around a cement walk or tile floor and take turns dropping the strips, one at a time, while everyone listens. They will discover that the pitch changes with the length of the strip and will be able to predict a sound by looking at a strip (the longer the strip, the lower the sound; the shorter the strip, the higher the sound). Students might test other materials (e.g., wood against wood, wood against metal, metal against metal) to hear what sounds are produced.

01 Gc

Making percussion instruments. Percussion instruments depend upon a vibrating membrane or other solid surface set into motion by being struck (e.g., drum, xylophone, bell, tuning fork). A variety of such instruments can be made. For some of them, students can note how the size and shape of each relates to the sounds produced.

02 Gc

a. *Drums.* Use empty large fruit cans, large coffee cans, cookie cans, tobacco cans, or lard containers. Carton drums can be made from round cereal cartons, salt boxes, or large ice cream containers. Keg drums can be made from wooden mixing bowls, nail kegs, wine kegs, or butter tubs. Have students remove one or both ends from each container. For drumheads, cut round pieces from an inner tube, rubber sheeting, or canvas to fit over the ends of the container and extend approximately 1½ in. (4 cm) down the side. If secondhand drumheads are obtained from a music store, they should be soaked in water before they are cut. The edges should be scalloped and have a hole punched in each scallop. Single drumheads can be tightly stretched and attached with tacks. Heavy cord or leather strips can be used to lace double drumheads together.

b. *Xylophones and Marimbas.* Cut bars of wood of different lengths from a long piece of hardwood or bamboo. Lay the lengths across two thin supports or suspend each from a length of string. If the following lengths are cut, the blocks will provide an approximation of the musical scale: 7, 7¼, 7¾, 8½, 8¾, 9½, 10 in. (18, 19, 20, 22, 23, 24, 26 cm). See Figure 324.02a (p. 264).

Figure 324.02a

c. *Bells.* Tie lengths of strong string around the middle of nails or through large buttons and thread them through the draining holes of different size flower pots so that the nails or buttons hold the pots suspended. Hang the pots in order of size from a crossbar as shown in Figure 324.02b. When struck, they will ring like bells. Similarly, eight identical drinking glasses can be filled with different volumes of water and tapped to play like bells. **Caution: Remind students to not strike glasses too hard. They can break and cause a hazard.**

Figure 324.02b

d. *Chimes.* Suspend different lengths of pipe from a crossbar of wood.

e. *Musical Tines.* Cut five straight pins to different lengths and hammer them into the bottom of an inverted cigar box. The pins can be struck with a rubber mallet and can be tuned by tapping them more deeply into the wood.

f. *Tambourines.* Punch holes in the edges of pie tins with a nail. Tie bells through the holes and play the instruments by striking the tins with the heel of a hand.

g. *Rattles and Maracas.* Place some dried beans or peas inside a tin can, box, or gourd that has been fastened to the end of a stick. To play, shake the stick. Various other materials can be placed inside the containers to make different sounds.

Contributing Idea B. Stringed instruments produce musical sounds when struck, plucked, or bowed (e.g. piano, banjo, violin).

Producing sounds by plucking strings. 03 Gc
Provide each student with a piece of strong thread, nylon fishing line, or thin string. The material should be long enough to tie around each student's desk. Tie the thread tightly with a square knot so that it will not slip. Next, tighten the thread at each desk by placing two blocks of wood between the thread and the desktop (Figure 324.03). Have students pluck the thread between the two blocks. (Note:

The blocks may need to be enlarged to produce a clear tone.) Experiment to see what types of sounds are produced by tapping the string, stroking it, or plucking it between two fingers. Investigate how the pitch varies by moving the blocks closer together or farther apart. Some students can tune their string to match a note on the musical scale. Students with different notes can learn to play simple tunes together.

Figure 324.03

Making stringed instruments. Stringed instruments depend upon a vibrating strand or string set into motion by plucking or bowing (e.g., violin, guitar, banjo). A variety of such instruments can be made. For each of the following, students can test different materials of different lengths, widths, and thicknesses, change the tautness of the materials, and vary the method used to produce a musical sound (e.g., plucked, bowed).

04
Gc

    a. *Violins.* Fasten rectangular wooden boxes to lengths of wood. Cut a circular hole in each box. Attach different instrument strings (obtained from a music supply store)

to the box so that they pass over two small blocks of wood fastened to the box and across the hole. Fasten them securely at the box end and around cotter-pins at the end of the piece of wood. The cotter-pins can be twisted (like violin screws) to adjust the tautness of the strings. The instrument can be plucked or bowed using a bow made from horsehair (Figure 324.04a).

Figure 324.04a

    b. *Guitars.* Stretch three rubber bands of different thicknesses across the opening of a cigar or chalk box (Figure 324.04b, p. 266). The bands can also be cut from an old inner tube with widths of ¼ in., ½ in., and ¾ in. (1, 2, and 3 cm). To play, students can use several variables at one time (e.g., thickness, length, tightness). A block of wood or pencil inserted near one end would compare to the frets on a guitar that shorten the length of the vibrating string (Figure 324.04c, p. 266).

Figure 324.04

The tightening of the bands with a piece of wood would compare to the screws which tighten guitar strings (Figure 324.04d). A one-string guitar can be made by attaching two small blocks of wood at opposite ends of a long board. Fasten a steel wire to the board, crossing the blocks, and let the free end hang over the side. Tie a weight to the free end to hold it taut. The instrument is played by plucking the wire or stroking it. Different tones can be produced by moving a third block of wood along the length of the wire (Figure 324.04e).

  c. *Harpsichords.* Pluck rubber bands stretched around rectangular cake tins, cigar boxes, or wooden chalk boxes. Set the bands at different tensions by twisting a piece of wood under each band.

  d. *Zither.* Hammer four pairs of nails into a wooden board approximately 15 in. × 15 in. (35 cm × 35 cm). The first pair should be set 3 in. (7.5 cm) apart, the second, 8 in. (20 cm), the third, 10 in. (25 cm), and the fourth, 12 in. (31 cm). Stretch rubber bands between each pair of nails and play by plucking the rubber bands.

Contributing Idea C. Wind instruments produce musical sounds when blown.

Producing sounds by blowing. Fill eight identical bottles with water and attempt to tune them to the musical scale by adding or removing some of the water. Simple tunes can be played on the containers by blowing across their tops to set the air column inside into vibration. For each container, compare the length of the air column to the sound that is produced. (Note: Students can tap the containers as well as blow across them. Tapping, however, causes the glass and the liquid in it to vibrate; thus when blowing across the bottles, the bottle with the least water has the lowest sound while the one with the most has the highest—conversely, when striking the bottles, the one with the most water produces the lowest sound while the one with the least produces the highest.) **05 Gc**

Making wind instruments. Wind instruments depend upon vibrating air columns set into motion by blowing air across a **06 Gc**

sharp edge (e.g., flute, piccolo, whistle), by vibrating the lips (e.g., coronet, trombone, trumpet, tuba), or by vibrating reeds (e.g., accordion, clarinet, harmonica, oboe, saxophone). In each case, the sound is amplified by the air column within the instrument. A variety of such instruments can be made. If possible, bring actual instruments to class and demonstrate how each works.

   a. *Flutes* (or flute-type instruments). Cut a row of holes in a dry, straight, empty piece of bamboo that is open at both ends. Similarly, potatoes can be carved into simple flutes.

   b. *Trombones* (or horn-type instruments). Obtain two cardboard tubes, one just fitting inside the other. Have students put the tubes together and blow across an open end while sliding the inner tube in and out. They will realize that the sound changes because the air column is lengthened and shortened. Similarly, a trombone can be made by placing a piece of glass or metal tubing approximately 1 ft. long and ½ in. (30 cm × 1 cm) diameter into a bottle nearly full of water.

Students can blow across the top of a tube while the bottle is moved up and down. They will note that the length of the air column in the tube varies and the sound changes as with a slide trombone.

   c. *Saxophones* (or reed-type instruments). Flatten ½ in. (1 cm) of one end of a paper drinking straw and cut away both its corners. Students can place the flat end into their mouths, close their lips around the straw, and blow very hard (moistening the flat end sometimes helps). They will realize that the flat end acts as a reed does in a wind instrument. Next, shorten the straws with scissors while blowing through them. (The pitch will change when a piece is snipped off.) Encourage students to tune eight straws to the musical scale. A team of eight students, each with a straw representing a different musical note, might practice some simple tunes together. Others might test to see what effect splitting the flat end, or making small holes have upon the sound produced.

330 Light

331 Characteristics

Generalization I. Light has identifiable characteristics.

Contributing Idea A. Light travels in all directions from a source.

Observing that light travels in all directions from a source. Have students pour **01 Aa** several in. or centimeters of sand into an oatmeal box. Turn on a small pen flashlight and insert it into the sand so that it stands facing upward. Cover the box, darken the room, and punch a hole in the top of the box with a large turkey needle or medium-size nail. Students will see that the light from the flashlight travels straight up through the hole to the ceiling. Now punch other holes in the box along the sides as well as the top. Students will find that a beam of light travels from each hole no matter where it is punched. Have them note that the spots of light appear in every direction, indicating that the light travels in all directions from its source.

Contributing Idea B. Light travels in a straight line.

Observing a straight line of light through the air. Cut a small hole in a large piece **02 Aa** of construction paper, and place the paper entirely over a sunlit window. Darken the room as much as possible, and have students look at the light coming through the hole. If the light cannot be seen clearly, and if chalkboard erasers are available, clap two dusty chalkboard erasers together near the beam. Ask if the light is traveling in a straight line. How would it look if it was not traveling in a straight line?

Observing that light travels in a straight 03 line. Use a paper punch to make holes in **Aa** the exact centers of three old playing cards or index cards. Find the center by drawing diagonal lines between opposite corners. The center will be at the point where the lines intersect. Now place the cards into chalkboard erasers, lumps of clay, or tack them to blocks of wood so they will stand upright. Next, light a candle that is just the height of the holes. Place it in the center of a table, and line up the cards so students can look through all three holes and see the flame. Ask them to slightly move any one of the cards. (The flame will no longer be seen.) Students will find that the flame can only be seen when the cards are in a straight line, no matter where they place the cards around the table.

Observing light passing through a nar- 04 row opening. Cut pieces of cardboard as **Aa** shown in Figure 331.04a. Glue a square of aluminum foil to each piece, cutting a narrow slit in it approximately $1/16$ in. (0.2 cm) wide and 1 in. (2 cm) long (Figure 331.04b). Set the arrangement into lumps of clay or pieces of grooved wood to hold it upright. Now write the numbers one through five approximately 1 ft. (30 cm) apart on a chalkboard or large sheet of paper. Let a few students walk back and forth in front of the numerals and note that they can be seen from many places, as light reflects from the numerals in every direction. Students can set the cardboard pieces on desks approximately 12 ft. (4 m) away from the numerals, and look through the narrow slits at the number 3. Place sheets of paper behind the slits, and have students mark the numeral 3 on their sheets directly in front of their eyes (Figure 331.04c). Without moving the cardboard, let students move their heads until the numeral 2 can be seen with the same eye; and then mark a 2 on the sheet of paper in front of their eyes. Repeat this for each of the remaining numerals. (Note: Be sure the aluminum foil is held steady.) When finished, compare what has been written. Ask students what they notice about the numerals they wrote. (The numerals will be the reverse of the ones on the chalkboard.) Next, have each student hold the cardboard between an eye and the numeral 1 on the chalkboard. Students will find that only the beam of light from the numeral that is in a straight line with the eye can be seen and that if they move an eye to the right or left, they will see more to the left or right side of the numeral. They should realize that because light travels in a straight line, objects on the right side of an opening are seen on the left, and objects on the left side of an opening are seen on the right.

Contributing Idea C. Light can be diffracted or refracted. White light is composed of different colors.

Figure 331.04a, b, c

Observing that white light can be separated into colors. In a darkened room, lean a small mirror in a full, clear glass of water. Shine a bright beam of light through the water at the mirror. Adjust the mirror so that the light reflects a number of colors on the ceiling or wall. Ask students what colors they see and whether or not the colors are spread out. From this experience, they will realize that the colors were made from ordinary light. You might tell them that the range of colors they observed is called the visible spectrum.   **05 Aa Bb**

Observing diffraction. Place a strip of cellophane tape across the lower halves of two identical needles approximately   **06 Aa Bb**

½ in. (1 cm) apart. Fasten the tape to a magnifying lens so that the tops of the needles are slightly higher than the middle of the lens. Shine a narrow beam of light from a pen flashlight from one end of the darkened room. At the other end, have students hold the lens with the needle side toward the light and take turns looking at the beam with one eye. (Note: They may have to move the lens back and forth until it is filled with light.) They will observe that there are colored shadow bands around the sharp edges of the needles. You might explain that the bands appear because light bends around the sharp edges of obstacles. You might also tell them that the bending is called diffraction.

Making a spectroscope. A spectroscope is an instrument used to separate light into its component parts. To build such an instrument, obtain a cardboard tube from a roll of paper toweling or wrapping paper. Cut two identical circles from a piece of cardboard so that they will just seal the ends of the tube. Punch a ¼ in. (0.5 cm) hole in one circle, and cut the other circle in half. Tape a piece of diffraction grating over the small hole and fasten it to one end of the tube so that the grating faces inward. (Note: Inexpensive diffraction grating replicas, which are made from a special film imprinted with about 15,000 to 30,000 parallel lines to the inch, are generally available from scientific supply

**07
Bb
Gc**

houses. If they cannot be obtained, a small prism can be substituted; however, it will refract the light rather than diffract it.) Next, tape the two half circles to the other end of the tube with a very narrow vertical slit left between them. Now use masking tape to seal both ends of the tube so that no other light enters. Aim the slit end at a lightbulb. Looking through the slit, students will see the spectrum along the inside of the tube. (Light is broken up into its component parts as it passes through the narrow spaces on the diffraction grating.) Let them aim the spectroscope at other light sources. **Caution: Do not aim it at the Sun. Warn students about the dangers of looking at the Sun.** They will soon realize that different light sources produce different patterns of light. You might tell them that a *continuous spectrum* shows all the colors of the rainbow, while a *line spectrum* shows only some of the colors.

Observing refraction. In a darkened room, shine the light from a slide projector through a prism. Have students locate the spectrum that is produced and hold a sheet of white paper over it so that the colors can be clearly seen. You might explain that when light passes into and out of a prism, the different colors (frequencies) are bent by different amounts—the blues the most and reds the least—thus appearing separated as in a rainbow. Have students look for examples of the spectrum

**08
Aa
Ga**

produced in more natural ways (e.g., rainbows, soap bubbles, oil slicks).

Making a prism. Tape the edges of three microscope slides together to form a triangle. Press the slides into some clay or plaster. When the triangle is filled with water (see Figure 331.09), the light transmitted through it will act like the light through a prism.

09
Gc

Microscope
Slides

Water

Tape
Edges

Clay

Figure 331.09

Observing that a spectrum of colors can be combined to make white light. You can show in several ways that white light is composed of the colors of the spectrum.

10
Aa

a. Place a shallow pan of water in direct sunlight or in front of a projector beam in a darkened room. Lean a mirror against the rim of the pan so that the light strikes part of the mirror beneath the water's surface. When the water is still, a spectrum will be found on a nearby wall or ceiling. Stir the water and note that the colors combine and white light appears on the wall.

b. In a darkened room, hold a prism in direct sunlight or in front of a projector beam and slowly rotate the prism until a spectrum appears on a wall or ceiling. Now place a second prism in the path of the light leaving the first prism so that all of the colored light strikes one facet of the second prism. Vary the angle of the second prism until the colored light passing through it is focused in a small spot. (Students can also try a hand lens in place of the second prism.) The spot of light will appear white. (Note: It may take some practice to set the second prism properly.) If three prisms and a very powerful light beam are available, challenge students to arrange them so that the light through two prisms is colored and the light from the third is white.

Contributing Idea D. Light can be reflected and absorbed; the color of objects depends on which colors are transmitted, reflected, and absorbed.

Observing the transmission and reflection of colors. In a darkened room, shine a projector beam through a prism set on a pile of books so that the spectrum appears on a white screen. Have students note the exact position of the red color in the spectrum, then place a double thickness of red

11
Aa

cellophane between the prism and the screen. Students will see that all but the red part of the spectrum disappears and will realize that the cellophane prevented all but the red light from getting through. Repeat this activity using green and then blue cellophane. (Note: It is difficult to obtain perfect filtering action with ordinary cellophanes, so some visual discrepancies may occur. Colored glass can be tested in place of the cellophane.)

Observing the transmission, reflection, and absorption of colors. In a very dark room, challenge students to detect the actual colors of squares of colored construction papers as they are held in various colored lights one at a time. The students can keep their eyes closed, while the squares of paper and the cellophanes (blue, green, red) over the lens of a projector are changed. Stay with one color of cellophane before switching to another so that all the squares can be observed. After each square is observed, have students write down their guesses for the actual color, then remove the cellophane and let them see the actual color in white light to check. From this experience, they will understand that color is a function of the light striking an object as well as the color it reflects. For an additional experience, they can use red and green crayons to lightly print their names on pieces of white paper. Have them make some letters green and some red, then look at their **12 Aa Ec**

names and at other red and green objects through the red and green cellophane pieces.

Generalization II. Characteristics of light can be classified.

Contributing Idea A. Some characteristics of light can be seriated.

Seriating colors of light. Have students list the sequence of colors produced in a spectrum of light from a prism. Let them use paints or crayons to reproduce the sequence on paper, and then compare their representations to other rainbows of light that they can find. They will note that the sequence of colors always remains the same. **13 Da**

Seriating light by intensity. In a darkened room, hold a light meter 1 ft. (30 cm) away from various light sources (e.g., burning candle, lightbulb, fluorescent tube) to measure the intensity of each. Let students order the sources from least to most intense. They might compare the intensity of one candle to the intensities of other sources of light. **14 Da**

Contributing Idea B. Some characteristics of light can be classified.

Categorizing luminous and nonluminous light sources. Have students make two lists of as many light sources as they can: (1) objects that produce their own light (e.g., the Sun, burning fuel); (2) **15 Bb Db**

objects that reflect light (e.g., the Moon, mirrors). Discuss each item on the lists. They will realize that reflective sources tend to be cooler. You might explain that the objects that produce their own light are called luminous objects while those that reflect light are called nonluminous objects.

Classifying materials by the way they transmit light. Have students hold different transparent, translucent, and opaque objects up to a light source and divide them into three categories based upon the way light does or does not pass through them.

16 Dc

332   Interactions

Generalization I. Light is a form of energy produced by different sources.

> *Contributing Idea A.* The Sun is a primary source of light (nuclear propagation).

Observing that the Sun is a source of light. While sitting in the classroom without the lights on, let students discuss from where they think the light comes. Ask how things look on dark cloudy days compared with clear sunny days. Have them close their eyes and tell why they cannot see anything (their eyelids block the light from entering their eyes). Make the room as dark as possible by covering the windows with shades and drapes. Ask what can be seen now as compared

01 Aa Ba

with when much light entered the room. If possible, take groups of students into a closet, ask from where the small sources of light come, and ask if anything could be seen if all the cracks were sealed up (without a source of light, nothing could be seen). From these experiences and discussions, students will realize that during the day, the primary source of light is the Sun.

> *Contributing Idea B.* Heating can be a source of light.

Observing light produced by heating. Hold a thin nail or wire with a pair of pliers and heat it in a flame until it glows. Let students describe how the appearance changes as the object is heated. Ask them to guess what would happen if the object could be made hotter (it would glow more brightly—from "red hot" to "white hot"). Explain that many rocks and minerals glow when heated, and materials can become white hot in the production of steel and other metals in factories. You might tell them that when a metal is glowing hot, it is said to be *incandescent.* Have students find pictures of glowing metals in magazines or reference books. **Caution: Follow safety guidelines when using an open flame and with objects that have been heated.**

02 Aa Bb

Observing light produced by glowing wires. Place a thin piece of copper wire across two battery terminals and observe what happens. **Caution: The wire will**

03 Aa Ec

become too hot to touch, and it can burn the skin. Discuss what caused the light to be emitted. Explain that electricity passing through the wire made it hot enough to glow. After students test other wires, tell them that light bulbs (sometimes called incandescent bulbs) work in a similar way. Let them examine the filament in a bulb to see that it performs similarly to their copper wire. (Note: Bulb filaments are usually made of tungsten rather than copper; however, platinum, carbon, and tantalum were used in early bulbs.)

> *Contributing Idea C.* Burning can be a source of light (chemical propagation).

Observing light produced by burning. 04 Aa Bd
Light a match and a candle. Discuss the appearance of the light that is emitted by each. Explain that when something burns, a chemical action (combustion) takes place and light is given off. Have students list other combustible materials that can be used as light sources (e.g., kerosene, gasoline, and oils in lamps; wax and wicks; wood). Some students might be interested in researching the history of artificial lighting from early campfires and torches, to oil and candles, to gas and electricity. **Caution: Follow safety guidelines when using an open flame.**

Comparing candlelight to sunlight. 05 Bb Ca
Light a 1 in. (2 cm) thick candle in a closet or darkened room and note the appearance of some objects that are 1 ft. (30 cm) away. Explain that the intensity of the light upon the object is a standard measurement for light called one foot-candle. Now light two, then three candles, and note the increase in brightness. Next, light one candle outdoors in the bright sunlight to see how effective one candle is. Tell students that on a clear day at noon, the intensity of sunlight is about the equivalent of 10,000 candles 1 ft. (30 cm) away. (Note: The intensity of sunlight 1 ft. or 30 cm from the Sun is about 2.5 billion billion billion candles.)

> *Contributing Idea D.* Electricity can be a source of light (electrical propagation).

Observing light produced by electricity. 06 Aa Bd
Have students examine neon lighting tubes. Have them note that compared to incandescent bulbs, the neon tubes have small separate filaments at each end. Light one tube, and let students describe how it lights up compared with an incandescent bulb. Discuss differences in the lighting (e.g., the incandescent light is yellower). Explain that neon tubes are filled with a gas (neon), and when electricity passes through the gas from one end to the other, it glows as light. The color of the light depends upon the kind of gas in the tube (e.g., neon gives off a red light; argon gives off blue). An interested committee of students can research to find out what other gases are put to use in lighting.

Some may wish to study fluorescent and mercury-vapor lights. (Note: Fluorescent bulbs were patented in the 1890s but only recently were they designed for use in receptacles used for incandescent bulbs. Today a fluorescent bulb is an energy-saving light called a compact fluorescent light (CFL). Compared to incandescent lights, CFLs use less power and have a longer life, although at half-life they begin to dim.) **Caution: The fluorescent lights contain mercury, are dangerous when broken, and must be properly recycled or discarded when used.**

> *Contributing Idea E.* The intensity of a light depends upon its energy source and the distance the light travels.

Observing that light intensity diminishes over distance. In a darkened room, light a lamp with its shade removed. Hold a book close to the lamp and observe the brightness of a page. Have one student walk from the light while holding the book, and let others note that the page becomes dimmer. Similarly, four identical pieces of white paper can be placed 1, 2, 3, and 4 ft. (20, 40, 60, and 80 cm) from the lighted lamp and observed for differences in brightness.

07 Ca

Determining factors that influence the intensity of light. Insert a piece of aluminum foil that is shiny on both sides between two identical blocks of paraffin wax. Be sure all three pieces are the

08 Ca Ec

same size. Hold them together with rubber bands. Set the blocks in the middle of a table and place a lighted birthday candle at one end and four identical candles the same distance away at the other end. Darken the room, and let students observe the blocks from the side to see which glows the most. Next, let them move the blocks back and forth between the two light sources until they glow equally brightly. They will find that the intensity of each glow depends on the energy source (four candles versus one candle) and on the distance the source is from the receiving object.

Generalization II. Adding or removing light affects many materials and organisms.

> *Contributing Idea A.* Adding or removing light causes changes in some materials.

Testing the effect of light upon some colored materials. Place one piece of dark blue construction paper or cloth on a windowsill in direct sunlight. After two days, compare the colors on each side. Next, test different colors and other materials to see if they fade differently in sunlight. Each of the colors of the spectrum can be ordered by the amount it fades. Students can also test other sources of light to see how they affect the colors and materials (e.g., fluorescent lights; incandescent lights).

09 Db Ec

Using blueprint paper. Have students take a piece of blueprint paper, place an object on it, cover the object and paper with clear glass, and expose it to direct sunlight for two to five minutes. (The time needed will vary with the brightness of the day.) After the paper has been washed in clear water, observe how the light affected the portion not covered by the object.

**10
Ga**

> *Contributing Idea B.* Adding or removing light influences plants and animals.

Testing the effect of light upon plants. Place a plant in a dark closet for an extended period of time and note the gradual changes in it. For comparative purposes, be sure an identical plant is kept in sunlight and that all other conditions (e.g., amount of water, temperature) remain identical for both plants.

**11
Ec**

Testing the effect of light upon animals. Obtain two glass jars, and paint the outside of one completely black so that no light can enter it. Fill the unpainted jar with houseflies or fruit flies, and cover it with a stiff piece of cardboard so they cannot escape. Set the painted jar upside down on top of the cardboard on the unpainted one, remove the cardboard, keep the jars on top of each other, and observe where the flies go. After about five minutes, turn the jars over so that the painted jar is below the unpainted one. After another five minutes, students will

**12
Ec**

be able to suggest why flies are usually found near windows. (Flies respond to light—that is, they move toward light.) If possible, test other animals such as mosquitos, spiders, or worms in the same way to see how light affects them.

Generalization III. **Light travels through some solids, liquids, and gases at different speeds.**

> *Contributing Idea A.* Light travels through some materials but not others.

Observing that some materials are transparent. Place a coin on a desk and cover it with a piece of clear plastic. Cover the plastic with clear cellophane, then an upright, clear drinking glass. Add water to the glass. Ask students if they could see the coin through each material. Tell them that materials that allow the light from an object to pass through them so that the object is clearly seen are called transparent materials. Next, have students observe the coin and other objects through colored glass or cellophane. They will realize that the colored materials are transparent, but allow only certain colors to pass through. Have them find examples of transparent materials in the classroom.

**13
Aa
Bb
Ga**

Observing that some materials are translucent. Shine a flashlight beam through various translucent materials such as oiled paper, frosted glass, or a glass of milk. Have students note that

**14
Aa
Bb
Ga**

although light is transmitted, one cannot clearly see through the materials. Tell them that materials that allow some light to pass through, but transmit no clear image, are called translucent materials. Let them find examples of translucent materials around the school.

Observing that some materials are **15** **opaque.** Stand a wooden ruler upright **Aa** between two books on a desk in a dark- **Bb** ened room. Lay a small narrow-beamed flashlight behind the ruler to make a shadow on a wall or screen. Have students describe what happens to the light beam. (It is blocked by the ruler and produces a shadow.) Tell them that objects or materials that block light so that none gets through are called opaque materials. Now have them move the flashlight closer to the ruler, then farther away. Let them try to explain why the shadow becomes taller and wider when they move the flashlight closer, and why it becomes shorter and thinner when they move the light farther away. Next, have them test various objects between the light source and the wall. They will find that most objects are opaque.

Contributing Idea B. Slanted light rays bend when traveling from one medium to another of a different density.

Observing refraction. From the fol- **16** lowing experiences, students will find **Aa** that light can be "bent" under certain **Bb** **Ca**

conditions. After the experiences, you might tell them that such bending of light rays is called refraction.

a. Set a lighted candle on a table approximately 2 ft. (60 cm) away from a wall in a darkened room. Have one student stand across the room and shine a flashlight beam on the wall above the candle flame. (The flashlight beam will seem to waver.) This can also be done across the top of a heated hot plate. Let students describe similarities with what they have seen near the surface of roads on hot days. **Caution: Follow safety guidelines when using a candle.**

b. Place a straight stick, pencil, or ruler in an empty clear thin-sided glass. Look at the object from all sides. (It will appear to be straight.) Now half-fill the glass with water, and look again. (From certain positions slightly above the water level, the object will appear to be bent.)

c. Stand a glass of water at the edge of a table. Look upward through the side of the glass at the top surface of the water. While looking, have a student stick the pointed end of a pencil down into the water. (The point will look larger than it really is.)

Observing that light rays can be **17** refracted as the rays move from a **Aa** denser to a less dense medium. Place **Ca** a lighted narrow-beamed flashlight into **Fc** a plastic bag, seal it with a rubber band, and submerge it (beam shining upward) in a large transparent container filled with milky water. In a darkened room, students can see what happens to the beam as it passes from the water to the air. Several additional activities can be experienced by students.

a. Have students work in pairs. Let one in each pair place a coin in the bottom of an empty, clear cup. Have the other stand up, look at the coin, and back up until it just disappears from view. While she keeps her head in this position, have the partner, without moving the cup or the coin, slowly pour water into the cup. (The viewer will see the coin reappear.) Let them switch places and repeat. Explain that the direct view from the eye would not detect the coin, but because the light rays from the coin leave the water and enter the less dense air at an angle, the rays that strike the air first travel faster than the rays still within the denser water—the result is the light rays are refracted (bent) into the viewing path.

b. Students can observe from various positions spoons or pencils placed in empty glasses of different thicknesses or glasses filled with different liquids. In each case, they can describe how the light travels from one medium to another. Let them decide from their observations which medium is more or less dense.

c. Some students might enjoy filling an aquarium with water and trying to touch objects at the bottom with a pencil or stick. Discuss why they are visually fooled. (The light is refracted as it leaves the water and enters the air; thus, the object in the aquarium is not in the position it appears to be.)

Generalization IV. Light can be controlled.

Contributing Idea A. Light can be refracted. Lenses in optical instruments refract light.

Observing the shapes of lenses. Obtain **18** several convex and concave lenses. Let **Aa** students feel the surfaces of each and note **Bb** that some are hollowed and others are **Ca** bulged outward on one or both sides. Let them look through the lenses at various objects and describe what they see. (Convex lenses magnify: double convex lenses provide more magnification than plano-convex (single convex) lenses. Concave lenses make things look smaller.) Tell students that a lens that curves outward on one or both sides is called a convex lens and that a lens that curves inward on one or both sides is called a concave lens.

Finding examples of how lenses are used. 19 Ga Have students research the topic of lenses in encyclopedias and other reference books. They may find that several different kinds of lenses are found in the eyes of animals and in manufactured devices such as telescopes, microscopes, projectors, and cameras. Have students find examples of how different lenses are put to use in optical equipment. Double-convex lenses are used in hand magnifiers, slide projectors, and telescopes because they provide more magnification than plano-convex lenses. Plano-convex lenses are used in eyeglasses to correct farsightedness. Double-concave lenses are used in eyeglasses for nearsighted people and in some binocular eyepieces. Artists also use these lenses as "reducing glasses" to make images smaller. Automobile headlights have many small lenses distributed over their surface in a complex pattern to control the light to obtain superior illumination. The lenses in some simple cameras are combinations of convex and concave lenses—the side away from the film is convex and the side nearest the film is concave—and expensive cameras may contain eight or more lens combinations either next to each other to obtain superior optical qualities, or separated by space as in the objective/ eyepiece combination used in refracting telescopes, binoculars, and microscopes.

Observing that an outward curving surface refracts light to magnify the appearance of objects. 20 Aa Ca Fill a tall, thin bottle, such as an olive bottle, three-quarters full with water. Let one student stick an index finger into the water and compare its appearance to his other index finger outside the bottle. Ask if the inserted finger appears larger near the back or front of the bottle. Point out that the outside curvature of the bottle is similar to that of a convex lens: as light travels from the water in the bottle to the less dense air, it is refracted by the curved surface between them. Next, cut a strip of graph paper or two strips of notebook paper— one with lines running lengthwise and one with lines running across the strip. Place the strip into the bottle of water and observe. Have students compare the spacing between the lines both vertically and horizontally, and relate any observable differences to the curvature of the bottle. Repeat these examinations using bottles of different curvatures (diameters). You might discuss which bottle students would use if they wanted a product to look larger (e.g., olives in a jar).

Observing that a convex lens refracts and magnifies light. 21 Aa Ca Have students print a small letter *F* on a piece of paper, measure its height and width, and look at the letter through a convex lens. (The letter will look larger; at times it will be clearly upside down.) Now have students remove the shade from a lamp, find the trademark on the bulb, face the trademark toward the ceiling, notice the arrangement of the numbers and letters in the trademark, then turn the lamp on. Have one student move a convex lens up and down over the top of the bulb until a clear image of the trademark is projected on the ceiling. (A magnified but reversed image will be seen.) Let students find examples of instruments in which convex lenses are used to magnify (e.g., binoculars, microscopes, telescopes), and discuss whether the viewed image is upside down or not.

Measuring the magnifying power of a convex lens. Focus a convex lens over some narrowly lined paper. Compare a single space seen through the lens with the number of spaces seen outside the lens. For example, if there are four spaces outside the lens to one through the lens, the power is four times (4×). **22 Cc**

Observing that a convex lens refracts and focuses light. In a darkened room, shine a narrow beam of light through a convex (magnifying) lens. Clap two chalkboard erasers together so that the light beam can be seen clearly. Students will see how the beam of light comes to a point after it passes through the lens. **23 Aa**

Locating the focal point of a convex lens. Hold a convex (magnifying) lens approximately 1 ft. (30 cm) above a large sheet of paper at such an angle that the **24 Aa Bb Cd**

direct rays of the Sun (or other bright light source that is at least 25 ft. away) pass through the lens. Tell students that the point where the light under the lens comes together at its greatest brightness is called the focus or focal point. Have them measure the distance between the paper and the magnifying lens when it is focused, and tell them that this distance is called the focal length of the lens.

Observing that a concave lens refracts and spreads out light. Hold a concave lens approximately 1 ft. (30 cm) above a large sheet of paper at such an angle that the direct rays of sunlight pass through the lens. Slowly move the lens back and forth to try to bring the light to a focus. Students will find that this cannot be done. (Convex lenses bend light inward while concave lenses bend light outward.) In a darkened room, shine a narrow beam of light through the lens, and if available, clap chalkboard erasers together to put some dust in the air, and observe that the beam is spread out after it passes through the lens. **25 Aa**

Testing to see how different pieces of optical equipment affect light rays. Obtain a thick sheet of corrugated cardboard that is approximately 1½ ft. × 1 ft. (1½ m × 1 m) in size. Mount the cardboard to a stand to hold it upright. Cut holes in the cardboard for the placement of different pieces of optical equipment such as lenses, prisms, and mirrors. Paint **26 Ec**

the face of the cardboard white so that it will serve as a viewing screen. (See Figure 332.26.) Now set a slide projector approximately 6 ft. (2 m) to one side of the cardboard so its beam just strikes the center of the screen at a very slight, glancing angle. A projector slide that will produce rays of light against the screen can be made in two ways: (1) Using a pen and India ink, rule a ¼ in. × 1 in. (1 cm × 3 cm) area of frosted acetate with fine, closely spaced lines; (2) Using a white background, tape strips of ½ in. (1 cm) black tape at ½ in. (1 cm) intervals, then photograph the strips with a camera from a distance of approximately 8 ft. (2.5 m). By either method, the slide that is made will produce parallel rays of light when placed horizontally in the projector's slide mount. Be sure any unlined area on the slide is blacked out with tape. Darken the room, project the rays so that they strike the screen, and then place pieces of optical equipment, singly or in combinations, in the screen openings and in the path of the rays. Observe the results. Students can test combinations of differently angled prisms, plano- and double-convex lenses, plano- and double-concave lenses, convex and concave mirrors. Many studies can be carried out with this simple equipment (e.g., colored glass or cellophane can be used to produce colored light rays; quantitative data can be obtained by attaching paper to the screen, tracing the rays, then measuring the angles and distances after the paper is removed; cylindrical liquid lenses can be tested by filling bottles with various liquids and placing them in the beams of parallel light rays).

Corrugated Cardboard
Painted White

Holes for Lenses
and Mirrors

Holes for Prisms

Block of Wood

Tacks

Figure 332.26

Contributing Idea B. Light can be reflected; mirrors in optical instruments reflect light.

Observing reflections. From the following experiences, students will find that light can be "bounced" under certain conditions. After the experiences, you might tell them that the bouncing of light rays is called reflection.

27
Aa
Bb

a. Fill a pan with water, set it on a table in sunlight, and look for a bright spot on the wall or ceiling. Students will realize that water can serve to reflect light.

b. Clean a piece of window glass, lay it on white paper, and let students try to see their reflections in it. They can repeat their observations after laying it on black paper. From this they will be able to explain why a window makes fairly good mirror reflections at night when it is bright inside and dark outside. Let them try other colored papers under the glass.

Reflecting light. Have students take turns holding a mirror in the sunlight and flashing the light on a wall or ceiling. Let other students take turns holding another mirror in the line of reflection. Using two mirrors, challenge them to direct a spot of light to particular locations in the room. You might tell them that signals are sometimes sent at sea from one ship to another in a similar way and that the U.S. Cavalry once used reflectors to send signals from one hill to another.

28
Aa

Making a seismograph using reflected light. Place a pan of water on a table in such a way that a beam of sunlight strikes the surface of the water and reflects a spot of light on the ceiling or a wall. Now have a student stamp a foot on the floor, and observe what happens to the spot of light. Explain that the device is similar to a seismograph that detects vibrations; every time there is a small quake, vibrations travel through the floor and air to the water and set up ripples on its surface, thus causing the spot on the wall to shimmer. If the quake is weak, the shimmering is slight, if it is strong, the shimmering is great. Students can set up vibrations in many ways (e.g., clapping their hands, closing a door or window,

29
Ga
Gc

dropping a book). Have them see if their seismograph is sensitive enough to detect the hum of a motor in a school appliance or the rumble of vehicles passing by the school.

Testing to see how different surfaces reflect light. Use poster paint to blacken the inside of a shoe box. Cut a slit $\frac{1}{3}$ in. × 3 in. (0.2 cm × 8 cm) in one end as shown in Figure 332.30. Stand the box on its long side in the sunlight, and observe the beam of light that enters through the slit. Now place a mirror in the bottom of the box and observe again. (The light will reflect and strike the opposite end.) Next, place the mirror with other materials such as white paper, black paper, colored paper, aluminum foil, and so forth to see how each reflects light. Students will see that some of the materials, like white paper, scatter the light in all directions (irregular reflections), while more polished surfaces reflect it with little scattering (regular reflections). Have students order the materials by the way they reflected the light.

30
Da
Ec

Figure 332.30

Observing that particles in gases (air) and liquids (water) reflect light. Prepare a flashlight so that it projects a thin beam. To do this, cover the bulb with masking tape, leaving a pinhole in the center. Next, tape a paper cup over the end of the flashlight, leaving a pinhole in the bottom. Now darken the inside of a shoe box with black paint and cut viewing holes in each end and the top. Place a white index card opposite one end and shine the thin beam from the flashlight through the box so that it can be seen on the card. (See Figure 332.31.) Have students take turns looking down into the box through the top hole at the passing beam of light. (The beam cannot be seen.) Explain that light is generally invisible and that we see it only at its source or when it is reflected. For example, when one looks into the sky at night, only the stars (sources of light) and the Moon and planets (reflectors of light) can be seen, while the light that fills the sky from the Sun and stars remains invisible. Next, blow some smoke into the box or clap two chalkboard erasers together to fill it with dust. Students can observe the interior of the box again. (The beam will be clearly visible.) They will realize that the beam is now visible because it is reflected from countless tiny particles in the air. Now shine the beam through a clear glass of water, and then add a spoonful of milk to the water. Students will see that the beam was invisible (except for the tiny dust particles) until the particles of milk were added.

**31
Aa**

Figure 332.31

Measuring angles of reflection. Prepare a flashlight so that it projects a thin beam (see entry 332.31). Tape mirrors inside three identical cardboard boxes at the center of one of the long sides. In one box, cut a hole in the opposite side so that the flashlight can be inserted. Paint the inside of the boxes black, and cover the open top of each with transparent plastic (e.g., sandwich wrap or a dry-cleaning bag). (See Figure 332.32.) Before closing the first box, set a burning string, piece of punk, or incense on a metal jar lid so that the box will fill with smoke (the smoke will make the light beam easier to see). If the flashlight holes are placed in different positions in the remaining two boxes, students can vary the angle at which incoming beams

**32
Cd
Ec**

Figure 332.32

strike the mirror. By looking straight down through the plastic, students will see how the light beam strikes and reflects from the mirror. A string can be stretched across the top of the plastic to match the lines that form the angles of incidence and reflection. A protractor can be used to measure the angles. Students will discover that the beam always travels in straight lines, and the angles of incidence and reflections are always equal no matter how the beam strikes the mirror. Test other materials in place of the mirror to see how they reflect. From the tests students will find that rougher surfaces tend to scatter or diffuse the light beams because of their varying angles of incidence.

Contributing Idea C. Light can be absorbed.

Observing that colored materials absorb most of the colors of the spectrum. Place a piece of green cloth in a completely dark room. Put a red bulb in a socket or cover a white bulb with several layers of red cellophane, and turn on the light. Let students describe the color of the cloth. Now repeat the observations using a green bulb in the socket. Students will see that when the red light falls on the green material, no light is reflected (it is absorbed), and the material appears black; but when the green light strikes the material, the color is reflected. Test other colored light sources and colored materials. (Note: Objects have different colors because they contain different

33
Aa
Ec

chemicals that have the ability to absorb [change into heat energy] certain colors [wavelengths of light] and reflect others.)

Observing what happens to light that is absorbed. Place a piece of black cloth about a foot beneath an electric lightbulb. Use books to support a pane of glass between the bulb and the cloth to prevent radiant heat from reaching the cloth. (See Figure 332.34.) Turn the light on; then after 15 minutes let students feel the cloth. Repeat this using a piece of white cloth, and compare the findings. Students will discover that when light is absorbed by a material, the light energy is changed into heat energy. As a supplemental activity, they can lay a thermometer under the black cloth, check its reading every three minutes for a half hour, then plot the change in temperature on a graph.

34
Ab
Bf
Ch

Figure 332.34

333 Theory

Generalization I. According to the particle theory, light energy is made up of tiny particles.

> *Contributing Idea A.* Light energy is made up of particles.

Using a marble model to represent light as particles. Have students shoot marbles through a narrow slit between two supported, upright sheets of cardboard. After a marble passes through, note that it continues to move in a straight line. Use this particle model in accompaniment with activities that indicate that light travels in a straight line. What is observed can also be compared to a water wave model (see entry 333.09). Let students decide whether a particle model or wave model best explains what they observe. Similarly, they can carry out activities dealing with the reflection of light to see how the two models explain the results. Some interested students might like to research the work of Sir Isaac Newton (1642–1727) who advocated a particle theory to explain light.

**01
Bd
Fc**

> *Contributing Idea B.* Some characteristics of light cannot be explained by the particle theory.

Observing a discrepancy in the particle model. Discuss the idea that if light is made up of particles, a disturbance would occur when two beams of light met. After the discussion, have students shine the beams of two flashlights across each other in a dark room and carefully look at the area where they cross to see if there is any evidence of particles hitting each other and bouncing off course. Ask students which theory of light, the particle theory or the wave theory, (see entry 333.09), best supports the observed evidence. Some students might be interested in researching the work of Christian Huygens (1629–1695) who suggested that light consisted of tiny waves.

**02
Bd
Fc**

Generalization II. According to the wave theory, light energy is thought of as vibrations that transfer energy in wavelike patterns through molecules.

> *Contributing Idea A.* Light energy travels in transverse waves.

Using a rope model to represent light as transverse waves. Tie one end of a 50 ft. (15 m) clothesline to a post. Extend it so that all the kinks are stretched out and the rope does not touch the ground. Let one student move the free end of the rope up and down rhythmically to make waves while others observe. Let students take turns producing waves in different ways (e.g., they might move the rope from side to side to make horizontal waves or strike the stretched rope in the center with a stick). If brightly colored pieces of yarn or cloth are tied on the rope at 6 in. (15 cm) intervals, the wave motions will be more visible. If the students are

**03
Bb
Fc**

challenged to make waves that have more or less energy, they will find that the rope waves are put into motion by some work on their part and that they can increase the energy of the waves by moving their hand up and down a greater distance or by increasing the force and rate of their hand's motion. To indicate the amount of energy carried by the waves, crease a sheet of paper to form a saddle over the rope. Students will see that when the rope is moved up and down a greater distance or when the force and velocity are increased, the folded paper will respond accordingly (low energy waves move the paper comparatively little; high energy waves can make it jump off the rope). Tell them that waves that travel up and down, such as those observed, are called transverse waves, and that such waves can be used to explain some behaviors of light.

Comparing longitudinal and transverse waves in a rope. Tie a 50 ft. (15 m) length of clothesline to a post and pull the line taut. Let one student tap the post with a hammer and ask a second student holding the free end of the line to tell if she feels the arrival of the wave. The first student can tap the post rhythmically, and the second student can feel the waves. Tell them that the energy from the hammer is being transmitted along the rope by *longitudinal* waves. Let students discover ways to make some longitudinal waves of low amplitude or high amplitude (by

**04
Bb
Fc**

tapping lightly or heavily) and high frequency or low frequency (by tapping rapidly or slowly). Now slacken the rope and let the student with the free end move the rope up and down. Tell the students that the waves they see now are called transverse waves. Discuss the ease of detecting each kind of wave, and then ask them to figure out a way to race longitudinal and transverse rope waves. (They can tie identical ropes to the same post and produce each kind simultaneously.) Also ask how they can make both kinds of waves with equal frequencies. (Note: Longitudinal waves [e.g., sound waves] travel in a back and forth movement in line with the particles that produce them, while transverse waves [e.g., light waves, electrical waves, radio waves, and all electromagnetic waves] move at right angles to the direction the wave is traveling.)

Observing transverse waves in water. Fill an aquarium or large rectangular glass dish with water and float a small cork or piece of wood on the surface. Have students watch from various positions as you release drops of water from a medicine dropper or touch the surface of the water repeatedly with a pencil point a short distance from the cork. The students will see that the cork moves up and down (oscillates), while the waves move away from their source of disturbance. Explain that the movement of the cork indicates that it is only the energy that moves horizontally

**05
Aa**

and not the water. If the water waves are viewed from the side, students will recognize their similarity to those produced in a rope: both are transverse waves. Whenever possible, relate the water wave model to the rope wave model.

Using a water wave model to explain diffraction. 06 Fc Gb Set a stick upright in a large container of water to see what happens when a wave is obstructed. Have students start a wave and observe. (A shadow of quiet water will extend beyond the stick, but it narrows as the waves on each side spread.) Now set up two broad barriers in the container with a 3 in. (8 cm) opening between. Have students start a wave and observe as the wave spreads out after passing beyond the opening. Let students invent other barriers with more openings and/or larger and smaller openings. Relate this model to observations of light diffraction.

Using a water wave model to explain reflection. 07 Ec Fc Use an aquarium or large rectangular glass dish with 1 in. (2 cm) of water in it. Start a transverse wave in the water and observe what happens when it hits the far side of the container (the wave returns). Now let students experiment with a semicircle coffee can rim at the far end to observe how waves collect and reflect. Other shapes can also be tested to see how they reflect and concentrate waves. The results can be used to explain reflections from some mirrors.

Making and using a ripple tank. 08 Ga Gc Build a 2 ft. × 4 ft. (60 cm × 120 cm) frame that is approximately 6 in. (15 cm) high. Set the frame on a large table or on the floor, and line it with a sheet of plastic. Add water to the sheet to a depth of 2 or 3 in. (5 or 7 cm). Cut a thin, flat board that is 1 ft., 10 in. (55 cm) long, and float it across one end. When the water is very still, tap the board, and watch the transverse wave move to the opposite end of the trough. Reflecting waves can be reduced by lining the far end of the tank with paper towels. A projector light can be cast on the waves to make them more distinct. (See Figure 333.08.) The light can also be reflected on a screen or the ceiling to show the ripple patterns. Students can use a camera to take photographs of the waves or the reflected patterns. Photographs will make it possible to study such characteristics as wavelengths or interferences. Experiment with the apparatus (e.g., students can make high and low frequency waves by moving the flat board up and down more times per minute; they

Figure 333.08

can make high amplitude waves by moving the board farther up and down; they can partition the tank in half and race high and low amplitude waves).

Contributing Idea B. Some characteristics of light energy cannot be explained by the wave theory.

Observing discrepancies in the water wave model. **09 Fc** Place two barriers opposite each other in a ripple tank. Let one student practice tapping the floating board until he can produce a steady series of straight waves. Let other students observe the waves as they hit the edges of the slit between the two barriers and observe what happens at the edges as the waves pass through. Ask students to use the model to explain what happens to light at a corner. They will realize that if the model is correct, light will go around corners as water and sound waves do. Have them note that light does not behave as the water model: it travels in straight lines and it produces sharp shadows.

Generalization III. According to a theory that combines the wave and particle theories, light energy, as a part of the electromagnetic spectrum, is made up of photons that travel in waves at a great speed.

Contributing Idea A. Light energy is made up of photons that travel at a great speed.

Researching the wave-particle theory. **10 Bd** The most recent theory to explain the nature of light came in 1900. Max Planck (1858–1947) described light as consisting of little packages of energy (photons) that move in waves. Have students explore encyclopedias and other reference books to see what they can find out about the man and his theory.

Observing that light travels at a great speed. **11 Ca** Have several students stand approximately 200 yd. away from the rest of the class. Let them blow up and pop several balloons while others observe. If they observe carefully, they will see the balloons pop before they hear the sound, thus indicating that the light from the balloons travels much faster than the sound. Students can share experiences they have had in lightning storms in which they first saw the flash, and then heard the crack.

Contributing Idea B. Light energy is a part of the electromagnetic spectrum.

Categorizing light energy. **12 Bb Dc** The electromagnetic spectrum is made up of radiations that travel at a great speed (approximately 186,000 mi. or 300,000 km per second). All the radiations can be refracted and reflected, and differ only in frequency and in wavelength. Use Chart 333.12 to point out to students that out of the total spectrum, light radiation represents only a small part. They should note that the radiations that have wave lengths

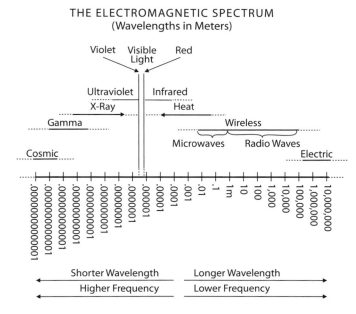

THE ELECTROMAGNETIC SPECTRUM
(Wavelengths in Meters)

Chart 333.12

just shorter than visible violet light are called ultraviolet, while radiations that have lengths just longer than visible red light are called infrared. You might also tell them that radiations with very short wave lengths behave more like particles than waves, and vice versa for radiations with very long wave lengths.

Contributing Idea C. Ultraviolet energy is a part of the electromagnetic spectrum.

Detecting ultraviolet radiation. Have students tape the edges of small glass slides, then tape the slides to a student's upper arm that is usually uncovered and exposed to sunlight for much of the day. After one day, remove the slides and observe. The students will notice that the **13 Bb Fb**

section under each slide is lighter in color than the surrounding skin. Tell them that the glass allowed light radiation to pass through, but blocked the *ultraviolet* portion of the electromagnetic spectrum. You may model this lesson to avoid exposing students to ultraviolet sunlight. **Caution: Follow safety guidelines when using glass slides.**

Contributing Idea D. Infrared energy is a part of the electromagnetic spectrum.

Detecting infrared radiation. Cover a sunlit window with black construction paper that has an approximately ⅖ in. × 2 in. (1 cm × 5 cm) slit in it. Darken the rest of the room as much as possible. Now set a prism in the beam of light, turning it until the light casts a spectrum on a piece of white paper or cardboard set close to the prism. Tape a thermometer that is at room temperature on the paper so that the red light of the spectrum is shining on the thermometer bulb. (See Figure 333.14, p. 290.) After five minutes, record the temperature that the thermometer shows. (Note: The paper may need to be moved to keep the red light exactly on the thermometer bulb.) Next, move the thermometer and tape it to the paper so that the bulb is *just past* the red light. After five more minutes, check the temperature. Students will find that there seems to be some radiation that cannot be seen beyond the red part of the spectrum. Tell them that this radiation **14 Bb Fb**

is called infrared, which means "below red." Infrared radiations are commonly referred to as *radiant heat* and are given off by all hot objects. After this experience, students may be interested in determining the temperatures of other colors of the spectrum. This can be done by keeping the thermometer within each color band for five minutes.

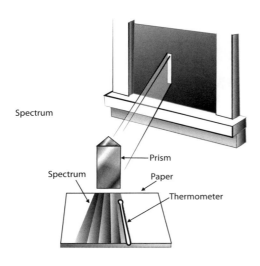

Figure 333.14

Contributing Idea E. Radio energy is part of the electromagnetic spectrum.

Detecting radiation in the form of radio waves. Tell students that *radio waves* have a longer wavelength than infrared radiation on the electromagnetic spectrum. Since they are invisible, ask students how they can be detected. (The waves are sent through the air by radio stations, thus can be detected by turning on a radio.) Have **15 Bb Fb**

students bring one or more pocket-size transistor radios to school. Divide students into as many groups as there are radios, and try to find out what kinds of materials block radio waves. A radio can be turned on and wrapped in a sheet of rubber, placed inside a metal can with a metal lid, or set in a large glass jar with a plastic bag and submerged in an aquarium to see if the radio waves travel through water. Another can be wrapped in a large sheet of aluminum foil (since this material seems to block radio waves, students can try cutting holes in the foil to see what happens). Let students generalize about the effect the materials have on radio waves.

334   Applications

Generalization. Instruments can be made to take and show pictures.

> *Contributing Idea A.* A camera is an instrument used to take pictures.

Making and using a pinhole camera. **01 Ga Gc** Obtain a sturdy cardboard box that is approximately 5 in. (13 cm) square and 3 in. (7 cm) high. Be sure it has a tight-fitting lid that comes down over the sides approximately 1 in. (3 cm). Paint the inside of the box and lid black, cut a ½ in. (1 cm) hole in the center of one side, glue a piece of aluminum foil over the hole on the inside, and punch a tiny hole in the center of it with a pin. Make a shutter for the camera by cutting a strip of masking tape or friction tape and pressing it lightly over the ½ in. (1 cm) hole on the outside of the box. Make a film holder by looping a 4 in. (10 cm) strip of masking tape and pressing it inside the box opposite the pinhole. (See Figure 334.01.) Now place the camera and a box of photographic film inside a dark room or portable darkroom. (Note: Outdated film is relatively inexpensive and available at most photography stores.) Tear open one end of the light-proof envelope containing the film, remove one sheet, and press its shiny side out against the loop of tape on the back wall of the camera. Keep the film edges parallel with those of the box. Cover the film box and the camera, and then be sure the pinhole of the camera is completely covered by the shutter tape. Students can now take a picture by pulling the shutter tape away from the pinhole to expose the film for a certain length of time. (Note: Because it is difficult to hold the camera steady for the 15–45 seconds of exposure time usually required, rest the camera on a chair or something stable.)

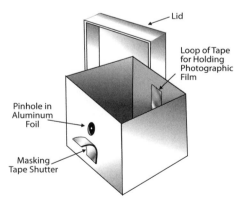

Figure 334.01

Contributing Idea B. Projectors are instruments used to show pictures.

Projecting an image. Have students work in small groups in a darkened room. Have one student place a sheet of white cardboard approximately 1 yd. (1 m) from a 40-watt clear bulb. Turn the bulb on and have a second student hold a magnifying lens between the bulb and the cardboard. Move the lens until a sharp image of the thin wire in the bulb appears on the screen. By testing, students can find out if there is more than one position of the lens that produces a sharp image. Let them see what happens to the size of the image when the lens or cardboard is moved. Position the bulb so that it produces a sharp image that is twice the distance from the lens as the bulb is. When this is done, measure the size of the image, and compare it to the size of the bulb. Now find and measure the position where a sharp image is four times larger than the bulb. See if there is a numerical pattern to the positioning in relation to the size of the image. Now put the bulb where the screen was and the screen where the bulb was to see what happens. Let students discuss how larger images can be projected on a screen. Next, replace the clear bulb with a 40-watt frosted bulb. **Caution: Follow safety guidelines, as the clear bulb will be very hot.** Turn the frosted bulb on and hold a 35mm slide approximately ½ in. (1 cm) in front of it. Adjust the cardboard until a sharp picture

02
Ec
Fb

appears. Students can realize that they have just made a model slide projector. Let them discuss why it is necessary to place a slide upside down in a projector.

Determining the number of frames flashed through a motion picture projector each second. Have students examine several frames of motion picture film. Explain that the holes are used to move the film through a projector and that they mark off each frame. Thread the film into a projector and lightly mark the edge of the frame closest to the projection slot. Run the projector for exactly 10 seconds, then mark the frame just beyond the slot. Students can count the number of frames between the crayon marks and determine the frames per second by dividing by 10. (Note: Old silent movies were projected at 16 frames per second, about the number of separate images the human eye can see in one second; sound films are projected at 24 frames per second to insure audio fidelity; and television pictures change at the rate of 30 per second.)

03 Cc Ch

Making "flip" movies. Provide students with small pads of paper or stacks of at least 25 index cards. In one corner, have students draw an object that slightly

04 Gb

changes on subsequent pages so that a movement is suggested (e.g., a person walking, bird flying, car moving). When the pages are flipped rapidly, the individual pictures will appear as a sequence of movement. You might explain that the human eye cannot see more than about 16 separate images in one second; when more than that number appear, the pictures seem to run together, producing one smooth continuous movement rather than many different images. After their first try, let students create other, improved "flip" movies.

Making movies on film. Obtain a reel of 16mm film leader, leave the first 4 ft. (125 cm) untouched, and let each student use felt pens to create designs on subsequent 2 ft. (62 cm) segments (about 80 frames) to produce a "movie" of lines and colors. Students can mark their segment by coding their first frame (by color, number, letter). Many students can work on the film at one time if it is carefully rolled out on the floor. Ink can be used instead of felt pens; however, the film must first be sanded lightly. When finished, hold a "Premier Showing." Subsequent experiences might include film editing and timing of images to match a sound track.

05 Gb

340 Heat

341 Characteristics

Generalization I. Heat has identifiable characteristics.

Contributing Idea A. Temperature is a characteristic that can be measured with a thermometer.

Feeling and describing temperatures. **01 Ab Ba** Prepare three bowls of water: one three-fourths filled with water that is about as hot as a student's hand can stand; one three-fourths filled with water that is about room temperature; one three-fourths filled with very cold water. Have students place one hand in the very hot water, one hand in the very cold water, and describe the sensation felt by each hand. Remove hands from the two bowls and place them simultaneously into the bowl of lukewarm water. Let them describe the sensations. (The hand from the hot water will feel cold while the hand from the cold water will feel hot.) Students will realize that telling temperatures by the sense of touch is relative and not accurate. For example, it may seem hot in a schoolroom, but after being out in the sunlight for a period of time, the same schoolroom will seem cool.

Observing how temperatures affect thermometers. **02 Aa** Obtain various kinds of thermometers (e.g., alcohol, gas, metal). Have students notice that if they touch a thermometer, the heat of their hands changes the temperature reading. Let them observe what happens to each thermometer as it is touched with an ice cube or when it is inserted into bowls of water of different temperatures.

Standardizing temperature measurements. **03 Ce** Prepare two or more containers of water that are very nearly the same temperature. Without using thermometers, let students ascertain which water is warmer. Try to obtain a general agreement, and then measure the temperature of each with a thermometer so that universal agreement can be obtained. Point out the need for universal agreements in measuring temperatures.

Measuring temperatures. **04 Ce** Have students use graph paper to prepare a map of the school grounds showing the arrangement of buildings, lawns, shrubs, trees, etc. Let them use thermometers to measure the temperatures of the air, water, and soil in different locations around the grounds. These measurements can be placed in the appropriate squares on the map. (Note: Air temperatures are more accurate if the thermometer is allowed to swing freely in the air from the end of a string. Ground temperatures can be taken by carefully inserting the bulb end of a thermometer into the soft earth. Surface temperatures are more accurate if the bulb is shaded from the sunlight.) Compare the temperatures. Temperatures can also be compared for different seasons of the year.

Making a liquid thermometer. Completely fill a milk carton with water colored with red dye. (The dye is used to make the water more visible.) Make a hole in the center of the carton's top, and insert a clear plastic straw. Use an eyedropper to add more colored water into the straw until it rises halfway up the tube. Seal the straw into the carton with clay, gum, or wax. Add a few drops of light machine oil to the top of the colored water in the tube to prevent evaporation. Fasten a card behind the tube, and mark the level of the liquid on the card each day. Test the instrument in various areas around the school grounds.

05 Gc

Calibrating a liquid thermometer. Have students fill a flask or soft drink bottle with colored water. Fit the container with a one-hole stopper and a plastic straw or glass tube. Press the stopper into the container so that the colored water rises in the tube approximately 3 in. (7 cm) above the stopper. Now place the container in a pan of water and heat it on a hot plate. When the colored water stops rising, mark the water level on the straw. Let the container cool to room temperature. Next, place it into a deep bowl filled with ice and pack the ice around the container. When the colored water stops dropping, mark the level. Students will realize that the two marks provide the high and low points for a temperature scale (the fixed points at which water expands when heated and

06 Bd Gc

contracts when cooled). Explain that the most common thermometer is the Fahrenheit thermometer. Gabriel Fahrenheit (1686–1736), a German physicist, established his scale by marking 0°F for a mixture of ice and salt. His high point was what he thought was the normal temperature of the human body (96°F). This range was extended for measuring other temperatures. On his scale, the freezing point of water is 32°F, the boiling point 212°F. Anders Celsius (1701–1744), a Swedish astronomer, established his scale by marking the freezing and boiling points of water as 0°C and 100°C. Scientists all over the world use the Celsius scale. (Note: This scale is also called the Centigrade scale.) Students can divide the range of their scales into tenths and hundredths and compare temperature readings with those from a commercial scale. Some students might be interested in researching the work of Fahrenheit and Celsius.

Making an air thermometer. Obtain a bottle with a screw cap. Punch a hole in the cap so that a plastic straw or tube will fit into it snugly. Screw the cap on the bottle and drip candle wax around all connections to seal them. Fasten the bottle upside down on a support so that the straw sticks into colored water in a second bottle. Have a student warm the first bottle with her hands to force some air from it. (Air bubbles will be seen in the

07 Gc

colored water.) When the bottle cools, a column of water will rise inside the straw to replace the air that was forced out. A scale can be attached behind the straw and calibrated. (See Figure 341.07.)

Figure 341.08

Air Thermometer

Figure 341.07

Making a copper-wire thermometer. **08** **Gc** Build a wooden stand as shown. Suspend a length of copper wire (#12 to #16 in size) from a nail that is bent slightly downward. Drill a hole approximately 1 in. (2.5 cm) deep in the base of the upright, just below and to the right of the lower end of the copper wire. Cut and bend a coat hanger wire and slip the bent end into the hole. Be sure it turns freely in the hole. Tape a scale to a small block of wood and set it at the far end of the coat hanger (Figure 341.08). As temperatures change, the copper wire will expand and contract causing the hanger to rise and fall.

Contributing Idea B. Temperature is a measure of the average amount of energy in a material; heat is the total amount of energy in a material.

Comparing differences between tem- **09** **perature and heat.** Obtain an aluminum **Ce** nail and an aquarium nearly filled with warm water. Have students compare the nail and the aquarium (which has the greatest amount of material?). Measure the temperature of the water in the aquarium with a thermometer. Ask how the temperature of the nail might be taken. (If the nail has been sitting untouched in the room for a period of time, it is probably the temperature of the air in the room.) Record the two temperatures. Use a clothespin or a pair of pliers to hold the nail in a flame until it glows red hot. Ask which now has the highest temperature: the nail or the aquarium. Plunge the hot nail into the aquarium and allow it to remain for a few minutes. Take the temperature of the aquarium again. Students can realize that even though the nail was extremely hot, it hardly affected the water because the water originally contained a greater amount of heat due to its quantity.

Determining which metals hold more heat. On one side of a balance arm, place five or six pennies. (Note: Although pennies are not made of pure copper, they can be used as a basis of comparison for other metals.) Next, fold several large sheets of aluminum foil into small lumps and place enough aluminum on the other balance arm to balance the pennies. Now place the pennies in a tea bag or small plastic bag with a string attached. Lower the bag into a pot of boiling water. While the pennies are warming, take the temperature of a ¼ c. (100 ml) of cold water and record it on Table 341.10. Remove the heated pennies and quickly lower them into the cold water. Stir, and record the highest temperature reached by the water. Calculate the number of degrees the water temperature rose because of the hot pennies. Next, let students repeat the activity using the aluminum foil, then equal weights of

**10
Bc
Ce**

iron or other metals. They might also see how "sandwich" type coins compare to "older" types in terms of heat. Challenge them to find a way to test which liquids, such as cooking oil and water, hold the most heat. They can try placing equal weights of metals in a freezer, then adding them to equal amounts of warm water and determining the cooling effect.

342   Interactions

Generalization I. Heat is a form of energy produced by different sources.

> *Contributing Idea A.* The Sun is a primary source of heat (nuclear propagation).

Feeling heat produced by sunlight. Have students sit in the sunlight for some time, then move to the shade to feel the difference in heat. Discuss how burned one can get if one stayed in the sun too long. (Note: Burning can also take place on a cloudy day and has nothing to do with apparent sunlight.)

**01
Ab**

Table 341.10. Measuring the Heat Held by Metals

	Water Temperature		Rise In Temperature
	Cold	Heated	
Copper			
Aluminum			
Silver			
Nickel			
Iron			

Comparing differences in tempera- **02** **tures from the Sun.** Have students use **Ce** thermometers to compare: (1) temperatures in sunlight and shade; (2) temperatures of a sunny day and a cloudy day; (3) temperatures of a summer day and a winter day; (4) temperatures at different times of the same day.

Focusing the Sun's rays to produce **03** **high temperatures.** Obtain magnify- **Aa** ing hand lenses, small aluminum pans, and small sheets of tissue paper. Have students hold the hand lenses in the sunlight to focus Sun rays on a ball of tissue paper in the aluminum pan until the paper bursts into flame. Hand lenses can also be used to focus Sun rays on a thermometer to observe the temperature rise. **Caution: Be sure the rise in temperature does not exceed the limits of the thermometer. Be prepared to handle any burning paper.**

> *Contributing Idea B.* Motion can be a source of heat (mechanical propagation).

Feeling heat produced by motion. Heat **04** produced by motion can be observed in **Ab** many common experiences. Have students feel the blade of a saw after sawing a piece of wood; feel the break hub of the rear wheel after applying the brakes while riding down a hill on a bicycle; feel the warmth after sliding down a rope or when a rope or string is pulled through the hands. **Caution: The heat generated**

in this manner can get hot enough to **02** burn. Have them feel the sides of an air **Ce** pump after it has been pumped briskly for a short time; feel how warm a nail gets after hammering it quickly several times or after it is pulled from a block of wood; feel a wire after bending it back and forth several times.

Rubbing objects to produce heat. Have **05** students rub various objects together: **Ab** rub hands together briskly until warmth is sensed; rub a brass button (or similar object) energetically against a piece of wool cloth, then touch the button; rub a small piece of metal on a piece of paper and sense how warm they get; rub a pencil eraser briskly against a piece of paper, then quickly touch the eraser to the upper lip or the tip of the nose (a sensitive part of the body) to feel the warmth produced. If possible, have the class observe a scout (or someone with similar experience) start a fire by rubbing pieces of wood together.

Measuring the heat produced by **06** **motion in a solid (sand).** Fill jars or tin **Bf** cans about one-fourth full of dry sand. **Cd** Let students measure and record the tem- **Ec** perature of the sand in each container (Table 342.06, p. 298). Cover the containers, and shake them vigorously about 100 times, then measure the temperature again. Compare the two temperatures. Let students experiment to see if shaking the containers more or less times changes the temperature. The data can be graphed in Graph 342.06.

Table 342.06. Measuring Heat Produced by Motion (jar filled with sand)

Number of Shakes	Temperature in °F (or °C)

MEASURING HEAT PRODUCED BY MOTION

Graph 342.06

Measuring the heat produced by motion in a liquid (water). Fill a mixing bowl three-fourths full of cold water, measure and record the temperature, then run an electric beater in the bowl for about 10 minutes. Measure the temperature again. Compare the temperatures. Students will realize that the motion of the beater produced the amount of heat that was measured. Experiment to see if a time difference in using the beater changes the measurements. **07 Bf Ce Ec**

Contributing Idea C. Burning materials can be a source of heat (chemical propagation); some burning materials can be used as fuels.

Feeling heat produced by burning. Light a match, then a candle. Students can feel the heat given off by the flames. Use pliers, forceps, or a long fork with a wooden handle to hold various flammable objects in the candle flame. Students will sense that heat is given off as the objects burn. **08 Ab**

Comparing differences in the ignition of materials. Light a candle and use pliers to hold various objects (e.g., celluloid, twists of various papers, wood, coal, cotton) in the flame one at a time. You might explain that the point at which a material bursts into flame is called its kindling point, and that heat-producing materials do not all burst into flame at the same temperature. Have students order the materials by the amount of time it takes to ignite each. **Caution: Follow safety guidelines for burning objects.** **09 Bb Ca Da**

Comparing kindling points. Kindling points can be compared by placing various objects (e.g., match head, coal, sulfur, wood, paper) on a sheet of copper, iron, or aluminum. Bridge the metal sheet across a flame source, make sure the objects are about the same size and equidistant from the flame, then have students note the order in which the materials ignite. (Note: Some materials may not ignite because **10 Ca**

their kindling points are higher than can be reached with this method.) **Caution: Follow safety guidelines when working with an open flame and heated objects.**

Contributing Idea D. Electricity can be a source of heat (electrical propagation).

Feeling heat produced by electricity. **11 Ab** Have students observe the filaments in various appliances (e.g., electric toaster, stove, heater, iron) and feel that heat is radiated from them when they are turned on. Students can also observe the filament in a nonfrosted 100-watt electric lightbulb. Place a sheet of paper against the bulb, turn it on, and observe as it scorches. **Caution: Follow safety guidelines when investigating heated objects.**

Comparing electrically produced temperatures in different materials. **12 Ca** Obtain two or more dry cell batteries and connect them in series (positive pole of one dry cell to the negative pole of another) by attaching, one at a time, pieces of copper wire that vary in thickness. Let students feel the differences in temperatures (the thicker the wire, the lower the temperature). **Caution: Some thin wires can get hot enough to burn fingers and melt.** Students might begin with two dry cells, test the wires, then add more dry cells, one at a time, to compare what happens as the current is increased.

Generalization II. Adding or removing heat affects materials and organisms.

Contributing Idea A. Adding heat causes nearly all solids to expand; removing heat causes them to contract.

Observing the expansion and contraction of some solids. **13 Aa Bb** Expansion and contraction can be observed through a variety of classroom activities. Following the suggested activities, you may wish to introduce the terms *expansion* and *contraction*.

a. Hammer a nail into the base of an empty can. Gently remove the nail, then replace it to make sure the hole is just large enough for it. Hold the nail with a clothespin or pair of pliers, heat it in a flame, then try to put the nail back into the hole.

b. Obtain two 1 ft. (30 cm) dowels with 1 in. (2.5 cm) diameters, one large eye screw, and a flat-head screw that barely passes through the eye screw. Screw the pieces into the ends of the two dowels, then using a candle flame, heat the flat-head screw and try to pass it through the eye screw. (Expansion will keep it from passing through.) Now heat the eye screw and try again. (Expansion will allow the flat-head screw to pass through.) Cool the eye screw and try again. (The solid eye screw contracts and keeps the expanded screw from passing through.)

Measuring the expansion and contraction of some solids. Build a stand as shown in Figure 342.14a. On block 1, place a wooden pencil so that it will roll easily. Put a pin in the eraser end of the pencil and hang a threaded fish weight from the pin. Let the weight hang freely over the edge. Mark a card in $1/3$ in. (3 mm) intervals for a scale and mount it to the block behind the weighted thread. Now as the pencil is rolled back and forth, the thread will move along the scale, and the distance it moves can be measured. To block 2, attach one end of a rod or strip of metal, such as a brass curtain rod, with U-shaped nails or straight nails that are bent over the rod. Set the other end **14 Cd**

of the metal rod so that it rests on the pencil near the inside edge of block 1 as shown in Figure 342.14b. Heat the metal with a flame. As the metal expands, students will see it move across the pencil and cause it to roll. The thread will move along with it, and the distance can be measured and recorded. Now place several different flame sources to the metal at the same time to see how far the metal can be made to expand. Other metals such as iron, copper, or aluminum can also be tested and compared.

Measuring the expansion and contraction of some wires. Obtain a board approximately ½ in. × 2 in. × 12 in. (1 cm × 5 cm × 30 cm), one large nail and two small nails, one drinking straw, a rubber band, and a white card. Assemble them as shown in Figure 342.15. A scale can be drawn on the card with the aid of a protractor. With this device, students can compare the expansions and contractions of different wires quite accurately. **15 Cd**

Figure 342.14a

Figure 342.15

Figure 342.14b

Observing how people adjust materials to allow for the expansion and contraction of solids. Take a field trip or bring in photographs to notice the spaces between the concrete slabs of sidewalks, the spaces between the steel rails of railroad tracks, or the spaces between the steel girders in bridges. Discuss the need for this allowance for expansion and contraction of solid objects.

16 Aa

Observing that expansion and contraction can break some solids. Thoroughly heat some small marbles or rocks in a pan over a heating unit. Using pliers, pick them from the pan one at a time, and plunge each into a glass or beaker of cold water. The expanded objects will crack or break as the cold water quickly contracts their exterior. Similarly students can observe in a demonstration that a hot liquid poured into a cold glass container will sometimes cause it to crack or break because the quickly heated inside surface suddenly expands, pushing out the outside unheated surface.

17 Aa

Contributing Idea B. Adding heat causes nearly all liquids to expand; removing heat causes them to contract.

Measuring the expansion and contraction of some liquids. Fill two or more flasks or bottles to the brim with various liquids such as colored water, alcohol, and oil. Press into the flasks one-hole stoppers fitted with approximately 12 in.

18 Cd Da

(30 cm) lengths of glass tubing. **Caution: Glass tubing is fragile; a paper towel wrapped around the tubing while it is being inserted will protect hands should the glass accidentally break.** As each stopper is pressed into a flask, the liquid will rise partway up the tube. Let the flasks sit in a shady part of the room for several hours so that the liquids will attain the same temperature, and then mark the levels of the liquids with a string or rubber band (or a card can be placed behind the tubes for marking). Now move the flasks into a sunny spot in the room or take them outside into the sunlight. After the liquids have stopped rising, mark the height of each liquid as before, and compare the expansions of the different liquids. Students can order them by degrees of expansion. (Note: A greater range between expansion and contraction can be found for each liquid by placing each flask first in a bowl of ice, to mark the near freezing point of water, then into warm water that is brought to a boil for several minutes, to mark the near boiling point of water.)

Contributing Idea C. Adding heat causes all gases to expand; removing heat causes them to contract.

Observing the expansion and contraction of a gas (air). Place the open end of a bottle under water. Heat the bottle with a flame or pour fairly hot water over it. Students will see air bubbles coming

19 Aa

out of the bottle. (The air in the bottle expands and forces some of the air out.)

Observing the expansion and contrac- **20** **tion of a gas (air) in different situa-** **Aa** **tions.** Stretch a sheet of rubber cut from a balloon over the mouth of a can or jar. Attach the rubber tightly to the can with a rubber band. Students can realize that the gas (air) in the can will now be in a closed system, isolated, and generally independent of the outside air. Influences upon the isolated gas (air) can create observable changes in the flexible rubber lid. Heat the container with a flame and observe the lid. (The air inside will expand and force the lid upward.) Next, cool the container with a damp cloth or ice cube and observe the lid. (The air inside will contract and the outside air will force the lid downward.) Several alternative or supplementary activities can be provided for the students.

  a. Fasten a rubber balloon over the opening of a flask, test tube, or pop bottle. Set the container in hot water or heat it gently with a flame. Have students observe the balloon. (It will become partially inflated.) Now cool the container, and observe again. (It will deflate.) (Note: If the balloon is stretched before attaching, it will expand and contract more easily during the activity.)

  b. Dip the mouth of a medicine bottle into soapy water to produce a film across the opening. The film will expand if warm hands are placed on the bottle.

  c. Students can discuss experiences with the popping of bottle tops. Have them recall the sequence of events prior to the popping. (Usually a cold bottle is taken from the refrigerator, used, and stoppered—as the bottle sits in the warm room, the air inside the bottle becomes warm, and as it expands, it presses harder against the sides and top of the bottle, causing the top to pop open.) If a refrigerator is available at school, have students see if they can cause the event to happen.

Contributing Idea D. Adding heat causes some solids to melt into liquids; removing heat causes some liquids to freeze into solids.

Observing phase changes. Basically, **21** matter exists in states—solid, liquid, **Aa** and gas. Adding or reducing heat causes **Ba** matter to change from one state to **Bb** another. You might explain to students that a change from one state to another is called a phase transformation. Observation of water best depicts the various phase transformations. Students can cite examples for and discuss each of the following: (liquid to solid) ponds, lakes, and rivers solidify in cold weather; (solid to liquid) ice melts in warm weather; (liquid to gas) puddles of water evaporate on warm days; (gas to liquid) unseen water vapor condenses against a cold mirror in the bathroom; (solid to gas) wet wash on a clothesline in freezing weather will freeze, then sublime dry; (gas to solid) water vapor in the air will frost on plants on cold mornings.

Observing freezing and melting (liquid ↔ solid). Completely cut the tops from several small milk cartons. Prepare each carton with the same amount of water. Add different concentrations of salt, measured in level spoonfuls, to the containers. Stir and label the containers, then place them in a freezer and check every hour to determine the order in which the solutions freeze. (Note: Some may not freeze.) Students will realize that liquids do not all freeze at the same temperature. In this activity the salt lowers the freezing point of water. You might explain that in the winter saltwater harbors are often unfrozen, while nearby freshwater lakes are frozen; it takes a much lower temperature to freeze salt water than freshwater. For further comparisons, students can repeat this activity using other liquids and solutions (e.g., oil, alcohol, sugar water, syrup). After the liquids have been frozen, see how long it takes for each to melt under the same temperature conditions.

22 Aa Ca

Contributing Idea E. Adding heat causes liquids to evaporate into gases; removing heat causes gases to condense into liquids.

Observing evaporation (liquid → gas). The phenomenon of evaporation can easily be observed in several ways.

23 Aa

a. Students can observe the effect of hot weather upon wet sidewalks, puddles, or spilled water. They can also observe wet clothes hung on a clothesline (or wet cloths on the school fence) and feel them periodically as they dry in the sunlight.

b. Students can set liquids such as alcohol, water, or milk in open dishes in the sunlight and watch them on a daily basis.

Measuring the cooling effect of evaporation. Wrap the bulbs of three identical thermometers with small pieces of cotton; one saturated with water, one with alcohol, and one with ether. Let students fan them rapidly with a sheet of cardboard. Observe the temperature changes. You might explain that people with high temperatures are sometimes given alcohol rubdowns to lower their temperatures.

24 Ce

Graphing evaporation rates of different liquids. Have students weigh two beakers or paper cups and record the weights in Table 342.25, p. 304. Fill one beaker with 4 oz. of water and the other with 4 oz. of alcohol. The cups and their contents

25 Bf Cf Ch

Table 342.25. Comparing Evaporation Rates (Beaker weight = ½ oz.)

Alcohol		Water		Remarks
Days	**Weight (oz.)**	**Days**	**Weight (oz.)**	
0	4	0	4	Started observations
1	3½	1	3¾	
2	3	2	3½	
3	2½	3	3¼	
4	2	4	3	
5	1½	5	2¾	Made a prediction

should then be measured at equal intervals—preferably daily at the same time. (Note: If a measurement is taken one day at noon and the next measurement is taken the following day at 3 p.m., the first point on the graph could be plotted at TIME = 0, and the second point on the graph could be plotted at TIME = 1⅛.) An alternative method of measurement for this activity would be to put the liquids in graduated cylinders or measuring cups. (The depth of each liquid could be measured with a ruler.) The volume could be recorded at successive intervals rather than the weight. (Note: The tabled data for this activity will produce a straight line graph [Graph 342.25]; if all conditions remain constant, predictions concerning total evaporation time for each liquid can be made after five points have been graphed.) Many thought-provoking questions can aid students in interpreting graphs of this type: Which liquid takes longer to evaporate? After four days, how much water and alcohol was left? When there was 1½ oz. of alcohol remaining, how many days had passed?

COMPARING EVAPORATION RATES

Weight (in oz.)

Time (in Days)

Beaker Weight

Graph 342.25

When the alcohol had evaporated, how much water was left?

Observing condensation (gas → liquid). 26 Ask students to exhale against a pane of Aa glass or a mirror. (Since the warm air in one's breath contains much moisture, the cool or cold glass will cause the moisture to condense, making it visible on the glass.) Some students can recall the fogging of car windows on cold nights or the sight of their own breath in the air on cold days. Students who wear glasses can relate some of their experiences.

Observing the effect of removing heat on condensation. Obtain two milk bottles or large coffee cans. Fill one with warm water and one with very cold water. (Water vapor in the air around the cool bottle will condense from the air as droplets of water on the surface of the bottle.) If students think the droplets came from the inside of the can, some dye can be added to the can's water. The colorless droplets on the outside of the can should convince students that the water came from the outside air. You may wish to discuss condensation on pitchers of ice water, bottles of cold soft drinks, and glasses of cold drinks. **27 Aa**

Contributing Idea F. Adding heat causes some solids to sublime into gases; removing heat causes some gases to frost into solids.

Observing subliming (solid → gas). Caution: Follow safety guidelines when working with dry ice. Put a small piece of dry ice into a small flask. Because the dry ice gas (carbon dioxide) is odorless and colorless, put a balloon over the neck of the flask and fasten it securely with a rubber band. As the dry ice sublimes, the balloon will inflate and perhaps pop. **28 Aa**

Observing subliming and frosting (solid ↔ gas). Caution: This activity should only be done by the teacher as a demo under a fume hood. Place iodine crystals in a flask, cover the flask with a saucer or water glass, and set the materials in the sunlight. Students will see that the heat from the sun causes the iodine to sublime (seen as a violet-colored gas). As the gas contacts the cooler saucer and sides of the flask, crystals of iodine will form. **Caution: Care should be taken in handling iodine; do not inhale the fumes or handle the crystals with bare hands.** Rinse all equipment thoroughly with cool water after use. The formation of morning frost can be compared to this activity. **29 Aa**

Contributing Idea G. Adding or removing heat influences plants and animals.

Testing the effect of heat upon seed germination. Have students plant identical seeds in three labeled flower pots. Place the pots respectively in cold, normal, and very hot locations. As an alternative, the temperatures can be created artificially using dry ice or crushed ice, a heater, or a lightbulb. Thermometers can be placed on each pot to take the temperatures in each location. Students should see that each condition is given equal measures of water. They can compare the germination pattern and growth in each pot and judge what effect heat or the lack of it has upon the plants. This activity can also be done without soil (see entry 641.01) so that students can observe the temperature effects on root growth. If measurements are taken, the data can be graphed. **30 Bf Ec**

Testing the effect of heat upon insect metamorphosis. Have students gather caterpillars that are feeding on plants. Place equal numbers of caterpillars, together with parts from the plants, into separate jars. Cover the jars with nylon mesh to keep the caterpillars from escaping. Now place one jar in a warm, but not hot, location and another in a cool location. Be sure all other conditions, such as the amount of sunlight and food, remain the same for both. Thermometers can be used to keep daily temperature records. Record any differences in the time it takes the caterpillars to go into pupation and for the pupas to change into adult butterflies or moths. (Note: Be sure to keep a wad of moist cotton in each jar during the pupa stage to prevent the insects from drying out.) From this experience students will be able to make some judgment concerning the relationship of heat to stages of metamorphosis.

31 Ec

Generalization III. Heat travels through solids, liquids, and gases in different ways and at different speeds.

Contributing Idea A. Heat sometimes travels through materials by conduction; some materials conduct heat better than others.

Feeling the conduction of heat. Have students recall that the metal handles of pans become hot as the pan is heated, that spoons become hot when placed into hot

32 Ab Bb

liquids, and that heat can travel gradually through an object's entire length. Several similar experiences can be carried out in the classroom.

a. Place spoons of different metals into cups of hot water. After several minutes let students feel the handle of each spoon to see which conducted the heat best. (Silver spoons are excellent conductors of heat.)

b. Fill an aluminum cup and a china cup with very hot water. Let students touch the handles to compare the heat flow through aluminum and china.

c. Have a student hold a nail or brass curtain rod in the flame of a candle to see how rapidly the heat is conducted throughout the length. **Caution: Let the student be ready to drop the item if it gets too hot.** Different kinds of nails (aluminum, galvanized, etc.) or rods can be compared.

Following these experiences, you may wish to tell students that when heat travels in this manner, the traveling is called conduction.

Observing differences in heat conduction through various materials. Several activities can help students realize that some materials conduct heat better than others.

33 Aa

a. Obtain a pencil with a metal cap on one end (or with a metal band around an eraser). Tightly wrap a piece of white paper around the end of the pencil so that it covers the wood and the metal. Heat the pencil in a flame at the metal tip end. Observe what happens, then remove the pencil from the flame when the paper starts to char. Open the paper and have students note that there is less char area where the paper was wrapped around the metal. (The heat was conducted away from the paper by the metal but not by the wood.) **Caution: Follow safety guidelines when working with heat sources and heated objects.**

b. Partially fill a nonwaxed paper cup with water. Hold or suspend it over a flame, and have students observe as it is brought to a boil. (The water will reach the boiling point before the cup is burned, because the heat is conducted away from the paper and dispersed through the water.)

c. Lower a small piece of aluminum screen over a candle flame. Have students observe how the flame is suddenly cut off even though the screen has many holes in it. (The metal wires conduct the heat away from the flame.) An interesting reversal of the phenomena can be observed if a Bunsen burner is available. Set the screen across a tripod or on a ring stand, and place the unlit burner under it. Turn on the gas and light the gas *above* the screen. The gas will burn only above the screen because the metal wires conduct the heat away from the gas below.

d. Place a wooden match between two tines of a fork, and light the match. Students will observe that the match burns only until the flame reaches the metal. (The metal conducts the heat away from the match so that part of the wood never reaches its burning point.)

Observing that liquids are generally poor conductors of heat. 34 Aa Drop a piece of ice into a test tube, and wedge it in securely with a piece of steel wool. Fill the tube with water and tilt the test tube diagonally in order to heat the water in the top half of the tube. Students can observe the water boiling at the top while the ice remains undisturbed at the bottom. Other liquids can be tested in a similar way to show that they are also poor conductors. (Note: Liquid metals are not poor conductors of heat.) A dramatic variation of this activity can be done by filling a test tube with water, holding it at the base with a bare hand, and heating the top of the tube. Students will observe the boiling water while the tube is held in a bare hand.

Determining that gases (air) are poor conductors of heat. Light a candle, and have students take turns holding their hands approximately 10 in. (23 cm) above the flame. Let them describe what they feel. Have them move their hands to 10 in. (23 cm) from the side of the flame, and describe what they feel. (If air were a good conductor, there would be no difference at the same distance above and to the side of the flame.) As a variation, hold the head of a wooden match approximately ½ in. (1 cm) from the side of a candle flame for about 10 seconds. (The match will not burst into flame.) Next, hold the match approximately ½ in. (1 cm) above the flame. (The match will burst into flame immediately.) (Note: Because gases are poor conductors of heat, porous and fibrous materials, such as asbestos, fur, and feathers, are usually good insulators because they have air spaces throughout their structures.) **Caution: Follow safety guidelines when working with an open flame.** **35 Ab**

> *Contributing Idea B.* Heat sometimes travels through materials by convection; the exchange of heated and cooler gases and liquids creates currents.

Determining the locations of heated and cooler air in the classroom. To help students realize that warmed air is lighter (thus near the ceiling) and cold air is heavier (thus near the floor), have them stand on ladders, hold their hands high up, and describe what they feel. Next, have them kneel on the floor and feel the temperature of the air for comparison. As an alternative experience, they can use individual thermometers to measure the temperature in different parts of the room. For example, a thermometer can be put near the floor of the room away from the radiator, while another can be put on a window pole and held near the ceiling for several minutes. A chart of the room's various temperatures can be made. Students will realize that the highest temperatures are generally in the highest places in the room because cool air is heavier and settles downward, pushing the lighter heated air upward. Thus heated air does not "rise." It is pushed away by the heavier cool air that is moving downward because of gravity. **36 Ab Be Ce**

Observing that cooler air falls and pushes heated air upward. Several experiences can help students realize that cooler air moves downward and pushes warmer air upward. (Note: In cooler air, molecules are closer together than in heated air, thus for a comparative volume of air, the cooler air is heavier and moves downward due to gravity. The warmer and lighter air is pushed out of the way.) **37 Aa**

a. Clap two chalkboard erasers over a hot radiator, and then do the same close to an open window on a cool or cold day.

b. Light a rope and blow out the flame so that it will smoke. Hold the rope a short distance above a candle flame and away from other air currents. The smoke will travel upward. This can be repeated over a hot radiator, electric hot plate, near an open refrigerator door, or at the top and bottom of an open window.

c. Hold thin strips of aluminum foil above a lit lamp chimney and observe what happens to them when they are dropped. Repeat near the base of the chimney. Students should note that the cooler air moves into the bottom of the chimney and the hotter air is pushed out of the top.

Locating air currents. Various individualized devices can aid students in making observations of air movements.

38
Aa
Be

a. Cut a 6 in. (15 cm) square of paper as shown in Figure 342.38a, and fold the corners toward the center. Put pinholes through the folded-over corners and the center of the pinwheel. Suspend the pinwheel from a knotted thread, and let students explore the room and school grounds for rising and falling air. They can chart the air currents on a school map. Several maps can be used to show the currents at different times of the day.

Figure 342.38a

Figure 342.38b

b. Cut a circle of paper about 6 in. (15 cm) in diameter and make a pinhole in the center. Cut the paper in a spiral as shown in Figure 342.38b, and hang the spiral from a knotted thread. The spiral can be held over a radiator or in other parts of the room or school yard to find the movements of air currents.

c. Tissue paper can be cut into narrow 6 in. (15 cm) long strips and attached to a stick or ruler with tacks, glue, or tape. The stick can then be held in various locations to aid seeing air movements.

Observing convection currents in gases. Several experiences can help students realize that warmer and cooler air tend to exchange places. After several experiences you may wish to tell them that when heat travels in this manner, the traveling is called convection.

**39
Aa
Bb
Ec**

a. Wrap a few turns of wire around a candle, allowing enough wire for a handle so that the candle can be lowered into a large bottle. Light the candle and lower it into the bottle. (The candle will go out quickly because the air in the bottle is heated, rises, blocks the mouth of the bottle, and prevents fresh air from entering.) Now cut out a T-shaped piece of cardboard with a stem that just fits into the neck of the bottle. Remove the candle from the bottle, turn the bottle upside-down so that the "candle air" (carbon dioxide) can escape, and swing the bottle in the air a few times to fill it with fresh air. Light the candle again, and lower it into the bottle. Quickly put the cardboard T in place and observe. Now light one end of a piece of rope, blow out the flame, and while the rope is smoldering, hold it first on one side of the cardboard T and then on the other side. (On the heated side the smoke will rise; on the cooler side the smoke will go down into the bottle.) From observing the drifts of smoke, students will begin to realize that nearly all upward and downward drafts of air are caused in similar ways and that such differences in temperatures cause winds. **Caution: Follow safety guidelines when using an open flame.**

b. Put three holes in a large wooden (or sturdy cardboard) box as shown in Figure 342.39. Plug the holes with corks or rubber stoppers. To the face of the box, attach a sheet of glass or transparent sandwich wrap so that it can be lifted as a door, and so that observations can be made of the interior when it is closed. Place a candle in the box under the top hole. Light the candle, remove any two plugs, and hold a smoking rope near the lowest opening. (The smoke will travel from the lowest opening through the box and out a higher opening.) The openings simulate some of the possible openings in a room for proper ventilation (e.g., Openings #1 and #3 simulate an

Figure 342.39

open window or an open chimney; openings #1 and #2 simulate a window opened at top and bottom). Students can check their own room for comparisons. Let them experiment with the box to create other air movements.

Observing convection currents in liquids. To help students understand that convection currents take place in liquids as well as gases, the following activities can be done using water.

40
Aa
Be

    a. Obtain a clear heat-resistant pot, fill it with cold water, and place it on a heating unit. To make the convection currents visible, shred some blotter paper into the water by rubbing it against the fine side of a food grater. Let the shreds settle to the bottom, turn on the heating unit, and have students observe the movements of the pieces of paper. Next, turn off the unit, and have students draw the movements they saw. After the water has cooled, repeat the activity, but this time, place the pot only partly on the heating unit. Have students observe and draw what they see. (In both instances the cooler water moves downward and pushes the warmer water upward.) As an alternative to blotter paper, sawdust or wood shavings from a pencil sharpener

can be used. Similarly, cold milk can be gently poured down the inside of the clear pot filled with warm water. If the water is still, the heavy cold milk will settle to the bottom. When the heat is turned on low, students will see the movements of the two liquids.

    b. Obtain two identical milk bottles, one filled with hot, deeply colored water, the other with uncolored, cool tap water. Put a card over the hot water bottle opening. Invert the bottle and place it gently over the second bottle. Remove the card. (There should be almost no mixture, because the cold water is heavier.) Now hold the bottles carefully at their mouths and reverse their positions. (The heavier, cold water will quickly displace the hot water.)

Contributing Idea C. Heat sometimes travels by radiation.

Feeling radiant heat energy. Obtain enough electric lamps so that students can work in small groups. Gooseneck lamps with shades removed work best, because they can be turned in various directions. Have students turn on the lightbulb, and put their hands near it but not touching it. If they hold their hands in different positions around the bulb, they will find that heat travels from the bulb in all directions and realize that the heat reaches their

41
Ab
Bb

hands by some means other than conduction or convection. (If the heat traveled by convection, it would be felt only above the bulb, and gases, such as air, are poor conductors.) By turning the bulb off and on, they will find that the heat they feel is immediate. (Heat traveling by conduction or convection takes time.) For alternative radiant heat sources, electric irons, toasters, or a warm radiator can be used. Have students recall and discuss the warmth of a fire after the fire has gone out or the warmth radiated from sidewalks and concrete buildings shortly after the Sun has set. You might explain that when heat travels in this manner, the traveling is called radiation.

Feeling that radiant heat energy will pass through transparent materials without heating them. **42 Ab Ec** Place a pane of glass between a lit bulb and bare hands. The hands will sense the heat immediately, but the pane of glass will remain cool. (Note: This experience also emphasizes that, because of the glass barrier, the heat must have traveled by a means other than conduction or convection.) Students might recall having felt heat through a closed window while the pane of glass remained cool. Additional tests can be tried using various transparent materials (e.g., sandwich wraps, plastics) or variously colored cellophanes.

Comparing the effect of dark and light materials upon radiant heat energy. **43 Ca**

Several activities will help students realize that dark objects absorb radiant heat more readily than light ones.

a. Place a sheet of white and a sheet of black paper on the ground in the sunlight. After several minutes, let students feel the sheets of paper. Ask them to describe what they feel. (The black paper will feel warmer than the white paper.) Similarly, pieces of light and dark cloth of identical size and material can be set on the ground or on snow in winter to note the differences in temperature. (The snow under the dark cloth will melt more rapidly.) These activities may bring about discussions on the effects of light and dark clothing on a hot summer day as compared with a cold winter day.

b. Obtain two identical soft drink bottles. Snap a balloon over each one, and paint one bottle with black paint. Place both bottles in the sunlight and have students observe and compare them. (The black bottle will absorb the Sun's rays more quickly, and its balloon will inflate first.)

c. Paint two tin cans, one black and the other white. Invert them over ice cubes in the sunlight. Uncover them every two minutes to let students observe and compare the effects on the ice cubes.

Observing that heat builds up within some materials. 44 Ce Obtain five identical sheets of black paper. Place the sheets, one at a time, in the sunlight at one-minute intervals. At the end of four minutes, have students feel the papers and judge which is the warmest. (The temperatures will range from warmest to least warm in relation to the time in the sunlight.) This activity can also be done with tin cans painted black and covered with cardboard lids that have thermometers inserted through them.

Determining whether dark or light materials reradiate heat faster. 45 Ce Paint two identical tin cans, one black inside and out, the other white inside and out (or leave it shiny). Pour hot water into the two cans and cover each with a cardboard lid that has a hole cut in it just large enough to hold a thermometer without slipping through. Have students record the temperature changes within both cans at regular intervals, then compare the results. (The darker color helps to increase the heat radiation; the water temperature drop is greatest in the dark colored container.) Students can also observe that the most efficient radiators (automobile and room radiators) are usually painted black so as to give up as much heat as possible (silvered or light colored ones are not as efficient).

Contributing Idea D. Heat travels through some materials faster than through others.

Comparing materials by conduction rates. 46 Ca Obtain rods of the same diameter and length, but of different materials (e.g., brass, iron, copper, glass, wood, rubber). Attach thumbtacks to them at 1 in. (2.5 cm) intervals using candle wax. Insert the rods vertically through holes in a coffee can lid. Add 1 in. (2.5 cm) of water to the can and place the lid on it so that the rods rest in the water at the same depth. Place the can on a heating unit. Students can note the speed of conduction by the dropping of the tacks.

Generalization IV. Heat can be controlled.

Contributing Idea A. Poor conductors of heat make good heat insulators.

Comparing the insulating differences of some materials. 47 Ce Have students fill four jars to the top with hot water, record their temperatures, and cover them tightly. Wrap three of the jars in different materials (e.g., wool, cotton, nylon). Leave the fourth jar unwrapped for later comparisons. Set the jars aside for about 30 minutes, then take the temperatures again and compare the changes. From their findings, students can discuss the best types of clothing to wear at certain times of the year. A similar activity can be done by comparing various vacuum bottles that students bring to school. Compare the better insulators for their common characteristics. Students can also examine and test hot pads, insulated bags to carry ice cream, and handles on pots and pans.

You might challenge them to use their understanding to see who can preserve an ice cube the longest.

Generalizing about the insulating quality of some materials. Obtain three or more large tin cans and three or more small cans that fit in the larger ones leaving approximately a 1 in. (2.5 cm) space between the sides. (Beakers or jars can be used instead of cans.) Obtain some materials that might be used for insulation (e.g., sawdust, rock wool, ground cork, Styrofoam pieces, or packing materials). Place approximately 1 in. (2.5 cm) of each material in the bottom of each of the three large cans. Set the smaller cans on top of the material and fill in around them with a 1 in (2.5 cm) thickness of the material. Use pieces of heavy cardboard to cover the large cans. Punch a small hole in the center of each piece and insert a thermometer so that it will reach about halfway into the small can, making sure the hole is small enough so that the thermometer does not fall through. Remove the cardboard pieces and pour equal amounts of boiling water into the small cans until they are almost full. Cover the cans with the cardboard pieces. (See Figure 342.48.) Let students observe the thermometers and record the temperature of the water in each can at one-minute intervals. Graph the results, and elicit some inferences about the insulating power of the tested materials. (The material that retained the heat in the water

48
Ce
Ec
Fa

for the longest period of time is the poorest heat conductor and the best insulator.) (Note: The best insulators are generally a combination of a poor conducting material and trapped air spaces.) Using the same cans, many other tests can be made on other materials such as fur, feathers, and water. Air can also be tested if the small can is kept from directly touching the larger can by placing three or four 1 in. (2.5 cm) high rubber stoppers or corks under the small can. The can will then be suspended from the larger can and surrounded by air. From these experiences, students will be able to state some generalizations concerning insulating materials.

Figure 342.48

Contributing Idea B. Heat can be refracted.

Observing that radiant heat energy can be focused and reflected. Have students hold magnifying glasses in the sunlight and focus the Sun's rays to a point. Now have them tilt a mirror about halfway between the point of focus and the magnifying glass. One student can adjust a sheet of paper until the new point of focus

49
Aa

is found. A sheet of paper can be placed at this new point and burned. Students will realize that the Sun's heat was refracted by the lens and reflected by the mirror.

Contributing Idea C. Heat can be reflected.

Observing that reflective materials can be used as insulators. Obtain a sturdy square wooden or cardboard box that will fit over an upright lightbulb with a few in. (5 to 6 cm) to spare on all sides. Obtain several rectangles of glass such as 2 in. × 2 in. (5 cm × 5 cm) or 3 in. × 5 in. (8 cm × 13 cm) mounting slides. Cut two square holes exactly opposite each other on the box. Be sure they are smaller than the pieces of glass. Cut a piece of aluminum foil to cover one glass pane. Glue or tape it as smoothly as possible to the pane. Mount the glass against one hole in the side of the box with tape with the aluminum on the outside. Attach the other glass, without aluminum, in the same way to the other hole. Use a drop of wax to fasten a tack to the center of each pane. Put two ventilation holes in the top of the box at opposite ends and place the box over **50 Ec**

the lightbulb. (See Figure 342.50.) Turn on the bulb and have students observe or time how long it takes the tacks to drop. (The tack on the reflective aluminum will drop last.) Similarly, other materials can be tested for their reflective power, and different bulb wattages can be tried. **Caution: Follow safety guidelines when handling glass.**

Contributing Idea D. Heat can be absorbed.

Observing the insulating quality of dark and light surfaces. Blacken one-half of a large tin can with paint, inside and out. Do not paint the other half (it should be shiny). Use small drops of wax to fasten tacks on the can at opposite sides. Place a lighted candle or lightbulb inside the can in the center (Figure 342.51), and have students observe which tack falls off first. The surfaces of the can may also be tested by touch. Students will realize that the dark surface absorbed the heat while the shiny surface reflected it. They can discuss the advantages and disadvantages of light and dark surfaces in building homes and clothing. **51 Aa Ga**

Figure 342.50

Figure 342.51

343 Theory

Generalization. According to theory, heat is a form of energy possessed by a material because of the motion of its molecules.

> *Contributing Idea A.* When a material is heated, the molecules in it begin to move about more violently; when heat is removed, the molecules move more slowly and are closer together.

Observing the influence of heat upon molecules. Place a drop of dark food coloring or black ink into a clear glass of cold water, and at the same time place another drop into a glass of hot, but not steaming, water. Explain that both the coloring and the water are composed of tiny particles called *molecules*. Let students note how long it takes the coloring to disperse in each container. Let them hypothesize why the coloring seems to move about more quickly without stirring in the hotter water. (The more rapidly moving molecules of the hot water bounce against the molecules of the coloring and scatter or diffuse them faster.) Now repeat this activity using water of various temperatures and let students speculate how fast the molecules of coloring will move in each case. Next, ask them to predict what would happen if they put equal spoonfuls of instant coffee or cocoa into identical cups of cold water and hot water. Let them check their predictions (the material

01
Bb
Ca
Fc

will mix faster in the hot water), then ask if they think odors would spread faster on hot or cold days.

> *Contributing Idea B.* Most materials expand when heated and contract when the heat is removed.

Using a model to explain expansion and contraction. Explain that when the movement of the molecules in a material increases, the molecules bump into each other with more force and knock each other farther apart. This can be demonstrated by having marbles represent molecules. Shoot the marbles into other marbles. Students will realize how this model can explain the expansion and contraction of materials.

02
Fc

Using a model to explain changes of state. Use marbles to represent molecules, and shoot them at each other. Students will see that when the force is increased, the marbles knock each other farther apart. Tell them that molecules in a material behave in a similar way when heat (the force) is added. For example, when a glass of water is heated, the molecules of water hit each other, and some strike with such force that they bounce right out of the glass into the air. Let students use this idea to explain evaporation. Tell them that when the molecules in a material are very far apart, as in this example, the material is called a gas. Now explain that when some heat is taken away from a material, the molecules do not hit each

03
Bb
Fc

other with as much force. Thus, the molecules in the material would move more slowly and be closer together. Tell them that when the molecules are in such a state, the material is called a liquid. Let students use this idea to explain condensation. Next, explain that when more heat is taken away, the molecules in a material move still more slowly and strike each other with still less force. Thus the molecules in the material would be much closer together. Tell them that when the molecules are in such a state, the material is called a solid. Students can use this idea to explain the presence of solid wax at the base of a burning candle. Other changes of state, such as melting, freezing, subliming, and frosting, can be explained using this model.

Contributing Idea C. Temperature is a measure of the average speed with which the molecules are moving within a material; heat is the average speed of moving molecules and their total quantity in a material.

Comparing differences between temperature and heat. Fill a large bucket with very warm water, pour some of the water into a glass, and then use two **04 Ce** thermometers to record the temperatures of each (the temperatures will be the same). Wait five minutes, and take the temperatures again. (The water in each container loses heat at about the same rate, but since the water in the bucket had a larger amount of heat to begin with, after several minutes it will still have more heat and a higher temperature than the water in the glass.)

Measuring differences between temperature and heat. Half-fill two beakers **05 Ce** with cold water and record the temperatures of each. Boil 1 c. (200 ml) of water, and pour one-fourth of it into one beaker and three-fourths into the other. Measure the temperatures again, and record them as shown in Table 343.05. Ask which beaker had more heat put into it. (Although the average speed of the added molecules was identical for each beaker, the greater quantity of rapidly moving molecules added to the second beaker produced a greater amount of heat.) You might explain that the amount of heat energy in a fuel or food is found by scientists in a similar way—a fuel or food is burned to see how hot it can make a certain volume of water.

Table 343.05. Comparing Temperature and Heat

	Amount of Water to Be Added	Temperature Before Adding Hot Water	Temperature After Adding Hot Water	Difference in Temperatures
Beaker 1	¼ cup	68°F	70°F	2°F
Beaker 2	¾ cup	68°F	73°F	5°F

344   Applications

Generalization. Instruments that are run by heat energy can be built to do work.

> *Contributing Idea.* Heated water can move objects.

Observing that heated water can move objects. Pour approximately 1 tbsp. (5 ml) of water into a test tube and place the test tube in a mound of clay as shown in Figure 344.01. Insert a rubber stopper firmly, but not too tightly, into the test tube. Heat the bottom of the test tube with a candle. **Caution: Be sure the stopper in the test tube is pointed safely away from students and other objects.** Students will see that as the water is heated, the pressure inside the test tube increases and fires the stopper out like a cannon shot. You might use this experience to explain that pistons and cylinders in gasoline and steam engines work in a similar way.

01 Aa Fc

Figure 344.01

Making a model steam turbine. Prepare a can with a tiny nail hole in its side (Figure 344.02a). Be sure the lid on the can is able to pop off if the steam pressure becomes too great. Out of another can lid, cut slits every ½ in. (1 cm) and bend them to form rotor blades (Figure 344.02b). Fasten the lid to a test tube with clay and mount it on a coat hanger (Figure 344.02c). Set the apparatus in front of the can so that the pressure of the steam from the hole will strike the blades. Now have students compare this model with pictures of steam turbines.

02 Aa Fc

Figure 344.02

350 Electricity

351 Characteristics

Generalization. Electricity has identifiable characteristics.

> *Contributing Idea A.* Electrical energy can be stationary (static electricity).

Seeing, feeling, and hearing evidence of electrical charges. In a darkened room on a dry, cool day, have a student pull a piece of tape quickly away from a roll of black, sticky, bicycle tape. (A spark will appear at the place where the tape pulls away from the roll.) Similarly, in a dark room, students can rub the leather soles of their shoes against a wool rug and touch a metallic object, or long hair can be combed with long strokes to produce visible sparks. When hair is stroked, students can often hear a crackling sound. (Stroking a cat or removing clothes recently tumbled in a dryer also produces the crackling sound.) If hair is stroked near a radio that is tuned between stations with the volume turned high, they will hear the crackling over the radio. The spark that is seen is similar to lightning (both are discharges of static electricity), and the sound is similar to thunder (but on a much smaller scale). You might ask what must happen to produce the phenomenon (certain materials must be rubbed or stroked).

01 Aa Ab Ac

Observing that rubbing charges some materials. Let students experience several of the following activities, and encourage

02 Aa Bb Fb

them to determine any similarities. (In each case, objects are rubbed and certain other objects are attracted to them.) Tell students that when this phenomenon takes place, the materials are said to be *electrically charged* and that this form of electricity is called static electricity. For each of the following, students can test various other materials to see which ones can produce charges and which ones cannot. (Note: The activities work best on dry, cool days.)

> a. Hold a newspaper flat against a table, a wall, or a chalkboard. Rub the entire surface with a wool cloth. (The paper will remain attached to the surface for quite some time.) Let students listen as they pull one corner loose, then quickly let it go. (They may hear a crackling sound, and the paper will be attracted back to the wall.)
>
> b. Turn on a water faucet to produce a slender stream, rub a comb against a wool cloth, and hold one edge close to the stream. (The static electricity in the comb will attract the water.)
>
> c. Set two books on a table approximately 4 in. (10 cm) apart. Place a sheet of glass across them. Cut confetti pieces out of tissue paper and put them on the surface between the books under the glass. When students rub the glass vigorously with a silk cloth, they will see

the pieces move. Similarly, place confetti pieces in small glasses or plastic dishes, such as petri dishes, cover them with plastic wrap or glass, and rub the covering surface. (The pieces will jump about and cling to the surface.)

d. Hold a hard rubber comb near confetti pieces made from tissue paper or grains of puffed rice (nonsugarcoated), then compare what happens when the movement is repeated after rubbing the comb vigorously with a piece of wool cloth. Challenge students to see if rubbing the comb harder or longer makes any difference in what they observe. Similarly, move a plastic ruler or glass rod near the pieces, then compare what happens when done again after rubbing the object with a piece of plastic wrap or silk cloth. Students can also test metal rods by rubbing them with a wool cloth, plastic wrap, or a silk cloth.

e. Blow up a balloon and close it with a rubber band or string. Rub the balloon with a piece of wool cloth and bring the balloon near the pile of confetti. Challenge students to see what happens when the rubbed balloon is touched to a wall, then released, or what happens when it is brought next to their hair.

Determining what materials can produce electrical charges. Place several sheets of newspaper on a flat, wooden table. Rub each sheet vigorously with a different material (e.g., wool, silk, fur, paper, plastic wrap, pencil, foil). After rubbing, try to lift each sheet from the table. (Some will have acquired an electrical charge and will tend to be attracted to the table.) Tell students that when certain materials are attracted to others after rubbing, they are said to be *electrically charged* and this form of electricity is called static electricity. Students can sort the materials according to whether or not static electricity was produced.   **03 Bb Ec Fa**

Determining that not all electrical charges are alike. Place two 6 inch (9 cm) lengths of wool yarn on a flat surface and rub them lengthwise several times with an inflated rubber balloon. When the lengths are held up by one end, approximately 1 in. (2.5 cm) apart, they will repel each other. Now prepare two 6 in. (9 cm), narrow lengths of rubber from a balloon and rub them with wool. When held approximately 1 in. (2.5 cm) apart, the lengths will repel each other. Students will find it reasonable to deduce that each of the paired lengths have the same kind of charge since each are of the same material and receive the same treatment. Next, hold up a charged length of wool near a charged length of rubber. Because the lengths behave differently   **04 Bb Ec Fa**

(i.e., they attract), students will realize that the charges must be different. Tell them that after the wool has been rubbed with rubber, the charge is called a *positive charge*; the charge on the rubber is called a *negative charge*. Knowing this, students can now identify charges produced when different materials are rubbed together.

> *Contributing Idea B.* Electrical energy can move (current electricity).

Generating a direct current. Obtain or build an electric cell and a galvanometer (see entry 352.15). When the cell and galvanometer are connected, the galvanometer will indicate a current moving in the wire. Tell students that when a current moves continuously in one direction it is called a direct current. Now have them reverse the wires on the cell and observe any changes in the galvanometer. (The galvanometer will indicate that the current reverses its direction.) **05 Aa Bb**

Generating an alternating current. Obtain or build a galvanometer (see entry 352.15). Wind 50 turns of insulated copper bell wire to make a coil. Tie the coil with string so it will not come apart, and then connect it to the galvanometer. Move one end of a bar magnet through the coil and notice that the galvanometer indicates a current moving in the wire. When the magnet is removed, students will observe that the galvanometer indicates the current moves in the opposite direction. They will also note that no **06 Aa Bb**

current is produced when the magnet and the coil are motionless. Tell them that a current moving in first one direction and then the other is called an alternating current. Now let them test to see if the current is greater when the movement of the magnet is vigorous, whether it matters if the magnet or the coil is moved, what happens when the other end of the magnet is used, and how different magnets of different strengths and coils with different numbers of loops affect the current. Interested students can research information about how electricity is generated to run machinery and light cities.

352 Interactions

Generalization I. Electricity is a form of energy produced by different sources.

> *Contributing Idea A.* Chemical reactions can be a source of electricity (electro-chemical propagation).

Making an electric cell. Have students bare approximately 1 in. (2.5 cm) at the ends of two 2 ft. (60 cm) lengths of insulated copper bell wire. Attach one end of one length to a silver knife. Attach one end of the other length to a sheet of aluminum foil. Now place a paper towel that has been soaked in salt water between the two metals. An electric current can be detected using a current detector (see entry 352.15). Tell students that what **01 Bb Gc**

they have made is called an electric cell. Explain that in an electric cell there are always two different metals called electrodes and a fluid called an electrolyte. Next, let them try making other cells by substituting magnesium or zinc for the aluminum and copper or gold for the silver. They can also substitute vinegar or boric acid for the salt solution.

Producing electricity from a "wet" cell. 02 Gc
Wrap one bared end of a 2 ft. (60 cm) length of insulated copper bell wire around a ½ in. × 6 in. (1 cm × 15 cm) strip of clean copper; then do the same with another wire and a piece of clean zinc (a strip of zinc can be obtained by cutting the outer casing of an old dry cell). Connect the free ends of the wires to a galvanometer (Figure 352.02). A slight deflection of the galvanometer will indicate a slight current (the saliva and the two dissimilar metals make an electric cell). Now use the galvanometer after suspending the two different metals in a glass of vinegar. Try other metals and other liquids such as cooking oil, sugar water, mouthwashes, detergents, and various concentrations of salt solution. Test to see if there is a stronger current when the liquid is warm or cold. (Note: Be sure the metals are washed and dried between each test. Students will find that almost any two dissimilar metals immersed in most chemical solutions will produce electricity.)

Figure 352.02

Producing electricity from a "dry" cell. 03 Bb Gc
Insert copper and zinc strips approximately ½ in. (1 cm) apart in a potato. Attach the bared ends of two 1 ft. (30 cm) lengths of insulated copper bell wire to the strips and to a current detector (see entry 352.15). (See Figure 352.03.) Students will see that a current is produced. (They can increase the number of potatoes to make the current stronger.) Explain that the potato is somewhat like a *dry cell* because, unlike "wet" cells, no chemicals can spill out regardless of how it is held. (Note: A dry cell is not really dry inside.)

Figure 352.03

Testing materials to make "dry" cells. 04
Roll a lemon on a table until it feels soft
and juicy inside. Bare approximately 1 in. Bc
(2.5 cm) at the ends of two 2 ft. (60 cm) Ec
pieces of insulated copper bell wire. Gc
Wrap one end tightly around the head of
an iron nail and insert the nail into the
lemon. Approximately ½ in. (1 cm) from
the nail, insert one end of the second
piece of wire. Use a current detector to
see if electricity is being produced (see
entry 352.15). Now have students carry
out various tests.

  a. They can see what other metals,
  such as aluminum, gold, lead,
  pencil "lead" (carbon), steel, zinc,
  and so forth, will produce electricity. They can also test a dime
  and a penny. Keep records of the
  results to see which combinations
  produce the strongest current.

  b. They can test to see what effect
  changing the distance between
  the two metals in the lemon has on
  the current. (The closer the metals
  are without touching, the greater
  the amount of current produced.)

  c. They can test other fruits or vegetables in place of the lemon.

  d. They can test nonmetal materials
  such as wood, plastic, or glass.

Examining a "dry" cell. Distribute 05
D-cell batteries (standard flashlight cells) Aa
to students. Place the cells on newspapers
and, using pliers and screwdrivers, pry

open the top edges, and remove the top
piece and the tarlike material beneath it.
Twist the center black (carbon) rod carefully, loosen it, and slowly pull it out.
Scrape out and examine the remaining
materials. (See Figure 352.05.) (Note:
The materials inside the cell are not harmful to the skin; however, they may stain
clothing so some care should be taken.)
As an additional experience, the cell can
be attached to a bulb in a circuit to see at
what stage of the dissection the cell stops
lighting the bulb. Conversely, students
can find out at what point a bulb begins to
light as the black rod is pushed back into
the cell. Students can test and list all the
materials that make up the cell that do not
conduct electricity. For study and display,
a large cell can be cut vertically or horizontally with a hacksaw.

Metal Cap (Positive Terminal)
Sealing Tar   Top
                          Carbon
                          Rod
                          Black
                          Paste
                          Wrapper
                          Zinc Case
                          (Negative
                          Terminal)

Figure 352.05

Making a battery. Polish a penny and 06
a dime with steel wool. (Note: Pennies Bb
dated prior to 1983 will work best for this Gc
activity. Pennies made before 1983 are
made from 95% copper and will be the

best conductors.) From blotter paper or paper toweling, cut three or four six-sided pieces that have a diameter no larger than a dime (Figure 352.06a). Sandwich the pieces between the penny and dime, and then bare approximately 1 in. (2.5 cm) from the ends of two 2 ft. (60 cm) lengths of insulated copper bell wire. Tape one end of one wire to the penny and one end of the other wire to the dime (Figure 352.06b). Use friction tape to hold the materials tightly together. With a medicine dropper filled with a salt water solution, moisten the papers between the coins and wipe any excess solution from the edges of the coins. The presence of an electrical current can be detected by connecting the free ends of the two wires to a current detector (see entry 352.15). Tell

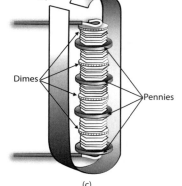

Figure 352.06

students that they have made an *electric cell*. Tell them that when several are put together, the collection is called a battery. Encourage them to find out if the electric power increases as the number of cells increases. This can be done by polishing more pennies and dimes, cutting more blotter pieces, and sandwiching them between alternating pennies and dimes. The battery can be held together with friction tape (Figure 352.06c).

Contributing Idea B. Motion can be a source of electricity (mechanical propagation).

Producing electricity by rubbing objects. Darken the classroom on a cool, dry day. Stretch a pair of rubber bands at right angles to each other across an aluminum pie pan. Place a plastic bag on a table, rub it vigorously with wool, and hold it up vertically by one edge. Hold the pie pan by the rubber bands, press it against the bag, and then touch it to one end of a burned-out fluorescent tube. (Note: Be sure that fingers do not touch the pan.) Repeat this activity several times, and let students touch the pan to their fingers, a nose, or other objects in the room. They will see, feel, and hear the electricity produced by the rubbing of the wool on the plastic. **07 Gc**

Producing electricity by moving a magnetic field. Loop 50 turns of insulated bell wire to make a coil that will pass easily over a strong bar magnet. **08 Bb Ec Gc**

Connect the free ends to a current detector (see entry 352.15). Move the magnet in and out of the coil. Students will see a current being registered on the detector. Now see what happens when the magnet is held still while the coil is moved, when both are moved simultaneously, or when the opposite end of the magnet is used. Test other types of magnets. Tell students that the process by which a current is produced by moving the magnetic field near a wire is called electromagnetic induction, and that the principle is used in most telephones and in radio and television speakers.

Generalization II. Current electricity produces a magnetic field.

> *Contributing Idea A.* An electric current carried by a wire produces a magnetic field around it.

Observing that an electric current produces a magnetic field. Remove the insulation from both ends of a 3 ft. (1 m) length of copper wire. Lay the wire flat on a table, and put a pencil on each side of it. Place a sheet of glass or stiff cardboard on the pencils and sprinkle iron filings on it. With a switch in the circuit, connect the wire to an electric cell. (See Figure 352.09.) Close the switch and tap the glass lightly. Students will see a pattern made by the magnetic field around the wire. **09 Aa**

Figure 352.09

Comparing magnetic and electric fields. Suspend two needles from threads: one magnetized and one unmagnetized. Bring a charged comb near each end of each suspended needle. (The needles will be equally attracted by the electric field of the charged comb.) Now bring one pole of a strong magnet near each end. (Both ends of the unmagnetized needle will be attracted; one end of the magnetized needle will be attracted, while the other will be repelled.) From this experience, students will realize that magnetic and electric fields are not the same. **10 Ca Fa**

Testing the effect of magnetic and electric fields on different materials. Use lengths of thread to suspend small objects of various materials (buttons, paperclips, pins). Be sure the suspended objects can swing freely. Test each by first bringing to it a magnet, then a charged object such as a comb rubbed with wool. Students can record their observations on Table 352.11, p. 326. They can deduce that magnetic and electric fields are not **11 Bc Ec**

the same (all materials are attracted in electric fields; only certain materials are attracted by magnets).

Table 352.11. Testing Magnetic and Electric Fields

Test Material	Moved By Electric Field	Moved By Magnetic Field
iron	Yes	Yes
steel	Yes	Yes
brass	Yes	No
plastic	Yes	No

Contributing Idea B. A compass is an instrument that can be used to detect magnetic fields.

Detecting the magnetic field produced by an electric current. Have students connect a switch to a circuit. With the switch open, place a compass beside one of the wires so that the needle on the compass and the wire point in the same direction. (See Figure 352.12.) Close the switch. (The compass needle will be influenced by the magnetic field.) Repeat this activity by holding the compass first over the wire, then under it, to see what happens. Students will realize that a wire carrying an electric current seems to have a magnetic field around it and that this field can be detected by a compass.

**12
Aa
Ec**

Compass

Electric Cell

Switch

Figure 352.12

Generalization III. Current electricity moves when there is a complete circuit.

Contributing Idea A. Current electricity can be detected.

Detecting electric currents. Have students touch the ends of wires from a flashlight cell a short distance apart on their tongues. If a current is produced, they will detect a metallic taste. When the current is stopped, the taste will disappear. **Caution: Follow safety guidelines when working with electricity.**

**13
Ae**

Using a radio to detect electric currents. Obtain a transistor radio, turn it on, and dial it so that it is between stations with the volume turned up. Now tap together two wires that are attached to an electric cell. Students will hear a clicking sound on the radio. This indicates an electric current is nearby.

**14
Ac**

Building a galvanometer. Use transparent tape to fasten a small compass to a piece of cardboard (Figure 352.15a). Cut two slots in the cardboard at the north and south markings on the compass, then wind about 50 turns of fine, insulated copper bell wire through the slots and around the compass and cardboard (Figure 352.15b). Leave approximately 2 ft. (60 cm) of wire free at each end. Now put two brass paper fasteners through the cardboard and twist the free ends of the wire around them once or twice to keep the wire from

**15
Bb
Gc**

Compass Taped to Cardboard

(a)

50 Turns of Wire

Brass Fasteners

(b)

Figure 352.15

unwinding. Scrape the insulation away from an inch of wire at each of the free ends and attach them to the terminals of an electric cell. (The needle of the compass will move, thus indicating that electricity is moving.) Tell students that the instrument is called a galvanometer and that it is used to detect electric currents. Now have them keep their eyes on the compass needle as you reverse the wires so that they touch the opposite terminals. Discuss what effect reversing the connections has on the compass needle. (The needle turns in the opposite direction.)

Contributing Idea B. A circuit is a continuous path through which electricity can move.

Arranging a circuit to light a bulb. Distribute to individuals or pairs of students, one D-cell battery (a flashlight battery), one #48 (flashlight) bulb, and two 1 ft (30 cm) lengths of #20 bare copper wire. Insulated wire can be used, but the ends **16 Bb Ec**

must be stripped or scraped so that contact can be made. Ask students to see if they can make the bulb light. (Note: This makes a fine "discovery" experience, and students will find several ways to make the bulb light.) Discuss similarities among different ways to light the bulb (the points of contact always remain the same). Next, challenge them to light the bulb using only one wire. As the students freely experiment, explain that an electric bulb lights when it is part of a continuous loop of materials through which electricity moves. Tell them that such a loop is called a circuit. Have them trace the circuit in each arrangement they make.

Making a holder for a D-cell battery and preparing wires for use in a circuit. Cell holders can make it easier for students to connect two or more D-cell batteries in a circuit. Simply press a brass paper fastener into each end of a wide rubber band (Figure 352.17a, p. 328), and stretch the band over a *D* cell so that the fasteners make proper contact. Connecting wires can be wrapped around the fasteners. Fahnestock clips, available at hardware stores, can be used instead of the fasteners, and wires can be easily inserted into their eyelets. Another type of cell holder can be made using paper clips and right angle brackets (Figure 352.17b, p. 328). (Note: When the cells are put away after a class, be sure that the wires are disconnected to prevent the **17 Gc**

Figure 352.17a, b

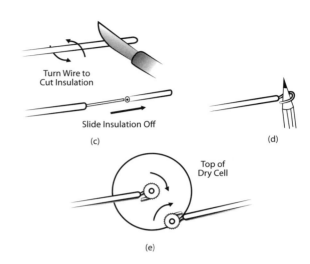

Figure 352.17c, d, e

cells from becoming "worn out" by short circuits.) If larger dry cells are used and if terminals are of the screw-type, it is best to prepare and use wires in a certain way. If students' insulation is lacquered, scrape it off with scissors or a knife blade. If it is made of a thick material, cut the material down to the wire, and pull or whittle it off (Figure 352.17c). Be careful that the wire is not cut in the process. Generally a removal of about an inch (2.5 cm) of insulation is sufficient. To connect the wires to terminals, bend the bare end around a pencil point to form a hook (Figure 352.17d). Fasten the hook clockwise around a terminal (i.e., in the same direction that the screw turns) (Figure 352.17e). Wires can also be spliced easily together. Such wires should then be taped.

Making a holder for a small (flashlight) bulb. Bulb holders can make it easier to connect two or more bulbs in a circuit. Have students spread a paper clip slightly apart, then wrap a 1 in. (2.5 cm) piece of masking tape around the small arm of the clip (Figure 352.18a). Remove approximately 1½ in. (4 cm) of insulation from a 1 ft. (30 cm) length of copper wire. Wind the bare portion around the masking tape and fasten the free end to a D-cell battery. Wind a second length of wire around the clip as close to the tape as possible (Figure 352.18b). Now turn the clip over and screw a small bulb into the large portion so that its tip touches the wire around the tape (Figure 352.18c). (Note: It may be necessary to bend the large arm of the clip to ensure a tight fit and a good contact for the bulb.) Another type of bulb holder can

18
Gc

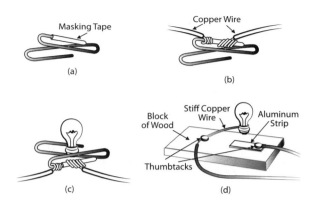

Figure 352.18

be made using paper clips, thumbtacks, and an aluminum strip (Figure 352.18d).

Exploring electric circuits. Provide small groups of students with two or more D-cell batteries with holders, two or more #41 bulbs with holders, and lengths of insulated copper wire. Allow them to explore different ways to put the materials together. They might try several bulbs and one cell, several cells and one bulb, or several bulbs and several cells. Whenever a bulb lights, have them trace the completed circuit. If they note differences in the brightness of the bulbs in their arrangements, challenge them to find out if there is any relationship between the brightness and the arrangement. Encourage further experimentation: they can find out how many cells it takes to light a household bulb (it takes about eight *D*-cells to dimly light a 60-watt bulb); they can find out how many bulbs they can light with one

**19
Ec
Fa**

cell; they can find out how brightly a bulb will shine when several cells are used.

Making a circuit tester. Using insulated copper wire, have students arrange a bulb, bulb holder, D-cell, and cell holder as shown in Figure 352.20. Various materials can now be touched by the two unattached bare ends to see whether or not the materials conduct electricity. Students will realize that if the electricity passes through a material, a circuit is completed, and the bulb will light. Conversely, if the bulb does not light, a circuit is not completed. The tester can also be used to test bulbs to see if they are "worn out" or not.

**20
Ec
Gc**

Figure 352.20

Locating hidden circuits. Students can use a circuit tester (see entry 352.20) to locate hidden circuits, much as an electrician checks electrical circuits in a home or appliance. To do this, prepare some "mystery" circuits as follows. Put four brass paper fasteners through a 4 in. × 6 in. (10 cm × 15 cm) piece of heavy cardboard, and label each with a letter (Figure 352.21a, p. 330). Connect lengths of

**21
Be
Eb
Ec**

of insulated copper wire to the backs of the fasteners (Figure 352.21b). Cover the arrangement with another 4 in. × 6 in. (10 cm × 15 cm) piece of cardboard. Fasten the two pieces together with staples and/or tape. Many possible "mystery" circuits can be made. For each, have students infer the arrangement by testing for connections with a circuit tester. They can keep a record of their tests by drawing a picture of the arrangement. Compare drawings prepared independently by different students. (Note: Some of the circuits can be connected several different ways.) After this experience, students can create "mystery" circuits of their own.

Figure 352.21

Contributing Idea C. Current electricity takes the shortest and easiest circuit back to the place where it started.

Observing a short circuit. Demonstrate that electricity will take the easiest pathway back to its starting place by removing some insulation from two wires connected to a D-cell and bulb. Touch the bare places together or place a length of thick copper wire across the bare places so that it makes a good contact. **Caution:** **22 Aa Bb**

Do not touch the bare wires at the contact points because they get very hot. The bulb will go out. It is best to do this quickly so as not to greatly drain the cell's energy. Have students trace the circuit. Tell them that such a pathway is called a short circuit. (Note: A short circuit may not always be the shortest path; electricity will follow the path of least resistance.) Now place a length of #26 Nichrome wire across the bare places. Students will see that the bulb remains lit. Next, shorten the Nichrome wire bit by bit, placing it across the copper wires each time. The bulb will become dimmer and dimmer, thus indicating that the electricity takes the easiest as well as shortest path in a circuit. Let students use insulated copper wire to put together various short circuit arrangements. Discuss the fact that some fires begin in homes due to short circuits. (Insulated wires often become worn, and the two wires of a circuit may touch.)

Observing a grounded circuit. Have students arrange a bulb and D-cell on an aluminum pan as shown in Figure 352.23. Place a thick copper wire across the bare portion of one wire to the aluminum pan. Students will see the light go out. Trace the circuit for them. Tell them that such a pathway is called a grounded circuit because the electricity travels back to its source through the ground. Discuss with them the danger in turning on an electric appliance that has defective wiring while **23 Aa Bb**

touching a radiator or other object that has pipes connected to the ground. **Caution: It is particularly dangerous if the body is wet (body salts and water make good conductors for electricity); electrocution is possible.**

Figure 352.23

Contributing Idea D. Switches are used to open and close circuits.

Making a switch. Have students prepare a circuit tester (see entry 352.20). Let them turn the bulb on and off by connecting and disconnecting the ends of the free wires. Tell them that a *switch* is a device designed to do this easily and safely. Now let them build a switch by inserting a screw through a rubber washer and fastening it to a block of wood. Next, bend a strip of copper or aluminum as shown in Figure 352.24a and punch a hole in **24 Bb Gc**

Figure 352.24a

one end. Push a second screw through the hole, then through a rubber washer, and then into the wooden block so that the raised end of the strip is over the first screw. Connect the end wires of the circuit tester to the screws and test the switch by pressing down on the raised end of the strip until it touches the screw underneath it (Figure 352.24a). Students can place their switch or combinations of switches in various parts of a circuit arrangement to see how switches function in turning appliances on or off (Figure 352.24b).

Figure 352.24b

Generalization IV. Current electricity travels through some materials better than others.

Contributing Idea A. Some materials allow electricity to pass through them easily (conductors); other materials tend to block the movement of electricity (insulators).

Identifying conductors and insulators. Let students build a circuit tester (see entry 352.20) to test several objects **25 Bb Bc Ec**

or materials to see which complete the circuit. They might test door hinges and knobs, coins, metal desks, faucets, paper clips, pins, or pipe cleaners. **Caution: Pliers should be used to hold the wires, which may heat up quickly and can burn the skin.** Results can be recorded on Table 352.25. Mention to students that materials that permit electricity to pass through them easily are called conductors, while those that do not permit easy passage are called insulators. Discuss why electrical wires, plugs, and switches are covered with insulating materials. As an extending experience, some students might try increasing the number of D-cells in a parallel circuit to test the conductivity of liquids such as water, cooking oil, vinegar, coffee, or various solutions of salt, baking soda, and so forth. They might also try varying the distance between the wires in the liquids.

Table 352.25. Testing Conductivity

Lights the Bulb (conductors)	Doesn't Light the Bulb (insulators)
aluminum foil	Rubber
carbon	Paper
graphite (pencil "lead")	Chalk
silver-plated knife	Glass
copper wire	Wool

Contributing Idea B. Thinner wires have more resistance than thicker wires of the same material; longer wires have more resistance than shorter wires of the same material.

Examining the influence of size factors on the conductivity of wires. Let students test various thick and thin wires (e.g., #22 and #36 copper wires) of equal length to see if thickness influences a circuit in any way. (Both wires will complete the circuit, but the thicker wire will cause the bulb to dim considerably.) (Note: Students might check each test wire using other bulbs and cells to make sure the effect is caused by the wires and not a "worn out" cell.) Now see if length makes any difference by placing a 2 ft. (30 cm) length of #32 Nichrome wire, available at hardware stores, in a circuit. Test each time as the wire is shortened. Now prepare a different

26
Ca
Ec

Copper Wire → ← Nichrome Wire

Figure 352.26a

circuit using both kinds of wires (Figure 352.26a). Students should note that while the Nichrome wire should form a short circuit, it does not because its length provides too much resistance for the electricity to travel through it. Gradually shorten the Nichrome wire, testing each time. (As the length is shortened, the bulb goes out and the wire gets hot.) Repeat this experience using other wires (e.g., #26 Nichrome and #36 copper wires). The

Figure 352.26b

influence of wire length can also be tested by stringing a test wire around the heads of paper fasteners attached to a board or stiff cardboard (Figure 352.26b). Test by touching the wire at different distances along its length.

Making a rheostat. Prepare a 1 ft. (30 cm) length of coat hanger wire by straightening it and sanding off any coating of paint on it. Now fasten one wire from a circuit tester to one end of the hanger wire. As the second tester wire is moved up and down along the hanger wire, students will see the brightness of the bulb change. They will realize that the electricity seems to move more easily when the distance traveled is shortened. Mention to them that the device they have made is called a *rheostat* and that it is used to control the amount of current. **27 Bb Gc**

Contributing Idea C. Some metals have more resistance to electricity than others.

Examining resistance in metals. Obtain equal lengths of iron picture wire and **28 Ca** copper bell wire of equal diameters. Using a circuit tester (see entry 352.20), compare the brightness of the bulb as the two different metals are tested. (Due to the resistance of the iron, the bulb will appear dimmer.)

Using resistance in metals to make a model lightbulb. Place two pieces of #20 bare copper wire through some clay so that the wires resemble the interior of a bulb. Fasten various thin materials across the upright wires to see which ones resist the passage of electricity, get hot, and give off light. (See Figure 352.29.) Students can test pieces of steel wool and very thin wires (e.g., #32 Nichrome wire, available at hardware stores, will get very hot and begin to glow). They can compare their results to observations of commercial lightbulbs. Interested students might research the work Thomas Edison (1847–1931) did while inventing the first practical incandescent bulb. Students might be interested in researching other types of bulbs: fluorescent, CFCs, diodes, and so on. **29 Bd Ec Gc**

Figure 352.29

Contributing Idea D. Overloading a circuit with too many resistors can overheat the wires.

Making a fuse. Have students cut a thin strip of foil from a chewing gum wrapper, and trim it into the shape as shown (Figure 352.30a). It is not necessary to remove the paper backing from the foil. Now place the strip on a block of wood and push a thumbtack through each end. Attach the bare ends of connecting wires from a D-cell to the two thumbtacks and

30
Bb
Ec
Fc

Figure 352.30

observe (Figure 352.30b). The foil strip will melt and break apart. Tell students that what they have made is called a fuse. Explain that when there is too much current in a circuit, the fuse overheats and melts. They will understand that a fuse acts like an automatic switch—it opens the circuit (to turn off the current) when the circuit is overloaded. Now let them experiment with various kinds and sizes of foil to see if they can also be made into fuses. (Note: Household foils are usually such good conductors that they are difficult to melt unless they are trimmed

very thin.) Students can also examine and compare a new fuse to a burned-out fuse.

Using fuses. To show that attaching too many appliances to a house circuit can cause the wires to overheat, have students make a fuse and place it in a circuit with two D-cells and a 2½-volt bulb as shown in Figure 352.31. Overheat the circuit by adding more 2½-volt bulbs, one at a time, until the fuse melts. Students will realize

31
Ga

Figure 352.31

that fuses keep the wires from overheating and causing fires. Now let them try trimming the center width of the fuse until it will melt according to a particular specification such as a "three-bulb" fuse, a "four-bulb" fuse, etc. Tell them that in a similar way, engineers design fuses that will melt at a specified temperature or amount of electrical current.

Generalization V. **Current electricity can be controlled.**

Contributing Idea A. Series circuits channel all the electricity through a single pathway; parallel circuits channel all the electricity through a main pathway and branching pathways.

Comparing series and parallel circuits. **32 Bb Ca Ec** Cut five 1 ft. (30 cm) lengths of insulated bell wire, remove the insulation from the ends, and connect them to three bulb holders, a switch, and a D-cell as shown in Figure 352.32a. Screw 1½-volt bulbs into the holders and close the circuit. Students will see what happens when they unscrew one bulb in the circuit. (The

Figure 352.32a

other bulbs go out.) Trace the circuit. Tell the students that when the electric current from the cell moves through each bulb in turn, the arrangement is called a series circuit. Ask them to imagine what would happen if the appliances in their homes were arranged in series. (If one went out, all would go out.) Now challenge them to design a circuit that will keep the remaining lights on after one goes out. If allowed to explore freely, they will discover that this can be done by connecting the three bulbs as shown in Figure 352.32b. Trace the circuit for them, and indicate that not all the current goes through each bulb: it divides with some going down each branching pathway. Tell them that such an arrangement is called a parallel circuit. If possible, obtain strings of Christmas tree lights for students to examine.

Figure 352.32b

Testing one electric cell and several bulbs. **33 Ec** Connect two bulbs in series, and then add more bulbs in the series, one at a time. Students will find that the more bulbs they connect, the dimmer each becomes. Explain that as the length of the circuit is increased, the resistance to the movement of the electricity is increased, and there is a corresponding cut down in the current moving in the circuit. Now have them connect two bulbs in parallel, then add more bulbs in parallel, one at a time. Trace the circuit, and indicate that not all the current goes through each bulb, but divides along each branching pathway. As more bulbs are added, students will find that there is no cut down in the current moving through any one bulb.

Contributing Idea B. Electric cells can be arranged to produce different voltages.

Testing several electric cells and one bulb. **34 Bb Ec** Have students hook up a 2½-volt bulb to a single D-cell, and observe the bulb's brightness. Now arrange two cells in series and observe again. Students will find that increasing the number of cells in series increases the brightness of the bulb. Explain that increasing the cells in series increases the electrical pressure in the wires causing the bulb to burn brighter. Tell them that the increase in pressure is called voltage. Next, have them arrange the cells in parallel. They will see that there is a return to the original brightness. As an additional experience, students can substitute a galvanometer for the bulb. Ask them what they can conclude about the force of the current in each arrangement.

Testing several electric cells and several bulbs. If allowed to experiment freely with 2½-volt bulbs and D-cells, students can discover that when connecting cells, the series arrangement gives more light, but when connecting bulbs, the parallel arrangement gives more. They can also discover that in the series arrangement of cells, the lifetime of the cells is no greater than a single cell, but in the parallel arrangement of two or more cells, the lifetime is at least twice as long as a single cell. You might explain that the series arrangement of cells builds up electrical pressure called *volts*. For example, two 1½-volt cells in series produce 3 volts of electrical pressure, but in the parallel arrangement they produce only 1½ volts and last twice as long.

35
Bb
Ec
Fa

Contributing Idea C. Switches can be used to control circuits and voltages easily and safely.

Turning an appliance on and off from two or more switches. Have students recall where they have used switches that turn lights on by flipping them up *or* pushing them down. (Such switches are usually used at the bottom and top of a stairway or at opposite ends of a hallway.) Have them make several switches, and challenge them to design an arrangement that can turn a bulb on and off by either of two switches. Challenge students to design a way to turn an appliance off and on using three switches.

36
Ga
Gb
Gc

Making a reversible switch. Students can build a switch that can change the current direction quickly and easily. Such a switch can be used to reverse a motor's direction from time to time without removing and rearranging the wires. (See Figure 352.37.)

37
Ga
Gb
Gc

Figure 352.37

Making a dimmer switch. Carve the **38** wood from a pencil to expose the "lead" **Gc** (graphite) inside. By sliding a contact wire from a circuit tester along the length of the "lead," the lightbulb will become brighter or dimmer. (See Figure 352.38.)

Figure 352.38

Listing safety precautions for use of **39** **electricity.** Have students discuss the **Ba** dangers related to electricity (it can hurt **Bc** or kill living things, and it can set things on fire), then let them develop a listing of guidelines to follow when using electricity. The following are a few suggestions that might be listed.

a. Electric wires or cords that have worn or frayed insulation should not be used in an electric circuit.

b. Electric wires, cords, switches, fuses, or appliances that are connected in a circuit should never be touched with wet hands.

c. Switches should be repaired immediately if you get a shock when you use them.

d. Electric circuits should be disconnected from the source of electricity before any work is done to them.

353 Theory

Generalization I. According to theory, all matter is made up of atoms that contain tiny particles of electricity.

> *Contributing Idea A.* Atomic particles can be accumulated into electrical charges.

Using drawings to explain the electri- **01** **cal components of atoms.** Rub various **Aa** objects to produce electric charges (e.g., **Bb** plastic wrap and plastic spoons; wool or cotton and balloons). Have students summarize the results of these experiences, then tell them that in experiments on hundreds of different kinds of materials, scientists have found that there are only two types of electric charge. One type they call positive and the other type they call negative. Objects that do not have an electric charge are said to be uncharged, or *neutral.* To explain what rubbing has to do with electricity, use Figure 353.01a–c on page 338. Begin by telling students that everything in the world is made out of tiny particles called atoms (there are more than 100 different kinds of atoms), but that atoms are made up of even tinier particles. Explain that two of these particles are electrical: the *proton,* located in the center or *nucleus* of the atom and the *electron*, which may spin in many different orbits around the nucleus (Figure 353.01a). Every electron has exactly the same negative charge

Two-Dimensional Model of an Atom

Electron   Proton

(a)

Model of Electrically Neutral Atoms

Hydrogen   Helium   Lithium

(b)

Model of Electrically Charged Atoms

Negatively Charged

Positively Charged

(c)

Figure 353.01

(–), and every proton the same positive charge (+). When an atom has one proton and one electron, it is said to be electrically neutral. (The positive charge of the proton exactly balances the negative charge of the electron.) Normal atoms are electrically uncharged or neutral (Figure 353.01b). The transfer of electrons from one object to another is one thing that causes objects to become charged. When two uncharged objects are rubbed together, some electrons are rubbed off

one object and left on the other; one loses electrons, the other gains extra electrons, and the objects are unbalanced. For example, when electrons are rubbed off neutral atoms, the atoms take on a positive charge because each has more protons than electrons; if neutral atoms gain some electrons, they take on a negative charge because each has more electrons than protons (Figure 353.01c). Tell students that both static and current electricity can be explained by the movement of electrons from negatively charged atoms to positively charged atoms until balance is achieved. Now let them build a device as in entry 352.07 and use their knowledge of protons and electrons to explain what happens when used.

Contributing Idea B. Unlike electric charges attract; like electric charges repel.

Building an electroscope. Tell students **02** that an *electroscope* is an instrument **Bb** that can show if an electrically charged **Ga** object is nearby and can provide some **Gc** indication as to how strong its charge is. One way to build an electroscope is to obtain a clean, clear bottle, and fit it with a one-hole rubber stopper. Push the end of a heavy, noninsulated copper wire or coat hanger wire that has been sanded, through the stopper and bend it (Figure 353.02a). Tape the wire to hold it in place. Notch a ¼ in. × 4½ in. (or 1 cm × 11 cm) aluminum strip (Figure 353.02b), and drape it over the wire. Insert the stopper back in the bottle (Figure 353.02c). Hold a charged comb or balloon near the top without touching the coil of wire. Students can observe the strip of aluminum foil. Explain that when the comb is held close to the loop, extra electrons on the comb push electrons from the copper coil down the wire and onto the leaves of the aluminum strip even though the comb's electrons don't move off the comb (the excess electrons on the leaves cause the leaves to push apart). Conversely, when the comb is moved away, the electrons on the leaves scatter throughout the copper wire, and the leaves hang down again. Now rub a glass rod with silk and slowly bring it to the loop without touching it. Explain that the rod has a shortage of electrons and attracts the electrons in the strip and wire to the top of the wire even though they don't actually leave the wire (the shortage of electrons in the strip causes the leaves to push apart). Students will realize that in either case, the instrument indicates when a charged object is nearby. Now charge the comb again by rubbing it three times on a piece of wool. This time touch it to the loop, and then pull it away (some of the comb's electrons move onto the wire giving it extra electrons ,which cause the leaves to stay apart after the comb is removed). After students note how far apart the leaves stand, drain off the electrons by touching the wire with a finger. Next, rub the

Figure 353.02

comb six times and repeat. Students will understand that the electroscope provides some indication of how strong a particular charge is. Let them experiment with various shapes and sizes of aluminum foil strips to compare the strips' sensitivity in detecting electric charges. Let them also test various lengths, thicknesses, and kinds of wires in the electroscope.

Contributing Idea C. Models can be used to explain the movement of electrons.

Using a marble model to explain the movement of electrons through materials. **03 Fc** Arrange a row of marbles. Students can observe that only the end marble moves away when a single marble is snapped into the row. Relate the movement of the marbles to the movement of electrons. For example, electrons move similarly to the pushing of marbles through a tube; when the tube is full, one needs to push only one marble into one end and a marble will immediately come out of the other. (Individual marbles, like electrons, do not move much, but the effect is almost instantaneous.)

Using a water-hose model to explain the movement of electrons. **04 Fc** Have students test the conductivity of various thick and thin wires (see entry 352.26). Compare what took place with two water hoses, both the same length, but one narrower in diameter than the other (e.g., a garden hose and a fire hose). Ask what would happen if both hoses were attached to the same fire hydrant (i.e., electrical source). Students will realize that the larger hose will carry more water and allow a larger amount of water to move out of the nozzle (similarly, thick copper wire will have more movement of electrons than a thin copper wire of the same length). Next, test various long and short wires, then compare to a garden hose: a very long hose would not have as much pressure at its nozzle end as a short hose of the same diameter. Students can realize that the friction taking place inside the hose (wire) as the water (electrons) moves along gradually reduces the force of the water (current). Now let them use the water hose model to make analogies to electric circuits.

Generalization II. Electrical energy can produce electromagnetic radiation.

> *Contributing Idea A.* Electrical energy can produce heat and light.

Producing heat and light from electricity. **05 Af** Unravel a piece of electric cord wire to obtain several of the very thin strands that make up the cord. Place one strand across the terminals of a large electric cell as shown in Figure 353.05. A strip of paper held against the strand will begin to smolder, and the strand should get hot enough to glow. **Caution: Follow safety guidelines when working with heated wires. Hot wires can burn the skin.** Students can feel that electricity produced heat and see that it produced light. Discuss how people have used this knowledge to develop such appliances as heaters, toasters, lightbulbs, and so on.

Clothespin

Figure 353.05

Contributing Idea B. Electrical energy can produce radio waves.

Producing radio waves from electricity. When an electrically charged object is moved very rapidly (e.g., a million times per second) electromagnetic radiation can be produced. The radiation travels outward from the object at the speed of light. Tell students that such radiation can be converted into radio waves. To do this, stretch approximately 25 ft. (8 m) of insulated copper wire to form an antenna. Fasten one end to the positive terminal on a large electric cell and a shorter piece of wire to the other terminal. Fasten the free end of the shorter piece to a ground such as a bare water pipe. Fasten another short piece to the handle of a coarse file and to the negative terminal. Lightly slide the free end of a fourth wire along the file. (Students will see sparks.) Now turn on a radio (see Figure 353.06) and tune it to a place on the dial where no station is heard, then turn the volume high. Slide the wire along the file again. Students will hear a scratchy sound over the radio. Test to see how far from the antenna the radio receiver can detect the radio waves. Test the effect of direction from the antenna, the influence of the number of cells arranged in series in the circuit, and differences in the material used to make the antenna. Students can experiment with longer and shorter antennas, straight and circular ones. Since the sounds heard are produced by radio waves, some students might learn the

**06
Ec
Gc**

International Code to send messages. Others might place a bell or buzzer in the circuit in place of the file. (They will see the sparks produced in each device and hear the static over the radio.) A discussion of lightning might also be appropriate. (Lightning produces radio waves that can be heard as a kind of static on radios.)

Figure 353.06

354 Applications

Generalization I. A magnetic field is generated around a wire carrying electricity; the strength of the magnetic field can be increased or decreased in several ways.

> *Contributing Idea A.* The electromagnet is an instrument used in the operation of many electrical systems.

Studying the presence of a magnetic field produced by an electric current. Place two lengths of insulated copper wire close together (Figure 354.01a, p. 342). When the switch is closed, the

**01
Aa
Ca**

parallel wires will carry the electric current in opposite directions, and students will see that the wires move apart. Rulers can be used to measure the distance between the wires before and after the switch is closed. By adding more electric cells, students will find that the distance of movement depends upon the strength of the current produced. Have them arrange the circuit so the wires can carry the current in the same direction (Figure 354.01b). They will see that the parallel wires are drawn closer together when the switch is closed and will realize that: (1) current-carrying wires produce a magnetic field around them, and (2) opposite-direction currents repel each other, while like-direction currents attract each other.

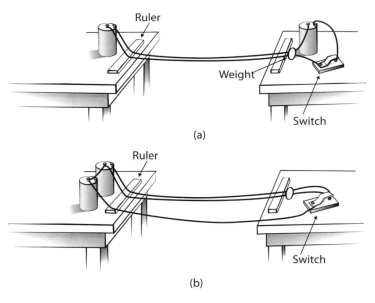

Figure 354.01

Making an electromagnet. Wind 50 loops of insulated copper bell wire around a large pencil to make a coil. Put a large, unmagnetized iron nail through the center of the coil, and connect the coil in a circuit with a D-cell and switch. Close the switch and dip the nail into a pile of paper clips or thumbtacks. (See Figure 354.02.) Tell students that the instrument they have made is called an electromagnet. Let them see how many paper clips the electromagnet will pick up when the iron nail is removed (not as many). See if the electromagnet attracts the same materials other magnets attract (it does). Now set up a second electromagnet using uninsulated wire to see how many paper clips it will pick up. Students can infer that the lack of insulation is responsible for the lack of magnetism. Next, try various arrangements using more or fewer loops of wire around the nail and two or more cells in series. Record observations on Table 354.02. Interested students might research the uses of electromagnets in industry.

02
Bb
Ec
Gc

Figure 354.02

Table 354.02. Testing Electromagnets

Test	Number of Loops of Wire	Number of Cells in Series	Number of Paper Clips Picked Up
1	25	1	
2	50	1	
3	25	2	
etc.			

Contributing Idea B. Electric circuit breakers and door chimes can operate using electromagnets.

Building a simple circuit breaker. Use plastic tubing or make a stiff paper tube into which a large iron nail fits loosely. Wind 50 loops of insulated copper bell wire around the tube leaving two free ends to attach to a D-cell and switch. Tape the coil so that it will not unwind. When the circuit is completed, the nail will be pulled up into the tube. (Note: If the nail moves "down" instead of "up," reverse the connections of the wires on the cell.) Tell students that the device they have made is called a *circuit breaker.* Explain that some circuit breakers are used instead of fuses to break an over-loaded circuit; when too much current moves through a circuit, the electromagnetic coil becomes strong enough to raise a metal core and the circuit is broken (a spring catch keeps the core from returning). If a bulb is included in the circuit, the opening and closing of the circuit will be obvious (see Figure 354.03a). As an interesting supplementary activity, wind

**03
Bb
Gc**

about 100 loops of insulated copper wire around a wide test tube containing water, insert an iron nail into a small cork, and place the cork into the water in the test tube (Figure 354.03b). When the circuit is completed, the cork and nail will dive into the water.

(a)

(b)

Figure 354.03

Building a simple electric bell. Prepare a circuit breaker as in entry 354.03. Hold the coil so the head of the nail rests on a metal pan. Hold another metal pan just above the coil. (See Figure 354.04, p. 344.) When the circuit is completed, the nail is "pulled" up into the tube and its

**04
Gc**

point strikes the metal pan above. When the circuit is broken, the nail drops back and strikes the metal pan below. Explain that door chimes work in a similar way. If possible, obtain a door chime, and compare its features.

Negative Terminal

Metal Pans

Figure 354.04

Generalization II. Many household appliances use highly resistant wires to produce heat and to control electric currents.

Contributing Idea. Highly resistant metal wires are commonly used to produce heat in such appliances as electric irons, toasters, and heaters.

Observing the application of the idea that a greater electrical resistance results in a greater production of heat. If possible, obtain various worn-out appliances such as electric hot plates, toasters, heaters, or irons. Let students take them apart to examine the lengths and thicknesses of the heating wires and to test their conductivity with a circuit tester. Ask them to hypothesize why some wires are partly coiled or zigzagged in some appliances (to provide more wire, thus more heat in a small space).

05
Aa
Eb
Ec

360 Magnetism

361 Characteristics

Generalization I. **Magnetism has identifiable characteristics.**

> *Contributing Idea A.* Magnetism exists as a magnetic field surrounding all magnets.

Observing magnetic fields. Have students place a sheet of cardboard, glass, or plastic over a bar magnet. Punch holes in the lid of an old jar and fill it with iron filings or cut-up pieces of steel wool. From approximately 1 ft. (30 cm) above the cardboard, sprinkle the filings lightly and evenly. Tap the cardboard gently to help the filings line up in the magnetic field. Students will see that some force moves the filings into a definite pattern. Tell them that the force is called a magnetic field and the place where the field is concentrated is called the pole. If they repeat this experience using magnets of different sizes and shapes, they will find that all magnets have a magnetic field surrounding them.

01 Aa Bb

Feeling magnetic fields. Have students work in pairs to push the ends of two bar magnets together in various ways. They will be able to feel the force of attraction or repulsion between the two magnets depending upon which ends they bring together. Let them also test the middle and sides of the magnets. Tell them that what they feel are the *magnetic fields* that surround the magnets.

02 Ab Bb

> *Contributing Idea B.* Magnetism extends from one end to the other in the same magnet.

Making permanent pictures of magnetic fields. The patterns produced by magnetic fields can be preserved in several ways for display or for further study. If students compare the preserved examples, they will find that in each case the magnetic field extends from one end of the magnet to the other.

03 Aa

a. Cover a magnet with cardboard or glass and place a sheet of waxed paper on top. After sprinkling iron filings over the paper, fix the patterns by warming the waxed paper near a heating unit. After the wax cools, the filings will stick well enough so that normal movement of the paper will not disturb the pattern. **Caution: Follow safety guidelines when using iron filings.**

b. Cover a magnet with a sheet of white cardboard and use an atomizer to spray the iron filings with a fine water mist. If the filings are kept damp for a short time (24–48 hours), they will rust, and the stains will leave a pattern on the cardboard.

c. Spread newspapers, place a magnet on them, then cover the magnet with a sheet of cardboard. Using a clear lacquer in a commercial spray can, spray the iron filings. When dry, the patterns can be displayed. (Note: Some practice may be necessary to properly use the spray can; if it is held too close, the force of the spray may disturb the pattern.)

d. Place a magnet in position beneath blueprint paper, scatter iron filings over it, then produce a print by following the directions on the blueprint paper package. Generally, the procedure is to expose the paper to strong sunlight for several minutes as soon as the iron filings have arranged themselves along the lines of force, then carefully pour the filings into a container, rinse the blueprint paper in a pan of water for about five minutes, and pat dry. The patterns of white on the blue background can be easily studied. Similarly, students can make ozalid prints that produce dark lines of force on a white background.

Generalization II. Materials can be organized by the way they are influenced by magnetism.

Contributing Idea A. Magnetism attracts some materials.

Sorting objects by the way they are affected by magnetic fields. Collect a variety of small objects such as coins, wires, matchsticks, nails, papers, rubber bands, thumbtacks, tin cans, small pieces **04 Bb Db** of aluminum foil, silk cloth, and woolen cloth. Touch the objects with the end of a bar magnet to see which are attracted to it. Let students sort the objects into groups: those that are attracted and those that are not. Tell them that the objects that are attracted to a magnet are called magnetic, while those that are not attracted are called nonmagnetic. The results of the sorting can be recorded in a table.

Contributing Idea B. Some materials can be magnetized.

Classifying materials according to which can and cannot be magnetized. **05 Dc Ec** Have students slowly stroke a large steel needle 20 to 25 times across one end of a bar magnet using the same end for each stroke, stroking the needle in the same direction, and lifting it completely away from the magnet at the end of each stroke. When finished, hold the needle by the other end, and stroke it slowly over the opposite pole of the bar magnet. Now lower the needle over some iron filings. (It should attract them.) Let students try making magnets out of other materials such as iron and steel nails, hacksaw blades, and so on. Through testing, they will find that magnets cannot be made out of any materials except iron, nickel, or combinations using these materials (e.g., steel). Students can classify the materials they test by the material's ability to become magnetized.

362   Interactions

Generalization I. Magnetism is a form of energy produced by different sources.

Contributing Idea A. The Earth is a source of magnetism.

Detecting the Earth's magnetism using a "horizontal lines of force indicator." **01 Aa Gc** Magnetize a large steel needle (see entries 362.18–19) and push it horizontally through the side of a small cork. Float the cork in a bowl of water. Be sure the needle is horizontal to the water's surface. (Several drops of sudsless detergent will keep the cork from floating toward the side of the bowl.) The needle will align itself with the Earth's magnetic field so that one end points north. Let students move and turn the cork, then move the bowl to different areas around the school grounds. (Note: If large metal objects or metal within the structure of buildings influences the position of the needle, do this activity outdoors.) When students are satisfied that the needle always returns to the same position, mark the edge of the dish for north. Tell them that the magnetized needle is affected by the Earth's magnetic lines of force. Now add the other points of the compass to the bowl, and use the floating needle to indicate directions. As an additional activity, set a compass so the indicator is directly in line with the north and south marks. Place a bar magnet to the side of the compass and adjust its distance so the compass indicator moves 45° toward the magnet. Measure and record the distance from the compass to the nearest end of the magnet. After moving the bar magnet closer to or farther away from the compass, students will develop some concept of the strength of the Earth's magnetic field compared with the magnetic field of a small bar magnet.

Detecting the Earth's magnetism using a "vertical lines of force indicator." **02 Aa Gc** Tell students that a compass only indicates the horizontal direction of the Earth's lines of magnetic force. Explain that at the equator a compass indicator would be horizontal, but as it is carried closer to the magnetic poles, it would dip down more and more, and would be vertical over the pole. To measure the dipping, insert a large steel sewing needle through a large cork, then push two smaller needles into the cork from opposite sides. Balance the cork by the protruding smaller needles between two glasses and place a scale beside the large needle so that it rests at 0° on a protractor (Figure 362.02). Now

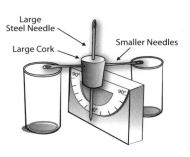

Figure 362.02

remove the large needle, magnetize it, then re-insert it in the cork. The angle at which the needle now dips can be measured by the protractor. Next, move the indicator to different parts of the school grounds to see if the angle remains the same. Students will realize that the angle of dip varies from place to place on the Earth. As an additional experience, they can use the indicator to locate magnetic materials buried in some sand. Discuss what practical use could be made of such an indicator.

"Seeing" the Earth's magnetic field. **03 Aa Be** Unroll large sheets of butcher paper on the school grounds. Set compasses at various places on the paper. When a compass needle stops moving, have a student put a dot on the paper at the north and south poles of the indicator. Remove the compass, draw a line between the two points, and then replace the compass so that the south pole of the indicator is at the top of the line. Put a dot at the north pole again, remove the compass, and connect the points with a line. Continue doing this for several ft. for each compass. Students will see that none of the lines ever cross; they follow the same direction and seem to be parallel. Tell them that they have been marking lines that represent the lines of force of the Earth's magnetic field, and that such lines of force exist everywhere on earth. Explain that if the lines were continued in each direction, they would

converge at the Earth's magnetic north and south poles.

Making a model to represent the Earth's magnetic poles. **04 Fc** Make a ball of clay, use a large ball of yarn, or obtain a rubber ball with a diameter the size of a bar magnet. Make an opening in the material and insert the magnet, then support the ball on a wooden meat skewer at an inclined angle that represents the axis of rotation of the Earth. Tell students that the ball represents the Earth, the skewer represents its axis of rotation, and the magnet represents its magnetic poles. Explain that the magnetic poles and the geographic poles are not located in the same place. Tell them that maps showing the magnetic poles must be periodically changed because the poles slowly change position. Students can use small compasses to study the lines of magnetic force surrounding the model.

> *Contributing Idea B.* Certain natural and artificial materials can be sources of magnetism.

Examining natural magnets. **05 Aa Bb** Obtain several lodestones. Let students use them to pick up iron and steel objects such as pins, needles, paper clips, and bobby pins. Now set a lodestone on a board floating in a bowl of water. Students will find that the stone will always turn to face one direction no matter how the board is placed. Tell them that many years ago, sailors noticed that when this natural magnetic rock was placed on a floating board, it tended to line up so that one end always pointed north. Because of this, they called that end of the rock the *North Pole*; and since the rock was used to lead the sailors to distant destinations, the rock was called "lead stone" or *lodestone*. (Note: Today geologists have decided that the end of any magnet that points north will be called north.)

Examining artificial magnets. Have students work individually with artificial magnets of various sizes and shapes to test an array of objects for reactions. When they have ascertained that iron and steel are the materials attracted to the magnets, let them use the magnets to determine what objects in the classroom contain iron and steel. Prepare a list of the objects. Students can also move a magnet back and forth through a quantity of sand to see what kinds of particles the magnet removes. (It will remove the iron particles.)

06 Bc Ec

Contributing Idea C. Electricity can be a source of magnetism.

"Seeing" the magnetic field produced by electricity. Have students draw a 4 in. (10 cm) diameter circle on an 8 in.(14 cm) square of white cardboard and make a small hole in its center. Support the square on two tall stacks of books. Remove an inch (2.5 cm) of insulation from the middle of a 1 ft. (30 cm) length of copper bell wire. Pull the wire vertically through the

07 Aa

cardboard so that the uninsulated section is at the hole. Now place four small compasses on the circle. Attach the length of wire to a switch and two dry cells that are connected in series. (See Figure 362.07.) When the circuit is closed, students will see that the four compass indicators outline the circle. Reverse the connections to the dry cells and repeat. (The compass indicators will reverse positions.) As a supplementary experience, sprinkle iron filings on the circle around the wire in place of the compasses. When the current is turned on and the cardboard is tapped gently, the filings will form a circular pattern. From these experiences students will realize that a magnetic field surrounds a wire when a current moves through it.

Figure 362.07

Using electricity to produce magnetism. Remove approximately 1 in. (2.5 cm) of insulation from a 1 ft. (30 cm) length of copper bell wire. Connect the length of wire to a dry cell and a switch.

08 Ga

Sprinkle iron filings on a sheet of paper (Figure 362.08), then, when the switch is closed, touch the bare part of the wire to the filings. Students will see that the wire attracts the filings. When the switch is turned off, the filings will fall back onto the paper. **Caution: Follow safety guidelines when using batteries and wires for an extended period of time. Bare wires get hot enough to burn the skin.**

Iron Filings

Figure 362.08

Generalization II. All magnetic sources are surrounded by a magnetic field.

> *Contributing Idea A.* Magnetic fields extend in unbroken lines from one pole of a magnetic source to the opposite pole of another magnetic source; magnetic fields from one pole of a magnetic source turn away from the same pole of another magnetic source.

Observing interactions between magnetic fields. Obtain a transparent, flat-sided bottle such as a hip flask. Fill it with clear glucose, and add a spoonful of iron filings. Cap the bottle, and then shake it to distribute the filings throughout the **09 Aa Ec**

liquid. Set the bottle on a table and bring one end of a bar magnet to one side. (The filings will arrange themselves into a three-dimensional representation of the magnetic field around the magnet.) Shake the bottle again, and repeat using like or unlike poles on opposite sides of the bottle, using magnets of various shapes, or by suspending an iron washer from the cap of the bottle to see the magnetic field induced by an approaching magnet. Students can also test other liquids in the bottle to see if they can improve the visual effect (e.g., clear molasses, white syrup).

Determining the polarity of magnets. Construct a wire support to hold a bar magnet. Tie a string to the support, and suspend a magnet from it so that the magnet is balanced. (See Figure 362.10.) When the magnet stops turning, compare the direction it points to the alignment of a compass indicator. Explain that the magnet, just like the compass indicator, lines up with the magnetic poles of the Earth. Tell students that the end that points north is labeled the *N* or *north pole* of the magnet while the end that points south is labeled the *S* or *south pole*. Now magnetize some iron nails or steel needles and determine the poles of each by suspending them from threads and observing how they line up with a compass. Red nail polish can be used to mark the north pole end of each magnetized object. **10 Aa Bb**

String
Magnet
Support
Wire
Stand
Wood
Block

Figure 362.10

Examining polarity. Have students **11** bring the north pole of a bar magnet to **Cd** the south pole of a suspended bar magnet. **Ec** Determine how far away from each other **Fa** the poles are when the suspended magnet begins to move. Compare the strengths of various magnets by bringing each toward the suspended one and measuring the distance at which it begins to move. Now place two other bar magnets beneath a sheet of white cardboard, glass, or plastic so that the north pole of one and the south pole of the other are approximately 1 in. (2.5 cm) apart. Sprinkle iron filings on the cardboard over the magnets, tap the cardboard, and observe the pattern that appears. Students will note that the lines of force indicate an attraction between the unlike poles. Next, bring the north pole of the first bar magnet toward the north pole of the suspended magnet. Students will find that the poles repel each other. Likewise, south poles will repel each other. Now place two like poles approximately 1 in. (2.5 cm) apart beneath the sheet of cardboard. Sprinkle iron filings over

them and tap the sheets. Students will find that there seems to be a wall between the like poles; the lines of force deflect away from the like poles, indicating that these poles repel each other. Have them devise a rule that explains what happens when various poles are brought together (unlike poles attract each other, like poles repel each other).

Determining the polarity of unmarked **12** **magnets.** Set one bar magnet on a support, **Bc** suspend it from a string, and bring another **Cc** bar magnet close to it to test different com- **Ec** binations of poles. From the results, students will be able to generalize that like poles repel and unlike poles attract. Now tape markings on several magnets so that students cannot identify the poles. Using a marked magnet, let students test to identify the poles of unmarked magnets. The tape can be removed to check answers. If unmagnetized iron or steel bars can be obtained, tape the ends and mix them with the bar magnets. Students will find that although the bars are attracted to another magnet, they are never repelled. They will realize that repulsion, rather than attraction, is the best test of whether or not a material is magnetic. Since large, stationary steel objects, such as cabinets or lockers, usually have magnetic poles, students can use their gained knowledge to locate and identify these poles. (They can bring a compass very close to all parts of the object and note which way the indicator points.)

Differentiating among magnetic, magnetized, and nonmagnetic objects. Tape each of various small objects between two squares of cardboard so that they cannot be seen. The cards should contain a variety of magnetic objects (e.g., iron washer, Canadian nickel), magnetized objects (e.g., small magnets), and nonmagnetic objects (e.g., pieces of plastic and wood). Students can test each card using a marked magnet and sort the cards into groups. (They may first sort them into two groups: magnetic and nonmagnetic. But if challenged to determine whether or not there is a magnet inside a card, they will find that there are two kinds of magnetic objects.)

13 Db

Contributing Idea B. Magnetic fields can be induced in some materials.

Inducing magnetic fields. Sprinkle some thumbtacks, paper clips, or bobby pins on a sheet of paper. Test the point of an iron nail to see if it will pick up any of the objects (Figure 362.14). If it doesn't, place one end of a bar magnet against the head of the nail, and test again. (The objects will be picked up by the nail.) Remove the magnet. (The objects will drop back on the paper.) Explain that the magnetic field surrounding a magnet can temporarily magnetize certain other objects. Tell students that when this happens, the object is said to be magnetized by *induction* and is called a temporary magnet. Now let them test other materials and keep a record to

14 Bb Bc Ec

see which can be temporarily magnetized by induction. They will find that magnetic fields can be induced only in materials made of iron or steel.

Figure 362.14

Contributing Idea C. The compass is an instrument used to detect magnetic fields, to determine the polarity of a magnetic source, and to indicate directions on Earth.

Making a compass. From the following experiences, students will find that a compass is simply a small magnet that is allowed to turn freely. It can be used to detect magnetic fields or to determine the polarity of a magnetic source; however, it is usually used to indicate directions on Earth. Simple compasses can be made in several ways. (Note: For proper functioning, be sure to use the compasses away from large metal objects and structures containing iron or steel.) The following compasses can be carried around and used outdoors even on windy days.

15 Gc

 a. Cut out two sides of a quart (liter) milk carton and suspend a small bar magnet from a string so that it is free to turn in the carton. Let the bar magnet align itself, and mark the four compass directions on the carton. (See Figure 362.15a.)

Figure 362.15a

b. Magnetize a large steel needle, fold in half a length of cardboard that is just a little shorter than the needle, push the needle through the cardboard, and suspend it from a thread within a wide-mouthed jar. A protractor can be used to prepare a circular directional disk that can be glued to the inside bottom of the jar. (See Figure 362.15b.)

Figure 362.15b

c. Place a magnetized needle in a cork and float the cork in a bowl of water. Add a few drops of sudsless detergent to keep the cork from being drawn to the sides of the bowl. You might tell students that Christopher Columbus used a floating compass when he arrived in North America.

d. Tie a thread to the center of a magnetized bobby pin, and suspend it in a glass jar to shield it from wind. Test to see if this compass will work as well when the jar is filled with water. You might tell students that airplane and ship compasses are liquid-filled to keep the indicator from swinging too much.

e. Push a wire through a hole in the lid of a widemouthed jar, make a hook at the lower end, and tape it securely to the lid at the upper end. Tie one end of a thread to the hook and the other end to the middle of a U-shaped magnet. Place the lid on the jar, and mark the points of the compass on the lid when the magnet lines up in a north and south position.

Discovering that not all compasses and magnets are correctly marked. When compass indicators line up in a north and south position, students can infer that the north pole of a compass is really

16
Ec
Fb

the "north-seeking" pole; however, if students use a marked magnet to test the polarity of several inexpensive compasses from different companies, they will be likely to find that some of the compasses are incorrectly marked. (There is no agreement among companies on which pole points north; and some companies try to avoid confusion by coloring one end instead of imprinting the words *north* and *south*. Thus, in some compasses, the colored end points north, and in others it points south.)

Using compasses. Have students work in groups of three. Provide each group with two large cardboard boxes with open tops and one compass. In an outdoor area, have two members from each group place the boxes over their heads. Give the compass to one of the two students, then have them both walk in a straight line for 300 steps, and then retrace their steps. The observing students will see that the student with the compass is able to come closest to the starting point by following the compass indicator in one direction, then in the opposite direction after turning around. You may wish to introduce map reading to the students and show them how to orient a map using a compass.

17
Ga

Generalization III. Magnetism can be transferred to some materials.

Contributing Idea A. Electricity or another magnet can be used to make a magnet.

Making a magnet using another magnet. Spread apart the prongs of a bobby pin so that they are in a straight line except for the small bend in the middle. Hold the bobby pin by the bend, and stroke its entire length about 50 times across one end of a strong bar magnet, always in the same direction. Test the bobby pin to see if it will pick up paper clips or thumbtacks. (If it doesn't, repeat the procedure.) Similarly, hold a steel needle by its eye end or an iron nail by its head, and stroke its entire length across one end of the magnet. Suspend the magnetized object from a thread or float it on a piece of aluminum foil in a bowl of water. Students can try turning the object to see if it always returns to a north and south position (the position can be checked with a compass). Mark the north-seeking pole of the object with some red nail polish. If several needles and nails are made into magnets and tested, students may find that the north-seeking pole is not always at the same end. (If the object is held by the point and stroked, or if the opposite pole of the magnet is used, the polarity of the object will be reversed.) Students can also make temporary magnets by inducing magnetism from a permanent magnet. To do this, touch an iron nail to one pole of a magnet and try to pick up a paper clip with it. Students will find that as long as the nail is in contact with the magnet, it also becomes a magnet.

18
Gc

Making a magnet using electricity. **19** Roll a strip of light cardboard to make a **Ga** **Gc** 4 in. (10 cm) long tube with a diameter of approximately ½ in. (2 cm). Hold the tube together with tape. Wind 100 turns of #22 or #26 insulated copper wire around the tube in a clockwise direction leaving approximately 1 ft. (30 cm) free at each end. Strip an inch (2.5 cm) of insulation from the ends, and mark the beginning end of the coil with adhesive tape (Figure 362.19a). Attach the coil to a switch and two dry cells (in series) with the beginning end on the negative terminal. Now insert

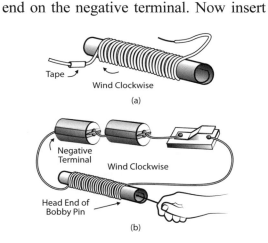

Tape
Wind Clockwise
(a)

Negative Terminal
Wind Clockwise

Head End of Bobby Pin
(b)

Figure 362.19

an entire bobby pin, steel needle, or iron nail into the tube from this end, head end first as shown in Figure 362.19b. Close the switch for five seconds. Open the switch and remove the bobby pin. Students can use a marked magnet to be sure the head end of the bobby pin is the north-seeking pole. Now magnetize a second bobby pin in the same way, mix the two magnetized

bobby pins with some unmagnetized ones, and challenge students to pick them out. Students can use the coil to magnetize other objects such as iron curtain rods, hacksaw blades, and screwdrivers.

Contributing Idea B. Permanent magnets retain their magnetism longer than temporary magnets.

Comparing a permanent magnet to **20** **a temporary magnet.** Using the same **Bb** **Ca** number of strokes, have students magnetize a large steel needle and an iron nail of about the same size. Keep a record of how many steel thumbtacks or paper clips each magnetized object will attract. After the magnets have been put aside for three days, test again, and compare how many tacks each now attracts. Explain that although any material attracted by a magnet can be made into a magnet, materials differ in how permanently they can be magnetized (e.g., iron loses its magnetism rapidly; steel retains its magnetism for a longer period of time). Now make magnets out of various other objects, and test each after several days to see which retain their magnetism the longest. Tell students that magnets made of materials that lose magnetism rapidly are called temporary magnets, while magnets that hold magnetism for a long time are called permanent magnets. (Note: Permanent magnets are not really permanent. They can lose their magnetism in a number of ways. See entry 362.21.)

Observing that a magnet can be demagnetized. Have students make several magnets out of steel needles, bobby pins, or iron nails. Test each to be sure it attracts paper clips or thumbtacks. Now place one of the magnets crosswise to a coil of wire and turn on the current for five seconds. Test the magnet for magnetism again. Hold a second magnet with a clothespin or pair of pliers, and heat one end in a flame. When cool, test it. Drop a third magnet several times on a hard surface or strike it several times with a hammer, then test it. Students will find that magnets can lose magnetism by influencing them with a strong magnetic field, by heating them, or by giving them a sharp blow.

Generalization IV. Magnetism travels through some materials better than others.

> *Contributing Idea A.* Magnetic fields travel through space.

Observing and comparing magnetic fields through space. Draw lines through a 36 in. (1 m) square of paper to divide it into quarters. Next, draw diagonal lines to divide it into eighths. Place a compass on one of the diagonal lines near the center of one of the quarters. Students can notice how the compass indicator moves when a magnet is pushed back and forth along the line on which the compass rests (Figure 362.22a). If a "vertical lines of force indicator" is constructed (see entry 362.02), students can move the magnet

21 Aa

22 Ca Cd

Figure 362.22a

vertically to see how it affects the indicator. Students will find that the magnetic field becomes weaker as the space between the compass and the magnet is increased. Now mark the place on the line under the compass where the magnet's field no longer disturbs the compass indicator. If the distance is recorded, other magnets can be tested in the same way and compared in terms of the distance the magnetic field extends through space. Next, set the magnet upright in the center of the paper and move the compass along each line toward it. Mark the place on each line under the compass to indicate where the magnet's field first disturbs the compass indicator, and then join the marks with a heavy line (Figure 362.22b). On identical 36 in. (1 m) squares of paper, students can plot and then compare the extent of the magnetic fields around the poles of other magnets. They can also try plotting the fields when the magnet is on its side or when magnets of other shapes are used. As a supplementary activity, suspend a U-shaped magnet by a string over a compass indicator. Spin the magnet, and observe what happens to the indicator. Students will realize that the magnetic field travels through space and induces the spinning motion in the compass indicator.

Figure 362.22b

Contributing Idea B. Magnetic fields pass through some materials, but are blocked by others.

Testing and comparing the penetration of magnetic fields through various materials. Suspend a magnet from a support. Fasten a string to a block of wood so that a paper clip tied on its end nearly reaches the magnet. Let students determine the greatest distance the magnet can be moved away and still hold the string and paper clip in the air. Now insert various materials between the paper clip and the magnet (e.g., aluminum foil, copper, glass, iron, paper, plastic, steel, wood). (See Figure 362.23.) Students will find that all materials are transparent to magnetism except **23 Ca Ec**

Figure 362.23

iron and steel. (Such materials block the magnetic field, and the paper clip falls.) By testing with the magnet, they will also find that any material that blocks the magnetic field *is* attracted by the magnet, while any material that is transparent to the magnetic field *is not* attracted.

Measuring and comparing the penetration of magnetic fields through various materials. Prepare a variety of barriers to place between an end of a bar magnet and some magnetic objects. Barriers can be made from items such as iron coat hangers, Canadian nickels, wooden rulers, and strips of corrugated cardboard. Each barrier should be made about the same size so that comparisons can be made. Let students place paper clips, thumbtacks, bobby pins, or iron filings on one side of the barrier, and slide the magnet toward the barrier from the other side. For each barrier, measure and record the distance between the paper clips and the magnet when the paper clips first move. From their tests, students will find that materials have no noticeable effect on the penetration of the magnetic field, except those that can be magnetized (e.g., iron, nickel, and their alloys). (Note: Canadian nickels are a good source of nickel as the coins are 100% nickel, while U.S. nickels are 75% copper and 25% nickel.) **24 Ca Cd**

Observing that magnetic fields can penetrate liquids. Submerge a magnet in an aluminum pan or heat-resistant dish **25 Aa**

of water. Put steel thumbtacks in a cork and float it on the water. Turn the cork in various ways to see if the magnetic field penetrates the water and influences the metal on the cork. Students can test other liquids in a similar way.

Contributing Idea C. The strength of a magnetic field can be measured.

Measuring the strength of a magnetic field. Set a bar magnet on a glass slide bridge, supported between two stacks of books. Open a paper clip to make a hook. Touch the paper clip to the underside of the glass slide so that it is held up by the magnetic field of the magnet above it. Now hang other paper clips, one at a time, on the first one until their weight pulls them away from the glass slide (see Figure 362.26). Record the number of paper clips held up by the magnet. Next, raise the magnet so that it rests on two glass slides, and repeat the tests. Continue adding slides, one at a time, each time recording the number of paper clips supported. Students can record results in Table 362.26 and graph the results on Graph 362.26.

**26
Bc
Bf
Cc**

Figure 362.26

Table 362.26. Measuring the Strength of Magnetic Fields

Number of Glass Slides	Number of Paper Clips
1	8
2	6
3	4

MEASURING THE STRENGTH OF MAGNETIC FIELDS

Graph 362.26

Testing the strength of magnetic fields through various materials. Measure the strength of magnetic fields through materials such as paper, cardboard, cloth, aluminum foil, or plastic wrap by stacking sheets of the material into sets of 1, 2, 3, 7, 10, 20, 30, 70, and 100. A magnet can be placed on one side of a set and a paper clip on the other side. The sets can be combined to increase the number of pieces between the magnet and the paper clip. Continue increasing the number of pieces until the paper clip no longer hangs from the material. The data can be tabled and graphed.

**27
Bf
Cc**

Measuring and comparing the strength of magnetic fields. Place a bar magnet on a sheet of lined paper so that one end of the magnet is on a line of paper. Push a paper clip slowly toward the end of the magnet, and count the number of spaces

**28
Cc
Cd
Da**

remaining at the point when the magnet moves the paper clip. If this is repeated using different magnets, students can order them by strength, from those that affect the paper clip from the greatest distance to those that affect it from the shortest distance.

363   Theory

Generalization. According to theory, magnetism comes from magnetic properties within atoms.

> *Contributing Idea A.* Atomic particles can be lined up to produce magnetic fields.

Observing that small parts of magnets possess magnetic characteristics. Make a magnet out of a steel needle or bobby pin. Use wire cutters to cut the magnet into two equal-length pieces. Test each of the four ends of the two pieces with a compass or suspend them from threads to see if the poles will attract and repel each other. Students will find that when a magnet is cut, the ends of each part still possess a north pole and a south pole. They can cut each part in half again and test. Tell them that magnetic characteristics remain in each part down to the smallest piece that can be cut. **01 Aa Ec**

Using drawings to explain the magnetic domains of atoms. Use Figures 363.02a–c to explain that most scientists believe that within objects there are small clusters of atoms, each containing north and south **02 Bb Fc**

poles. The clusters, called domains, are normally randomly arranged (Figure 363.02a). When the object to be magnetized is stroked in one direction with a magnet or otherwise magnetized, the domains tend to line up in a single direction, and each acts like a tiny magnet (Figure 363.02b). Tell students that when an object is heated or jarred, the domains are knocked out of line again, and the object loses its magnetism. You might also tell them that when magnets are stored with like poles together, the domains are pushed out of alignment, causing the magnets to lose some of their strength (Figure 363.02c). For preservation, it is best to store magnets in pairs with opposite poles together.

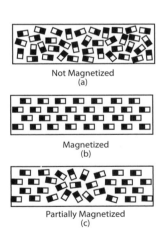

Not Magnetized
(a)

Magnetized
(b)

Partially Magnetized
(c)

Figure 363.02

Observing a model of magnetic domains. Have a student fill a test tube about two-thirds full of iron filings and put a stopper in the end. Be careful not to shake the tube. Tell the students that the **03 Aa Bb Fc**

tube could represent an iron nail and that each iron filing could represent a cluster of atoms. Tell them that each cluster is called a domain and each has a north and south pole. Stroke the test tube in one direction with one pole of a strong bar magnet, then bring a compass near it. Observe that the test tube now has magnetic characteristics. Tell students that the domains within magnetic objects are thought to line up somewhat like the filings in the test tube. Next, shake the test tube, and bring the compass near it. Students will find that it has lost its magnetic characteristics. Tell them that jumbled domains cancel each other out, and there is no net magnetism that can be detected.

Contributing Idea B. Atomic particles in the Earth can produce electricity and magnetism.

Using drawings to explain a theory of the Earth's magnetic interior. Tell students that no one knows why the Earth acts like a huge magnet; however, one theory suggests that the Earth is composed of several liquid or plastic parts. Use Figure 363.04 to explain that the several parts of the Earth's interior may rotate at different speeds and thus slip by each other. The resulting friction between the parts rubs electrons from atoms, causing an electric current; this current, in turn, produces a magnetic field. Point out that the huge iron and nickel core, thought to be at the Earth's center, probably acts like a

04
Aa
Fc

huge electromagnet. The result is that the Earth's magnetic field exists everywhere and its presence can be indicated by magnets and compasses whether on land, in the air, or under water. You might also tell them that the slippage between different parts of the interior may also cause the Earth's magnetic pole to change position.

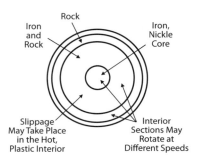

Figure 363.04

364 Applications

Generalization I. A magnetic field can induce an electric current in a wire.

Contributing Idea A. An electric current is produced in a coil of wire moved through a magnetic field.

Producing electricity using a magnet. Make a 50-loop coil of insulated copper bell wire. Attach the end wires of the coil to a current detector. Now move one pole of a strong magnet in and out of the coil. Students will observe a movement in the current detector. Now put the other pole of the magnet in and out of the coil. (The current detector will indicate a movement

01
Aa

of the current in the opposite direction.) Next, try holding the magnet stationary and moving the coil over one of its poles. Students will find that whenever a coil of wire passes by a magnetic field, a current is set up in the coil.

Contributing Idea B. The interaction of the magnetic fields around magnets and electric wires produces the mechanical motion of electric motors.

Making a model to represent the motion within an electric motor. Stand a cover-less shoe box on end and set a U-shaped magnet inside with its prongs upward. Hold it in place with modeling clay. Use fine insulated copper wire to make a coil small enough to fit between the poles of the magnet without touching them. Leave a foot of wire free at each end. Tie the coil with string so that it will not unwind. Cut a hole the size of a dime at the top of the box, and pull the end wires through it until the coil hangs between the poles of the magnet. Connect the free ends to a dry cell and switch. (See Figure 364.02.) Close the switch and observe the coil. (It will turn until its north pole is opposite the south pole of the U-shaped magnet.) Let students speculate what would happen if the current in the coil were reversed. (The polarity would reverse, and the coil would turn again until the opposite poles in the coil and magnet lined up.) Explain that what happens is similar to what takes place in an electric motor.

02
Fc

Coil

Figure 364.02

Generalization II. Magnetism can be used for play or for practical purposes.

Contributing Idea A. Magnetic fields are put to use in some toys and tools.

Finding examples of how magnetic fields are used in toys and tools. Encourage students to bring to class any magnetized toys they might have (e.g., magnetized dogs, horseshoe magnets, doughnut magnets on posts). Have them show how each works. Next, have them find examples of magnetized tools that can be used at home, and discuss the value of having them magnetized (e.g., screwdrivers, tack hammers, scissors).

03
Ga

Playing with magnetic fields. The idea that like poles repel and unlike poles attract can be used to make several interesting devices for play.

04
Gc

a. Attach four upright sticks to a block of wood that is the same size as a bar magnet. Set the magnet on the wood, and place an identical second magnet over, but not touching the first, so that the like poles are above each other as shown in Figure 364.04. Students will have fun playing with the top magnet that seems to float above the bottom one.

Figure 364.04

b. Magnetize six steel needles so that their points have the same polarity. Insert each vertically through a small cork or thin slice of a larger cork. Float the corks with the needles pointed in the same direction in a bowl with sloping sides. Students will see that the needles repel each other. Now turn one or two needles over, and observe again. Try bringing different ends of a bar magnet near the floating needles to see what happens. Next, insert the needles horizontally through the sides of the corks. Students will find that they can play with the magnetized needles to arrange the corks into various geometric patterns.

c. Build a simple cardboard stage and fasten paper clips to the bases of various cardboard figures. From under the stage floor, move magnets to make the figures perform. Similarly, put an iron nail in the hull of a small boat, float it in an aluminum or glass dish, and control it by moving a magnet beneath the dish.

Contributing Idea B. Magnetic fields are used in many electrical appliances.

Finding examples of how magnetic fields are used in household appliances. Have students make an electromagnet and see how the magnetic field it produces can be put to use. List examples of where electromagnets are used in their homes. If possible, let them take apart an old buzzer, bell, telephone receiver, or motor to see how it works.

05
Bc
Ga

400–499
Inference Models

410 Atoms and Molecules

411 Characteristics

Generalization I. Atoms are extremely small.

> *Contributing Idea A.* All evidence of the characteristics of atoms is indirect.

Inferring that particles exist even though they cannot be seen. Heat a container of water on a hot plate. Have students observe the surface of the water from the side as it begins to boil. They will see small droplets of water in the air above the container but none in the space below the droplets. Let them discuss why. (The heated water particles are too small to be seen, but when they are cooled and collect together, they become visible as droplets.)

**01
Aa
Fa**

Using the sense of smell to determine that particles exist even though they are too small to be seen. Fill a tall jar with a fragrant liquid, and then pour half into an empty jar. Pour half of what is left into another jar and continue doing this until it cannot be divided any more. Discuss how the liquid might be divided into even smaller particles. One way to do this is to pour a small bit into a perfume atomizer and pump a fine spray into the air. Discuss how the sense of smell can "see" the particles better than the eyes.

**02
Ad
Fa**

Using the sense of taste to determine that particles exist even though they are too small to be seen. Set a lump of sugar on a sheet of black paper and cut it in half with a knife. Set half the lump aside and cut the remaining portion in half again. Cut each new half in half until it is not possible to continue. Discuss how the sugar might be divided into even smaller particles. One way to do this is to take the half lump that was set aside and drop it into a glass of warm water. Students will see the lump gradually diminish until the sugar can no longer be seen. Explain that the lump breaks up into very tiny particles that cannot be seen even through a microscope. (A drop can be placed on a glass slide and observed through a microscope.) The students can tell that the sugar is still in the water and that it did not disappear by tasting the water. This activity can be repeated using a spoonful of salt. Discuss how the sense of taste can "see" the particles better than the eyes.

**03
Ab
Fa**

Determining that some particles are extremely small. Put 1 oz. (30 ml) of ink or liquid dye in a transparent quart (liter) container of water. Shake the container until the color is evenly distributed. Ask students how they know the particles of ink are still in the container (by the color). Now mark the middle of the container with a piece of tape, pour away half of the solution and refill the container by adding clear water. Shake the jar and observe the color. Ask if there are as many particles as before (the lighter color indicates fewer particles). Next, pour out half the solution and refill the container with clear

**04
Cc
Cg**

water. Students will realize that each time this is done, the amount of ink is cut in half. Challenge them to see how many times they can repeat this procedure and still see some of the color in the solution. (Note: For easier viewing when the solution becomes lighter, place the container on a piece of white paper and observe it through the top.) This activity can be repeated using other colorful liquids such as egg dye, vegetable coloring, and iodine. (Note: Atoms are so small that one ordinary drop of water contains more than 100 billion billion atoms. They are so small that it would take all the people in the world all their lifetimes, without taking time to eat or sleep, to count the number in a pinhead.)

Defining what an atom is. Discuss with students what would happen if you could take a very small piece of a substance and tear it in half and keep on tearing it in half, could it be torn in half forever or is there one last tiny piece that you would come to? Explain that if you could keep tearing a piece of copper in half until you came to the last tiny piece, you would find (if you could see it) that the last piece would still have the physical characteristics of copper. If you could tear a piece of iron in the same way, the last piece would still resemble iron. Tell the students that the scientists call the last piece of a substance an *atom*. The smallest piece of copper is a copper atom. The smallest piece of iron is an iron atom.

**05
Bb
Fa**

Contributing Idea B. Atoms join together to form molecules.

Defining what a molecule is. Have students construct models of elements and compounds and compare them for similarities and differences. From the comparisons, students will find that some models are made up of atoms that are all the same kind (elements), while others are made up of different kinds of atoms (compounds). You might then tell them that when two or more atoms join together, they form a *molecule*. The following are sample models of the two types of molecules.

**06
Bb
Fc**

a. *Elements.* Burn a piece of paper in a dish and have students look at what is left. When it has cooled, let them feel the ashes and rub some on a white piece of paper. Now let a wooden match burn in the dish and compare the remains with the burnt paper. Tell students that the black material left after burning the paper and the match is an element called carbon. Students can burn other materials such as cloth or bread to see if they also contain carbon. Next show students four medium-size Styrofoam balls. Tell them that each represents a carbon atom. Use 2 in. (5 cm) lengths of heavy wire to join the balls together as shown in Figure 411.06a on page 366. Explain that when four carbon atoms join together in this way, they form one molecule of carbon. (It takes billions of these molecules to form a small piece of black carbon.) Emphasize that the molecular structure is composed only of one kind of atom and that there are basically 92 elements that can be formed from the 92 kinds of atoms.

Figure 411.06a, b, c

b. *Compounds.* Have students look at a small grain of salt under a hand lens or microscope and describe its shape. Explain that salt is made up of two different kinds of atoms: One sodium atom and one chlorine atom joined side by side make one molecule of salt (Figure 411.06b). Construct several models of this molecule using Styrofoam balls (a small one for sodium, and a large one for chlorine). Put them together with wire so that a sodium and chlorine atom are always side by side, up and down, in front and in back of each other (the molecules will always form a cube as shown in Figure

411.06c). Have students compare the shape of the model with the small grains of salt they observed. Emphasize that the molecular structure is composed of more than one kind of atom and that the possible combinations of different atoms are almost limitless.

Defining what an element is. Obtain some objects made of various natural elements (e.g., iron nails, copper wire, aluminum foil, lead pipe). Have students describe these materials and compare as many of their physical characteristics as they can. Explain that each material has its own physical characteristics, and thus is described in a special way. Tell the students that when each material is made up of only one kind of atom—copper is made up of copper atoms, aluminum is made up of aluminum atoms—the material is called an element.

07 Aa Bb

Learning the chemical symbols for the elements. Tell students that scientists use shorthand to write about atoms and elements. For carbon they use the letter C, for oxygen they use O. Ask what might be used for iodine (I), uranium (U), and hydrogen (H). Point out that the names for some atoms begin with the same letter (hydrogen and helium). Since H is used for hydrogen, ask what symbol might be used for helium (He). If C is used for carbon, what could be used for calcium (Ca)? If S is for sulfur,

08 Bb Bd

what can be used for silicon (Si)? Some students might be interested in researching the eleven "unusual" symbols in the listing of atoms. In early times, Romans and Greeks made use of some substances such as gold, silver, and iron. Since they did not speak English, they used words in their own language to name the substances: gold was aurum (Au); silver was argentum (Ar); iron was ferrum (Fe).

Examining the characteristics and uses of elements. Obtain samples of as many elements as possible (tin, copper, sulfur, gold, silver, zinc, lead). Let students examine and record the characteristics of each. Guide them to look for such aspects as color, hardness, and texture. Students can then compare their independently obtained listings. Some might be interested in playing a game whereby one student describes the characteristics and has another identify the element. Next, challenge them to find examples and list uses of as many of the 92 elements as they can.

09
Af
Ga

Using a flame test to identify some metallic elements. Straighten a paper clip and make a small loop at one end to hold materials. Use a pair of pliers to hold the clip at the unlooped end in a flame until it does not cause a change in the flame's color. (If there is a color, it will mean that the clip is not clean. To clean the clip, hold it in the flame until the color is gone.) Now dip the loop into table salt so that some sticks to it. When the loop is placed in the flame, students will observe a change in the flame's color. Explain that scientists have learned that certain metallic elements burn with characteristic colors. Sodium is a metallic element that burns with a characteristic yellow color. You might tell the students that two elements make up table salt—sodium and chlorine (NaCl)—but only sodium is metallic and provides the color. Next, students can test other materials that contain metallic elements and develop a table, like Table 411.10, indicating the characteristic flame color of each. The materials

10
Aa
Fb

Table **411.10.** Using a Flame Test to Determine the Color Characteristic of Some Elements

Material to Be Tested	Element That Makes the Color	Color of the Flame
Barium nitrate	Barium (Ba)	Yellow green
Boric acid	Boron (B)	Green
Calcium chloride	Calcium (Ca)	Orange
Copper sulfate	Copper (Cu)	Bright green
Lithium nitrate	Lithium (Li)	Dark red
Potassium dichromate	Potassium (K)	Violet
Sodium chloride	Sodium (Na)	Yellow
Strontium nitrate	Strontium (Sr)	Crimson

containing the elements can be obtained from most drug stores.

Defining what a compound is. Put some sugar in the bottom of a test tube, hold the tube at an angle with pinchers, and heat the sugar slowly over a flame. Students will see a black substance form in the bottom of the tube and should recognize it as carbon. They will also see moisture on the side of the tube and realize that sugar must also contain the elements found in water. Tell them that when two or more different atoms are joined (in this example, carbon, hydrogen, and oxygen), they form a *compound*.

11
Aa
Bb

Generalization II. Atoms can be organized on the basis of their characteristics.

Contributing Idea A. Atoms can be seriated.

Seriating atoms. Prepare a set of about 25 cards, each providing the name, symbol, weight, and number of electrons and protons of a common atom. Ask students to order the cards by one or more of the characteristics. They will most likely seriate the cards from the lightest atom to the heaviest or from the one containing the least electrons and protons to the one containing the most. Some students might be interested in researching the work of Jöns Berzelius (1779–1848), a Swedish chemist who worked out a system of atomic weights.

12
Bd
Da

Contributing Idea B. Atoms can be classified.

Developing classification schemes analogous to the periodic table. Put the numerals from 1 to 50 in one long line on a chalkboard. Have students discuss whether or not there is a special sequence to the numerals (from the symbol representing the least to the symbol representing the most). Make an analogy to a listing of the 92 natural elements (they could be seriated from the lightest to the heaviest or from the element made up of the fewest protons and electrons to the element made up of the most). Now rearrange the numerals into columns. Students will realize that the arrangement not only indicates the sequence previously discussed, but adds a set of patterns that reveal some commonalities among numerals in vertical sequences. Students can make analogies between the numerals and the symbols on a periodic table. (Commonalities among elements are revealed in vertical rows: the elements in the first row react with water [lithium reacts slowly; sodium, quickly; potassium, very quickly; rubidium, violently]; the elements in the last row are very stable, rare gases, difficult to combine with other elements.) Next, show an arrangement of the alphabet and ask students to indicate any patterns they can find (e.g., the vowels are lined up in the first row; letters that produce the same sound in certain words are found in the third row, no

13
Bd
Dc
Gb

letters are left over). Challenge students to create other arrangements of the alphabet to reveal different patterns. Some students might be interested in researching the work of Demitri Mendeleev (1834–1907), a Russian chemist who discovered that every seventh element was similar. Since similar patterns repeated periodically, his arrangement became known as the *periodic table of the elements*.

412 Interactions

Generalization. Heat causes atomic particles to move faster; cooling slows their motion.

> *Contributing Idea A.* Atomic particles are always in motion.

Observing that particles move. Fill a container with water and place a drop of ink or dye on the surface. Students will see that the particles gradually spread throughout the whole glass without stirring. Let them develop an explanation for what happens. Scientists believe the spreading is caused by particles bouncing against each other in a random fashion (much like marbles bouncing together if shaken in a box). You might tell them that the movement is called the Brownian movement. Some students might be interested in researching the work of Robert Brown (1773–1858), a Scottish botanist whose observations provided evidence that small particles are always in motion. Now close the doors and **01 Af Bb Bd**

windows to the room and have everyone sit as still as possible so that there is very little wind motion in the room. Place several drops of perfume on a handkerchief and let students raise their hands when they are sure they can smell the perfume. Ask them to compare this experience with the previous one. (In both cases, the particles of the material gradually diffused through the water or air seemingly of their own accord.)

> *Contributing Idea B.* Heat affects the movement of atomic particles.

Using heat to break materials into particles that are too small to be seen. Weigh two dishes and record the weight of each. Place six mothballs into one. Weigh the dish with mothballs in it and determine the weight of the mothballs by subtracting the weight of the dish from the total weight. Into the second dish, place some camphor and determine its weight. Set the dishes near a sunny window ledge and weigh them each day at about the same time. Let students discuss what any change in weight might indicate. (Heat can break solid objects into tiny particles that cannot be seen, yet they can be detected by the sense of smell.) **02 Ad Cf Fa**

Using heat to break liquids into particles that are too small to be seen. Place some water in a beaker and mark the level with a grease pencil. Bring the water to a boil for several minutes on a hot plate. Remove the container from the heat so **03 Bb Fa**

that the boiling will stop, then check the water level (it will be lower). Discuss where the water might have gone and why it was not seen. Now put the beaker back on the hot plate and bring the water to a boil again. Hold a mirror in the highest part of the cloud of water vapor for two or three seconds, then remove it (the mirror will have small beads of liquid on it). Explain that if one could imagine the water to be made up of atomic particles (atoms or molecules), the particles might be pictured as bouncing against each other. When the water is heated, the molecules bounce even harder and as they hit each other, some strike with a force that causes others to bounce right out of the glass into the air. If many are bounced out of the container, scientists say that the liquid is *evaporating*. Conversely, when heat is removed, the liquid is said to be *condensing*. (The particles do not strike each other with as much force, thus are closer together.)

Testing the effect of heat upon different materials. Prepare three identical glass containers with water. Set one in a pan on a heating unit, leave one in a pan at room temperature, and place one in a pan of ice cubes. Hang a tea bag or drop ink or dye onto the water in each. Students will observe differences in the diffusion of the material. Similarly, perfume can be placed on a handkerchief and students can time how long it takes

04
Bb
Ec
Fc

before they can smell it. Next, a different perfume on a different handkerchief can be held over a radiator or a lightbulb, and the traveling of the odor can again be timed. Students will realize that the small particles of the materials move at an increased speed with increased heat. Explain that if one can imagine the materials being made up of atomic particles (atoms or molecules), one could picture them bouncing against each other. When they hit very hard and are knocked far apart, scientists say that the material is a *gas*. When heat is removed, the particles do not hit each other with as much force, thus are closer together, and the scientists say the material is a *liquid*. If more heat is removed, they move more slowly and bounce together with less force. A material in which particles are close together is a *solid*. Scientists have never been able to completely stop atomic particles from moving (even in ice, they are moving and bumping into each other). You might also explain that the movement in these ways causes *expansion* and *contraction*: a heated material expands or gets larger, a cooled material contracts or gets smaller.

413   Theory

Generalization. According to atomic theory, all matter is composed of a limited number of fundamental particles (atoms) that are not altered during ordinary physical and chemical changes.

Contributing Idea A. Models help us to understand the atom.

Developing a model of something that cannot be seen. Provide students with numbered, sealed boxes containing a marble and a wooden block glued in place. The shape of the block should be simple for beginners (Figure 413.01a) and more complex for experienced stu-

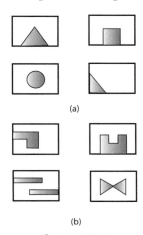

(a)

(b)

Figure 413.01

dents (Figure 413.01b). Tell the students they can roll the marble but cannot look inside. Have them draw a picture depicting what they think the shape of the block is. Students can compare pictures and try to refine their drawings. Let them discuss how it is possible to describe an object without seeing it. Explain that scientists, in a similar way, make inferences about things they cannot see, such as atoms, the interior of the Earth, and phenomena in outer space (quasars). Now provide students with identical empty boxes, some blocks, and marbles. Ask them to try to

01
Af
Be
Fc

construct a box that is like the sealed one. You might explain that scientists often construct models to see if the models behave in the same way as indirectly observed phenomena.

Constructing atomic models. Various atomic structures can be modeled.

02
Bb
Fc

a. *Hydrogen Atom.* You might tell students that even though the smallest atom is hydrogen, scientists have found that it is made up of two smaller particles. The particle in the center is called a proton, much larger than the other particle, called an electron (about 1,837 electrons equal the size of 1 proton). To show the spatial and size relationships within an atom, set a table-tennis ball or other sphere approximately 1 in. (2.5 cm) in diameter on the ground outdoors. Now place a common pin in the ground 400 ft. (122 m) from the sphere (about 133 footsteps). Tell the students that the sphere represents the proton in the center of the atom, and the pinhead represents the electron that moves about it. They will easily realize that the atom is mostly made up of space. Tell them that the electron moves rapidly throughout all the space in a large, imaginary sphere (a radius equal to the distance from the sphere to the pinhead) surrounding the proton. Emphasize that the movement is three-dimensional and not two-dimensional. (See Figure 413.02a.)

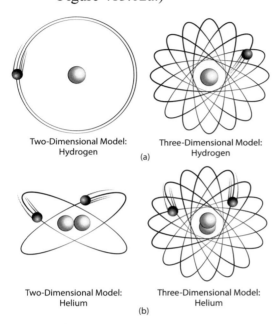

Two-Dimensional Model: Hydrogen

(a)

Three-Dimensional Model: Hydrogen

Two-Dimensional Model: Helium

(b)

Three-Dimensional Model: Helium

Figure 413.02

b. *Other Atoms.* The next smallest atom is helium, made up of two protons in the center and two electrons orbiting around them (Figure 413.02b). The third smallest is lithium, composed of three protons and three electrons. Students will quickly realize that the next atomic model must have four protons and four electrons (beryllium). Explain that there are 92 naturally found atoms on Earth, the largest having 92 protons with

92 electrons orbiting around them (uranium). Tell students that each is given an atomic number indicating how many protons and electrons it has (e.g., oxygen has eight protons and eight electrons and has the atomic number eight).

Making an analogy to show that rapidly moving electrons occupy a great deal of space. Let students observe a wheel with spokes on an overturned bicycle and note that it is made up mostly of space. Tell them that the spokes could represent electrons that spin rapidly around the center or *nucleus* of an atom. Set a table tennis ball behind the wheel to represent the nucleus. Now spin the wheel and have the students try to throw beans or wads of paper through the spokes. Even though the spokes occupy only a small fraction of the space within the wheel, they stop the beans from passing through due to their rapid movement. In a similar way, electrons in an atom move and occupy the space surrounding the nucleus.

03 Bb Fc

Using an atomic model to understand electrical charges. Tell students that when the numbers of protons and electrons in an atom are the same, scientists say that the atom is balanced. It is possible, however, to unbalance atoms by brushing away some electrons. Unbalanced atoms occur when materials rub together, as when people slide across the plastic seat of an automobile or walk across a wool

04 Fa Fc

rug. Because of the rubbing, electrons are brushed away from some atoms. When atoms are unbalanced, there is a tendency for electrons to move until balance is regained. The shock that is felt when one touches a door handle is caused by such movement of electrons. On a chalkboard, draw a picture of a carbon atom that is balanced (six protons and six electrons). Tell the students that electrons and protons in all atoms are electrically charged (electrons, negatively charged; protons, positively charged). When there are as many electrons as protons, the atom is said to be neutral (no charge). Now brush away one electron in the drawing, and explain that there are now more positive charges than negative charges, thus the unbalanced atom is said to have a positive charge. Replace the erased electron in the drawing and add another electron. Explain that if an electron is picked up by an atom, it becomes unbalanced and is said to have a negative charge.

Theorizing that atoms can be given two kinds of electrical charges. Tie an 8 in. (20 cm) length of string around a plastic spoon and label it spoon 1. Suspend it from a ruler or stick secured on a table so that it hangs on its side. Label a second plastic spoon 2, and bring it close to the bowl of the first until it almost touches. Now rub both sides of the bowl of spoon 1 several times with a piece of sandwich wrap, then rebalance the spoon.

05
Ec
Fc

Rub spoon 2 in the same way and bring the bowls of both spoons close together (they should move apart). Explain that the particles that make up atoms have electrical charges. Scientists say that each proton has a positive charge and each electron has a negative charge. When plastic spoons are rubbed with sandwich wrap, electrons from the atoms in the spoons are transferred to the wrap, leaving the spoons with more protons (positive charges) and giving the wrap more electrons (negative charges). From this, students will realize that when two positively charged spoons are brought together, they repel each other. Now number two balloons (i.e., balloon 1 and balloon 2) and hang spoon 1 from a ruler with a string. Rub it with a piece of wool. (Try not to make too much wind near the balloon because it will blow around and make it difficult to observe what happens.) Rub balloon 2 in the same way and bring the balloons together (they will repel each other). Explain that when balloons are rubbed with wool, electrons are brushed from the atoms in the wool and are transferred to the balloons, leaving the wool with a positive charge and giving the balloons a negative charge. Next, rub spoon 1 with sandwich wrap and make sure it is balanced; then, rub balloon 2 with the wool and slowly bring it close to the spoon (the objects will attract each other). From these tests, students will realize that when the electrical charges are alike, they repel each other; when they are different, they attract each other. You might tell them that in the atom, the electron is attracted to the proton because their charges are not alike.

Contributing Idea B. Radioactive elements disintegrate naturally, giving off atomic particles and radiation.

Constructing and using a cloud chamber. Wrap a large piece of dry ice in a towel and cut a circle in the towel to fit a quart (liter) jar lid. (The dry ice is used to cause an extreme temperature difference between the top and bottom of the container.) Cut a circle of black velvet to cover the inside of the jar lid and glue it in place. (The black velvet provides a good background for observing vapor trails.) Cut a circle from blotter paper to cover the inside bottom of the jar. Hold it in place with glue or a bent piece of coat hanger wire. Now rinse the outside of the jar with hot water to warm it. Saturate the blotter with rubbing alcohol, swish it around the side, and pour off any excess. (Rubbing alcohol will form vapor better than most other liquids.) Screw the jar into the lid. Shine a bright light (at least 200 watts) from a projector or other source, directly into the jar. (See Figure 413.06.) Students will see vapor trails forming when they look into the container at the velvet. You might tell them that the device is called a *cloud chamber*, and that radiation particles enter the jar and travel through the alcohol

06
Bb
Ga
Gc

vapor. When particles collide with the vapor molecules, droplets form, and cloud trails can be seen. Scientists can recognize certain particles by the kinds of trails they produce. For example, nuclei (alpha particles) are heavy and leave straight, dense trails; electrons (beta particles) are light and leave irregular trails because they are easily deflected by other particles. Some students might try photographing the trails using ASA 200-rated film and test different lens openings and shutter speeds. They might also research the work of Charles Wilson (1869–1959), the Scottish physicist who invented the cloud chamber and photographed vapor trails.

Figure 413.06

Contributing Idea C. Models help us to understand molecules.

Constructing molecular models. Obtain three sizes of Styrofoam balls, 12 of each size. Tell the students that each of the smallest balls represents a hydrogen atom, each middle-size ball represents a carbon atom, and each large ball represents an oxygen

07
Fc
Gc

atom. Various molecular models can be constructed using these representations.

a. *Water Molecule.* Cut 2 in. (5 cm) lengths of heavy wire and insert them into the centers of two small balls. Attach them to one of the largest balls (Figure 413.07a). Explain that a single molecule of water is made from two atoms of hydrogen (the smallest atom) and one of oxygen. Scientists describe this molecule as H_2O. Let students discuss the properties of a drop of water made up of billions of these molecules.

Styrofoam Models

Figure 413.07a

b. *Hydrogen-Peroxide Molecule.* Tell students that hydrogen peroxide is a liquid used as a bleaching agent and disinfectant. A model of this molecule is made by fastening two small balls with two large ones (Figure 413.07b). Scientists describe this molecule as H_2O_2 because it is made up of two hydrogen atoms and two oxygen atoms. Compare the properties of this substance with others depicted in this activity.

Figure 413.07b

c. *Carbon-Dioxide Molecule.* Tell students that carbon dioxide is a heavy, colorless gas used in soft drinks. A model of this molecule can be made by attaching one middle-size ball to two large ones (Figure 413.07c). Scientists describe this molecule as CO_2. It is made up of one carbon atom and two oxygen atoms.

Figure 413.07c

d. *Ethyl-Alcohol Molecule.* Ethyl alcohol (C_2H_5OH) is a more complicated molecule (Figure 413.07d). It is a liquid found in some medicines, wines, and other liquors.

Figure 413.07d

e. *Simple-Sugar Molecule.* Sugar is a common household substance that students are familiar with. Its molecular structure can be in several forms. Dextrose ($C_6H_{12}O_6$) is one form that can be constructed (Figure 413.07e).

Figure 413.07e

From these models students will realize that not only are there many possible substances that can be made using these three kinds of atoms, but that the possible combinations using other atoms is beyond counting.

Theorizing that there are spaces between molecules. Various activities provide evidence that molecules are extremely small, but that there is a great amount of space between them.

08
Fc

   a. Students can fill one 100 ml graduated cylinder with water and another with alcohol. Ask where the level of the mixture will be when the two are poured into a 200 ml cylinder. When the two are poured together, the volume will be visibly less than 200 ml. Challenge the students to develop

an explanation for what happened. An analogy might be made by mixing one large jar of walnuts with an identical jar filled with dried peas. When poured together, the mixture will be considerably less than expected because the peas will fit in the spaces between the walnuts. Students can realize that the walnuts might represent molecules of alcohol (the larger molecules), and the peas the water molecules (the smaller molecules).

   b. Students can fill one 100 ml graduated cylinder with water and another with cotton. Ask them to predict what might happen when the water is added to the cotton. After students speculate, slowly add the water a little at a time to the cotton. The cotton should not cause the water to overflow. Students can discuss possible explanations for what happened.

   c. Students can fill a glass to the brim with water. When not a single drop can be added without causing an overflow, slowly add sugar a little bit at a time. (The water will still not overflow.)

420 Astronomy

421　Characteristics

Generalization I. The universe is extremely large.

> *Contributing Idea A.* The telescope is an instrument used to view objects in the universe.

Constructing a telescope. Obtain two lenses, one with a long focal length (approximately 8 in. or 20 cm) and one with a short focal length (approximately 1 in. or 2.5 cm). Students can hold the small (thicker) lens (the eyepiece) close to their eyes and the larger one (the objective lens) at arm's length. By bringing the larger lens closer, an image of some object across the room will come into focus through the lenses. When focused, have another student measure the distance between the two lenses. Cut a length of cardboard tubing, such as a mailing tube, in half. Slit one section lengthwise and remove a ¼ in. (1 cm) strip down the side, so that by squeezing and taping it closed, the tube will be slightly smaller than the other section (Figure 421.01a). Both sections can be wrapped with masking tape to make them sturdier, but be sure the smaller one slides easily inside the larger. Cut two rings of cardboard for each end and cement the lenses between them (Figure 421.01b). Tape the lenses to the tube sections (Figure 421.01c). The fit should make the tubing as lightproof as possible. By looking through the eyepiece lens and moving the smaller tube in

01
Bb
Gc

and out, students can magnify and focus on distant objects. You might tell them that the instrument they have made is called a *refracting telescope.* **Caution: Warn students that they should never look directly at the Sun with or without a telescope.**

Figure 421.01

> *Contributing Idea B.* Stars, planets, moons, and other objects make up part of the universe.

Defining some types of objects in the universe. Use Styrofoam balls of different sizes and a bright light source to explain the differences between *stars* and *planets.* (Stars produce their own light, planets reflect light.) Show students how our solar system's planets revolve around one star, our Sun. Explain that smaller objects, called moons, also reflect light, but revolve around some planets. (Note: At the time of this writing the Earth has 1 Moon, Mars 2, Jupiter 63, Saturn 62, Uranus 27; and Neptune 13. It is likely that more will be

02
Bb
Bd

found.) Tell students that the planets and moons orbiting around the Sun make up the *solar system*, which is but one tiny part of the universe. Some students might be interested in researching information on other objects in the solar system such as asteroids, comets, and meteors. (Note: Pluto was discovered in 1930 and was thought to be the solar system's ninth planet. However, in 2006 it was reclassified as a "dwarf planet" because it did not have all the characteristics of the other planets. Pluto has three moons.)

Locating the North Star. On a clear night, have students connect an imaginary line between the two end stars in the bowl of the Big Dipper. By extending the line about five times, they will find an average-looking star, the North Star. (Note: Even though the Big Dipper changes its position during the night and year, the two end stars always point to the North Star. Smog conditions may keep the North Star from being seen.) Now have the students stand a 5 ft. (1.5 m) stick with an eye screw in one end into a large can of sand or soil. Move the can until the North Star can be seen through the eye screw and is in line with the top of a pole, tree, TV antennae, or other landmark. By sighting through the eye screw at regular intervals, students can see if there is any shift in the North Star's position. This can be compared with sightings of other stars.

03
Aa
Ga

Using instruments to determine the altitude of the North Star. Use tape to hinge two rulers together end to end at a 90° angle. Hold one so that it points straight out to the horizon and the other to the zenith. Tape a protractor to the rulers so that the base is on the horizon line and the zenith line cuts the 90° mark (Figure 421.04a). To determine the altitude of the

04
Ga
Gc

Figure 421.04a

North Star where you live, hold the rulers horizontally at eye level. Look at the North Star and move the top ruler to point at it. The number of degrees or altitude of the star can be read on the protractor (Figure 421.04b).

Figure 421.04b

Using a star map to locate constella- **05** some of them. To use a map, hold it verti-
tions. Numerous constellations can be **Ga** cally and turn it so that the point of the
seen on a clear night. The star maps in compass toward which you are facing
Figures 421.05a–d can be used to locate shows on the bottom of the map.

THE NIGHT SKY IN SUMMER

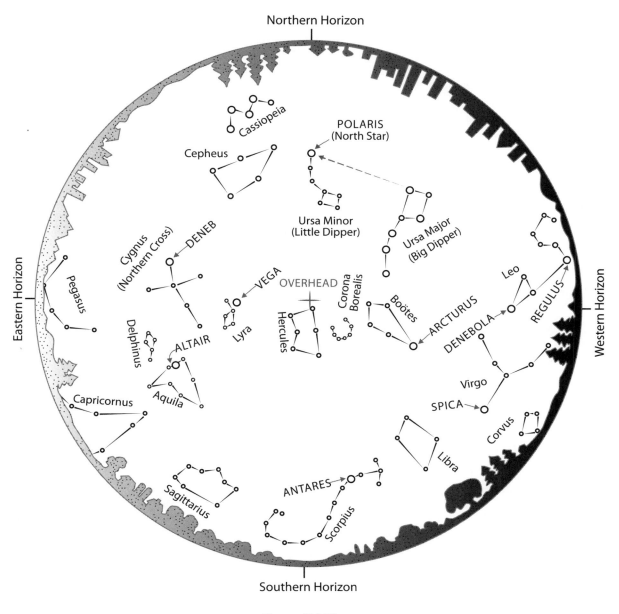

Figure 421.05a

THE NIGHT SKY IN FALL

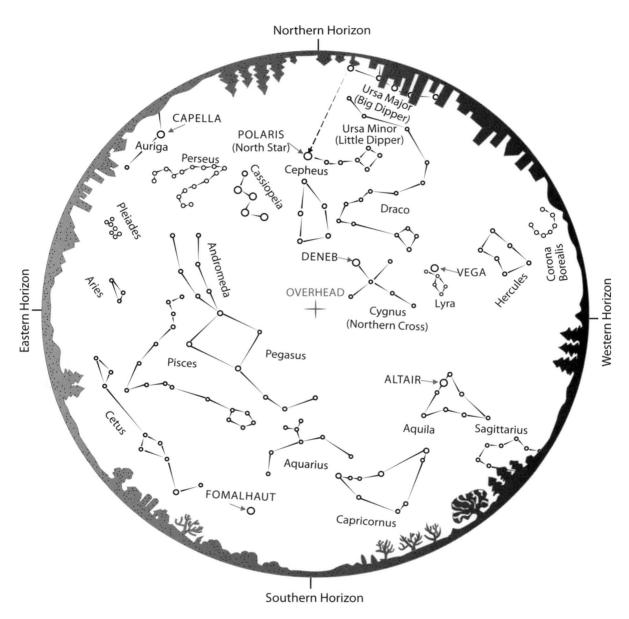

Figure 421.05b

THE NIGHT SKY IN WINTER

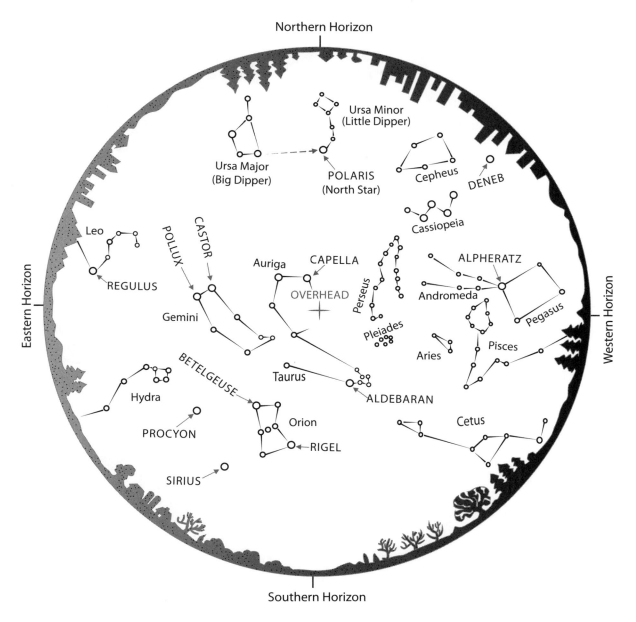

Figure 421.05c

THE NIGHT SKY IN SPRING

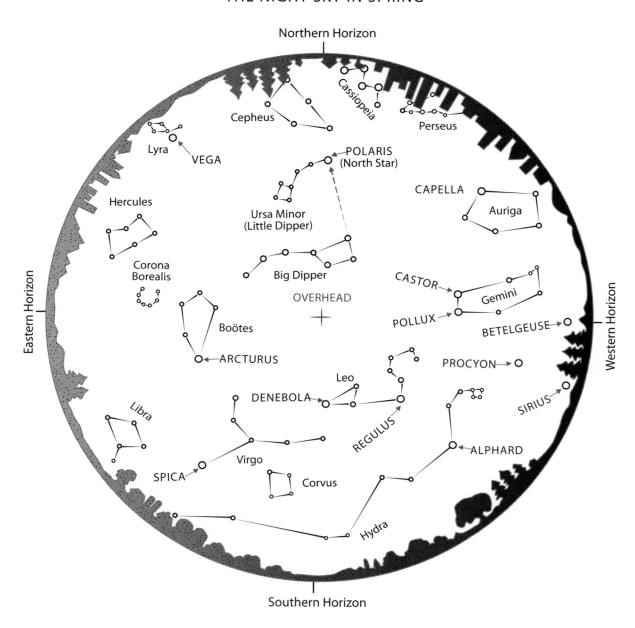

Figure 421.05d

Making a constellation projector. Have students choose a constellation and use a pin to punch holes in the lid of a large oatmeal carton, shoe box, or saltbox in the pattern of the constellation. Slightly larger holes can be made to represent brighter stars. A lid can also be made to depict the whole night sky. When the container is placed over a lightbulb or flashlight, the images can be projected in a darkened room. Students can try to identify the constellations.

**06
Ga
Gc**

Observing the Sun. The Sun can be observed by having students use a pin or small nail to punch a hole in the center of a sheet of cardboard. With their backs to the Sun, they can focus the Sun's rays through the hole onto another sheet of cardboard. The tiny image cast will be that of the Sun. Any small telescope with an external focal plane can be used in a similar way to project an image of the Sun. During a solar eclipse, it is possible to watch the image gradually become obscured by the Moon. **Caution: No direct observation techniques for viewing the Sun are safe. Looking through exposed photographic film, sun glasses, smoked glass, or similar materials are also not safe. The only advised technique is to view the Sun indirectly using a pinhole device.**

**07
Aa**

Measuring the size of the Sun. Let sunlight pass through a pinhole in a card to form a small image of the Sun a yard

**08
Cd**

(meter) or more away. Draw a pair of similar triangles on the chalkboard to diagram how the image is made. Students can see from the diagram that the ratio of the image's diameter to its distance from the pinhole is the same as the ratio of the Sun's diameter to its distance from the Earth. **Caution: Direct viewing of the Sun, even for a short time, can cause burns to the eye's retina. Burns will not be felt but can produce a permanent blank spot in the field of vision.** This experience might be preceded using a frosted bulb as a light source. The size of the bulb can be calculated, and then measured to compare the actual size to the calculation. (See Figure 421.08.)

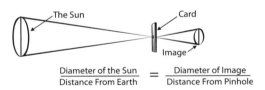

$$\frac{\text{Diameter of the Sun}}{\text{Distance From Earth}} = \frac{\text{Diameter of Image}}{\text{Distance From Pinhole}}$$

Figure 421.08

Using a model to represent the distances between planets and the Sun. Have students research the distances of the planets from the Sun and challenge them to develop a scale to represent them. For example, if a scale of 1 in.= 1,000,000 miles is used, the size of the Sun can be represented by a quarter and Jupiter (the largest planet) by a pinhead. Other planets would be almost too small to be seen. On a playground, the quarter and pin can be placed 483 in. apart (40 ft. and 3 in.).

**09
Bd
Cd
Fc**

Markers can be placed for the other planets to indicate their mean distances from the Sun. (See Table 421.09.)

Contributing Idea C. Nearly all information about the characteristics of the universe is indirect.

Using models to see how the temperatures of stars can be determined. Astronomers use several techniques to determine the temperatures of stars. The following suggest two of the techniques.

10
Ce
Fc

a. Students can use a pair of pliers to hold an iron nail, pin, or needle in a flame. Observe and note what happens to the color as it gets hotter. Explain that in an analogous way, astronomers compare the colors of stars to colors of heated objects on Earth to estimate temperatures. The "hottest" stars are a blue-white color, "cooler" stars are yellow, and the "coolest" stars are red.

b. Students can hold a thermometer approximately 1 ft. (30 cm) away from an unshaded lightbulb. Record the temperature reading after three minutes. Now hold a magnifying glass so that the light focuses on the bulb of the thermometer. After three minutes, record the temperature again. Repeat the measurement by moving the thermometer greater distances from the bulb. Students will realize that as the distance increases, more sensitive instruments are needed. They can graph the relationship between the distance in in. (centimeters) and degrees in temperature. Explain that in a similar way, astronomers use the lenses of telescopes and other sensitive instruments to measure the temperatures of stars.

Table 421.09. Scaling the Distances of Planets From the Sun

Planet	Mean Distance From Sun (to nearest million miles)	Scaled Distance (1 in. = 1,000,000 miles)
Mercury	36,000,000	3 ft.
Venus	67,000,000	5 ft. 7 in.
Earth	93,000,000	7 ft. 10 in.
Mars	141,000,000	11 ft. 9 in.
Jupiter	483,000,000	40 ft. 3 in.
Saturn	888,000,000	74 ft.
Uranus	1,783,000,000	148 ft. 7 in.
Neptune	2,795,000,000	231 ft. 23 in.

Constructing a simple spectroscope to see how the composition of stars can be determined. Cut a circle of black paper to fit the end of a cardboard tube. Cut the circle in half, tape one half onto one end of the tube and the other half next to the first, leaving a narrow slit between the two pieces. Hold a piece of diffraction grating up to the open end and look through it at the vertical slit at the opposite end and toward a bright electric light. (Diffraction grating can be obtained from a scientific supply house.) You might explain that diffraction grating has parallel lines on it (15,000 to 30,000 per inch) that cause the light passing between them to spread out into a band of colors (the spectrum). Slowly rotate the grating until a bright color band is seen on a side of the slit, then tape the grating in place. Now have students look through the instrument at a lighted fluorescent tube. They will see a spectrum on either side of the slit and can notice narrow bright lines in the yellow, green, or blue portions of the spectrum. Explain that the lines are caused by the glowing gases in the fluorescent tube and that every element produces its own characteristic spectrum lines when heated to a point where it glows. Tell them that the instrument they have made is called a spectroscope. Astronomers can look through a spectroscope at any glowing body in space. By comparing the color patterns of known elements with the spectrum of a star, they can determine what

11
Bb
Fb
Gc

elements are present in the star. Now let students hold a looped paper clip in a flame to clean it, wet the loop slightly, dip it into chalk dust, and hold it in the flame again while examining the glow through the spectroscope. (They will see the spectrum that is characteristic of calcium.) Similarly, they can test baking soda (they will see the spectrum that is characteristic of sodium) and other materials.

Calculating the distance to objects by triangulation. Cut two pieces of drawing paper to fit the bottoms of two sturdy cardboard boxes. Draw a 90° angle with 8 in. (20 cm) sides on one piece of paper. Mark off and label every 5° of arc within the angle and label the base *WX* as shown in Figure 421.12a (p. 386). Turn one box with bottom side up and fasten the paper to it. Insert a pin at each 5° mark on the arc. Do the same on the second paper, but reverse the angle and label the base *YZ* as shown in Figure 421.12b (p. 386). Place the boxes facing some distant object such as a telephone pole, tree, or television antennae. Line up the boxes so that the pins *WXYZ* are in a straight line. Have students measure the distance from *W* to *Z* and record it as the base of an imaginary triangle. Have students look from point *W* to the distant object and decide what angle on the arc is directly between the observer and the object. (Several students might check this to be sure.) Do the same from point *Z* (see

12
Cd

Figure 421.12c). Now have them make a scale drawing of line *WXYZ* and the angles measured at *W* and *Z*. They can extend the angles of their drawing until the lines intersect, then draw a line from the base line perpendicular through the intersection. By measuring this line and converting the scale, they will know the approximate distance to the object. They can check this by actually measuring the distance. They will realize that this method allows them to measure the distance to objects without actually going to them. If they use the method to measure the distance to other objects, they might discover that the longer the distance to be measured, the more closely parallel the lines become and the greater the chance for error. (Note: Since the moon is very far away, astronomers must use a very

long base line such as the diameter of the Earth.)

Using the parallax effect to calculate the distance to objects. Draw vertical lines at 1 in. (2 cm) intervals on a chalkboard. Have students hold a pencil upright at arm's length and line it up with one of the lines. Without moving the pencil or the observer's head, have each student look at it first with one eye, then with the other and note how many vertical lines it seems to shift. You might tell them that the apparent shift of position of the pencil is called the parallax effect. Have them check the effect when the pencil is closer or farther from their eyes to see if the parallax effect is greater or smaller. Now fasten a pencil upright on a desk. On another desk farther from the chalkboard, fasten two more pencils in upright positions and 6 in. (15 cm) apart. The added pencils can be used as sighting points. Have students sight on the single pencil from one of the added pencils and note which vertical line it is near. Next, sight from the second added pencil and record the parallax effect (the number of vertical lines the pencil seems to shift). Repeat the procedure with the pencils 12 and 18 in. (30 cm and 45 cm) apart. From these experiences, students will find that two factors influence the parallax effect: (1) the farther the object is from the observer, the smaller the parallax, and (2) the greater the distance between sighting

**13
Bb
Cd**

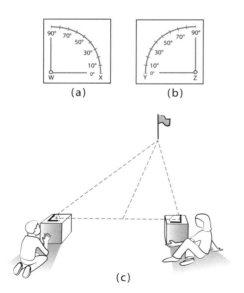

(a)   (b)

(c)

Figure 421.12

points, the greater the parallax. Explain that astronomers can measure the distance to the Moon in a similar way. The stars that are billions of miles away provide the background (much like the stationary vertical lines on the chalkboard). Observers on opposite sides of the Earth sight on the Moon (much like the sightings from the two pencils) in relation to the stars. Astronomers have found there is a difference of 1° between the background star and the Moon for each observer; therefore, the base angle for each is 89° and the parallax angle for the Moon is 2°. Students can draw this to scale by drawing a line that is 1 yd. (1 m) long, making a 2° angle at one end, and continuing this line until the two are exactly 1 in. (2.5 cm) apart (approximately 30 in. or 75 cm distant). Since this inch (2.5 cm) represents the diameter of the Earth (approximately 7,900 mi. or 12,719 km), the scale is 1 in. (2.5 cm) = 7,900 mi. (12,719 km). From this, students can calculate the distance to the Moon.

Calculating the diameter of the Moon. **14 Cd** Students can put two pieces of masking tape 1 in. (2.5 cm) apart, horizontally one above the other, on a window through which a full Moon can be seen. Move back from the pieces of tape until the Moon's diameter exactly fills the space between them, then measure the distance from the eye to the pieces of tape. Repeat this a few times and determine an average distance.

Knowing that the Moon is approximately 240,000 mi. (actually 238,900 mi. or 384,629 km) from the Earth, and realizing that the distance of the Moon from the Earth is to the diameter of the Moon as the distance of the tape from the eye is to the diameter of the image between the tape, students can calculate the diameter of the Moon by simple proportion. For example, if the average distance to the tape was 110 in., then

$$\frac{\text{diameter of image}}{\text{distance to eye}} = \frac{\text{diameter of Moon}}{\text{distance to Moon}}$$

$$\frac{1 \text{ in.}}{110 \text{ in.}} = \frac{n}{240,000 \text{ miles}}$$

Similarly, students can measure the diameter of a coin, hold it between an eye and the full Moon, then measure the distance it is held (from the eye to the coin) when it covers the Moon exactly. The ratio of the diameter of the coin and its distance from the eye will be the same as the diameter of the Moon and its distance from the Earth.

Determining the difference between real size and apparent size. **15 Bb Ca** Have students measure the diameter of a 50-cent piece (1½ in. or 3 cm across), then hold the coin at a distance of more than 20 ft. (6 m). Although students know it to be the same size, they will realize that the coin appears to be only a fraction of an inch (cm) across. Explain that the measurement taken was the object's *real* size and that the observation was of its *apparent* size. Whenever the size of distant objects is measured, astronomers must remember that they never see the real size of an object, but only its apparent size. Now have students hold a coin (or their thumbs) in front of them, close one eye and sight on a clock or basketball at the front end of the room. Have them move the coin nearer or farther until it exactly hides the object (the apparent sizes of the coin and the clock are now the same). An analogy can be made to the apparent sizes of the Sun (the clock) and Moon (the coin). Students can discuss the fact that the Sun and Moon often appear to be the same size. Next, have them note what happens when the coin is moved nearer or farther away from the eye. (The apparent size changes as it moves nearer and farther away—an inch appears shorter as distance increases and larger as distance decreases.)

Measuring the angular diameter of an object. Place a 50-cent piece on a piece of paper so that its edge is near one edge of the paper. With a pencil, make a dot on the edge of the opposite side of the paper and use a ruler to draw straight lines from the dot to each side of the coin as shown in Figure 421.16a. Now move the coin to the middle of the paper and do the same. Next, move the coin to within 2 in. (5 cm) of the dot and draw the lines as shown in Figure 421.16b. Use protractors to measure the size of each angle. Explain that each angle is the apparent size of the coin

16
Bb
Cd

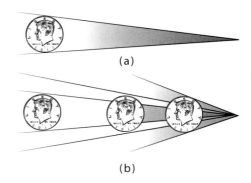

(a)

(b)

Figure 421.16

as seen from a different distance from the dot. Students will note that the angle decreases as the distance increases and vice versa. Tell them that the angle determined by the apparent size of an object is called the object's angular diameter.

Making and using a circumferentor. Attach an upright piece of wood to a sturdy base. Tape a protractor to the upright and use a pin to fasten a drinking straw to the center of the protractor. Students can sight through the straw to the top of a distant object and read the figure on the protractor at the bottom edge of the straw. They can then sight on the bottom edge of the object and note the reading. The difference between the two readings is the angular diameter of the object being observed. By sighting on objects of various sizes from various distances, students will discover that objects with the same angular diameter are not always the same size, that the angular diameter becomes smaller as the distance increases, and that angular diameter depends both on the

17
Cd
Ga
Gc

distance and the real size of the object. You might tell the students that the instrument they have constructed is called a circumferentor. To determine the real size of the object, students can draw the angle to scale. For example, if a basketball is 10 ft. (3 m) away when its angular diameter is measured, students can draw a 10 in. (25 cm) line on a sheet of paper (1 in. or 2.5 cm = 1 ft. or 30 cm), use the circumferentor to measure the angular diameter of the basketball (e.g., 10°), and draw the angle from the 10 in. (25 cm) line. When the angle is extended to the same length (10 in. or 25 cm), an imaginary triangle is formed that is the exact ratio of the imaginary triangle formed by the viewer and the basketball. Since 1 in. (2.5 cm) equals 1 ft. (30 cm) in the scale, the distance between the ends of the two lines represents the diameter of the object. If this distance is 1½ in., then in this scale, the diameter of the basketball is 1½ ft.. (See Figure 421.17.)

Figure 421.17

Using angular diameter to calculate the diameter of the Moon. Tell the students that astronomers have used instruments **18 Cd Ga** such as the circumferentor to determine that the angular diameter of the Moon is 0.5°. Have them use protractors to draw an angle 0.5° on a long sheet of paper. Extend the sides of the angle to represent the distance to the moon (about 240,000 mi. or 38,000 km). A scale of 1 in. for each 10,000 mi. (or 1 cm for each 1,000 km) would produce an angle with sides 24 in. (60 cm) long. When the imaginary triangle is completed between the two sides, students will find the diameter to be approximately ⅕ in. (5 mm) long. This scale would indicate that the diameter of the Moon is approximately 2,000 mi. (actually 2,160 mi. or 3478 km).

Using a model to compare the sizes and distances between objects in the solar system. Cut a 2 ft., 7⅛ in. diameter circle from red or orange construction paper to represent the Sun. Using the accompanying table (Table 421.19, p. 391), have students cut out other objects to scale. By placing the circles together, students will gain some notion concerning the relative sizes of the Moon, Sun, and planets. Now have them place the circle representing the Sun on the ground outdoors (a football field works well for this activity). Set the circles for each of the first three planets (Mercury, Venus, Earth) at the scaled distances from the Sun. From this, students will develop some notion concerning the vast distances between these objects. Older students might develop **19 Cd Fc**

their own scale system. (Note: The relative sizes and distances between the Sun, planets and Earth's Moon are accurate to the nearest million miles (million kilometers) on the sample table (Table 421.19). It is important that students realize that both the distance and size scales are the same, thus making it possible to look at both factors at the same time.)

Defining a light-year. Explain that distances to stars are so great that astronomers use a light-year (the distance light traveling at 186,000 miles per second reaches in one year) as a unit of measure. Students might be interested in calculating this distance in miles: **20 Bb Cc**

186,000 miles (speed of light per second)
× 86,400 seconds (number of seconds in one day)
× 365 days (number of days in one year)
_____
5,865,696,000,000 miles

This figure is usually rounded to read six trillion miles. A few students might be interested in calculating the distance in miles to some close stars: our Sun (8 seconds away); Alpha Centauri, our next nearest star (4.3 light-years away); Polaris, the north star (300 light-years away). (Note: If a scale of 1 in. = 1,000,000 mi. is used to develop a model of the solar system on the playground (see entry 421.19), then Alpha Centauri would be over 400 miles away! You might add that if people could travel in a spaceship at 25,000 mi. per hour, it would take about 10,000 years to reach this star.)

Defining what a galaxy is. Some students might have noticed a bright band of hazy light in the night sky. Tell them that this band is called the Milky Way and that it is actually a somewhat flat spiral made up of many stars. Explain that there are millions of other clusters of stars of different sizes and shapes scattered throughout the universe and that these clusters are called galaxies. Use a projector to show an illustration of the face view and end view of a spiral galaxy. Tell students that the Sun is one star within the picture. Locate its general position for them. Help them imagine that the Milky Way is the view we see when we look through our own galaxy. (We are on the inside looking out, thus it is difficult to perceive our galaxy's form.) You might also explain that our galaxy is about 100,000 light-years across and 7,000 light-years thick at the center. **21 Bb Ca**

Generalization II. Objects in the universe can be organized on the basis of their characteristics.

> *Contributing Idea.* Objects in the universe can be seriated.

Seriating planets by size. Students can research the sizes of planets, determine a scale to represent all of them, construct models for each, and order them by size. A good scale for such construction is 1 in. = 8,000 mi. (1 cm = 1,000 km). Spherical or circular models can be painted and arranged for display. **22 Bd Da**

Table 421.19. Scaling the Diameters of and Distances Between the Sun, Planets, and Earth's Moon

Object	Mean Diameter		Scaled Diameter		Mean Distance From the Sun		Scaled Diameter	
	Nearest 100 mi.	Nearest 100 km	1 yd. = 1 million mi.	1 m = 1 million km	Nearest million mi.	Nearest million km	1 yd. = 1 million mi.	1 m = 1 million km
Sun	865,000	1,400,000	2 ft. 7 in.	1.4 m				
Mercury	3,000	4,800	$\frac{3}{32}$ in.	4.8 mm	36	58	36 yd.	58 m
Venus	7,500	12,100	$\frac{9}{32}$ in.	12.1 mm	67	108	67 yd.	108 m
Earth	7,900	12,700	$\frac{5}{16}$ in.	12.7 mm	93	150	93 yd.	150 m
Mars	4,200	6,800	$\frac{5}{32}$ in.	6.8 mm	141	227	141 yd.	227 m
Jupiter	88,600	142,600	$3\frac{3}{16}$ in.	14.26 cm	483	777	483 yd.	777 m
Saturn	74,700	120,200	$\frac{23}{32}$ in.	12.02 cm	888	1,429	888 yd.	1,429 m
Uranus	30,500	49,100	$1\frac{3}{32}$ in.	4.9 cm	1,783	2,869	1,783 yd.	2,869 m
Neptune	31,200	50,200	$1\frac{1}{8}$ in.	5.02 cm	2,795	4,497	2,795 yd.	4,497 m
Earth's Moon	2,200	3,500	$\frac{3}{32}$ in.	3.5 mm	238,900 miles from Earth	384,600 km from Earth	$8\frac{19}{32}$ in.	38.44 cm

Table 421.23. Seriation of Planets by Average Temperatures and Distances From the Sun

Planet	Average Daytime Temperature (s = Surface; c = Clouds)		Average Distance From the Sun	
	°F	°C	Nearest Million Mi.	Nearest Million Km
Mercury	662 (s)	350 (s)	36,000,000	58,000,000
Venus	896 (s) –27 (c)	430 (s) –33 (c)	67,000,000	108,000,000
Earth	71 (s)	22 (s)	93,000,000	150,000,000
Mars	15 (s)	–23 (s)	141,000,000	227,000,000
Jupiter	–238 (c)	–150 (c)	483,000,000	777,000,000
Saturn	–292 (c)	–180 (c)	888,000,000	1,429,000,000
Uranus	–346 (c)	–210 (c)	1,783,000,000	2,869,000,000
Neptune	–364 (c)	–220 (c)	2,795,000,000	4,497,000,000

Seriating planets by temperatures. Have several students hold their hands at various distances from an unshaded bulb. They will find that they feel warmer when close to the bulb and cooler when farther away. Make an analogy between the bulb and the Sun and the hand and planets. Now have students research the temperatures of the planets and list them in the order of their average temperatures. They will find that the listing coincides with the order of the planets in terms of distance from the Sun, and realize that the temperature pattern is analogous to the relationship of their hands to the bulb. Some students might research the distances from the planets to the Sun and add this information to their listing (see Table 421.23). If the average temperatures of planets are transferred to a bar graph (see Graph 421.23), students can readily note some interesting relationships. For example, the temperature of Venus

23
Bb
Bd
Da

(second closest to the Sun) is significantly higher than other planets; there is a great difference in temperature between Mars and Jupiter (with a corresponding increase in the distance from the Sun at this point).

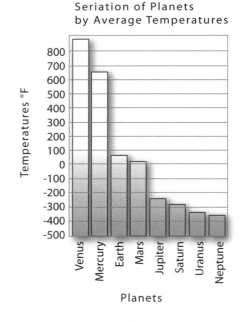

Seriation of Planets by Average Temperatures

Graph 421.23

You might tell the students that because of the great distance between Mars and Jupiter, the first four planets are called the inner planets while the others are called the outer planets. Some students might be interested in reading about the asteroids found between Mars and Jupiter.

422   Interactions

Generalization I. The Sun, Moon, and stars appear to change positions in the sky when viewed from the Earth.

> *Contributing Idea A.* The Sun seems to follow a path across the sky from east to west; the Sun's daily path gradually changes with the seasons.

Observing that the Sun seems to change position. Push a long nail, point up, through the center of a 1 ft. (30 cm) square of heavy cardboard. Place the cardboard on a sunny windowsill and do not move it again until this whole experience is completed. Mark a dot at the tip of the nail's shadow every day at the same time for several weeks. Students will realize that the shadow movement is related to changes in the Sun's position and find that the Sun does not travel in the same path each day. They might compare the shadow curves for widely different times of the year (e.g., September, January, May) or exchange similarly obtained information with schools farther to the south or north. This activity can also be done using the shadow of a flagpole, telephone pole, or tall tree. Students can determine what features change or stay the same from day to day.

01 Ca

Observing the apparent motion of the Sun. Make a pinhole in a piece of black construction paper and fasten the paper to a sunny window. When the rest of the room is darkened, the light from the Sun will shine clearly through the hole. Stand a piece of white cardboard approximately 3 ft. (1 m) from the window so that the Sun makes a small bright spot on it. (This spot is an image of the Sun.) Have students mark the location of the spot with a pencil and watch it for several minutes. They can soon extrapolate what path the Sun's image would make on the paper from sunrise to sunset.

02 Aa Ch

> *Contributing Idea B.* The Moon seems to follow a path across the sky in the same general direction as the Sun.

Observing that the Moon seems to change position. Have students choose a window at home from which they can see the Moon. On a clear night, they can line up the edge of the window frame with an object outdoors, such as a telephone pole, tree, or edge of a building. Mark the Moon's position on the window pane with tape. If observations are repeated every 15 minutes, students will realize that the Moon apparently changes its position. (Note: Students should be sure to hold their heads in exactly the same position for every observation.)

03 Ca

Observing the apparent motion of the Moon. Label a yardstick or meterstick stick A, and drill a hole near one end. Label a second stick stick B, and drill a hole in the center. Fasten them together with a bolt and wing nut. Make a grid of 1 in. (2.5 cm) squares on a transparent plastic sheet and attach it to one end of stick B (Figure 422.04a). Fasten stick A to the back of a chair or other support as shown in Figure 422.04b. Sight along the upper edge of stick B and adjust the support so that the Moon appears to be sitting right on the end of stick B. Do not move the stick for five minutes, then sight along it again. (Students will find that the Moon appears to change its position.) The instrument can be used to sight on various stars to see if they also move.

**04
Ca**

Figure 422.04

> *Contributing Idea C.* The stars seem to follow a path across the sky and keep their positions in relation to each other.

Observing that stars seem to change position. Draw a circle and divide it into four equal parts by drawing two lines through the center. Put a star in the center of the circle to represent the North Star. In each of the four parts of the circle, draw the Big Dipper, making sure the pointer stars are in line with the North Star in each drawing. Number the drawings. (See Figure 422.05.) At night, students can hold the paper circle so that first drawing is in the same position as the Big Dipper in

**05
Ca**

the sky. Mark the time by the Big Dipper. Predict at what time the Big Dipper will be in the second position, and then check the prediction. Let the students discuss where it will be in the daytime.

Figure 422.05

Observing the apparent movement of stars. On a clear evening in an open area away from bright lights, have each student pick out a star for herself, walk around while observing it until it appears to touch the tip of a tree, pole, TV antennae, or other prominent landmark, and place a marker at the spot where she is standing. Repeat, using the same star and sighting point, at 10-minute intervals. Have students compare marks for different stars. They will realize an overall pattern to the apparent movement of stars.

**06
Aa
Ch**

Generalization II. **The relative positions of the Sun and Earth relate to time and seasonal changes.**

> *Contributing Idea A.* The Sun's light can be used to mark time during the day.

Making and using an indoor sundial. Fix a small mirror on a windowsill so that light from the Sun is reflected on a large sheet of graph paper on the wall inside. If the Sun does not shine directly through the window, a mirror can be attached to a tree or some other fixed object to reflect it inside. Students can mark the location of the reflected sunlight on the graph paper each day. If students have the opportunity to observe a solar eclipse, it is interesting to begin marking several days before and continue marking several days after the eclipse.

**07
Ga
Gc**

Making and using an outdoor sundial. Use a protractor to make a half circle on a 10 in. (25 cm) square of cardboard. Divide the circle into 12 15° angles and number them. Determine the latitude of your school. Some latitudes are given below:

**08
Cd
Ga
Gc**

St. Paul, Minnesota   45°
Philadelphia, Pennsylvania   40°
Los Angeles, California   34°
Miami, Florida   26°

Out of stiff cardboard, cut an angle that is the same as the number of degrees of latitude. Fasten the angle to the half circle with tape. Place the instrument in sunlight so that the triangle points directly north (see Figure 422.08). North is best determined by noting the direction of the

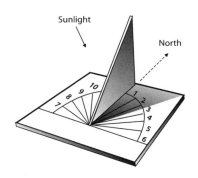

Figure 422.08

line made when the shadow is at its shortest length. The shadow line is along the north–south line. The shadow cast will indicate the time of day in your location. Similar sundials can be made by sticking any upright object such as a pencil or dowel into the ground and slanting it to the angle of latitude in the direction of north. Students can mark the top of the shadow every hour for many days and connect the marks to see changes in the apparent course of the Sun.

Making and using a Sun clock. Cut a round cardboard carton in half lengthwise. Glue a bead to a length of thread. Fasten the thread through the centers of the carton's ends as shown in Figure 422.09. Place the instrument on a level windowsill or outdoors in precisely the same position each day by lining the thread up in a north–south direction. The thread's shadow will indicate Sun time. Students can mark the interior of the carton at 15-minute intervals where the bead's shadow is cast. By connecting these marks, students will note a shift in the Sun's apparent path with the seasons.

**09
Ch
Ga
Gc**

Figure 422.09

Contributing Idea B. Changes in the length of day and seasonal changes are related to the tilt of the Earth's axis and its revolution around the Sun.

Orienting a model of the Earth to the Sun. On a sunny day, set a globe of the Earth so that its axis points toward the North Star's position. Rotate it until the state in which students live is at the highest part of the globe and parallel to the ground. (The globe is now in the same position as is the Earth, relative to the Sun.) Have students locate where it is daytime and nighttime on the Earth. Place a small lump of modeling clay on the globe to represent the location of the school. Stand a toothpick straight up in the clay. The direction of the toothpick's shadow can be compared to that of a nearby flagpole, and students can see how their shadows move throughout the day.

**10
Aa
Fc**

Using a model to depict day and night. Darken a room, turn on a slide projector, and slowly rotate a globe of the Earth counterclockwise in the light beam. Tell the students that the turning of the Earth is called rotation. One complete rotation takes 24 hours (one complete day). Now have students imagine how the eastern portion of the United States experiences sunrise as the Earth turns into the light and how the western portion eventually disappears in the shadow at sunset. Try reversing the rotation and compare the images.

**11
Bb
Ca
Fc**

Using a model to depict seasonal changes. Place a piece of metal window screen into a 2 in. × 2 in. (5 cm × 5 cm) slide frame and project it onto a globe of the Earth. Tell the students that

**12
Aa
Bb
Fc**

the projector represents the Sun and the globe represents the Earth in its summer position. Students will see that the squares of the grid elongate toward the top and bottom of the globe. Using this model, they should realize that the Sun's radiation spreads out more toward the poles because of the greater angle at which it strikes the globe, and infer that light and heat are less intense toward the poles. Now have a student place a square piece of paper, the size of one square of the projected grid, over the city where your school is located. With a grease pencil, trace the square. Next, turn the globe so that it moves to its winter position. You might explain that the Earth's tilted axis continually points 23½° in one direction throughout its *revolution* and that one revolution takes about 365 rotations (days). Discuss any differences between the shape of the square and the square of light now cast on the same spot. (Students will note that the light is more spread out and can infer that vertical radiation probably produces more warmth and light than slanted radiation.) Other times of the year can be compared as can other locations on the globe (e.g., equator, Tropic of Cancer, Tropic of Capricorn).

Generalization III. The relative positions of the Sun, Earth, and Moon relate to Moon phases and eclipses.

Contributing Idea A. The appearance of the Moon seems to change as it revolves around the Earth.

Observing Moon phases in the daytime. Students can observe the Moon in the daytime and draw its apparent shape on a calendar. When it cannot be seen, mark the calendar with an explanation (e.g., rain, cloudy sky). Now have them take a tennis or Styrofoam ball outdoors and hold it at arm's length directly in front of the Moon. The sunlit portion of the ball will appear similar in shape to the sunlit portion of the Moon. You might tell them that the changes in the sunlit portion from day to day are called phases. Now have them move the ball slowly to the right or left and note the changes. They can realize the relative position of the Sun to the Moon phases by extending one arm toward the Sun and the other toward the Moon and determining the angle on successive days.

13
Bb
Be
Ca

Using a model to demonstrate Moon phases. Have a student hold a white volleyball higher than his head. Tell other students that the ball represents the Moon. To represent the Sun, point a slide projector at the ball approximately 6 ft. (2 m) above the floor and at least 10 ft. (3 m) away. Now have another student stand behind the ball and in a direct line with the projector. This person represents the Earth. Darken the room and have the student with the Moon slowly walk

14
Bb
Ca
Fc

around the Earth until one full circle (revolution) is completed. Other students can observe apparent changes in the Moon's lighted surface and compare their observations with those made from the Earth. The view from the Earth can be drawn to represent different positions of the Moon during rotation. Students will realize that the Moon's apparent shape goes through changes when seen in different positions of its orbit.

Using a model to depict the Moon's orbit around the Earth. Have students make one complete turn in place. Tell them that when they or any object faces all directions during one complete turn, the turn is called a rotation. Now place a student or globe of the Earth in the center of a large circle drawn on the school ground. Have a second student stand on the line of the circle facing the center. Explain that the person in the center represents the Earth and the person on the circle represents the Moon. Since most students have noticed that they see only one side of the Moon, have the student on the circle move counterclockwise around the circle so that she is always facing the Earth at the center. After one complete orbit, let the students discuss whether or not the Moon rotated. By repeating the orbit, students will realize that the Moon faced all directions as it moved around the Earth; therefore, it must have rotated. This activity can be repeated by having

15
Bb
Fc

the Moon face in a direction other than the center. (Students will see all sides of the Moon during the orbit.)

> *Contributing Idea B.* A lunar eclipse occurs when the Earth's shadow falls upon the Moon; a solar eclipse occurs when the Moon's shadow falls upon the Earth.

Using a model to show eclipses. From a distance of 10 ft. (3 m), shine a slide projector on a globe of the Earth. Hang a Styrofoam ball from a string and slowly move it counterclockwise around the globe. Students will see that when the ball, which represents the Moon, is between the globe and the light source, a shadow is cast on the globe. Compare this to an eclipse of the Sun by telling students that when the Sun, Moon, and Earth are in such positions, a *solar eclipse* occurs. Now continue the revolution of the ball until it is behind the globe. Make an analogy to an eclipse of the moon or *lunar eclipse.* Students can try moving the three objects to find a way to explain why eclipses are not observed at each new Moon and full Moon. (Only a Moon orbit tilted relative to the Earth's orbit around the Sun will produce infrequent solar and lunar eclipses.)

16
Bb
Ec
Fc

Using a model to explain eclipses. Hold the narrow end of a key between two stacks of books. Use a shaded desk lamp to shine a bright light from approximately 1 ft. (30 cm) height directly down

17
Bb
Fc

on the top of the key. Students can note if the shadow cast is sharp or fuzzy. Now make the light source smaller by moving the light farther away or by covering the shade of the lamp with a heavy piece of cardboard that has a small hole punched in the center. Shine the light on the key again. Students will discover that when the light source is larger than the object upon which it shines, the shadow cast has two parts. You might tell them that the dark, inner part is called the umbra and the lighter, gray part is called the penumbra. Use Figure 422.17 to make an analogy to the Earth (the key) and the Sun (the light). Explain that the umbra is dark because all light is blocked from it by the object, while the penumbra is lighter because some light rays from the

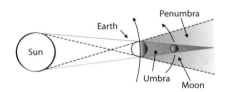

Figure 422.17

larger light source get past the edges of the object. Let the students try to draw the shadows cast if the Sun were smaller than the Earth's diameter. Next, add the Moon to the diagram, first in a lunar eclipse, then in a solar eclipse position. Students can discuss the effects of the shadows cast upon the eclipses.

Observing an eclipse of the Sun. About **18** a week in advance of a solar eclipse, stu- **Ca** dents can draw a picture of the eastern horizon early in the morning (moonrise and sunrise). Every week on the same day, the location of the Moon and Sun can be marked on the picture. Students will see that as the week of the eclipse approaches, the setting points get closer and closer together (they will eventually coincide exactly if there is a total eclipse). If the plotting is continued for several weeks after the eclipse, observing the evening western horizon (sunset and moonset), students will see the two paths separate. **Caution: Students should never observe the Sun directly.**

423   Theory

Generalization. According to the heliocentric theory of the solar system, the Earth and other planets revolve around the Sun.

> *Contributing Idea A.* Until the 16th century, it was generally believed that the Earth was the center of the universe.

Discussing an Earth-centered theory. **01** Have students discuss whether or not the **Ba** Earth is moving, and if it is, ask for evi- **Fc** dence (this is difficult). From the discussion, students will appreciate why it was generally believed that the Earth was a stationary object at the center of the universe. Most of the students' observations of the sky suggest that the Sun, Moon, planets, and stars move around the Earth.

Using an Earth-centered model to explain the movement of planets. 02 Bb Ca Fc
Explain that early records indicated that planets moved from west to east among the stars, but from time to time, one would seem to go backward and appear brightest halfway along the backward path. Students can see how an Earth-centered theory might explain the phenomena by putting a clay ball on one spoke of an umbrella to represent a planet, having a student hold the umbrella above his head and slowly rotate it while walking in a circle around another student who represents the Earth. Students can describe when the planet goes in the same direction that the student is walking and when it goes in the opposite direction. Discuss when it would seem to be brightest to an Earth observer if it reflected light. You might explain that according to an Earth-centered theory, the planet moved along a complicated path called an epicycle. (See Figure 423.02.) Students can research how a Sun-centered theory explained the same phenomena differently and in a less complicated way.

> *Contributing Idea B.* It is currently believed that there are eight planets that revolve at different distances around the Sun.

Making different theoretical models of the solar system. Have students use empty cardboard boxes and Styrofoam 03 Bb Bd Fc

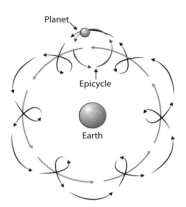

Figure 423.02

balls or clay to make models of the solar system according to an Earth-centered theory and a Sun-centered theory. Students can research and compare the two theories and discuss why astronomers now universally accept the Sun-centered theory. You might have students research the work of Claudium Ptolemy (second century AD), an Alexandrian astronomer who made the final major refinement of a centuries-old Earth-centered (*geocentric*) theory, and compare it to the work of Nicolaus Copernicus (1473–1543), a Polish astronomer who is credited for the Sun-centered (*heliocentric*) theory.

Making a Sun-centered model of the solar system. Use a 40 ft. (13 m) length of string and chalk to draw a circle on the playground. Within the circle, draw eight more circles at intervals that represent the average scale distance of planets from the Sun. Have eight students line up in a row, each on a different line. At 04 Bb Bd Fc a signal, let them move in counterclock-wise orbits. Observers will see the outer planets fall behind and that the various planets change in their distances from the Earth. Tell the students that when a planet makes one complete orbit around the Sun, the orbit is called a revolution. Some students might be interested in research-ing the revolution periods of the planets (see Table 423.04). The periods can be compared to the distances each planet is from the Sun.

Table 423.04. Listing of Revolution Periods of Planets

Planet	Time (in Earth Time)
Mercury	88 days
Venus	226 days
Earth	365 days (1 year)
Mars	688 days
Jupiter	12 years
Saturn	29 years
Uranus	84 years
Neptune	165 years

500–599
Technology and Engineering

510 Machines

511   Simple Machines

Generalization I. A machine is a human-made device that helps to make better use of forces.

> *Contributing Idea A.* Force is any push or pull on an object that causes that object to move.

Identifying some characteristics of force. Have students push and pull various objects such as books, tables, chairs, and desks to make them move. Let them describe their efforts (e.g., shove, tug, jerk, yank). Explain that scientists use the word *force* to describe all of the efforts they made. **01 Ab Bb**

Feeling force. Have students put the palms of their hands together, push, and describe what they feel. Have them hook two forefingers together, pull, and describe what they feel. Explain that in each case a force was exerted and that the force was either a push or a pull. **02 Ab**

> *Contributing Idea B.* An applied force is the effort used to move something; a counter force is anything opposing an applied force.

Identifying some characteristics of applied force and counter force. Have each student push a book with one finger. Explain that the effort used to move the book is called force. Now let **03 Ab Bb** students apply one finger of force to various objects in the classroom, and list the objects as being easy, hard, or impossible to move. Have them describe the different amounts of force they exerted. Explain that the objects they tried to move provided a *counter force*. Ask them to tell which objects in their listing provided the greatest or least counter force.

Feeling applied force and counter force. Have students manipulate various simple machines to feel the advantage each provides. For example, they can carry books across the room, and then repeat by carrying them in a wagon. Similarly, some students can lift a fairly heavy object by hand, and then repeat the action by using a pulley or lever. From several such experiences, they will realize that a certain amount of applied force is needed to overcome the counter force of an object. **04 Ab**

> *Contributing Idea C.* All machines lose some efficiency because of friction.

Feeling friction. Have students rub two blocks of wood together rapidly for a few minutes, then feel the blocks (they will be warm). Have them rub their hands together rapidly to feel the warming effect of the rubbing. Now have them rub various surfaces together (e.g., cotton over sandpaper, rough wood over rough wood) **05 Ab Bb**

and note the counter force in each case. Tell them that the counter force caused by one surface rubbing against another is called friction. Explain that as machines work, some of their parts rub together, the machines become less efficient, and the parts often become heated and wear out. This can be demonstrated by cutting out a cardboard wheel and putting a round pencil through the center of it. Be sure the wheel turns freely on the pencil. Spin the wheel several times and note each time how long it takes the wheel to slow down and stop. (If a mark is made on the wheel, students can count the number of revolutions it makes.) Now wrap a strip of sandpaper around the pencil, and spin the wheel again. Compare the spinning times (or revolutions) with those found in the earlier trials. Set the wheel so that its rim rests on a tabletop. Push gently downward and make the wheel roll across the table. Students can observe what happens to the center hole as you increase the downward pressure (as if the wheel were carrying a heavy load).

Finding evidence of friction. If students note worn objects such as shoe soles, flooring, eraser ends, and concave steps, they will be able to explain that each example is worn due to its rubbing against some other object. Let them find worn parts of some machines (e.g., tires on wagons and cars, axles on various toys, pivot or fulcrum points on levers **06 Ga**

such as seesaws). Have them feel the heat produced in machines due to friction (e.g., saw blades after sawing, motors after running, screws after being quickly unscrewed from a block of wood). From such experiences they will realize that friction produces heat and wear and that heat and wear are evidences of friction.

Using lubrication to reduce friction in machines. Various experiences can help students understand the effectiveness of lubrication in reducing friction. **07 Ga**

a. Students can note how a lubricant can reduce friction by first pressing a dry hand downward against a tabletop and pushing forward, then wetting the hand and repeating the action. The second attempt should be much easier due to the reduction of friction by the lubrication.

b. If students find a door hinge that squeaks, they will discover that the squeak is caused by two parts of the door (a second-class lever) rubbing together. Place a few drops of light oil on the squeaking hinge, and swing the door a few times. The squeak should be eliminated.

c. Bring a rusty wagon to class. Place a load in it and have students listen to the rubbing surfaces as the load is pulled. Place some oil on the surfaces to reduce the friction. Not only should there be a difference in the sound, but the load should be easier to pull.

d. Turn a rusty wagon or scooter upside down. Make a chalk mark on the rim of one wheel. Spin the wheel and have students note how many revolutions it makes. Add a few drops of oil to the axle and turn the wheel a few times to distribute the oil. Spin the wheel again with a force equal to the first spin. Students can count the revolutions. (The number will increase due to the reduction of friction.) Find other simple machines that will work more smoothly if they are oiled (e.g., scissors, shears, various wheels and axles). If students try to unscrew a jar lid or turn a doorknob with wet or soapy hands, they will realize that reducing friction is not always beneficial. Friction does help to keep nails in wood and people from sliding as they walk or climb slopes.

Using bearings to reduce friction. Have students try pushing a large book across a piece of sandpaper on a tabletop. Let them place a few marbles beneath the book and push again. (They will note that the marbles make pushing the book easier because one surface rolls over another instead of sliding across it.) By tying a **08 Ga** piece of string around the book and pulling it with a spring scale, a mathematical comparison of the effort can be made. Now substitute a few round pencils for the marbles to show that the rolling objects can be spherical or roller shaped. Using the spring scale, numerical comparisons between the two kinds of rolling objects (bearings) can be made. Another comparison can be made by rolling six pieces of modeling clay: three into a ball shape and three into a roller shape. Set a book on the first three, then on the second three. Students can judge which type of bearing could carry the heavier load without being flattened.

Making a model ball bearing. Have students try to spin a book on a tabletop or smooth floor. (It will not spin easily due to friction.) Next, place 15–20 marbles of uniform size on the table and cover them with a coffee can lid to hold them in place. Set the book on the lid, and spin it again. Explain that the device used is called a ball bearing. The advantage of the ball bearing can be measured by tying a string around the book, setting it on the table, and trying to pull it by the string with a spring scale. Repeat the procedure after placing the book on the ball bearing. If possible, obtain some commercial ball bearings to see how they are constructed. Students might also listen to the ball bearings in roller skates as you shake them. **09 Bb Fc**

Generalization II. Levers are simple machines that can be used to make work easier by helping to lift loads with less effort. The force needed to use a lever changes as the length of the applied-force arm is changed.

> *Contributing Idea A.* A first-class lever is one in which the pivot point (fulcrum) is between the applied force (effort) and the load or counter force (resistance).

Identifying the characteristics of a first-class lever. Obtain a sturdy board (approximately 1 in. × 4 in. or 2.5 cm × 10 cm) that is the same height as a table. Place a strong stick of the same length across the board and under the edge of the table as shown in Figure 511.10a. Let

10
Ab
Bb

(a)

First-Class Lever

(b)

Figure 511.10

several students press down on the stick to lift the table and discuss the effort it took. They will realize that the stick makes it easier to lift the table and that the closer to the end of the stick one presses, the easier it is to lift the table. Tell them that the device they used is called a first-class lever (see Figure 511.10b). Locate for them the *pivot point* (fulcrum), the *load* or *counter-force arm* (the portion of the stick on which the table or resistance rests), and the *applied-force arm* (the portion of the stick on which the students pushed).

Determining numerical patterns using the first-class lever. From a lumber yard, obtain sticks (similar to the wood used in yardsticks or metersticks) for individual students or small groups of students. Balance the sticks on blocks of wood so that they function as a first-class lever (see Figure 511.11). Let students place one checker (or other weight such as a marble

11
Bb
Cf
Fb

Figure 511.11

or a jack) in a cup on one end of the lever, and ask where the same weight must be placed on the other side to lift and balance the first one. Students can test to find out. Repeat the procedure by having students place the first checker in different positions to achieve balance. Next, place two or more checkers on top of each

Table 511.11. Determining Numerical Patterns Using the First-Class Lever

Load or Counter-Force Arm		Applied-Force Arm		Conclusions
Number of Weights	Distance From Pivot Point	Distance From Pivot Point	Number of Weights	
2	1	—	—	
2	2	—	—	
2	3	—	—	
—	—	—	—	

other, and have students test to see what is needed to achieve balance again. They will realize that balance is achieved when the same amount of weight is placed in the same position on the opposing arm. Now put two checkers 2 in. (5 cm) from the pivot point, and balance them using only one checker. Have students balance three, four, five, and then six checkers using only one checker. They will discover that the greater the load, the greater the distance needed if the balancing force remains the same. These tests can be reversed (balance one checker at one end with two, three, four, or more checkers on the other side), and combinations of distances can be tried. If the unmarked sticks are next marked at 1 in. (2 cm) intervals and the above experiences are repeated and the information tabled (see Table 511.11), students will discover that the distance times the load (weight) on one arm is equal to the distance times the applied force (weight) on the other arm. These experiences can also be done using a more sophisticated balance scale, and

measurements can also be made using a spring scale. Students can determine the mechanical advantage from the numerical patterns in the table. *Mechanical advantage* is the ratio of the force that performs useful work of a machine to the force applied.

Finding examples of first-class levers. 12 Ga
Bring to class tools that are variations of first-class levers (e.g., crowbar, hand can opener, claw hammer, tack puller). Students can find the pivot point, load or counter-force arm, and applied-force arm for each tool. They can compare the relative distances of the load and applied-force arms, and discuss the mechanical advantages of each tool. Some tools are made of double first-class levers (e.g., scissors, garden shears, wire cutters, tin or metal snips, forceps, pliers). Have students bring examples of double first-class levers to class. Show them how to use each kind of tool properly, and locate the pivot, applied-force, and counter-force points for each example.

Contributing Idea B. A second-class lever is one in which the load or counter force (resistance) is between the pivot point (fulcrum) and the applied force (effort).

Identifying the characteristics of a second-class lever. Obtain a wooden stick similar to a yardstick or meterstick and attach a weight to the center of it. Rest one end of the stick on a desk and raise the weight by lifting the other end as shown in Figure 511.13a. Explain that the device is called a second-class lever (Figure 511.13b). Students can locate the *pivot,* the *applied-force,* and the *counter-force* points. Let them compare and note differences between this and a first-class lever.

**13
Ab
Bb**

the stick between two uprights on a stand (Figure 511.14a). Place a small eye screw at the other end of the stick so that it can be lifted by a spring scale as shown in Figure 511.14b. Now hang a weight from different positions along the stick and note how much applied force on the spring scale is needed to lift the weight. Vary the position and continue testing; then repeat by varying the amount of weight to be lifted. If the measurements are tabled, students can note numerical patterns and derive the mechanical advantage. They should see that the closer the weight is to the pivot point, the less applied force is needed to lift it (or the farther the applied force is from the pivot point, the easier it is to lift the weight).

Figure 511.13

Figure 511.14

Determining numerical patterns using the second-class lever. Cut notches at 1 in. (2 cm) intervals along a wooden yardstick or meterstick. Attach one end of

**14
Cd
Cf
Fb**

Finding examples of second-class levers. Bring to class some tools and/or pictures of devices that are variations of second-class levers (e.g., bottle opener,

**15
Ga**

crowbar, rowboat oars, wheelbarrow, post puller, paper cutter). Students can find the pivot, applied-force, and counter-force points for each tool. Let them compare relative distances of the arms with the amount of force needed to work the tools. Have them also note that doors are second-class levers. They might speculate on why doorknobs are usually placed at the edge of the door, far from the fulcrum. Some tools are made up of two second-class levers put together (e.g., nutcracker, lemon squeezer). Have students bring examples to class. They can find the pivot, applied-force, and load or counter-force points for each example.

> *Contributing Idea C.* A third-class lever is one in which the applied force (effort) is between the pivot point (fulcrum) and the load or counter force (resistance).

Identifying the characteristics of a third-class lever. Obtain a wooden yardstick or meterstick, cut notches along it at 1 in. (2 cm) intervals, and set it between two uprights. Hang a weight from the free end, and have a student lift the weight by applying her effort to the center of the stick as shown in Figure 511.16a. Discuss differences in the effort when the weight is lifted from various positions along the stick. Tell students that the device is called a third-class lever (see Figure 511.16b). They can locate the *pivot,* the *applied-force*, and the *load* or *counter-force* **16 Ab Bb**

points. Compare the points with those of first and second-class levers.

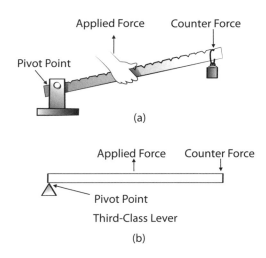

Figure 511.16

Determining numerical patterns using the third-class lever. Attach a weight to a third-class lever and lift the lever using a spring scale. Vary the position of the spring scale along the arm of the lever, and then repeat the procedure by varying the amount of weight to be lifted. If the measurements are tabled, students can note numerical patterns. They should also note that by applying the force at certain positions, the advantage is in the speed at which the lever moves rather than in a reduction of effort. **17 Cd Cf Fb**

Finding examples of third-class levers. Bring to class some tools and/or pictures of devices that are variations of third-class levers (e.g., shovel, pitchfork, broom, fishing pole, fly swatter, tennis **18 Ga**

and badminton rackets, golf club, spoon, baseball bat). Students can find the pivot, applied-force, and load or counter-force points for each device. By manipulating the various devices, they will find that the devices provide for more speed and distance, rather than more force. You might explain that the human arm is a version of the third-class lever and that a mouse trap, slingshot, and catapult are other variations. Some tools are made up of two third-class levers put together (e.g., ice cube tongs, sugar tongs, tweezers). Bring some examples to class, and let students find the pivot, applied-force, and load or counter-force points in each example.

Generalization III. Wheels and axles are simple machines that can be used to move a load farther than a lever can. The force needed to use a wheel and axle changes as the size of the applied force (effort) wheel changes.

>   *Contributing Idea A.* Wheels and axles are turning levers.

Identifying the characteristics of the wheel and axle. Use a compass to draw a 3 in. (5 cm) and a 6 in. (10 cm) diameter circle on double corrugated cardboard. Carefully cut out the two circles. Make sure the edges are smoothly and cleanly cut. Glue or staple the smaller circle to the center of the larger circle. Use a nail to punch a hole in the center of the joined circles. The circles are now like two

**19
Ab
Bb**

wheels joined together. Gently press the nail into the rim of each wheel to make a groove. Suspend the wheels from a long nail in a board, making sure they turn freely on the nail. Hang a long piece of twine or string over each wheel, and attach each piece to the groove with a pin. Suspend three weights, such as clothespins, from the free end of the string on the smallest wheel (see Figure 511.19a). Test to see how many weights are needed

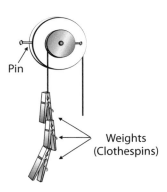

Pin

Weights
(Clothespins)

Figure 511.19a

on the other string to lift the first weights. Students will see that when one set of weights is pulled down, the other set goes up. When compared to a first-class lever, students will realize that the apparatus is a turning lever and has the advantage of being able to move a load farther than a first-class lever can (Figure 511.19b, p. 412). Point out that the larger of the two wheels turns the smaller and that the larger is called the wheel, while the smaller is called the axle. It is only when a wheel is fastened to an axle (or smaller

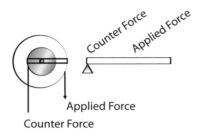

Figure 511.19b

wheel) in such a way that the turning of the wheel turns the axle, that we have a simple machine called the wheel and axle. Point out that the pivot point is at the center of the axle, the load is the weights suspended from the smaller wheel (the radius of the axle corresponds to the load or counter-force arm), and the applied force is on the larger wheel (the radius of the wheel corresponds to the applied-force arm) (Figure 511.19c). If possible, bring to class various kinds of wheels that turn axles (e.g., round-handled faucet dials, radio dials, doorknobs, bicycle pedals). Let students manipulate each kind of wheel and axle.

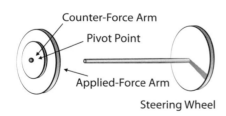

Figure 511.19c

Finding examples of wheels and axles. **20** **Ga** Bring to class several different forms of the wheel and axle (e.g., faucets without round handles, rolling pin, screwdriver,

pipe wrench, handlebars). Show how each is used. Students can locate the wheel and axle of each. Remove the cover from a manual pencil sharpener and point out that the handle is turned in the same way as a wheel turns an axle. Tie a piece of twine to the axle of the sharpener and lift a weight, such as a book, by turning the crank of the pencil sharpener. Students can describe the force it takes to lift the weight this way.

> *Contributing Idea B.* Large wheels can be used to turn smaller wheels with less applied force.

Determining numerical patterns using **21** **the wheel and axle.** Use the materi- **Bc** als from entry 511.19 and glue a 9 in. **Cf** (15 cm) diameter cardboard circle to the **Fb** back of the 6 in. (10 cm) diameter wheel. Tie a piece of twine to it, and let students determine how many weights must be attached to this twine to support four, six, or eight weights suspended from the smaller wheel. The measurements can be recorded, compared, and a mathematical rule derived. Other comparisons can be made between the large and middle size wheels or by reversing the starting positions of the weights (e.g., how many weights are needed on the small wheel twine to support or lift two, four, or six weights on the middle size or large wheel?) Students will discover that the mechanical advantage depends on the ratio of the radius of the wheel to the radius of the axle (or small wheel), and they will sense that the smaller wheel will take a greater amount of applied force to turn the larger wheel to lift the weights. To further emphasize this principle, have students try turning on a faucet when the handle (wheel) is removed. Add the wheel, and have them try again. Similarly, have them try to open a door by first turning the axle of the doorknob, then by turning the knob (wheel).

Testing the advantages of cranks. To help students realize the mechanical advantage of various handles or cranks, divide the class into pairs and give each pair a paper clip to straighten out. Have one student hold one end, the partner the other. Let each try to make the wire turn in the other's fingers without bending the wire. Now bend the wire at a right angle approximately 1 in. (2 cm) from the end (Figure 511.22a). Have one student turn the bent part as a crank while the other squeezes the unbent part and tries to turn it in the opposite direction. Discuss who is the most successful and why. Now have the student with the longer part of the wire use it as a crank to see if the length has any effect (Figure 511.22b). Students will find that length makes a difference. Next, have them make a second bend in some cranks to form handles, and test again. They will find that the second bend makes the cranks more convenient to turn. From these experiences they will

22
Ab
Ec

Figure 511.22

discover that the turning effect of the force depends not only on the strength of the force, but also on how far from the axle the force is applied. You might tell them that the distance is called the force arm and that a crank is simply a means of providing a longer force arm for a greater turning effect.

Generalization IV. Pulleys are simple machines that can be used to increase force and/or change the direction of force. The force needed to use a pulley changes as the number of ropes supporting the load or counter force is changed.

> *Contributing Idea A.* The pulley is a grooved wheel over which a rope is passed.

Identifying the characteristics of a pulley. Obtain an old pulley, such as a clothesline pulley, and demonstrate how it works. Let students note the groove around the wheel, its axle, and the way it can be suspended. Show them how a rope or cord passes around the wheel and sits in the groove. Suspend the pulley and let students lift some objects with it. Tell them that this simple machine is called a pulley.

23
Aa
Bb

Comparing pulleys with levers. Show students that the pulley is a modified form of the wheel and axle (it has a movable wheel and stationary axle much like wheels on skates and wagons), and thus is a variation of the lever. Let students locate the positions of the load or counter force, applied force, and pivot point on a pulley. If each kind of pulley is used, students will realize that the pulleys are similar either to a first-class lever (e.g., seesaw) or a second-class lever (e.g., wheelbarrow). In one case the pivot point is the pulley axle, in the other the load or counter force is at the axle.

24 Ca

Finding examples of pulleys. Have students find examples of pulleys at home or near school and report on what they find. They can collect pictures of people using pulleys (dockworkers loading ships, mechanics removing an engine from an automobile, sailors manipulating the boom and sail on a sailboat, operators using steam shovels or derricks, farmers using barn hoists or wells). They can arrange the pictures on a bulletin board by similarities in the uses of the pulleys.

25 Ga

Making a pulley. Students can make a simple pulley from a light wire clothes hanger and a large empty thread spool. Cut the hanger approximately 8 in. (20 cm) from either side of the hook and bend the ends at right angles so that they can be slipped through the spool (Figure 511.26a). Make sure the spools turn

26 Gc

easily, and then bend the wire ends down to keep them from spreading apart. Similarly, any stiff wire can be bent to hold a spool (Figure 511.26b), Pulleys can also be made by placing a nail through a wooden spool and attaching lightweight wire to the nail (Figure 511.26c). These pulleys can be used singly or in combinations. Due to a great amount of friction, they are not useful in showing how pulleys reduce work.

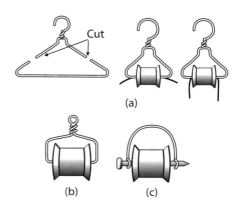

Figure 511.26

Contributing Idea B. A fixed pulley is one that is attached to a support and does not move; it changes the direction of the force, but does not change the force, the distance traveled, or the speed.

Examining a single fixed pulley. To study a single fixed pulley, distribute pulleys and strong twine, string, or pulley cord to individuals or small groups of students. Clothesline pulleys can be used and are fairly common. Inexpensive small pulleys can be obtained from

27 Ab Bb

hardware or variety stores. Mount pulleys to a hook on a wall, in a beam, or door frame. A sturdy board set across the high backs of two heavy chairs can also be used. Let students lift a book, rock, or similar object by tying it to one end of the twine. Run the other end over the pulley wheel, and balance the object by holding the free end. Lift an object (Figure 511.27), and have students describe the force needed to balance, raise, or lower it. Let them discuss if it takes less force to lift the object with the pulley or without it (it tends to be easier to pull downward to lift an object than upward because we can usually use the weight of our bodies to pull). From these activities students will realize that the single fixed pulley has an advantage only in changing the direction of the pull, such as when a flag is raised by pulling a rope downward. They will also note that the pulley is fixed and does not move from its attached position; thus, it is called a fixed pulley.

Figure 511.27

Using two single fixed pulleys. Have students note that in addition to moving objects vertically, fixed pulleys can be used to move objects horizontally. Put up a clothesline in the classroom or across the school yard using two fixed pulleys. Students can move materials from one end of the line to the other. Discuss the convenience of moving an object in this way. (Ski lifts operate in this manner.) **28 Ga**

Finding examples of single fixed pulleys. Have students find pictures or examples of fixed pulleys (e.g., flagpole pulley, window shade pulley, venetian blind pulley, stage curtain pulley, hay hoist, window weight pulley, clothesline pulleys). **29 Ga**

> *Contributing Idea C.* A movable pulley is one that is attached to a load or counter force (resistance) and moves as the load moves; it increases the force, but decreases the distance traveled and reduces the speed.

Examining a single movable pulley. Attach one end of some strong twine to a fixed hook and suspend a single movable pulley on the twine as shown in Figure 511.30 (p. 416). Hang a heavy object, such as a brick, from the pulley. Pulling upward on the twine will now raise the object. Have students locate the load or counter force, pivot, and applied-force points on this pulley. They will note that the pulley moves with the weight; thus it is called a movable pulley. **30 Ab Bb**

Figure 511.30

Determining numerical patterns using the single movable pulley. Several kinds of measurements can be made of a single movable pulley. The following suggest a few kinds. **31 Cd Cf Fb**

a. Attach a spring scale to the free end of a fixed pulley, then a movable pulley. Lift an object, and use rulers to measure the distance the object rises relative to the distance the twine is pulled. The measurements can be recorded in Table 511.31a.

b. Measure and record the relative speeds of the downward movement of the twine with the upward movement of the object. Stopwatches and rulers can be helpful in making observations. The data in Table 511.31a and Table 511.31b can be combined and/or graphed.

From the information, students will learn that single pulleys have no advantage; however, they offer a wide choice of directions from which a force can be applied to a load.

Contributing Idea D. The force needed to move a load or counter force is decreased as the number of pulleys in a system is increased (within limits).

Examining a simple block and tackle. Arrange a single fixed and a single movable pulley. This system of pulleys makes **32 Aa Bb Cf**

Table 511.31a. Determining Numerical Patterns Using the Single Movable Pulley

	Fixed Pulley	Movable Pulley	Conclusions
Distance Twine Was Pulled			
Distance Object Was Raised			
Force Needed to Lift Object			

Table 511.31b. Determining Numerical Patterns Using the Single Movable Pulley

	Fixed Pulley	Movable Pulley	Conclusions
Speed of Pull (Applied Force)			
Speed of Lift (Counter Force)			

up a simple *block and tackle*. Tie cup A to the movable pulley and cup B to the free end of the twine. Put four identical marbles (same size and weight) into cup A, and then add marbles to cup B, one at a time, until cup A rises (Figure 511.32). Record the number of marbles placed in cup B. Repeat this procedure using six marbles in cup A, then eight marbles, and so on. As a variation, the pulley system can be arranged to hang two identical books (or some known unit of weight) from the movable pulley. Students can find out how many identical books (weights) must be attached to the free end of the twine to balance the books. Still another variation would be to measure with a spring scale the force needed to lift an object.

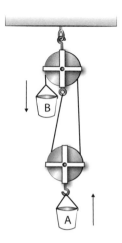

Figure 511.32

Determining numerical patterns using the simple block and tackle. Using any of the variations in entry 511.32, students can measure the distance through which the load or counter force and applied force move. All the gathered information can be recorded in Table 511.33a and 511.33b. By looking for numerical

**33
Bf
Cf
Fb**

Table 511.33a. Determining Numerical Patterns Using the Simple Block and Tackle

	Cup A		Cup B		
	Weight	Distance Moved	Weight	Distance Moved	Conclusions
1st Test	2 marbles				
2nd Test	4 marbles				
3rd Test	6 marbles				

Table 511.33b. Determining Numerical Patterns Using the Simple Block and Tackle

	Movable Pulley		Fixed Pulley		
	Weight	Distance Moved	Weight	Distance Moved	Conclusions
1st Test	2 books				
2nd Test	4 books				
3rd Test	6 books				

patterns in the data, students will discover that with a fixed and movable pulley system, a greater load can be moved with less applied force (e.g., four marbles can be raised using the weight of only two marbles); however, the distance traveled is reduced (e.g., for every two units the applied force moves, the load moves only one unit), and the speed by which it moves is reduced. Students can derive rules, and state them in their own words: The amount of applied force times the distance it moves (work input: 2 marbles × 2 units) is the same as the amount of load times the distance it moves (work output: 4 marbles × 1 unit).

Testing various pulley systems. If possible, obtain multiple pulleys, and let students test them in systematic combinations. Test each kind of pulley several times, and take an average of the findings. Dual wheels on the pulleys (either placed side by side or one above the other) simply allow the rope to pass over the same pulley several times without binding the

34
Bc
Ec
Fb

strands. Forces, distances, and speeds can be measured for each pulley arrangement and recorded in Table 511.34. Representations of the information on graphs will aid interpretations. From the tabled and graphed information students will realize mathematical rules pertaining to the pulley systems (e.g., applied force × distance moved = load or counter force × distance moved, but distance and speed are sacrificed for decreased effort; the advantage is proportional to the number of strands supporting the load).

Contributing Idea E. Drive belts are a form of pulley system that can be used to turn wheels and gears.

Using drive belts to turn gears, wheels, and pulleys. Hammer two nails into a board far enough apart to slightly stretch a rubber band between them. Place a small wooden spool over one nail and a larger spool over the other. Be sure the spools turn freely, and then slip the rubber band around both spools so that when one spool is turned, the other is also turned. Place a

35
Ga

Table 511.34. Testing Pulley Systems

		Test 1: Single Pulley			
		Number of Marbles	Distance Moved	(s = d/t) Speed of Movement	Conclusions
Trial 1	Cup A				
	Cup B				
Trial 2	Cup A				
	Cup B				
Trial 3	Cup A				
	Cup B				

mark on the edge of each spool with a pencil or crayon. Beginning with the mark, turn the large spool through one complete turn. Students can see how many times the small spool turns. They can notice that the smaller spool makes more than one full turn, seems to turn faster, and both spools turn in the same direction. To see if the length of a drive belt has anything to do with these factors, drive another nail farther away from the large spool and move the small spool to it. The rubber band will stretch tighter around both spools. Turn the large spool around once again to see if the smaller spool turns the same distance as before. Now twist the rubber band so that it forms a cross between the spools. Turn the larger spool again, and have students note what happens to the smaller spool (it makes more than one full turn, turns faster, and turns in the opposite direction). Students can try more spools and drive belts in creative arrangements to see what can be done with them. They can look for machines that use drive belts (e.g., clothesline pulley, bicycle chain, some motors).

Generalization V. Gears can be used to transfer forces from one part of a machine to another part.

> *Contributing Idea A.* Gears are toothed wheels.

Identifying the characteristics of gears. **36 Aa Bb** Cut gears out of heavy cardboard as shown in Figure 511.36. Let each student mount a gear on a board or heavy sheet of

cardboard so that it turns freely on a thin nail. Tell students that this object is called a gear. Let them compare the gear with a wheel or cardboard circle of the same diameter. They will realize that a gear is simply a wheel with teeth on it.

Figure 511.36

Comparing a gear to a lever. **37 Ca** Cut a gear and a lever out of heavy cardboard. Let each student mount the gear, then the lever on a cardboard sheet so that both turn freely on a thin nail. Note that when one gear tooth is pushed, the action is similar to the pushing on one end of a lever. Students will realize that opposite teeth on a gear form imaginary levers. They can locate the pivot, load, or counter force, and applied-force points on the gear (Figure 511.37).

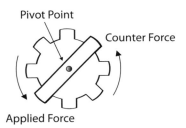

Figure 511.37

Contributing Idea B. With gears, the direction or speed of rotation of other objects can be changed.

Comparing the interactions of two gears to two levers. Cut two levers out of heavy cardboard: one 3 in. (7 cm), one 6 in. (14 cm). Mount them so that when one end of the smaller is pushed down, the other end will lift one end of the larger. Now prepare two cardboard gears to fit over the levers. Let students explore the movements of the gears and levers simultaneously (opposite teeth act as levers). They will realize that a gear acts like a turning lever and has the advantage of being able to move a load farther than a lever can. You might explain that in this example, a 1 lb. (0.5 kg) force applied to a tooth of the smaller gear makes it possible to push a tooth of the larger gear with a force of 1 lb. (0.5 kg), but since the larger gear is twice the diameter (its lever equivalent is twice as long), the 1 lb. (0.5 kg) of force provides 2 lb. (1 kg) of force to the larger gear. The mechanical advantage is compensated for as the smaller gear must go around twice to turn the larger gear once. Conversely, if the larger gear were used to turn the smaller, each turn would turn the smaller gear twice, but each pound of force would only provide ½ lb. (0.25 kg) of force to the smaller gear. You might wish to relate this to the gears in an automobile or bicycle. Low gear is the same as the largest gear and provides much power but little speed; high gear is

38 Ca

a smaller gear that provides little power but much speed.

Determining numerical patterns using gears. Cut two gears out of heavy cardboard (3 in. and 6 in. diameters or 5 cm and 10 cm diameters). Mount them so that their teeth mesh. (See Figure 511.39.) Be sure the gears turn freely on nails. Now turn the larger gear slightly to the right, then to the left and note how the smaller gear turns (it will always turn in the opposite direction). Mark one tooth on each gear so that students can keep track of the distance each moves. If they turn the large gear around once, they can keep count of how many times the smaller gear turns and whether it turns faster or slower. If they turn the smaller gear around once, they can note the effect it has on the larger gear. From these tests students can decide to which gear they would apply force to make something turn faster or slower. Have them make an even larger gear with

39 Bc Cc Fb

Figure 511.39

Table 511.39. Determining Numerical Patterns Using Gears

Number of Teeth on Largest Gear 32	Number of Teeth on Middle-Size Gear 16	Number of Teeth on Smallest Gear 8	Conclusions
Number of Turns	Number of Turns	Number of Turns	
1	—	—	
2	—	—	
3	—	—	
—	—	—	

32 teeth, 12 in. (30 cm) diameter. Turn this large gear and record its relationship to the smaller ones. Record information in Table 511.39, and students will discover the relationships between numbers of teeth on gears and the relative numbers of rotation each makes. They will realize that the mechanical advantage is determined from the ratio of the number of teeth on each gear. The gear ratio in this example is 8 to 16 to 32; the middle sized gear rotates twice for every full turn of the larger gear, while the smaller turns four times.

Generalization VI. Inclined planes are simple machines that can be used to raise an object from one level to another with less force; the force needed to use an inclined plane changes as the tilt of the plane changes.

> *Contributing Idea A.* Inclined planes are flat, sloping surfaces along which an object can be pushed or pulled to move it to a higher level; the shallower the slope, the easier the work.

Identifying the characteristics of an inclined plane. Lay one very wide board, or two less wide boards, from the ground to the top of three or four steps. Take a fairly heavy, wheeled object (e.g., wagon) or round object (e.g., barrel) and compare the exertion involved in pulling or pushing it up the board with that of lifting the object to the same height. Next, have students use wooden planks to answer such questions as the following: If you make the slope longer but to the same height, will it be harder or easier to pull something up it? If you have two sloping boards of the same length, but different heights, which will be easier to walk up? Tell students that a sloping or slanting surface that connects a lower level to a higher level is called an inclined plane. **40 Ab Bb**

Finding examples of inclined planes. Have students locate some examples of inclined planes around home, school, or in pictures from magazines (e.g., sloping floors in theaters or auditoriums, straight roads up hills, planks, ramps). Have students find two or more objects in the **41 Ga**

classroom that were probably moved up an inclined plane to get them inside the school.

Determining numerical patterns using inclined planes. Have a student prepare an inclined plane by stacking several books to raise one end of a 4 ft. (120 cm) board to a height of 1 ft. (30 cm). Have another student attach a spring scale to a wheeled object such as a toy dump truck or roller skate. By holding the spring scale, lift the object vertically to the 1 ft. (30 cm) height of the board. Record the amount of pull needed to lift the object and the distance it moved. Now slowly pull the object up the inclined plane to the top. Record the amount of pull and the distance traveled. Compare this information with the previous information, and let students describe any difference in the amount of work in each situation. They will see that the inclined plane reduces the amount of force needed to lift the object, but the distance traveled is greater. They should note that the second reading is about one-fourth that of the first reading; hence, the advantage of this inclined plane is four: the length of the ramp (4 ft. or 120 cm) divided by the height (1 ft. or 30 cm). The work in both cases is the same; however, some differences in measuring may appear due to friction. This activity can be varied by making the slope greater, increasing its length, or by increasing the weight of the

42 Bc Cd Fb

object to be moved (e.g., a brick can be placed in the toy truck or tied onto the roller skate). In each case, the amount of force times the distance traveled ($f \times d$) can be compared. Students will see that by raising the board to different heights or increasing its length, different advantages will be produced. If such tests are done systematically (e.g., raising the board 6 in. or 15 cm at a time for each test), and measurements are carefully recorded and tabled, mathematical patterns can be obtained and statements of a rule can be derived.

Contributing Idea B. The wedge is two inclined planes placed back to back.

Identifying the characteristics of the wedge. Glue two identical inclined planes together. Show how this "new" shape can be tapped under the leg of a table or edge of some heavy object to lift it easily. Explain that this object is a double inclined plane and is called a wedge. If possible, obtain a hammer and wedge and split a log or piece of wood with it, then split the wood with an axe or hatchet. Students can compare the shape of the wedge with the shape of the axe head (both are double inclined planes). **Caution: When using such tools, keep students a safe distance from the operation.**

43 Aa Bb

Recognizing varieties of wedges. Bring a variety of wedge-type tools to the classroom for students to handle and use

44 Ga

(e.g., chisels, needles, pins, nails, knives, saws, can openers). They will realize that most cutting tools are various forms of the wedge or double inclined plane. Students can also realize that the main difference between the inclined plane and wedge-type tools is that the inclined plane remains stationary while an object is moved over it and the wedge is moved or forced into an object that remains stationary. Let students observe how the blades of scissors force their way into a piece of cardboard, examine the edges of the blades, and note that a pair of scissors is a combination of two wedges (the cutting edges) that pivot as first-class levers. You might instruct in how to use a saw, having students note that the teeth are wedge-shaped. Students can find other examples of wedges at home or in pictures (e.g., trowel, spade, hoe, sickle, door stop, airplane wheel block, carpenter's plane, fork, front of bulldozer, bow of ship, nose of airplane, woodpecker's bill, certain teeth).

Sensing the advantage of wedges. For each of the following experiences, have students note that the steepness of slopes is related to the ease with which the wedge-type machine is operated.

45
Af

    a. Look at the slopes at the points of different nails of the same thickness. Drive the nails into a block of wood and compare the force

needed in relation to the slope of the point.

    b. Obtain a dull-bladed knife and a sharp-bladed knife. Examine each knife blade by pressing one side flat against a table and noting that it forms an inclined plane. Turn the knife blade over and note that this side also forms an inclined plane. Students will realize that a knife blade is a form of the wedge. Use the knives to cut a piece of wood. Ask if the slopes of the blades, which differ due to dullness, seem to make any difference in the ease with which each cuts. **Caution: Demonstrate the proper handling of a knife and point out that carving is done away from the body.**

    c. Cut two wedges from a piece of wood. Both wedges should be the same thickness; however, the slopes on one should be about four times as long as the slopes on the other. Let students take turns seeing which is the easier wedge to drive into the ground. Students will realize that a gradual slope reduces the effort but increases the distance traveled to spread the earth a given amount. Such an advantage and disadvantage can be related to real experiences. For example, students can share experiences they have had on hikes (walking straight up a hill versus zigzagging up the hill) or bike rides (riding straight up a hill versus winding up the hill).

Contributing Idea C. The screw is a special kind of inclined plane that is wound or threaded around a shaft.

Identifying the characteristics of the screw (winding inclined plane). Have half the class cut right angle triangles from paper (5 in. base and 4 in. side or 15 cm base and 10 cm side). Have the other half of the class cut a different set of right angle triangles (10 in. base and 4 in. side or 20 cm base and 10 cm side). Point out how the sloping sides are like those of an inclined plane. Discuss the advantage provided by a shallow slope over a steep slope. Now have students roll their triangles around a pencil beginning at the short sides and rolling toward the far points. Make sure the baselines of the triangles are kept even. Hold the paper in place with a piece of tape. When finished, students can note that the length of the inclined plane spirals up and down the pencil. (Suggestion: If the longest side of each triangle is colored first, it will be easier for the students to follow the spiral.) Tell them that this form of the inclined plane is called a screw. An analogy can be made to wood screws. Students can predict which screw would be easier to turn by observing the slopes of the spirals. Another analogy can be made to roads and staircases that spiral.

46 Aa Bb

Finding examples of screws. Bring to class different forms of the screw (e.g., wood and metal screws, nuts and bolts, automobile jacks, C-clamps) and various machines that make use of the screw (e.g., vises, meat grinders, faucets, brace and bit). You might explain that propellers are another form of the screw, although this form is less recognizable.

47 Ga

512   Complex Machines

Generalization. A complex machine is made up of two or more simple machines.

> *Contributing Idea.* Some complex machines can do work.

Defining work. Work involves moving something. For example, one does work when carrying a book across the room. Work is a product of a force moving some distance. Since force is usually measured in pounds, ounces, or Newtons, and distance is measured in ft., in., or meters, work, as a product of the two, is measured in foot/pounds, inch/ounces, or Newton/meters. To help students understand this concept, obtain an object that weighs 1 lb. (0.5 kg). Many items in grocery stores come in 1 lb. packages or cans. Place the object on the floor and have them lift it to the top of the table. Tell them that when a force is used to move an object, the result is called work. Now have students hold the weight in their hands without lifting or lowering it. Ask if they are doing any work (no) and if they are exerting any

01 Bb Cd Cf

force (yes, 1 lb. of force). Explain that the work can be measured. For example, if the table is 3 ft. high, the student did 3 foot/pounds of work (1 lb. lifted 3 ft.; 1 lb. × 3 ft. = 3 foot/pounds). Ask how much work would have been done if the book had been lifted 10 ft. (10 foot/pounds) or 100 ft. (100 foot/pounds).

Measuring work. It is possible to determine how much work is involved in climbing stairs or a ladder by having each student write his weight on a sheet of paper and walk up a flight of stairs. Each student can calculate the amount of work done (weight × height of stairs = amount of work).

02
Cd
Cf

Identifying the components of a complex machine. Bring various complex machines to class and have students examine and identify the various simple machines from which they are made (shovels, hoes, and axes have lever handles and wedge blades; lawn mowers, pencil sharpeners, and meat grinders are made up of screws, wedges, wheels, and axles; the jaws of pipe wrenches and monkey wrenches open and close with a screw and act as a wheel and lever when used).

03
Ga

Making a water-powered machine that will do work. The following complex machine is a combination of a wheel and axle and pulleys (drive belts). Have students use a compass to draw two circles

04
Ga
Gc

with 3 in. (7.5 cm) diameters on the sides of a milk carton. Keeping the compass open at 1½ in. (3.75 cm), let them mark the circumference of each circle into six equal parts and draw lines across the circle to connect opposite marks. From another side of the milk carton, cut six 2 in. × 1 in. (4 cm by 2 cm) strips and fold them to form tabs ½ in. (1 cm) from each end as shown in Figure 512.04a. Glue or staple the folded strips between the two circles (Figure 512.04b). Carefully insert a six-sided pencil through the center of the circles so that it fits tightly and turns as the circles turn. The apparatus is now a waterwheel and can be inserted into slots cut into another milk carton (Figure 512.04c, p. 426). The waterwheel will turn if it is placed under a running faucet. A string tied to the end of the pencil can be used to lift various objects by water power (Figure 512.04d, p. 426). Have students cut a second slot into the carton and insert another pencil that has a spool glued to one end of it. Slip a rubber band

(a)

(b)

Figure 512.04a–b

Figure 512.04c–e

(not too tight or too loose) around the spool and the pencil as shown in Figure 512.04e. Challenge students to design the spool so that it will do some work, then measure what work it does.

520 Communications

521 Simple Devices

Generalization I. Communication is the interchange of thoughts and ideas.

> *Contributing Idea A.*
> Communication can be silent.

Communicating without language. **01 Ba Bd Gb** Using colored cocktail toothpicks, have students devise ways to place them on paper to communicate an idea or story. The toothpicks can be broken, bent, or combined in any way. When finished, let students try to decode each other's idea or story. They can discuss the advantages and disadvantages of trying to communicate without using the symbols of our language. Some might be interested in looking up information on Egyptian hieroglyphics or Asian characters. Others might research information on smoke signals.

Communicating with flags. **02 Ba** Have students make several sets of flags out of sticks and cloth or paper. They can send messages to each other across a playground using a basic signal code such as the semaphore alphabet. Some might be interested in researching information on semaphore signals and the uses of flags in communication.

Communicating with light. **03 Ga** Have students stand at opposite ends of the school grounds and flash messages to each other using mirrors. With practice, they can send "dots" and "dashes" and use the Morse or International Codes for relaying ideas. They will find that when the Sun is behind them, they can use two mirrors to send a message.

Writing invisible messages. **04 Bc Gb** Have students use a solution on the ends of a match, toothpick, or cotton swab to write an "invisible ink" message. When dry, such writing disappears but becomes visible again when held over a heat source such as a hot plate or lightbulb. "Invisible ink" can be prepared in several ways.

   a. Write a message using milk or lemon juice. Letters will turn brown when held near heat. Students can also try various household bleaches (e.g., chlorine bleach) to see which make good "inks." **Caution: Follow all safety guidelines when using bleach in the classroom.**

   b. Dissolve $1/3$ oz. (3.5 g) of cobalt chloride and $1/3$ oz. (3.5 g) of gum arabic in 1 oz. (28 g) of water. Stir thoroughly. The writing will turn blue when heated and will disappear again when it cools.

> *Contributing Idea B.* Nonverbal and verbal communication can be achieved using sound.

Communicating nonverbally with sound. **05 Ba Bd** Students can blow long and short blasts on various whistles to send coded messages to each other. The Morse or International Codes can be used. A simple signal whistle can be made by cutting a 5 in. (13 cm) long twig that is nearly round and smooth from either a willow or green sycamore tree. Slice a slanting piece from one end to form the lip of the whistle (Figure 521.05a). Cut a notch at the top of the lip and a ring just through the bark at the other end (Figure 521.05b). Soak the twig in water for an hour, occasionally tapping the bark to loosen it. Slip off the bark from in front of the ring in one piece. Dry the surface of the underwood and enlarge the notch by cutting wood away from the pointed end (Figure 521.05c). Now cut a thin strip from the top surface of the underwood between the notch and the pointed end as shown in Figure 521.05d. When the bark is replaced (Figure 521.05e),

Figure 521.05

the whistle can be blown to give a clear note. Some students might be interested in researching how drums are used for communication.

Making and using a simple telegraph key. Students can build a telegraph key as shown in Figure 521.06. Messages can be sent by clicking the bottle caps together. **06 Ga Gc**

Figure 521.06

Making and using a simple telephone. Obtain approximately 30 ft. (10 m) of string. Make a tiny hole in the bottoms of two empty cans, paper cups, or round cartons. Pull one end of the string through the hole in each from the inside out. Tie the string ends to a button or nail to hold them in place. Now have students hold the cans at their rims and pull the string straight and tight. You can talk into one can while someone listens at the other. Experiment with the materials by trying fishlines or different wires. Try waxing the string by rubbing along it with a candle. Students will find that the more solid materials are better carriers of sound. Challenge them to devise a way for four students to communicate on the same line. **07 Ga Gb Gc**

Generalization II. Mechanical devices can be constructed to aid the communication of thoughts and ideas.

> *Contributing Idea A.* Some mechanical devices can play a part in the interchange of ideas.

Making a device to code and decode written messages. Students can make two cardboard circles with identical diameters. Evenly space the letters of the alphabet around the edge of one circle as shown in Figure 521.08a. Place the second circle on top of the first and cut out two squares opposite each other as shown in Figure 521.08b. Mount the circles on a board with a pin or small nail (Figure 521.08c). To code a message, set one hole over the letters of the words one wishes to send, but write the letters that appear in the opposite hole (e.g., COME QUICK = PBZR DHVPX). To decode the message, reverse the procedure. Let students create other code devices. Some might place

08
Bc
Ga
Gb

the holes in different positions, and others might use other symbols in the hole opposite the letter hole.

Making a device to decode written messages. Students can type or write (double-spaced) many independent words on a page and insert among them the words of a message. When finished, they can place a sheet of paper over the page and cut out rectangles to reveal the words of the message. To decode the message, place the decoder sheet over the page and read the message that appears in the spaces.

09
Bc
Ga

> *Contributing Idea B.* The heliograph is a device that uses light to send messages.

Building and using a heliograph. Students can construct an apparatus to send light messages by fastening a horizontal board to an upright 2 ft. × 4 ft. (60 cm × 120 cm) stake. The horizontal board should be 6 ft. (180 cm) long and mounted so that it can rotate. Scratch a $^3/_8$ in. (1 cm) peephole in the center of a 4 in. × 4 in. (10 cm by 10 cm) mirror, set it in a picture-frame molding, and fasten the molding to a U-shaped frame so that it can be tilted (see Figure 521.10a, p. 430). Mount the U-shaped frame to one end of the horizontal board so that it can be rotated. Build Frame #1 out of light wood or cardboard with a 3 in. (7.5 cm) square hole cut in its center. Fasten wires or string across the hole so that they cross accurately in the center as

10
Bb
Ga
Gc

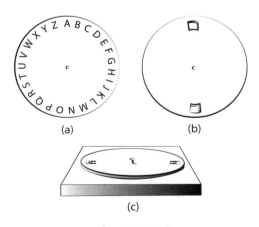

(a)   (b)

(c)

Figure 521.08

shown in Figure 521.10b. Set the frame in a strip of wood so that it can be moved back and forth on the horizontal board. Build Frame #2 in the same way except that the hole in the center should be 2 in. (5 cm) square. Mount it at the other end of the board (see Figure 521.10c). After construction, pick a location to which students would like to send a message.

Figure 521.10

Have them look through the peephole in the mirror and adjust the horizontal piece of the framework and the two frames so that the receiving location appears where the two wires cross in each frame. Now hold a sheet of paper over Frame #1, and turn the mirror until the dark spot formed by the peephole shows on the place where the wires cross. To signal, shut off the rays of light by placing cardboard or

wood in front of Frame #2. With practice, a series of long and short flashes can be made to send messages using the Morse or International Codes. (Note: If the Sun is behind the sender, an additional mirror is needed to reflect a beam of light onto the mirror on the horizontal board.) You might tell students that the device they have made is called a heliograph (from the Greek words meaning "sun-writer"). Two heliographs can be used to send messages between rooftops or hilltops.

522   Complex Devices

Generalization. Electrical devices can be constructed to aid the communication of thoughts and ideas.

> *Contributing Idea A.* The telegraph is an electrical device for communicating at a distance by signals.

Building and using a model telegraph system. Arrange four batteries in series and attach to them two telegraph keys made from clothespins. Attach two bulbs into the system. Provide enough wire so that one bulb and key can be placed in another room. (See Figure 522.01.) The Morse or International Codes can be used to send messages by flashing the bulb in short and long "dots" and "dashes." As a variation, place receiving keys or buzzers into the system in place of the bulbs. Some students might research the work

01
Ba
Gc

of Samuel Morse (1791–1872) who built the first practical telegraph.

Figure 522.01

Contributing Idea B. The telephone is an electrical device for reproducing sounds at a distance.

Hearing sounds through a telephone receiver. Obtain a telephone receiver from a surplus store. Fasten one wire from it to a battery and the other to the end of a metal file. Attach one more wire to the negative pole of the battery and scrape the free end across the parallel grooves on the file. Students will hear the sound that is made and realize that the current varies because of the interruption of the grooves, thus causing the disk in the receiver to vibrate and produce sounds. Students can take a receiver apart to see how the diaphragm vibrates.

02 Ac

Building and using a model telephone system. Cut two grooves in the top of a hollow box such as a cigar box. Insert the back of a razor blade in each and glue each firmly in place. Prepare a second box in the same way. Fasten wires to the razor blades, to two telephone receivers (available from surplus stores), and to

03 Ga Gc

four batteries arranged in series as shown in Figure 522.03. Set one length of pencil lead across each set of razor blades. **Caution: Take precautions when handling razor blades. Do not allow students to handle the razor blades or the system.**

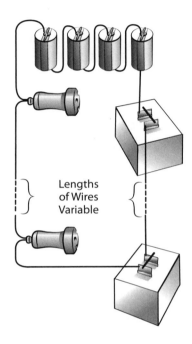

Lengths of Wires Variable

Figure 522.03

Students will be able to hear the contact through the receivers. Now talk against the top of the box. (This will cause the box to vibrate, which in turn causes the pencil lead to vibrate on the razor blades. The vibrating lead interrupts the electric current, which causes the diaphragm in the receiver to vibrate in the same way to produce the sound.) Students can also watch as sand is poured onto one box or a loudly ticking clock is brought near it to hear the sound made through the receiver. Adding longer wires to the system will allow communication between different rooms. Challenge students to suggest various improvements to the system. (They might suggest adding more batteries or placing paper megaphones into the boxes.)

> *Contributing Idea C.* The radio is an electrical device for transmitting signals without means of connecting wires.

Building and using a radio. Interested students can obtain the parts necessary to build an inexpensive crystal set from most radio stores. Let them see if there are some areas of the playground that pick up programs better than others. Discuss how the radio and television have speeded up communications, and list the advantages and disadvantages of the increased speed.

04
Ga
Gc
Fa

> *Contributing Idea D.* The computer is a programmable electronic device.

Comparing electronic devices. Provide a variety of comparable electronic devices and have students compare their features. Data on each can be obtained from the internet. Have them decide which is "best" (e.g., rank them) based on particular usages. Have them note that different devices might be "best" for different purposes. Some possible items to compare: desktops, laptops, digital cameras, cell phones, tablets, audio players, and printers.

05
Ca
Da

Experiencing how a simple binary program works in a computer. Have students line up side-by-side and facing you. Tell them that they will arrange themselves by their birthdates with the youngest person being at the far right end of the line and the oldest at the left. The rules for doing this are to have students: turn to a person next to him/her; compare their birthdates (year, month, date). The "older" person moves one place to his/her left, the "younger," one place to the right. When next to another person, compare again. Students keep moving position one at a time until no more moves can be made. Have students say their birthdates beginning with the youngest. Explain that this is the way a binary program works (one "yes" or "no" decision at a time) to sort information by one-to-one correspondences. Students might be surprised when they find two or more people were born on the same date.

06
Fc

Using a computer for different purposes. Student can use computers in several ways. They can learn important computing skills using utility programs like word processing, spreadsheets, and presentation software. Some examples are below.

07
Ga
Ba
Bb
Bc
Bd
Be
Bf
Bg

   a. *Locating Information.* The internet makes available much more information than you can obtain in any one source. Activities that require internet research are limitless. Students can be asked to research the life of a particular scientist; examine the life during a historical time period; see time-lapse photography of important events; visit locations that are distant in time and space. Locating information can be attached to assignments requiring students to report findings as written documents or PowerPoint presentations. **Caution: Students should be taught how to tell accurate information from incorrect or unsubstantiated information. They should also be instructed on plagiarism. Spend time teaching students about computer viruses and the importance of firewalls and antivirus programs. Teach them computer courtesies. Warn them about chatting with strangers.**

  b. *Word Processing.* It is valuable to teach students the fingering for typing on a computer keyboard. Research shows that this improves the speed of production on a computer and improves spelling (without a spell checker). Formatting and learning how to insert images improves the appearance and readability of documents. Many of the findings from activities in this book can be written as reports.

  c. *Visual Presentations.* Have students prepare a slide show using a program such as PowerPoint. This can be done individually or in groups. Preparing a visual presentation develops communication skills and invites creativity. Such presentations can be done in reporting the findings of many of the activities in this book.

  d. *Mathematical Calculations.* Computers can store and manipulate numerical data in several ways. The production of tables, spreadsheets, and graphs can accompany many of the activities in this book.

  e. *Collaboration.* Computer data can be collected and shared among different classes and schools. Teacher planning is needed to accomplish this. Here are a few collaborative studies that make use of computers:

    • *Studying weather:* Link many schools studying weather across a large area. Pool data, track weather phenomena, and make predictions. Local weather stations can link to the schools to share data and to use data from students. Schools might also link to schools in other countries. Through e-mail exchanges, they can share weather data about their own locations and learn about weather in other locations.

- *Tracking illnesses:* If schools are linked across a large area, students can enter some information regarding illnesses (e.g., coughs, sneezes, colds, flu symptoms, and so on.). Some illnesses can be tracked as they move across an area.

Local medical facilities can be invited to link with this research and to provide medical information to schools.

These suggestions are starter ideas. Creative teachers will springboard from these suggestions to other topics of science in which a computer can be effectively used.

530 Transportation

531 Simple Vehicles

Generalization. Transportation is the carrying of objects from one place to another.

> *Contributing Idea A.* Some vehicles can be powered by mechanical means.

Building a vehicle to travel on land. 01 Ec Gc
Hammer a finishing nail into one end of a wooden spool. Be sure it is midway between the hole and rim and that it protrudes approximately ⅓ in. (0.5 cm). With a file, make eight equidistant notches on each end of the spool. Obtain a candle with a ¾ in. (2 cm) or 1 in. (2.5 cm) diameter. Cut a ½ in. (1 cm) slice from its base and remove the wick. Put a thick rubber band through the wick's hole and the spool so that the slice of candle is against the end without the nail. Insert a dowel that is shorter than the diameter of the spool through the rubber band on the nail side of the spool. Through the other end of the rubber band, insert a second dowel that is three times longer than the diameter of the spool. (See Figure 531.01.) Use the longer dowel as a lever to wind up the vehicle. Observe how it travels across different surfaces. Challenge students to improve the vehicle (e.g., who can build one to push or pull the most weight, climb the steepest incline, or travel the greatest distance). They can also compare the working of larger and smaller spools.

Some might alter the vehicle by attaching paddles so that it will travel in water.

Figure 531.01

> *Contributing Idea B.* Some vehicles can be powered by action and reaction.

Building a vehicle to travel on water. 02 Gc
Punch a small hole at one edge of the base of a toothpowder can or similar can with a screw top. Half-fill the can with water, cap it, and then suspend it horizontally above a candle in a plastic dish. Light the candle and place the vehicle in a large container of water. (See Figure 531.02.) Students will see that when the water boils, steam escapes from the small hole, and the vehicle moves on the water like a boat.

Figure 531.02

Building a vehicle to travel in air. Inflate 03 Gc
a sausage-shaped balloon, and hold the air in by placing a clothespin on the opening.

Tape a straw on the side near the top of the balloon, then fasten approximately 20 ft. (6 m) of string to a post and thread the string through the straw. Hold the string firmly, and remove the clothespin. Students will see that when the clothespin is removed, air escapes from the balloon's opening, and the vehicle travels through the air like a jet or rocket (Figure 531.03).

Figure 531.03

532 Complex Vehicles

Generalization I. Various structural elements of an aircraft influence its ability to fly and the nature of its flight.

Contributing Idea A. The wind tunnel is a chamber through which air is forced at controlled velocities in order to study the airflow around objects suspended within it.

Building and using a wind tunnel. Build a honeycomb from quart (liter) milk cartons with both ends removed, or obtain separations from egg cartons and reinforce their corners with tape. The honeycomb separators will straighten swirling air currents from an electric fan. Now push the flaps inward at both ends of a corrugated box to make the box sturdier. Fit the separators into one end of the box. Cut a window in the side of a 4 ft. (120 cm) long piece of furnace pipe and cover the window with an overhead transparency. Fasten hooks at the top and bottom of the pipe opposite the window. Next, place a small fan that has several speeds in the box facing the

**01
Ga
Gc**

Figure 532.01

Labels: Box With Fan in It; Egg Carton or Milk Carton Separators; Window Covered With Acetate; Test Wing; Wedges to Keep Pipe From Rolling; Pan of Dry Ice and Hot Water; Test Stand; Furnace Pipe separators, and push the separators against the pipe at the end away from the window. Various test objects can be placed in the pipe opposite the window or suspended from the hooks. The velocity of the wind in the tunnel can be measured with a wind-speed indicator. A source of fog or smoke can be added to make the air in the tunnel more visible as it moves across the parts of the test object. This can be done by (1) putting dry ice and hot water in a low pan between the separators and the object and (2) setting several lit punks in front of the object. (See Figure 532.01.) (Note: The tunnel will work fairly well without the section of furnace pipe.)

> *Contributing Idea B.* Aircraft wings are shaped so that when air blows under and over them, the upward pressure is greater than the downward pressure.

Observing the shapes of wings. Have students observe the wings of aircraft in photographs and on model airplanes. They will note that the top of a wing is somewhat curved while the underside is generally straight. Slow-moving planes such as gliders have wings shaped for great lifting power. Moderate-speed planes have wings shaped for moderate lifting power. High-speed planes, such as jets, have wings shaped for very little lifting power. Tell students that the front edge of a wing is called the leading edge and the back is called the trailing edge. As a plane moves,

**02
Aa
Bb**

air flows across the wing from the leading edge to the trailing edge.

Building and testing wings of different shapes. Students can cut two identical wing shapes from cardboard. Fold a piece of cardboard with slots cut in it to support the shapes (Figure 532.03a). Glue toothpicks between the wing cardboard pieces to make a wing frame as shown in Figure 532.03b. After the glue dries, remove the frame from the cardboard, and wrap the frame with paper by beginning at the trailing edge, going around the leading edge, and then returning to the trailing edge (Figure 532.03c). Now sand one

**03
Ec
Ga
Gc**

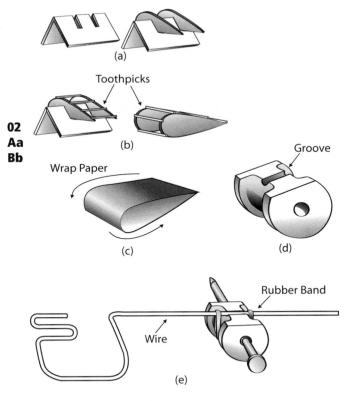

(a)

Toothpicks

(b)

Wrap Paper

Groove

(c)   (d)

Rubber Band

Wire

(e)

Figure 532.03

side of a wooden spool to flatten it, and then cut a small groove across the center (Figure 532.03d, p. 437), Bend a clothes hanger and fasten it to the spool with a rubber band (Figure 532.03e, p. 437). The wire works best if it has three spring tension pressure points on the inside of a test wing. Next, nail the spool to a stand, place a test wing on the wire, and set it in a wind tunnel (see entry 532.01).

Observing that air blowing against the underside of a wing helps to lift it. 04 Aa Have students hold a stiff sheet of paper slanted downward from front to back under the palm of one hand and run with it. They will find that it will not fall because the air pushes against it as they run. They can understand that if the air was blowing hard enough, they could stand still and the sheet would not fall. Make an analogy to an aircraft wing. Explain that when an aircraft moves, air pushes against the tilted underside of the wing and helps to lift it just as it did the piece of paper.

Observing that air moving rapidly across the top surface of a paper tube can cause the tube to rise. 05 Aa Fa Roll a sheet of paper into a tube and set it horizontally on a table against two upright pencils or sticks. Have a student blow hard through a large diameter straw so that the air passes just over the tube. (The tube will rise.) Explain that the rapidly moving air above the tube caused a decrease in air pressure above the tube, thus the greater air pressure below lifted the tube. Now challenge students to see who can make the tube rise the highest. Similarly, students can note the reduction in air pressure of a rapidly moving air stream by blowing air between two suspended strips of paper, table tennis balls, spoons, or other objects.

Observing that air moving rapidly across the top surface of a wing helps to lift it. 06 Aa Fa Place a 2 in. × 10 in. (5 cm × 25 cm) strip of paper between the pages of an upright book so that it hangs out over the top. Use a large diameter straw and have students blow a stream of air across the top surface of the piece of paper. (The paper will rise.) Fasten a paper clip to the end of the strip and blow again. Repeat to see how many paper clips can be lifted by the stream of air. Explain that when air moves rapidly, it is accompanied by a decrease in air pressure and since the decrease on the top side of the paper is less than on the lower side, the greater air pressure underneath pushes the paper upward. Now make an analogy between the lifting of the strip of paper to an aircraft wing by making a section of wing from the strip of paper. Place a pencil through the wing, and use the straw to blow across the top of it.

Observing that air tends to hold back forward movement of an aircraft wing if it is improperly designed. 07 Aa Bb Fa Place a lit candle or burning punk on a table and

(a)

(b)

Figure 532.07

hold a 3 in. × 3 in. (7.5 cm × 7.5 cm) piece of cardboard approximately 2 in. (5 cm) from the candle. Have a student blow hard against the card as shown in Figure 532.07 (the flame will flicker toward the card). Explain that swirls of air eddy around the edges of the card and slow down the air flow to the extent that a backward pull, called drag, is created. Now let students see how drag can be minimized by placing the candle or punk at the trailing edge of a wing made by curving a strip of cardboard over and fastening the edges with staples or glue. A student can blow hard against the cardboard wing as shown in Figure 532.07b (the flame will move away from the cardboard). Explain that the air currents now flow smoothly along the streamlined cardboard and the flame moves in the direction of the flow.

Experimenting to see what effect differently shaped wings have upon flight. **08** **Ec**
Have students experiment with the wing designs of paper gliders shown in Figure 532.08. Students can test broad, narrow, or unusually shaped wings to see how well each provides lift for the craft.

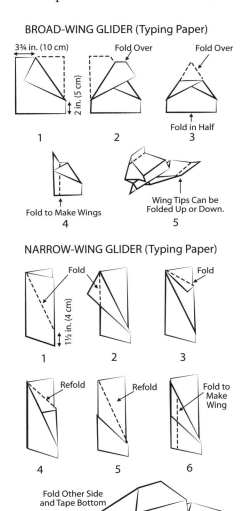

BROAD-WING GLIDER (Typing Paper)

NARROW-WING GLIDER (Typing Paper)

Figure 532.08

Contributing Idea C. The stabilizers, fin, rudder, ailerons, and elevators control the directional movements of a moving aircraft with air pressure.

Feeling the three basic directional movements of an aircraft. Place a marble in a small milk carton with a flat top. Insert knitting needles or thin dowels through the ends and sides, and fasten cardboard wings, tail, and propeller. Have a student hold the ends of any needle and slowly rotate it (Figure 532.09). The model will *pitch* (dive and climb), *yaw* (turn to the left and right), or *roll* (spin to the left and right), depending on which needle is turned. Students will feel a corresponding shift of the marble inside the carton. With the help of other students, the model can be turned in several directions at once to make the plane *bank*.

09 Ab Bb

Figure 532.09

Making a model to observe the function of stabilizers. Students can cut out an aircraft shape from a filing card and tape a knitting needle or thin dowel across the wing spread as shown in Figure 532.10a. Suspend the needle on bent paper clips

10 Bb Fc

hooked on a wire so that it can rock easily (Figure 532.10b). Let students blow through a large diameter straw against the tail of the model or place it in a wind tunnel. (The model will rise into a flying position as long as the air is moving.) Tell them that the tail of the model functions much like *stabilizers* (the horizontal unmovable parts of an aircraft tail). Explain that whenever the tail of a plane goes up or down, moving air against the stabilizers pushes the tail back into position. The stabilizers control the steadiness of the plane and keep it flying level.

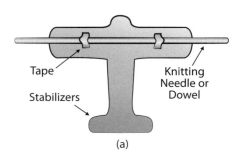

Tape

Knitting Needle or Dowel

Stabilizers

(a)

Paper Clips Suspended on Wire

(b)

Figure 532.10

Making a model to observe the function of the fin. Have students cut a tail piece from a filing card and tape it to another card. Balance the cards on the cork in a bottle, mounting them with

11 Bb Fc

a pin. Let students use a large diameter straw to blow across the horizontal card or place the bottle in a wind tunnel. (See Figure 532.11.) They will see that the card always turns to face the moving air even if the card is moved to one side or the other. Tell them that the upright card functions much like the *fin* (the vertical unmovable part of an aircraft tail). Explain that whenever the tail of a plane starts to swing to one side, moving air against the fin pushes the tail back into line. The fin controls the steadiness of the plane and keeps it facing into the moving air. Students can also observe a wind vane, and note that it always points toward the moving wind in the same way.

Figure 532.11

Making a model to observe the function of the rudder. Have students cut a tail piece from a filing card, and tape it to another card. Mount the cards on the cork of a bottle with a pin. If students fold and then bend the back half of the tail piece to the right or left and blow against it with a large diameter straw or place the bottle in a wind tunnel, they will see that the card turns to the right or left. (See Figure

12
Bb
Fc

532.12.) Tell them that the card functions much like the *rudder* (the movable part of an aircraft tail piece). Explain that when the pilot wants to turn the aircraft to the right, he moves the rudder to the right, and the moving air pushes the tail to the left, causing the plane to head toward the right. The process is reversed to turn to the left.

Figure 532.12

Making a model to observe the function of ailerons. Have students cut an aircraft shape from a filing card and fasten thread to its nose. Let them pull the model plane through the air by the thread or place it in a wind tunnel. Observe its movements. Now cut and fold the edges of the wings, bending one flap down and one flap up as shown in Figure 532.13. Pull the model

13
Bb
Fc

Figure 532.13

through the air again. (Students will see it spin.) When the bent parts are reversed, the model will spin in the other direction. Tell students that the bent parts function much like *ailerons* (the movable parts on aircraft wings). Explain that when a pilot wants the plane to tilt to the right, the pilot tilts the right aileron up and the left down (the ailerons are connected so that when one tilts up, the other tilts down). When this is done, the moving air pushes the right wing down and the left wing up, causing the plane to roll to the right. The procedure is reversed to roll to the left.

Making a model to observe the function of elevators. Prepare an aircraft shape as in entry 532.10 (p. 440), and bend the tail down. Let students blow against the tail through a straw with a large diameter or place the model in a wind tunnel. They will see the model point up or down depending on how the tail is bent. Tell them that the bent tail functions much like *elevators* (the moveable parts of an aircraft tail). Explain that when a pilot wants to dive, he tilts the elevators down, and the moving air against the elevators pushes the tail up—therefore the nose points down. To climb, the elevators are tilted up.

14 Bb Fc

Experimenting to see what effect the movable parts of an aircraft have upon flight. Have students fold paper gliders, and bend different parts on them to see how flight is influenced. For example, when one wing edge is bent up and one

15 Ec

down (like ailerons), the glider will roll or spin. When both wing edges are bent in the same direction (like elevators), the glider will dive or climb. When the tail piece is bent to one side (like a rudder), the glider will turn to the left or right. Students can experiment with combinations of bends and designs. See who can keep a glider in flight the longest, who can design one to travel the greatest distance, and who can design one that does the best acrobatics.

Contributing Idea D. Propellers, turned by an engine, drive some aircraft forward by pushing the air backward.

Observing that a propeller creates thrust. Use a small electric fan for a propeller, and attach it to a wagon or two roller skates fastened together by a board. Add a long extension cord to the fan. When turned on, the wagon or skates will move backward because the blades are set to throw the air in front of the fan. **Caution: Be ready to pull the electric plug before the fan reaches the end of the cord.**

16 Aa

Making and flying propellers. Push a pencil point through the center of a rectangular piece of cardboard. Cut the cardboard to make blades as shown in Figure 532.17a. Bend the blades at an angle to form the propeller as shown in Figure 532.17b. Students can spin the pencil between the palms of their hands and feel the breeze that is produced. Let them try bending the blades in the opposite direction to see if the

17 Ga Gc

direction of the breeze changes. Another propeller can be carved from balsa wood (Figure 532.17c). After it is carved, fasten it to a stick or the eraser end of a pencil as shown in Figure 532.17d. Hold the stick or pencil between the palms of both hands, propeller up, roll it back and forth quickly several times, then push it into the air. Because the apparatus flew up into the air, students will realize that a revolving propeller creates thrust.

Figure 532.17

Contributing Idea E. Reaction engines are used to drive some aircraft.

Observing action and reaction caused by the pressure of steam. Suspend a test tube horizontally from two wires. Put a **18 Aa Bd Fa** small amount of water into it, and loosely insert a cork. Heat the water with a candle. The pressure of the steam (gas) inside will cause the cork to pop out. Repeat this several times, and have students observe what happens to the test tube when the cork pops. (The action of the cork moving in one direction will cause the test tube to move in the opposite direction.) Explain that the action and reaction is comparable to how jets and rockets are propelled. Students can research the differences between jet and rocket engines. (Rockets carry their own oxygen supply to support combustion, and jets get oxygen from the air.)

Measuring the reaction to an action. **19 Cf** Use bathroom scales and a basketball to measure the reaction to the action of throwing the ball. To do this, have a student stand on the scales and throw the ball. Note the deflection of the scale. Now have the student throw the ball sidearm to see what happens.

Experimenting to see how jets and rockets can be stabilized. **20 Ec** Have students blow air into a sausage-shaped balloon, and then feel the air coming out. Explain that this sort of action stimulates the compressed gases that escape through the rear of jets and rockets. Now blow up the balloon again and place it on the edge of a table. When released, it will fly off in a zigzag path. Challenge students to design ways to control the flight of the balloon. They might tie a length of string to it (to somewhat stabilize the balloon much as a tail stabilizes a kite). They can also place a few short plastic straws, the glass portion of a medicine dropper, or other nozzles into the mouth of the balloon and hold them in place with a rubber band (the size and shape of the nozzles will control the amount of thrust). Students can compare thrusts of different nozzles by fastening a straw to the balloon and threading it on a string to guide the direction of flight.

Building a model action/reaction engine. Use the end of a paper clip, make a small hole in the center of the top of an empty, small milk carton. Put a thread through the hole, and tie a matchstick to it so that it will not slip out of the carton. Put clay around the thread hole so that it will not leak. Now make a small hole in one side of the carton and on the opposite side. Pour water into it until it is approximately 1 in. (2.5 cm) below the two holes. Suspend the carton by the thread. Using tongs or tweezers, put several pieces of

21
Fc
Gc

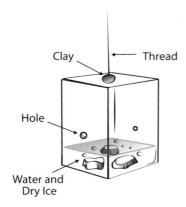

Figure 532.21

dry ice into the water and close the carton tightly. (See Figure 532.21.) When released, the carton will move back and forth like a pendulum. (The water in the carton is warm enough to change the dry ice into carbon dioxide gas that escapes through the holes.)

Contributing Idea F. The parachute is a device used for making a safe descent through the air from aircraft.

Feeling the pressure relationships on a parachute. Have students hold an umbrella high over their heads while they jump from a chair. (They will feel the pressure of the air against the underside of the umbrella.) Explain that as a parachute falls through the air, the pressure above it is reduced, thus the greater pressure below tends to hold it aloft.

22
Ab

Designing parachutes. Have students make parachutes out of various materials (cotton, silk, nylon) by tying string or thread to the materials and hanging weights or toy figures from the string. They can experiment with sizes and shapes of materials, lengths of string, and different weights by dropping them down stairwells or from high windows. A contest might be held to see whose parachute will stay aloft longest or whose will support the greatest weight. An egg drop contest might also be held. This can be done by challenging students to design parachutes for carrying containers

23
Ec
Gb

to safely land an uncooked egg from an agreed-upon height.

Generalization II. Various structural elements of space vehicles allow people to travel into space.

> *Contributing Idea A.* Space vehicles remain in orbit because of a balance between gravitational attraction and the thrust of the vehicle.

Making a model to represent an orbit- **24** **ing space vehicle.** Tie four metal wash- **Fc** ers to a string, thread the string through a spool, and tie one washer on the free end. Hold the spool in one hand and whirl the single washer in a circle. (See Figure 532.24a.) Explain that the four washers

Fish Weight

N

Figure 532.24

hanging down from the spool represent gravitational attraction and the single washer represents an orbiting space vehicle. Discuss what happens as the speed of the single washer increases and decreases. Another model can be made by hanging an iron weight on a string from the ceiling. Stand a strong bar magnet on end directly under the weight and almost touching it. Start the weight in a circular motion to represent the orbit of a space vehicle. (See Figure 532.24b.) Students will see that the speed of orbit increases as the weight gets closer to the magnet.

> *Contributing Idea B.* Insulating and reflective materials can be used to protect space vehicles from too much space radiation.

Testing to see the effect of insulation **25** **upon temperatures.** Line a nonburnable **Ce** box (e.g., an oven- or microwave-safe box) with insulation material. Place an oven thermometer in the box and seal it. Set the box and an identical thermometer in an oven and bring the heat to 300°F (150°C). After five minutes, use oven gloves to remove the box. Quickly open it and read the temperature on the thermometer inside. Compare the reading with that on the other thermometer. Interested students might want to research the hazards of outer space to see how designers have tried to solve such problems as overheating.

Testing to see the effect of reflective **26** **materials upon temperatures.** Use a **Ca**

stove to heat a black iron frying pan and a piece of aluminum foil that has been folded into a pan shape. Drop a piece of butter in each. Students will see that the butter sputters in the frying pan, but is not so quickly affected in the aluminum foil. Discuss how dark materials absorb solar radiation, while reflective materials do not.

600–699
Instructional Apparatus, Materials, and Systems

610 Safety Precautions

611 Guidelines

Generalization. Science learning requires active participation with equipment, thus safety practices are essential.

Contributing Idea A. Some general precautions are important when using equipment in the classroom.

Practicing safety in the classroom. Various precautions must be considered by the teacher prior to permitting students to use equipment in science experiences. The teacher should

   a. handle the equipment and materials prior to student usage to check out possible hazards;

   b. organize the classroom so that there can be constant supervision during individual or group work with equipment;

   c. limit the number of students in groups when there is a limited amount of equipment, because large groups can cause confusion among students and result in accidents;

   d. allow sufficient time for students to carry out experiments because haste can cause accidents;

   e. safety glasses should be considered for certain activities. In many school districts they are mandatory; and

01 Ga

   f. long hair should be tied back or kept in a hair net when students are working near an open flame.

Contributing Idea B. Some precautions are important when using heat sources.

Practicing safety when using heat. Various precautions should be taken before using heat in a classroom science experience. The teacher should

   a. become familiar with the school's regulations regarding fire, personally practice general safety procedures when using heat, and instruct students in the same procedures;

   b. take extreme care to see that volatile or flammable liquids are kept a safe distance from heat sources;

   c. always place heat sources on flat surfaces away from student traffic and be sure electrical cords cannot tip over equipment by looping them around the legs of sturdy furniture;

   d. use an oven mitt, pot holder, or other device when handling hot objects;

   e. set hot objects on insulated pads to protect surfaces; and

   f. provide small containers of water for matches after they have been lit.

02 Ga

Contributing Idea C. Some precautions are important when using electricity.

Practicing safety with electricity. Various precautions should be taken when studying electricity. The teacher should   **03 Ga**

a. tell students not to experiment with electric current at home or at school;

b. be sure students do not handle electric devices immediately after use because such devices sometimes retain a high temperature; and

c. instruct students on the proper way to remove electric plugs from sockets by pulling the plug and not the cord.

Contributing Idea D. Some precautions are important when using glassware.

Practicing safety when using glassware. Various precautions should be taken when using glassware. The teacher should   **04 Ga**

a. label all bottles to identify their contents;

b. tell students that only heat-treated glassware can be heated;

c. use soap or petroleum jelly for lubrication when inserting tubing into a stopper. The tubing should be wrapped with several layers of cloth, held as close to the stopper as possible, and inserted with

a twisting motion. Tubing that is stuck in stoppers can be removed by splitting the stopper with a single-edge razor blade. The stopper can be reclosed with glue or rubber cement;

d. tape sharp or chipped edges of mirrors and sheets of glass;

e. wrap tape around the base of glass objects that might break when dropped. The tape will keep fragments from scattering;

f. never pick up broken glass with fingers. A whisk broom and dustpan should be used for large pieces and wet cotton should be used to pick up small pieces; and

g. be sure that broken glassware is disposed in a container clearly marked *BROKEN GLASS.*

Contributing Idea E. Some precautions are important when working with animals and plants.

Practicing safety when studying animals. Various precautions should be taken when animals are brought into the classroom for study. The teacher should   **05 Ga**

a. be sure proper habitat and food are available for an animal before it is brought into the classroom. The living quarters should be kept clean, and plans should be made for care over weekends and holidays;

b. be sure all mammals brought to the classroom have been inoculated for rabies. Scratches or bites should be reported immediately to the school nurse. Check the school's policy on having animals in the classroom;

c. caution students against teasing animals and inserting fingers or objects into cages;

d. see that students handle animals only when necessary. Handling should be done properly according to the particular animal. Special handling is important if the animal is nervous, pregnant, or with its young; and

e. be sure students wash their hands after handling fish, amphibians, and reptiles. Water from their habitats should be disposed of carefully because of bacterial growth.

Practicing safety when studying plants. **06 Ga**
Various precautions should be taken when plants are studied. The teacher should

a. help children learn, before going on field trips, to identify plants that can produce poisonous effects;

b. be careful not to use certain flowers and molds for study if some children are allergic to them; and

c. when growing plants in the classroom, be aware of and caution children against, any parts of the plants that may be poisonous.

620 General Equipment

621 Heat Sources

(Note: These entries are for teachers only. Students are not to conduct these activities.)

Generalization. Heat sources are essential for many science experiences.

> *Contributing Idea A.* Some heating equipment is inexpensive and easily obtained.

Identifying inexpensive heating sources. **01 Ga**
Heat is essential for many science experiences. It can be obtained from candles, electric lightbulbs, electric hot plates, alcohol lamps, and canned-heat cooking fuels. Liquefied petroleum burners are valuable when very hot temperatures are required.

622 Support Stands

Generalization. Support stands are useful for many science experiences.

> *Contributing Idea A.* Some support stands can be constructed from inexpensive materials.

Constructing support stands. Many sci- **01 Gc**
ence experiences require support stands to hold and suspend objects. Such stands can be easily constructed from scrap materials.

a. *Wire Stands.* Insert coat hanger wire into holes drilled into blocks of wood. Be sure the drilled holes are slightly smaller than the diameter of the wire so that the wire will fit snugly. Make the base of each stand large enough so that it cannot be tipped over easily when used. (See Figure 622.01a.)

Figure 622.01a

b. *Wood Stands.* Drill a hole through a small block of wood just large enough to fit a heavy dowel through it. Screw the block to a larger one, then fasten a crossbeam to the dowel. Clothespins can be used to suspend objects from or hold objects to the stand. (See Figure 622.01b.)

Figure 622.01b

c. *Test-Tube Stands.* Wooden blocks with ¾ in. (2 cm) holes drilled into them serve well as individual test tube holders. Stands for several test tubes can also be constructed. (See Figure 622.01c.)

Figure 622.01c

Contributing Idea B. Special stands are necessary to support heated objects.

Constructing a heating stand. Cut arch-shaped holes from the sides of a tin can to form three or four legs. A heat source can be placed beneath the can and objects can be heated on its tin top. Differently sized cans can be made to fit differently sized heating equipment. **02 Gc**

623 Glassware

Generalization. Various glassware are useful for many science experiences.

Contributing Idea. Glass tubing can be shaped for specific purposes.

Cutting glass tubing. To cut tubing, draw a triangular file across one side of the glass where it is to be cut. With leather gloves on, hold tubing at arm's length with thumbs together behind the cut. Push toward the cut and the tubing should snap cleanly. If it does not, draw the file across the cut again and repeat. Next, hold the cut end in a flame to smooth the edges. **01 Gc**

Bending glass tubing. To bend, hold tubing horizontally in a flame at the point to be bent. Rotate it slowly and allow the tube to bend into a right angle by gravity. (Such natural bending will keep the corner from flattening out.) Other angles can be achieved by holding the tubing in different positions. To make a U-shaped bend, set tubing that has been bent at a right angle onto an asbestos sheet while it is still very hot. Slowly curve the angle with pliers. **02 Gc**

630 Measuring Systems and Instruments

631 Measuring Systems

Generalization I. **Measurements can be estimated and/or depicted in various ways.**

Contributing Idea A. Measurements can be estimated.

Estimating. Obtain six identical quart (liter) glass jars. Fill five of them, each with a different material that can be counted such as marbles, breakfast cereal, peas, raisins, rice, beans, or candies. Fill the sixth container with salt or sand. Let students quickly guess how many individual pieces are in each jar, then have them think of ways to find out how accurate their guesses were. (Note: Guesses arenot hte same as reasoned estimates. The following activities show how to make reasoned estimates and not guesses. With experience, the ability to estimate improves.)

01 Cb

   a. Students might count each item one by one (the most accurate way to know how many items there are—but people often lose count or give up if there are many items).
   b. They can count how many it takes to fill a small paper cup, then see how many cups are in the container.
   c. They can weigh 10 objects from a jar one at a time, to get the average weight for one object. Next, they can weigh the jar with the objects inside, then again when it is empty. By subtracting the weight of the jar from the total weight and dividing by the average weight of one object, they can tell how many objects the jar holds.
   d. They can pour some objects from one jar into a square baking pan, and distribute the objects evenly to form one layer. By counting the number along one side, then squaring the number, they can determine how many there are in one layer.

When finished, students can compare their original guesses with their estimates. Let them try estimating other measurable objects such as the number of books in the school library, letters on the page of a book, students in the school, people in a photograph. With practice, they can become very skilled at estimating numbers of objects.

Contributing Idea B. Measurements can be depicted pictorially.

Graphing. Perhaps the most visual means of presenting quantitative data is through graphing. Graphs enable learners to see

02 Bf

relationships among quantities through a pictorial form, thus offering a clearer presentation of data.

a. *Histograms.* A histogram is a form of graph that is made up of tallied observations showing relative frequencies. Students can count the number of seeds in a sample of pods and tally them on a histogram as shown in Histogram 631.02. The results provide a pictorial representation of the natural distribution of seeds in the pods of a particular plant. Other histograms can be produced by counting the number of raisins in slices of bread in a loaf, paper clips a magnet can pick up, drops squeezed from a medicine dropper with one squeeze, students absent each day for a month, words on a page or letters in a line, seeds in a specific kind of fruit, different makes of cars seen in 30 minutes, seeds that sprout in a germination test, and so on. Anything that can be counted can be developed into a histogram.

COMPARING GROWTH OF
RADISH WITH LIMA BEAN

Graph 631.02a

b. *Bar Graphs.* A bar graph uses a solid bar to represent some measured observation. The growth of plants or heights of students can be converted into bar graphs as shown in Graphs 631.02a and 631.02b.

COMPARING GROWTH OF
RADISH WITH LIMA BEAN

Graph 631.02b

c. *Line Graphs.* Intermittent measurements plotted on a grid produce a line graph. When the measurements are connected by lines, inferences can be made about changes between points and in some cases predictions can be made. To prepare such

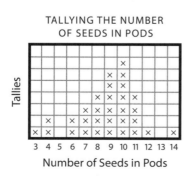

TALLYING THE NUMBER
OF SEEDS IN PODS

Number of Seeds in Pods

HISTOGRAM 631.02

graphs, horizontal and vertical axes should correspond with the columns of data on a table; thus, each tabled recording represents a point on the graph.

1. Some tabled data produce straight-line graphs. Predictions can be made from such graphs. For example, if students burn a candle, record the time it takes to burn each ¼ in. for several minutes (see Table 631.02). Then plot the data on a graph like the one shown in Graph 631.02c. Students can make a prediction telling when the candle would burn out (if the conditions remain the same), because the data produce a straight line. Similarly, stu-

dents can predict how long it will take a liquid to evaporate by weighing cups of each liquid on a daily basis for a week, then graphing the data. They can make predictions about the flow of water by measuring at 10-second intervals the volume or weight of water collected in a container filled at a drinking fountain.

Graph 631.02c

Table 631.02. Burning a Candle (Diameter of candle = one-quarter inch)

Length (inches)	Time of Day	Burning Time (minutes)	Remarks
2½	1:10	0	lit candle
2¼	1:12	2	
2	1:15	5	
1¾	1:18	8	
1½	1:20	10	
1¼	1:23	13	
1	1:25	15	blew out candle made a prediction
1	1:37	15	lit candle again
¾	1:39	17	
½	1:42	20	
¼	1:45	23	
0	1:46	24	candle burned out

2. Some tabled data do not produce straight line graphs. Most graphs of this type cannot be used for predictive purposes, but they do produce interesting information that can be discussed. For example, students can heat water, record the temperature change at one-minute intervals, and then graph the data after boiling point is reached. The graph can be compared with graphs made after boiling salt water or sugar water. Plant and animal growth also produce irregular curves on graphs.

Generalization II. Scientists throughout the world measure lengths, weights, and other values by a standard system.

> *Contributing Idea A.* Units of measure are arbitrary.

Creating measuring systems. Students can develop and use their own systems of measurement. To measure lengths, they might use unsharpened pencils, crayons, erasers, or edges of cards. To measure weights, they might use nails, pins, sequins, or other objects on a balance scale. To measure liquid capacities, they might use unmarked containers, paper cups of different sizes, or thimbles. As they measure various aspects of their environment, encourage them to make up words for each unit they devise, and then have them describe the sizes of desktops, tables, chairs, their own heights, weights, and so forth. You can guide them toward realizing that the different measuring systems used in the classroom are analogous to different, widely accepted systems developed by people. Students will discover that some systems are more accurate than others, and that some standards are necessary if people are to communicate with each other about measurements. You might explain that the metric system is designed to be a single system for all people.

> *Contributing Idea B.* No one system of units is inherently more accurate than another, but some, such as the metric system, are more convenient to use.

Converting units of measure to different systems. The following tables can be used to convert the more frequently used measurements in the U.S. system to the metric system. Some students might be interested in researching the development and use of metric units. (See Tables 631.04a and 631.04b [p. 458].)

03
Cc
Gb

04
Bd
Ga

Table 631.04a. Tables of the Metric System

Units of Length	A kilometer	(km) =	1,000	meters (m)
	A hectometer	(hm) =	100	meters
	A dekameter	(dm) =	10	meters
		A METER		
	A decimeter	(dm) =	0.1	of a meter
	A centimeter	(cm) =	0.01	of a meter
	A millimeter	(mm) =	0.001	of a meter
Units of Liquid Capacity	A hectoliter	(hl) =	100	liters (L)
	A dekaliter	(dal) =	10	liters
		A LITER		
	A deciliter	(dl) =	0.1	of a liter
	A centiliter	(cl) =	0.01	of a liter
	A milliliter	(ml) =	0.001	of a liter
Units of Weight	A kilogram	(kg) =	1,000	grams (g)
	A hectogram	(hg) =	100	grams
	A dekagram	(dag) =	10	grams
		A GRAM		
	A decigram	(dg) =	0.1	of a gram
	A centigram	(cg) =	0.01	of a gram
	A milligram	(mg) =	0.001	of a gram
Units of Volume	A cubic hectometer	(hm^3) =	1,000,000	cubic meters (m^3)
	A cubic dekameter	(dam^3) =	1,000	cubic meters
		A CUBIC METER		
	A cubic decimeter	(dm^3) =	0.001	of a cubic meter
	A cubic centimeter	(cm^3) =	0.000,001	of a cubic meter
	A cubic millimeter	(mm^3) =	0.000,000,001	of a cubic meter

Table 631.04b. U.S. → Metric and Metric → U.S. Conversion Tables

	U.S. System to Metric Conversion Table		Metric to U.S. System Conversion Table	
Units of Length	1 inch	25.4 millimeters (mm)	1 millimeter	0.039 inch (in.)
		2.54 centimeters (cm)	1 centimeter	0.394 in.
	1 foot	0.305 meter (m)	1 meter	39.37 in.
	1 yard	0.914 meter		3.281 feet (ft.)
	1 mile	1609.347 m		1.093 yards (yd)
		1.609 kilometers (km)	1 kilometer	0.621 mile (mi.)
Units of Liquid Capacity	1 fluid ounce	29.573 milliliters (ml)	1 milliliter	0.034 fluid ounce
		0.03 liters (L)	1 liter	2.113 pints
	1 pint	473.167 ml = 0.473 L		1.057 quarts
	1 quart	946.33 ml = 0.946 L		0.264 gallon
	1 gallon	3785.33 ml = 3.785 L		
Units of Weight	1 ounce	28349.527 milligrams (mg)	1 gram	0.035 ounce (oz.)
			1 kilogram	35.274 oz.
		28.35 grams (g)		2.205 pounds (lb.)
	1 pound	453.592 g	1 metric ton	2204.62 lb.
		0.454 kilogram (kg)		1.102 short tons
	1 short ton	907.185 kg		
		0.907 metric ton		
Units of Volume	1 cubic inch	16.387 cubic centimeters (cm³)	1 cubic centimeter	0.061 cubic inch (in.³)
		0.016 cubic decimeter (dm³)	1 cubic decimeter	61.023 in.³
				0.035 cubic foot (ft.³)
	1 cubic foot	28.317 dm³	1 cubic meter	35.314 ft.³
		0.028 cubic meter (m³)		1.308 cubic yards
	1 cubic yard	764.559 dm³		
		0.765 m³		

632 Measuring Instruments

Generalization. Measuring instruments can be used to compare any object or event with others of known or accepted dimensions.

Contributing Idea A. Some instruments are designed to measure distances.

Constructing a sextant. Attach two blocks of wood on the ends of a 1ft. (30 cm) long ruler or stick. (The blocks can be used as handles.) Tape a plastic straw to the top of the ruler and fasten a protractor to its side with a thumbtack. Hang a weight on a length of thread and suspend it from the thumbtack. Be sure that the thread hangs freely and parallel to the protractor's base. When the sextant is tilted upward, the weighted thread will indicate the angle in relation to the ground (Figure 631.01a). Students can

01
Bb
Cd
Gc

Figure 632.01a

use this instrument to measure the heights of various structures by triangulation. For example, they can look at the top of a flagpole through the straw on the sextant,

determine the angle, then measure the distance (baseline) they are standing from the pole. Next, draw on a piece of graph paper the angle found and add the baseline distance in a scale that fits on the paper. On the other end of the baseline, draw a perpendicular line to represent the pole. The height of the pole (in scale) is determined by the point where the angle line intersects the perpendicular line (Figure 632.01b). (Note: Students must add their own heights to this distance since they sighted on the pole several ft. above the baseline.) This sextant can be used to determine the heights of structures whenever a baseline (the dis-

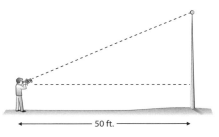

50 ft.

Figure 632.01b

tance to the flagpole) and two angles are known (the angle of the sextant and the angle of the flagpole—90°—in relation to the ground), simply by drawing the imaginary triangle to scale. You might tell them that the instrument they constructed is called a sextant.

Constructing a range finder. Fasten two small protractors and plastic straws at the 3 in. and 33 in. marks on a yardstick (5 cm

02
Bb
Cd
Gc

and 95 cm on a meterstick). The distance between the straws represents a baseline of 30 in. (90 cm) (Figure 632.02a). Set the stick on the ground and look through the straws at a tree or other object some distance away as shown in Figure 632.02b. Mark a corresponding 3 in. (7 cm) baseline on graph paper and draw the angles at each end. When the two lines intersect, measure the vertical distance from the baseline to the intersection. In scale, this is the distance to the viewed object. Students can use a tape measure to check. You might tell them that such an instrument is called a range finder.

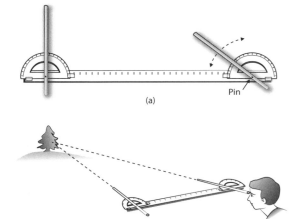

(a)

(b)

Figure 632.02

Contributing Idea B. Some instruments are designed to measure liquid capacity.

Making a graduated cylinder. Cut a strip of paper approximately ½ in. (2 cm) wide and fasten it to the side of a test tube or tall, **03 Cg Gc**

thin jar such as an olive jar. Use a measuring cup or laboratory graduated cylinder to pour equal volumes of water into the container. Mark the water level with a fine pen and waterproof ink for each amount. The space between each mark can be divided into 10 equal divisions. When the scale is finished, cover it completely with waterproof cellulose tape.

Contributing Idea C. Some instruments are designed to measure weight.

Constructing a spring scale. Suspend a spring from a support stand and hang a cup or jar lid from its base. Fasten a short plastic ruler to the support with rubber bands. Adjust the ruler so that the bottom of the spring is opposite the ¼ in. (1 cm) mark. (See Figure 632.04.) (A wire pointer can be attached to the base of the spring to make readings of the scale easier.) Objects can now be placed in the lid and the weight read on the ruler (subtract 1 from the reading and record the weight in ¼ in. or centimeters). To calibrate the scale so that the readings can be converted into grams, place gram weights on the lid until the bottom of the spring reaches the 11 cm mark. Subtract 1 and divide the remainder (10) into the number of grams on the scale. The result will be the number of grams per centimeter. This number can be printed at the base of the scale. To change any readings to grams, simply **04 Cf Gc**

multiply the number of centimeters the pointer moves by this number.

Figure 632.04

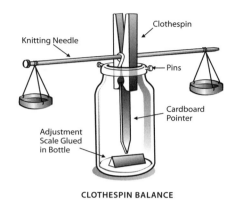

CLOTHESPIN BALANCE

Figure 632.05b

Constructing a balance scale. Balance scales can be made in numerous ways. Many variations can be created as shown in Figures 632.05a–d.

05
Cf
Gc

PEGBOARD BALANCE

Figure 632.05c

SODA STRAW BALANCES

Figure 632.05a

WEIGHING PANS

Figure 632.05d

Using a balance scale. Balance scales are used to compare unknown weights to known weights. To prepare a set of known weights, obtain a set of gram weights (e.g., grams, decigrams, centigrams). Let students balance each weight by cutting segments of wire or rolling tinfoil together until balance is attained. The wires or tinfoil can then be used in place of the gram weights. Various measurements can be made using these units of measure.

06
Bc
Bf
Cf

a. Very small dry particles such as salt, sugar, talcum, or soap powder can be weighed with the balance scale. To do this, cut two square pieces of waxed paper or aluminum foil the same size. Fold each from corner to corner twice. Place one on each balance pan and balance the beam. When small particles are poured, the weighing paper makes it easy to remove them from the pans.

b. Objects can be counted with a balance scale. To do this, obtain 100 small nails, pins, paper clips, and staples. Balance the scale, place a 1 g weight in one pan, then weigh out 1 g of the nails or pins in the other. Count the number of nails or pins in 1 g. Now place an unknown number of nails or pins in one pan and weigh them. Without counting, the number can be calculated by multiplying the number of objects in 1 g by the number of grams.

c. The liquid content of objects can be measured with a balance scale. To do this, obtain different foods such as bread, apples, pears, lemons, meat, peas, crackers, and so on. Put 10 g of fresh bread or other food on a weighing paper in one of the pans. Do the same for other foods, and use a fresh piece of paper each time. Record the weights on a table, and put the papers of food in the sunlight to dry for a few days; then, when dried, weigh them again. The difference between the fresh weight and the dry weight indicates the amount of moisture (liquid) in each food. By starting with 10 g of each food, percentages are easy to figure.

d. Evaporation rates can be measured with a balance scale by placing the scale in a warm airy place where it will not be disturbed. Prepare two weighing papers and put them on the balance pans. Set a small piece of wet sponge on one dish. Weigh the sponge and record the weight and the time of day. Check the weight every 30 minutes, and record it on a table.

e. Amounts of absorption can be measured with a balance scale. To do this, obtain pieces of different materials such as sponges, blotters, cloths, and paper towels. Make weighing papers, and put one in each balance pan. Balance the scale, then weigh each of the sample materials and record the dry weight on a table. Now saturate each material with water. Shake off any excess water and weigh each when wet. Compare the dry weight with the wet weight. Students can compare different brands of paper towels to see which absorb more than others. They can also test other materials such as napkins and facial tissues.

Contributing Idea D. Some instruments are designed to measure temperature.

Making a sensitive thermometer. Obtain a dowel the same size as a thermometer bulb and a 1½ in. × 3 in. (3 cm × 6 cm) strip of copper. Bend the strip of copper tightly around the dowel (see Figure 632.07a), and fold the ends back to form a flat surface as shown in Figure 632.07b. Slide the copper under the bulb of the thermometer and gently pinch it around the bulb as in Figure 632.07c. Set it in the shade for several minutes, and then place it in sunlight. The copper should absorb enough heat energy to quickly affect the thermometer. The instrument can be improved by removing the copper strip, blackening it

07
Ce
Gc

with soot from a candle flame (see Figure 632.07d), and attaching it to a stand so that the black surface faces outward as shown in Figure 632.07e. Use the instrument to measure the heat from electric bulbs by setting it so the blackened surface is about 1 ft. (20 cm) from a single 100-watt bulb. After some time, the temperature of the thermometer will stop rising. Now let students test different factors that affect the temperature, such as the length of time the lamp is on, the area of blackened surface, the distance the surface is from the bulb, and the wattage of the bulb. They might also try other metals in place of the copper (aluminum foil), or determine what happens to the energy output of a test bulb when others are added in either parallel or series circuits.

(a)

(b)

(c)

(d)

(e)

Figure 632.07

Contributing Idea E. Some instruments are designed to measure time.

Making a water clock. Use a pin to punch a hole in the bottom of a quart (liter) milk carton. Fill it with water, and set it on top of a quart (liter) glass jar that has straight sides. See how long it takes for the water to drip out by timing it with a clock that has a second hand. Now use a safety pin to punch a larger hole in another carton. Time the flow to see how long it runs. Tell students that they have made simple *water clocks*. Challenge them to make clocks that will run for 5 minutes, 10 minutes, or 30 minutes. To calibrate a clock, attach a strip of tape that can be written on to the side of the jar. Hold a finger over the hole in the carton and fill it almost to the top. Put a mark in the carton at this level so that it can always be filled with the same amount of water. Hold the carton above the jar, and when the second hand of the clock reaches 12, start the clock running. At one-minute intervals, use a fine-tipped, waterproof pen to mark the water level on the tape. Students will discover that as the water level gets lower, the water comes out slower and the spacing between the marks changes. (Note: An unclear band will be seen at the water level because the water tends to climb part way up the side of the jar.) Place a mark at the lower edge of the band because it is easier to see than the top level.

08
Bb
Ch
Gc

Making a pendulum clock. Tie a piece of thread to a metal weight such as a fishing weight or washer. Fasten the free end to a pin pushed into a block of wood. Set the block at the edge of a table so that the thread swings freely from the side as shown in Figure 632.09a. Pull the weight to one side and allow it to swing for one minute. Check this several times. If the pendulum does not swing exactly 60 times in one minute, challenge the students to change it until it does (the thread can be lengthened or shortened). When the pendulum is adjusted, each swing (back and forth motion) will represent one second of time. A similar timer can be made by suspending the thread and weight from the cap on a transparent jug or bottle. The pendulum swinging inside will not be influenced by passing breezes (Figure 632.09b).

09
Ch
Gc

(a)   (b)

Figure 632.09

640 Plant and Animal Containers

641 Planters

Generalization. Planters can be used to control factors that influence the growth of plants.

> *Contributing Idea A.* Soilless planters are designed for observations of growth of all parts of a plant for short periods of time.

Constructing soilless containers. Growing plants in soilless containers has the advantage of keeping the seed and the germinating process visible for observations and measurements. Seeds sprouted in such gardens, however, will not grow long under these conditions. During the brief growth period, students can observe how seeds swell and crack, what happens to the seed coat as the embryo pushes through, how the roots and stem begin, how the first leaves develop, and what happens to the seed itself. Generally it is best to soak seeds overnight before placing them in a soilless container. Each of the following methods requires only water and a means of transmitting it to the seed. Other creative variations can be made from these examples.

01
Gc

a. Obtain a strip of gauze or sheeting approximately 6 in. × 8 in. (15 cm × 20 cm). Place seeds upon the strip 1 in. (2.5 cm) apart. Cover the strip with another dampened strip. Carefully roll the strips and fasten them at the ends with rubber bands. Set the rolled strips in a shallow dish of water. Unroll them every few days to observe.

b. Set a wet sponge in a saucer of water and sprinkle some seeds such as grass seed, radish seed, bird seed, or any individual seeds on it. If the sponge is set in a deep bowl, the bowl can be covered with plastic sheeting to create a greenhouse effect. A porous brick or wad of cotton can be used in place of the sponge.

c. Set a block of wood across a pan of water. Fold a blotter so that it rests across the block like a saddle and so the ends dip into the water in the pan. Place seeds on the blotter. A greenhouse effect can be obtained by inverting a glass jar over the seeds.

d. Place a blotter or layer of cotton on a sheet of glass such as a lantern slide glass. Set seeds on the blotter approximately 2 in. (5 cm) up from a long side base. Place another sheet of glass on top and fasten the pieces together with several rubber bands. If the selected seeds are large, small strips of wood along the edges will keep the pieces of glass separated. Stand the materials in a pan or tray of water to keep the center moist.

e. Roll a blotter, paper toweling, or cloth and slip it inside a jar or other glass container. Fill the center of the container with peat moss, cotton, excelsior, sawdust, sand, or some similar material. (Note: Some materials, such as sawdust, tend to discolor the water and blotter.) Place seeds between the glass and the blotter. Space the seeds evenly about a quarter of the way down the side. Moisten the material in the center of the glass. A little water can be kept in the bottom of the glass, but do not let the water touch the seeds directly. Occasionally, it might be necessary to replace the water that is lost by evaporation.

f. Tie a piece of cloth over the mouth of a small jar. Set the jar in a larger jar or pan, and let the extra cloth length hang down the sides into 1 or 2 in. (3–5 cm) of water. A sheet of glass can be placed across the large jar to keep the inside air moist. Scatter seeds onto the part of the cloth that covers the mouth of the small jar.

Contributing Idea B. Soil planters are designed to allow for observations of growth of plants over long periods of time.

Preparing small soil containers. Success in seed planting and germination in soil containers depends upon several variables. The following are suggestions that have provided a great amount of success in classroom experiences. (Note: Seeds will germinate and grow with less care than described here; however, an oversight of any one of the following factors can hinder germination and growth.) Many experiments can be designed by controlling for all factors except the one being tested.

02 Gc

a. *Containers.* Seeds can be grown in many kinds of common containers such as waxed paper cups, milk or cream cartons, cigar boxes, wooden cheese boxes, flower pots, and seed flats. Most containers, especially milk and cream cartons, should be thoroughly cleaned before using. If clay pots are used, it is helpful to soak them in water just before use or they might draw much moisture from the soil and away from the seeds.

b. *Drainage.* Containers should have proper drainage for good plant growth. A hole should be punched in containers that do not have holes so that excess water will drain out. The hole should be covered, but not blocked, with a small rock or piece of pottery so that the soil will not wash out. A drainage saucer such as a pie or cake tin or an aluminum foil pan should be placed underneath the container. A coarse-gravel layer in the saucer will aid in the drainage and diffusion of excess water. Because proper drainage is important, do not use glass or other sealed containers. Seeds planted in such containers usually do not thrive, for it is difficult to keep the soil from becoming too soggy or too dry. Soggy soil keeps air from the seeds, while dry soil will not bring enough moisture. If for some reason a container without a hole must be used, drainage can be aided by placing a layer of coarse pebbles approximately 1 in. (2.5 cm) deep in the bottom of the container.

c. *Soil.* Unless a special soil experiment is being attempted, several layers of soil should be placed in the container.

1. The first layer, approximately ½ in. (1 cm) deep, should be gravel.

2. The second layer should be of loam or good sandy garden soil. The loam or garden soil should be sifted to remove rocks and other debris. Loam is composed of sand (which allows water to drain through), organic matter (dead plant or animal matter), and clay. The layer should nearly fill the container. Tap the bottom of the container until the particles settle to within ½ in. (1 cm) of the top. If the layer is not high enough, the plants might get too much water and/or be too shaded. If it is too high, the topsoil might wash away, and the plants might not get enough water.

3. The third or top layer should be a sprinkling of fine soil or sand to cover the surface. Vermiculite or other commercial materials can be used in place of soil. Such materials can be obtained from local nurseries or florists. Vermiculite is a material made from mica, and it holds water better than most soils. Because of this, germination is generally speeded up when it is used. It does not, however, contain nutrients needed for sustained plant growth.

d. *Seeds.* Germination will be more rapid if seeds are soaked overnight before planting. For approximate germination time for common seeds, see Graph 641.02. There are several ways in which seeds can be planted.

APPROXIMATE GERMINATION TIMES
FOR SOME COMMON SEEDS

Graph 641.02

1. Seeds can be added to the top of the layer of loam, and then covered with a ½ in. (1 cm) layer of fine soil or sand. The soil should be pressed firmly with the bottom of a milk bottle or similar implement. Pressing with fingers tends to compact the soil too firmly about the seeds.

2. Seeds can be inserted into the soil. The depth for planting should be in accordance with the depth prescribed on seed packages. If the proper depth for planting is not known, a general rule of thumb is to plant a seed to a depth of one and a half times its length. A mark of the depth to be planted can be made on an unsharpened pencil or stick. The pencil can be pressed into the soil to the mark. Seeds can be dropped into the holes and covered with humus. If seeds are sown onto the soil rather than placed individually, overcrowding might induce rot. On the other hand, too few seeds in an activity will not allow for casualties or nongerminating seeds. As soon as seeds sprout, place the container in a sunny place. Plants should have as much direct sun as possible unless an experiment measuring the effect of sun energy is being conducted. Lack of sunlight will make seedlings weak and spindly.

e. *Watering.* Soil can be moistened before or after it has been placed in a container.

1. To moisten the soil before it is placed in the container,

knead enough water into the soil to form a soft, but not muddy, ball that will hold its shape in the palm of your hand. This consistency will be right for planting.

2. To moisten the soil after it has been placed in the container, water the soil from the top *before* seeds are planted. Enough water should be added so that it drains from the base. Subsequent watering is best done by adding water to the drainage saucer before all moisture is gone from it. Watering from the base will not disturb seeds or plants, for the water will move up through the hole in the container and through soil by capillary attraction. If, however, the container must be watered from the top, it is best to water thoroughly every four or five days rather than a little every day. Frequent light watering tends to draw the moisture out of the soil by capillary attraction and evaporation. Water added to the top of the container should be carefully poured against the side so that the seeds or plants are not disturbed.

f. *Greenhouses.* In the classroom, weekends and vacations can pose a watering problem. Greenhouses will help retain moisture over such periods. Plastic wrap sheets and glass covers can be placed over some of the previously suggested containers to obtain a greenhouse or hotbed effect. With such an effect, temperatures will be raised and evaporation will be reduced.

Preparing large soil containers. Large planters can be obtained commercially. They can also be made from a large flower pot, 8 in. (20 cm) or more in width at the top, and a small flower pot, 3 in. (8 cm) or less at the top. Arrange the pots as shown in Figure 641.03. Place a cork in the bottom hole of the small pot and keep the small pot filled with water. Seeds can be planted and grown in the soil in the large pot. **03 Gc**

Gravel

Figure 641.03

Preparing outdoor planting areas. The care of outdoor school or home gardens can provide interesting activities for students, but careful planning is necessary **04 Gc**

to make the activities fruitful learning experiences. Through such experiences, students can carry out their plans, work independently with various phases of gardening, and implement their knowledge about soils, plants and tools. Before planting an outdoor garden, they should find out how much work is involved, and then decide whether or not they wish to undertake the job. Outdoor gardening requires time and effort when the climate and other conditions are suitable, and not just when the gardener is ready. It should be noted that many problems concerning soil, climate, altitude, and seed selection can arise because of geographic locations. Because of the great variety of considerations involved in outdoor gardening, the following suggestions are general in nature.

a. *Locale.* A planting area might be found on the school grounds, on a nearby lot, or on any land area that can be cleared and protected from vandals. The best location is one that receives sunlight all day, is level so that topsoil and seeds will not wash away, has proper drainage even after heavy rain, and has sandy or loamy soil. After a decision is made about the size of the area to be planted and the kinds of seeds to be grown, a plan should be made for the garden. The choice of seeds will determine the spacing and arrangement

needed. (See Figures 641.04a and 641.04b.)

(a)

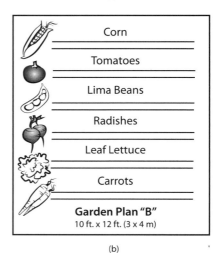

(b)

Figure 641.04

b. *Soil.* Proper preparation of the soil for an outdoor garden is important. When it is dry enough to crumble easily, the soil should be broken up with a spade to a depth of at least 6 in. (15 cm). Turn over each spadeful and break up the largest lumps as they are dug. A hoe and rake should be used to break up smaller lumps to make a fine, loose soil. Unbreakable lumps, stones, sticks, and other rubbish should be removed. The condition of the soil should be examined. Some soils become acid through time because leaves accumulate in them. Some become alkaline, the opposite of acid soils. The kind of soil needed for proper growth depends upon the kinds of plants to be grown. It is best to obtain information and advice from a local nursery. Generally, soils can be made acid by adding aluminum sulfate or can be rendered neutral by applying lime. Fertilizer is also important, but the kinds of fertilizer the soil needs depend upon what is already in the soil. Again local nurseries can help. Any fertilizer that is added to a soil should be applied according to the directions that accompany the fertilizer. Too much fertilizer can damage plants. Usually it is added to the soil in the spring when it can be worked into the ground.

c. *Planting.* The locale and choice of seeds determine the planting time. For most seeds, planting begins after the soil is prepared and when the weather is warm and not too wet. Because of differences in seeds, not all can be planted at the same time. Follow the directions for planting on seed packages.

d. *Watering.* Do not sprinkle the surface of the soil lightly. This will cause the roots of plants to grow too close to the surface. When the soil is dry beneath the surface, soak the garden slowly and thoroughly. Thorough soaking penetrates the soil deeply and keeps the roots at a proper depth. Such watering might be done only once a week, depending upon the weather. It is usually best not to water during the heat of the day because much of the water evaporates.

e. *Weeding.* Weeds in an outdoor garden take food from the soil and moisture needed by the growing plants. If weeds are pulled out as soon as they appear, it is easier to keep the plot free of weeds. The general appearance of the garden will also be improved.

f. *Transplanting.* At times, it might be necessary to move a plant from a smaller container to a larger container or area. Transplanting should be done before plants are very large. Large plants have extensive root systems and more roots are injured when they are transplanted. Smaller plants suffer less damage than larger plants and begin renewed growth much sooner. It is preferable to either transplant in the evening or on an overcast day. If the plant to be moved is in a pot, water the pot thoroughly. Place a hand across the rim with fingers spread and turn the pot over. Tap the pot against something hard. The contents should drop out. If several plants are grown in a flat container, gently separate them. Roots tend to bind the contents of the soil together, so keep as much soil as possible with each plant. Have the new position for the plant prepared ahead of time. The soil should be moist, but not wet. Prepare a hole in the damp soil deep and wide enough to take all the roots. Place the seedling so that the roots are just below the ground level. Firm the soil by gently pressing inward and downward against the roots. Make a saucer-shaped depression around each seedling and give it a good watering. It might help to shade the seedlings for a few days if the weather is hot and sunny. Leafy branches, stiff cardboard, or shingles can be used for this purpose. Water frequently for the first few days until the plants are growing

strongly. Frost-susceptible plants should be covered at night if the danger of frost is present.

642 Vivariums

Generalization. Vivariums can be used to control factors that influence environmental conditions.

> *Contributing Idea A.* The aquarium is a simulated environment designed for observing marine plants and animals.

Building aquariums. Almost any clean glass container works well for housing aquatic life. As a general rule, the surface of the water in the container should allow for at least 20 in.^{2} (50 cm^2) of air surface for each inch (0.5 cm) of body length of fish. Set the container in a strong light, but not in direct sunlight. Cover the bottom with 1 or 2 in. (3 cm) of clean sand mixed with gravel. Goldfish, guppies, and a variety of plants can be kept in these simple aquariums. They can be fed commercial fish food obtained from a pet store. Tropical or saltwater aquariums require special equipment (see entry 241.01). **01 Gc**

> *Contributing Idea B.* The terrarium is a simulated environment designed for observing land plants and animals.

Building terrariums. Terrariums can be built from sheets of glass taped together and set in a baking pan filled with plaster of paris for permanent support. A glass **02 Gc**

top should be used. An aquarium tank or widemouthed jar can also serve as a terrarium. If a jar is used, place it on its side to provide a larger land surface, and make a plaster, sand, or wood base to keep it from rolling. Various other containers can be used to create different environments (see entry 241.02).

650 Equipment for Collecting

651 Collections

Generalization. Collections show ways by which objects can be organized.

> *Contributing Idea A.* Living objects can be collected, preserved, and organized on the basis of similarities and differences.

Collecting and preserving animals. Because of possible damage to habitats and the depletion of species, it is not recommended that students pick up samples of animals for collections. If seashore or other animals are temporarily studied, be sure they are replaced into the ecological niche from which they were taken. A possible exception to this recommendation might be made for insects that are abundant and that generally reproduce in quantity.

01 Dc Gd

Collecting and preserving plants. Because of possible damage to habitats and the depletion of species, it is not recommended that samples of whole plants be collected. Parts of plants, however, can be collected without endangering an area if students are cautioned against damaging plants and property.

02 Dc Gd

    a. *Seeds.* A great variety of seeds can be obtained from a nursery. Others can be found scattered outdoors. Collected seeds can be kept in small baby food jars. Egg cartons also make fine containers because of their separate compartments. Hosiery boxes and shallow department store boxes make good containers when they are lined with cotton. Students can develop their own rationales for collections, and labels should reflect the rationale.

    b. *Leaves.* Leaf specimens should be preserved as soon as possible after picking because they become dry and brittle very quickly. Until they can be mounted, keep them between sheets of moist newspapers in a flat, but natural position. Place a few sheets of another newspaper on top of them. These papers will absorb the moisture as the specimens dry. Place other leaves on top of the second layer of newspapers. Continue this arrangement for several layers, then place flat boards on the last layer of newspapers. These boards can be weighted down by stacks of heavy books. Make sure the weight is heavy enough to keep the specimens from wrinkling. If the specimens are very moist, the procedure might need to be repeated with fresh newspaper. An alternative method is to place the layers of newspapers and leaves between two flat boards. The boards can then be clamped or strapped tightly together, pressing the leaves and papers between them. After 24 hours, the specimens can be mounted to fairly heavy sheets of paper with tape, glue, or staples. The sheets can be prepared for scrapbooks or individually framed. Specimens can be labeled and organized into classifications determined by the students.

c. *Flowers.* Flower specimens can be pressed between sheets of waxed paper until they are dry, then mounted and arranged in some orderly way. Similarly, they can be placed immediately on tag paper and covered with transparent shelf paper. Either method preserves the coloration of the flowers for long periods of time.

Contributing Idea B. Nonliving objects can be collected and organized on the basis of similarities and differences.

Collecting rocks. Students can take a nature walk or a field trip to an excavation or rock quarry to collect samples of rocks. Collections can be housed in a variety of boxes (e.g., shoe boxes, cigar boxes, egg cartons). Each can be properly titled (e.g., smooth rocks, red rocks, sedimentary rocks). Individual labels (e.g., shale, quartz) might be added later after checking reference books or identification keys. A local rock collector might be invited to speak to the class and to share some of his or her collection. A list of students' questions prepared beforehand will help the collector with the talk. **03 Dc Gd**

Index Guide

Absorption
  of heat, 163.04–05
  of light, 331.12, 332.33–34
  of liquids, 122.34–35, 632.06e
  of sound, 321.10, 322.25–26
Acceleration (*see also* Deceleration)
  definition of, operational, 312.11–12
  influence on mass, 312.22
Action/reaction
  applications of
    in aircraft, 531.03, 512.16–21
    in everyday use, 313.10
    in seacraft, 314.02, 531.02
  measurement of, 313.08–09
Ailerons on aircraft, 532.13
Air (*see also* Air pressure; Wind)
  characteristics of, 131.05–07, 162.07
  currents
    detection of, 132.17–18
    heat influence, 342.36–39
    pressure influence, 163.08–11
  measurement of
    movement, 162.04–05, 09
    pressure, 163.08–11
    temperature, 162.07–09
    weight, 131.17
Air barometer
  construction and use of, 132.15
Air conditioner, 162.13
Aircraft
  airplane
    directional movements of, 532.09–15
    parts of, 532.02–17, 532.20
  jets/rockets, 532.18–21
  parachutes, 532.22–23
  space vehicles, 532.24–26
  wind tunnel for testing, 532.01
Air pressure
  changes in, 132.11–12
  definition of, operational, 132.06
  effect upon
    aircraft, 532.04–06
    ears, 132.06
    weather, 161.08, 161.13
  measurement
    at altitudes, 132.07–08
    by barometers, 132.13–15, 161.06–07

Algae
  characteristics of, 231.19
  classification of, 151.23
  culturing, 231.18
  measurement of growth, 231.02
  observations of, 151.10
  reproduction of, 232.01
Alligators, 211.37
Alternating current (electricity), 351.06
Altimeter
  construction and use of, 132.07
Altitude
  pressure differences, 132.07–08
  temperature differences, 161.03
Amoeba
  observations of, 231.12
Amphibians
  characteristics of, 211.31–36
  definition of, operational, 211.30
Amplitude
  of sound waves, 323.07
Anemometer
  Construction and use of, 162.04–05
Angular diameter
  measurement technique, 421.16–18
ANIMALS, 210 (*see* Zoology; *see also* names of
  specific animals)
Anthers in flowers, 242.12
Ants, 211.23
Apple, 221.24
Applied force in machines
  definition of, operational, 511.03–04
  in gears, 511.37–38
  in levers, 511.10, 511.13, 511.16
  in pulleys, 511.24, 511.30–34
  in wheels and axles, 511.19
Aquariums
  construction of, 241.01, 642.01
Arthropods, 211.12–14
Ash tree, 221.19
ASTRONOMY, 420
  characteristics of the universe, 421.01–21
  classification of objects, 421.22–23
  eclipses, 422.13–18
  measurement in
    distances, 421.12–13, 421.19–20
    sizes, 421.14–19, 421.22
    moon, 421.14, 422.03–04, 422.13–18

in mud samples, 151.20–21
natural selection of, 243.03
in ocean samples, 151.22–23
outdoor gardening, 641.04
parts of
    cotyledons, 221.14
    flowers, 221.21–22, 242.11–16
    leaves, 221.20, 242.10
    roots, 221.14, 242.01–06
    stems, 221.15–19, 242.07–09
pollination of, 242.11–16
reproduction of, 221.01–02, 242.11–16
responses to environmental conditions,
    141.21, 221.05–07, 221.17–31, 332.11
safety precautions in handling, 611.06
soil containers for, 641.01
soilless containers for, 641.01
spores, 221.08–09
terrarium habitats, 241.02, 642.02
theory of evolution, 243.01, 243.03–04
types with seeds, 221.01, 221.03, 221.12,
    221.26, 222.01, 242.17–18
types without seeds
    ferns, 221.10–11
    fungi, 221.08–09
    mosses, 221.10–11
    mushrooms, 221.08–09
use of, 244.01–04
Bread making, 231.17–22
Brown, Robert, 412.01
Brownian movement
    observations of, 412.01
Budding of yeast cells, 232.02
Buds of plants
    arrangements on stems, 221.20
Building (*see* Models, making; Science
    equipment)
Buoyancy
    characteristics of, 122.18–21
    definition of, operational, 122.17
    of ice, 151.06
    ocean vs. freshwater, 151.05–06
Burning
    heat, as a source of, 342.08
    kindling point, 342.09–10
    light, as a source of, 332.04–05
Butterflies, 211.23
Butterwort, 242.10b

Calcium
    test for, 411.10
    spectrum analysis of, 421.11
Camera, pinhole
    construction and use of, 334.01, 421.07–08
Canary, 242.20b
Candles
    graphing burning times of, 631.02
Capillary action
    characteristics of, 122.35
    definition of, operational, 122.34
    in soils, 641.03c
Carbon
    in compounds, 411.11, 413.07–10
    model of, atomic, 411.06a
Carbonate
    test for, 111.09
Carbon dioxide
    applications of, 131.19–21, 132.10
    collecting, 131.11
    measurement of, 131.18–20
    model of, molecular, 413.07c–10c
    production of, 131.10
    yeast, as an action of, 232.07–08
Carrots, 221.23
Catfish, 242.19
Cedar waxwings, 211.46
Cell division, 232.01
Celsius, Anders, 341.06
Celsius/centigrade temperature scale, 341.06,
    631.04
Changes of state
    of gases, 121.01–03, 131.01–04
    of liquids, 111.01–03, 121.01–03, 131.03
    model of, theoretical, 343.03
    phases, 342.21–29
    of solids, 111.01–03, 131.04
Chemical symbols
    for elements, 411.08
Cherry tree, 221.15
Chickadees, 211.46
Chimes, musical percussion instrument
    construction of, 324.02d
Chlorine
    model of, atomic, 411.06b
Circuit, electrical
    breaker, 354.03
    characteristics of, 352.16–24

Earth formation, models of, 143.01–08,
153.01–04
erosion/deposition
by chemicals, 142.29
by heat, 142.26
by plants, 142.28
by water, 142.07–28
by wind, 142.01–06
minerals, 141.13–15
rocks, 141.01–12, 141.22–24
soils, 141.16–21
Geotropism, 22.17–19
Geranium, 221.22, 222.22
Germination
environmental conditions' effect upon,
22.08–16
observations of, 221.08–16
ratios of, 221.02–03
table of wait-time for, 641.02
Glaciers
erosion by, 142.24–25
icebergs from, 151.06
Glassware, construction techniques
bending tubing, 623.02
cutting tubing, 623.01
making containers, 632.03
safety in handling, 611.04
Gneiss, 141.08
Goldfish, 242.19
Graduated cylinders
construction and use of, 632.03
Graphing techniques
bar graphs
definition of, operational, 631.02b
examples of, 222.06, 332.09
curved-line graphs
definition of, operational, 631.02c
examples of, 211.05, 221.05, 222.24,
631.02a
histograms
definition of, operational, 631.02a
examples of, 121.17, 221.17, 221.24,
222.03, 631.02
straight-line graphs
definition of, operational, 632.02c
examples of, 121.02, 311.07, 311.10–11,
342.06, 342.25, 362.26–27, 631.02b
Grasses, 221.20

Grasshoppers, 211.23, 212.10
Gravity
motion, as a source of, 312.05
plant growth, effect upon, 222.17–19
sensing, 312.04
tides, as a source of, 152.12–13
Greenhouses
construction and use of, 641.02f
Growth
of animals, 211.04–05
measurements of, 211.05
of microorganisms, 231.02–06
rings of trees, 221.18–19
Guinea pigs, 211.48
Guitars, musical string instruments
construction of, 324.04b
Guppies, 211.02

Hail, 162.29
Hamster, 211.05, 211.48
Hard water, 122.39–41
Harpsichord, musical string instrument
construction of, 324.04c
Hawk, 242.20c, 242.20g
Hearing, using the sense of hearing
characteristics of
liquids, 121.25
solids, 111.04, 111.06, 111.16
communication messages, 521.01–05,
522.01–03
echoes, 321.09, 322.24
electricity, 351.01, 352.14
moving water, 122.25–26
sounds, 321.01–15, 322.07, 323.11–16,
522.02
sounds through materials, 322.11–15, 323.01,
323.08
HEAT, 340
applications of, 344.01–02
behavior of
absorption, 161.05, 163.04–05, 342.51
reflection, 342.50
refraction, 342.49
changes of state, effect upon
gases, 131.02–04, 132.16–18, 342.19–20,
342.28–29
liquids, 121.01–03, 342.18, 342.23–27

mass and momentum, 313.05
Infrared energy, 333.14
Inheritance
    physical characteristics in animals, 211.03–07
INORGANIC MATTER, 100
    gases, 131.01–132.20
    geology, 141.01–143.07
    liquids, 121.01–122.52
    weather, 161.01–164.05
    oceans, 151.01–154.04
    solids, 111.01–112.05
Insects
    care of, 211.24
    collecting, 211.23
    respiration of, 242.23
    responses to environmental conditions,
        212.05, 342.31
INSTRUCTIONAL APPARATUS,
    MATERIALS, AND SYSTEMS, 600
Insulation
    from electricity
        definition of, operational, 352.25
        materials, characteristics of, 352.26–29
        tester for, 352.20
    from heat
        in space vehicles, 332.25–26
        testing materials, 342.47–48
Internodes, 221.15
Invisible ink, 521.04
Iodine
    as an indicator for starch, 111.09
    safety precautions in handling, 111.09
Iron
    as an indicator for oxygen, 131.14b

Jays, 211.26
Jets/rockets, 313.10, 531.03, 532.18–21

Kindling point
    definition of, operational, 342.09
    measurement of, 342.10

Ladybug, 211.13
Lateral bud, 221.15
Lava, 141.02
Leaves
    classification key, 221.20
    collecting and preserving, 651.02b

as insect traps, 242.10
responses to environmental conditions,
    222.22–24, 222.29–30
Leeuwenhoek, Anton, 231.08
Lenses (see also Concave lenses; Convex lenses)
    applications of
        binoculars, 332.19, 332.21
        microscopes, 231.08, 332.19, 332.21
        telescopes, 332.19, 332.21, 421.01
    characteristics of, 332.18
    focal points of, 332.24
    focus, 332.23–24
    magnification by, 332.20–22
    to produce high temperatures, 342.03
Lenticels, 221.15
Levers
    compared to
        gears, 511.37–38
        pulleys, 511.24
    types of
        first-class, 511.10–12
        second-class, 511.13–15
        third-class, 511.16–18
LIGHT, 330
    applications of
        pinhole camera, 334.01
        projector, 334.02–03, 334.05
    behavior of
        absorption, 331.12, 332.33–34
        diffraction, 331.05–07
        reflection, 331.11–12, 332.27–32
        refraction, 151.07, 331.08–10, 332.16–26
    characteristics of, 331.01–16
    control of, 332.18–34
    definition of, theoretical, 331.01–11
    intensity, 331.14, 332.05, 332.07–08
    and lenses
        focus of, 332.23–24
        magnification of, 332.20–22
        optical instruments, 332.18–32
    materials, effect upon
        blueprint paper, 332.10, 361.03d
        fading colors, 332.09–10
    measurement of
        intensity, 332.05
        speed, 322.18–19, 333.11, 421.20
    organisms, effect upon
        animals, 212.09, 332.12

telephone, 521.07, 522.02–03
characteristics of, 321.01–10
classifying, 321.11–15
control of, 322.22–24
decibels, 321.11
definition of, operational, 321.01–10
definition of, theoretical, 323.01–09
echoes, 321.09, 322.24, 323.04
effects, 322.06
frequency, 322.04, 322.09, 323.06
longitudinal waves, 323.01–07
loudness, 322.07
musical instruments, 324.01–06
pitch, 321.03–05, 321.11–12, 322.09–10
quality, 321.08
radio waves, 333.15
reflection of, 321.09
sensing, 322.01–04
sources of, 322.01–06, 324.01, 324.03, 324.05
speed of, 322.15–19, 333.10–11
thunder, 322.19
transmission through
    gases, 322.13–14, 322.23
    liquids, 322.12
    model of, 323.09
    solids, 111.16, 322.11, 521.07
types of, 321.01–02
vibrations, 322.20–22
volume, 321.03–05, 321.11, 322.07–08
Sounding board, 321.05
South pole, 362.10
Sowbugs, 211.13, 211.18–19
Sparrows, 211.46
Specific gravity
definition of, operational, 122.07
measurement of, 122.08–09
Spectroscope
construction and use of, 331.07, 421.11
Spectrum
analysis of, 421.11
electromagnetic, 333.12–15
Speed
changes in, 311.12
definition of, operational, 311.03
uniform, 311.10–11, 311.14
Spiders, 211.21–22, 332.12
Spores
definition of, operational, 232.02

growth from, 221.02, 221.04
in molds, 231.14
on mushrooms, 221.08–09
prints from, 221.09
Spring scale
construction and use of, 632.04
Stalactites/stalagmites, 142.29b
Stamens, 242.11–14
Starch
test for, 111.09
Star maps, 421.05
Stars
definition of, operational, 421.02
composition of, 421.11
constellations, 421.05–06
distances between, 421.20
motion of, 422.05–06
North Star, 421.03–04
Static electricity, 351.01–04
Steam turbine, 344.02
Stems
characteristics of, 221.15–19
conduction tubes in, 242.08
function of, 242.07–09
growth of, 222.06
responses to environmental conditions,
    222.17–19, 222.21, 222.26
uses of, 244.04
Stigma, 242.12–13
Stipules, 221.20
Storms, 152.19
Straight-line motion, 311.04–05
String telephone
construction and use of, 521.07
Strontium
test for, 411.10
Subliming/frosting, 131.04, 162.11, 342.28–29
Submarine
construction of, 152.02
Sugar
as a compound, 411.11, 413.07
model of, molecular, 413.07e
test for simple, 111.09
Sun
definition of, operational, 421.02
distance to, 421.09, 421.19
heat energy, as a source of, 161.04–05,
    342.01–03

definition of, operational, 341.09
effect of
    altitude upon, 161.03
    Earth's axis upon, 163.01
    Earth's curved surface upon, 163.02–03
effect upon
    air movement, 163.08–11
    animals, 212.10–13
    condensation, 162.18–20
    evaporation, 162.10–11
    microorganisms, 231.07, 232.09–14
    plants, 222.10–11, 222.29–31
    rocks, 141.18b, 142.26–27
    solubility, 122.44
feeling, 341.01
heat, compared to, 341.09–10, 343.04–05
measurement of
    atmosphere, 161.02–03, 163.06–07
    planets, 421.23
    stars, 421.10
Sun as a source of, 161.04–05
thermometers, 161.01, 341.05–08
Tensile strength, 111.23b
Tensiometer
    construction and use of, 121.17
Terminal bud, 221.15
Termites, 211.23
Terrariums, preparation of
    desert environment, 241.02c
    for ferns and mosses, 221.11
    swamp environment, 241.02b
    woodland environment, 241.02a
Testing
    air pressures, 132.08
    aircraft parts, 532.03, 532.08, 532.15, 532.20
    to amplify and mute sounds, 322.21, 322.26
    for colors animals can see, 243.04
    for compass markings, 362.11–12, 362.14, 362.16
    for electrical charges, 413.05
    electric circuit arrangements, 352.16, 352.19–21, 352.25–26, 352.29–30, 352.32–35
    objects for effect
        by electric fields, 352.11
        by heat, 142.26–27, 342.30–31, 412.04
        by light, 333.09–12
    optical equipment, 332.06
    parachute designs, 532.23

    for the presence of
        carbonates, 111.09
        carbon dioxide, 131.12
        metallic elements, 411.10
        oxygen, 131.14
        starch, 111.09
        simple sugars, 111.09
    pulley arrangements, 511.34
    for root functions, 242.04, 242.06
    soap powders, 122.41
    soil compaction, 142.10
    for stem functions, 242.09
    trained animals, 244.07–09
    types of food to attract birds, 211.46
    water pressures, 122.13–14
Test tube stands
    construction and use of, 622.01c
Thermometer
    air, 341.07
    copper-wire, 341.08
    liquid, 161.01, 341.05–06, 632.07
    use of, 341.02–04
Third-class lever (*see also* Levers)
    definition of, operational, 511.10–16
    examples of, 511.18
    mechanical advantages of, 511.17
Thistle, 242.18c
Thunder, 322.19, 351.01
Tidal basin, 152.14
Tidal wave, 152.10
Tides
    definition of, operational, 152.11
    source of, 152.12–14
Time
    measurement of, 422.07–09, 632.08–09
Tines, musical percussion instruments
    construction of, 324.02e
Toads, 211.33–36
Tobacco seeds, 221.23
Tornado
    model of, 152.19, 163.09
Tortoise, 211.42–43
Touching (*see* Feeling)
Translucent objects, 332.14
Transmission
    light, 221.11–12, 331.16, 332.14, 332.31
    sound, 111.16, 322.23
Transparent objects, 332.13

rocks, effect upon, 141.18a, 142.26–27, 142.29
in soils, 142.07–12
in terrariums, 641.02e
transparency of, 151.07–08, 151.16–19
waterborne materials, 142.17–20
waves, 151.11–14, 152.08–10
Water barometer
construction and use of, 632.08
Water clock, 632.08
Water cycle, 152.18
Water sampler
construction and use of, 151.19
Waterspout
model of, 152.20
Waterwheel
construction and use of, 122.34–35, 512.04
Wave theory
amplitude, 323.07
frequency, 323.06
light, 333.01–15
longitudinal wave, 323.01–07
sound, 323.01–09
transverse wave, 333.05
Waves, water
characteristics of, 151.12, 152.08
determining velocity, 151.12
earthquakes, as a source of, 152.10
relationship to depth, 151.13
shoreline erosion, 142.23, 151.11, 151.14
wind, as a source of, 152.10
WEATHER, 160
characteristics of, 161.01–13
measurement of factors
air pressure, 161.06–08
humidity, 161.09–13
temperature, 161.01–05, 162.07
wind, 162.01–06
measuring instruments for
anemometer, 162.04
barometer, 132.14–15, 161.06–07
hygrometer, 161.09
nephoscope, 162.02
rain gauge, 162.15
thermometer, 161.01, 341.05–08, 632.07
wind vane, 162.01
predictions of weather and climate, 164.01–05
water cycle

model of, 152.18, 163.01–12
temperature, effect of, 162.07–09
water, effect of, 162.10–31
wind, effect of, 162.01–06
Wedges
definition of, operational, 511.43
examples of, 511.44
mechanical advantages of, 511.45
Weighing (*see* Measuring techniques)
Wet cell
construction and use of, 352.01–02
Wheels
with drive belts, 511.35
friction in, 511.05–07
as pulleys, 511.23–24
and rotary motion, 311.08–09
Wheels and axles
in complex machines, 512.04
cranks, 511.22
definition of, operational, 511.19
examples of, 511.20
mechanical advantages of, 511.21–22
pulley, compared to, 511.24
Willow, 221.16
Wilson, Charles, 413.06
Wind (*see also* Air)
air movement indicator, 162.09, 342.38
applications of, 132.19–20
Beaufort wind scale, 162.06
cloud direction indicator, 163.02–03
definition of, operational, 132.17
deposition by, 142.02–04
Earth's rotation, effect of, 163.11
erosion by, 142.04–06
ocean currents, as a source of, 152.05–06
rocks, effect upon, 152.16–17
shorelines, effect upon, 156.16–17
temperature/pressure, effect of, 163.08–11
tornado, 163.09
windborne materials, 142.01–04
windsock, 162.01
wind speed indicator, 162.04–05
wind vane, 162.01, 162.03
Wind tunnel
construction and use of, 532.01, 532.03
testing aircraft in, 532.10–12
Wings (on aircraft), 532.10–12
Witch hazel fruit, 242.18b

Index

overheating due to overloading a circuit with too many resistors, 334, **334**
Work, 424–425
    complex machines to do, 425–426
    definition of, 424–425
    measurement of, 425
Worms
    camouflage characteristics of, 212
    respiration in, 208, 210
    response to light, 164, 276
    response to smell, 163
    response to touch, 162–163
    responses to cold, 164
    segmented, 149–150, **150**
    training of, 215–217, **216**
Written messages
    devices for coding and decoding, 429, **429**
    in "invisible ink," 427

X
Xylophones, 263, **264**

Y
Yeast(s), 186, 191–192
    for bread making, 192, 195
    budding of, 193–194, **194**
    culture of, 187
    culturing of, 191–192
    fermentation of, 195
    growth of, 186
        effect of temperature changes on, 192
        food for, 187

Z
Zither, 266
Zoology, 148–165. *See also* Animals

DATE DUE

NOV 1 4 2016 IU# 17202 0678 ANTC#

PRINTED IN U.S.A.